W9-BXP-600

RANDALL DALE ADAMS
Former Death Row Inmate

The most extensive collection of videos available to enhance your lectures and help bring criminal justice concepts to life for students!

Available to instructors on adoption of a Cengage Learning text*:

▶ **NEW!** The CJ Files
▶ Career Profile Videos
▶ ABC® Videos for Criminal Justice
▶ Moments in Time: The Oral History of Criminology and Criminal Justice
▶ Wadsworth Customized Films for the Humanities Videos
▶ Cengage Learning Video Library

Video is also integrated into these Cengage Learning resources:

▶ PowerLecture with ExamView® and JoinIn™ Student Response System
▶ CengageNOW™ for Criminal Justice
▶ WebTutor™ for Criminal Justice

<<<<< **SEE INSIDE FOR DETAILS!**

And visit us online at
www.cengage.com/criminaljustice

ABC® Videos for Criminal Justice <<<<<<<<

ABC® Videos feature short, high-interest clips from current news events as well as historic raw footage going back 40 years. Perfect as discussion starters or to enrich your lectures and spark interest in the material in the text, these brief videos provide students with a new lens through which to view the past and present, one that will greatly enhance their knowledge and understanding of significant events and open up to them new dimensions in learning. Clips are drawn from such programs as *World News Tonight*, *Good Morning America*, *This Week*, *PrimeTime Live*, *20/20*, and *Nightline*, as well as numerous ABC News specials and material from the Associated Press Television News and British Movietone News collections.

ABC Videos are available for the following courses:

▶ Introduction to Criminal Justice
▶ Criminology
▶ Corrections
▶ Terrorism
▶ Criminal Procedure
▶ Issues in Criminal Justice

Moments in Time: The Oral History of Criminology and Criminal Justice <<<

Moments in Time videos were created from the Oral History Project videos from the American Society of Criminology and the Academy of Criminal Justice Sciences.

Wadsworth Customized Films for the Humanities Videos <<<<<<<<

Short 5- to 10-minute segments provide faculty with a method for building interest and classroom discussion without losing an entire class to watching a video. The organization of the videos follows that of the main sections of our introductory criminal justice texts.

>>>>>>>>> NEW! The CJ Files Videos

Do your students come to class expecting that life as a criminal justice major will be as exciting as what they see on television crime shows? Do they have unrealistic expectations about what it takes to become a criminal justice professional because it looks so easy in the movies? **The CJ Files Videos** follow three students as they discover that although real life might not be as glamorous as the world Hollywood creates, working towards a career in criminal justice comes with its own very real rewards. These videos are accessible from our Careers in Criminal Justice Website, CengageNOW, and WebTutor™, as well as our PowerLecture CD-ROMs for instructors.

>>>>>>>>> Career Profile Videos

Cengage Learning's **Career Profile Videos** give unique insight into the realities of life in a variety of criminal justice careers. Real professionals answer questions about how they got started in their careers—including educational background—as well as the most challenging and most interesting parts of their jobs. These videos give students a concrete sense of what to expect from various criminal justice occupations, and can be a powerful tool in the decision-making process. Career Profile videos are available on the Careers in Criminal Justice Website and in other online resources.

>>> ALSO AVAILABLE: The Careers in Criminal Justice Website

The **Careers in Criminal Justice Website** provides students with extensive career profiling information and self assessments, and is designed to help them investigate and focus on the criminal justice career choices that are right for them. With links and tools to assist students in finding a professional position, this new website includes over 50 career profiles and more than 25 video interviews. The website also features a career rolodex, interest assessment quiz, and a career planner with sample resumes, letters, interview questions, and more. Ask your Cengage Learning representative about packaging access with the Wadsworth Criminal Justice text of your choice.

View a demo at **www.cengage.com/criminaljustice/careers**

Cengage Learning Video Library

Video Policy: Cengage Learning Criminal Justice adopters may request one video per 100 new books ordered. Titles subject to availability. For a complete list of available videos, please contact your local Cengage Learning sales representative.

Court TV® Videos

Court TV videos feature provocative one-hour court cases to illustrating seminal and high-profile cases in depth. We offer many videos from the Court TV library, including the following:

Florida v. Wuornos—Trial of America's First Female Serial Killer

ISBN-10: 0-534-52981-X • ISBN-13: 978-0-534-52981-9

Aileen Wuornos admitted killing a man after soliciting him for sex. She admitted to six other killings under similar circumstances, but she claimed they were all in self-defense.

Maximum Security

ISBN-10: 0-534-52738-8 • ISBN-13: 978-0-534-52738-9

The video takes viewers behind the walls of Massachusetts' Walpole Penitentiary, following a team of corrections officers whose task it is to investigate crime among the state's most violent offenders.

Florida v. Campbell—Driving While Black

ISBN-10: 0-534-52846-5 • ISBN-13: 978-0-534-52846-1

Nathan Campbell is stopped by white members of the Orlando Sheriff's Office for two alleged traffic violations. Campbell, an African-American police officer, who was off-duty at the time, claims he was really stopped because of his race.

A&E Videos

A sampling of the videos we offer from A&E includes:

Deadly Force DVD (American Justice)

Revisit some of the most infamous incidents in the history of law enforcement, from the MOVE bombing to Waco, in this hard-hitting look at the controversial use of deadly force. 50 minutes.

Ma Barker: Crime Family Values DVD (Biography)

Ma Barker: criminal mastermind or blindly devoted mother? This is a fascinating look at one of the nation's most enigmatic anti-heroes. 50 minutes.

The Cop and the Criminal: The Whitey Bulger Story DVD (Investigative Report)

Find out why the FBI cultivated a 15-year relationship with a notorious New England gangster. 50 minutes.

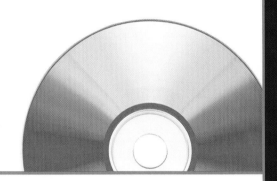

Films for the Humanities and Sciences® Videos

Cengage Learning will purchase videos from Films for the Humanities and Sciences on your behalf as per our video policy outlined above. Go to **www.films.com** to search for videos by topic.

Some of the videos offered by Films for the Humanities and Sciences include:

Legal Limbo: The War on Terror and the Judicial Process (BVL33636)

Does the U.S. have the judicial measures in place to combat terrorism or do the events of 9/11 require a fundamental shift in the judicial process? This *ABC News* program examines whether the U.S. judicial process was sidestepped by the George W. Bush administration in the interests of the war on terror. It highlights two case studies: Zacharias Moussaoui, a French citizen arrested on immigration violations before the 9/11 attacks, for his role as the alleged "20th hijacker"; and Jose Padilla, a U.S. citizen held as an enemy combatant for his alleged plan to detonate a dirty bomb. 23 minutes.

School Shootings: America's Tragedy (EFA10755)

This program provides an in-depth analysis of the causes and long-term effects of school shootings. Six of these horrific crimes, which culminated in numerous deaths—from the Barry Loukaitis case in Moses Lake, Washington, to the copycat atrocities in Colorado, Oregon, Arkansas, Kentucky, and Mississippi—these profiles reveal the fault lines running beneath the surface of many suburban communities. 48 minutes.

Crime Tech: New Tools for Law Enforcement (CLJ7958)

Law enforcement officers demonstrate the state-of-the-art crime-fighting weapons that make apprehending criminals less dangerous. 52 minutes.

ISBN-10: 1-4390-3795-7 • ISBN-13: 978-1-4390-3795-9

Compelling, balanced, and objective...

Explore a text as fast-paced and vital as the field of criminal justice

This best-selling brief introduction to the criminal justice system provides students with thorough, objective coverage of all the latest research in the field, cutting-edge topical and case discussions, and the richest examination of career options ever.

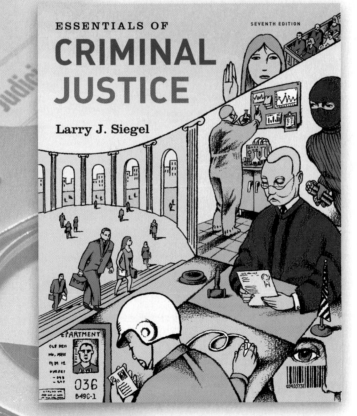

Essentials of Criminal Justice is perfectly tailored to meet the needs of today's students with the help of integrated learning objectives, plentiful visuals, and a **unique new RealityCheck theme**. Found only in Siegel's text, *RealityCheck* separates myth from reality to help students correct the false notions, perceptions, and biases they bring to the class as a result of misleading or misinformed statements they may hear on television or read on the Internet.

Supported by a powerful suite of teaching and learning resources, *Essentials of Criminal Justice* is the ideal solution for instructors looking for the proven reliability of Larry Siegel's authorship in a shorter paperback presentation. Explore the Seventh Edition with this preview, and discover a text that reveals the dynamic nature of criminal justice today.

New! In an effort to be brief and to the point, the book has been pared down to 14 chapters.

Separating criminal justice myth from reality

Fueled by the popularity of the television series, the "CSI effect" deals many instructors one of their greatest challenges when it comes to teaching students about the realities of criminal justice in America today—and the **all-new** *RealityCheck* theme ensures that the Siegel text meets that challenge head on. The *RealityCheck* theme is first introduced in Chapter 1, so students start to understand just how misinformed they might be about criminal justice if television or the Internet has influenced their knowledge. Then, each part opener provides a ripped-from-the-headlines vignette that sets straight a prevalent misconception. Each chapter opens with a list of "myth or reality" statements highlighting common misperceptions about crime related to that chapter's topic.

RealityCheck

MYTH or REALITY?

- ▶ We live in a very violent society; there is more crime today than ever before.
- ▶ Police departments are an American creation, the first having been formed in New York City after the Civil War.
- ▶ At its core, the justice system is designed to protect the public from those people who cannot abide by or obey the law.
- ▶ Just as on *Law and Order* and similar shows, the agencies of the justice system work closely together to solve cases, process offenders, and punish the guilty.
- ▶ There is equal justice under the law, and everyone can expect to get their day in court.

RealityCheck

MYTH or REALITY?

- ▶ We live in a very violent society; there is more crime today than ever before.
- ▶ Police departments are an American creation, the first having been formed in New York City after the Civil War.
- ▶ At its core, the justice system is designed to protect the public from those people who cannot abide by or obey the law.
- ▶ Just as on *Law and Order* and similar shows, the agencies of the justice system work closely together to solve cases, process offenders, and punish the guilty.
- ▶ There is equal justice under the law, and everyone can expect to get their day in court.
- ▶ Justice tends to be objective rather than subjective; agents of the justice system put their personal feelings aside in the course of their duties.
- ▶ Seeking justice is often confounded by ethical dilemmas that may be difficult to resolve.

Learning Objectives

1. Be able to define the concept of criminal justice
2. Be aware of the long history of crime in America
3. Discuss the formation of the criminal justice system
4. Name the three basic component agencies of criminal justice
5. Comprehend the size and scope of the contemporary justice system
6. Trace the formal criminal justice process
7. Know what is meant by the term "criminal justice assembly line"
8. Discuss the "wedding cake" model of justice
9. Be familiar with the various perspectives on justice
10. Understand the ethical issues involved in criminal justice

1

CRIME AND CRIMINAL JUSTICE

"Myth or Reality" statements posed to students include:

▶ We live in a very violent society; there is more crime today than ever before.

▶ Just like on "Law and Order" and similar shows, the agencies of the justice system work closely together to solve cases, process offenders and punish the guilty.

▶ Seeking justice is often confounded by ethical dilemmas that are often difficult to resolve.

▶ Police work primarily involves crime fighting.

▶ The more serious the crime, the more likely it is that detectives will solve it.

▶ Elected state judges can be affiliated with a political party.

▶ Inmates lose all civil rights once they enter a high security correctional facility.

▶ Most released inmates fail on parole.

▶ Convicted criminals can be forced to surrender their homes and cars.

REALITY CHECK

MYTH OR REALITY? We live in a very violent society; there is more crime today than ever before.

MYTH: There was more crime and violence in the nineteenth century than there is today.

Despite what you may read in the newspapers or see on TV, America was a more violent place in years gone by. Those familiar media images of frontiersmen carrying six guns and getting into bar fights is not far from the truth. Are the conditions that produce violence today similar to what made the country violent in the nineteenth century, or have conditions changed?

Throughout the chapter, *RealityCheck* insets spotlight where these myths are countered or dispelled. Focusing questions are also provided to encourage critical thinking and discussion.

RealityCheck Revisited sections at the end of each chapter direct students to web sites that expand on the myths and realities discussed in the chapter.

RealityCheck Revisited

To learn more about the myths and realities related to the justice system that were presented in this chapter, visit the following websites.

- To read more about Wyatt Earp and other famous nineteenth-century lawmen and outlaws, go to

http://www.wyattearp.net/

http://oldwesthistory.net/oldwest2.html/

http://www.legendsofamerica.com/WE-Outlaws.html

- To read more about the development of the first police agency in the United States, go to

http://www.cityofboston.gov/police/glance.asp

- If you are interested in criminal justice ethics, you might want to check out this site, which has links to a variety of sources:

http://www.llrx.com/features/criminaljusticeethics.htm#criminal%20defense

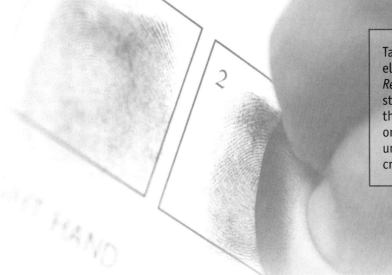

Taken together, the elements of this all-new *RealityCheck* theme help students replace the fiction they've seen on television or the Internet with a solid understanding of today's criminal justice system.

3

Timely careers coverage that meets today's teaching challenges and exceeds expectations

Exposing students to the myriad career options available, each chapter starts with a *Career Profile* describing the background and activities of a working member of the criminal justice system. With 12 of 14 career profiles **new** to this edition, these vignettes highlight professionals in the criminal justice system. Students gain valuable insight into how people chose their careers, their educational background, daily activities, and greatest challenges. For example, Chapter 2 features an Investigator with the New Hampshire public defender's office; a Juvenile Probation Officer is featured in Chapter 13; and Chapter 14 features a Special Agent with the Department of Homeland Security.

Career Profile

Daisy Mongeau is an Investigator with the New Hampshire Public Defender's Office in Concord. Her job involves interviewing witnesses, writing reports, obtaining medical/court records, subpoenaing witnesses, taking pictures, interacting with clients,

helping attorneys in trial preparation, and testifying at hearings. She finds that a lot of her friends just can't understand why she works so hard to defend people who are guilty, even those who have confessed to the crime. They don't seem to realize that all defendants are entitled to a criminal defense, even if they actually committed the crime!

After Daisy earned her bachelor's degree in Sociology and Justice Studies from the University of New Hampshire, she chose her career in criminal justice because she likes fighting for the "underdog" who would have no chance in the legal system without representation. The job is challenging. She has to locate witnesses who may not have a phone or permanent address by tracking them down through neighbors, friends, acquaintances, or anyone else who might know their location. She also has to work with the mentally ill in the course of defending them effectively when they are charged with a crime. When public defenders suspect that someone is mentally ill, they try to get help for their client through therapy, medication, or (if necessary) admission to the state hospital.

What is Mongeau's greatest reward? "Getting the prosecutor to drop the case nolle prosequi because of what a witness has told me during an investigation." She finds that clients are thrilled that someone actually believed them and helped them win the case. These are people not used to being given a helping hand.

Careers in Criminal Justice

FORENSIC SCIENTIST

Duties and Characteristics of the Job	• Forensic scientists perform comprehensive chemical and physical analyses on evidence submitted by law enforcement agencies.
	• Forensic scientists analyze the physical evidence they receive from police and then prepare reports describing the results of their analysis. Those documents, along with forensic scientists' expert testimony, can be important prosecutorial tools for convicting the accused. Therefore, their work is often instrumental in apprehending and convicting criminals.
	• Although most forensic scientists focus on criminal cases and are sometimes called criminalists, others work in the civil justice system—performing duties such as comparing handwriting to determine the validity of a signature on a will.
	• Forensic scientists perform two roles in their work. One is to analyze physical evidence found on a victim, at the scene. The other is to provide expert testimony in a court of law.
	• Most forensic scientists work in crime laboratories run by city, county, or state governments; the next largest group work for federal agencies, including the justice department (FBI, DEA, and Secret Service) and the treasury department; a smaller number work in private labs and colleges and universities.
	• Forensic scientists usually work a regular 40-hour week. Sometimes they have to travel and work long, irregular hours.
	• They spend much time in laboratories analyzing evidence, but they also work in offices to record and draft reports on the results of their analyses.
Job Outlook	• Job opportunities are expected to increase as a result of the judicial system's continuing need for corroborating evidence in prosecutions.
	• Forensic scientists can expect competition for jobs at the Department [of] Treasury, and other federal law enforcement agencies.
	• Job opportunities will be best for crime lab professionals who have a degree or certification.
Salary	• About 13,000 forensic scientists are now employed, with starting sal[ary in the] $45,000 range.
	• Experienced crime lab professionals can earn upwards of $100,000 a ye[ar.]
	• Lab directors earn in the low to mid-$100,000 range.
Opportunities	• Job opportunities will be best for crime lab professionals who have a degree or certification.
	• The Bureau of Labor Statistics projects that there may be 17,000 positio[ns for foren-] sic scientists in 1016, so growth is anticipated.
Qualifications	• Employment of most crime lab professionals is contingent upon satis[factory com-] pletion of a background investigation and random drug testing.
	• Those who work in large labs may use technologically advanced equipment such as chromatographs to analyze drugs, alcohol, arson evidence, and fibers; spectrographs to identify chemicals; and computerized laboratory equipment.
	• Crime lab professionals may be exposed to health or safety hazards when working in the lab or handling certain chemicals, but there is little risk if procedures are followed.

(continued)

Word to the Wise

• A career in forensics is not what it is made out to be on television, in such programs as *CSI*, *Cold Case*, *Bones*, and *Criminal Minds*. Much time is spent in a laboratory, and little (if any at all) on the streets chasing down criminals.

• Forensics experts are often employed in criminal justice agencies, so certain criminal activities and convictions in one's past can serve as a bar to employment.

• A degree in the social sciences is generally not enough for success as a forensic scientist. The very term "scientist" calls for training, and generally a degree, in the natural sciences.

• Compared to the nearly 700,000 sworn law enforcement personnel in the United States, there are very few forensic scientists (around 13,000).

• Most job opportunities will be found in and around large cities.

Each chapter includes a *Careers in Criminal Justice* feature that provides detailed information on a specific career, including job duties and characteristics, future outlook, salary, qualifications, required education, and training. Careers profiled in these features include:

- ▶ Criminologist
- ▶ Attorney
- ▶ Prosecutor
- ▶ Border Patrol Agent
- ▶ Forensic Scientist
- ▶ Forensic Psychologist
- ▶ Corrections Counselor
- ▶ Correctional Officer

New! As part of every *Careers in Criminal Justice* profile, **wholly unique** *Word to the Wise* sections identify potential pitfalls of each career area as well as what might disqualify a person from the career or job highlighted.

Designed to help students understand the many facets of criminal justice

Policies, Programs, and Issues in Criminal Justice

The *CSI* Effect

When *CSI: Crime Scene Investigation*, debuted, it was a surprise television hit. At one point, it was labeled the most popular show in the world. Its spinoff programs, *CSI: Miami* and *CSI: New York*, were also popular. *CSI* spawned an entire genre of similar programs, including *Cold Case*, *Bones*, and *NUMBERS*. In 2006, five of the top 10 television programs involved criminal investigations.

The criminal investigations genre is but the latest to evolve in the long history of television programming that has featured (and sensationalized) criminal investigations and courtroom proceedings. More than most other shows, though, *CSI* and its progeny may have started to blur the lines between reality and fiction. And this effect may be enhanced by the popularity of crime magazine shows such as *48 Hours Mystery*, *American Justice*, and (sometimes) *Dateline NBC*, which feature real cases. But it's *not* that these entertainment programs portray the criminal justice system so accurately that they seem more realistic than fictional. Read on.

Many attorneys, judges, and journalists have started to claim that *CSI*-like programs have influenced jurors' expectations. Some have alleged that jurors sometimes acquit defendants when no scientific evidence is presented. Others have alleged that jurors have developed unrealistic expectations about just what information scientific investigations can bring to bear on a case. As one prosecutor put it, "Jurors now expect us to have a DNA test for just about every case. They expect us to have the most advanced technology possible, and they expect it to look like it does on television."

Does a *CSI* Effect Really Exist?

Donald Shelton, a judge, and his colleagues, criminology professors at Eastern Michigan University, surveyed 1,000 prospective jurors in an effort to determine whether there is a real "*CSI* effect." They asked questions concerning expectations and demands for scientific evidence and the television programs that the respondents regularly watched. The respondents were asked about several crime types and then asked to report what scientific evidence they would expect to see presented at trial. Choices for the latter ranged from eyewitness testimony and circumstantial evidence to DNA, ballistics, and fingerprint evidence. They were even asked how likely they would be to find the defendant guilty or not guilty based on the evidence presented by the prosecution. What did the researchers find?

- 46 percent expected to see scientific evidence presented in *every* criminal case.
- 22 percent expected to see DNA evidence in *every* criminal case.
- 36 percent expected to see fingerprint evidence in *every* criminal case.
- 32 percent expected to see ballistic or other firearms evidence in *every* criminal case.

What do the percentages mean? Are expectations unrealistic? In one-third of all criminal cases, it is virtually impossible to gather fingerprint evidence. It appears, indeed, that the respondents' expectations were driven somewhat by their television-watching habits. For all the categories of evidence, *CSI* viewers tended to have higher expectations for being presented with scientific evidence. This suggests there is evidence of a *CSI* effect, but Shelton and his colleagues also found that respondents were only somewhat likely to alter their verdicts based on the presence or absence of scientific evidence in a trial. They found, for example, that

- *CSI* viewers were more likely than their non-*CSI*-viewing counterparts to convict without scientific evidence if eyewitness testimony was available.
- In rape cases, *CSI* viewers were less likely to convict if DNA evidence was not presented.
- In breaking-and-entering and theft scenarios, victim or other testimony was sufficient to convict.

Shelton and his colleagues concluded, in short, that there *is* a *CSI* effect, but it may not be as influential as was previously thought. Not everyone agrees, however. The National Academy of Sciences report presented in the Policies, Programs, and Issues feature "*Forensics under the Microscope*" in Chapter 5 revealed that a number of prosecutors are concerned about a supposedly real *CSI*-like effect.

Critical Thinking

It is said that life imitates art. As the popularity of the crime scene investigator profession grows, more students will probably be drawn into forensics, and more police and law enforcement agencies are likely to use forensic specialists in their daily operations. Do you think that crime is better solved in the lab or on the beat?

© Mike Kemp/Rubberball Productions/Getty Images

Policy, Programs, and Issues in Criminal Justice boxes help students think critically about current issues and practices. For example, the feature in Chapter 8 looks at the "The CSI Effect," while Chapter 12's feature gives students a look at life in a female prison.

Criminal Justice and Technology boxes review the impact of recent scientific advances, with features on "Monitoring Probationers with Technology" (Chapter 10), "Technocorrections: Contemporary Correctional Technology" (Chapter 11), and "Using Biometrics to Fight Terrorism" (Chapter 14).

Criminal Justice and Technology

Monitoring Probationers with Technology

It is a myth that supervising people on probation is merely a form of social work and that probation officers spend all their time dispensing counseling to clients. The fact is that monitoring and control are also a significant aspect of the probation officer's job. Many probationers have substance abuse problems that can interfere with their community sentence. Several newly developed technologies may help uncover and curb these behaviors and provide probation officers with tools to better manage their caseloads by doing their jobs more effectively and efficiently.

Sleep Pattern Analysis

Sleep pattern analysis technology, already used by some jurisdictions, can provide preliminary indications of substance abuse and help community corrections officials determine whether more testing is warranted. Sleep disruption due to substance abuse can occur in several ways, including altering the sequence and duration of various stages of sleep, total sleep time, and the amount of time needed to fall asleep. The technology consists of a small device, secured to an offender's wrist with a tamper-evident band, that measures sleep quality by recording gross motor activity. Analysis of the data collected may indicate sleep disorders, which might be caused by substance abuse. The device passively collects and records body movement information, and when the offender reports to the probation office or drug court, data can be downloaded and analyzed in a matter of minutes. If data analysis indicates possible substance abuse, the offender can be required to immediately provide a urine specimen for further testing.

Infrared Spectroscopy

Currently in field tests, this technology seeks to modify a glucose-monitoring device into an alcohol-testing product. The device uses a light source, an optical detector, and spectrometers to conduct chemical analysis of tissue and measure alcohol levels. Results, available within just 1 minute, have accuracy comparable to that of breathalyzers and blood tests. The technology uses infrared spectroscopy to make a nonintrusive examination of a subject's inner forearm; the device also could be modified to examine other parts of the body. The analysis process incorporates a biometric component that identifies an individual's unique tissue structure and tissue chemistry, thus ensuring accurate identification of the person being tested.

Driver Monitoring and Surveillance

This surveillance technology consists of a pair of ankle bracelets that collect data on the unique patterns of movement associated with foot-to-brake, foot-to-gas pedal, and acceleration and deceleration of a motor vehicle. Data analysis can then indicate whether and when a subject has been driving. In the case of an individual whose license is restricted rather than suspended, it can also indicate whether the driving took place during a prohibited time (such as outside the normal workday). The bracelets can store and process data for up to 30 days, allowing a community corrections officer to upload data during a scheduled monthly visit. This technology would help community corrections professionals deal with a widespread and long-standing problem: research indicates that up to 75 percent of all drivers with suspended or restricted licenses continue to drive.

Critical Thinking

1. Does this type of monitoring interfere with the treatment aspects of probation? Is it possible to help people who believe they are regarded as untrustworthy and must be monitored 24/7?

2. Even though it might pay to closely monitor probationers soon after their community sentence begins, does it pay to continue close control two, three, or even five years after they have been in the community? If they haven't violated probation in years, aren't they a safe bet?

ETHICAL CHALLENGES IN CRIMINAL JUSTICE

A Writing Assignment

A criminologist proposes a research project to test the association between IQ and crime. She wants to look at the association among race, intelligence, and delinquent behavior. To carry out the project, she wants to conduct IQ tests with K–12 students in the local school district, use a self-report instrument, and gather arrest data from local police. She guarantees that all data will be confidential. Take the role of a school board member who must approve of the project. Would you grant her permission to conduct the research? Explain your answer in detail. What possible harm could be done by her project and to whom?

Ethical Challenge writing assignments are found near the end of each chapter. These assignments pose a thought-provoking essay question that ties together the substantive material covered in the chapter with a real-life event or hypothetical situation. Students are asked to write a critical essay on the topic; helpful web links are provided.

Multimedia resources to enliven your course and advance student understanding

New! Cengage Learning Criminal Justice Media Library

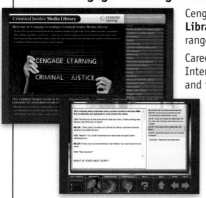

Cengage Learning's **Criminal Justice Media Library** includes nearly 300 media assets on a wide range of topics, including:

Careers in Criminal Justice • Comparative/ International • Corrections • Courts • Crime and the Media • Criminal Evidence/Procedure • Criminal Investigation • Criminal Law • Criminology • Cybercrime • Drugs • Ethics • Forensics • Fundamentals of Criminal Justice • History of Criminal Justice • Juvenile Justice • Organized Crime • Policing • Research Methods • Security • Serial Killers • Statistics • Terrorism • Victimology • White-Collar Crime • Women and Criminal Justice

Available to stream from any Web-enabled computer, the **Criminal Justice Media Library**'s assets include such valuable resources as:

▶ **Career Profile videos** featuring interviews with criminal justice professionals from a range of roles and locations

▶ **Simulations** that allow students to step into various roles and practice their decision-making skills

▶ **Video clips** on current topics and **Animations** that illustrate key concepts

▶ **Interactive learning modules** that help students check their knowledge of important topics

▶ **RealityCheck exercises** that compare expectations and preconceived notions against the real-life thoughts and experiences of criminal justice professionals

▶ **Interactive Timelines** for Criminal Justice Technology and Legal Landmarks

View a demo of the Criminal Justice Media Library

Log into your account on Single Sign On at login.cengage.com/sso/ and use **ISBN 0-495-80998-5** to add the Criminal Justice Media Library to your dashboard. If you do not have a Cengage Learning Single Sign On account, you may also register for one at the site.

Please contact your Cengage Learning sales representative for more information, including pricing.

Careers in Criminal Justice Website

Designed to help students investigate and focus on the criminal justice career choices that are right for them, this site provides students with extensive career profiling information and self-assessment testing. With links and tools to assist students in finding a professional position, this website includes 20 new *Career Profiles* and two new video Interviews. The website also features a career Rolodex, interest assessments, and a career planner with sample resumes, letter, interview questions, and more. View a demo at **academic.cengage. com/criminaljustice/careers**. Ask your Cengage Learning representative about packaging access with this text.

Book Companion Website

www.cengage.com/criminaljustice

 The book-specific website offers students a variety of study tools and useful resources such as quizzing, web links, Internet exercises, glossary, flashcards, and more. Website quizzes are linked to chapter learning objectives to maximize student mastery of key concepts.

Also available for your course...

CengageNOW for Criminal Justice

ISBN: 978-0-538-49206-5

CengageNOW is an online teaching and learning resource that gives you more control in less time and delivers better outcomes NOW. **CengageNOW** offers all of your teaching and learning resources in one intuitive program organized around the essential activities you perform for class—lecturing, creating assignments, grading, quizzing, and tracking student progress and performance. For more information visit **www. cengagenow.com**.

WebTutor™

Jumpstart your online course with customizable, rich, text-specific content—all easily and immediately accessible within your existing learning management system. Simply load a **WebTutor** cartridge into your course management system and add/edit/reorganize/delete content—quizzes, learning objectives, flashcards, videos, learning modules, animations, web links, games, exercises, and more—as you see fit. Plus, use the book's test bank and your own grade book to make assessment easier than ever. Whether you want to Web-enable your class or put an entire course online, **WebTutor** *delivers*. Visit **www.cengage.com/webtutor** to learn more.

Plan, teach, and assess with a complete suite of instructor resources

Instructor's Resource Manual with Test Bank
ISBN 13: 978-0-538-73835-4

By Lisa Anne Zilney, Montclair State University. This improved and completely updated resource includes learning objectives, detailed chapter outlines, key terms and figures, class discussion exercises, lecture suggestions, a detailed transition guide to make it even easier to switch from your current textbook to Siegel's, and a complete Test Bank. Each chapter's test bank contains approximately 80 questions in multiple- choice, true false, fill-in-the-blank, and essay formats, with a full answer key. The test bank is coded to the learning objectives that appear in the main text and includes the page numbers in the main text where the answers can be found. Finally, as part of our **Test Bank** Review Program, experienced criminal justice instructors have carefully reviewed each question for quality, accuracy, and content coverage. Our "Instructor Approved" seal on the front cover assures that you are working with an assessment and grading resource of the highest caliber.

PowerLecture™ with JoinIn Student Response System and ExamView®
ISBN 13: 978-0-538-73840-8

This one-stop lecture and class preparation tool makes it easy for you to assemble, edit, publish, and present custom lectures for your course, using Microsoft® PowerPoint®. Based on the learning objectives outlined at the beginning of each chapter, the enhanced **PowerLecture** lets you bring together text-specific lecture outlines and art from this text, along with new "myth-busting" video clips, animations, and learning modules from the web or your own materials—culminating in a powerful, personalized, media-enhanced presentation. The **PowerLecture** DVD also includes video-based polling and quiz questions that can be used with the **JoinIn on TurningPoint**® personal response system and integrates **ExamView**® testing software for customizing tests of up to 250 items that can be delivered in print or online.

eBank Lesson Plan Development
ISBN: 978-0-538-73839-2

By Todd Scott, Schoolcraft College. This new **Lesson Plan** brings accessible, masterful suggestions to every lesson. The lesson plans include a sample syllabus, learning objectives, lecture notes, discussion topics, in-class activities, tips for classroom presentation of chapter material, a detailed lecture outline, and assignments. Lesson plans are available on the **PowerLecture** resource and the instructor website or by emailing your local Cengage representative and asking for a download of the eBank files.

Distance Learning Instructor's Resource Manual
ISBN: 978-0-495-80469-7

By Kenneth Mentor. Your best guide for setting up a distance learning course in criminal justice, this manual features coverage of the pedagogy of distance education, tips and strategies for managing an online course, purposes/objectives, grading policy, how to post assignments, and much more.

Classroom Activities for Criminal Justice
ISBN: 978-0-495-10382-0

Stimulate student engagement with a compilation of the best of the best in criminal justice classroom activities. Novice and seasoned instructors will appreciate this powerful course customization tool containing tried-and-true favorites and exciting new projects drawn from the spectrum of criminal justice subjects, including introduction to criminal justice, criminology, corrections, criminal law, policing, and juvenile justice.

Criminal Justice Faculty Development: Teaching Professors to Teach
ISBN: 978-0-534-57264-8

This helpful guide includes suggested teaching tips and lecture outlines for the introduction to criminal justice course. In 50 pages the author proposes a teaching model, which can be used to develop a teaching course in criminal justice graduate curricula, to assist graduate students who do not have the benefit of such courses, and to help veteran faculty members improve their teaching skills.

Learning aids that expand student understanding

Study Guide

ISBN: 978-0-538-73833-0

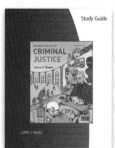

By Todd Scott, Schoolcraft College. The Study Guide features a variety of elements to help students get the most out of their classroom experience, including learning objectives, a chapter outline and summary, key terms, and a self-test. The self-test consists of multiple-choice, fill-in-the-blank, true/false, and essay questions coded to the learning objectives for maximum reinforcement.

Guide to Careers in Criminal Justice

ISBN: 978-0-495-13038-3

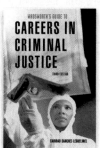

By Caridad Sanchez-Leguelinel, John Jay College of Criminal Justice. This guide gives students information on a wide variety of career paths, including requirements, salaries, training, contact information for key agencies, and employment outlooks.

Writing and Communicating for Criminal Justice

ISBN: 978-0-495-00041-9

Provide students with a basic introduction to academic, professional, and research writing in criminal justice. This text contains articles on writing skills, a basic grammar review, and a survey of verbal communication on the job that will benefit students in their professional careers.

Centering on VALUE.
Centering on CHOICE.
Centering on ENGAGEMENT.

From results-oriented course materials to effective faculty training, from personalized student study plans to state-of-the-art online tools, our products and services satisfy a full spectrum of instructor, student and institutional needs. Cengage Learning produces solutions centered on engagement that offer students and faculty the broadest set of options in our industry.

We're here to help by offering you and your students the best content available, with the support you deserve, in a format you choose. By partnering with us, you can be confident that what you've chosen will provide the most value to your students.

PRINT FORMAT

If you prefer a traditional text, we have the book you need in a paperbound printed format. Siegel's *Essentials of Criminal Justice,* **Seventh Edition** is also available in a 3-hole punched loose-leaf version to offer you another money-saving option. Contact your local Cengage Learning sales representation for ordering information.

DIGITAL FORMAT

The majority of our print offerings are also available in digital formats. You can choose an e-book in its entirety, purchase individual digital chapters, at fraction of the cost, as well as a suite of online assets.

CLeBook allows students to access Siegel's *Essentials of Criminal Justice,* **Seventh Edition** in an easy-to-use online format. Highlight, take notes, bookmark, search your text, and, in some titles, link directly into multimedia: CLeBook combines the best aspects of paper books and ebooks in one package. Contact your local Cengage Learning representative to learn more.

 **Save your students time and money. Tell them about** www.iChapters.com **for choice, savings...and a better chance to succeed in your class.**

Please consult your Cengage Learning representative for pricing details and more information regarding any of these offerings.

ESSENTIALS OF
CRIMINAL
JUSTICE

ESSENTIALS OF CRIMINAL JUSTICE

SEVENTH EDITION

Larry J. Siegel

University of Massachusetts, Lowell

WADSWORTH
CENGAGE Learning

Australia • Brazil • Japan • Korea • Mexico • Singapore • Spain • United Kingdom • United States

ESSENTIALS OF CRIMINAL JUSTICE
Seventh Edition
Larry J. Siegel

SENIOR PUBLISHER: LINDA SCHREIBER-GANSTER

SENIOR ACQUISITIONS EDITOR: CAROLYN HENDERSON MEIER

ASSISTANT EDITOR: MEGAN POWER

EDITORIAL ASSISTANT: JOHN CHELL

MEDIA EDITOR: TING JIAN YAP

SENIOR MARKETING MANAGER: MICHELLE WILLIAMS

MARKETING ASSISTANT: JILLIAN MYERS

SENIOR MARKETING COMMUNICATIONS MANAGER:
    TAMI STRANG

CONTENT PROJECT MANAGER: CHRISTY FRAME

CREATIVE DIRECTOR: ROB HUGEL

SENIOR ART DIRECTOR: MARIA EPES

SENIOR PRINT BUYER: BECKY CROSS

RIGHTS ACQUISITIONS ACCOUNT MANAGER, TEXT:
    BOB KAUSER

RIGHTS ACQUISITIONS ACCOUNT MANAGER, IMAGES:
    LEITHA ETHERIDGE-SIMS

PRODUCTION SERVICE: AARON DOWNEY,
    MATRIX PRODUCTIONS INC.

PHOTO EDITOR: LINDA L. RILL

COPY EDITOR: CONNIE DAY

COVER DESIGNER: RIEZEBOS HOLZBAUR DESIGN GROUP

COVER IMAGE: © PEDRO SCASSA

COMPOSITOR: PRE-PRESSPMG

For product information and technology assistance, contact us at **Cengage Learning Customer & Sales Support, 1-800-354-9706**. For permission to use material from this text or product, submit all requests online at **www.cengage.com/permissions**. Further permissions questions can be e-mailed to **permissionrequest@cengage.com**.

Library of Congress Control Number: 2009933735

ISBN-13: 978-0-495-81099-5

ISBN-10: 0-495-81099-1

Wadsworth
20 Davis Drive
Belmont, CA 94002
USA

Cengage Learning is a leading provider of customized learning solutions with office locations around the globe, including Singapore, the United Kingdom, Australia, Mexico, Brazil, and Japan. Locate your local office at **www.cengage.com/global.**

Cengage Learning products are represented in Canada by Nelson Education, Ltd.

To learn more about Wadsworth, visit **www.cengage. com/wadsworth**

Purchase any of our products at your local college store or at our preferred online store **www.ichapters.com.**

Printed in the United States of America
1 2 3 4 5 6 7 13 12 11 10 09

Dedication

This book is dedicated to

my kids Eric, Andrew, Julie, and Rachel;

my grandkids Jack, Kayla, and Brooke;

and to my wife Therese J. Libby.

The author with his wife, Therese, in Italy

Larry J. Siegel was born in the Bronx in 1947. While living on Jerome Avenue and attending City College of New York in the 1960s, he was swept up in the social and political currents of the time. He became intrigued with the influence contemporary culture had on individual behavior: Did people shape society or did society shape people? He applied his interest in social forces and human behavior to the study of crime and justice. After graduating CCNY, he attended the newly opened program in criminal justice at the State University of New York at Albany, earning both his M.A. and Ph.D. degrees there. After completing his graduate work, Dr. Siegel began his teaching career at Northeastern University, where he was a faculty member for nine years. After leaving Northeastern, he held teaching positions at the University of Nebraska–Omaha and Saint Anselm College in New Hampshire. He is currently a professor at the University of Massachusetts–Lowell. Dr. Siegel has written extensively in the area of crime and justice, including books on juvenile law, delinquency, criminology, criminal justice, and criminal procedure. He is a court certified expert on police conduct and has testified in numerous legal cases. The father of four and grandfather of three, Larry Siegel and his wife, Terry, now reside in Bedford, New Hampshire, with their two dogs, Watson and Cody.

CONTENTS

CHAPTER 3

Criminal Law: Substance and Procedure | 80

PART II
The Police and Law Enforcement 111

CHAPTER 4

Police in Society: History and Organization | 112

CHAPTER 5

The Police: Role and Function | 140

CHAPTER 6

Issues in Policing: Professional, Social, and Legal | 172

PART III
Courts and Adjudication   209

CHAPTER 7

Courts, Prosecution, and the Defense | 210

CHAPTER 8

Pretrial and Trial Procedures | 248

CHAPTER 9

Punishment and Sentencing | 292

PART IV
Corrections and Alternative Sanctions   331

CHAPTER 10

Community Sentences: Probation, Intermediate Sanctions, and Restorative Justice | 332

CHAPTER 11

Corrections: History, Institutions, and Populations | 370

CHAPTER 14

Criminal Justice in the New Millennium: Terrorism, Homeland Security, and Cyber Crime | 484

CHAPTER 1 *Oris Buckner*

Municipal Police Officer, New Orleans, Louisiana

CHAPTER 2 *Daisy Mongeau*

Investigator, New Hampshire Public Defender's Office, Concord, New Hampshire

CHAPTER 3 *Ralph C. Martin 77*

Attorney, Managing Partner at Bingham McCutchen LLP and Leader of the Bingham McCutchen Diversity Task Force, Boston, Massachusetts

CHAPTER 4 *John Sullivan*

Massachusetts State Trooper, Revere, Massachusetts

CHAPTER 5 *Larry Napolitano*

Patrol Officer, Shrewsbury, Massachusetts Police Department, Shrewsbury, Massachusetts

CHAPTER 6 *Stephen Bishopp*

Sergeant, Patrol Division Training Coordinator, Dallas, Texas

CHAPTER 7 *Carlos Martinez*

Court Reporter, Sonoma County Superior Courts, California

CHAPTER 8 *Patricia Sullivan*

Social Worker with the Commonwealth of Massachusetts Department of Children and Family Services

CHAPTER 9 *Ruben Andres Martino*

Presiding Justice, Harlem Community Justice Center, Harlem, New York

CHAPTER 10 *Ann Beranis*

Probation Officer Supervisor, DuPage County Probation and Court Services, Wheaton, Illinois

CHAPTER 11 *Gina Curcio*

Correctional Officer, Essex County House of Corrections, Middleton, Massachusetts

CHAPTER 12 *Rachel Anita Jung*

Executive Development Program Manager, Arizona Department of Corrections, Phoenix, Arizona

CHAPTER 13 *Kevin Kellems*

Intensive Juvenile Probation Officer, Calhoun County, Michigan

CHAPTER 14 *Mark O.*

Special Agent, Department of Homeland Security, Immigration and Customs Office of Investigations

On March 12, 2009, financier Bernard Madoff pled guilty to an 11-count criminal complaint, charging that he had defrauded thousands of investors out of billions of dollars in the most elaborate financial crime in the nation's history. How did Madoff manage to separate sophisticated investors from their hard-earned money?

Madoff founded the Wall Street firm Bernard L. Madoff Investment Securities LLC in 1960, and it soon became one of Wall Street's largest "specialist" trading firms. He became the darling of the jet set and was trusted by many wealthy people, including director Steven Spielberg, as well as sophisticated financial managers and investors. They were taken in by his promise of high returns and his long track record of success. However, when the market crashed in 2007–2008 and people wanted to withdraw their money, they found that the cupboard was bare. It seems that the "asset management arm" of his firm was a giant Ponzi scheme. Madoff had not invested any of his clients' money; instead, he had deposited it in various banks and used the interest and principal to pay off investors who needed cash. But until the crash, most people left their money in the account because they were making fantastic paper profits. When Madoff's house of cards fell apart, billions of dollars were missing, and no one seems to know where it all went.

Madoff later claimed that he merely wanted to satisfy his clients' demand for high returns and that their expectations simply could not be met by legal means. Instead, he resorted to an illegal scheme involving false trading activities, illegal foreign transfers, and false SEC filings. Madoff's Ponzi scheme has been estimated to have cost his clients an estimated *$65 billion*, perhaps the largest criminal conspiracy in history. On June 29, 2009, Madoff was sentenced to 150 years in prison, a life sentence.[1]

The Madoff case reminds us of the enormous impact that crime, law, and justice have had on the American psyche. Crime can range from a random mugging in the park to a multi-billion-dollar fraud involving highly educated corporate executives. As folksinger Woody Guthrie once put it,

> *. . . through this world I've wandered*
> *I've seen lots of funny men*
> *Some will rob you with a six-gun*
> *And some with a fountain pen.*[2]

The criminal justice system has been empowered by case law and legislation to protect us from these "funny men" who prey upon us with gun or pen. Each year the criminal justice system routinely processes millions of cases involving fraud, theft, violence, drug trafficking, and other crimes. How does this vast enterprise, which costs billions of dollars and involves millions of people, operate? What are its most recent trends and policies? How effective are its efforts to control crime? What efforts are being made to improve its efficiency? I have written the seventh edition of *Essentials of Criminal Justice* in an attempt to help answer these questions in a concise, forthright, and objective manner.

---

[1] Securities and Exchange Commission, "SEC charges Bernard L. Madoff for multi-billion-dollar Ponzi scheme," December. 11, 2008, http://www.sec.gov/news/press/2008/2008-293.htm (accessed April 30, 2009); Joe Lauria, "Life inside the weird world of Bernard Madoff," Timesonline, March 22, 2009, http://businesstimesonline .co.uk/tol/business/industry_sectors/banking_and_finance/article5949961.ece (accessed April 28, 2009).

[2] Woody Guthrie, "Ballad of Pretty Boy Floyd," http://www.woodyguthrie.org/Lyrics/Pretty_Boy_Floyd.htm.

GOALS AND OBJECTIVES

Because the study of criminal justice is a dynamic, ever-changing field of scientific inquiry, and because the concepts and processes of justice are constantly evolving, I have updated *Essentials of Criminal Justice* to reflect the most critical legal cases, research studies, and policy initiatives that have taken place during the past few years. *Essentials* lays a foundation for the study of criminal justice by analyzing and describing the agencies of justice and the procedures they use to identify and treat criminal offenders. It covers what most experts believe are the crucial issues in criminal justice and analyzes their impact on the justice system. This edition focuses on critical policy issues in the criminal justice system, including efforts to control and contain terrorism.

Thus my primary goals in writing this seventh edition remain the same as they have been for the previous six editions. They are that this book should

1. Provide students with a thorough knowledge of the criminal justice system
2. Be as readable and interesting as possible
3. Be objective and unbiased
4. Describe current methods of social control and analyze their strengths and weaknesses

Every attempt has been made to make the presentation of material interesting, balanced, and objective. No single political or theoretical position dominates the text; I try to be as objective as possible. Accordingly, I have included the many diverse views that are represented within criminal justice and that characterize its interdisciplinary nature.

NEW THEME

A main goal of this new edition is to expose some of the myths that persist about crime, criminals, and the criminal justice system. Given the popularity of television series such as *CSI* and *Law and Order*, which purport to strip away the veneer of the justice system and expose the truth, it has become essential to help students separate rhetoric from reality in the criminal justice system: Is the crime rate really out of control? Are unemployed people more likely than others to commit crime? Do detectives solve the most serious crimes? Do prisons really work? Does the death penalty deter people from committing murder? Making it clear what is true and what is merely legend is one of the greatest challenges for instructors teaching the first course in criminal justice. The all-new **RealityCheck** feature in *Essentials of Criminal Justice* meets that challenge head on. Its purpose is to separate myth from reality and thereby inform students of the incorrect notions, perceptions, and biases they bring to class as a result of what they see on television or read in fiction and on the Internet.

The **RealityCheck** theme is introduced in Chapter 1 so that students will realize just how misinformed they may be about criminal justice if their knowledge has been accumulated largely by Web surfing or watching television. Then, each part opener provides a ripped-from-the-headlines vignette that sets straight a prevalent misconception about crime, policing, courts and the law, or corrections. And each chapter opens with a **RealityCheck** feature that consists of a list of "Myth or Reality?" statements highlighting common misconceptions about crime that are related to the subject of the chapter. As the chapter proceeds, these topics are discussed, and each statement is either revealed as a myth and corrected with true information or confirmed as an accurate statement about criminal justice today.

ORGANIZATION OF THE TEXT

My major goal when creating the seventh edition of *Essentials of Criminal Justice* was to simplify the presentation and write as clearly and concisely as possible. Therefore, I have streamlined the text while maintaining the essential features of past editions. I have made every effort to ensure that the book is informative, comprehensive, interesting, well organized, and impartial, yet stimulating and thought-provoking.

PART 1 gives the student a basic introduction to crime, law, and justice. The first chapter covers the agencies of justice, outlines the formal justice process, and introduces the concept of the informal justice system, which involves discretion, deal making, and plea bargains. Chapter 1 examines the major perspectives on justice and shows how they shape justice policy. Chapter 2 discusses the nature and extent of crime and victimization: How is crime measured? Where and when does it occur? Who commits crime? Who are its victims? What social factors influence the crime rate? Chapter 3 provides a discussion of the criminal law and its relationship to criminal justice. It covers the legal definition of crime, the types of defenses available to those charged with having committed a crime, as well as issues in constitutional procedural law.

PART 2 offers an overview of law enforcement. Three chapters cover the history and development of police departments, the functions of police in modern society, issues in policing, and the police and the rule of law. Special emphasis is placed on community policing and crime prevention, technology and policing, and changes in police procedures.

PART 3 is devoted to the court process, from pretrial indictment to the sentencing of criminal offenders. In this section, individual chapters focus on the organization of the court system and the roles of its major participants (judge, prosecutor, and defense attorney), pretrial procedures, the criminal trial, and sentencing. The topics explored include bail, court reorganization, sentencing, and capital punishment.

PART 4 focuses on the correctional system, including probation and the intermediate sanctions of house arrest, intensive supervision, and electronic monitoring. Although the traditional correctional system of jails, prisons, community-based corrections, and parole is discussed at length, there is also a new focus on restorative justice programs. Such issues as the crisis of overcrowding in prisons and jails, house arrest, correctional workers, super-maximum-security prisons, and parole effectiveness are discussed.

PART 5 explores current issues in justice. One chapter deals with the problem of juveniles who break the law. What should be done with them and how should they be treated? There is information on the development of juvenile justice, on waiving youth to the adult court, and on the death penalty for children. Chapter 14, which appears for the first time in this edition, focuses on two of the critical issues currently facing the justice system: terrorism and cyber crime. It illustrates the dynamic nature of the justice process and the fact that the problems it faces are constantly evolving.

KEY CHANGES IN THE SEVENTH EDITION

In addition to infusing the new **RealityCheck** theme into the seventh edition, I have thoroughly updated and revised each chapter. Discussions are more concise—leaner than ever before. And the book contains many new graphs, figures, charts, and tables that make the presentation easier to understand. Finally, I have made the following key changes to the text.

- **Chapter 1, Crime and Criminal Justice**, has been thoroughly revised and has been updated with new data on criminal justice expenditures and the numbers of people in the correctional system.

- **Chapter 2, The Nature of Crime and Victimization**, contains new data on immigration and crime and shows how crime rates among immigrants may actually be lower than those found in the general population. There is a new concept summary on the definitions of crime. Data on child abuse and hate crimes has been updated and expanded. The sections on crime data have been expanded. The section on international crime has been revised and updated.

- **Chapter 3, Criminal Law: Substance and Procedure**, has a boxed feature on gun control that has been substantially revised in the aftermath of the Heller decision prohibiting governmental jurisdictions from banning guns outright. There is also a new section on neurolegal defenses to crime that rely on showing that neurological activity or the lack of it, measured through brain scan devices, can cause a person to commit crime.

- **Chapter 4, Police in Society: History and Organization**, has a reorganized section on police history. More federal law enforcement agencies are covered. Now the federal law enforcement agencies are organized into two categories: Justice Department agencies and Homeland Security agencies. There is a new *Careers in Criminal Justice* box featuring the position of Border Patrol agent.

- **Chapter 5, The Police: Role and Function**, has a new section titled "Improving Patrol" that features a discussion of rapid response and broken windows policing. There is also a new section on the effectiveness of community policing. A new *Policies, Programs, and Issues* box features the National Academy of Sciences report *Strengthening Forensic Science in the United States*.

- **Chapter 6, Issues in Policing: Professional, Social, and Legal**, contains a new section on police fatigue and another new section titled "Use of Force." The *International Justice* box is also new and features interrogation law in three other countries. The section "Police and the Rule of Law" has been updated and reorganized.

- **Chapter 7, Courts, Prosecution, and the Defense**, now has a dedicated section on problem-solving courts, as well as a new exhibit featuring court staff. Updated caseload statistics appear, as does a new section on the appointment of federal judges, including U.S. magistrate judges.

- **Chapter 8, Pretrial and Trial Procedures**, is a new chapter that combines material from former Chapters 9 and 10, thus ensuring balanced coverage, with three chapters each in Parts 2, 3, and 4 on policing, the courts, and corrections. This took the book down to 14 manageable chapters. Chapter 8 also includes an expanded "Legal Rights during Trial" section and a new *Policies, Programs, and Issues* box featuring the so-called *CSI* effect.

- **Chapter 9, Punishment and Sentencing**, includes the latest punishment statistics and an expanded treatment of how race affects sentencing. It also includes a dedicated section on error and wrongful convictions in the death penalty context. The three-strikes and capital punishment sections have been revised and updated to include the latest research.

- **Chapter 10, Community Sentences: Probation, Intermediate Sanctions, and Restorative Justice,** features a new *Criminal Justice and Technology* box that discusses monitoring probationers with technology. The section on administration of probation services has been redone. There is a section on specialized probation: teams of probation officers who focus on clients convicted of one specific type of crime, such as drug offenses or domestic violence, rather than working with a wide variety of offenders. Privatization of probation services is also discussed.

- **Chapter 11, Corrections: History, Institutions, and Populations**, contains revised and updated data on prison and jail populations. There is more material on jail populations and new-generation jails. A new section covers the development of parole. A new Concept Summary focuses on defining early correctional systems. And a new *Criminal Justice and Technology* box looks at contemporary correctional technology.

- **Chapter 12, Prison Life: Living in and Leaving Prison**, has a new section on sexual coercion, long considered common in penal institutions. New sections cover anger management and efforts to control violent criminal behavior both in the institution and upon prisoners' release into the community. Another new section looks at faith-based programs and reviews research suggesting that inmates involved in religious programs and education do better following release than those in comparison groups. The problems of reentry are reviewed in some detail.

- **Chapter 13, Juvenile Justice in the Twenty-first Century**, updates data on juvenile court processing. The section titled "Waiver of Jurisdiction" has also been improved and reorganized.

- **Chapter 14, Criminal Justice in the New Millennium: Terrorism, Homeland Security, and Cyber Crime**, is an all-new chapter that addresses such topics as the definitions of terrorism and cyber crime. It covers the debate over the utility and problems associated with the USA Patriot Act. There is much information on the various forms of cyber crime (including cyber terrorism) and on what law enforcement agencies are doing to thwart cyber criminals. A Concept Summary table provides an overview of the types of cyber crime. A *Criminal Justice and Technology* feature discusses how biometrics is being used to fight terrorism in the US-VISIT program.

BOXED FEATURES

The boxed features that address **Policies, Programs, and Issues** *in Criminal Justice* help students to think critically about current justice issues, policies, and practices. For example, "Forensics under the Microscope" looks at the critical field of forensic science and some of its problems.

- **Criminal Justice and Technology** boxes review some of the more recent scientific advances that can aid the justice system. In Chapter 10, for example, a feature titled "Monitoring Probationers with Technology" describes such technologies as ankle bracelets that collect data on the unique patterns of movement associated with foot-to-brake, foot-to-gas pedal, and acceleration and deceleration of a motor vehicle.

- **Careers in Criminal Justice** We have updated this very popular feature of the previous edition with information on the latest career paths in criminal justice. These boxes contain detailed information on salaries, educational requirements, and future prospects, and we have added to each of these boxes a new "Word to the Wise" section, discussing the potential pitfalls of that career area, as well as what might disqualify a person from the career or job highlighted.

- **International Justice** boxes look at crime and crime control efforts in other countries. For example, Chapter 6 features a new box that compares interrogation laws in three countries.

OTHER IMPORTANT CHAPTER FEATURES

Every chapter of *Essentials of Criminal Justice* also contains learning tools to enhance student mastery of the material.

- **Learning Objectives**. Each chapter begins with a list of key learning objectives. These objectives are then revisited in the **Summary**, where they are directly tied to the material covered in the text.

- **Career Profiles**. Each chapter starts with a vignette describing in detail the background and activities of a working member of the criminal justice system. This feature is designed to give students insight into criminal justice careers. It traces how the people profiled chose their careers, their educational background, what they do on the job, and what they see as their greatest challenges.

- **Research Links**. Throughout the book there are a variety of weblinks that help students do further research and reading on the Internet. Some of these are links to websites containing information that can enrich the textual material.

- **Ethical Challenges in Criminal Justice: A Writing Assignment**. Each chapter presents a writing assignment that challenges students to solve an ethical dilemma they may someday confront while working within the justice system. For example, the ethical challenge posed in Chapter 2 concerns a criminologist who believes there may be an association between IQ and crime. She wants to do research investigating this possible association. The assignment is for students to decide—and explain—whether they would grant this criminologist permission to conduct her research.

ANCILLARIES

For the Instructor

Instructor's Resource Manual with Test Bank. The manual, written by Lisa Zilney of Montclair State University, includes learning objectives, key terms, a detailed chapter outline, a chapter summary, discussion topics, student activities, and a test bank. Each chapter's Test Bank contains questions in multiple-choice, true/false, fill-in-the-blank, and essay formats, with a full answer key. The Test Bank is coded to the learning objectives that appear in the main text, and it includes the page numbers in the main text where the answers can be found. Finally, each question in the Test Bank has been carefully reviewed by experienced criminal justice instructors for quality, accuracy, and content coverage. Our Instructor Approved seal, which appears on the front cover, is our assurance that you are working with an assessment and grading resource of the highest caliber.

PowerLecture DVD. This one-stop digital library and presentation tool includes preassembled Microsoft® PowerPoint® lecture slides—now linked to the text's learning objectives and featuring all-new animations and simulations—as well as the full Instructor's Manual and Test Bank, ExamView, JoinIn, video, and image libraries.

ExamView® Computerized Testing. The comprehensive Instructor's Resource Manual described above is backed up by ExamView, a computerized test bank available for IBM-PC compatibles and Macintosh computers. With ExamView you can create, deliver, and customize tests and study guides (both print and online) in minutes. You can easily edit and import your own questions and graphics, change test layouts, and reorganize questions. And, using ExamView's complete word processing capabilities, you can enter an unlimited number of new questions or edit existing questions.

ABC Video Program. ABC videos feature short, high-interest clips from current news events, as well as historic raw footage going back 40 years. Perfect for discussion starters or to enrich your lectures and spark interest in the material in the text, these brief videos provide students with a new lens through which to view the past and present, one that will greatly enhance their knowledge and understanding of significant events and open up new dimensions in learning. Clips are drawn from such programs as *World News Tonight, Good Morning America, This Week, PrimeTime Live, 20/20,* and *Nightline,* as well as numerous ABC News specials and material from the Associated Press Television News and British Movietone News collections.

JoinIn™ on TurningPoint®. Spark discussion and assess your students' comprehension of chapter concepts with interactive classroom quizzes and background polls developed specifically for use with this edition of *Essentials of Criminal Justice.* Also available are polling and quiz questions that enable you to maximize the educational benefits of the ABC News video clips that we custom-selected to accompany this textbook. Cengage Wadsworth's exclusive agreement with TurningPoint software lets you run our tailor-made Microsoft® PowerPoint® slides in conjunction with the "clicker" hardware of your choice. Enhance the way your students interact with you, your lecture, and each other. For college and university adopters only. Contact your local Cengage representative to learn more.

WebTutor™. Jump-start your course with customizable, rich, text-specific content within your Course Management System. Whether you want to Web-enable your class or put an entire course online, WebTutor™ delivers.

WebTutor™ offers a wide array of resources, including media assets, test bank, practice quizzes, and additional study aids. Visit webtutor.cengage.com to learn more.

Lesson Plans. The Lesson Plans, created by Todd Scott of Schoolcraft College, bring accessible, masterful suggestions to every lesson. The Lesson Plans include a sample syllabus, learning objectives, lecture notes, discussion topics, in-class activities, a detailed lecture outline, and assignments. Lesson Plans are available on the **PowerLecture** resource and the instructor website, or you may email your local representative and ask for a download of the eBank files.

Website. The book-specific website at www.cengage.com/criminaljustice/siegel offers students a variety of study tools and useful resources, such as quizzing, weblinks, Internet exercises, glossary, flashcards, and more.

Criminal Justice Media Library. Available to stream from any Web-enabled computer, the Media Library includes nearly 300 media assets on a wide range of topics. These include Careers in Criminal Justice, Comparative/International, Corrections, Courts, Crime and the Media, Criminal Evidence / Procedure, Criminal Investigation, Criminal Law, Criminology, Cyber Crime, Drugs, Ethics, Forensics, Fundamentals of Criminal Justice, History of Criminal Justice, Juvenile Justice, Organized Crime, Policing, Research Methods, Security, Serial Killers, Statistics, Terrorism, Victimology, White-Collar Crime, Women and Criminal Justice.

Course360. This resource is a complete turnkey solution that teaches course outcomes through student interaction in a highly customizable online learning environment. **Course360** blends relevant content with rich media and builds on your course design, needs, and objectives. With a wide variety of media elements, including audio, video, interactives, simulations, and more, **Course360** is the way today's students learn best.

For the Student

Study Guide. An extensive student guide has been developed for this edition by Todd Scott of Schoolcraft College. Because students learn in different ways, the guide includes a variety of pedagogical aids to help them. Each chapter is outlined and summarized, major terms and figures are defined, and self-tests are provided.

CengageNOW. This unique, interactive online resource has the student take a chapter pretest and then offers him or her a personalized study plan. Once the student has completed the personalized study plan, a posttest evaluates her or his improved comprehension of chapter content.

Careers in Criminal Justice website *available bundled with this text at no additional charge*. Featuring plenty of self-exploration and profiling activities, the interactive Careers in Criminal Justice website helps students investigate and focus on the criminal justice career choices that are right for them. Includes interest assessment, video testimonials from career professionals, résumé and interview tips, and links for reference.

CLeBook. CLeBook allows students to access Cengage Learning textbooks in an easy-to-use online format. Highlight, take notes, bookmark, search your text, and (in some titles) link directly into multimedia: CLeBook combines the best aspects of paper books and ebooks in one package.

ACKNOWLEDGMENTS

Many people helped make this book possible. The following reviewers of this edition made suggestions that I attempted to follow to the best of my ability:

Cary D. Adkinson, Fayetteville State University

Sherree R. B. Davis, Hampton University

Kelly Enos, Los Angeles Mission College

Charles B. Noel, Community College of Allegheny County

Stacy Parker, Muskingum College

Laurie Rosenzweig, Castleton State College

Cathy Schuh, Bismarck State College

Amy B. Thistlethwaite, Northern Kentucky University

Thanks to my terrific editor, Carolyn Henderson Meier, who is always at my side with ideas, suggestions, and a shoulder to cry on. A lot of credit for getting this book out must go to my fabulous developmental editor, Shelley Murphy, who has two shoulders to cry on. Special thanks to my outstanding production manager, Christy Frame; to my new albeit wonderful production editor, Aaron Downey; to the precise and knowledgeable copyeditor, Connie Day, who did a thorough and professional job; and to the incredible marketing manager, the astonishing Michelle Williams; all of whom do great and magnificent jobs. As always, my BFF and photo editor Linda Rill worked her special magic on the photo program. Special thanks for all his help to John Worrall, a great scholar and friend.

LARRY SIEGEL
Bedford, New Hampshire

Teaching Using Learning Objectives

Section One:

Introduction and Overview of Supplements that Contain Learning Objectives

Cengage Learning recognizes the challenges of teaching and seeks to support faculty in their efforts to educate students. In pursuit of this goal, this supplement has been provided to aid faculty in using the Learning Objectives included in the textbooks and supplementary materials adopted for your class. Learning Objectives can make teaching and learning an easier and more profitable exercise. This supplement is intended to assist you in incorporating the Learning Objectives into your classroom.

How do Learning Objectives make teaching easier? Learning Objectives can be the organizing framework for all of the information taught in class. This supplement will show you how the ancillary materials tie all of the textbook information together for you using the Learning Objectives for each chapter in our instructor and student resources. These resources are available in print and electronically via various products, downloads, and companion websites provided by Cengage Learning.

How do Learning Objectives make learning easier? Students who know what is expected of them are more likely to succeed. Learning Objectives let the student know exactly what you expect them to learn, while the Study Guide and various tutorials available in our products and on our companion websites show them how to achieve the Learning Objectives. Making students aware of these materials provides them with a roadmap to successful completion of the class.

Learning Objectives make it a simple process to communicate what students are expected to know by the end of the class, thus making your job easier. Additionally, the Learning Objectives are used repeatedly in the textbook and study materials, and on the companion website available to each student. Repetition of this information promotes student success.

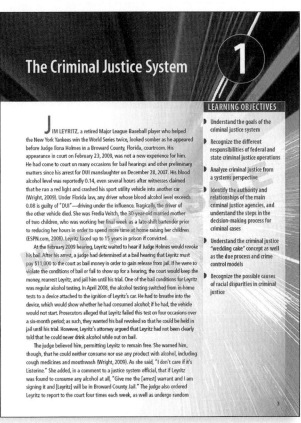

The Criminal Justice System

1

JIM LEYRITZ, a retired Major League Baseball player who helped the New York Yankees win the World Series twice, looked somber as he appeared before Judge Ilona Holmes in a Broward County, Florida, courtroom. His appearance in court on February 23, 2009, was not a new experience for him. He had come to court on many occasions for bail hearings and other preliminary matters since his arrest for DUI manslaughter on December 28, 2007. His blood alcohol level was reportedly 0.14, even several hours after witnesses claimed that he ran a red light and crashed his sport utility vehicle into another car (Wright, 2009). Under Florida law, any driver whose blood alcohol level exceeds 0.08 is guilty of "DUI"—driving under the influence. Tragically, the driver of the other vehicle died. She was Fredia Veitch, the 30-year-old married mother of two children, who was working her final week as a late-shift bartender prior to reducing her hours in order to spend more time at home raising her children (ESPN.com, 2008). Leyritz faced up to 15 years in prison if convicted.

At the February 2009 hearing, Leyritz waited to hear if Judge Holmes would revoke his bail. After his arrest, a judge had determined at a bail hearing that Leyritz must pay $11,000 to the court as bail money in order to gain release from jail. If he were to violate the conditions of bail or fail to show up for a hearing, the court would keep the money, rearrest Leyritz, and jail him until his trial. One of the bail conditions for Leyritz was regular alcohol testing. In April 2008, the alcohol testing switched from in-home tests to a device attached to the ignition of Leyritz's car. He had to breathe into the device, which would show whether he had consumed alcohol; if he had, the vehicle would not start. Prosecutors alleged that Leyritz failed this test on four occasions over a six-month period; as such, they wanted his bail revoked so that he could be held in jail until his trial. However, Leyritz's attorney argued that Leyritz had not been clearly told that he could never drink alcohol while out on bail.

The judge believed him, permitting Leyritz to remain free. She warned him, though, that he could neither consume nor use any product with alcohol, including cough medicines and mouthwash (Wright, 2009). As she said, "I don't care if it's Listerine." She added, in a comment to a justice system official, that if Leyritz was found to consume any alcohol at all, "Give me the [arrest] warrant and I am signing it and [Leyritz] will be in Broward County Jail." The judge also ordered Leyritz to report to the court four times each week, as well as undergo random

LEARNING OBJECTIVES

▸ Understand the goals of the criminal justice system

▸ Recognize the different responsibilities of federal and state criminal justice operations

▸ Analyze criminal justice from a systems perspective

▸ Identify the authority and relationships of the main criminal justice agencies, and understand the steps in the decision-making process for criminal cases

▸ Understand the criminal justice "wedding cake" concept as well as the due process and crime control models

▸ Recognize the possible causes of racial disparities in criminal justice

Instructor Resources

Learning Objectives are available in a variety of materials for you and your students. An Annotated Instructor's Edition is available for some titles, and includes a list of all of the tools we offer for instructors and students. Some of the key features of the **Annotated Instructor's Edition** include Teaching Tips, Discussion Tips, Web Tips, and Media Tips for each chapter. These tips are specifically designed to assist you in incorporating the Learning Objectives into the classroom through assignments, discussion, and use of the internet. Additionally, these tips are highlighted in blue in the margins of the textbook to help you spot them easily when preparing for classes.

The **Instructor's Manual with Test Bank** includes Learning Objectives, a Chapter Outline, Key Terms, and a Test Bank. Each question in the Test Bank is coded to the appropriate Learning Objective for that question. This allows you the opportunity to focus on the Learning Objectives you feel are most important for your students to understand.

▶ The Lesson Plans include two sample syllabi, Learning Objectives, Lecture Notes, Discussion Topics, Class Activities, tips for classroom presentation of the chapter material, and Assignments.

Instructor Resources Cont.

Power**Lecture**™

The **PowerLecture DVD** is a compilation of all of the above tools except the Annotated Instructor's Edition, plus some additional resources. Included on the **PowerLecture DVD** are PowerPoint slides, an Image Library, the Instructor's Manual, the Test Bank, the Lesson Plans, ExamView, JoinIn for Clickers, and videos. ExamView includes all of the Test Bank questions from the Instructor's Manual with Test Bank in customizable electronic format. It creates tests for you and allows you to choose multiple choice, true/false, fill-in-the-blank and essay questions that focus on the Learning Objectives of your choice. Using ExamView, you can view the test results as you create the test, and edit the test as you create it.

▶ Microsoft® PowerPoint® slide presentations are available for each chapter of the textbook and provide a lecture presentation focused on the Learning Objectives.

What is Crime?

Crime:
1. Violates criminal law.

2. Is punishable by criminal sanctions.

Student Resources

The **Study Guide** is the student's version of the Instructor's Manual. It provides the student with the Learning Objectives for each chapter, a Chapter Outline, Key Terms and the pages on which they can be found in the textbook, special projects that can be used as assignments for class, and a Practice Test Bank with answers coded to the Learning Objectives.

CengageNOW is an interactive online learning resource for students. This tool provides students with study tools for each chapter such as essay questions, flashcards, and tutorial quizzes, all of which are centered on the Learning Objectives to ensure that students understand what material to focus on while studying.

Both the Study Guide and CengageNOW allow you to target your students' study time on the Learning Objectives while enabling you to communicate the focus of each chapter in the text to your students, as well as where you want them to be at the end of the term.

Learning Objectives

After reading this chapter, you should be able to:

LO1: Describe the two most common models of how society determines which acts are criminal.
LO2: Define "crime" and list the different types of crime.
LO3: Outline the three levels of law enforcement.
LO4: List the essential elements of the correctional system.
LO5: Explain the difference between the formal and informal criminal justice processes.
LO6: Describe the layers of the "wedding cake" model.
LO7: Contrast the crime control and due process models.
LO8: List the major issues in criminal justice today.

Chapter Outline

Section Two:

Using the Supplements to Integrate Learning Objectives into Your Classroom

One of the first tasks for you in teaching using Learning Objectives is to tie them into the Chapter Outline and lecture materials. This process is made easy through the use of the supplementary materials discussed in Section One. Let's take a look at how each of these supplements can work for you.

The Instructor's Manual with Test Bank is available to instructors in print and electronically. The Instructor's Manual portion can be downloaded from the companion website for the book, and the full version is available electronically as part of the PowerLecture DVD or through a download by contacting your Cengage Learning sales representative. The Lesson Plans and PowerPoint slides are both available

electronically as a download by contacting your Cengage Learning sales representative, or as part of the PowerLecture DVD.

The Instructor's Manual with Test Bank includes a Chapter Outline for each chapter of the textbook adopted for your class. A quick look at each of the headings for the Outline provides you with the ability to tie each section of the Outline to the Learning Objectives for that chapter. For example, in *Criminal Justice in Action: The Core*, the Learning Objectives for Chapter One can be linked directly to the sections in the Outline. Table 2.1 demonstrates how each of the Learning Objectives for this chapter connects to the Outline in the Instructor's Manual.

Table 2.1 Connection Between Learning Objectives and Outline Sections

Learning Objective	Outline Section
1. Describe the two most common models that show how society determines which acts are criminal.	3. Values of the Criminal Justice System
2. Define crime and identify the different types of crime.	1. What is Crime
3. Outline the three levels of law enforcement.	2. The Criminal Justice System
4. List the essential elements of the corrections system.	2. The Criminal Justice System
5. Explain the difference between the formal and informal criminal justice processes.	2. The Criminal Justice System
6. Describe the layers of the "wedding cake" model.	2. The Criminal Justice System
7. Contrast the crime control and due process models.	3. Values of the Criminal Justice System

The Annotated Instructor's Edition is another powerful tool to help you teach using Learning Objectives. The marginal callouts mentioned in the first section (Teaching Tips, Discussion Tips, Web Tips, and Media Tips) correlate to the Learning Objectives, and can provide you with ideas as to how to generate discussion on the Learning Objectives and be creative in incorporating them into your classes. For example, regarding Learning Objective One from above, one of the Teaching Tips suggests having students research how violent crimes are classified in your state. It suggests asking students to name the specific circumstances required for each degree of an offense. Such an assignment not only explores the deeper meaning of crime but also investigates the criminal justice system in a way that can be more meaningful to the student as she or he considers the criminal justice system in her or his own local area.

Discussion Tips also help focus the class on Learning Objectives by providing topics for group and class discussion directly related to the Learning Objectives. One such Discussion Tip relates to Learning Objectives One and Three from above. The Discussion Tip suggests having students work in small groups to brainstorm examples of offenses that fit the conflict model of criminal justice, focusing on which groups hold the power and which do not. A discussion such as this not only focuses the students on the Learning Objectives, but also helps them understand how the different concepts in the Learning Objectives are applied in the criminal justice system.

The Annotated Instructor's Edition also provides an End of Chapter Summary with links to the Learning Objectives. This summary offers a synopsis of all of the Learning Objectives, providing a quick reference for review of the Learning Objectives prior to class discussion. Additionally, the End of Chapter Summary can be used as a tool in class to review the topics covered with students at the end of class, and reinforce discussion of any or all of the Learning Objectives covered.

The Study Guide incorporates the Learning Objectives as well as a Chapter Outline, Key Terms, and Practice Test Bank. Students can be assigned to group the Learning Objectives to the Outline, per the example above, prior to each class so they will come prepared. Additionally, just as the Instructor's Manual includes a Test Bank with answers mapped to the Learning Objectives, the Study Guide also provides the appropriate Learning Objectives with each answer to the Practice Test Bank questions, and the questions in the CengageNOW online tutorials test the student's knowledge of the Learning Objectives as well.

Using the PowerPoint slides allows you to lecture based on a PowerPoint presentation created specifically for each of the chapters in the book. The slides are prepared for you by instructors who teach the material, so they reflect what instructors using the book want to see in their classrooms. The Learning Objectives

are incorporated into the PowerPoint slides, making it quick and easy for you to lecture in the classroom using the Learning Objectives as your focus.

For those who prefer not to use PowerPoint slides, the Lesson Plans also include the Learning Objectives as the foundation for lectures, as well as discussion questions and possible activities to use in the classroom.

Including the Learning Objectives in your syllabus can also aid students in understanding the focus for each class session and help them to be prepared prior to class. These materials can all work together to allow you to organize classes easily and enable you to have a greater impact. See Figure 2.1 below for an example of a syllabus based on the information from Table 2.1. The materials included in the Instructor's Manual with

---

Figure 2.1 – Incorporating the Learning Objectives into a Class Syllabus

Professor Bell   Fall Semester – 2009

Syllabus – Criminal Justice in Action

Date	Text Book Chapter	Topics	Learning Objective(s)
9/12/2009	One	What is Crime?	Two
		The Criminal Justice System	Three, Four, Five, Six
		Values of the Criminal Justice System	One, Seven

Test Bank can differ slightly from book to book. They always include Learning Objectives, Key Terms, a Chapter Outline, Discussion Topics, Student Activities, and the Test Bank, but can also include Activity Suggestions for Online Courses, Internet Connections, and Using Media in the Classroom resources.

The Lesson Plans can help you integrate Learning Objectives into your teaching style in the classroom. The Learning Objectives are included in the sample syllabi and can also easily be integrated into the Chapter Outline as shown above.

Now that we have covered some of the materials available to assist you in Teaching Using Learning Objectives, we will discuss some other ways you can use the material included in these resources in your classroom.

Key Terms

Key Terms are a very helpful tool for implementing Learning Objectives while teaching in the classroom, and are provided in almost all of the supplemental materials we've discussed. As you read this supplement, think about the different classes you took as a student in college. In order to acquire an undergraduate degree it is almost always necessary to take classes known as "core" classes. These classes are not directly related to the major you are taking, but are required of many undergraduate programs to ensure that students are well-rounded when they receive their degree.

One of the first things necessary when taking a class in a field you are not familiar with is to learn the language. Medical students must learn medical terminology, psychology students must learn psychological terminology, and criminal justice students must learn criminal justice terminology. Therefore, for a student to be able to gain a firm grasp of the concepts in the Learning Objectives, it is necessary to understand the language of that material. One of the best ways to understand the language is to first learn the Key Terms.

Sociological theories of crime explain the causes of criminal behavior the social conditions that bear on the individual. Three types of sociological theory are social structure theories, social process theories, and critical theories, including social conflict theories.

Feminist theories call attention to scholars' neglect of women's criminal behavior. Such theories often take a

Analyze crime causation theories and women offenders

The criminality of women has only recently been studied. Some argue that, as society increasingly treats women and men as equals, the number of crimes committed by women will increase.

Theories of criminality are criticized for focusing too exclusively on lower-class and male perpetrators.

Questions for Review

1. What are the six types of crimes?
2. What are the positive and negative attributes of the two major sources of crime data?
3. Who is most likely to be victimized by crime?
4. What are the costs of crime?
5. How does the criminal justice system treat victims?
6. What are the major theories of criminality?
7. What have scholars learned about the criminal behavior of women?

Key Terms and Cases

anomie (p. 00)
biological explanations (p. 00)
classical criminology (p. 00)
control theories (p. 00)
crimes without victims (p. 00)
criminogenic (p. 00)
critical criminology (p. 00)
cyber crimes (p. 00)
dark figure of crime (p. 00)
feminist theories (p. 00)
integrated theories (p. 00)
labeling theories (p. 00)

learning theories (p. 00)
life course theories (p. 00)
mala in se (p. 00)
mala prohibita (p. 00)
money laundering (p. 00)
National Crime Victimization Surveys (NCVS) (p. 00)
National Incident-Based Reporting System (NIBRS) (p. 00)
occupational crimes (p. 00)
organized crime (p. 00)
political crime (p. 00)

positivist criminology (p. 00)
psychological explanations (p. 00)
social conflict theories (p. 00)
social process theories (p. 00)
social structure theories (p. 00)
sociological explanations (p. 00)
theory of differential association (p. 00)
Uniform Crime Reports (UCR) (p. 00)
victimology (p. 00)
visible crime (p. 00)

Each of the Key Terms can be directly categorized under a Learning Objective. Although each of the Key Terms are directly related to one particular Learning Objective, some of them may apply to more than one. Table 3.1 shows an example of how the Key Terms connect to the Learning Objectives in Chapter One of *Criminal Justice in Action: The Core*.

Table 3.1 Connection between Learning Objectives and Key Terms

Learning Objective	Key Terms
1. Describe the two most common models that show how society determines which acts are criminal.	Consensus model, conflict model
2. Define crime and identify the different types of crime.	Crime, deviance, murder, sexual assault, assault, larceny, battery, public order crime, white-collar crime, organized crime, terrorism
3. Outline the three levels of law enforcement.	Homeland Security
4. List the essential elements of the criminal justice system.	Federalism, criminal justice system
5. Explain the difference between the formal and informal criminal justice processes.	Federalism, criminal justice system, discretion, Civil Rights
6. Describe the layers of the "wedding cake" model.	"Wedding Cake" Model
7. Contrast the crime control and due process models.	Crime Control Model, Due Process Model

A good example of an ongoing homework assignment is to have the students list each Learning Objective with the Key Terms that are related to it and explain how they are related. The assignment should be due on the day of class that each topic is to be covered. This provides an opportunity for class discussion as well as opening students up to interject a fresh perspective on the material. Although the Key Terms do apply to some Learning Objectives more than others, it is important to remember that such an assignment is primarily about getting the student to think about the Key Terms and the Learning Objectives, and how they apply to the subject of that particular chapter. Thus, it is possible that more than one answer is correct in such an assignment.

The Key Terms can also be used in class or as a homework assignment using some of the study tools available to the student through CengageNOW.

Flashcards of Key Terms are available for students and instructors, and can be used as an activity in class to keep students involved.

Students can be asked to define a Key Term and then relate it to the appropriate Learning Objective. One way to increase participation with this kind of exercise is to offer extra credit points for correlating the definitions with the correct Learning Objectives. The amount of extra credit does not have to be large, and an activity such as this accomplishes several goals at the same time. First, students quickly learn that the way to gain extra credit is to come to class. Second, the students will relate the Key Terms to the Learning Objectives and develop an understanding of the language necessary to understand the information. Finally, students are encouraged to participate in class. It's a good idea to limit the number of times each student can answer, so as to allow all students the opportunity to participate.

Section Four:

Online Study Tools

CengageNOW provides online study tools that allow students to take Pre- and Post-tests with questions that correlate directly to the Learning Objectives. As you can see in the figure below, the student can take a Pre-test on material related to the Learning Objectives, and the program offers them a personalized study plan based on the results of the Pre-test. After the student has completed the personalized study plan, a Post-test evaluates her or his improved comprehension of the chapter content. The student has electronic access to all of the information from the chapter as he or she is studying, and can access video information as well.

Use of tools such as these can not only help you incorporate Learning Objectives into your teaching in the classroom, but can also help make the material more compelling for the student. Reviewing material in more than one format can help students gain a better grasp of the material by reinforcing the same information in various contexts.

Additionally, making the material available to students in more than one format helps ensure that all students are presented the material in a format which is most conducive to their learning style.

Section Five:

Conclusion

Although we have covered a number of ways that Learning Objectives can be used as part of teaching in the classroom, there are many more possibilities. The goal of this supplement is to provide you with a few examples of how you can incorporate Learning Objectives into your teaching style to make teaching easier and more productive.

All of the tools provided to instructors by Cengage Learning can aid you in teaching using Learning Objectives. These tools are available in a number of different platforms to enable you to choose the version you're most comfortable with, that best suits your teaching style and the various learning styles of your students. Whether you prefer using print supplements such as the Instructor's Manual with Test Bank or Annotated Instructor's Edition, the electronic option of the PowerLecture that includes everything on a single DVD, or the CengageNOW convenience of interactive online tools, Cengage Learning has a resource for you and your students. Incorporating the tools created specifically for use with the textbook you use in your class can make teaching more rewarding for you and more effective for your students.

Teaching using Learning Objectives has the potential to make your classroom, whether traditional or online, a learning-friendly environment in which students can get the most out of the academic experience. Providing students with alternatives to traditional lecture formats can make for a more dynamic and successful learning experience. Teaching a class that is enjoyable for students makes the teaching experience enjoyable as well. We hope that this supplement has provided you with some ideas on how to incorporate Learning Objectives into your classroom and how to make better use of the tools available to you to help your students learn the material you present in class.

Part I

THE NATURE of CRIME, LAW, and CRIMINAL JUSTICE

On April 29, 2009, Mohamad Ibrahim Shnewer was sentenced to life in a federal prison, and his partner Serdar Tatar received a sentence of 33 years; there is no parole in the federal system. What did these men do to earn such a harsh punishment? They, along with four other co-conspirators, were convicted of plotting to kill members of the U.S. military during an armed attack on U.S. military personnel at Fort Dix in New Jersey. The defendants were arrested on May 7, 2007, after they attempted to purchase four automatic M-16 rifles and three semi-automatic AK-47 rifles, which they planned to use in this attack. The gun dealer was in reality a confidential federal informant. During their trial, evidence showed that group members conducted surveillance at Fort Dix and Fort Monmouth in New Jersey, Dover Air Force Base in Delaware, and the U.S. Coast Guard base in Philadelphia. The co-conspirators obtained a detailed map of Fort Dix, where they hoped to use assault rifles to kill as many soldiers as possible, according to trial testimony. During the trial, the jury viewed secretly recorded videotapes of the defendants engaging in small-arms training at a shooting range in the Pocono Mountains in Pennsylvania and watching, among themselves, training videos that included depictions of American soldiers being killed and of known foreign Islamic radicals urging jihad against the United States.

Photo credit: © Rick Friedman/Corbis

> It is therefore more important than ever for students of criminal justice to understand what the facts of the justice process are—and what popularly held beliefs are merely fiction. Are acts of violence skyrocketing, or is that merely an impression created by the media? Do all criminal defendants enjoy equal protection under the law and assurances of a fair trial, or are these rights reserved only for American citizens?

This case illustrates the complex types of crimes that agents of the justice system are now facing. It is therefore more important than ever for students of criminal justice to understand what the facts of the justice process are—and what popularly held beliefs are merely fiction. Are acts of violence skyrocketing, or is that merely an impression created by the media? Do all criminal defendants enjoy equal protection under the law and assurances of a fair trial, or are these rights reserved only for American citizens? The first section of *Essentials of Criminal Justice* deals with these issues in some detail. Chapter 1 reviews the criminal justice process, Chapter 2 analyzes the nature and extent of crime in the United States, and Chapter 3 looks at the substance and procedures of criminal law.

Chapter 1
Crime and Criminal Justice

Chapter 2
The Nature of Crime and Victimization

Chapter 3
Criminal Law: Substance and Procedure

1

CRIME AND CRIMINAL JUSTICE

RealityCheck

MYTH or REALITY?

▶ We live in a very violent society; there is more crime today than ever before.

▶ Police departments are an American creation, the first having been formed in New York City after the Civil War.

▶ At its core, the justice system is designed to protect the public from those people who cannot abide by or obey the law.

▶ Just as on *Law and Order* and similar shows, the agencies of the justice system work closely together to solve cases, process offenders, and punish the guilty.

▶ There is equal justice under the law, and everyone can expect to get their day in court.

▶ Justice tends to be objective rather than subjective; agents of the justice system put their personal feelings aside in the course of their duties.

▶ Seeking justice is often confounded by ethical dilemmas that may be difficult to resolve.

Learning Objectives

1. Be able to define the concept of criminal justice
2. Be aware of the long history of crime in America
3. Discuss the formation of the criminal justice system
4. Name the three basic component agencies of criminal justice
5. Comprehend the size and scope of the contemporary justice system
6. Trace the formal criminal justice process
7. Know what is meant by the term "criminal justice assembly line"
8. Discuss the "wedding cake" model of justice
9. Be familiar with the various perspectives on justice
10. Understand the ethical issues involved in criminal justice

Chapter Outline

© VCL/Chris Ryan/Taxi/Getty Images

Career Profile

Oris Buckner is a municipal police officer in New Orleans. Otis got involved in criminal justice through his mother, who also was associated with the New Orleans Police Department and heard about a cadet program for young people between the ages of 17 and 19. These cadets would work for the police department during the day and attend college at night. A government grant was awarded to each cadet, and one of the stipulations was that cadets who remained in the criminal justice field for two years after receiving an undergraduate degree would not have to repay the grant. Buckner used the program for both an education and a job: He now holds a bachelor's degree in Criminal Justice from Loyola University of the South, in New Orleans, and a master's degree in Criminal Justice from Southern University at New Orleans.

Buckner found police work challenging. He had to succeed in a police department where African American police officers were not well received by some of their white coworkers *or* by the African American community. To overcome these challenges, he had to stay focused on the reasons why he went into law enforcement in the first place: to make a difference; to be respected; and to be ethical, moral, fair, sincere, and committed.

Buckner claims that the greatest reward he gets from police work is knowing that he has made a difference in someone's world. Police officers, he believes, are society's vanguard against those who would prey on others or disrupt the social order. A man of strong beliefs, he is grateful for the opportunity to serve his fellow citizens. He recognizes that police are humans who make mistakes. Yet, he knows that most police officers are willing to put their lives on the line to protect citizens, their property, their rights, and the social order, so that all can feel safe and secure in their daily lives.

Buckner is a strong advocate of education. By being exposed to different viewpoints and experiences, police officers can come to understand why some people are involved in criminality. Education also taught him to appreciate the concepts of deterrence, treatment, therapy, prevention, and restoration. He learned that there are alternatives to incarceration that are more cost-effective and beneficial to both the offender and society. Criminal justice education taught him to be a more critical and analytical thinker, which helps him make on-the-job decisions.

Police officers such as Oris Buckner are the backbone of the criminal justice system.

Criminal justice may be defined as *the system of law enforcement, adjudication, and correction that is directly involved in the apprehension, prosecution, and control of those charged with criminal offenses*. This loosely organized collection of agencies is responsible for, among other matters, protecting the public, maintaining order, enforcing the law, identifying transgressors, bringing the guilty to justice, and treating criminal behavior. The public depends on this vast system not only to protect them from evil-doers and to bring justice to their lives but also to maintain order and protect the fabric of society.

This textbook serves as an introduction to the study of criminal justice. This area of research and scholarship includes describing, analyzing, and explaining the behavior of those agencies authorized by law and statute to dispense justice—police departments, courts, and correctional agencies—and helping these institutions to identify effective and efficient methods of crime control.

As we engage in this study, we also wish to set straight some of the myths and legends that have grown up about the justice system. Many people form opinions about criminal justice from the media, which often leads to false impressions and unrealized expectations. In the movies and on TV, it takes police about an hour to catch even the most wily criminal, shootouts and car chases are routine, and every criminal defendant receives a lengthy trial in front of an attentive jury. Journalists help perpetuate these myths: Newspaper headlines routinely feature stories exposing brutal cops and violent prisons. How true are these images of justice? How can we separate myth from reality? Throughout this textbook we will confront such myths and legends and try to sort out the facts from the fiction.

criminal justice process
The decision-making points, from the initial investigation or arrest by police to the eventual release of the offender and his or her reentry into society; the various sequential criminal justice stages through which the offender passes.

This chapter introduces some basic issues, beginning with a discussion of the history of crime in America and the development of criminal justice. The major organizations and **criminal justice processes** of the criminal justice system are then introduced as an overview of how the system functions. Because there is no single view of the underlying goals that help shape criminal justice, the varying perspectives on what criminal justice really is, or should be, are set out in some detail.

Is Crime a Recent Development?

Crime and violence have existed in the United States for more than 200 years. In fact, the crime rate may actually have been much higher in the nineteenth and early twentieth centuries than it is today.[1] Guerilla activity was frequent before, during, and after the Revolutionary War. Bands supporting the British—the Tories—and the American revolutionaries engaged in savage attacks on each other, using hit-and-run tactics, burning, and looting.

The struggle over slavery during the mid-nineteenth century generated decades of conflict, crimes, and violence, including a civil war. After the war, night riders and the Ku Klux Klan were active in the South, using vigilante methods to maintain the status quo and terrorize former slaves. The violence spilled over into bloody local feuds in the hill country of southern Appalachia. Factional hatreds, magnified by the lack of formal law enforcement and grinding poverty, gave rise to violent attacks and family feuding.

After the Civil War, former Union and Confederate soldiers headed west with the dream of finding gold or starting a cattle ranch. Some even resorted to murder, theft, and robbery, such as outlaws like John Wesley Hardin (who is alleged to have killed 30 men, studied law in prison, and became a practicing attorney before his death), Billy the Kid, and Johnny Ringo. Opposing them were famous lawmen such as Wyatt Earp (who, along with his brothers Virgil and Morgan and gunfighter Doc Holliday, fought the Cowboy gang led by Johnny Ringo and Curly Bill Brocius, killing three Cowboys at the famous gunfight at the O.K. Corral in Tombstone, Arizona, on October 26, 1881), and Bat Masterson, who became a sports columnist in New York after hanging up his guns!

Just as the Civil War generated western gunslingers, it also produced widespread business crime. The great robber barons bribed government officials and managed to corner markets and obtain concessions for railroads, favorable land deals, and mining and mineral rights on government land. The administration of President Ulysses Grant was tainted by numerous corruption scandals.

REALITYCHECK

MYTH OR REALITY? We live in a very violent society; there is more crime today than ever before.

MYTH: There was more crime and violence in the nineteenth century than there is today.

Despite what you may read in the newspapers or see on TV, America was a more violent place in years gone by. Those familiar media images of frontiersmen carrying six guns and getting into bar fights is not far from the truth. Are the conditions that produce violence today similar to what made the country violent in the nineteenth century, or have conditions changed?

Crime at the Turn of the Twentieth Century

From 1900 to 1935, the nation experienced a sustained increase in criminal activity. This period was dominated by Depression-era outlaws, including the infamous "Ma" Barker (and her sons Lloyd, Herman, Fred, and Arthur), Bonnie Parker and Clyde Barrow, and Lester Gillis (also known as Baby Face

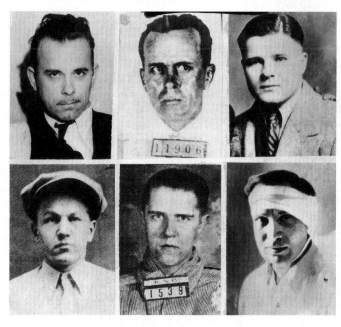

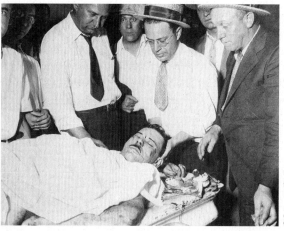

At the turn of the last century, rural outlaws became mythic figures. Here are photos of the FBI's six most wanted men in 1934. Charles "Pretty Boy" Floyd (left photo, top right of the group) was a folk hero among the sharecroppers of eastern Oklahoma. Floyd robbed as many as 30 banks, filing a notch in his pocket watch for each of the 10 men he killed. Floyd was shot dead by police on October 19, 1934. John Dillinger (right photo and left photo, top left of the group) became the nation's premier bank robber until he was killed in front of a Chicago movie house on July 22, 1934. After his death, his body was put on view at the morgue. Hordes of people came to view America's most notorious criminal.

Nelson), George "Machine Gun" Kelly, and Charles "Pretty Boy" Floyd. The most notorious of the bunch, bank robber John Dillinger, cut a swath through the Midwest until he was slain on Sunday, July 22, 1934, in a shootout with federal agents in front of a Chicago movie house.

While these relatively small and mobile outlaw gangs were operating in the Midwest, organized gangs flourished in the nation's largest cities. The first criminal gangs formed before the Civil War in urban slums, such as the Five Points and Bowery neighborhoods in New York City. Although they sported colorful names, such as the Plug Uglies, the Hudson Dusters, and the Dead Rabbits, they engaged in mayhem, murder, and extortion. These gangs were the forerunners of the organized crime families that developed in New York and then spread to Philadelphia, Chicago, New Orleans, and other major urban areas.

Developing the Criminal Justice System

The emergence of criminal gangs and groups in the nineteenth century coincided with the development of formal agencies of criminal justice. In 1829 the first police agency, the London Metropolitan Police, was developed to keep the peace and identify criminal suspects. In the United States, the first police agencies were created in Boston (1838), New York (1844), and Philadelphia (1854). The penitentiary, or prison, was created to provide nonphysical

REALITYCHECK

correctional treatment for convicted offenders; these were considered "liberal" innovations that replaced corporal or capital punishment.

Although significant and far-reaching, these changes were rather isolated developments. As criminal justice developed over the next century, these fledgling agencies of justice rarely worked together in a systematic fashion. It was not until 1919—when the Chicago Crime Commission, a professional association funded by private contributions, was created—that the work of the criminal justice system began to be recognized.[2] This organization acted as a citizens' advocate group and kept track of the activities of local justice agencies. The commission still carries out its work today.

In 1931 President Herbert Hoover appointed the National Commission of Law Observance and Enforcement, which is commonly known today as the Wickersham Commission. This national study group made a detailed analysis of the U.S. justice system and helped usher in the era of treatment and rehabilitation. The final report found that thousands of rules and regulations governed the system and made it difficult for justice personnel to keep track of the system's legal and administrative complexity.[3]

The Modern Era of Justice

The modern era of criminal justice can be traced to a series of research projects begun in the 1950s under the sponsorship of the American Bar Foundation.[4] Originally designed to provide in-depth analysis of the organization, administration, and operation of criminal justice agencies, the ABF project discovered that the justice system contained many procedures that had been hidden from the public view. The research focus then shifted to an examination of these previously obscure processes and their interrelationship—investigation, arrest, prosecution, and plea negotiations. It became apparent that justice professionals used a great deal of personal choice in decision making, and showing how this discretion was used became a prime focus of the research effort. For the first time, the term "criminal justice system" began to be used, reflecting a view that justice agencies could be connected in an intricate yet often unobserved network of decision-making processes.

Federal Involvement in Criminal Justice

In 1967 the President's Commission on Law Enforcement and Administration of Justice (the Crime Commission), which had been appointed by President Lyndon Johnson, published its final report, entitled *The Challenge of Crime in a Free Society*.[5] This group of practitioners, educators, and attorneys was given the responsibility of creating a comprehensive view of the criminal justice process and recommending reforms. In 1968 Congress passed the Safe Streets and Crime Control Act, providing for the expenditure of federal funds for state and local crime control efforts and launching a massive campaign to restructure the justice system.[6] It funded the National Institute of Law Enforcement and Criminal Justice (NILECJ), which encouraged research and development in criminal justice. Renamed the National Institute of Justice (NIJ) in 1979, it has continued its mission as a major source of funding for the implementation and evaluation of innovative experimental and demonstration projects in the criminal justice system.[7]

Careers in Criminal Justice

MUNICIPAL POLICE OFFICER

Duties

- Enforcing the written laws and ordinances of the jurisdiction.
- Duties may be routine, such as writing a speeding ticket, or more involved, such as responding to a domestic disturbance or investigating a robbery.
- Testifying in court; writing reports of law enforcement actions.
- May choose or be chosen to work in specialized units such as Special Weapons and Tactics (SWAT) or canine corps (K9).

Job Characteristics

- Intense and stressful at times; may entail encounters with hostile and potentially violent people.
- Shifts may fall on weekends and holidays; younger police officers often take these less desirable shifts.
- Overtime; 45-hour work weeks are common.

Job Outlook

- Opportunities are expected to grow at an average rate; positions open regularly through attrition and retirement in most departments.
- Officers are usually employed at the local level, often in larger urban or suburban areas; most opportunities exist in areas with comparatively higher crime rates or lower salaries.

Salary

- Median annual salary is almost 50,000; most officers earn between $35,000 and $60,000. Those who ascend the ranks of their department to lieutenant or go into a specialization will earn higher salaries. Median annual salary of detectives is about $60,000 and of detective supervisors is about $70,000.

Opportunities

- Excellent benefits and retirement policies.
- College education improves one's chances of being hired.
- With job experience and a reputation for good work, officers can rise in the ranks of their department or be assigned to desirable positions such as detective or investigator.

Qualifications

- Physical and mental fitness is necessary.
- Candidates must pass written tests and can expect to be administered lie detector and drug tests.
- Key personal qualities include responsibility, good communications skills, good judgment, and the ability to make quick decisions.
- A high school diploma is sufficient in some jurisdictions, but many are requiring at least some college education.

Education and Training

- Higher education, generally in the form of a bachelor's degree in a relevant field, is often required or at least suggested for promotion to senior rank.
- Rigorous training and testing are required before officers are allowed on the streets, normally 12–14 weeks of police academy training.
- Recruits are trained in diverse skills, including self-defense and first aid, as well as knowledge of laws, procedures, and citizens' rights.

Word to the Wise

- The job often has long hours, including weekends and holidays.
- There is stress related to exposure to traumatic incidents and violence.
- If you plan a police career, stay out of trouble. Don't get involved in any form of substance abuse, including DWI/DUI.
- Don't borrow money you can't afford to repay (e.g., have a poor credit history).
- If you do get into trouble, do not lie about it during the hiring process.

than 14 million people are still being arrested each year, including more than 2 million for serious felony offenses.[9] In addition, about 1.5 million juveniles are handled by the juvenile courts. Today, state and federal courts convict a combined total of over 1 million adults on felony charges.[10]

Today, more than 7.3 million people are under some form of correctional supervision, including 2.3 million men and women in the nation's jails and prisons and an additional 5.1 million adult men and women being supervised in the community while on probation or parole (see Exhibit 1.1). Even though the crime rate has been in decline for most of the past decade, this correctional population continues to grow, and the number of people in the correctional system has trended upward (Figure 1.3). How can this trend be explained? There is less crime, but people are more likely to be convicted than in the past and, if sent to prison or jail, to serve more of their sentence (Figure 1.4).

Adult Correctional Populations (millions), 1980–2007

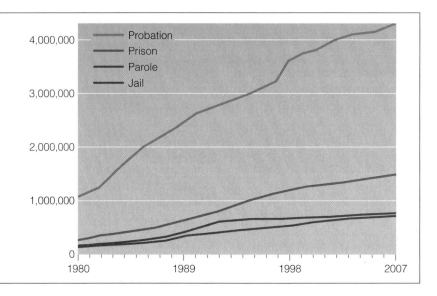

FIGURE 1.3

Felony Convictions in State Courts

Source: *Felony Sentences in State Courts, 2004*

http://www.ojp.usdoj.gov/bjs/glance/felconv.htm.

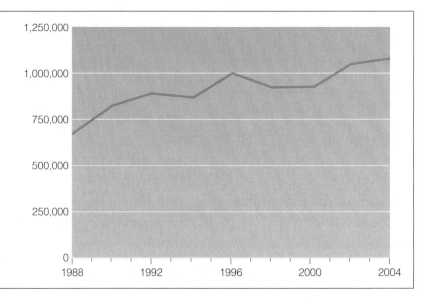

FIGURE 1.4

EXHIBIT 1.1

Elements of the Correctional System

Probation Court-ordered community supervision of convicted offenders by a probation agency. Offenders on probation are required to obey specific rules of conduct while in the community.

Prison A state or federal correctional facility that houses convicted criminals who have been sentenced to a period of confinement that is typically more than 1 year.

Jail A county correctional facility that holds people pending trial, awaiting sentencing, serving a sentence that is usually less than 1 year, or awaiting transfer to other facilities after conviction.

Parole Community supervision after a period of incarceration.

The Formal Criminal Justice Process

Another way of understanding criminal justice is to view it as a process that takes an offender through a series of decision points beginning with arrest and concluding with reentry into society. During this process, key decision makers resolve whether to maintain the offender in the system or discharge the suspect without further action. This decision making is often a matter of individual discretion, based on a variety of factors and perceptions. Legal factors, including the seriousness of the charges, available evidence, and the suspect's prior record, are usually considered legitimate influences on decision making. Troubling is the fact that such extralegal factors as the suspect's race, gender, class, and age may also influence decision outcomes. Some critics believe that a suspect's race, class, and gender largely determine the direction a case will take, whereas supporters argue that the system is relatively fair and unbiased.[11]

In reality, few cases actually are processed through the entire formal justice system. Most are handled informally and with dispatch. The system of justice has been roundly criticized for its "backroom deals" and bargain justice. Although informality and deal making are in fact the rule, the concept of the formal justice process is important because it implies that every criminal defendant charged with a serious crime is entitled to a full range of rights under law. The fact that most criminal suspects are actually treated informally may be less important than the fact that all criminal defendants are entitled to a full range of legal rights and constitutional protections.

A comprehensive view of the formal criminal process would normally include the following:

1. ***Initial contact.*** In most instances, an offender's initial contact with the criminal justice system takes place as a result of a police action:

   • Patrol officers observe a person acting suspiciously, conclude the suspect is under the influence of drugs, and take her into custody.

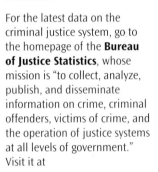

Bureau of Justice Statistics

For the latest data on the criminal justice system, go to the homepage of the **Bureau of Justice Statistics**, whose mission is "to collect, analyze, publish, and disseminate information on crime, criminal offenders, victims of crime, and the operation of justice systems at all levels of government." Visit it at

www.cengage.com/criminaljustice/siegel

MYTH OR REALITY? Just as on *Law and Order* and similar shows, the agencies of the justice system work closely together to solve cases, process offenders, and punish the guilty.

MYTH: There is actually little contact among the agencies of justice.

The police are seldom consulted when a prosecutor decides to offer the defendant a deal or when a judge sentences the convicted offender to probation instead of prison. And the judge and prosecutor may have little knowledge of how the corrections system decides to deal with convicted offenders or when they release them on parole. What would you do to improve communications among these agencies of the law?

- Police officers are contacted by a victim who reports a robbery; they respond by going to the scene of the crime and apprehend a suspect.
- An informer tells police about some ongoing criminal activity in order to receive favorable treatment.
- Responding to a request by the mayor or other political figure, the local department may initiate an investigation into an ongoing criminal enterprise such as gambling, prostitution, or drug trafficking.
- A person walks into the police station and confesses to committing a crime—for example, killing his wife after an altercation.

2. *Investigation.* The purpose of the criminal investigation is to gather sufficient evidence to identify a suspect and support a legal arrest. An investigation can take only a few minutes, as in the case where a police officer sees a crime in progress and can apprehend the suspect quickly. Or it can take many years and involve hundreds of law enforcement agents. Dennis Rader, the notorious BTK ("Bind, Torture, Kill") serial killer began his murderous streak in 1974 and was finally apprehended in 2005 after an investigation that lasted more than 20 years.[12]

3. *Arrest.* An arrest is considered legal when all of the following conditions exist: (1) the police officer believes there is sufficient evidence, referred to as *probable cause*, that a crime is being or has been committed and the suspect is the person who committed it; (2) the officer deprives the individual of freedom; and (3) the suspect believes that he is now in the custody of the police and has lost his liberty. The police officer is not required to use the word "arrest" or any similar term to initiate an arrest, nor does the officer have to bring the suspect to the police station. In most cases, to make an arrest in a misdemeanor, the officer must have witnessed the crime personally, a provision known as the **in-presence requirement**. Arrests can also be made when a magistrate, presented with sufficient evidence by police, issues a warrant authorizing the arrest of the suspect.

4. *Custody.* After an arrest and while the suspect is being detained, the police may wish to search for evidence, conduct an interrogation, or even encourage a confession. Witnesses may be brought to view the suspect in a lineup or in a one-on-one confrontation. Because these procedures are so crucial and can have a great impact at trial, the U.S. Supreme Court has granted suspects in police custody protection from the unconstitutional abuse of police power, such as illegal searches and intimidating interrogations.

5. *Charging.* If the arresting officers or their superiors believe that sufficient evidence exists to charge a person with a crime, the case will be turned over to the prosecutor's office. The prosecutor's decision to charge the suspect with a specific criminal act involves many factors, including evidence sufficiency, crime seriousness, case pressure, and political issues, as well as personal factors such as a prosecutor's own specific interests and biases. After conducting a preliminary investigation of its legal merits, prosecutors may decide to take no further action in a case; this is referred to as dropping the case **nolle prosequi**.

6. *Preliminary hearing/grand jury.* The U.S. Constitution mandates that before a trial can take place, the government must first prove probable cause that the accused committed the crime for which he is being charged. In about half the states and in the federal system, this determination is made by a **grand jury** in a closed hearing. If the prosecution can present sufficient evidence, the grand jury will issue a **true bill of indictment**, which specifies the exact charges on which the accused must stand trial. In the remaining states, the prosecution will file a charging document (usually called an *information*) before a lower trial court, which then conducts an open hearing on the merits of the case. During this procedure, which is sometimes referred to as a *probable cause hearing*, the defendant and

in-presence requirement
The condition that in order to make an arrest in a misdemeanor, the arresting officer must have personally witnessed the crime being committed.

nolle prosequi
The term used when a prosecutor decides to drop a case after a complaint has been formally made. Reasons for a nolle prosequi include evidence insufficiency, reluctance of witnesses to testify, police error, and office policy.

grand jury
A type of jury responsible for investigating alleged crimes, examining evidence, and issuing indictments.

true bill of indictment
A written statement charging a defendant with the commission of a crime, drawn up by a prosecuting attorney and considered by a grand jury. If the grand jury finds sufficient evidence to support the indictment, it will issue a true bill of indictment.

Some jurisdictions maintain the grand jury system for indictments while others now use preliminary hearings. The federal justice system is one that still employs the grand jury. Former San Francisco Giants baseball player Barry Bonds arrives at the federal courthouse in San Francisco, California, on June 6, 2008. Bonds pleaded not guilty to 15 felony charges of lying to a federal grand jury about his use of performance-enhancing drugs. At the time of this writing, his trial has not taken place.

© AP Images/Marcio Jose Sanchez

the defendant's attorney may appear and dispute the prosecutor's charges. The suspect will be called to stand trial if the presiding magistrate or judge accepts the prosecutor's evidence as factual and sufficient.

7. ***Arraignment.*** Before the trial begins, the defendant will be arraigned, or brought before the court that will hear the case. At this time, formal charges are read, the defendant is informed of his constitutional rights (for example, the right to be represented by legal counsel), an initial plea (not guilty or guilty), is entered, a trial date set, and bail issues are considered.

8. ***Bail/detention.*** Bail is a money bond levied to ensure the return of a criminal defendant for trial, allowing the defendant to remain in the community prior to trial. Defendants who do not show up for trial forfeit their bail. Those people who cannot afford to put up bail or who cannot borrow sufficient funds for it will remain in state custody prior to trial. In most instances, this means an extended stay in a county jail or house of correction. If they are stable members of the community and have committed nonviolent crimes, defendants may be released on their own recognizance (promise to the court), without bail.

9. ***Plea bargaining.*** After an arraignment, or even before, the defense and prosecution will discuss a possible guilty plea in exchange for the prosecution's reducing or dropping some of the charges or agreeing to a request for a more lenient sentence. It is generally accepted that almost 90 percent of all cases end in a plea bargain, rather than a criminal trial.

10. ***Trial/adjudication.*** If an agreement cannot be reached or if the prosecution does not wish to arrange a negotiated settlement of the case, a criminal trial will be held before a judge (bench trial) or jury, who will decide whether the prosecution's evidence against the defendant is sufficient beyond a reasonable doubt to prove guilt. If a jury cannot reach a decision—that is, if it is deadlocked—the case is left unresolved, leaving the prosecution to decide whether it should be retried at a later date.

11. ***Sentencing/disposition.*** If after a criminal trial the accused has been found guilty as charged, he will be returned to court for sentencing. Possible dispositions may include a fine, probation, some form of community-based corrections, a period of incarceration in a penal institution, or, in rare instances, the death penalty.

12. *Appeal/postconviction remedies.* After conviction, the defense can ask the trial judge to set aside the jury's verdict because the jury has made a mistake of law—for example, by misinterpreting the judge's instructions or convicting on a charge that was not supported by the evidence. Failing that, an appeal may be filed if after conviction the defendant believes that her constitutional rights were violated by errors in the trial process. Appellate courts review such issues as whether evidence was used properly, the judge conducted the trial in an approved fashion, jury selection was properly done, and the attorneys in the case acted appropriately. If the court rules that the appeal has merit, it can hold that the defendant be given a new trial or, in some instances, order his outright release.

13. *Correctional treatment.* After sentencing, the offender is placed within the jurisdiction of state or federal correctional authorities. The offender may serve a probationary term, be placed in a community correctional facility, serve a term in a county jail, or be housed in a prison. During this stage of the criminal justice process, the offender may be asked to participate in rehabilitation programs designed to help her make a successful readjustment to society.

14. *Release.* Upon completion of the sentence and period of correction, the offender will be free to return to society. Most inmates do not serve the full term of their sentence but are freed through an early-release mechanism, such as parole or pardon or by earning time off for good behavior. Offenders sentenced to community supervision simply finish their term and resume their lives in the community.

15. *Postrelease.* After termination of their correctional treatment, offenders may be asked to spend some time in a community correctional center, which acts as a bridge between a secure treatment facility and absolute freedom. Offenders may find that their conviction has cost them some personal privileges, such as the right to hold certain kinds of employment. These privileges may be restored by court order once the offenders have proved their trustworthiness and willingness to adjust to society's rules.

The Criminal Justice Assembly Line

To justice expert Herbert Packer, the image that this process evokes is an assembly line conveyor belt down which moves an endless stream of cases, never stopping.[13] According to this view, each of the 15 stages is actually a *decision point* through which cases flow. At the investigatory stage, police must decide whether to pursue the case or terminate involvement because there is insufficient evidence to identify a suspect, the case is considered trivial, the victim decides not to press charges, and so on. At the bail stage, a decision must be made whether to set bail so high that the defendant remains in custody, to set a reasonable bail, or to release the defendant on his or her own recognizance without requiring any bail at all. Each of these decisions can have a critical effect on the defendant, the justice system, and society. If an error is made, an innocent person may suffer or a dangerous individual may be released to continue to prey upon society.

Figure 1.5 illustrates the approximate number of offenders removed from the criminal justice system at each stage of the process. As the figure shows, most people who commit crime escape detection, and of those who do not, relatively few are bound over for trial, convicted, and eventually sentenced to prison. About 30 percent of people arrested on felony charges are eventually convicted in criminal court; however, nearly a third of those convicted on felony charges are sentenced to probation and released back into the community without doing time in prison.[14] For every 1,000 crimes, about 20 people are sent to prison.

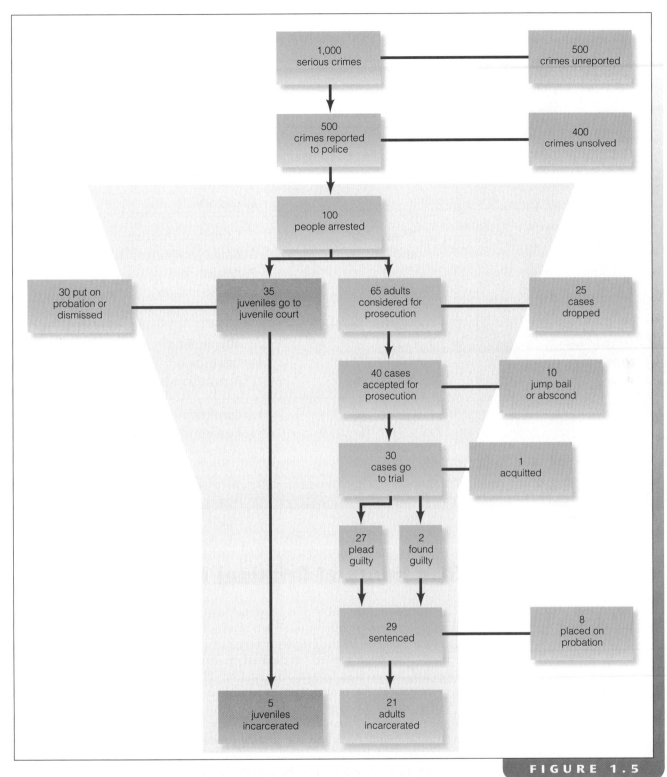

FIGURE 1.5

The Criminal Justice Funnel

Sources: Matthew Durose and Patrick Langan, *Felony Sentences in State Courts, 2004* (Washington, D.C.: Bureau of Justice Statistics, 2007); Thomas Cohen and Brian Reaves, *Felony Defendants in Large Urban Counties, 2002* (Washington, D.C.: Bureau of Justice Statistics, 2006).

In actual practice, many suspects are released before trial because of a procedural error, evidence problems, or other reasons that result in a case dismissal by the prosecutor, or nolle prosequi. Although most cases that go to trial end in a conviction, others are dismissed by the presiding judge because of a witness or a complainant's failure to appear or procedural irregularities. Thus the justice process can be viewed as a funnel that holds many cases at its mouth and relatively few at its end. Concept Summary 1.1 shows the interrelationship of the component agencies of the criminal justice system and the criminal justice process.

Concept Summary 1.1

The Interrelationship of the Criminal Justice System and the Criminal Justice Process

The System: Agencies of Crime Control	The Process
1. Police	1. Contact
	2. Investigation
	3. Arrest
	4. Custody
2. Prosecution and Defense	5. Complaint/charging
	6. Grand jury/preliminary hearing
	7. Arraignment
	8. Bail/detention
	9. Plea negotiations
3. Court	10. Adjudication
	11. Disposition
	12. Appeal/postconviction remedies
4. Corrections	13. Correction
	14. Release
	15. Postrelease

The Informal Criminal Justice System

The traditional model of the criminal justice system depicts the legal process as a series of fifteen decision points through which cases flow. Each stage of the system, beginning with investigation and arrest and ending after a sentence has been served, is defined by time-honored administrative procedures and controlled by the rule of law. This "ideal" model of justice still merits concern and attention, but it would be overly simplistic to assume that the system works this way for every case. Although a few cases exhibit the full array of procedures, many are settled in an informal pattern of cooperation between the major actors in the justice process. For example, police may be willing to make a deal with a suspect in order to gain his cooperation, and the prosecutor may bargain with the defense attorney to gain a plea of guilty as charged in return for a promise of leniency. Law enforcement agents and court officers are allowed tremendous discretion in deciding whether to make an arrest, bring formal charges, handle a case informally, substitute charges, and so on. Crowded courts operate in a spirit of getting the matter settled quickly and cleanly, rather than engaging in long, drawn-out criminal proceedings with an uncertain outcome.

Whereas the traditional model regards the justice process as an adversarial proceeding in which the prosecution and defense are combatants, most criminal cases are actually cooperative ventures in which all parties get together to work out a deal; this is often referred to as the **courtroom work group**.[15] Made up of the prosecutor, defense attorney, judge, and other court personnel, the courtroom work group helps streamline the process of justice through the extensive use of deal making and plea negotiation. Rather than looking to provide a spirited defense or prosecution, the defense attorney and prosecutor usually focus much more on cooperation than on conflict. It is only in a few widely publicized criminal cases involving rape or murder that the adversarial process is called into play. Consequently, upward of 80 percent of all felony cases and over 90 percent of misdemeanors are settled without trial.

courtroom work group
The phrase used to indicate that all parties in the adversary process work together cooperatively to settle cases with the least amount of effort and conflict.

The "Wedding Cake" Model of Justice

Samuel Walker, a justice historian and scholar, has come up with a rather unique way of describing this informal justice process: He compares it to a four-layer cake, as depicted in Figure 1.6.[16]

LEVEL I ● The first layer of Walker's model is made up of celebrated cases involving the wealthy and famous, such as O. J. Simpson and Michael Vick, or the not-so-powerful who victimize a famous person—for example, John Hinckley, Jr., who shot President Ronald Reagan. Other cases fall into the first layer because they are widely reported in the media and become the subject of a TV investigation, one such defendant was Scott Peterson, convicted of killing his wife, Laci.

REALITYCHECK

MYTH OR REALITY? There is equal justice under the law, and everyone can expect to get their day in court.

MYTH: In practice, few cases find their way to court, and most are settled informally with a plea bargain.

Do you have an alternative to the plea bargaining system? What would happen if all criminal cases were settled with a formal trial rather than a plea agreement?

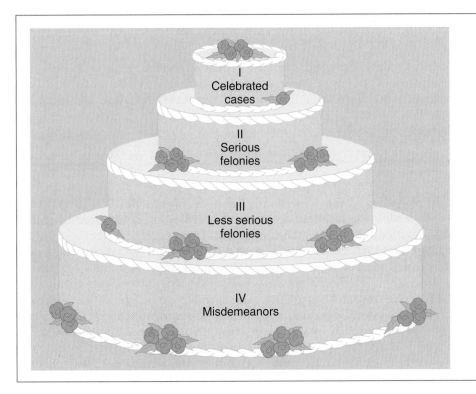

The Criminal Justice "Wedding Cake"

Source: Based on Samuel Walker, *Sense and Nonsense about Crime* (Belmont, Calif.: Wadsworth, 2001).

I
Celebrated cases

II
Serious felonies

III
Less serious felonies

IV
Misdemeanors

FIGURE 1.6

High-profile cases garner the greatest amount of criminal justice attention and effort. No recent case has attracted more national attention than the July 16, 2009, arrest of Harvard professor Henry Louis Gates. Returning home from a trip to China, Gates found the door to his house jammed. As he and his driver attempted to gain entrance, a neighbor called police and reported a possible break-in. When Cambridge, Massachusetts, police officers arrived, a confrontation developed, resulting in Gates being arrested and charged with disorderly conduct. Prosecutors later dropped the charges. The fact that a very prominent African American academic was suspected of breaking into his own home and then taken away in handcuffs sparked a great deal of discussion about race relations and the police. The arresting officer, police sergeant James Crowley, an 11-year veteran of the force, was accused of racism, even though, as one of the responsibilities entrusted to him during his career, he had been in charge of training officers to avoid such practices as racial profiling in their police work. In the aftermath of the incident, Sergeant Crowley and Professor Gates were invited by President Barack Obama "for a beer" at the White House to discuss race relations.

Cases in the first layer of the criminal justice wedding cake usually receive the full array of criminal justice procedures, including competent defense attorneys, expert witnesses, jury trials, and elaborate appeals. Because of the media focus on Level I cases and the Hollywood treatment of them, the public is given the impression that most criminals are sober, intelligent people and most victims are members of the upper classes, a patently false impression.

LEVEL II • The second layer contains serious felonies—rapes, robberies, and burglaries. Police, prosecutors, and judges all agree that these are serious cases, worthy of the full attention of the justice system. The seriousness of the offense places them in the Level II category:

- They are committed by experienced, repeat offenders.
- The amount of money stolen in a burglary or larceny is significant.
- Violent acts are committed by a stranger who uses a weapon.
- Robberies involve large amounts of money taken by a weapon-wielding criminal.

Offenders in Level II cases receive a full jury trial and, if convicted, can look forward to a prison sentence.

LEVEL III • Although they can also be felonies, crimes that fall in the third layer of the wedding cake either are less serious offenses, committed by young or first-time offenders, or involve people who knew each other or were otherwise related. Level III crimes may be dealt with by an outright dismissal, a plea bargain, reduction in charges, or (most commonly) a probationary sentence.

LEVEL IV • The fourth layer of the cake is made up of the millions of misdemeanors—disorderly conduct, shoplifting, public drunkenness, and minor assault—that are handled by the lower criminal courts in assembly-line fashion. Few defendants insist on exercising their constitutional rights, because the delay would cost them valuable time and money, and punishment is typically a fine or probation.[17]

The wedding cake model of informal justice is an intriguing alternative to the traditional criminal justice flowchart. Criminal justice officials handle individual cases quite differently, yet there is a high degree of consistency with which particular types or classes of cases are handled in every legal jurisdiction. For example, police and prosecutors in Los Angeles and Boston will handle the murder of a prominent citizen in similar fashion. They will also deal with the death of an unemployed street person killed in a brawl in a similar manner. The wedding cake model is useful because it helps us realize that public opinion about criminal justice is often formed on the basis of what happened in an atypical case.

Perspectives on Justice

Even though it has been more than 35 years since the field of criminal justice began to be the subject of both serious academic study and attempts at unified policy formation, significant debate continues over the actual meaning of *criminal justice* and how the problem of crime control should be approached. After decades of effort in research and policy analysis, it is clear that criminal justice is far from a unified field. Practitioners, academics, and commentators alike have expressed irreconcilable differences concerning its goals, purpose, and direction. Considering the complexity of criminal justice, it is not surprising that no single perspective or philosophy dominates the field. What are the dominant views of the criminal justice system today? What is the role of the justice system, and how should it approach its tasks? The different perspectives on criminal justice are discussed next.

Crime Control Perspective

People who hold the **crime control perspective** believe that the proper role of the justice system is to prevent crime through the judicious use of criminal sanctions. Because the public is outraged by violent crimes, it demands an efficient justice system that hands out tough sanctions to those who choose to violate the law.[18] If the justice system were allowed to operate in an effective manner, unhampered by legal controls, potential criminals would be deterred from violating the law. Those who did commit a crime would be apprehended, tried, and punished so that they would never dare commit a crime again. Crime rates trend upward, the argument goes, when criminals do not sufficiently fear apprehension and punishment. If the efficiency of the system could be increased and the criminal law could be toughened, crime rates would eventually decline. Effective law enforcement, strict mandatory punishment, incarceration of dangerous criminals, and the judicious use of capital punishment are the keys to reducing crime rates. Crime control may be expensive, but reducing the pain inflicted by criminal activity is well worth the price. If punishment were swift, certain, and severe, few would be tempted to break the law.

Crime control advocates do not want legal technicalities to help the guilty go free and tie the hands of justice. They lobby for the abolition of legal restrictions on a police officer's ability to search for evidence and interrogate suspects. They want law enforcement officers to be able to profile people at an airport in order to identify terrorists, even if it means singling out individuals because of their gender, race, or ethnic origin. They are angry at judges who let obviously guilty people go free because a law enforcement officer made an unintentional procedural error.

crime control perspective
A model of criminal justice that emphasizes the control of dangerous offenders and the protection of society. Its advocates call for harsh punishments as a deterrent to crime and support availability of the death penalty.

In sum, the key positions of the crime control perspective are these:

- The purpose of the justice system is to deter crime through the application of punishment.
- The more efficient the system, the greater its effectiveness.
- The justice system is not equipped to treat people but, rather, to investigate crimes, apprehend suspects, and punish the guilty.

Rehabilitation Perspective

rehabilitation perspective
The view that the primary purpose of criminal justice is helping to care for people who cannot manage themselves. Crime is an expression of frustration and anger that is created by social inequality and can be controlled by giving people the means to improve their lifestyle through conventional endeavors.

Whereas the crime control perspective views the justice system in terms of protecting the public and controlling criminal elements, advocates of the **rehabilitation perspective** view crime as an expression of frustration and anger created by social inequality and see the justice system as a means of caring for and treating people who have been the victims of this inequity. According to this view, crime can be controlled by giving people the means to improve their lifestyle and helping them overcome any personal and or psychological problems caused by their life circumstances.

The rehabilitation concept assumes that people are at the mercy of social, economic, and interpersonal conditions and interactions. Criminals themselves are the victims of racism, poverty, strain, blocked opportunities, alienation, family disruption, and other social problems. Many (such as Seung-Hui Cho, who killed more than 30 students and teachers at Virginia Tech in 2007) seem mentally and emotionally unstable. They live in socially disorganized neighborhoods that are incapable of providing proper education, health care, or civil services. Society must help them in order to compensate for their social problems. Punishment cannot deter these people but proper treatment may prevent their crimes.

Rehabilitation advocates believe that government programs can help reduce crime on both a societal (macro-) and individual (micro-) level. On the macro-, or societal, level, rehabilitation efforts are aimed at preventing crimes before they occur. If legitimate opportunities increase, crime rates decline.[19] This goal may be achieved at the neighborhood level by increasing economic opportunities through job training, family counseling, educational services, and crisis intervention. On a micro-, or individual, level, rehabilitation efforts are aimed at known offenders who have already violated the law. The best way to reduce crime and recidivism (repeat offending) rates is to help offenders, through intensive one-on-one counseling, adopt prosocial changes in attitudes and improved cognitive thinking patterns.[20] Although the public may want to "get tough" on crime, many are willing to make exceptions—for example, by advocating leniency for younger offenders.[21]

The key provisions of the rehabilitation model are these:

- In the long run, it is better to treat than punish.
- Criminals are society's victims.
- Helping others is part of the American culture.
- Convicted criminals can be successfully treated within the confines of the justice system.

Due Process Perspective

due process perspective
Due process is a basic constitutional principle based on the concept of the privacy of the individual and the complementary concept of limitation on governmental power; it is a safeguard against arbitrary and unfair state procedures in judicial or administrative proceedings. Embodied in the due process concept are the basic rights of a defendant in criminal proceedings and the requirements for a fair trial. See the Glossary for further details.

According to the **due process perspective**, the justice system should be dedicated to providing fair and equitable treatment to those accused of crime.[22] This means providing impartial hearings, competent legal counsel, evenhanded treatment, and reasonable sanctions to ensure that no one suffers from racial, religious, or ethnic discrimination and that their basic constitutional rights are respected.

Those who advocate the due process orientation are quick to point out that the justice system remains an adversarial process that pits the forces of an all-powerful state against those of a solitary individual accused of a crime. If concern for justice and fairness did not exist, the defendant who lacked resources could easily be overwhelmed; miscarriages of justice are common. Numerous criminal convictions have been overturned because newly developed DNA evidence later showed that the accused could not have committed the crimes; many of the falsely convicted spend years in prison before their release.[23] Evidence also shows that many innocent people have been executed for crimes they did not commit.[24] Because such mistakes can happen, even the most apparently guilty offender deserves all the protection the justice system can offer.

The key positions advocated by due process supporters include the following:

- Every person deserves her or his full array of constitutional rights and privileges.
- Preserving the democratic ideals of American society takes precedence over the need to punish the guilty.
- Because of potential errors, decisions made within the justice system must be carefully scrutinized.
- Steps must be taken to treat all defendants fairly regardless of their sex, socioeconomic status, race, religion, or ethnicity.

A 2003 case decided by the Supreme Court, *Sattazahn v. Pennsylvania* (see the Policies, Programs, and Issues in Criminal Justice feature on page 24, addresses two issues of key concern to advocates of the due process model: double jeopardy and imposition of the death penalty. The decision in the case

Those who are concerned about due process fear that innocent people are routinely convicted of crimes they did not commit, so the criminal justice system must be carefully monitored. Here, on January 30, 2009, in New Lisbon, Wisconsin, Robert Lee Stinson (facing camera) hugs a family friend as his sister Charlene Stinson, right, wipes her tears. Stinson, 44, had just walked out of the New Lisbon Correctional Institution after serving 23 years in prison for a crime he did not commit. A judge vacated the sentence after reviewing new bite-mark analysis and DNA evidence that proved Stinson's innocence.

© AP Images/Andy Manis

(1) shows how issues of due process influence the application of criminal justice and (2) illustrates that what seems fair and just to one decision maker may appear to another to be unfair and a violation of due process.

Policy, Programs, and Issues in Criminal Justice

Due Process in Action: *Sattazahn v. Pennsylvania*

One of the myths of criminal justice is that all people are treated equally under the law and that every citizen is entitled to due process. However, the interpretations of due process of law are not fixed but rather reflect what society deems fair and just at a particular time and place. The degree of loss suffered by the individual (victim or offender) balanced against the state's interests also determines which and how many due process requirements are ordinarily applied. When the Supreme Court justices are conservative, as they are now, they are less likely to create new rights and privileges under the guise of due process.

The Court's decision in the case of *Sattazahn v. Pennsylvania* (2003) helps define the concept of due process within the context of the double-jeopardy clause of the Fifth Amendment. Sattazahn had been sentenced to death under a Pennsylvania law that requires that the sentencing jury must unanimously find that the case warranted capital punishment. If the jury cannot unanimously agree on the sentence, then the court must enter a life sentence. After he was convicted of murder, Sattazahn's jury became deadlocked on the sentence; the trial judge discharged them and entered a life sentence. Later, Sattazahn appealed the conviction and received a new trial. At the second trial, the prosecutor again sought the death penalty and Sattazahn was again convicted, but this time the jury imposed a death sentence. Sattazahn appealed once again on the grounds that imposition of the death sentence after he had originally

received a life sentence was a violation of double jeopardy. However, the Supreme Court disagreed, finding that jeopardy was not compromised in this case. When a defendant is convicted of murder and sentenced to life imprisonment but succeeds in having the conviction set aside on appeal, jeopardy has not terminated, so a life sentence imposed in connection with the initial conviction raises no double-jeopardy bar to a death sentence on retrial. If the jury had met in a trial-like hearing and decided against imposition of the death penalty, then the outcome would have been different. But the fact that they deadlocked meant that no final decision had been reached; the result could not be called an "acquittal" within the context of double jeopardy. Sattazahn had gambled by appealing his conviction and lost.

SATTAZAHN V. PENNSYLVANIA aptly illustrates how due process demands that the individual's rights must be balanced against the state's interests. In this case, the Supreme Court decided to interpret the double-jeopardy clause very narrowly, ruling that it applied only when a jury decides that an actual element of the prosecutor's case has not been proved. A more liberal Court might have decided that due process demands that Sattazahn be spared the death penalty because the life sentence, mandated by law in the first trial, terminated the proceedings in his favor and barred the imposition of the death penalty in the second trial.

© Mike Kemp/Rubberball Productions/Getty Images

Critical Thinking

1. Do you believe Sattazahn was treated shabbily by the Court? Does this decision inhibit the appellate process if people can receive a much more severe sentence at a second trial? Or did Sattazahn reap what he sowed?

2. Does due process include rights not mentioned in the Constitution? For example, the Sixth Amendment allows one to have legal representation at trial. Should a free lawyer be provided to indigent people? The Constitution doesn't say anything about providing free lawyers.

Sources: *Sattazahn v. Pennsylvania*, 537 U.S. 101 (2003).

Nonintervention Perspective

Supporters of the **nonintervention perspective** believe that justice agencies should limit their involvement with criminal defendants. They believe that regardless of whether intervention is designed to punish people or to treat them, the ultimate effect of any involvement is harmful and will have long-term negative consequences. Once involved with the justice system, criminal defendants develop a permanent record that follows them for the rest of their lives. They may be watched and kept under surveillance. Bearing an official label disrupts their personal and family life and harms their own self-image; they may view themselves as bad, evil, outcasts, troublemakers, or crazy. Official labels then may promote rather than reduce the continuity in antisocial activities.[25] When people are given less stigmatized forms of punishment, such as probation, they are less likely to become repeat offenders.[26]

Fearing the harmful effects of stigma and labels, noninterventionists have tried to place limitations on the government's ability to control people's lives. They have called for the **decriminalization** (reduction of penalties) and **legalization** (lawful and noncriminal) of nonserious **victimless crimes**, such as the possession of small amounts of marijuana. Noninterventionists have sponsored the removal of nonviolent offenders from the nation's correctional system, a policy referred to as **deinstitutionalization**. They support the placement of first offenders who commit minor crimes in informal, community-based treatment programs, a process referred to as **pretrial diversion**.

Noninterventionists fear that efforts to help or treat offenders may actually stigmatize them beyond the scope of their actual offense; this is referred to as **widening the net of justice**. Their efforts have resulted in rulings stating that these laws can be damaging to the reputation and the future of offenders who have not been given an opportunity to defend themselves from the charge that they are chronic criminal sex offenders.[27] As a group, noninterventionist initiatives have been implemented to help people avoid the stigma associated with contact with the criminal justice system.

The key elements of the nonintervention perspective include the following:

- The justice process stigmatizes offenders.
- Stigma locks people into a criminal way of life.
- Less is better. Decriminalize, divert, and deinstitutionalize whenever possible.

Equal Justice Perspective

According to those who take the **equal justice perspective**, the greatest challenge facing the American criminal justice system is its responsibility to dispense fair and equal justice to those who come before the law. It is unfair for police to issue a summons to one person for a traffic violation, while letting a second offender off with a warning, or to have two people commit the same crime but receive different sentences or punishments. Unequal and inconsistent treatment produces disrespect for the system, suspiciousness, and frustration; it also increases the likelihood of recidivism. Therefore, law violators should be evaluated on the basis of their current behavior, not on what they have done in the past (they have already paid for that behavior) or on what they may do in the future (because future behavior cannot be accurately predicted). The treatment of criminal offenders must be based solely on their present behavior: Punishment must be equitably administered and based on "just desserts."

nonintervention perspective
A view of criminal justice that emphasizes the least intrusive treatment possible. Among its central policies are decarceration, diversion, and decriminalization. In other words, less is better.

decriminalization
Reducing the penalty for a criminal act but not actually legalizing it.

legalization
The removal of all criminal penalties from a previously outlawed act.

victimless crime
An act that is in violation of society's moral code and therefore has been outlawed—for example, drug abuse, gambling, and prostitution. These acts are linked because, although they have no external victim, they are considered harmful to the social fabric.

deinstitutionalization
The policy of removing as many offenders as possible from secure confinement and treating them in the community.

pretrial diversion
A program that provides nonpunitive, community-based alternatives to more intrusive forms of punishment such as jail or prison.

widening the net of justice
The view that programs designed to divert offenders from the justice system actually enmesh them further in the process by substituting more intrusive treatment programs for less intrusive punishment-oriented outcomes.

equal justice perspective
The view that all people should be treated equally before the law. Equality may best be achieved through individual discretion in the justice process.

The equal justice perspective has had considerable influence in molding the nation's sentencing policy. There has been an ongoing effort to reduce discretion and to guarantee that every offender convicted of a particular crime receives equal punishment. There have been a number of initiatives designed to achieve this result, including mandatory sentences requiring that all people convicted of a crime receive the same prison sentence. **Truth-in-sentencing laws** now require offenders to serve a substantial portion of their prison sentence behind bars, limiting their eligibility for early release on parole.[28]

The key elements of the equal justice perspective are these:

* People should receive equal treatment for equal crimes.
* Decision making in the justice system must be standardized and structured by rules and regulations.
* Whenever possible, individual discretion must be reduced and controlled.
* Inconsistent treatment produces disrespect for the system.

Restorative Justice Perspective

According to the concept of restorative justice, the criminal justice system should promote a peaceful and just society; the justice system should aim for peacemaking, not punishment.[29]

The **restorative justice perspective** draws its inspiration from religious and philosophical teachings ranging from Quakerism to Zen. Advocates of restorative justice view the efforts of the state to punish and control as encouraging crime rather than discouraging it. The violent, punishing acts of the state are not dissimilar to the violent acts of individuals.[30] Therefore, mutual aid rather than coercive punishment is the key to a harmonious society. Without the capacity to restore damaged social relations, society's response to crime has been almost exclusively punitive.

According to restorative justice, resolution of the conflict between criminal and victim should take place in the community in which it originated,

truth-in-sentencing laws
A sentencing scheme requiring that offenders serve at least 85 percent of their original sentence before being eligible for parole or other forms of early release.

restorative justice perspective
A view of criminal justice that advocates peaceful solutions and mediation rather than coercive punishments.

Inmate James Burton Jr. waters the "Restorative Justice Gardens" at the Southeast Correctional Center in Charleston, Missouri, on September 5, 2007. Inmates have produced tens of thousands of pounds of fresh vegetables from a six-acre garden at the state prison complex, all of it donated to the Bootheel Food Bank in Sikeston, Missouri, which serves some of the poorest counties in the state. Should society attempt to restore law violators back to the community, or should violators merely be punished for their misdeeds?

© AP Images/Jeff Roberson

not in some far-off prison. Under these conditions, the victim has a chance to tell his story, and the offender can directly communicate his need for social reintegration and treatment. The goal is to enable the offender to appreciate the damage he has caused, to make amends, and to be reintegrated into society.

Restorative justice programs are now being devised to reflect to these principles. Police officers, as elements of community policing programs, are beginning to use mediation techniques to settle disputes, rather than resorting to formal arrest.[31] Mediation and conflict resolution programs are common features in many communities and are being used in efforts to resolve harmful human interactions ranging from domestic violence to hate crimes.[32] Financial and community service restitution programs as an alternative to imprisonment have been in operation for more than two decades.

The most important elements of the restorative justice model are the following:

- Offenders should be reintegrated into society.
- Coercive punishments are self-defeating.
- The justice system must become more humane.

Perspectives in Perspective

Advocates of each view have attempted to promote their vision of what justice is all about and how it should be enforced. During the past decade, the crime control and justice models have dominated. Laws have been toughened and the rights of the accused curtailed, the prison population has grown, and the death penalty has been employed against convicted murderers. Because the crime rate has been dropping, these policies seem to be effective; they may be questioned if crime rates once again begin to rise. At the same time, efforts to rehabilitate offenders, to provide them with elements of due process, and to give them the least intrusive treatment have not been abandoned. Police, courts, and correctional agencies supply a wide range of treatment and rehabilitation programs to offenders in all stages of the criminal justice system. Whenever possible, those accused of crime are treated informally in nonrestrictive, community-based programs, and the effects of stigma are guarded against. Although the legal rights of offenders are being closely scrutinized by the courts, the basic constitutional rights of the accused remain inviolate. Guardians of the process have made sure that defendants are allowed the maximum protection possible under the law. For example, criminal defendants have been awarded the right to competent legal counsel at trial; merely having a lawyer to defend them is not considered sufficient legal protection.

In sum, understanding the justice system today requires analyzing a variety of occupational roles, institutional processes, legal rules, and administrative doctrines. Each predominant view of criminal justice provides a vantage point for understanding and interpreting these rather complex issues. No single view is *the* right or correct one. Each individual must choose the perspective that best fits his or her own ideas and judgment—or to propose a different

REALITY CHECK

MYTH OR REALITY? Justice tends to be objective rather than subjective; agents of the justice system put their personal feelings aside in the course of their duties.

MYTH: Agents of the justice system have varied and differing perspectives on what justice is all about and how they should approach their role and duties.

Some police officers, court officers, and correctional personnel practice a "law and order" orientation, whereas others are more interested in helping and treating offenders. What other professions maintain competing values and viewpoints?

view that combines elements of all the perspectives or expresses the individual's own view in a new and unique way.

Ethics in Criminal Justice

The general public and criminal justice professionals are also concerned with the application of ethics in the criminal justice system.[33] Both would like every police officer on the street, every district attorney in court, and every correctional administrator in prison to be able to discern what is right, proper, and moral, to be committed to ethical standards, and to apply equal and fair justice. These demands are difficult because justice system personnel are often forced to work in an environment where moral ambiguity is the norm. For example, should a police officer be forced to arrest, a prosecutor charge, and a correctional official punish a woman who for many years was the victim of domestic abuse and who in desperation retaliated against her abusive spouse? Who is the victim here and who is the aggressor? And what about the parent who attacks the man who has sexually abused her young child? Should she be prosecuted as a felon? But what happens if the parent mistakenly attacks and injures the wrong person? Can a clear line be drawn between righteous retribution and vigilante justice? As students of justice, we are concerned with identifying the behavioral standards that should govern each of the elements of justice. If these can be identified, is it possible to find ways to apply these standards to police, court, and correctional agencies around the nation?

Ethics in criminal justice is an especially important topic today because of the power granted to those who control the justice system. We rely on the justice system to exert power over people's lives and to be society's instrument of social control, so we grant the system and its agents the authority to deny people their personal liberty on a routine basis. A police officer's ability to arrest and use force, a judge's power to sentence, and a correctional administrator's ability to punish an inmate give them considerable personal power that must be governed by ethical considerations. Without ethical decision making, it is possible that individual civil rights will suffer and that personal liberties guaranteed by the U.S. Constitution will be trampled upon. The need for an ethical criminal justice system is further enhanced by cyber-age advances in record keeping and data recording. Agents of the criminal justice system now have immediate access to our most personal information, ranging from arrest records to medical history. Issues of privacy and confidentiality—which can have enormous economic, social, and political consequences—are now more critical than ever. Take the case of Seung-Hui Cho, the Virginia

Ethics violations taint the criminal justice system and undermine its credibility. If we can't trust the keepers, whom can we trust? Here, on June 5, 2007, former state Supreme Court Justice Gerald Garson, center, and a member of his legal team react as he is sentenced to three to ten years in prison in Brooklyn for accepting cash, cigars, and other expensive gifts in exchange for helping fix divorce cases.

Tech killer. Did the authorities go too far to protect his privacy and hide his psychological problems? Should students be warned about peers who are unstable or who have court orders requiring they get psychological treatment? We now maintain sex offender registration lists. Should we register the mentally unstable as well?

Ethical issues transcend all elements of the justice system. Yet each branch has specific issues that shape its ethical standards, as we will see in the following sections.

Ethics and Law Enforcement

Ethical behavior is particularly important in law enforcement because, quite simply, police officers have the authority to deprive people of their liberty. And, in carrying out their daily activities, they also have the right to use physical and even deadly force.

Depriving people of liberty and using force are not the only police behaviors that require ethical consideration. Police officers exercise considerable discretion when they choose whom to investigate, how far the investigation should go, and how much effort is required—for example, undercover work, listening devices, or surveillance. In carrying out their duties, police officers must be responsive to the public's demand for protection, while at the same time remaining sensitive to the rights and liberties of those they must deter and/or control. In this capacity, they serve as the interface between the power of the state and the citizens it governs. This duality creates many ethical dilemmas. Consider the following:

- Should law enforcement agents target groups who they suspect are heavily involved in crime and violence, or does this lead to racial/ethnic profiling? Is it unethical for a security agent to pay closer attention to a young Arab male getting on an airline flight than she pays to a well-groomed American soldier from upstate New York? After all, there have been no terrorist activities among army personnel, and the 9/11 terrorists were of Arab descent. But don't forget that the clean-cut Tim McVeigh, who grew up in rural Pendleton, New York, and spent more than three years in the army, went on to become the Oklahoma City bomber. How can police officers balance their need to protect public security with the ethical requirement that they safeguard citizens' legal rights?
- Should police officers tell the truth even if it means that a guilty person goes free? For example, a police officer stops a car for a traffic violation and searches it illegally. He finds a weapon used in a particularly heinous shooting in which three children were killed. Would it be ethical for the officer to lie on the witness stand and say the gun was resting on the car seat in plain sight (thereby rendering its seizure legal and proper)? Or should he tell the truth and risk having the charges dismissed, leaving the offender free to kill again?
- Should police officers be loyal to their peers even when they know a colleague has violated the law? A new officer soon becomes aware that his partner is taking gratuities from local gangsters in return for looking the other way and allowing their prostitution and

REALITY CHECK

MYTH OR REALITY?   Seeking justice is often confounded by ethical dilemmas that may be difficult to resolve.

REALITY: Agents of the justice system face ethical dilemmas on a daily basis.

Consider what you would do in this situation: As a police officer, you spy a fellow officer smoking marijuana at a party. Would you report her behavior to your superiors?

bookmaking operations to flourish. Should the rookie file a complaint and turn in his partner? Will she be labeled a "rat" and lose the respect of her fellow officers? After all, gambling and prostitution are not violent crimes and don't really hurt anyone. Or do they?

What help is available to law enforcement officers in making ethical decisions? Various national organizations have produced model codes of conduct that can serve as behavioral guides. One well-known document created by the International Association of Chiefs of Police says, in part,

> As a law enforcement officer my fundamental duty is to serve mankind; to safeguard lives and property; to protect the innocent against deception, the weak against oppression or intimidation, and the peaceful against violence or disorder; and to respect the constitutional rights of all men to liberty, equality, and justice . . .[34]

Ethics and the Courts

Ethical concerns do not stop with an arrest. As an officer of the court and the "people's attorney," the prosecutor must seek justice for all parties in a criminal matter and should not merely be targeting a conviction. To be fair, prosecutors must share evidence with the defense, must not use scare tactics or intimidation, and must represent the public interest. It would be inexcusable and illegal for prosecutors to suppress critical evidence, a practice that might mean the guilty walked free and the innocent were convicted.

Prosecutorial ethics become tested when the dual role of prosecutors cause them to experience role conflict. On the one hand, a prosecutor represents the people and has an obligation to present evidence, uphold the law, and obtain convictions as vigorously as possible. In the adversary system, it is the prosecutor who takes the side of victims and on whom they rely for justice.

But as a fair and impartial officer of the court, the prosecutor must oversee the investigation of crime and make sure that all aspects of the investigation meet constitutional standards. If during the investigation it appears that the police have violated the constitutional rights of suspects—for example, by extracting an illegal confession or conducting an illegal search—then the prosecutor has an ethical obligation to take whatever action is necessary and appropriate to remedy legal or technical errors, even if it means rejecting a case in which the defendant's rights have been violated. Moreover, the canon of legal ethics in most states forbids the prosecutor from pursuing charges when there is no probable cause and mandates that all evidence that might mitigate guilt or reduce the punishment be turned over to the defense.

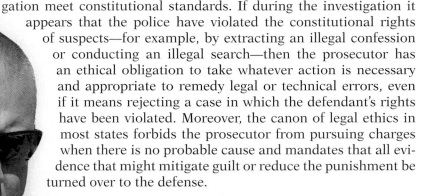

© moodboard/Corbis

DEFENSE ATTORNEY ● As an officer of the court, along with the judge, prosecutors, and other trial participants, the defense attorney seeks to uncover the basic facts and elements of the criminal act. In this dual capacity of being both a defensive advocate and an officer of the court, the attorney is often confronted with conflicting obligations to his client and profession. Suppose, for example, a client confides that she is planning to commit a crime. What are the defense attorney's ethical responsibilities in this case? Obviously, the attorney would have to counsel the client to obey the law; if the attorney assisted the client in engaging in illegal behavior, the attorney would be subject to charges of unprofessional conduct and even criminal liability.

What about the situation where an attorney knows that his or her client is guilty because the client admitted as much during pretrial conferences? Should the defense lawyer still try for an acquittal? What is said privately before trial, even at a plea discussion, is never admissible during trial. An attorney would be accused of incompetence if she or he did not try to raise reasonable doubt in every case. The attorney's job is not to decide whether the client committed the offense but to provide a vigorous defense and ensure that the client is not convicted unless the prosecution can prove its case beyond a reasonable doubt. And it is impossible to make the prosecution meet its burden without aggressively challenging the evidence, even if the defender believes the client committed the crime. However, if a client attempted to take the stand and lie about his involvement in the crime, then the attorney would be required to tell the judge.[35]

Ethics and Corrections

Ethical issues do not disappear once a defendant has been convicted. All the ethical issues in punishment are too vast to discuss here, but they include the following:

- Is it fair and ethical to execute a criminal? Can capital punishment ever be considered a moral choice?
- Should people be given different punishments for the same criminal law violation? Is it fair and just when some convicted murderers and rapists receive probation for their crimes while others are sentenced to prison for the same offense?
- Is it fair to grant leniency to criminals who agree to testify against their co-conspirators and therefore allow them to benefit from their perfidy, while others, who are not given the opportunity to "squeal," are forced to bear the full brunt of the law?
- Should some criminal inmates be granted early release because they can persuade the parole board that they have been rehabilitated, while others, who are not as glib, convincing, or well spoken, are forced to serve their entire sentence behind bars?
- Should technology be used to monitor offenders in the community? Would it be ethical to track a probationer's movements with a GPS unit attached to an ankle bracelet she is required to wear at all times? Should her Internet use and computer downloads be monitored.

Ethics is also challenged by the discretion afforded to correctional workers and administrators. Discretion is involved when a correctional officer decides whether to report an inmate for disorderly conduct, which might jeopardize his or her parole. And although the Supreme Court has issued many rulings related to prisoners' rights, no justices are at the scene of the prison to make sure that their mandates are carried out reliably and consistently.

Correctional officers have significant coercive power over offenders. They are under a legal and professional obligation not to use unnecessary force or take advantage of inmate powerlessness. Examples of abuse would be an officer who beats an inmate, or a staff member who coerces sex from an inmate. The possibility that these abuses of power will be perpetrated exists because of the powerlessness of the offender relative to the correctional professional. A recent national survey uncovered evidence that this breach of ethics is significant: An estimated 8,210 allegations of sexual violence were reported by correctional inmates. About 42 percent of the reported allegations of sexual violence involved staff-on-inmate sexual misconduct, and 11 percent involved staff sexual harassment of inmates. In other words, staff members were involved in more cases of sexual violence and harassment in correctional facilities than were inmates![36]

Ethical considerations transcend all elements of the justice system. Making ethical decisions is an increasingly important task in a society that is becoming more diverse, pluralistic, and complex every day.

ETHICAL CHALLENGES IN CRIMINAL JUSTICE

A Writing Assignment

Some experts believe that the justice system could operate more effectively if drugs were legalized and their trade controlled so that they could not fall into the hands of adolescents. This would be similar to the way we now regulate the sale of alcohol and cigarettes.

Write an essay addressing this issue. Remember to consider such topics as the consequences of regulating the sale of drugs: If juveniles, criminals, and members of other at-risk groups were forbidden to buy drugs, who would be the customers? Noncriminal, nonabusing, middle-aged adults? And would not those adolescents prohibited from legally buying drugs create an underground market almost as vast as the one for illegal alcohol?

RealityCheck Revisited

To learn more about the myths and realities related to the justice system that were presented in this chapter, visit the following websites.

- To read more about Wyatt Earp and other famous nineteenth-century lawmen and outlaws, go to

http://www.wyattearp.net/

http://oldwesthistory.net/oldwest2.html/

http://www.legendsofamerica.com/WE-Outlaws.html

- To read more about the development of the first police agency in the United States, go to

http://www.cityofboston.gov/police/glance.asp

- If you are interested in criminal justice ethics, you might want to check out this site, which has links to a variety of sources:

http://www.llrx.com/features/criminaljusticeethics.htm#criminal%20defense

SUMMARY

© VCL/Chris Ryan/Taxi/Getty Images

1. Be Able to Define the Concept of Criminal Justice

- The term "criminal justice" refers to the agencies that dispense justice and the process in which justice is carried out.

2. Be aware of the long history of crime and justice in America

- America has experienced crime throughout most of its history.

- In the Old West, justice was administered by legendary lawmen such as Wyatt Earp.

3. Discuss the formation of the criminal justice system

- There was little in the way of a formal criminal justice system until the nineteenth century when the first police agencies were created.

- The term "criminal justice system" became prominent around 1967, when the President's Commission on Law Enforcement and the Administration of Justice began a nationwide study of the nation's crime problem.

- Criminal justice is a field that uses knowledge from various disciplines in an attempt to understand what causes people to commit crimes and how to deal with the crime problem.

4. Name the three basic component agencies of criminal justice

- Criminal justice consists of the study of crime and of the agencies concerned with its prevention and control.

- On an ideal level, the criminal justice system functions as a cooperative effort among the primary agencies—police, courts, and corrections.

5. Comprehend the size and scope of the contemporary justice system

- The contemporary criminal justice system in the United States is monumental in size.

- It now costs federal, state, and local governments more than $200 billion per year for civil and criminal justice.

- The criminal justice system employs more than 2 million people.

- The system is massive because it must process, treat, and care for millions of people. More than 14 million people are still being arrested each year.

- There are more than 7 million people in the correctional system.

6. Trace the formal criminal justice process

- The process consists of the actual steps the offender takes from the initial investigation through trial, sentencing, and appeal.

- The justice process contains 15 stages, each of which is a *decision point* through which cases flow.

- Each of these decisions can have a critical effect on the defendant, the justice system, and society.

7. Know what is meant by the term "criminal justice assembly line"

- Some experts believe that the justice system processes cases in a routine, ritualized manner resembling an assembly line.

- Because justice is often dispensed in a hasty fashion, an innocent person may suffer or

(continued)

a dangerous individual may be released to continue to prey upon society.

- The system acts as a "funnel": Most people who commit crime escape detection, and of those who do not, relatively few are bound over for trial, convicted, and eventually sentenced to prison.

8. *Discuss the "wedding cake" model of justice*

- In many instances, the criminal justice system works informally to expedite the disposal of cases.

- Criminal acts that are very serious or notorious may receive the full complement of criminal justice processes, from arrest to trial. However, less serious cases are often settled when a bargain is reached between the prosecution and the defense.

9. *Be familiar with the various perspectives on justice*

- The role of criminal justice can be interpreted in many ways. People who study the field or work in its agencies bring their own ideas and feelings to bear when they try to decide on the right course of action to take or recommend. Thus there are a number of different perspectives on criminal justice today.

- The crime control perspective is oriented toward deterring criminal behavior and incapacitating serious criminal offenders.

- The rehabilitation model views the justice system as a treatment agency focused on helping offenders. Counseling programs are stressed over punishment and deterrence strategies.

- The due process perspective sees the justice system as a legal process. The concern of this view is that every defendant receive the full share of legal rights granted under law.

- The nonintervention model is concerned about stigma and helping defendants avoid a widening net of justice; these advocates call for the least intrusive methods possible.

- The justice model is concerned with making the system equitable. The arrest, sentencing, and correctional process should be structured so that every person is treated equally.

- The restorative justice model focuses on finding peaceful and humanitarian solutions to crime.

10. *Understand the ethical issues involved in criminal justice*

- The justice system must deal with many ethical issues. It is sometimes difficult to determine what is fair and just and to balance it with the need to protect the public.

Key Terms

criminal justice process, 6

Law Enforcement Assistance Administration (LEAA), 9

social control, 9

in-presence requirement, 14

nolle prosequi, 14

grand jury, 14

true bill of indictment, 14

courtroom work group, 19

crime control perspective, 21

rehabilitation perspective, 22

due process perspective, 22

nonintervention perspective, 25

decriminalization, 25

legalization, 25

victimless crime, 25

deinstitutionalization, 25

pretrial diversion, 25

widening the net of justice, 25

equal justice perspective 25

truth-in-sentencing laws, 26

restorative justice perspective 26

Review Questions

1. Can a single standard of ethics be applied to all criminal justice agencies? Or is the world too complex to legislate morality and ethics?

2. Describe the differences between the formal and informal justice systems. Is it fair to treat some offenders informally?

3. What are the layers of the criminal justice "wedding cake"? Give an example of a crime for each layer.

4. What are the basic elements of each model or perspective on justice? Which best represents your own point of view?

5. How would each perspective on criminal justice consider the use of the death penalty as a punishment for first-degree murder?

6. What amendments to the Constitution are the most important for the administration of justice?

THEY TOOK
HIS HOPES & DR
GIVE "EVREN
SO HE C
REST IN P

BEAUTIFUL LIFE
TAKEN FOR
NOTHING
LIFE IS FOR LIVING
NOT FOR
KILLING.....

2.

THE NATURE OF CRIME AND VICTIMIZATION

RealityCheck

MYTH or REALITY?

▶ The content of the criminal law is often shaped by moral crusaders and not by the will of the majority.

▶ Most crimes get reported to the police.

▶ Crime and violence rates are out of control and getting worse every day.

▶ A poor economy and high unemployment cause crime rates to increase.

▶ Becoming a crime victim is a matter of being "in the wrong place at the wrong time."

▶ Kids who watch a lot of violence on TV are more likely to get involved in violent behavior themselves.

Learning Objectives

1. Be able to discuss how crime is defined

2. Be familiar with the methods used to measure crime

3. Discuss the strengths and weaknesses of crime measures

4. Recognize the trends in the crime rate

5. Comment on the factors that influence crime rates

6. Be familiar with international crime trends

7. Know the various crime patterns

8. Understand the concept of the criminal career

9. Be able to discuss the characteristics of crime victims

10. Distinguish among the various views of crime causation

Chapter Outline

© Janine Wiedel Photolibrary/Alamy

Career Profile

Daisy Mongeau is an Investigator with the New Hampshire Public Defender's Office in Concord. Her job involves interviewing witnesses, writing reports, obtaining medical/court records, subpoenaing witnesses, taking pictures, interacting with clients, helping attorneys in trial preparation, and testifying at hearings. She finds that a lot of her friends just can't understand why she works so hard to defend people who are guilty, even those who have confessed to the crime. They don't seem to realize that all defendants are entitled to a criminal defense, even if they actually committed the crime!

After Daisy earned her bachelor's degree in Sociology and Justice Studies from the University of New Hampshire, she chose her career in criminal justice because she likes fighting for the "underdog" who would have no chance in the legal system without representation. The job is challenging. She has to locate witnesses who may not have a phone or permanent address by tracking them down through neighbors, friends, acquaintances, or anyone else who might know their location. She also has to work with the mentally ill in the course of defending them effectively when they are charged with a crime. When public defenders suspect that someone is mentally ill, they try to get help for their client through therapy, medication, or (if necessary) admission to the state hospital.

What is Mongeau's greatest reward? "Getting the prosecutor to drop the case nolle prosequi because of what a witness has told me during an investigation." She finds that clients are thrilled that someone actually believed them and helped them win the case. These are people not used to being given a helping hand.

People like Daisy Mongeau, who work on the front lines of the justice system, depend on accurate information about crime—where it occurs, who commits it, and why—in order for them to carry out their jobs in an effective and efficient manner.

For example, in the aftermath of a highly publicized mass killing, such as the 2007 Virginia Tech massacre by student Seung-Hui Cho, state legislators may want to pass legislation not only making it more difficult to buy firearms but also imposing mandatory prison terms on anyone caught with an illegally obtained handgun. The effectiveness of such legal measures could not be determined without accurate data measuring change in violent crime rates. Without the ability to measure crime accurately, it would be impossible to assess the effectiveness of crime control policy. Similarly, understanding the causes of crime is needed in order to plan effective measures for its elimination. Was Seung-Hui Cho's rampage motivated by exposure to violent media, alienation from society, or an inferior upbringing? It is difficult to prevent crime or treat criminals unless we can understand criminal motivation.

This chapter reviews some basic questions about crime addressed by criminal justice professionals: How is crime defined? How is crime measured? How much crime is there, and what are its trends and patterns? Why do people commit crime? How many people become victims of crime, and under what circumstances does victimization take place?

HOW IS CRIME DEFINED?

The justice system revolves around crime and its control. Although for most of us the concept of "crime" seems rather simple—a violation of criminal law—the question remains: Why are some acts considered a violation of the law while others, seemingly more serious and dangerous, remain legal and noncriminal? There are three views of how and why some behaviors become illegal and are considered crimes whereas others remain noncriminal.

Consensus View

consensus view of crime
The majority of citizens in a society share common ideals and work toward a common good and that crimes are acts that are outlawed because they conflict with the rules of the majority and are harmful to society.

According to what is known as the **consensus view of crime**, crimes are behaviors that are essentially harmful to a majority of citizens living in society and therefore have been controlled or prohibited by the existing criminal law. Using this definition, criminal law is a set of rules, codified by state authorities, that express the norms, goals, and values of the *vast majority of society*. The definition implies that criminal law, and the behaviors it defines as crimes, represent the *consensus* of public opinion and that there is general agreement about which behaviors society needs to control and which should be beyond state regulation.

The consensus view rests on the assumption that criminal law has a social control function—restraining those who might otherwise engage in antisocial behavior. Criminal law works to control behaviors that are inherently destructive and dangerous in order to maintain the existing social fabric and ensure the peaceful functioning of society.

Conflict View

conflict view of crime (or critical view of crime)
The law is controlled by the rich and powerful who shape its content to ensure their continued economic domination of society. The criminal justice system is an instrument of social and economic repression.

According to the **conflict view of crime**, the content of criminal law, and consequently the definition of crime, are shaped and controlled by the ongoing class struggle between the rich and poor, the haves and have-nots. According to this view, criminal law is created and enforced by the ruling class as a mechanism for controlling dissatisfied, have-not members of society. The law is the instrument that enables the wealthy to maintain their position of power and to control the behavior of those who oppose their ideas and values or who might rebel against the unequal distribution of wealth.[1] Laws defining property crimes, such as larceny and burglary, are created to protect the wealth of the affluent. Drug laws are developed to ensure that workers will be productive, clearheaded, and sober. Laws defining violent crimes are enacted to keep the angry and frustrated lower classes under control. People who violate these laws are subject to severe punishments. In contrast, business and white-collar crimes receive lenient punishments, relative to the extent of the harm and damage they cause. So it is perfectly legal for greedy bankers to award their employees millions in bonuses, while at the same time it is a crime for an indigent person to steal $50 in order to buy food for her family.

Interactionist View

interactionist view of crime
Criminal law reflects the values of people who use their social and political power to shape the legal system.

moral crusade
A concerted action for some cause or idea, or against some perceived abuse, taken on by a committed individual or group.

moral entrepreneur
People who wage moral crusades to control criminal law so that it reflects their own personal values.

According to the **interactionist view of crime,** the criminal law is structured to reflect the preferences and opinions of people who hold social power and use their influence to shape the legal process.[2] These so called **moral entrepreneurs** wage campaigns (**moral crusades**) to control behaviors they view as immoral and wrong (such as abortion) or, conversely, to legalize behaviors they consider harmless social eccentricities (such as smoking marijuana). In essence, they dedicate themselves to molding the law to reflect their own world views. According to the interactionist view then, many crimes are not inherently evil or immoral acts, but are illegal because they are in conflict with social norms. So, for example, it is illegal to purchase marijuana and hashish, whereas liquor and cigarettes are sold openly, even though far more people die from the effects of alcoholism and smoking than from drug abuse each year.[3]

DEFINING CRIME • The basics of these views are set out in Concept Summary 2.1. Although these views of crime differ, they generally agree on four points: (1) Criminal law defines crime; (2) the definition of crime is constantly changing and evolving; (3) social forces mold the definition of crimes; and (4) criminal law has a social control function. Therefore, as used in this text, the term **crime** is defined as follows:

> Crime is a violation of social rules of conduct, interpreted and expressed by a written criminal code, created by people holding social and political power. Its content may be influenced by prevailing public sentiments, historically developed moral beliefs, and the need to protect public safety. Individuals who violate these rules may be subject to sanctions administered by state authority, which include social stigma and loss of status, freedom, and, on occasion, their lives.

REALITY CHECK

MYTH OR REALITY? The content of the criminal law is often shaped by moral crusaders and not by the will of the majority.

REALITY: A great deal of the criminal law reflects the values of a small group of moral crusaders.

Can you think of some moral crusades that have occurred during your lifetime that have resulted in changing the content of the law?

crime
A violation of societal rules of behavior as interpreted and expressed by a criminal legal code created by people holding social and political power. Individuals who violate these rules are subject to sanctions by state authority, social stigma, and loss of status.

Three Views of Crime

Consensus View	• The law defines crime. • Consensus exists on what is right and wrong. • Laws apply to all citizens equally
Conflict View	• The law is a tool of the ruling class. • Crime is a politically defined concept. • "Real crimes" are not outlawed. • The law is used to control the underclass.
Interactionist View	• Moral entrepreneurs define crime. • The definition of crime is subjective and reflects contemporary values and morals. • Criminal labels are life-transforming events.

Concept Summary 2.1

How Is Crime Measured?

In addition to understanding how crime is defined, it is important for criminal justice scholars to measure the nature, extent, and trends in the crime rate. They use a variety of techniques to study crime and its consequences. Three principal types of crime data have been developed—official data, victim data, and self-report data—each having particular strengths and weaknesses. The following sections review these methods in some detail and show what they tell us about the crime problem in the United States and abroad.

Official Crime Data: The Uniform Crime Reports (UCR)

The FBI's **Uniform Crime Reports (UCR)** is the best known and most widely cited source of criminal records.[4] Data from the UCR is published in an annual volume called *Crime in the United States* and serves as the nation's **official crime statistics**.

How is the UCR compiled? The FBI receives records and reports from over 17,000 police departments serving a majority of the U.S. population. Its main unit of analysis involves **Part I crimes**: criminal homicide, forcible rape, robbery, aggravated assault, burglary, larceny/theft, motor vehicle theft, and arson. Exhibit 2.1 defines these crimes. Local police departments enter into their database all reported incidents involving these crimes and send the information to the FBI. The Bureau tallies the local police reports and then compiles the numbers of known offenses by city, county, standard metropolitan statistical area, and geographical divisions of the United States. Besides these statistics, the UCR also provides a number of other pieces of crime data. Most important, it calculates the number and characteristics (age, race, and gender) of individuals who have been arrested for these and all other crimes—**Part II crimes**—such as prostitution and drug trafficking.

Uniform Crime Reports (UCR)
The FBI's yearly publication of where, when, and how much serious crime occurred in the prior year.

official crime statistics
Compiled by the FBI in its Uniform Crime Reports, these are a tally of serious crimes reported to police agencies each year.

Part I crimes
The eight crimes for which, because of their seriousness and frequency, the FBI reports their incidence in its annual Uniform Crime Reports. The Part I crimes are murder, rape, assault, robbery, burglary, arson, larceny, and motor vehicle theft.

Part II crimes
All other crimes except the eight Part I crimes. The FBI records all arrests made for Part II crimes, including race, gender, and age information.

Using pepper spray, Pittsburgh police arrest antiwar demonstrators during an unpermitted march as they protest U.S. involvement in the war in Iraq. The FBI's Uniform Crime Report program tallies arrests and reports them on a yearly basis.

© AP Images/John Heller

EXHIBIT 2.1

FBI Part I Crimes

Criminal Homicide

Murder and Nonnegligent Manslaughter The willful (nonnegligent) killing of one human being by another. Deaths caused by negligence, attempts to kill, assaults to kill, suicides, accidental deaths, and justifiable homicides are excluded. Justifiable homicides are limited to the killing of a felon by a law enforcement officer in the line of duty and the killing of a felon by a private citizen.

Manslaughter by Negligence The killing of another person through gross negligence. Traffic fatalities are excluded. Although manslaughter by negligence is a Part I crime, it is not included in the crime index.

Forcible Rape
The carnal knowledge of a female forcibly and against her will. Included are rapes by force and attempts or assaults to rape. Statutory offenses (no force used—victim under age of consent) are excluded.

Robbery
The taking or attempting to take anything of value from the care, custody, or control of a person or persons by force or threat of force or violence and/or by putting the victim in fear.

Aggravated Assault
An unlawful attack by one person on another for the purpose of inflicting severe or aggravated bodily injury. This type of assault is usually accompanied by the use of a weapon or by means likely to produce death or great bodily harm. Simple assaults are excluded.

Burglary
Breaking or entering. The unlawful entry of a structure to commit a felony or a theft. Attempted forcible entry is included.

Larceny/Theft (except motor vehicle theft)
The unlawful taking, carrying, leading, or riding away of property from the possession or constructive possession of another. Examples are thefts of bicycles or automobile accessories, shoplifting, pocket picking, or the stealing of any property or article that is not taken by force and violence or by fraud. Attempted larcenies are included. Embezzlement, "con" games, forgery, worthless checks, etc., are excluded.

Motor Vehicle Theft
The theft or attempted theft of a motor vehicle. A motor vehicle is self-propelled and runs on the surface and not on rails. Specifically excluded from this category are motorboats, construction equipment, airplanes, and farming equipment.

Arson
Any willful or malicious burning or attempt to burn, with or without intent to defraud, a dwelling, house, public building, motor vehicle or aircraft, personal property of another, and so on.

Source: FBI, *Uniform Crime Reports*, http://www.fbi.gov/ucr/cius2007/index.html

The UCR uses three methods to express crime data. First, the number of crimes reported to the police and arrests made are expressed as raw figures (for example, in 2007, 16,929 murders occurred). Second, crime rates per 100,000 people are computed. That is, when the UCR indicates that the murder rate was about 5.6 in 2007, it means that almost 6 people in every 100,000 were murdered between January 1 and December 31, 2007. This is the equation used:

$$\frac{\text{Number of Reported Crimes}}{\text{Total U.S. Population}} \times 100{,}000 = \text{Rate per } 100{,}000$$

Third, the FBI computes changes in the number and rate of crime over time. Even though the murder rate decreased by 0.6 percent between 2006 and 2007, the 2007 figure was still 2.4 percent above the 2003 level.

Crime in the United States

Access **Crime in the United States** via

www.cengage.com/criminaljustice/siegel

HOW ACCURATE IS THE UCR? ● The UCR's accuracy has long been suspect. Many serious crimes are not reported to police and therefore are not counted by the UCR. The reasons for not reporting vary:

- Victims consider the crime trivial or unimportant and therefore choose not to call the police.
- Some victims fail to report because they do not trust the police or have little confidence in their ability to solve crime.
- People without property insurance believe it is useless to report theft.
- Victims fear reprisals from an offender's friends or family.
- Victims have "dirty hands" and are involved in illegal activities themselves. They do not want to get involved with the police.

Because of these and other factors, less than half of all criminal incidents are reported to the police.

The way police departments record and report criminal activity also affects the validity of UCR statistics. Some departments may define crimes loosely—reporting a trespass as a burglary or an assault on a woman as an attempted rape—whereas others pay strict attention to FBI guidelines. Some make systematic errors in UCR reporting—for example, counting an arrest only after a formal booking procedure, even though the UCR requires arrests to be counted when the suspect is released without a formal charge. These reporting practices may help explain interjurisdictional differences in crime.

Some critics take issue with the way the FBI records data and counts crimes. According to the "Hierarchy Rule," in a multiple-offense incident, only the most serious crime is counted. So if an armed bank robber commits a robbery, assaults a patron as he flees, steals a car to get away, and damages property during a police chase, only the robbery is reported because it is the most serious offense.

Although these issues are troubling, the UCR continues to be one of the most widely used sources of criminal statistics. Because the UCR is collected in a careful and systematic way, it is considered a highly reliable indicator of crime patterns and trends. That is, even if reporting problems compromise the precision of any count of total crimes committed in a single year, measurement of changes from year to year should be accurate because these problems are stable over time. Thus, if the UCR reports that the murder rate decreased 4.4 between 2007 and 2008, that assessment is probably accurate because the reporting and counting problems that influenced data collection in 2007 had the same effect in 2008.

The National Crime Victimization Survey (NCVS)

Another important source of crime data is the **National Crime Victimization Survey (NCVS)**. This federally sponsored yearly survey uses a large, carefully drawn sample of citizens who are queried about their experiences with criminal activity during the past year. By assessing the number of victimizations, the NCVS enables crime experts to estimate the total number of criminal incidents that occur each year, including those that are never reported to police.[5]

How is the NCVS conducted? Samples of housing units are selected using a complex, multistage sampling technique. Victimization rates are based on data collected during the calendar year. At present time, the NCVS interviews almost 75,000 people in more than 40,000 households biannually.[6] Those contacted are asked to report on the frequency, characteristics, and consequences of criminal victimization for such crimes as rape, sexual assault, robbery, assault, theft, household burglary, and motor vehicle theft.

Because of the care with which the samples are drawn and the high completion rate, NCVS data is considered a relatively unbiased, valid estimate of all

UCR

Access the **UCR** via

www.cengage.com/ criminaljustice/siegel

National Crime Victimization Survey (NCVS)

The ongoing victimization study conducted jointly by the Justice Department and the U.S. Census Bureau that surveys victims about their experiences with law violation.

EXHIBIT 2.2

Validity Issues in the NCVS

- Victims may overreport as a consequence of their misinterpretation of events; for example, a lost wallet may be reported as stolen, or an open door may be viewed as a burglary attempt.
- Victims may underreport because they are embarrassed about reporting crime to interviewers, fear getting in trouble, or simply forget an incident.
- There may be an inability to record the personal criminal activity of those interviewed,

such as drug use or gambling; murder is not included for obvious reasons.
- Sampling errors may produce a group of respondents that does not represent the nation as a whole.
- A faulty question format may invalidate responses; some groups, such as adolescents, may be particularly susceptible to error because of question format.

victimizations for the target crimes included in the survey. Yet, like the UCR, the NCVS may suffer from methodological problems. As a result, its findings must be interpreted with caution. Some of the potential problems are listed in Exhibit 2.2.

Self-Report Surveys

Self-report surveys, the third source of crime data, ask subjects to describe their past and current criminal activities, including whether they have ever been involved in substance abuse, theft, and/or violence; how often they engage in these activities; what specific kinds of drugs they took; and whether they acted alone or in groups. It is assumed that respondents will be willing to describe their illegal activities accurately because self-report surveys are typically administered in groups, anonymously and unsigned. The idea is to measure crimes that would neither be reported to the police nor show up in victim surveys, such as using cocaine. The ability of self-reports to get at these "dark figures of crime" makes it possible to track the incidence of criminal acts that are not reflected in official statistics.

Many self-report studies, such as the ongoing Monitoring the Future (MTF) study conducted by the Institute of Survey Research at the University of Michigan, are administered among middle school and high school youth.[7] Because school attendance is universal in the United States, a school-based self-report survey represents a cross section of the community. However, self-reports are not restricted to youth crime. They are also used to examine the offense histories of prison inmates, drug users, and other segments of the population.

ARE SELF-REPORTS VALID? ● Critics of self-report studies frequently suggest that it is unreasonable to expect people to candidly admit illegal acts. They have nothing to gain, and the ones who would be taking the greatest risk are the ones with official records, who may be engaging in the most criminality. Some people may exaggerate their criminal acts, forget some of them, or be confused about what is being asked. Some surveys contain an overabundance of trivial offenses, such as shoplifting small amounts of items or using false identification, and often lump these together with more serious crimes to form a total crime index. Consequently, comparisons between groups can be highly misleading.

Response rate is also critical. Even if 90 percent of a school population voluntarily participates in a self-report survey, researchers can never be sure

NCVS

To access data from the **NCVS** on the Web, go to **www.cengage.com/criminaljustice/siegel**

self-report survey

A survey designed to measure past and current criminal activities that relies on confidentiality and anonymity to insure response validity.

Monitoring the Future

To access the **Monitoring the Future** website, go to **www.cengage.com/criminaljustice/siegel**

whether the few who refuse to participate or are absent that day account for a significant portion of the school's population of persistent, high-rate offenders.[8] It is also unlikely that the most serious chronic offenders in the teenage population are the most willing to cooperate with university-based criminologists administering self-report tests.[9] Although these drawbacks are troubling, criminologists have used a variety of techniques to verify self-report data.[10] The "known group" method compares youths who are known to be offenders with those who are not, to see whether the former report more delinquency. There is evidence that kids known to be active delinquents self-report more crime than those who are not involved in criminality.[11] Research shows that when kids are asked whether they have ever been arrested or sent to court, their responses accurately reflect their true life experiences.[12]

Compatibility of Crime Data Sources

Are the various sources of crime data compatible? Each has strengths and weaknesses. The FBI survey is carefully tallied and contains data on the number of murders and people arrested—information that the other data sources lack. However, this survey omits the many crimes that victims choose not to report to police, and it is subject to the reporting caprices of individual police departments.

REALITYCHECK

MYTH OR REALITY? Most crimes get reported to the police.

MYTH: Most crime victims fail to contact police, and for obvious reasons, many crimes, such as drug possession and use, are never reported.

Considering this problem, which crime is the one most likely to be reported?

The NCVS contains unreported crime and important information on the personal characteristics of victims, but the data consists of estimates made from relatively limited samples of the total U.S. population, so that even narrow fluctuations in the rates of some crimes can have a major impact on findings. It also relies on personal recollections that may be inaccurate. Furthermore, the NCVS does not include data on important crime patterns, including murder and drug abuse.

Self-report surveys can provide information on the personal characteristics of offenders that is not available from any other source, such as their attitudes, values, beliefs, and psychological profiles. Yet, at their core, self-reports rely on the honesty of criminal offenders and drug abusers, a population not generally known for accuracy and integrity.

Despite these differences, the data sources seem more compatible than was first believed. Although their tallies of crimes are certainly not in sync, the crime patterns and trends they record are often similar.[13] All three sources generally agree about the personal characteristics of serious criminals (such as age and gender) and about where and when crime occurs (such as urban areas, nighttime, and summer months). Concept Summary 2.2 summarizes the strengths and weaknesses of the three primary methods of collecting crime statistics.

CRIME TRENDS

What do the various sources of crime data tell us about the nature, extent, and trends in crime? As you learned in Chapter 1, criminal behavior is not new to this century.[14] Studies have indicated that a gradual increase in the crime rate, especially in violent crime, occurred from 1830 to 1860. Following the Civil War, this rate increased significantly for about 15 years. Then,

Data Collection Methods

Concept
Summary
2.2

Uniform Crime Reports
- Data is collected from records from police departments across the nation, crimes reported to police, and arrests.
- The strengths of the UCR are its reliable measurements of homicides and arrests. It is a consistent, national sample.
- The weaknesses of the UCR are that it omits crimes not reported to police, omits most drug usage, and contains reporting errors.

National Crime Victimization Survey
- Data is collected from a large national survey.
- The strengths of the NCVS are that it includes crimes not reported to the police, uses careful sampling techniques, and is a yearly survey.
- The weaknesses of the NCVS are that it relies on victims' memory and honesty and omits substance abuse.

Self-Report Surveys
- Data is collected from local surveys.
- The strengths of self-report surveys are that they include nonreported crimes, substance abuse, and offenders' personal information.
- The weaknesses of self-report surveys are that they rely on the honesty of offenders and that they omit offenders who refuse (or are unable) to participate and those who may be the most deviant.

© X Brand Images/Getty Images

Even though crime rates have been in decline for some time, spectacular headlines convince the public that crime is everywhere, even in small-town America. Here firefighters spray water on burning row houses in Coatesville, Pennsylvania, a town of about 10,000, on January 24, 2009. At least 30 arsons have been reported in the area since the beginning of 2008. There was no clear indication who was committing the crimes or why.

© AP Images/*Daily Local News,* Tom Kelly IV

1960
Total Crimes: 3.4 million
Violent Crimes: 288,000
Property Crimes: 3.1 million

1991
Total Crimes: 14.8 million
Violent Crimes: 1.9 million
Property Crimes: 12.9 million

2008
Total Crimes: 10.7 Million
Violent Crimes: 1.3 million
Property Crimes: 9.4 million

Crime Rate Change: 1960–2008

Source: *Sourcebook of Criminal Justice Statistics*

http://www.albany.edu/sourcebook/pdf/t31062006.pdf.

FIGURE 2.1

from 1880 up to the time of World War I—with the possible exception of the years immediately preceding and following the war—the number of reported crimes decreased. After a period of readjustment, the crime rate steadily declined until the Depression (about 1930), when another crime wave was recorded. Crime rates increased gradually following the 1930s until the 1960s, when the growth rate became much greater. The homicide rate, which had actually declined from the 1930s to the 1960s, also began a sharp increase.

As Figure 2.1 shows, the number of reported crimes rose from 3.3 million in 1960 to a peak in of 14.8 million in 1991. Since then the number of crimes has been in decline; in 2008 about 11 million crimes were reported to the police, a decline of about 25 percent from the peak. Even teenage criminality, a source of national concern, has decreased by about one-third over the past 20 years.[15]

Especially welcome has been a significant drop in violent crimes: murder, rape, robbery, and assault. About 1.3 million violent crimes are now being reported to the police each year, a rate of around 460 per 100,000 Americans. Although people are still disturbed by media reports of violent incidents, in reality there are 500,000 fewer violent crimes being reported today than in 1991, when almost 2 million incidents occurred—a violence rate of 758 per 100,000. This means that the violence rate has dropped almost 40 percent from its peak.

Not only has violent crime been in decline, but so have theft offenses. The property crimes reported in the UCR include larceny, motor vehicle theft, and arson. Property crime rates have also declined in recent years, dropping more than 10 percent during the past decade. In 1991, at their peak, about 13 million property crimes were reported, a rate of almost 5,000 per 100,000 citizens. In 2008, about 9.4 million property crimes were reported to police, a rate of about 3,300 per 100,000 population. Nonetheless, property crimes remain a serious national problem, and an estimated 18 billion dollars in losses result from property crimes annually.

Trends in Victimization Data

According to the latest NCVS survey, residents age 12 or older experienced about 23 million violent and property victimizations. About 16 million households experienced one or more property crimes or had a member age 12 or older who experienced one or more violent crimes.[16]

Similar to the UCR, NCVS data shows that criminal victimizations have declined significantly during the past 30 years. In 1973 an estimated 44 million victimizations were recorded, compared to 23 million today. Figure 2.2 shows the recent trends in violent crime, and Figure 2.3 tracks property victimizations.

REALITY CHECK

MYTH OR REALITY? Crime and violence rates are out of control and getting worse every day.

MYTH: Crime rates have been declining recently. Despite what the evening news tells us, crime rates have been down for almost 20 years.

Do you think this trend will continue?

Trends in Self-Reporting

Over the past decade, the MTF surveys indicate that, with a few exceptions, the trend in self-reported participation in theft, violence, and damage-related crimes seems to be more stable than the trends reported in the UCR and NCVS. When the results of recent self-report surveys are compared with various studies conducted over a 20-year period, a uniform pattern emerges: The use of most drugs has been in decline, whereas theft, violence, and

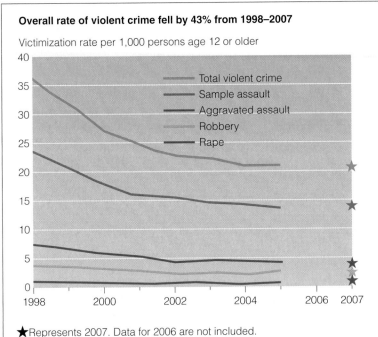

Overall rate of violent crime fell by 43% from 1998–2007

Victimization rate per 1,000 persons age 12 or older

- Total violent crime
- Sample assault
- Aggravated assault
- Robbery
- Rape

★Represents 2007. Data for 2006 are not included.

Trends in Violent Crime

Source: Rand, *Criminal Victimization, 2007*

http://www.ojp.usdoj.gov/bjs/pub/pdf/cv07.pdf.

FIGURE 2.2

Property crime rates overall fell by 33% from 1998–2007

Property crime rate per 1,000 households

- Total property crime
- Theft
- Burglary
- Motor vehicle theft

★ Represents 2007. Data for 2006 are not included.

Trends in Property Crimes

Source: Rand, *Criminal Victimization, 2007*

http://www.ojp.usdoj.gov/bjs/pub/pdf/cv07.pdf.

FIGURE 2.3

damage-related crimes seem more stable. Although a self-reported crime wave has not occurred, neither has there been any visible reduction in self-reported criminality. Table 2.1 contains data from the most recent (2008) Monitoring the Future survey. A surprising number of these "typical" teenagers reported involvement in serious criminal behavior: About 13 percent reported hurting someone badly enough that the victim needed medical care (6 percent said they did it more than once); about 29 percent reported stealing something

TABLE 2.1

Monitoring the Future Survey of Criminal Activity of High School Seniors

Percentage Engaging in Offenses

Crime	Committed at Least Once	Committed More than Once
Set fire on purpose	1	2
Damaged school property	5	7
Damaged work property	3	3
Auto theft	2	3
Auto part theft	2	2
Break and enter	12	13
Theft, less than $50	12	17
Theft, more than $50	4	5
Shoplift	12	16
Gang or group fight	9	7
Hurt someone badly enough to require medical care	7	6
Used force or a weapon to steal	1	2
Hit teacher or supervisor	1	2
Participated in serious fight	7	6

Source: *Monitoring the Future, 2008* (Ann Arbor, MI: Institute for Social Research, 2009).

worth less than $50, and another 9 percent stole something worth more than $50; 28 percent reported shoplifting; 12 percent damaged school property.

If the MTF data is accurate, the crime problem is much greater than UCR and NCVS data would lead us to believe. There are approximately 20 million high school age youths between the ages of 15 and 19, and 3 percent of the students in this age group say they have used a weapon to steal one or more times in the past year.[17] This suggests that high school students committed a minimum of 600,000 armed robberies during the past 12 months; in comparison, the UCR tallied about 450,000 armed robberies for all age groups.

What factors help explain the upward and downward movement in crime rates? Some of the more important ones are set out in Exhibit 2.3.

Although crime has been in a general decline in the United States, it is increasing abroad. The International Justice feature on page 54 discusses this trend.

REALITYCHECK

MYTH OR REALITY?　A poor economy and high unemployment cause crime rates to increase.

MYTH:　Crime rates tend to decline during an economic downturn.

Does it seem possible that one of your relatives or family members would suddenly become a criminal or rob a bank just because they got laid off from their job during a recession?

Coming Trends in Crime

Speculating about the future of crime trends is always risky because current conditions can change rapidly. Some criminologists predict that a significant increase

EXHIBIT 2.3

Factors That Influence the Direction of Crime Rates

Age Structure of the Population Teenagers have extremely high crime rates, whereas seniors rarely commit crime. The age composition of the population has a significant influence on crime trends: The greater the proportion of young males in the population, the higher the crime rate and the greater the number of persistent offenders. Because the number of senior citizens is expanding and the population aging, crime rates may remain relatively low for some time.

Immigration Immigration has become one of the most controversial issues in American society, and some people believe that immigrants have high crime rates and should be prevented from entering the country. However, research does not support any link between immigration and crime. And some scholars, such as Harvard sociologist Robert Sampson, find that immigrants are actually less violent than the general population. Sampson and colleagues discovered that Mexican immigrants experience lower rates of violence than their native-born counterparts. When Ramiro Martinez and his colleagues examined the association between drug crimes and immigration in Miami and San Diego, they also found that immigration has a *negative* effect on homicides, and especially on drug-related homicides. This research indicates that as the number of immigrants in the population increases, the crime rate may actually decline; that is, immigration has a suppressor effect on crime.

Economy/Jobs Although it seems logical that high unemployment should increase crime rates and that a good economy should reduce criminal activity, there is actually significant debate about the association between the economy and crime rates. Some crime experts believe a poor economy actually helps lower crime rates, because unemployed parents are at home to supervise children and guard their possessions. Because there is less to spend, a poor economy reduces the number of valuables worth stealing. Also, it seems unlikely that law-abiding, middle-aged workers will suddenly turn to a life of crime if they are laid off during an economic downturn. However, it is possible that over the long haul, a strong economy will help lower crime rates, whereas long periods of sustained economic weakness and unemployment may eventually lead to increased rates. (Crime skyrocketed in the 1930s during the Great Depression, and crime rates fell when the economy surged for almost a decade during the 1990s.) Some local police chiefs claim that a poor local economy has led to higher crime rates during the recent economic downturn, but national data still indicates that crime rates are declining even though the economy has nosedived.

Abortion There is evidence that the recent drop in the crime rate can be attributed to the availability of legalized abortion. In 1973, *Roe v. Wade* legalized abortion nationwide, and the drop in crime rate began approximately 18 years later, in 1991. Crime rates began to decline when the first groups of potential offenders affected by the abortion decision began reaching the peak age of criminal activity. It is possible that the link between crime rates and abortion is the result of two mechanisms: (1) selective abortion on the part of women most at risk of having children who would engage in criminal activity, and (2) improved child rearing or environmental circumstances caused by better maternal, familial, or fetal care because women are having fewer children.

Gun Availability As the number of guns in the population increases, so do violent crime rates. There is evidence that more guns than ever before are finding their way into the hands of young people. Surveys of high school students indicate that up to 10 percent carry guns at least some of the time. As the number of gun-toting students increases, so does the seriousness of violent crime, as happens when a schoolyard fight turns into murder.

Gang Membership According to government sources, there are now more than a million gang members in the United States. Criminal gangs commit as much as 80 percent of the crime in many communities, including armed robbery, assault, auto theft, drug trafficking, extortion, fraud, home invasions, identity theft, murder, and weapons trafficking. Gang members are far more likely to possess guns than non-gang members; criminal activity increases when kids join gangs. Drug-dealing gangs are heavily armed, a condition that persuades non–gang-affiliated kids to arm themselves for self-protection. The result is an arms race that produces an increasing spiral of violence.

(continued)

Drug Use As drug use increases, crime rates increase. The surge in the violent crime rate between 1985 and 1993 has been tied directly to the crack cocaine epidemic that swept the nation's largest cities. Well-armed drug gangs did not hesitate to use violence to control territory, intimidate rivals, and increase market share. When crack use declined in urban areas after 1993, so too did crime rates. A sudden increase in drug use may be a harbinger of future increases in the crime rate, especially if guns are easily obtained and the economy is weak.

Media The jury is still out, but some experts believe that media portrayal of violence can influence the direction of crime rates. As the availability of media with a violent theme skyrocketed with the introduction of home video players, DVDs, cable TV, and computer and video games, teen violence spiked as well.

Medical Technology Some crime experts believe that the presence and quality of health care can have a significant impact on murder rates, simply because fewer victims die. The big breakthrough occurred in the 1970s, when technology that was developed to treat injured soldiers in Vietnam was applied to trauma care in the nation's hospitals. Since then, fluctuations in the murder rate can be linked to the level and availability of emergency medical services.

Aggressive Law Enforcement Reductions in crime rates may be attributed to adding large numbers of police officers and using them in aggressive police practices that target "quality of life" crimes, such as panhandling, graffiti, petty drug dealing, and loitering. By showing that even the smallest infractions will be dealt with seriously, aggressive police departments may be able to discourage potential criminals from committing more serious crimes. Cities employing aggressive, focused police work may be able to lower homicide rates in the area.

Tough Sentences It is also possible that tough laws imposing lengthy prison terms on drug dealers and repeat offenders can affect crime rates. The fear of punishment may inhibit some would-be criminals and place a significant number of potentially high-rate offenders behind bars, lowering crime rates. As the nation's prison population has expanded, the crime rate has fallen. In the long run, however, increasing punishments may backfire: Putting more people in prison may take some dangerous offenders off the street temporarily, but eventually most get out. The recidivism rate of paroled inmates is quite high; about two-thirds of those released from state custody will eventually return to prison. Inmates reentering society may have a significant effect on local crime rates.

Cultural Change In contemporary society, cultural change, such as a reduction in the number of single-parent families, high school dropout rates, racial conflict, and teen pregnancies, can influence crime rates.

Criminal Opportunity As criminal opportunities increase, so do crime rates. Conversely, crime rates may drop when an alternative to criminal opportunity develops. The decline in the burglary rate over the past decade may be explained in part by the abundance of certain commonly stolen merchandise, such as cell phones, and the subsequent decline in their price. Improving home and commercial security devices may also discourage would-be burglars, convincing them to turn to other forms of crime, such as theft from motor vehicles. On the other hand, new targets may increase crime rates: Subway crime increased in New York when thieves began targeting people carrying iPods and expensive cell phones.

Source: Amy Anderson and Lorine Hughes, "Exposure to Situations Conducive to Delinquent Behavior: The Effects of Time Use, Income, and Transportation," *Journal of Research in Crime and Delinquency* 46 (2009): 5–34; The National Gang Intelligence Center, National Gang Threat Assessment, 2009, http://www.atf.gov/pub/gang_related/2009_nat_gang_threat_assessment.pdf; Scott Decker, Charles Katz, and Vincent Webb, "Understanding the Black Box of Gang Organization: Implications for Involvement in Violent Crime, Drug Sales, and Violent Victimization, *Crime and Delinquency* 54 (2008): 153–172; Robert Sampson and Lydia Bean, "Cultural Mechanisms and Killing Fields: A Revised Theory of Community-Level Racial Inequality," in *The Many Colors of Crime: Inequalities of Race, Ethnicity, and Crime in America*, eds. Ruth D. Peterson, Lauren Krivo, and John Hagan (New York: New York University Press, 2006): 8–36; Ramiro Martinez Jr., Matthew Amie Nielsen, "Local Context and Determinants of Drug Violence in Miami and San Diego: Does Ethnicity and Immigration Matter?" *International Migration Review* 38 (2004): 131–157; Martin Killias, "The Opening and Closing of Breaches: A Theory on Crime Waves, Law Creation and Crime Prevention," *European Journal of Criminology* 3 (2006): 11–31; Matthew Miller, David Hemenway, and Deborah Azrael, "State-Level Homicide Victimization Rates in the U.S. in Relation to Survey Measures of Household Firearm Ownership, 2001–2003," *Social Science & Medicine* 64 (2007): 656–664; Alfred Blumstein, "The Crime Drop in America: An Exploration of Some Recent Crime Trends," *Journal of Scandinavian Studies in Criminology & Crime Prevention* 7 (2006): 17–35; Thomas Arvanites and Robert Defina, "Business Cycles and Street Crime," *Criminology* 44 (2006): 139–164; Fahui Wang, "Job Access and Homicide Patterns in Chicago: An Analysis at Multiple Geographic Levels Based on Scale-Space Theory," *Journal of Quantitative Criminology* 21 (2005): 195–217; John J. Donohue and Steven D. Levitt, "The Impact of Legalized Abortion on Crime," *The Quarterly Journal of Economics* 116 (2001): 379–420.

Gun availability has been linked to violent crime rates. People can purchase guns at gun shows such as this one at the South Florida Fairgrounds in West Palm Beach. At the show, guns on sale to the general public range from all varieties of handguns to assault rifles and accessories such as flash suppressors or silencers. Should these shows be regulated more closely? If guns were banned, would violent crime rates decline?

© Robert Wallis/Corbis

© SuperStock RF/SuperStock

in teen violence may soon occur. There are approximately 60 million school-age children in the United States, many under age 10; this is more than we have had for decades. Though many come from stable homes, others lack stable families and adequate supervision. These are some of the children who will soon enter the prime crime-committing years.[18]

Other experts dispute the fact that we are in for a big upswing in the crime rate. Even if teens commit more crime in the future, their contribution may be offset by the growing senior citizen and elderly population, a group with a relatively low crime rate.[19]

It is also possible that economic, technological, and social factors could help moderate the crime rate.[20] Technological developments such as the rapid expansion of e-commerce on the Internet have created new classes of crime that may increase crime rates in the near future.

Crime Patterns

By studying crime data, experts can determine whether there are table patterns in the crime rate, which may help us to better understand where crime occurs, who commits crime, and why they violate the law. What are these enduring and stable patterns?

Ecological Patterns

There are distinct ecological patterns in the crime rate:

- Rural and suburban areas have much lower crime rates than large metropolitan centers, suggesting that urban problems—overcrowding, poverty, social inequality, narcotics use, and racial conflict—are related to crime rates.

International Justice

Crime Trends around the World

One of the great "myths" of crime is that the United States is more crime prone and certainly more violent than any other industrial society. How true is that assumption? Well, it may have been true at one time, but not any more.

While the United States has been experiencing a significant drop in crime, other nations have not been so fortunate. Asian countries now report an upswing in serious criminal activities. Cambodian officials are concerned with drug production/trafficking and human trafficking. Drugs produced in neighboring countries are being trafficked into Cambodia for local consumption, and drug traffickers routinely use it as a transit country for distributing narcotics around the world. Other major concerns include the trafficking of Cambodian women into Thailand for sexual activities and the presence of a large number of Vietnamese women in Cambodia who are engaged in prostitution. Even Japan, a nation renowned for its low crime rate, has experienced an upswing in crime linked to its economy. Japan's economic bubble burst in 1990, and more than 15 years of economic stagnation have resulted in climbing numbers of reported crime. Similarly, China, another relatively safe nation, has experienced an upswing in violent crime. Theft and robbery remain a serious problem, especially in public places. Railway stations, long-distance bus stations, and passenger docks were rated as the most dangerous places.

Violence Is Booming Abroad

Many people think of the United States as an extremely violent nation, but sadly, the rest of the world is now catching up, and some nations far exceed the United States in violent crime. Underdeveloped nations, especially those experiencing social or economic upheaval, have murder rates much higher than the United States. Colombia has about 63 homicides per 100,000 people, and South Africa 51, compared to less than 6 in the United States. During the 1990s there were more homicides in Brazil than in the United States, Canada, Italy, Japan, Australia, Portugal, Britain, Austria, and Germany *taken together*. Why are murder rates so high in Brazil and other nations? Law enforcement officials link the upsurge in violence to drug trafficking, gang feuds, vigilantism, and disputes over trivial matters among young, unmarried, uneducated males.

In some countries, local customs and practices underpin the homicide rate. India has experienced a shocking form of violence against women known as bride burning. A woman may be burned to death if her family fails to provide the expected dowry to the groom's family or if she is suspected of premarital infidelity; many Indian women commit suicide to escape the brutality of their situation.

Other nations are also surpassing us in the rate of sexual violence. Until 1990, U.S. rape rates were higher than those of any Western nation, but by 2000, Canada had taken the lead. Violence against women is related to economic hardship and the social status of women. Rates are high in poor nations in which women are oppressed. Sexual violence has significant health consequences, including suicide, stress, mental illnesses, unwanted pregnancy, sexually transmitted diseases, HIV/AIDS, self-inflicted injuries, and (in the case of child sexual abuse) adoption of high-risk behaviors such as multiple sexual partners and drug use.

Why the Change?

Why are crime rates increasing in some nations just as they are leveling off in the United States? Crime rates may be

- Crime rates are highest in the summer months, probably because people spend so much time outdoors and are less likely to secure their homes, and because schools are closed and young people have greater opportunity for criminal activity.
- Crime rates are also related to the region of the country. The West and South usually have significantly higher rates than the Midwest and New England.

Gender Patterns

UCR arrest data consistently shows that males have a much higher crime rate than females. The UCR arrest statistics indicate that the overall male–female spiraling upward in nations undergoing rapid changes in their social and economic makeup. In Eastern Europe, the fall of communism has brought about a transformation of the family, religion, education, and the economy. These changes increase social pressures and result in crime rate increases. Some Asian societies, such as China, are undergoing rapid industrialization, urbanization, and social change. The shift from agricultural to industrial and service economies has produced political turmoil and a surge in their crime rates. The island of Hong Kong, long a British possession but now part of the People's Republic of China, is experiencing an upsurge in club drugs.

What the Future Holds

What does the future hold for international crime rates? There is both good news and bad news. Some nations, such as England, report a stabilization or even decline in crime rates. The most recent British Crime Survey indicates that the number of crimes recorded by the police fell by 6 percent for the period April to June 2008, compared with the same quarter a year earlier. Some individual crime patterns have experienced a startling reversal: Since 1995, the number of burglaries in England and Wales has fallen by more than half (59%) from 1,770,000 to 729,000 today. Although this news is encouraging, globalization and technological innovation will continue to change the nature of international crime and to expand its reach. Large criminal syndicates, such as Russian organized crime groups, will remain powerful players with worldwide networks, but individuals or small groups empowered by high-tech computer skills and telecommunications capabilities may be the future wave of international crime. They would not require the infrastructure or protection of large criminal syndicates to mastermind and implement wide-ranging and sophisticated schemes. Through electronic theft or computer manipulation of markets, individuals or small crime groups could cause substantial public- and private-sector losses. In the next decade the international crime rate may skyrocket as these smaller, independent organizations begin to cooperate. Crime groups within these networks would specialize in specific activities, trading or selling expertise as benefits their criminal interests or criminal joint ventures. Criminal groups are also most likely to take advantage of scientific and manufacturing advances to produce new synthetic drugs or more high-quality counterfeit products, including high-tech components that may find their way into commercial transportation or military programs. Already, counterfeit DVDs of Hollywood blockbusters are flooding the market before the films open in movie theaters. Successful eradication efforts against narcotics crops may spur criminal organizations to exploit scientific pharmaceutical advances to produce synthetic heroin and cocaine for the illicit drug market.

Critical Thinking

1. Although risk factors at all levels of social and personal life contribute to youth violence, kids in all nations who experience change in societal-level factors (such as economic inequalities, rapid social change, and the availability of firearms, alcohol, and drugs) seem the most likely to get involved in violence. Can anything be done to help alleviate these social problems?

2. The United States is notorious for employing much tougher penal measures than Europe. Do you believe our tougher measures explain why crime is declining here while it increases abroad?

arrest ratio is about 3 male offenders to 1 female offender; for serious violent crimes, the ratio is closer to 4 males to 1 female.

Male–female arrest ratios have been much higher in the past. For example, prior to 1994, the violent crime ratio was 8:1 in favor of males. However, female arrest rates rose more rapidly than male arrests between 1970 and 1995, leading some criminologists to proclaim the emergence of a "new female criminal" whose antisocial behaviors were similar to those of their male counterparts.[21] The thinking was that as gender role differences at home, school, and the workplace narrowed, female participation in traditionally male-oriented forms of criminality such as violent crime and juvenile gang membership would increase.[22] The male–female arrest ratio has stabilized over the past 15 years, and there seems to be little indication that it will soon reach parity.

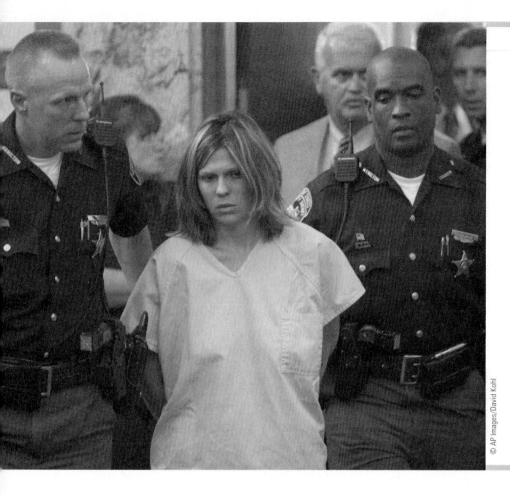

Women are now committing more violent crimes, and the gender ratio in crime has been reduced. Liz Carroll, foster parent of Marcus Fiesel, is led into Hamilton County Court on August 30, 2006, in Cincinnati, Ohio. Liz and David Carroll Jr., pleaded not guilty to charges in the death of the 3-year-old boy. The couple, who moved frequently and relied on child care payments for support, were accused of binding the foster child in a cocoon-like wrapping, leaving him to die in a closet, and then burning his body. Liz Carroll acknowledged those events to a grand jury, was convicted in February 2007, and sentenced to life in prison with no chance for parole for 54 years. David Carroll accepted a deal in which he pleaded guilty and was sentenced to 15 years to life, with an additional year for his plea to gross abuse of a corpse.

© AP Images/David Kohl

How can gender differences in the crime rates be explained? A number of views have been put forward:

- Males are stronger and better able to commit violent crime.
- Hormonal differences make males more aggressive.
- Girls are socialized to be less aggressive than boys and consequently develop moral values that strongly discourage antisocial behavior.[23]
- Girls have better verbal skills and use them to diffuse conflict.
- Males are granted greater personal freedom and therefore have more opportunities to commit crime. Girls are subject to greater parental control.

Racial Patterns

Official crime data indicates that members of minority groups are involved in a disproportionate share of criminal activity. According to UCR reports, African Americans make up almost 14 percent of the general population, yet they account for about 39 percent of Part I violent crime arrests and about 30 percent of property crime arrests.[24] How can these racial differences in the crime rate be explained? There are a number of competing views on this issue:

- Police are more likely to arrest racial minorities because of discriminatory patterns such as racial profiling.
- Differential opportunity, powerlessness, and other social problems in the United States have resulted in a higher African American crime rate. The high rate of crime committed by African Americans is an expression of their anger and frustration at an unfair social order.[25]

- African American families are forced to live in some of the nation's poorest communities that cannot provide economic opportunities. The resulting sense of hopelessness increases the incentive to commit crime.

According to most experts, if and when interracial economic, social, and educational differences converge, so too will crime rates.

Class Patterns

Official data indicates that crime rates are highest in deprived, inner-city areas and that the level of poverty and social disorganization in an area can predict its crime rate. Why are lower-class neighborhoods more likely than affluent communities to be afflicted by crime?

- Communities that lack economic and social opportunities also produce high levels of stress and strain, and residents may then turn to criminal behavior to relieve their frustration.[26]
- Family life is disrupted, and law-violating youth groups and gangs thrive in a climate where adult supervision has been undermined.[27]
- Socially disorganized neighborhoods lack the ability to exert social control over their residents. Lack of informal social control significantly increases the likelihood that residents will engage in criminality.
- Crime rates are high in deteriorated areas where the disadvantaged and the affluent live in close proximity. In these neighborhoods, social differences are magnified, and less affluent residents experience a feeling of relative deprivation that results in a higher crime rate.[28]
- People living in lower-class neighborhoods experience poverty, dilapidated housing, poor schools, broken families, drugs, and street gangs. Deteriorating neighborhoods attract law violators (i.e., the "broken windows" have been linked to high crime rates).

Whatever the reason, the crime data tells us that rates of violent and property crime are higher in impoverished areas.

Age Patterns

Official statistics tell us that young people are arrested at a rate disproportionate to their numbers in the population; victim surveys generate similar findings for crimes in which assailant age can be determined. As a general rule, the peak age for property crime is believed to be 16, and for violence 18. In contrast, the elderly are particularly resistant to the temptations of crime; elderly males age 65 and over are arrested predominantly for alcohol-related matters (public drunkenness and drunk driving) and elderly females for larceny (shoplifting). The elderly crime rate has remained stable for the past 20 years.

When violence rates surged in the 1980s, the increase was due almost entirely to young people; the adult violence rate remained stable. How can the age–crime relationship be explained?

- Young people are part of a youth culture that favors risk taking, short-run hedonism, and other behaviors that may involve them in law violation. The high-risk lifestyle of most youths ends as they mature and become involved in forming a family and a career.[29]
- Adolescents are psychologically immature and are therefore unlikely to appreciate the wrongfulness or destructive consequences of their antisocial acts.
- Youths have limited financial resources and may resort to theft and drug dealing for income.

- Young people have the energy, strength, and physical skill needed to commit crime, and all of these erode with age.[30]
- Adolescents are aware that the juvenile justice system is not as punitive as the adult court system and are therefore more likely to risk committing criminal acts.

Career Patterns: The Chronic Offender

One of the most important patterns discovered in the crime rate is that some people who begin committing crime at a very early age maintain a high rate of criminal violations throughout their lifetime. These chronic offenders are immune to both the ravages of age and the punishments of the justice system. More important, this small group may be responsible for a significant portion of all serious criminal behavior.

Chronic offenders can be distinguished from conventional criminals. The latter category contains law violators who may commit and be apprehended for a single instance of criminal behavior, usually of relatively minor seriousness—shoplifting, simple assault, petty larceny, and so on. The **chronic offender** is one who has serious and persistent brushes with the law, who is building a career in crime, and whose behavior may be excessively violent and destructive.

The concept of the chronic offender is most closely associated with the research efforts of Marvin Wolfgang and his associates at the University of Pennsylvania. In 1972 Wolfgang, Robert Figlio, and Thorsten Sellin published a landmark study entitled *Delinquency in a Birth Cohort*.[31] The researchers used official records to follow the criminal careers of a cohort of 9,945 boys born in Philadelphia in 1945 until they reached age 18 in 1963. Here is what they found:

- About two-thirds of the cohort (6,470) never had contact with police authorities.
- About one-third (3,475) had at least one contact with the police during their minority.
- Of the repeat offenders, a relatively small subgroup (627 boys) were arrested five times or more. These were the chronic offenders, who made up 6 percent of the total (600 out of 10,000).
- The chronic offenders were responsible for 5,305 arrests, or 51.9 percent of the total arrests. They committed 71 percent of the homicides, 73 percent of the rapes, 82 percent of the robberies, and 69 percent of the aggravated assaults.
- Arrest and punishment did little to deter chronic offenders. In fact, punishment was inversely related to chronicity—the stricter the sanctions they received, the more likely they were to engage in repeated criminal behavior.

Since the Philadelphia survey was carried out, a number of other independent studies, including one of a larger Philadelphia cohort of children born in 1958, have confirmed the existence of a repeat offender.[32] Here are some of the key findings about chronic offenders:

- Chronic offender research indicates that young persistent offenders grow up to become adult repeat offenders. This phenomenon is referred to as persistence or continuity of crime.
- Chronic delinquents who commit the most serious violent acts as youngsters have the greatest chance of later becoming adult offenders.[33]
- Youthful offenders who persist are more likely to abuse alcohol, to get into trouble while in military service, to become economically dependent, to

chronic offender
A delinquent offender who is arrested five or more times before he or she is 18 and who stands a good chance of becoming an adult criminal; these offenders are responsible for more than half of all serious crimes.

have lower aspirations, to get divorced or separated, and to have a weak employment record.

The chronic offender concept has had a great impact on the criminal justice system. If a small group of offenders commits almost all of the serious crime, then it stands to reason that their incarceration might have an appreciable influence on the crime rate. This thought pattern has been responsible for the "get-tough" laws designed to put habitual offenders behind bars for long periods of time. As a consequence of these get-tough sentences, the prison population has trended upward even as crime rates have fallen.

Victim Patterns

There are about 23 million victimizations each year.[34] The NCVS data provides a snapshot of the social and demographic characteristics of crime victims.

GENDER ● Gender affects one's risk of victimization. Men are much more likely than women to be victims of robbery and aggravated assault; they are also more likely to experience theft, but the differences are less pronounced. Although females are far more likely to be victims of sexual assault, thousands of men are sexually assaulted each year.

When men are the victims of violent crime, the perpetrator is usually described as a stranger. Women are much more likely to be attacked by a relative than men are; about two-thirds of all attacks against women are committed by a husband or boyfriend, family member, or acquaintance. In two-thirds of sexual assaults as well, the victim knows the attacker.

AGE ● Young people face a much greater victimization risk than older persons do. Victim risk diminishes rapidly after age 25. The elderly, who are thought of as being the helpless targets of predatory criminals, are actually much safer than their grandchildren. People over age 65, who make up 14 percent of the population, account for 1 percent of violent victimizations; teens aged 12 to 19, who also make up 14 percent of the population, typically account for more than 30 percent of crime victims.

What factors explain the age–victimization association?

- Adolescents often stay out late at night, go to public places, and hang out in places where crime is most likely to occur.
- Teens spend a great deal of time in the presence of their adolescent peers, the group most likely to commit crime.

INCOME ● The poorest Americans might be expected to be the most likely victims of crime, since they live in areas that are crime-prone: inner-city, urban neighborhoods. The NCVS does in fact show that the least affluent (annual incomes of less than $7,500) are by far the most likely to be victims of violent crimes, and this association occurs across all gender, racial, and age groups.

MARITAL STATUS ● Unmarried or never married people are victimized more often

REALITYCHECK

MYTH OR REALITY? Becoming a crime victim is a matter of being "in the wrong place at the wrong time."

MYTH: The risks people take do in fact affect the likelihood of their becoming a crime victim.

Comment on how a risky lifestyle influences the chances of becoming a victim. How can a college student avoid victimization risks?

than married people or widows and widowers. These relationships are probably influenced by age, gender, and lifestyle:

- Unmarried people tend to be younger, and young people have the highest victim risk.
- Widows, who are more likely to be older women, suffer much lower victimization rates because they interact with older people, are more likely to stay home at night, and avoid public places.

RACE ● African Americans are victimized by violent crime at a higher rate than other groups. NCVS data shows that African Americans have strikingly higher rates of violent personal crime victimizations than whites. Although these two groups are more similar in their risk of theft victimization, African Americans are still more likely to be victimized than whites.

Crimes committed against African Americans tend to be more serious than those committed against whites. African Americans experience higher rates of aggravated assault, whereas whites are more often the victims of simple assault. African Americans are about three times as likely to become robbery victims as whites. Young African American males are also at great risk for homicide victimization. They face a murder risk 4 or 5 times greater than that of young African American females, 5 to 8 times higher than that of young white males, and 16 to 22 times higher than that of young white females.[35]

Why do these discrepancies exist? One clear reason is that young black males tend to live in the largest U.S. cities, in areas beset by alcohol and drug abuse, poverty, racial discrimination, and violence. Because they are forced to live in the most dangerous areas, their lifestyle places them in the highest at-risk population group.

ECOLOGICAL FACTORS ● There are distinct ecological patterns in the victim rate:

- Most victimizations occur in large urban areas; rural and suburban victim rates are far lower.
- Most incidents occur during the evening hours (6:00 P.M. to 6:00 A.M.). More serious crimes take place after 6:00 P.M., less serious crimes before 6:00 P.M.
- The most likely site for a victimization—especially a violent crime such as rape, robbery, or aggravated assault—is an open, public area such as a street, park, or field.
- One of the most dangerous public places is a public school building. Each year about 10 percent of all U.S. youths aged 12 to 19 (approximately 2 million) are crime victims while on school grounds.
- An overwhelming number of criminal incidents involve a solo victim.
- Most victims report that their assailant was not armed (except for the crime of robbery, where about half the offenders carry weapons). The use of guns and the use of knives are about equal, and there does not seem to be a pattern of a particular weapon being used for a particular crime.

VICTIM–OFFENDER RELATIONSHIPS ● The NCVS can tell us something about the characteristics of people who commit crime. This information is available only on criminals who actually came in contact with the victim through such crimes as rape, assault, or robbery.

- About 50 percent of all violent crimes are committed by strangers. The other half of violent crimes are committed by people who were known to the victim, including family members, spouses, parents, children, and siblings.
- Women seem much more likely than men to be victimized by acquaintances; a majority of female assault victims know their assailants.

All too often victims know, are acquainted with, or are related to their attackers. Pall bearers load the casket of Bianca Revelus, 5, into a hearse, as the casket of her brother Kerby Revelus, 23, is wheeled from the Jubilee Christian Church in Boston, Massachusetts, on April 4, 2009. Samantha Revelus, 17, and Bianca Revelus were stabbed to death by their brother Kerby Revelus before he was shot and killed by police. As police burst into the family's apartment, they allegedly saw Kerby Revelus decapitating his 5-year-old sister. Police say they shot Kerby Revelus dead as he tried to attack another sister, 9-year-old Sarafina.

© AP Images/Josh Reynolds

- A majority of victims report that the crime was committed by a single offender over the age of 20.
- About 25 percent of victims indicate that their assailant was a young person 12 to 20 years of age. This may reflect the criminal activities of youth gangs and groups in the United States.
- Whites are the offenders in a majority of single-offender rapes and assaults; there is no racial pattern in single-offender robberies. However, multiple-offender robberies are more likely to be committed by African Americans.

REPEAT VICTIMIZATION ● Does prior victimization enhance or reduce the chances of future victimization? Stable patterns of behavior may encourage victimization, and a few people who maintain these patterns may become "chronic victims," constantly the target of predatory crimes.

Most research does in fact show that individuals who have had prior victimization experiences have a significantly higher chance of repeat victimization than people who have not been victims.[36] Research also shows that households that have experienced victimization are the ones most likely to experience it again.[37] Repeat victimizations are most likely to occur in areas with high crime rates; one study found that during a four-year period, 40 percent of all trauma patients in an urban medical center in Ohio were repeat victims.[38]

Some combination of personal and social factors may possibly encourage victimization risk. Most revictimizations happen soon after a previous crime, suggesting that repeat victims share some personal characteristics that make them a magnet for predators.[39] Not fighting back, not reporting crime to police, and repurchasing stolen goods may encourage repeat victimization.

Causes of Crime and Victimization

Although the various sources of crime statistics can tell us about the nature of crime patterns and trends, knowing why an individual commits crime in the first place is also important. Such knowledge is critical if programs are to be devised to deter or prevent crime. If, for example, people commit crime because they are poor and desperate, the key to crime prevention might be a job program and government economic aid. If, however, the root cause of crime is a poor family life marked by conflict and abuse, then providing jobs will not help lower the crime rate; family counseling and parenting skills courses are likely to be more effective.

Criminologists study the nature and cause of crime (see the Careers in Criminal Justice feature on page 63). Some criminologists view crime as a social phenomenon and study the social and economic factors that influence human behavior. Others view crime as an individual-level phenomenon and attempt to identify the cognitive and psychological processes that result in antisocial behavior. Regardless of their point of view, criminologists study crime data in order to identify the factors and motivations that predict crime and to assess the most effective responses to crime by various methods of law enforcement. Because there is still a great deal of uncertainty about the "real" cause of crime and the most effective methods of crime prevention, some of the more popular explanations are discussed in the following sections.

Choice Theory

choice theory
The school of thought holding that people will engage in delinquent and criminal behavior after weighing the consequences and benefits of their actions. People break the law based on a rational choice made by a motivated offender who perceives that the chances of gain outweigh any perceived punishment or loss.

The origins of **choice theory** can be traced to the writings of Cesare Beccaria (1738–1794), who believed that human behavior was motivated by people's desire to achieve pleasure and avoid pain. Because crime can bring benefits to the criminal, it can be eliminated by supplying sufficient pain to counterbalance the pleasure obtained from crime.[40]

According to this rational choice theory (or simply choice theory),

1. All people of their own free will can choose between conventional and criminal behaviors.

2. Most people have the potential to violate the law because crime promises great rewards and requires less effort for greater gain.

3. Before deciding to act, motivated offenders balance the risks and rewards of crime. Among the factors they consider are

   ● Personal factors such as the need for money, excitement, experience, or revenge
   ● Situational factors (e.g., how well a target is protected, the risk of apprehension, or the chance for hurting bystanders)
   ● Legal factors (the efficiency of police, the threat of legal punishment, or the effect of a prior criminal record on future punishment)

4. People will avoid doing antisocial acts if they believe

   ● That the severity of the punishment they will receive for their actions will outweigh any potential gain.
   ● That there is a substantial likelihood or certainty that they will be caught and punished.
   ● Punishment will be swift and timely.

5. The punishments threatened by the existing criminal law are the primary deterrent to crime.

According to rational choice theory, motivated people, after thoughtful consideration, will commit crime if they believe that it will provide immediate benefits without the threat of long-term risks.[41] Before concluding a drug sale, experienced traffickers will mentally balance the chances of making a large profit with the consequences of being apprehended and punished for drug dealing. They know that most drug deals are not detected and that the potential for enormous, untaxed profits is great. They evaluate their lifestyle

Careers in Criminal Justice

CRIMINOLOGIST

Duties and Characteristics of the Job

- Criminologists are academics who analyze patterns in criminal activity and attempt to determine the causes of, future trends in, and potential solutions to crime in society.
- They are concerned with questions such as how to effectively deter crime, who will commit crime and why, and how to predict and prevent criminal behavior.
- Criminologists often work with law enforcement at the local, state, or federal level.
- Some criminologists seek positions at universities and colleges, where they conduct research, write books and articles, and teach courses about crime and criminal justice.
- In general, criminologists work 40-hour weeks in office settings.

Job Outlook

- There is great demand for criminologists working in the university setting. Those with more education can expect better job opportunities and higher salaries.

Salary

- Criminologists' median annual earnings are about $60,000
- Salaries vary widely depending on employer and personal level of advancement.
- Starting pay for an assistant professor ranges from $45,000 to $70,000, depending on the institution.
- A full professor has an average annual salary of about $110,000.

Opportunities

- Predicted increases in retirement in the near future will most likely open up new positions.
- There is more opportunity in the university setting for criminologists than for specialists in other fields, such as psychology or sociology.
- Many individuals who get a degree in criminology or work as criminologists can use their education and experience to successfully launch careers in related jobs, such as police officer, federal agent, or psychologist.

Qualifications

- Educational requirements usually include courses on human behavior and the criminal justice system, and they usually involve developing skills in statistics and writing.
- Training typically includes familiarity with computer programs used for statistical analysis, such as SAS or SPSS.
- Because criminology requires collecting and examining data, conducting research, and presenting these ideas to others, personal qualities such as intellectual curiosity and strong communicative and analytical skills are important.
- Certain states require potential criminologists to pass a written test to become licensed before they can work. Additionally, those working with law enforcement agencies will have to pass background and security checks.

Education and Training

- Typically, this means a master's degree in criminology and/or criminal justice. Other social science degrees can be acceptable. This is generally enough for those desiring work at law enforcement agencies. Teaching at the university level requires a doctorate in one of the previously mentioned fields.

Word to the Wise

- Getting tenure can be difficult, and you must be ready to "publish or perish" at most universities.
- Teaching has its rewards, but assistant professors face large classes with many papers to grade.
- Research today requires highly sophisticated methodological skills, so be prepared to take advanced statistics classes.

and determine how much cash they need to maintain their standard of living, which is usually extravagant. They may have borrowed to finance the drug deal, and their creditors are not usually reasonable if loans cannot be repaid promptly. They also realize that they could be the target of a "sting" operation by undercover agents and, if caught, would get a long mandatory sentence in a forbidding federal penitentiary. They may be aware that law enforcement agents are now using sophisticated technology such as hidden cameras and facial recognition technology to monitor their whereabouts and spy on their drug deals.[42]

If they conclude that the potential for profits is great enough, their need for cash urgent, and the chances of apprehension minimal, they will carry out the deal. If, however, they believe that the transaction will bring them only a small profit and a large risk of apprehension and punishment, they may forgo the deal as too risky. The more often they are arrested, the less likely they are to engage in a risky deal.[43]

When deciding to commit crime, a potential offender balances her perceptions of getting caught and punished against the perceived benefits of crime. Benefits include not only monetary gains but also psychic rewards such as excitement and increased social status among their peers.[44] Experience may play a hand in the decision-making process. Veteran criminals may not fear some future punishment because they know firsthand that apprehension risk is actually quite low.[45] Some may be deterred in the short run but soon return to their criminal ways.[46] Others, convinced that the pains of punishment outweigh the benefits of crime, may become more wary and willing to desist from a criminal career.[47]

Biosocial Theory

positive stage
According to Comte, during the positive stage of human social development, people embrace rational scientific explanations for observed phenomena.

During the nineteenth century, the first social scientists began to apply the scientific method to the study of society. Auguste Comte (1798–1857), a founder of social science, described how as society progressed, people embraced a rational, scientific view of the world. Comte called this final stage the **positive stage**, and those who followed his writings became known as positivists. Those who embraced positivism relied on the strict use of empirical methods—factual, firsthand observation and measurement of conditions and events—to test hypotheses.

The first positivists to study crime focused on biological factors that caused people to become violent and antisocial. This approach was abandoned in the twentieth century, but in recent years there has been renewed interest in finding a biological basis of crime.

biosocial theory
Human behavior is a function of the interaction of biochemical, neurological, and genetic factors with environmental stimuli.

Today, those who believe that crime has a biological basis maintain that personal traits and biological makeup, not parenting or social environment, explain behavioral choices.[48] According to this **biosocial theory,** elements of the environment (family life, community factors) interact with biological factors (neurological makeup) to control and influence behavior. For example, children who suffer deficits caused by birth complications will be predisposed to committing violent acts as they mature if they are also forced to grow up in a dysfunctional and negative home environment.[49]

Biosocial theories can be divided into three broad areas of focus: biochemical factors, neurological problems, and genetic abnormalities.

BIOCHEMICAL THEORY ● Some criminologists believe that biochemical abnormality may lead to antisocial behaviors. Such biochemical factors as vitamin and mineral deficiencies, hormone imbalance, and environmental contaminants (such as the presence of lead and other metals) have been linked to antisocial behavior.[50] The influence of damaging chemical and biological contaminants may begin before birth: Maternal alcohol abuse and or smoking during gestation has long been linked to prenatal damage and subsequent antisocial behavior in adolescence.[51]

Adolescents exposed to harmful chemicals and poor diet may be prone to antisocial behavior choices.[52] If biochemical makeup can influence behavior, it stands to reason that there may be a link between diet and crime.[53] Those biocriminologists who believe in a diet–aggression association claim that in every segment of society there are violent, aggressive, and amoral people whose improper food, vitamin, and mineral intake may be responsible for their antisocial behavior. They believe that if diet could be improved, the frequency of violent behavior would be reduced.[54] Researchers have found these other biochemical links to crime:

- *Alcohol intake.* Research now shows that people who start drinking by the age of 14 are five times more likely to become alcoholics than people who hold off on drinking until the age of 21. Early exposure of the brain to alcohol can short-circuit the growth of brain cells, impairing the learning and memory processes that protect against addiction, and can have a direct influence on antisocial behavior.[55]
- *Environmental contaminants.* Overexposure to environmental contaminants such as metals (including lead, iron, and manganese) has been linked to neurological dysfunction. Exposure to environmental contaminants is believed to be a precursor of delinquent and criminal behaviors.[56]
- *Hormones.* Organic factors linked to crime and aggression include abnormal hormonal activity. Some criminologists argue that gender differences in the crime rate can be linked to the male hormone testosterone and its assumed effect on the behavior of adolescent males.[57] Although girls have only trace levels of testosterone, those who have the highest levels or are exposed to testosterone in utero stand a greater chance of becoming more aggressive in adolescence than their female peers.[58]

NEUROLOGICAL THEORY ● Another area of interest to biocriminologists is the relationship of brain activity to behavior. Biocriminologists have used the electroencephalogram to record the electrical impulses given off by the brain. Preliminary studies indicate that 50 percent to 60 percent of those with behavior disorders display abnormal recordings.[59]

People with an abnormal cerebral structure, referred to as "minimal brain dysfunction," may experience periods of explosive rage that can lead to violent episodes.[60] There is now evidence that self-control may in fact be regulated and controlled by the prefrontal cortex of the brain.[61] In this scenario, neurological impairment reduces impulse control and self-control, which then leads people to make damaging behavioral choices.

Brain dysfunction is sometimes manifested as attention deficit/hyperactivity disorder (ADHD), which has been linked to antisocial behavior. About 3 percent of all U.S. children, primarily boys, are believed to suffer from this disorder, and it is the most common reason why children are referred to mental health clinics. Some psychologists believe that the syndrome is essentially a chemical problem, specifically an impairment in the chemical system that supports rapid and efficient communication in the brain's management system.[62] The condition may result in poor school performance, bullying, stubbornness, and a lack of response to discipline.[63]

GENETIC THEORY ● Violent behavior is possibly inherited and a function of a person's genetic makeup. One approach to testing this theory has been to evaluate the behavior of adopted children. If an adopted child's behavior patterns ran parallel to those of his or her biological parents, it would be strong evidence to support a genetic basis for crime. Studies conducted in Europe have indicated that the criminality of the biological father is in fact a strong predictor of a child's antisocial behavior.[64] The probability that a youth will engage in crime is significantly enhanced when both biological and adoptive parents exhibit criminal tendencies.

A more rigorous test of genetic theory involves comparing the behavior of identical monozygotic (MZ) twins with that of fraternal dizygotic (DZ) twins; the former have an identical genetic makeup, whereas the latter share about 50 percent of their genetic combinations. Research has shown that MZ twins are significantly closer in their personal characteristics, such as intelligence, than are DZ twins.[65] When Sara Jaffee and her colleagues compared the behavior similarities of identical (MZ) with fraternal (DZ) twins, they found a strong genetic association in the development of such conduct disorders as persistent lying, bullying, violence, physical cruelty, and stealing; there was significantly more concordance among MZ twins than among DZ twins.[66]

Psychological Theory

Soon after Seung-Hui Cho's rampage at Virginia Tech, pundits began to diagnose his behavior from afar. Terms such as "paranoid schizophrenia," "paranoid ideation," "disorganized thinking," and "acute psychotic exacerbation" were tossed about. Cho's behavior was linked to several psychological symptoms: withdrawal from society, self-imposed isolation from peers and family, violent fantasies, unusual personal habits, and a monotonic voice and flat affect. Considering incidents such as the Virginia Tech massacre, it comes as no surprise that some experts believe criminality is caused by psychological factors. There are actually a number of views on the psychological basis of crime.

psychoanalytic view
Criminals are driven by unconscious thought patterns, developed in early childhood, that control behaviors over the life course.

PSYCHOANALYTIC THEORY ● According to the **psychoanalytic view**, some people encounter problems during their early development that cause an imbalance in their personality. The most deeply disturbed are referred to as psychotics, who cannot restrain their impulsive behavior. One type of psychosis is schizophrenia, a condition marked by incoherent thought processes, a lack of insight, hallucinations, and feelings of persecution. Schizophrenics may suffer delusions and feel persecuted, worthless, and alienated.[67] Other offenders may suffer from a wide variety of mood and behavior disorders that render them histrionic, depressed, antisocial, or narcissistic.[68] They may suffer from conduct disorders, which include long histories of antisocial behavior, or mood disorders characterized by disturbance in expressed emotions. Among the latter is **bipolar disorder**, in which moods alternate between wild elation and deep depression.[69] Some offenders are driven by an unconscious desire to be punished for prior sins, either real or imaginary. As a result, they may violate the law or even harm their parents to gain attention.

bipolar disorder
A psychological condition marked by mood swings between periods of wild elation and deep depression.

According to the psychoanalytic view, crime is a manifestation of feelings of oppression and of the individual's inability to develop the proper psychological defenses and rationales to keep these feelings under control. Criminality may allow these troubled people to survive by producing positive psychic results: It helps them to feel free and independent, and confers an opportunity for excitement and the chance to use their skills and imagination. It also provides them with the promise of positive gain, as well as allowing them to blame others (such as the police) for their predicament. Finally, it gives them a chance to rationalize their sense of failure ("If I hadn't gotten into trouble, I could have been a success").[70]

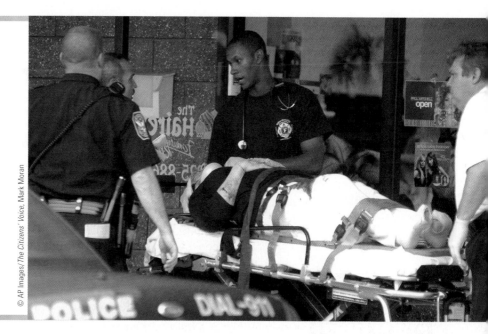

Some criminologists link violent, aggressive crime to an underlying neurological abnormality. Here, medics from Wilkes-Barre City and Plains Township police attend to a victim of a hammer assault at the Hairem Hair and Nail Salon in Plains Township, Pennsylvania, on August 10, 2007. According to police, a man entered the salon Friday morning with a hammer and randomly assaulted four people. It is hard to believe that such an unprovoked attack be the work of a mentally competent person.

© AP Images/*The Citizens' Voice*, Mark Moran

This view has great appeal, but research results are conflicting. Some studies find a link between mental disturbance and crime; others indicate that the mentally ill are not any more crime-prone than the mentally sound. The mentally ill who are violent or criminal typically manifest other problems such as drug abuse and alcoholism, conditions that have been linked to criminality.[71]

ATTACHMENT THEORY ● According to **attachment theory**, the ability to form an emotional bond to another person has important, lasting psychological implications that follow people across the life span.[72] Failing to develop proper attachments may cause kids to fall prey to a number of psychological disorders, including attention deficit/hyperactivity disorder (ADHD), impulsivity, and poor concentration. As adults, they often have difficulty initiating and sustaining relationships. Criminologists have linked people who have detachment problems with a variety of antisocial behaviors, including sexual assault and child abuse.[73] It has been suggested that boys disproportionately experience disrupted attachment and that these disruptions are related to disproportionate rates of male offending.[74]

behavioral theory
Behavior patterns are modeled and learned in interactions with others.

attachment theory
Psychological theory that people who had close, caring bonds with a caregiver while growing up are more likely to develop prosocial interpersonal relationships in adulthood.

BEHAVIORAL THEORY ● Another psychological view is that criminal behavior is learned through interactions with others. One assumption is that people act aggressively because as children they experienced violence firsthand, either observing it at home or being a target of violent parents. Children model their behavior after the violent acts of adults. Observed and experienced violence may have an interactive effect: Kids who live in high-crime neighborhoods and witness violence in the community and at home, who are the direct victims of domestic and community-based violence, are the ones most likely to commit crime.[75]

One area of particular interest to **behavioral theory** theorists is whether the media can influence violence. Studies have shown that youths exposed to aggressive, antisocial behavior on television and in movies are likely to copy that violent behavior. Laboratory studies generally conclude that violence on television can lead to aggressive behavior by children and teenagers who watch such programs.[76] Sociologist George Comstock has identified attributes that make some people especially prone to the effects of media violence:

- predisposition toward aggressive or antisocial behavior
- rigid or indifferent parenting
- unsatisfactory social relationships
- low psychological well-being
- having been diagnosed as suffering from DBDs—disruptive behavior disorders[77]

Whether the evidence obtained in controlled laboratory studies can be applied to the real world is still being debated.[78] Considering that the average child watches more than 20 hours of TV a week, and that the average child views 8,000 TV murders before finishing elementary school, any possible link between TV violence and criminal behavior is important.[79]

REALITYCHECK

MYTH OR REALITY? Kids who watch a lot of violence on TV are more likely to get involved in violent behavior themselves.

MYTH: Millions of kids watch violent TV shows and remain nonviolent. The link between violent media and violent behavior is still being debated.

In the meantime, should young children be prevented from watching media violence?

COGNITIVE THEORY • Law violators may lack the ability to perform cognitive functions in a normal and orderly fashion.[80] Because they have inadequate cognitive processing, criminals perceive the world as stacked against them; they believe they have little control over the negative events in their life.[81] Some may be sensation seekers who are constantly looking for novel experiences, whereas others lack deliberation and rarely think through problems. Some may give up easily, whereas others act without thinking when they get upset.[82]

This distorted view of the world shapes their thinking and colors their judgments. Crime is viewed as an appropriate means to satisfy their immediate personal needs, which take precedence over more distant social needs and such abstract moral concepts as "obey the law" and "respect the rights of others."[83]

Because they have difficulty making the "right" decision while under stress, people with poor cognitive ability pursue behaviors that they perceive as beneficial and satisfying but that turn out to be harmful and detrimental.[84] They find it difficult to understand or sympathize with other people's feelings and emotions, and this leads them to blame their victims for their problems.[85] Rapists may believe their target either "led them on" or secretly wanted the forcible sex to occur: "She was asking for it."[86] Child abusers may misperceive children as being able to and wanting to engage in sexual activity with adults and also as not harmed by such sexual contact.[87]

psychopathic (antisocial, sociopathic) personality
Psychopaths are chronically antisocial individuals who are always in trouble and who do not learn from either experience or punishment. They are loners who engage in frequent callous and hedonistic behaviors, are emotionally immature, and lack responsibility, judgment, and empathy.

CRIMINAL PERSONALITY • Psychologists have explored the link between personality and crime. Evidence shows that aggressive youths have unstable personality structures often marked by hyperactivity, impulsiveness, and instability.

One area of particular interest to criminology is identification of the **psychopathic** (sometimes referred to as the **antisocial** or **sociopathic**) **personality**. Psychopaths are believed to be dangerous, aggressive, antisocial individuals who act in a callous manner. They neither learn from their mistakes nor are deterred by punishment.[88] From an early age, psychopaths have had home lives filled with frustrations, bitterness, and quarreling.[89] They exhibit low levels of guilt and anxiety and persistently violate the rights of others.

Although they may exhibit charm and be highly intelligent, these qualities mask a disturbed personality that makes them incapable of forming enduring relationships.[90] Their intelligence may alter their criminal career development and render it quite different from that of nonpsychopathic criminals; high intelligence appears to enhance the destructive potential of a psychopath, while intelligence may mediate the criminality of the nonpsychopath.[91]

The concept of the psychopathic personality is important for criminology because it has been estimated that somewhere between 10 and 30 percent of all prison inmates can be classified as psychopaths or sociopaths or as having similar character disorders.[92] Psychopathy has also been linked to the phenomenon of serial murder.[93]

What causes a psychopathic personality to develop?

- Having a psychopathic parent, parental rejection and lack of love during childhood, and inconsistent discipline are all contributing factors.[94]
- Physical abnormality, especially the activity of the autonomic nervous system, may be a factor. Psychopaths may have lower arousal levels than normal.[95]
- Another view is that the psychopathic personality is imprinted at birth and is relatively unaffected by socialization or experience.[96]

According to this view of the causes of crime, the personality is the key to understanding antisocial behavior. The more severe the disorder, the greater the likelihood that the individual will engage in serious and repeat antisocial acts. [97]

Social Structure Theory

At the same time that biological positivists were dominating criminology, others were developing the field of sociology to scientifically study the major social changes taking place in nineteenth-century society. Émile Durkheim (1858–1917), one of the founders of sociology, considered crime normal and necessary because it produced social change. Without crime, society was doomed to conformity and inertia.[98] The social positivist tradition is still alive today. Because crime patterns have a decidedly social orientation, sociological explanations of crime have predominated in criminology.

According to one branch of social positivism, **social structure theory**, the United States is a stratified society. Recent surveys indicate that the number of "super rich" U.S. households with a net worth of more than $5 million, excluding their primary residence, now surpasses the 1 million mark.[99] In contrast, almost 40 million Americans live beneath the poverty line, which is now calculated at about $20,000 per year for a family of four.[100]

Those living in poverty face dead-end jobs, unemployment, and social failure. Because of their meager economic resources, lower-class citizens are often forced to live in poor areas marked by substandard housing, inadequate health care, renters rather than homeowners, poor educational opportunities, underemployment, and despair. These indicators of neighborhood disorder are highly predictive of crime rates.[101]

The problems of lower-class culture are particularly acute for racial and ethnic minorities who have an income level significantly below that of whites and an unemployment rate almost twice as high. In the inner cities, more than half of all black men do not finish high school. In addition, they face the burden of racism and racial stereotyping. Research shows that whites are averse to living in or visiting black neighborhoods because they consider them crime-ridden, even if these neighborhoods actually have relatively low crime rates.[102] In their book *There Goes the Neighborhood*, sociologists William Julius Wilson and Richard Taub assess the race relations in four Chicago neighborhoods and find that racism is still an active part of people's lives. People are

social structure theory
A person's position in the social structure controls his or her behavior. Those in the lowest socioeconomic tier are more likely to succumb to crime-promoting elements in their environment, whereas those in the highest tier enjoy social and economic advantages that insulate them from crime-producing forces.

Two abandoned homes sit across the street from new low-income housing being built in North Philadelphia. This section of the city is known for high levels of urban poverty and high levels of drug-related crime. These abandoned homes are two of an estimated 35,000 in Philadelphia. When crime rates are high in such areas, criminologists blame social disorganization, fear, and lack of informal social control.

© Mark Ludak/The Image Works

unusually hostile when outsiders move into their enclave. If they have a choice, they move; if not, they are angry and sullen. In a white middle-class neighborhood, people are angry when black and Latino newcomers arrive, believing they threaten property values and neighborhood stability. Fear and suspicion may keep the races apart.[103]

The crushing burden of urban poverty results in the development of a **culture of poverty**.[104] This culture is marked by apathy, cynicism, helplessness, and distrust. The culture is passed from one generation to another such that its members become part of a permanent underclass, "the truly disadvantaged."[105] In these areas people live in constant fear and suffer social and physical incivilities—rowdy youths, trash and litter, graffiti, abandoned storefronts, burned-out buildings, littered lots, strangers, drunks, vagabonds, loiterers, prostitutes, noise, congestion, angry words, dirt, and stench.[106] Forced to endure substandard housing and schools in deteriorated inner-city, socially disorganized neighborhoods, and cut off from conventional society, the urban poor face a constant assault on their self-image and sense of worth. Criminal acts and drug dealing provide a means of survival in an otherwise bleak existence. Those living in impoverished neighborhoods are continuously exposed to the opportunity to buy drugs and engage in antisocial acts.[107]

There are three independent yet overlapping branches within the social structure perspective: social disorganization, strain theory, and cultural deviance theory.

SOCIAL DISORGANIZATION THEORY • A socially disorganized area is one in which institutions of social control, such as the family, commercial establishments, and schools, have broken down and can no longer carry out their expected or stated functions.[108] Living in deteriorated, crime-ridden neighborhoods exerts a powerful influence that is strong enough to neutralize any positive effects of a supportive family and close social ties.[109]

Socially disorganized areas are characterized by high unemployment and school dropout rates, deteriorated housing, low income levels, and large

culture of poverty

The crushing lifestyle of slum areas produces a culture of poverty, passed from one generation to the next, marked by apathy, cynicism, feelings of helplessness, and mistrust of social institutions, such as schools, government agencies, and the police.

numbers of single-parent households. Delinquent gangs and youth groups soon form and lure members with respect, protection, and financial security.[110] As gangs actively recruit new members and grow larger, area residents are constantly being exposed to violence.[111] Not surprisingly, they experience conflict, despair, and hopelessness.[112]

As conditions deteriorate, those who can move out do, further destabilizing the neighborhood. Those who remain feel powerless and incapable of acting cooperatively with neighbors to solve community problems; they lack the ability to create what is known as **collective efficacy**.[113] Residents in communities that maintain collective efficacy are more active in informal crime control activities.[114] They may engage in surveillance practices by "keeping an eye out" for intruders when their neighbors go out of town.[115] In these more stable areas, kids use their wits to avoid violent confrontations and to feel safe in their own neighborhood, a concept referred to as **street efficacy**.[116] In contrast, adolescents who live in neighborhoods with concentrated disadvantage and low collective efficacy not only lose confidence in their ability to avoid violence but begin using violence themselves to solve problems.[117]

STRAIN THEORY ● Strain theory holds that crime is a function of the conflict between the *goals* people have and the *means* they can use to obtain them legally.[118] Social and economic goals are common to people in all economic strata, but ability to obtain these goals is class dependent. Most people in the United States desire wealth, material possessions, power, prestige, and other comforts. People are willing to do anything to get ahead, from cheating on tests to get higher grades, to engaging in corporate fraud and tax evasion.[119] Those who cannot succeed become willing to risk everything, including a prison sentence. Members of the lower class are unable to achieve these symbols of success through conventional means. Consequently, they feel anger, frustration, and resentment. Lower-class citizens either can accept their condition, and live out their days as socially responsible, if unrewarded, citizens, or can choose an alternative means of achieving success, such as theft, violence, or drug trafficking. Although there are other sources of strain, such as negative life experiences or losing a loved one, the strain imposed by limited opportunities may help explain why lower-class areas have such high crime rates.[120]

CULTURAL DEVIANCE THEORY ● Combining elements of both strain and social disorganization, cultural deviance theory holds that because of strain and social isolation, a unique lower-class culture has developed in disorganized, poverty-ridden neighborhoods. The independent **subcultures** maintain a unique set of values and beliefs that are in conflict with conventional social norms. Criminal behavior is an expression of conformity to lower-class subcultural values, which stress toughness, independence, and standing up to authority. These subcultural values are handed down from one generation to the next in a process called **cultural transmission**. Neighborhood youths who hold these values and incorporate them into their own personal code of behavior are much more likely to join gangs and violate the law than those who reject the deviant subculture.

Social Process Theory

A second branch of social positivism maintains that people commit crime as a result of the experiences they have while they are being socialized by the various

collective efficacy
The ability of neighborhood residents to act cooperatively to maintain social control within communities.

street efficacy
Using one's wits to avoid violent confrontations and to feel safe.

subculture
A substratum of society that maintains a unique set of values and beliefs.

cultural transmission
The passing of cultural values from one generation to the next.

© SuperStock RF/SuperStock

organizations, institutions, and processes of society. People are most strongly impelled toward criminal behavior by poor family relationships, destructive peer-group relations, educational failure, and labeling by agents of the justice system. Although lower-class citizens bear the added burdens of poverty and strain, even middle-class or upper-class citizens may turn to crime if their socialization is poor or destructive.

social process theory
An individual's behavior is shaped by interactions with key social institutions—family, school, peer group, and the like.

Social process theory points to research efforts linking family problems to crime as evidence that socialization, not social structure, is the key to understanding the onset of criminality. Family problems linked to criminality include inconsistent discipline, poor supervision, and the lack of a warm, loving, supportive parent-child relationship.[121] Parents who are supportive and who effectively control their children in a noncoercive fashion—**parental efficacy**—are more likely to raise children who refrain from delinquency.[122] In contrast, the likelihood of delinquency increases when parents are unable to provide the type of family structure that gives children the ability to assert their individuality and regulate their own behavior.[123]

parental efficacy
The ability of parents to provide support and discipline in a noncoercive manner.

Educational experience has also been found to have a significant impact on criminality. Youths who fail at school and eventually drop out are the ones most likely to engage in criminal behavior; academic performance is a significant predictor of crime and delinquency.[124] One reason is that many schools are troubled and cannot provide an adequate academic experience.

In a similar fashion, socialization within the peer group is also a significant influence on behavior. Children who maintain ties with a deviant peer group are the ones most likely to persist in criminal behavior into their adulthood.[125]

The social process approach has several independent branches. The first branch, social learning theory, suggests that people learn the techniques and attitudes of crime from close and intimate relationships with criminal peers; crime is a learned behavior. The second branch, social control theory, maintains that everyone has the potential to become a criminal but that most people are controlled by their bond to society. Crime occurs when the forces that bind people to society are weakened or broken. The third branch, social reaction (labeling) theory, says people become criminals when significant members of society label them as such and they accept those labels as a personal identity.

Put another way, social learning theory assumes people are born "good" and learn to be "bad"; social control theory assumes people are born "bad" and must be controlled in order to be "good"; social reaction theory assumes that whether "good" or "bad," people are controlled by the reactions of others.

Conflict Theory

In Europe, the writings of another social thinker, Karl Marx (1818–1883), described how economic, social, and political forces controlled human behavior and shaped society.[126] His thoughts were soon being applied to the study of crime and conflict.

conflict theory
Human behavior is shaped by interpersonal conflict, and those who maintain social power use it to further their own interests.

Contemporary **conflict theory** views the economic and political forces operating in society as the fundamental causes of criminality. The criminal law and criminal justice systems are viewed as vehicles for controlling the poor members of society. The criminal justice system is believed to help the powerful and rich impose their particular morality and standards of good behavior on the entire

© Kris Legg/Alamy

society, while it protects their property and physical safety from the have-nots, even though the cost may be the legal rights of the lower class. Those in power control the content and direction of the law and legal system.

Crimes are defined in a way that meets the needs of the ruling classes. The theft of property worth $5 by a poor person can be punished much more severely than the misappropriation of millions by a large corporation. Those in the middle class are drawn into this pattern of control because they are led to believe that they too have a stake in maintaining the status quo and should support the views of the upper-class owners of production.[127]

An important aspect of conflict theory, radical feminist theory, tries to explain how capitalism places particular stress on women and to explicate the role of male dominance in female criminality.[128] Radical feminists view female crime as originating with the onset of male supremacy (patriarchy), the subsequent subordination of women, male aggression, and efforts of men to control women sexually.[129] They focus on the social forces that shape women's lives and experiences to explain female criminality. For example, they attempt to show how the sexual victimization of females is a function of male socialization because so many young males learn to be aggressive and exploitive of women. Exploited at home, female victims try to cope by running away and by engaging in premarital sex and substance abuse. The double standard means that female adolescents have a much narrower range of acceptable behavior than male adolescents. Any sign of misbehavior is viewed as a substantial challenge to authority that requires immediate control. Feminist scholars view the female criminal as a victim of gender inequality.

Developmental Theory

While at Harvard University in the 1930s, Sheldon Glueck and Eleanor Glueck popularized research on the life cycle of delinquent careers. In a series of longitudinal research studies, they followed the careers of known delinquents to determine the factors that predicted persistent offending.[130] The Gluecks made extensive use of interviews and records in their elaborate comparisons of delinquents and nondelinquents.[131] Their work serves as the cornerstone for contemporary **developmental theory**.

According to developmental theory, even as toddlers, people begin relationships and behaviors that will determine their adult life course.[132] These transitions are expected to take place in a prescribed order—beginning with completing school, entering the workforce, getting married, and having children. Some individuals, however, are incapable of maturing in a reasonable and timely fashion because of family, environmental, or personal problems. In some cases, transitions can occur too early—for example, when adolescents engage in precocious sex. In other cases, transitions may occur too late, such as when a student fails to graduate on time because of bad grades. Sometimes disruption of one trajectory can harm another. For example, teenage childbirth is likely to disrupt educational and career development. And kids who are schoolyard bullies may later engage in aggressive behavior and crime.[133] Because developmental theories focus on the associations between life events and deviant behaviors, they are sometimes referred to as life-course theories.

Disruptions in life's major transitions can be destructive and ultimately can promote criminality. Those who are already at risk because of socioeconomic problems or family dysfunction are the most susceptible to these awkward transitions. The cumulative impact of these disruptions sustains criminality from childhood into adulthood.

Because a transition from one stage of life to another can be a bumpy ride, the propensity to commit crimes is neither stable nor constant; it is a developmental process. A positive life experience may help some criminals desist from

developmental theory
Social interactions that are developed over the life course shape behavior. Some interactions (such as involvement with deviant peers) encourage law violations, whereas others (such as marriage and military service) may help people desist from crime.

crime for a while, whereas a negative one may cause them to resume their activities. Criminal careers are said to be developmental because people are influenced by the behavior of those around them and in turn influence others' behavior. A youth's antisocial behavior may turn his more conventional friends against him; their rejection solidifies and escalates his antisocial behavior.

Developmental theory also recognizes that as people mature, the factors that influence their behavior change.[134] One vision is that development is controlled by a master trait, such as impulsivity and lack of self-control.[135] This master trait colors and shapes human relationships, including relationships with peers, family, and social institutions.[136]

Another view holds that all people go through different phases of development and that the influences on their behavior are constantly shifting. At first, family relations may be most influential; in later adolescence, school and peer relations predominate; in adulthood, vocational achievement and marital relations may be the most critical influences.[137] For example, some antisocial children who are in trouble during adolescence manage to find stable work and maintain stable marriages as adults; these life events help them desist from crime. In contrast, the less fortunate adolescents who develop arrest records and get involved with the wrong crowd may find themselves limited to menial jobs and at risk for criminal careers.[138]

A Final Word

There are probably so many views of crime causation because there are so many types of crimes. It is possible that all explanations are partially correct: Some people commit crime because they are poorly socialized; some succumb to the obstacles placed in their path by lower-class life; others have psychological or biological problems; some are victims of class conflict. There may also be interaction among the various theories of criminology: Impulsivity and low self-control may be genetically determined, kids who live in disorganized neighborhoods may receive improper socialization, and so on.[139] The various theories of criminology are summarized in Concept Summary 2.3.

Concept
Summary
2.3

© X Brand Images/Getty Images

Concepts and Theories of Criminology: A Review

Theory	Major Premise
Choice Theory	People commit crime when they perceive that the benefits of law violation outweigh the threat and pain of punishment.
Biosocial Theory	
Biochemical Theory	Crime, especially violence, is a function of diet, vitamin intake, hormonal imbalance, or food allergies.
Neurological Theory	Criminals and delinquents often suffer brain impairment. Attention deficit disorder and minimum brain dysfunction are related to antisocial behavior.

Genetic Theory	Criminal traits and predispositions are inherited. The criminality of parents can predict the delinquency of children.

Psychological Theory

Psychoanalytic Theory	The development of personality early in childhood influences behavior for the rest of a person's life. Criminals have weak egos and damaged personalities. Some suffer from mental illnesses and disorders.
Attachment Theory	The ability to form an emotional bond to another person in childhood follows people across the lifespan. People who lack attachment fall prey to psychological conditions related to criminality.
Behavioral Theory	People commit crime when they model their behavior after others whom they see being rewarded for the same acts. Behavior is reinforced by rewards and extinguished by punishment.
Cognitive Theory	Because they have distorted cognitive reasoning skills, criminals perceive the world as stacked against them and believe they have little control over the negative events in their lives.

Social Structure Theory

Social Disorganization Theory	The conflicts and problems of urban social life and communities control the crime rate. Crime is a product of transitional neighborhoods that manifest social disorganization and value conflict.
Strain Theory	People who adopt the goals of society but lack the means to attain them seek alternatives, such as crime.
Cultural Deviance Theory	Because of strain and social isolation, a unique lower-class subculture develops in disorganized, poverty-ridden neighborhoods whose norms put residents in conflict with conventional social norms, leading to law violations.

Social Process Theory

Social Learning Theory	People learn to commit crime from exposure to antisocial behaviors. Criminal behavior depends on the person's experiences with rewards for conventional behaviors and punishments for deviant ones. Being rewarded for deviance leads to crime.

(continued)

Concept Summary 2.3 (Continued)

© X Brand Images/Getty Images

Concepts and Theories of Criminology: A Review

Social Control Theory	A person's bond to society prevents him or her from violating social rules. If the bond weakens, the person is free to commit crime.
Self-control Theory	Crime and criminality are separate concepts. People choose to commit crime when they lack self-control. People lacking self-control will seize criminal opportunities.
Social Reaction Theory	People become criminals when significant members of society label them as such and they accept those labels as a personal identity.

Conflict Theory

Conflict Theory	People commit crime when the law, controlled by the rich and powerful, defines their behavior as illegal. The immoral actions of the powerful go unpunished.
Radical Feminist Theory	The capitalist system creates patriarchy, which oppresses women. Male dominance explains gender bias, violence against women, and repression.

Developmental Theory

Developmental Theory	Early in life people begin relationships that determine their behavior through their life course. Life transitions control the probability of offending.

ETHICAL CHALLENGES IN CRIMINAL JUSTICE

A Writing Assignment

A criminologist proposes a research project to test the association between IQ and crime. She wants to look at the association among race, intelligence, and delinquent behavior. To carry out the project, she wants to conduct IQ tests with K–12 students in the local school district, use a self-report instrument, and gather arrest data from local police. She guarantees that all data will be confidential. Take the role of a school board member who must approve of the project. Would you grant her permission to conduct the research? Explain your answer in detail. What possible harm could be done by her project and to whom?

RealityCheck Revisited

To learn more about the myths and realities related to crime and the justice system that were presented in this chapter, visit the following websites.

- For information on crime rates and trends, go to

The Bureau of Justice Statistics http://www.ojp .usdoj.gov/bjs/

The FBI's Uniform Crime Reports http://www.fbi .gov/ucr/ucr.htm#cius

- To learn more about the association between media and violence, go to

http://www.apa.org/releases/media_violence.html

http://aappolicy.aappublications.org/cgi/content/ full/pediatrics;108/5/1222

- How does the economy influence crime rates? Learn more at

http://www.heritage.org/press/commentary/ ed111500a.cfm

http://www.npr.org/templates/story/story .php?storyId=97234406

SUMMARY

© Janine Wiedel Photolibrary/Alamy

1. Be able to discuss how crime is defined

- There are three views on how behaviors become crimes: consensus, conflict, and interactionist.
- The consensus view holds that criminal behavior is defined by laws that reflect the values and morals of a majority of citizens.
- The conflict view states that criminal behavior is defined in such a way that economically powerful groups can retain their control over society.

- The interactionist view portrays criminal behavior as a relativistic, constantly changing concept that reflects society's current moral values.

2. Be familiar with the methods used to measure crime

- We get our information on crime from a number of sources, including surveys, records, interviews, and observations.
- One of the most important sources is the Uniform Crime Reports (UCR) compiled by the FBI. This national survey compiles criminal acts reported to local police. The acts are called Part I crimes (murder, rape, burglary, robbery, assault, larceny/theft, and motor vehicle theft).
- The federal government also sponsors the National Crime Victimization Survey (NCVS), which asks people about their experiences with crime.
- A third form of information is self-report surveys, which ask offenders themselves to tell about their criminal behaviors.

3. Discuss the strengths and weaknesses of crime measures

- The validity of the UCR has been suspect because many people fail to report crime to police because of fear, apathy, or lack of respect for law enforcement.

(continued)

- Many crime victims also do not report criminal incidents to the police because they believe that nothing can be done or that they should not get involved.

- Self-reports depend on the accuracy of respondents, many of whom are using drugs or delinquent.

- The crime patterns found in all three data sources may be more similar than some critics believe.

4. *Recognize the trends in the crime rate*

- Crime rates were high in the 1930s, declined afterward, and then began a rapid increase in the 1960s.

- Crime rates have been in a downward trend for about a decade.

5. *Comment on the factors that influence crime rates*

- Changes in the crime rate have been attributed to social factors, including the age structure of society.

- Crime rate increases have been tied to drug epidemics.

- The effect of the economy is less certain.

- Crime trends have been linked to the legalization of abortion.

- Criminal justice policy seems to influence crime rates.

6. *Be familiar with international crime trends*

- Crime rates have traditionally been higher in the United States than abroad.

- In recent years, crime rates have been climbing overseas while declining in the United States.

- Crime rates may be spiraling upward in nations undergoing rapid changes in their social and economic makeup.

7. *Know the various crime patterns*

- Crime occurs more often in large cities during the summer and at night. Some geographic areas (the South and West) have higher crime rates than others (the Midwest and New England).

- Arrest data indicates that males, minorities, the poor, and the young have relatively high rates of criminality.

- About 20 percent of all reported crimes are solved by police. However, a positive relationship exists between crime seriousness and the probability of a successful clearance; that is, murders and rapes are much more often solved than car thefts or larcenies.

- Victims of crime tend to be poor, young, male, and members of minority groups.

8. *Understand the concept of the criminal career*

- One of the most important findings in the crime statistics is the existence of the chronic offender.

- Repeat, career criminals are responsible for a significant amount of all law violations.

- Career criminals begin their careers early in life and, instead of aging out of crime, continue to commit crimes in adulthood.

9. *Be able to discuss the characteristics of crime victims*

- About 23 million U.S. citizens are victims of crime each year.

- Like crime, victimization has stable patterns and trends.

- Violent crime victims tend to be young, poor, single males living in large cities.

- Females are more likely than males to be victimized by someone they know.

- Adolescents maintain a high risk of being physically and sexually victimized.

10. *Distinguish among the various views of crime causation*

- Diverse schools of criminological theory approach the understanding of the cause of crime and its consequences.

- Some theories focus on the individual, whereas others view social factors as the most important element in producing crime.

- Developmental theories integrate variables at the social, individual, and societal levels.

Key Terms

Review Questions

1. Why are crime rates higher in the summer than during other seasons?

2. What factors account for crime rate trends?

3. What factors that are present in poverty-stricken urban areas produce high crime rates?

4. It seems logical that biological and psychological factors might explain why some people commit crime. How would a biologist or a psychologist explain the fact that crime rates are higher in the West than in the Midwest? Or that there is more crime in the summer than in the winter?

5. Considering the patterns that victimization takes, what steps should you take to avoid becoming a crime victim?

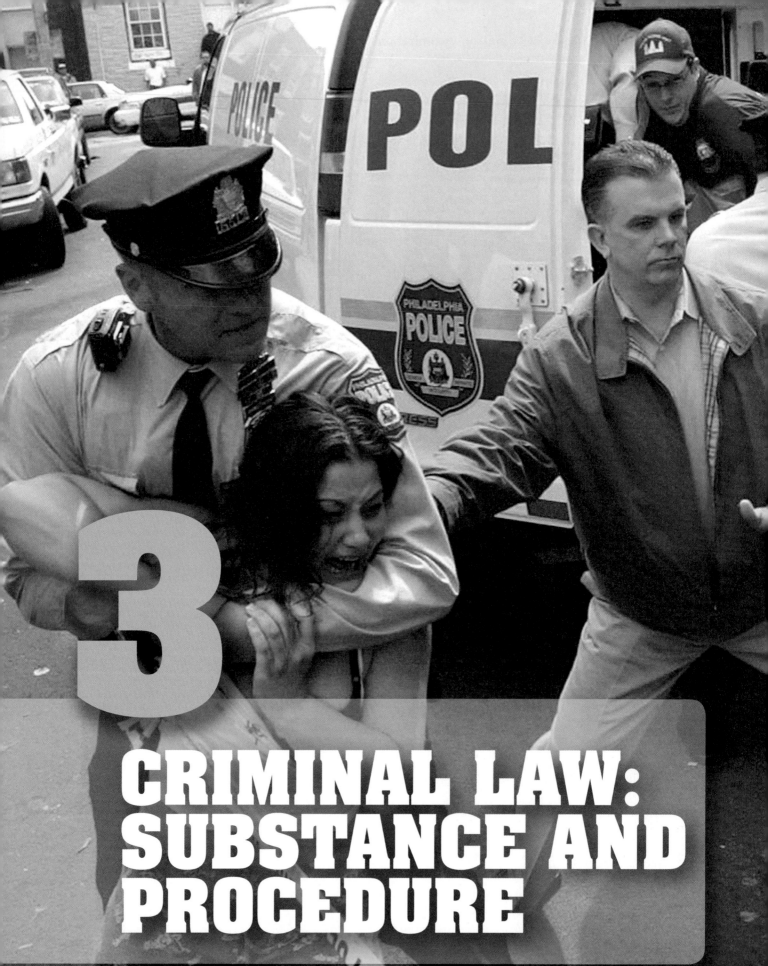

3

CRIMINAL LAW: SUBSTANCE AND PROCEDURE

© AP Images/Joseph Kaczmarek

RealityCheck

MYTH or REALITY?

▶ A person who is convicted of a crime cannot be sued for damages also, because that would be double jeopardy.

▶ The criminal law is constantly evolving and changing.

▶ To commit crime, not only must a person engage in a harmful act but he or she must also have the mental intent to commit crime.

▶ People who are mentally ill cannot be found guilty of a crime.

▶ Under the Fourth Amendment, in order to search a person, the police must first obtain a search warrant.

▶ All U.S. citizens accused of a crime have the right to be released on bail before trial.

Learning Objectives

1. Know the similarities and differences between criminal law and civil law

2. Understand the concept of substantive criminal law and its history

3. Discuss the sources of the criminal law

4. Be familiar with the elements of a crime

5. Define the term "strict liability"

6. Be able to discuss excuses and justification defenses for crime

7. Discuss the concept of criminal procedure

8. Describe the role of the Bill of Rights in shaping criminal procedure

9. Know which amendments to the Constitution are the most important to the justice system

10. List the elements of due process of law

© AP Images/Joseph Kaczmarek

Chapter Outline

Career Profile

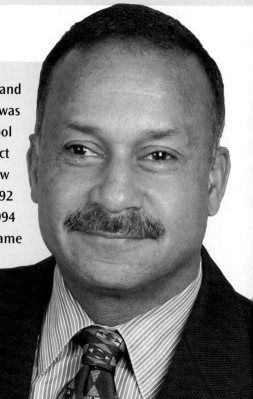

Ralph C. Martin II graduated from Brandeis University in 1974 and entered the criminal justice program at Northeastern University (where he was one of my students!) before receiving his law degree at Northeastern School of Law in 1978. His career has been unique. Martin served as the district attorney of Suffolk County and, in that capacity, was the chief elected law enforcement official for Boston, Chelsea, Revere, and Winthrop from 1992 to 2002. He was appointed in 1992 and won election to the office in 1994 by a margin of almost 20 percent. He ran unopposed in 1998 and became the first African American and Republican district attorney in Suffolk County's history. As district attorney he oversaw a $15 million budget and an office of 300 people, including 135 prosecutors. Ralph Martin was a highly respected court officer. He was recognized for his leadership by President Bill Clinton and Attorney General Janet Reno and has traveled across the country to lecture and consult on the business and strategy of managing and reducing crime.

Now a managing partner at the Bingham McCutchen law firm in Boston, Martin put his more than 20 years of experience as a trial lawyer and prosecutor to good use in his practice, which covers the areas of corporate governance and investigations, white-collar defense, and general civil litigation. He also leads Bingham McCutchen's Diversity Task Force with the goal of recruitment, retention, and advancement of lawyers from diverse backgrounds. Here are some of Ralph's present and past legal engagements:

- Member of defense team representing principals of Suffolk County Sheriff's Department in a two-year federal investigation that ended with the dissolution of the grand jury and no indictments.
- Member of defense team in an 18-month attorney general investigation of two Massachusetts corporations and several individuals accused of pension fraud abuses. The investigation was concluded after one corporate subject pled guilty to a misdemeanor charge of failure to keep proper records.
- Lead defense counsel for a major financial services institution defending a $42 million NASD securities arbitration claim brought by two former broker-dealers. After a four-week arbitration, the claim was denied in its entirety.
- One of two counsel representing a major public authority in connection with a $600 million air rights development project.
- Representation of a world-class research institution in connection with an internal investigation and assessment of its compliance with federal requirements.
- In May of 2006, Ralph was elected to a two-year term as chairman of the Greater Boston Chamber of Commerce. The Chamber is a broad-based association representing more than 1,700 businesses of all sizes from virtually every industry and profession in the region; it provides leadership in establishing a healthy climate for economic development and job creation. Most recently, the Chamber has played key roles in the passage of legislation promoting stem-cell research in Massachusetts and landmark health-care reform.

substantive criminal law
A body of specific rules that declare what conduct is criminal and prescribe the punishment to be imposed for such conduct.

criminal procedure
The rules and laws that define the operation of the criminal proceedings. Procedural law describes the methods that must be followed in obtaining warrants, investigating offenses, effecting lawful arrests, conducting trials, introducing evidence, sentencing convicted offenders, and reviewing cases by appellate courts.

ttorneys such as Ralph Martin are the guardians of the legal system who interpret the criminal law and apply it at critical decision-making stages within the justice system. Today, the rule of law governs almost all phases of human enterprise, including crimes, family life, property transfer, and the regulation of interpersonal conflict. It can generally be divided into three broad categories:

- *Substantive criminal law.* The branch of the law that defines crimes and their punishment. It involves such issues as the mental and physical elements of crime, crime categories, and criminal defenses. Exhibit 3.1 sets out the main goals of the **substantive criminal law**.
- *Procedural criminal law.* Those laws that set out the basic rules of practice in the criminal justice system. Some elements of the law of **criminal procedure** are the rules of evidence, the law of arrest, the law of search and seizure, questions of appeal, jury selection, and the right to counsel.

civil law
All law that is not criminal, including the law of torts (personal wrongs) and contract, property, maritime, and commercial law.

tort
A personal injury or wrong for which an action for damages may be brought.

● *Civil law.* The set of rules governing relations between private parties, including both individuals and organizations (such as business enterprises and/or corporations). **Civil law** is used to resolve, control, and shape such personal interactions as contracts, wills and trusts, property ownership, and commerce. The element of civil law most relevant to criminal justice is **torts**, or the law of personal injuries. (Exhibit 3.2 sets out the various types of torts.) If you are interested in becoming involved in this process and want to become an attorney, read the Careers in Criminal Justice feature on page 85.

EXHIBIT 3.1

The Goals of the Substantive Criminal Law

Enforce Social Control The substantive criminal law is the main instrument of control at the disposal of an existing government. It is used by those who hold political power to eliminate behaviors they believe pose a threat to society or challenge the government's authority.

Distribute Retribution By punishing people who infringe on the rights, property, and freedom of others, the law shifts the burden of revenge from the individual to the state. Although the thought of state-sponsored retribution may be offensive to some, it is greatly preferable to a system in which injured parties or their friends and relatives would seek to redress their injuries through personal vengeance or revenge.

Express Public Opinion and Morality Criminal law reflects public opinions and moral values. It expresses both traditional and contemporary moral values, and it may undergo change according to existing social conditions and attitudes. The criminal law is used to codify changing social values and to educate the public about what is expected of them.

Deter Criminal Behavior Criminal law is designed, through its application of punishment, to control,

restrain, and deter illegal acts before they actually occur. During the Middle Ages, public executions drove this point home; today long prison sentences and an occasional execution are designed to achieve the same result.

Punish Wrongdoing If the deterrent power of criminal law fails to prevent crime, the law gives the state the right to sanction or punish offenders. Those who violate criminal law are subject to physical coercion and punishment.

Maintain Social Order All legal systems are designed to support and maintain the boundaries of the social system they serve. The free enterprise system is supported and sustained by criminal laws that protect property transfer and control market operations.

Restoration Victims deserve restitution or compensation for their pain and loss. The criminal law can be used to restore to the victims what they have lost. Because we believe in equity and justice, it is only fair that the guilty help repair the harm they have caused others by their crimes. Punishments such as fines, forfeiture, and restitution are connected to this legal goal.

EXHIBIT 3.2

Three Categories of Torts

Intentional Tort Injury that the person knew or should have known would occur through his or her actions. Example: a person attacks and injures another (assault and battery) after a dispute.

Negligent Tort Injury caused because a person's actions were unreasonably unsafe or careless.

Example: a traffic accident is caused by a reckless driver.

Strict Liability Tort A particular action causes damage prohibited by statute. Example: a victim is injured because a manufacturer made a defective product.

Careers in Criminal Justice

ATTORNEY

Duties and Characteristics of the Job

- Attorneys use their experience and extensive knowledge of the law and the legal system to defend the rights of their clients and protect their best interests either in a legal setting, during a trial, or by settling their grievances in or out of court.
- They also act as legal advisors and engage in such activities as drawing up and/ or interpreting a legal document or contract, and they advise clients of changes in existing laws.
- Attorneys will often choose a field of specialization such as tax law or intellectual property and typically work in firms or start their own practice.
- Some work for the federal, state, or local government; others take advantage of increasing opportunities for employment within businesses.
- Attorneys work long hours; especially if a case goes to trial, a work week of more than 60 hours is not uncommon.

Job Outlook

- Job opportunities are expected to grow at an average rate for the next several years.
- A good academic record from a prestigious law school, as well as work experience, mobility, and additional education in a field of specialty, are especially helpful.
- Jobs will be most plentiful in urban areas, where there tend to be more law firms, big businesses, and government offices.

Salary

- Attorneys have a median annual salary of about $95,000.
- The majority of attorneys earn between $64,620 and $143,620.
- Partners in large national firms in Chicago or New York may have an annual salary in the millions.
- An attorney's salary will depend on type of employer, experience, region, and type of law being practiced. Extremely successful sole practitioners can win millions in tort actions.

Opportunities

- Competition for jobs with prestigious firms is fierce because there are more graduating lawyers than there are job positions.
- Making the law review, publishing law review articles while in school, and obtaining prestigious internships can be helpful in securing coveted jobs.
- Many lawyers use their education and experience as a means of launching careers in business, politics, government, or academia.

Qualifications

- A bachelor's degree in a program that develops strong analytical and writing skills is recommended for preparation for law school.
- Graduating from an accredited law school and passing the bar are required.

Education and Training

- Attorneys must stay informed of the latest developments in law and often attend conferences; many states have continuing legal education (CLE) requirements that must be met.
- For certain positions, such as law school professor and positions focusing on a specialty such as patent law, further experience and education will be needed.

Word to the Wise

- Gaining entrance to a law school takes not only hard work and discipline but also good grades and a desirable score on the Law School Admissions Test. Start preparing now.
- Be prepared for some long hours at work.
- Be realistic about pay. Not all lawyers start at $160,000 per year, but those hired by top metropolitan firms can expect substantial starting salaries.

In some instances, a person who has been the victim of a criminal act may also sue the perpetrator for damages in a civil tort; some crime victims may forgo criminal action and choose to file a tort claim alone. It is also possible to seek civil damages from a perpetrator even if he or she is found not guilty of crime, because the evidentiary standard in a tort action (by a preponderance of the evidence) is less than is needed for a criminal conviction (beyond a reasonable doubt). In one famous case, the families of Nicole Brown and Ron Goldman successfully sued O. J. Simpson for damages, even though he was found not guilty of murder.

The government has the option to pursue a legal matter through the criminal process, file a tort action, or both. White-collar crimes, including mail, wire, tax-related, computer fraud, and money-laundering violations, often involve both criminal and civil penalties, giving the government the choice of pursuing one type of action or both.

Concept Summary 3.1 summarizes the main similarities and differences between criminal law and tort law.

REALITYCHECK

MYTH OR REALITY?   A person who is convicted of a crime cannot be sued for damages also, because that would be double jeopardy.

MYTH: It is indeed difficult to try a person criminally for the same act twice, but it is common for victims to file tort actions against convicted criminals.

Why don't victims sue more often? Because most criminals are indigent and therefore "judgment proof."

Concept Summary 3.1

A Comparison of Criminal and Tort Law

Similarities

- Both share the goal of controlling unwanted behavior.
- Both impose legal sanctions.
- Both are involved in some of the same areas of legal action—for example, personal assault and control of white-collar offenses such as environmental pollution.
- The payment of damages to the victim in a tort case serves some of the same purposes as the payment of a fine in a criminal case.

Differences

- Crime is a public offense. Tort is a civil or private wrong.
- The sanction associated with tort law is monetary damages. Only a violation of criminal law can result in incarceration or even death.
- In criminal law, the right of enforcement belongs to the state. The individual brings the action in civil law.
- In criminal law, monetary damages (fines) go to the state. In civil law, the individual receives damages as compensation for harm done.
- The standard of proof is different. Criminal law, beyond reasonable doubt; tort law, preponderance of the evidence.

HISTORICAL DEVELOPMENT OF THE CRIMINAL LAW

The roots of the criminal codes used in the United States can be traced to such early legal charters as the Babylonian Code of Hammurabi (2000 B.C.E.), the Mosaic Code of the Israelites (1200 B.C.E.), and the Roman Twelve Tables (451 B.C.E.). Some of the elements of these codes still influence contemporary legal regulations. For example, Hammurabi's concept of **lex talionis** (an eye for an eye) still guides proportionality in punishment; the Ten Commandments' prohibition against theft, violence, and perjury still holds sway.

The early formal legal codes were lost during the Dark Ages after the fall of Rome (500–1000 C.E.). Emerging Germanic societies developed legal systems featuring monetary compensation, called *wergild* (*wer* means "worth" and refers to what the person, and therefore the crime, was worth), for criminal violations. Guilt was determined by two methods: "compurgation," which involved having the accused person swear an oath of innocence while being backed up by a group of 12 to 25 oath-helpers, who would attest to his or

lex talionis

(Latin for "law as retaliation.") From Hammurabi's ancient legal code, the belief that the purpose of the law is to provide retaliation for an offended party and that the punishment should fit the crime.

Internet Medieval Sourcebook

For a site with links and information on the early history of the law, go to the **Internet Medieval Sourcebook** via **www.cengage.com/criminaljustice/siegel**

According to the principle of stare decisis, legal precedents followed common custom and practice. Before the trial by jury, legal disputes could be settled by a duel in which the survivor was considered the innocent party. It was believed that God intervened on behalf of the victor. The "wager of battle" was introduced in England by the Normans and was used in both civil and criminal disputes.

"Wager of Battel," from *Le Coutum de Mormandie*, an illuminated manuscript (1450–1470)

stare decisis

To stand by decided cases. The legal principle by which the decision or holding in an earlier case becomes the standard by which subsequent similar cases are judged.

common law

Early English law, developed by judges, that incorporated Anglo-Saxon tribal custom, feudal rules and practices, and the everyday rules of behavior of local villages. Common law became the standardized law of the land in England and eventually formed the basis of the criminal law in the United States.

mala in se

A term that refers to acts that society considers inherently evil, such as murder and rape, and that violate the basic principles of Judeo-Christian morality.

mala prohibitum

Crimes created by legislative bodies that reflect prevailing moral beliefs and practices.

Buffalo Law Center

The **Buffalo Law Center** provides online access to criminal law materials from the United States and throughout the world, including (among other things) criminal codes, criminal procedure codes, and enforcement codes. You can access the website via

www.cengage.com/criminaljustice/siegel

her character and claims of innocence, and "ordeal," which was based on the principle that divine forces would not allow an innocent person to be harmed.

Determining guilt by ordeal involved such measures as having the accused place his or her hand in boiling water or hold a hot iron. If the wound healed, the person was found innocent; if the wound did not heal, the accused was deemed guilty. Another ordeal, trial by combat, allowed the accused to challenge his accuser to a duel, with the outcome determining the legitimacy of the accusation. Punishments included public flogging, branding, beheading, and burning.

Common Law and the Principle of Stare Decisis

Soon after Duke William of Normandy conquered England in 1066, a feat that transformed him into William the Conqueror, he sent his royal judges/administrators to travel throughout the land, holding court in each county of his new domain. When court was in session, the royal administrator, or judge, summoned a number of citizens who would, on their oath, tell of the crimes and serious breaches of the peace that had occurred since the judge's last visit. The royal judge then decided what to do in each case, using local custom and rules of conduct as his guide in a system known as **stare decisis** (Latin for "to stand by decided cases").

The present English system of law came into existence during the reign of Henry II (1154–1189), when royal judges began to publish their decisions in local cases. This allowed judicial precedents to be established and a national law to accumulate. Other judges began to use these written decisions as a basis for their decision making, and eventually a fixed body of legal rules and principles emerged. If the new rules were successfully applied in a number of different cases, they would become precedents, which would then be commonly applied in all similar cases. This unified system evolved into a **common law** of the country that incorporated local custom and practice into a national code. Crimes that were **mala in se**, inherently evil and depraved (such as murder, burglary, and arson), and were the cornerstone of the common law, were joined by new **mala prohibitum** crimes such as embezzlement, which reflected existing social and economic conditions.

Before the American Revolution, the colonies, then under British rule, were subject to the common law. After the colonies acquired their independence, state legislatures standardized common-law crimes such as murder, burglary, arson, and rape by codifying them (putting them into statutory form in criminal codes). As in England, whenever common law proved inadequate to deal with changing social and moral issues, the states and Congress supplemented it with legislative statutes, creating new elements in the various state and federal legal codes. Similarly, statutes prohibiting such offenses as identity theft and the pirating of videotapes have recently been passed to control human behavior unknown at the time the common law was formulated.

Sources of the Criminal Law

The contemporary American legal system is codified by state and federal legislatures. Each jurisdiction precisely defines crime in its legal code and sets out the appropriate punishments. However, like its English common-law roots, American criminal law is not static and is constantly evolving. A state statute based on common law may define first-degree murder as the "unlawful

EXHIBIT 3.3

Louisiana: Feticide in the First Degree

First degree feticide is defined as follows:

The killing of an unborn child when the offender has a specific intent to kill or to inflict great bodily harm.

The killing of an unborn child when the offender is engaged in the perpetration or attempted perpetration of aggravated rape, forcible rape, aggravated arson, aggravated burglary, aggra- vated kidnapping, second-degree kidnapping, assault by drive-by shooting, aggravated es- cape, armed robbery, first-degree robbery, or simple robbery, even though [the offender] has no intent to kill or inflict great bodily harm.

Whoever commits the crime of first-degree fe- ticide shall be imprisoned at hard labor for not more than 15 years.

SOURCE: Louisiana First-Degree Feticide Law, La. Rev. Stat. Ann. §§14:32.5–14.32.8, read with §§14:2(1), (7), (11) (West 1997).

killing, with malice and premeditation, of one human being by another." Over time, state court decisions might help explain the meaning of the term "mal- ice" or clarify whether "human being" refers only to someone "born and alive" or whether it can also refer to an unborn fe- tus. More than half the states have expanded their legal codes to include feticide law, which makes killing of an unborn fetus murder (see Exhibit 3.3 for an example).

The content of the law may also be influ- enced by judicial decision making. A criminal offense is no longer enforceable when an ap- pellate judge rules that the statute is vague, deals with an act no longer of interest to the public, or is an unfair exercise of state control over an individual. Conversely, a judicial ruling may expand the scope of an existing criminal law, thereby allowing control over behaviors heretofore beyond its reach.

MYTH OR REALITY? The criminal law is constantly evolving and changing.

REALITY: The criminal law changes all the time.

Can you think of acts that have been criminalized during your lifetime? What about those that have been decriminalized or legalized?

Constitutional Limits

Regardless of its source, all criminal law in the United States must conform to the rules and dictates of the Constitution.[1] Any criminal law that conflicts with the various provisions and articles of the Constitution will eventually be challenged in the appellate courts and stricken from the legal code by judicial order (or modified to adhere to constitutional principles). The Constitution has been interpreted to forbid any criminal law that violates a person's right to be treated fairly and equally; this principle is referred to as substantive due process. This means that before a new law can be created, the state must show a compelling need to protect public safety or morals.[2]

Criminal laws have been interpreted as violating constitutional principles if they are too vague or broad for their intent to be clear. A law forbidding adults to engage in "immoral behavior" could not be enforced, because it does not use clear and precise language or give adequate notice as to which conduct is forbidden.[3] The Constitution also prohibits laws that make a person's status a crime. Being a heroin addict is not a crime, although laws can forbid the sale,

The Supreme Court rulings help define the line between personal freedom and state control. Here Savana Redding, age 19, is seen in front of the Supreme Court after oral arguments were made in her case on April 21, 2009. At right is her mother April. Redding, age 13 at the time, was strip-searched at her Arizona school after another student accused her of giving out prescription-strength ibuprofen, the equivalent of two over-the-counter Advils, when she was in eighth grade. No pills were found. The Supreme Court found that the search was unconstitutional. The majority said a search of Savana's backpack and outer garments did not violate the Fourth Amendment's ban on unreasonable searches. But the pills in question did not justify the "embarrassing, frightening, and humiliating search," she was forced to endure.

© UPI Photo/Landov

possession, and manufacture of heroin. Finally, the Constitution limits laws that are overly cruel and/or capricious.[4]

The Constitution also forbids bills of attainder, which are legislative acts that inflict punishment without a judicial trial. This device, used by the English kings to punish rebels and seize their property, was particularly troublesome to American colonials when it was used to seize the property of people considered disloyal to the crown; hence, attainder is forbidden in the Constitution. Nor does the Constitution permit the government to pass ex post facto laws, which are defined as follows:

- A law that makes an action that was done before the passing of the law, and that was innocent when done, criminal and punishes such action
- A law that makes a crime more serious after the fact than it was when first committed
- A law that inflicts a greater punishment than was available when the crime was committed
- A law that makes it easier to convict the offender than it was at the time the crime was committed[5]

Sometimes there is great debate over what the Constitution actually means, and no issue has inspired more debate than the Second Amendment's instruction: "A well regulated Militia, being necessary to the security of a free State, the right of the people to keep and bear Arms, shall not be infringed." As a result, the policy and practice of gun control has been a topic of significant national debate. It is discussed in the Policies, Programs, and Issues in Criminal Justice feature on page 92.

www

Gunlaws.com

To read more about issues related to gun control, go to **Gunlaws.com** via

www.cengage.com/ criminaljustice/siegel

Crimes and Classifications

All states and the federal government have developed their own body of criminal law that defines and grades offenses, sets levels of punishment, and classifies crimes into categories. Crimes are generally grouped into three categories

- Felonies, the most serious crimes punishable by imprisonment, such as criminal homicide, robbery, and rape, as well as such crimes against property as burglary and larceny.
- Misdemeanors, less serious crimes punishable by a jail term, including petit (or petty) larceny, assault and battery, and the unlawful possession of marijuana.
- Violations (also called infractions), which are violations of city or town ordinances such as traffic violations or public intoxication, punishable by a fine. Some states consider violations civil matters, whereas others classify them as crimes.

Distinguishing between a **felony** and a **misdemeanor** is sometimes difficult. Simply put, a felony is a serious offense, and a misdemeanor is a less serious one.

The felony/misdemeanor classification has a direct effect on the way an offender is treated within the justice system. Police may arrest a felon if there is an arrest warrant issued by a court and/or probable cause that he or she committed a crime. In contrast, misdemeanants may be taken into custody only with an arrest warrant or if the police officer observed the infraction personally; this is known as the *in-presence requirement*. There are, however, some instances when police can make a misdemeanor arrest without observing its occurrence. For example, a number of jurisdictions have passed domestic violence prevention acts, which allow arrests based merely on the accusation of the injured party. These laws have been created in an effort to protect the target of the abuse from further attacks.[6]

If convicted, a person charged with a felony may be barred from certain fields of employment or some professions, such as law and medicine. A felony offender's status as an alien in the United States might also be affected, or the offender might be denied the right to hold public office, vote, or serve on a jury.[7] These and other civil liabilities exist only when a person is convicted of a felony offense, not of a misdemeanor.

felony
A more serious offense that carries a penalty of incarceration in a state prison, usually for one year or more. Persons convicted of felony offenses lose such rights as the right to vote, hold elective office, or maintain certain licenses.

misdemeanor
A minor crime usually punished by less than one year's imprisonment in a local institution, such as a county jail.

The Legal Definition of a Crime

Almost all common-law crime contains both mental and physical elements. Take, for example, the common-law crime of burglary in the first degree. Alabama's is defined as shown in Exhibit 3.4.

Note that in order to commit the crime of armed burglary in Alabama (and elsewhere), offenders must do the following things:

- Willfully enter a dwelling
- Be armed or arm themselves after entering the house, or commit an actual assault on a person who is lawfully in the house
- Knowingly and intentionally commit the crime

For the prosecutor to prove a crime occurred, and that the defendant committed it, the prosecutor must show (a) that the accused engaged in the guilty act (**actus reus**, or guilty act) and (b) that the act was intentional and purposeful (**mens rea**, or guilty mind). Under common law, both the actus reus and the mens rea must be present for the act to be considered a crime. Thoughts of

actus reus
An illegal act. The actus reus can be an affirmative act, such as taking money or shooting someone, or a failure to act, such as failing to take proper precautions while driving a car.

mens rea
Guilty mind. The mental element of a crime or the intent to commit a criminal act.

Policies, Programs, and Issues in Criminal Justice

Gun Control and the Constitution

To millions of Americans, the Second Amendment to the U.S. Constitution protects the right to bear arms, and the average American has a right to buy and possess a rifle and a handgun. Is this myth or reality?

The Second Amendment states that "a well regulated Militia, being necessary to the security of a free State, the right of the people to keep and bear Arms, shall not be infringed." What exactly does this mean? Seventy years ago, in *United States v. Miller* 307 U.S. 174 (1939), the Supreme Court ruled that the Second Amendment must be interpreted as intending to guarantee the states' rights to maintain and train a militia, and not a personal right to bear arms. Miller had wanted to avoid registering a "sawed-off shotgun" which he possessed for personal use. The Court ruled, "In the absence of any evidence tending to show that possession or use of a shotgun having a barrel of less than 18 inches in length at this time has some reasonable relationship to the preservation or efficiency of a well-regulated militia, we cannot say that the Second Amendment guarantees the right to keep and bear such an instrument." The Court's decision also mentioned that weapons appropriate for the militia at the time were in "common use" and that a sawed-off shotgun was not a weapon that was commonly used or widely possessed.

Because the Miller case applied only to sawed-off shotguns, it left the gun possession issue unsettled for seven decades. Then, in the landmark 2008 case *District of Columbia v. Heller*, the Supreme Court put this issue to rest when it held that the Second Amendment to the United States Constitution protects an individual's right to possess a firearm for private use. Its decision ruled that Washington, D.C.'s Firearms Control Regulations Act of 1975 was unconstitutional and determined that handguns are "Arms that may not be banned by a local jurisdiction. It also struck down the portion of the law that required that all firearms, including rifles and shotguns, be kept "unloaded and disassembled or bound by a trigger lock." The decision clearly declares the Second Amendment protection of "an individual right to possess a firearm unconnected with service in a militia, and to use that arm for traditionally lawful purposes, such as self-defense within the home." It goes on to clarify specific limitations on those Second Amendment protections, and it concludes with a characterization of the District's "total ban on handgun possession in the home (as) amount(ing) to a prohibition on an entire class of 'arms' that Americans overwhelmingly choose for the lawful purpose of self-defense." Because handguns are commonly used, the *Heller* decision does not conflict with the Miller decision's ban on sawed-off shotguns.

Gun Control Laws

Although the *Heller* decision prohibits governmental jurisdictions from banning guns outright, the ruling does not prohibit the state and federal governments from regulating gun use and possession. The decision stated: "*nothing in our opinion should be taken to cast doubt on longstanding prohibitions on the*

EXHIBIT 3.4

Alabama Definition of Burglary in the First Degree

Section 13A-7-5, Burglary in the First Degree

A person commits the crime of burglary in the first degree if he knowingly and unlawfully enters or remains unlawfully in a dwelling with intent to commit a crime therein, and if, in effecting entry or while in dwelling or in immediate flight there from, he or another participant in the crime: (1) is armed with explosives or a deadly weapon, or (2) causes physical injury to any person who is not a participant in the crime, or (3) uses or threatens the immediate use of a dangerous instrument. Burglary in the first degree is a Class A felony.

Sources: Alabama Criminal Code, Acts 1977, No. 607, p. 812, and sec. 2610; Acts 1979, No. 79–471, p. 862, and sec. 1; LegalTips.org, www.legaltips .org/Alabama/alabama_code/13A-7-5.aspx (accessed June 21, 2007).

possession of firearms by felons and the mentally ill, or laws forbidding the carrying of firearms in sensitive places such as schools and government buildings, or laws imposing conditions on the commercial sale of arms." This paragraph has been interpreted by the courts as suggesting that although governments cannot ban gun ownership, they are still entitled to its regulation.

The Heller decision does not conflict with the Federal Gun Control Act of 1968 that prohibits the direct mail order of firearms (except antique firearms) by consumers and mandates that anyone who wants to buy a gun from a source other than a private individual must do so through a federally licensed firearms dealer. It requires that all dealers be licensed, fill out forms detailing each trade, and avoid selling to people prohibited from owning guns, such as minors, ex-felons, and drug users. Dealers must record the source and properties of all guns they sell and carefully account for their purchase. Gun buyers must provide identification and sign waivers attesting to their ability to possess guns. The act also bans unlicensed individuals from acquiring handguns outside their state of residence, although long guns (rifles and shotguns) may (under federal law) be acquired from federally licensed firearms dealers located in other states, provided that this is allowed by both the state of purchase and the state of residence.

The Brady Handgun Violence Prevention Act of 1993, amending the Gun Control Act of 1968, imposed a waiting period of five days before a licensed importer, manufacturer, or dealer may sell, deliver, or transfer a handgun to an unlicensed individual. On November 30, 1998, the Brady Law changed, substituting an instant check based on the FBI's National Instant Criminal Background Check System (NICS) on whether a prospective buyer is prohibited from purchasing a weapon. Gun purchases by people convicted of or under indictment for felony charges, fugitives, the mentally ill, those with dishonorable military discharges, those who have renounced U.S. citizenship, undocumented aliens, illegal drug users, and those who have been convicted of domestic violence misdemeanors or are under domestic violence restraining orders are prohibited.

In addition to the federal controls, a number of states have instituted laws restricting access to firearms by individuals who are subject to a restraining order or have been convicted of a domestic violence misdemeanor, or allowing law enforcement officers to confiscate firearms at a domestic violence scene. The most famous attempt to regulate handguns using this method is the Massachusetts Bartley-Fox Law, which provides a mandatory one-year prison term for possessing a handgun (outside the home) without a permit.

The *Heller* ruling helps answer the question of whether gun ownership is a constitutional right (it is), it does not shut the door on governmental regulation and control of that right.

© Mike Kemp/Rubberball Productions/Getty Images

Critical Thinking

1. Despite the *Heller* ruling, do you believe that the sale and possession of handguns should be banned outright? Remember, drugs are illegal and yet are commonly possessed. Would a ban on guns take them out of the hands of citizens and place them in the hands of criminals?

committing an act do not alone constitute a crime; there must also be an illegal act. Let us now look more closely at these issues.

Actus Reus

The actus reus is a *voluntary and deliberate* illegal act, such as taking someone's money, burning a building, or shooting someone; an accident or involuntary act would not be considered criminal. However, even an unintentional act can be considered a crime if it is the result of negligence and/or disregard for the rights of others. A person cannot be held criminally liable for assault if while walking down the street he has a seizure and as a result his arm strikes another person in the face; his act was not voluntary and therefore not criminal. However, if this same person knew beforehand that he might have a seizure and unreasonably put himself in a position where he was likely to harm others—for instance, by driving a car—he could be criminally liable for his behavior because his actions were negligent and disregarded the rights of others.

Actus reas refers to the guilty act: dealing drugs, stabbing a victim, burning a home. In the case of Josephine Martinez it involved fraud and racketeering. Here she is shown being taken into custody by a member of the Miami-Dade police Mortgage Fraud Task Force on July 17, 2008, in Miami, Florida. Martinez was arrested during Operation "Life is Good," which included the arrest of 15 people suspected of being involved in mortgage fraud. The individuals were arrested for activity that included racketeering, conspiracy to racketeer, use of personal identification information, grand theft, and money laundering.

© Joe Raedle/Getty Images

In addition, there are occasions when the failure, or omission, to act can be considered a crime:

- *Failure to perform a legally required duty that is based on relationship or status.* These relationships include parent and child and husband and wife. If a husband finds his wife unconscious because she took an overdose of sleeping pills, he is obligated to save her life by seeking medical aid. If he fails to do so and she dies, he can be held responsible for her death. Parents are required to look after the welfare of their children; failure to provide adequate care can be a criminal offense.

- *Imposition by statute.* Some states have passed laws that require a person who observes an automobile accident to stop and help the other parties involved.

- *Contractual relationship.* These relationships include lifeguard and swimmer, doctor and patient, and babysitter or au pair and child. Because lifeguards have been hired to ensure the safety of swimmers, they have a legal duty to come to the aid of drowning persons. If a lifeguard knows a swimmer is in danger and does nothing about it, and the swimmer drowns, the lifeguard can be held legally responsible for the swimmer's death.

In these cases, the duty to act is a legal and not a moral duty. The obligation arises from the relationship between the parties or from explicit legal requirements. In contrast, a private citizen who sees a person drowning is under no legal obligation to save that person. Although we may find it morally reprehensible, the private citizen could walk away and let the swimmer drown without facing legal sanctions.

Mens Rea

For an act to constitute a crime, it must be done with deliberate purpose or criminal intent. A person who enters a store with a gun with the intention of stealing money indicates by his actions the intent to commit a robbery. Criminal intent is implied if the results of a person's action, though originally unintended, are certain to occur. When Mohammed Atta and his terrorist band crashed an aircraft into the World Trade Center on September 11, 2001, they did not intend to kill any particular person in the building. Yet the law would hold that Atta, and any others conspiring with him, would be substantially certain that people in the building would be killed in the blast and that they therefore had the criminal intent to commit the crime of murder.

In some situations intent is derived from recklessness or negligence. A drunk driver may not have intended to kill her specific victim, yet her negligent and reckless behavior—driving while drunk—creates a condition that a reasonable person can assume may lead to injury.

The Relationship of Mens Rea and Actus Reus

For an act to constitute a crime, the law requires a connection be made between the mens rea and the actus reas, thereby showing that the offender's conduct was the proximate cause of the criminal act. If a man chases a woman into the street intending to assault her, and the victim is struck by a car and killed, the accused cannot claim at trial that the death was an accident caused by the inopportune passing of the motor vehicle. The law holds that the victim would never have run into the street had she not been pursued by the defendant, and that, therefore, (a) the defendant's reckless disregard for the victim's safety makes him responsible for her death, and (b) his action was the proximate cause of her death.

CRIMINAL HARM • Thought alone is not a crime. For a person to be considered to have committed a crime, some act is required to prove the actor's willingness to cause harm. It is the nature of the harm that ultimately determines what crime the person committed. If someone trips another with the intent of making the person fall down and be embarrassed in public, he has committed the crime of battery. If by some chance the victim dies from the fall, the harm caused elevates the crime to manslaughter, even if that was not the intended result.

In the crime of robbery, the actus reas is taking the property from the person or presence of another. In order to satisfy the harm requirement, the robber must acquire the victim's possessions, referred to as "asportation." The legal definition of robbery is satisfied when even for a brief moment possession of the property is transferred to the robber. If a robber removes a victim's wallet from his pocket and immediately tosses it over a fence when he spies a police officer approaching, the robbery is complete because even the slightest change in possession of the property is sufficient to cause harm. Nor is the value of the property important: Actual value is unimportant as long as the property had some value to the victim.

Strict Liability

There are certain statutory offenses in which mens rea is not essential. These offenses fall in a category known as public safety or **strict liability crimes**. A person can be held responsible for such a violation independent of the existence of intent to commit the offense. Strict liability criminal statutes generally include narcotics control laws, traffic laws, health and safety regulations, sanitation laws, and other regulatory statutes. A motorist could not defend herself against a speeding ticket by claiming that she was unaware of how fast she was going and did not intend to speed, nor could a bartender claim that a juvenile to whom he sold liquor looked quite a bit older. No state of mind is generally required

The actus reas and the mens rea

To learn more about the relationship between **the actus reas and the mens rea**, go to the following website:

www.cengage.com/ criminaljustice/siegel

strict liability crime
Illegal act whose elements do not contain the need for intent, or mens rea; usually, an act that endangers the public welfare, such as illegal dumping of toxic wastes.

© Radius Images/Alamy

EXHIBIT 3.5

New York State Law S 270.10: Creating a Hazard

A person is guilty of creating a hazard when:

1. Having discarded in any place where it might attract children, a container which has a compartment of more than one and one-half cubic feet capacity and a door or lid which locks or fastens automatically when closed and which cannot easily be opened from the inside, he fails to remove the door, lid, locking or fastening device; or

2. Being the owner or otherwise having possession of property upon which an abandoned well or cesspool is located, he fails to cover the same with suitable protective construction.

Creating a hazard is a class B misdemeanor.

Source: New York State Consolidated Laws, Article 270, Other Offenses Relating to Public Safety, Section 270.10, Creating a Hazard (2002).

where a strict liability statute is violated.[8] Consider the New York State law S 270.10: Creating a hazard, which is laid out in Exhibit 3.5.[9] Note that intent to commit this crime is not required for a conviction on charges of creating a hazardous condition.

Criminal Defenses

In 1884 two British sailors, desperate after being shipwrecked for days, made the decision to kill and eat a suffering cabin boy who was on their lifeboat. Four days later, they were rescued by a passing ship and returned to England. English authorities, wanting to end the practice of shipwreck cannibalism, tried the two men and convicted them of murder. Clemency was considered, and a reluctant Queen Victoria commuted the death sentences to six months.[10] Were the seamen justified in killing a shipmate to save their lives? If they had not done so, it is likely they all would have died. Did they act out of necessity or malice? Can there ever be a good reason to take a life? Can we ever justify killing another? Before you answer, remember that we can kill in self-defense, to prevent lethal crimes, or in times of war (more on necessity defenses later).

When people defend themselves against criminal charges, they must refute one or more of the elements of the crime of which they have been accused. Defendants may deny the actus reus by arguing that they were falsely accused and the real culprit has yet to be identified. Defendants may also claim that although they did engage in the criminal act they are accused of, they lacked the mens rea, or mental intent, needed to be found guilty of the crime. If a person whose mental state is impaired commits a criminal act, it is possible for the person to excuse his criminal actions by claiming he lacked the capacity to form

REALITYCHECK

MYTH OR REALITY? To commit crime, not only must a person engage in a harmful act but he or she must also have the mental intent to commit crime.

MYTH: Although most common-law crimes require intent, strict liability crimes do not have a mental requirement. Telling a police officer you did not "intend" to be speeding when you are stopped on the highway does not help you avoid a ticket.

Should a person on her or his way to a hospital emergency room be exempt from a speeding ticket? Is there any such a thing as an excuse when you violate traffic laws? After all, you are endangering other motorists, no matter what your reason for speeding.

sufficient intent to be held criminally responsible. **Insanity**, intoxication, and ignorance are also among the types of excuse defenses.[11]

Another type of defense is justification. Here, the individual admits committing the criminal act, but maintains that the act was justified and that, given the circumstances, anyone would have acted in a similar manner; because her act was justified, she should not be held criminally liable. Among the justification defenses are necessity, duress, **self-defense**, and **entrapment**. We will now examine some of these defenses and justifications in greater detail.

Excuse Defenses

Excuses refer to situations in which the criminal defendants admit to performing the physical act of crime but claim they are not responsible for it because they lacked free will. It is not their fault, they claim, because they had no control over their actions; therefore, they should be "excused" from criminal responsibility.

IGNORANCE OR MISTAKE • People sometimes defend themselves by claiming either that their actions were a mistake or that they were unaware (ignorant) of the fact that their behavior was a crime. For example, they did not realize they had stepped onto private property and were guilty of trespassing.

As a general rule, ignorance of the law is no excuse. According to the great legal scholar William Blackstone, "Ignorance of the law, which everyone is bound to know, excuses no man."[12] Consequently, a defendant cannot present a legitimate defense by saying he was unaware of a criminal law, had misinterpreted the law, or believed the law to be unconstitutional.

In some instances, mistake of fact, such as taking someone else's coat that is similar to your own, may be a valid defense. If the jury or judge, as trier of fact, determines that criminal intent was absent, such an honest mistake may remove the defendant's criminal responsibility. Mistake can also be used as a defense when the government failed to make enactment of a new law public or when the offender relies on an official statement of the law that is later deemed incorrect.

insanity
A legal defense that maintains a defendant was incapable of forming criminal intent because he or she suffers from a defect of reason or mental illness.

self-defense
A legal defense in which defendants claim that their behavior was legally justified by the necessity to protect their own life and property, or that of another victim, from potential harm.

entrapment
A criminal defense that maintains the police originated the criminal idea or initiated the criminal action.

For a defendant who committed a criminal act to be considered insane, a jury must believe that mental instability made it impossible for him or her to have had the intent to commit crime. Even some bizarre cases do not qualify as insanity. Take, for instance, Sheila LaBarre, who on June 20, 2008, was found guilty of murder in Rockingham County Superior Court in New Hampshire. LaBarre, who claimed she was an angel sent from God to punish pedophiles, was convicted of murdering two boyfriends by a jury that rejected her insanity plea.

© AP Images/Thomas Roy

INSANITY ● Insanity is a defense to criminal prosecution in which the defendant's state of mind negates his or her criminal responsibility. A successful insanity defense results in a verdict of "not guilty by reason of insanity."[13]

Insanity is a legal category. As used in U.S. courts, it does not necessarily mean that everyone who suffers from a form of mental illness can be excused from legal responsibility. Many people who are depressed, suffer mood disorders, or have a psychopathic personality can be found legally sane. Instead, insanity means that the defendant's state of mind at the time the crime was committed made it impossible for that person to have the necessary mens rea to satisfy the legal definition of a crime. Thus, a person can be undergoing treatment for a psychological disorder but still be judged legally sane if it can be proved that at the time he committed the crime, he had the capacity to understand the wrongfulness of his actions.

If a defendant uses the insanity plea, it is usually left to psychiatric testimony to prove that the person understood the wrongfulness of her actions and was therefore legally sane, or conversely, was mentally incapable of forming intent. The jury then must weigh the evidence in light of the test for sanity currently used in the jurisdiction.

Such tests vary throughout the United States; the commonly used tests are listed in Exhibit 3.6.

REALITYCHECK

MYTH OR REALITY? People who are mentally ill cannot be found guilty of a crime.

MYTH: Mentally ill people, even those receiving psychiatric treatment, can be found guilty of crime. Only the legally insane cannot be found guilty of crime.

Do you agree? Or do you think mental illness should excuse crime? Is it really possible to be suffering from severe mental illness and yet have the intent to commit crime? Can we really say someone like Jeffrey Dahmer, the cannibal who raped, killed, and ate 17 men and boys, was not "insane"? Yet Dahmer was found guilty of his crimes and received 15 life sentences; he was killed in prison.

INTOXICATION ● As a general rule, intoxication, which may include drunkenness or being under the influence of drugs, is not considered a defense. However, a defendant who becomes involuntarily intoxicated under duress or by mistake may be excused for crimes committed. Involuntary intoxication may also reduce the degree of the crime; a judgment may be decreased from first- to second-degree murder because the defendant uses intoxication to prove the lack of the critical element of mens rea.

AGE ● The law holds that a child is not criminally responsible for actions committed at an age that precludes full realization of the gravity of certain types of behavior. Under common law, there is generally a conclusive presumption of incapacity for a child under age 7, a reliable presumption for a child between the ages of 7 and 14, and no presumption for a child over the age of 14. This generally means that a child under age 7 who commits a crime will not be held criminally responsible for these actions and that a child between ages 7 and 14 may be held responsible. These common-law rules have been changed by statute in most jurisdictions. Today, the maximum age of criminal responsibility for children ranges from age 14 to 17 or 18, and the minimum age may be set by statute at age 7 or under age 14.[14]

Justification Defenses

Justifications arise in situations in which the defendants don't deny they committed a crime but claim that anyone in their situation would have acted in a similar fashion. Justification defenses deny mens rea: "I did a bad act, but I did it for all the right reasons."

www

insanity defense

To read up on the **insanity defense**, go to

www.cengage.com/ criminaljustice/siegel

EXHIBIT 3.6

Various Insanity Defense Standards

The M'Naghten Rule The M'Naghten rule, first formulated in England in 1843, defines a person as insane if, at the time she commited the act she stands accused of, she was laboring under such a defect of reason, arising from a disease of the mind, that she could not tell or know the nature and quality of the act or, if she did know it, that she did not know what she was doing was wrong. In other words, she could not "tell right from wrong." The M'Naghten rule is used in the majority of the states.

The Irresistible Impulse The irresistible impulse test was formulated in Ohio in 1834. It is used quite often in conjunction with M'Naghten and defines a person as insane if she should or did know that her actions were illegal but, because of a mental impairment, could not control her behavior. Her act was a result of an uncontrollable or irresistible impulse. A person who commits a crime during a "fit of passion" would be considered insane under this test. The most famous use of this defense occurred in 1994, when Lorena Bobbitt successfully defended herself against charges that she cut off the penis of her husband, John, after suffering abuse at his hands.

The Durham Rule The Durham rule, or "product test," was set forth by the U.S. Court of Appeals for the District of Columbia Circuit in 1954 and states that "an accused is not criminally responsible if her unlawful act was the product of mental disease or defect." It was used for some time in the state of New Hampshire.

The Insanity Defense Reform Act (US) The Insanity Defense Reform Act, Title 18, U.S. Code, Section 17, was enacted by Congress in 1984 and states that a person accused of a crime can be judged not guilty by reason of insanity if "the defendant, as a result of a severe mental disease or defect, was unable to appreciate the nature and quality or the wrongfulness of her acts."

The Substantial Capacity Test The substantial capacity test was defined by the American Law Institute in its Model Penal Code. This argues that insanity should be defined as a lack of substantial capacity to control one's behavior. Substantial capacity is defined as "the mental capacity needed to understand the wrongfulness of [an] act, or to conform … behavior to the … law." This rule combines elements of the M'Naghten rule with the concept of irresistible impulse.

CONSENT ● A person may not be convicted of a crime if the victim consented to the act in question. In other words, a rape does not occur if the victim consents to sexual relations; a larceny cannot occur if the owner voluntarily consents to the taking of property. Consent is an essential element of these crimes, and it is a valid defense where it can be proved or shown that consent existed at the time the act was committed. In some crimes, such as statutory rape, however, consent is not an element of the crime and is considered irrelevant because the state presumes that young people are not capable of providing consent.

SELF-DEFENSE ● Defendants may justify their actions by saying they acted in self-defense. To establish the necessary elements to constitute self-defense, the defendant must have acted under a reasonable belief that he was in danger of death or great harm and had no means of escape from the assailant.

As a general legal rule, a person defending himself may use only such force as is reasonably necessary to prevent personal harm. A person who is assaulted by another with no weapon is ordinarily not justified in hitting the assailant with a baseball bat; a person verbally threatened is not justified in striking the other party. Persons can be found guilty of murder in the first degree if, after being attacked during a brawl, they shot and killed an unarmed person in self-defense. Despite the fact that it was the victim who initiated the fray and pummeled his opponent first; the imbalance in weaponry (gun versus fist) would mitigate a finding of self-defense.[15]

To exercise the self-defense privilege, the danger to the defendant must be immediate; it is not justifiable to kill someone who threatened you with death a year ago. In addition, most jurisdictions require that the defendants prove that they sought alternative means of avoiding the danger, such as escape, retreat, or assistance from others, before they defended themselves with force.

In some instances women (or men) may kill their mates after years of abuse; this is known as battered-wife syndrome (or, in cases involving child abuse, battered-child syndrome). Although a history of battering can be used to mitigate the seriousness of the crime, a finding of not guilty most often requires the presence of imminent danger and the inability of the accused to escape from the assailant.

STAND YOUR GROUND ● Most self-defense statutes require a duty to retreat before reacting to a threat with physical violence. An exception is one's own home. According to the "castle exception" ("every man's home is his castle"), a person is not obligated to retreat within his or her residence before fighting back. Some states, most notably Florida, now have "Stand Your Ground" laws, which allow people to use force in a wide variety of circumstances and eliminate or curtail the need to retreat, even if they are not in their own home but in a public place.

Florida's law, enacted on October 1, 2005, allows the use of deadly force when a person reasonably believes it necessary to prevent the commission of a "forcible felony," including carjacking, robbery, and assault.[16] The new law allows average citizens to use deadly force when they reasonably believe that their homes or vehicles have been illegally invaded. The Florida law authorizes the use of defensive force by anyone "who is not engaged in an unlawful activity and who is attacked in any other place where he or she has a right to be." Furthermore, under the law, such a person has no duty to retreat and can stand his or her ground and meet force with force. The statute also grants civil and criminal immunity to anyone found to have had such a reasonable belief.[17]

ENTRAPMENT ● Defendants can claim their criminal activity was justified because law enforcement agents used traps, decoys, and deception to induce criminal action; this is referred to as entrapment. It is generally legitimate for law enforcement officers to set traps for criminals by getting information about crimes from informers, undercover agents, and codefendants. Police officers are allowed to use ordinary opportunities for defendants to commit crime and to create opportunities that might involve a defendant in a crime. However, entrapment occurs when the police instigate the crime, implant criminal ideas, and coerce individuals into bringing about crime. In *Sherman v. United States* the Supreme Court found that the function of law enforcement is to prevent crime and apprehend criminals, not to implant a criminal design originating with officials of the government in the mind of an innocent person.[18]

DURESS ● To prove duress, defendants must show they have been forced into committing a crime in order to prevent death or serious harm to self or others. For example, a bank employee might be excused from taking bank funds if she can prove that her family was being threatened and that consequently she was acting under duress. But there is widespread general agreement that duress is no defense for an intentional killing.

NECESSITY ● Sometimes criminal defendants, like the two sailors who killed and ate the cabin boy after their ship sank and they were set adrift in a lifeboat, argue that they acted out of "necessity." To be successful, a defense of necessity must show that considering the circumstances and conditions at the time the crime occurred, the defendant (or any reasonable person) could not have behaved in any other way. For example, a husband steals a car to take his pregnant wife to the hospital for an emergency delivery, or a hunter shoots an animal of an endangered species that was about to attack his child. The defense has been found inapplicable in cases where defendants sought to shut down nuclear power plants or abortion clinics or to destroy missile components under the belief that the action was necessary to save lives or prevent a nuclear war.

Reforming the Criminal Law

In recent years, many states and the federal government have been examining their substantive criminal law. In some instances, what was formerly legal is now a crime, and in other instances, what was previously considered illegal has been legalized or decriminalized (in other words, the penalties have been reduced). An example of the former can be found in changes to the law of rape. In seven states, including California, it is now considered rape when the following sequence of events occurs: (1) The woman consents to sex, (2) the sex act begins, (3) she changes her mind during the act and tells her partner to stop, and (4) he refuses and continues. Before the legal change, such a circumstance was not considered rape.[19]

There are also many instances in which the law has been changed so that what was considered illegal is now legal and noncriminal. Until recently, sexual relations between consenting same-sex adults was punished as a serious felony under sodomy statutes. In an important 2003 case, *Lawrence v. Texas*, the Supreme Court declared that laws banning sodomy are unconstitutional if they restrict adults' private sexual behavior and impose on their personal dignity. As a result of this decision, laws banning same-sex relations between consenting adults in the United States are now unconstitutional and therefore nonenforceable.[20]

Creating New Crimes

In some instances, new laws have been created to conform to emerging social issues. The ones discussed below illustrate the evolving nature of the criminal law.

PHYSICIAN-ASSISTED SUICIDE ● Doctors helping people to end their life became the subject of a national debate when Dr. Jack Kevorkian began practicing what he calls **obitiatry**, helping people to take their lives.[21] In an attempt to stop Kevorkian, Michigan passed a statutory ban on assisted suicide, reflecting what lawmakers believed to be prevailing public opinion; Kevorkian was convicted and imprisoned.[22] He was released on parole on June 1, 2007, in recognition of good behavior and now gives lectures on college campuses. Forty-four states, including Michigan, now disallow assisted suicide either by statute or by common law.[23]

obitiatry
Helping people take their own lives.

© UpperCut Images/Getty Images

stalking
The willful, malicious, and repeated following and harassing of another person.

STALKING ● More than 25 states have enacted **stalking** statutes, which prohibit and punish acts described typically as "the willful, malicious, and repeated following and harassing of another person."[24] Stalking laws were originally formulated to protect women terrorized by former husbands and boyfriends, although celebrities often are plagued by stalkers as well. In celebrity cases, these laws often apply to stalkers who are strangers or casual acquaintances of their victims.

COMMUNITY NOTIFICATION LAWS ● These laws require the registration of people convicted of sex-related crimes; they were enacted in response to concern about sexual predators moving into neighborhoods. One of the best-known such statutes, New Jersey's "Megan's Law," was named after seven-year-old Megan Kanka of Hamilton Township, New Jersey, who was killed in 1994. Charged with the crime was a convicted sex offender who (unknown to the Kankas) lived across the street. On May 17, 1996, President Clinton signed Megan's Law, which contained two components:

- *Sex offender registration.* Requires the states to register individuals convicted of sex crimes against children.
- *Community notification.* Compels the states to make private and personal information on registered sex offenders available to the public.

© AP Images/Elise Amendola

New laws are constantly being created to protect people from emerging social harm. Here, Marie and Bernie Kane react as they speak about their youngest son, Kevin (in photo), at their home in Ashland, Massachusetts, on April 27, 2006. In 1998, Kevin, 26, died of a rare type of cancer. Public health authorities now link his death to exposure to toxic waste dumped by a former chemical and dye facility in the town. Environmental crimes, unknown in the common law, are unique to contemporary society.

ENVIRONMENTAL CRIMES ● In response to the concerns of environmentalists, the federal government has passed numerous acts designed to protect the nation's well-being. The Environmental Protection Agency has successfully prosecuted significant violations of these and other new laws, including data fraud cases (such as private laboratories submitting false environmental data to state and federal environmental agencies); indiscriminate hazardous waste dumping that resulted in serious injuries and death; industrywide ocean dumping by cruise ships; oil spills that caused significant damage to waterways, wetlands, and beaches; and illegal handling of hazardous substances, such as pesticides and asbestos, that exposed children, the poor, and other especially vulnerable groups to potentially serious illness.[25]

Creating New Defenses

Criminal defenses are also undergoing rapid change. As society becomes more aware of existing social problems that may contribute to crime, it has become commonplace for defense attorneys to defend their clients by raising a variety of new defenses based on preexisting conditions or syndromes with which their clients were afflicted. Examples include "battered-woman syndrome," "Vietnam syndrome," "child sexual abuse syndrome," "Holocaust survivor syndrome," and "adopted child syndrome."

Now being developed are **neurolegal defenses** that rely on using sophisticated brain scan devices to measure neural activity. Because research shows that people suffering neurological abnormality, such as brain lesions, tumors, and frontal lobe damage, may be crime prone, criminal defenses built around their inability to control their behavior are now being developed.

This line of defense is relatively new, but there have already been cases in which the defense has been allowed to link violent behavior to a neurological impairment, such as a brain cyst.[26] Defense lawyers routinely make use of brain scans to suggest their clients were not competent or use brain abnormality to mitigate the seriousness of the charges. As neurological imaging techniques improve, their incorporation into legal defenses should likewise grow more common.[27]

neurolegal defense
A criminal defense that relies on showing that neurological activity or lack of it, measured through brain scan devices, caused a person to commit crime. Therefore, she or he lacked the intent to commit crime and cannot be held criminally liable.

Constitutional Criminal Procedure

Whereas substantive criminal law primarily defines crimes, the law of criminal procedure consists of the rules and procedures that govern the pretrial processing of criminal suspects and the conduct of criminal trials. The main source of the procedural law is the body of the Constitution and the first ten amendments added to the Constitution on December 15, 1791, which are collectively known as the **Bill of Rights**. The purpose of these amendments is to prevent the government from usurping the personal freedoms of citizens. The U.S. Supreme Court's interpretation of these amendments has served as the basis for the creation of legal rights of the accused. Of primary concern are the Fourth, Fifth, Sixth, and Eighth Amendments, which limit and control the manner in which the federal government operates the justice system. In addition, the due process clause of the Fourteenth Amendment has been interpreted to apply these limits on governmental action to the state and local levels:

Bill of Rights
The first ten amendments to the U.S. Constitution.

Cornell University Law School

The **Cornell University Law School** provides a website with much useful information on criminal procedure. You can access it via

www.cengage.com/ criminaljustice/siegel

- The Fourth Amendment bars illegal "searches and seizures," a right especially important for the criminal justice system because it means that police officers cannot indiscriminately use their authority to investigate a possible crime or arrest a suspect. Stopping, questioning, or searching an individual without legal justification represents a serious violation of

REALITY CHECK

MYTH OR REALITY? Under the Fourth Amendment, in order to search a person, the police must first obtain a search warrant.

MYTH: Police can search without a warrant in emergency circumstances or if the courts have granted them permission to do so. This loophole has spurred many legal cases defining when and where police can conduct warrantless searches.

Should a guilty person be allowed to go free simply because a police officer made a mistake when conducting a search? (For example, say the officer illegally opened the trunk of a car and found a dead body in the vehicle.) Is there some other possible remedy?

exclusionary rule
Evidence seized in violation of the Fourth Amendment cannot be used in a court of law.

the Fourth Amendment right to personal privacy. Under the **exclusionary rule**, evidence seized in violation of the Fourth Amendment cannot be used in a court of law; it is as though it never existed.

- The Fifth Amendment limits the admissibility of confessions that have been obtained unfairly. In the 1966 landmark case *Miranda v. Arizona*, the Supreme Court held that a person accused of a crime has the right to refuse to answer questions when placed in police custody.[28] The Fifth Amendment also guarantees defendants the right to a grand jury hearing and to protection from being tried twice for the same crime (double jeopardy). Its due process clause guarantees defendants the right to fundamental fairness and the expectation of fair trials, fair hearings, and similar procedural safeguards.

- The Sixth Amendment guarantees the defendant the right to a speedy and public trial by an impartial jury, the right to be informed of the nature of the charges, and the right to confront any prosecution witnesses. It also contains the right of a defendant to be represented by an attorney—a privilege that has been extended to numerous stages of the criminal justice process, including pretrial custody, identification and lineup procedures, preliminary hearing, submission of a guilty plea, trial, sentencing, and postconviction appeal.

- According to the Eighth Amendment, "Excessive bail shall not be required, nor excessive fines imposed, nor cruel and unusual punishments inflicted." Bail is a money bond put up by the accused to attain freedom between arrest and trial. Bail is meant to ensure a trial appearance, because the bail money is forfeited if the defendant misses the trial date. The Eighth Amendment does not guarantee a constitutional right to bail but, rather, prohibits the use of excessive bail, which is typically defined as an amount far greater than that imposed on similar defendants who are accused of committing similar crimes. The Eighth Amendment also forbids the use of cruel and unusual punishment. This prohibition protects both the accused and convicted offenders from actions regarded as unacceptable by a civilized society, including corporal punishment and torture. Capital punishment, however, is legal unless it is employed in a random, haphazard fashion or if especially cruel means of execution were used.[29] One method used to avoid "cruelty" is lethal injection. In the 2008 case *Baze and Bowling v. Rees*, the Court upheld the use of this method unless there is a "substantial risk of serious harm" that the drugs will not work effectively.[30]

REALITY CHECK

MYTH OR REALITY? All U.S. citizens accused of a crime have the right to be released on bail before trial.

MYTH: Criminal defendants do not have a right to be released on bail, only a right to reasonable bail if pretrial release is granted. Dangerous offenders and those who are a flight risk can be denied bail.

Should a person accused of murder ever be given bail? What about rapists? What message does that send to crime victims who have to testify against attackers who are free in the community?

• The Fourteenth Amendment is the vehicle used by the courts to apply the protection of the Bill of Rights to the states. It affirms that no state shall "deprive any person of life, liberty, or property, without due process of law." In essence, the same general constitutional restrictions applicable to the federal government can be imposed on the states.

Due Process of Law

The concept of due process, found in both the Fifth and Fourteenth Amendments, has been used to evaluate the constitutionality of legal statutes and to set standards and guidelines for fair procedures in the criminal justice system. As you may recall from Chapter 1, some criminal justice experts believe that the concept of due process is the lens through which the criminal justice system must be examined. Without the application of due process, civil rights and Constitutional protections are meaningless. In seeking to define the term, most legal experts believe that it refers to the essential elements of fairness under law.[31] This definition basically refers to the legal system's need for rules and regulations that protect individual rights.

Due process can actually be divided into two distinct categories, substantive and procedural. Substantive due process refers to the citizen's right to be protected from criminal laws that may be biased, discriminatory, and otherwise unfair. These laws may be vague or may apply unfairly to one group and not others.

In contrast, procedural due process seeks to ensure that no person will be deprived of life, liberty, or property without proper and legal criminal process. Basically, procedural due process is intended to guarantee that fundamental fairness exists in each individual case. Specific due process procedures include the following:

1. Freedom from illegal searches and interrogations
2. Prompt notice of charges and a formal hearing
3. The right to counsel or some other representation
4. The opportunity to respond to charges
5. The opportunity to confront and cross-examine witnesses and accusers
6. The privilege to be free from self-incrimination

The right to due process of law extends to all people who come before the court. Here Samuel Komba Kambo is interviewed at an Immigration and Customs Enforcement contract facility in San Antonio, Texas, where he was being detained by U.S. Immigration authorities. Kambo, a legal immigrant, spent nearly a year in jail while fighting deportation as the government tried to revoke his visa. He was released from custody in October 2007 after a U.S. district judge ruled that U.S. Immigration and Customs Enforcement violated his due process rights. Kambo is a retired captain in the Republic of Sierra Leone Armed Forces and was one of six young soldiers in the Sierra Leonean Army that ousted President Joseph Saidu Momoh and the All People's Congress (APC) government on April 29, 1992.

© AP Images/Gloria Ferniz

7. The opportunity to present one's own witnesses
8. A decision made on the basis of substantial evidence and facts produced at the hearing
9. A written statement of the reasons for the decision
10. An appellate review procedure

Interpreting the Constitution

Within the context of due process, how the Supreme Court decides a specific case depends on the facts of the case, the federal and state constitutional and statutory provisions, previous court decisions, judicial philosophy, and the ideas and principles that society considers important at a given time and in a given place.[32] The judicial interpretation of the Constitution is not fixed but rather reflect what society deems fair and just at a particular time and place. The degree of loss suffered by the individual (victim or offender), balanced against the state's interests, also determines how many constitutional requirements are ordinarily applied. When the Supreme Court justices are conservative, as they are now, they are less likely to create new rights and privileges and more likely to restrict civil liberties. Take the 2009 case of *Herring v. U.S.*, which involved interpretation of the exclusionary rule.[33] Bennie Dean Herring had been searched after the police were informed that there was an outstanding warrant against him on a felony charge. The search turned up methamphetamine and a pistol. Soon after, it was discovered that the warrant had actually been withdrawn five months earlier and had been left in the computer system by mistake. Should the evidence be discarded because the police made an error? Or should it be allowed at trial because they acted in good faith based on existing information that later proved inaccurate? The majority ruled that "When police mistakes leading to an unlawful search are the result of isolated negligence attenuated from the search, rather than systemic error or reckless disregard of constitutional requirements, the exclusionary rule does not apply." The court ruled that the errors in the *Herring* case did not amount to deliberate police misconduct that should trigger the exclusionary rule.

ETHICAL CHALLENGES IN CRIMINAL JUSTICE

A Writing Assignment

In 1997 Louise Woodward, a teenage British nanny, was accused of first-degree murder; she was alleged to have shaken to death Matthew Eappen, the infant she was babysitting. Prosecutors claimed that Woodward was so frustrated by the crying child that she first shook him and then slammed the infant against a hard surface to silence him. Woodward's defense claimed that she did not cause Eappen's death and that a prior incident must have caused the baby's skull fracture.

After the jury found Woodward guilty of second-degree murder, Hiller B. Zobel, the trial judge, reduced Woodward's sentence to manslaughter because he concluded that the intent to do bodily harm or act with malice was not present. Involuntary manslaughter is a killing with no intention to cause serious bodily harm, such as acting without proper caution.

Write an essay commenting on the judge's behavior: Is it fair for a trial judge to overturn a jury verdict and impose his will on the people? Does that allow a single person to control the content of the law? What are some harmful outcomes that might occur if this became a common practice? What are some of the benefits?

RealityCheck Revisited

To learn more about the myths and realities related to the justice system that were raised in this chapter, visit the following websites.

- To read more about the insanity defense, go to

http://www.enotes.com/everyday-law-encyclopedia/ insanity-defense

- The need for a search warrant is discussed at

http://www.nolo.com/article.cfm/pg/2/objectId/ DED24689-ADA8-4785-887A0B4A19A694DE/ catId/268BB6A8-8884-4677-89869B6AD8A75A DA/104/143/127/ART/

- And the exclusionary rule is discussed at

http://legal-dictionary.thefreedictionary.com/ exclusionary+rule

- Where does the right to bail come from? Check out

http://www.bail.com/history.htm

SUMMARY

© AP Images/Joseph Kaczmarek

1. Know the similarities and differences between criminal law and civil law

- The law today can generally be divided into three broad categories.
- Substantive criminal law defines crimes and their punishment.
- Procedural criminal law sets out the basic rules of practice in the criminal justice system.
- Civil law governs relations between private parties, including both individuals and organizations (such as business enterprises and/or corporations).

- The goals of the substantive criminal law are to enforce social control, distribute retribution, express public opinion and morality, deter criminal behavior, punish wrongdoing, maintain social order, and provide for restoration.

2. Understand the concept of substantive criminal law and its history

- The roots of the criminal codes used in the United States can be traced to such early legal charters as the Babylonian Code of Hammurabi (2000 B.C.E.), the Mosaic Code of the Israelites (1200 B.C.E.), and the Roman Twelve Tables (451 B.C.E.).
- Emerging Germanic societies developed legal systems featuring monetary compensation, called *wergild*.
- After the Norman Conquest, royal judges would decide what to do in each case, using local custom and rules of conduct as a guide in a system known as stare decisis (Latin for "to stand by decided cases").
- Eventually this system evolved into a common law of the country that incorporated local custom and practice into a national code.
- Crimes were mala in se, "inherently evil and depraved" (such as murder, burglary, and ar-

(continued)

son), or mala prohibitum, which reflected existing social and economic conditions.

3. Discuss the sources of the criminal law

- Our legal code is directly tied to England.

- The contemporary American legal system was codified by state and federal legislatures.

- The content of the law may also be influenced by judicial decision making.

- Regardless of its source, all criminal law in the United States must conform to the rules and dictates of the Constitution.

- Criminal laws have been interpreted as violating constitutional principles if they are too vague or broad for their meaning to be clear.

- All the states and the federal government have developed their own body of criminal law that defines and grades offenses, sets levels of punishment, and classifies crimes into categories.

4. Be familiar with the elements of a crime

- Almost all common-law crime contains both mental and physical elements.

- The actus reus is a voluntary and deliberate illegal act, such as taking someone's money, burning a building, or shooting someone.

- For an act to constitute a crime, it must be done with deliberate purpose or criminal intent, or mens rea.

- To constitute a crime, the law requires a connection be made between the mens rea and the actus reus, thereby showing that the offender's conduct was the proximate cause of the criminal act.

5. Define the term "strict liability"

- Thought alone is not a crime. For a person to be considered to have committed a crime, some act is required to prove her or his willingness to cause harm.

- Certain statutory offenses exist in which mens rea is not essential. These offenses fall in a category known as public safety or strict liability crimes.

6. Be able to discuss excuses and justification defenses for crime

- When people defend themselves against criminal charges, they must refute one or more of the elements of the crime of which they have been accused.

- Defendants may deny the actus reus by arguing that they were falsely accused and the real culprit has yet to be identified.

- Defendants may also claim that even though they did engage in the criminal act they are accused of, they should be excused because they lacked mens rea.

- Insanity and intoxication are types of excuse defenses.

- Another type of defense is justification.

- A person claiming justification argues that anyone in a similar situation would act as they did, even if it meant breaking the law.

- Self-defense is a justification for crime.

7. Discuss the concept of criminal procedure

- The law of criminal procedure consists of the rules and procedures that govern the pretrial processing of criminal suspects and the conduct of criminal trials.

8. Describe the role of the Bill of Rights in shaping criminal procedure

- The main source of the procedural law is the body of the Constitution and the first ten amendments—the Bill of Rights—added to the Constitution on December 15, 1791.

- The purpose of these amendments is to prevent the government from usurping the personal freedoms of citizens.

9. Know which amendments to the Constitution are the most important to the justice system

- Of primary concern are the Fourth, Fifth, Sixth, and Eighth Amendments, which limit and control the manner in which the federal government operates the justice system.

- The Fourteenth Amendment applies these rights to the state and local governments.

10. List the elements of due process of law

- The concept of due process is found in both the Fifth and Fourteenth Amendments.

- Due process has been used to evaluate the constitutionality of legal statutes and to set standards and guidelines for fair procedures in the criminal justice system.

Key Terms

substantive criminal law, 83
criminal procedure, 83
civil law, 84
tort, 84
lex talionis, 87
stare decisis, 88
common law, 88
mala in se, 88
mala prohibitum, 88
National Instant Criminal Background Check System (NICS)?, 93
felony, 91

misdemeanor, 91
actus reus, 91
mens rea, 91
strict liability crime, 95
insanity, 97
self-defense, 97
entrapment, 97
obitiatry, 101
stalking, 102
neurolegal defense, 103
Bill of Rights, 103
exclusionary rule, 104

Review Questions

1. What are the specific aims and purposes of the criminal law? To what extent does the criminal law control behavior?

2. What kinds of activities should be labeled criminal in contemporary society? Why?

3. What is a criminal act? What is a criminal state of mind? When are individuals liable for their actions?

4. Discuss the various kinds of crime classifications. To what extent or degree are they distinguishable?

5. Numerous states are revising their penal codes. Which major categories of substantive crimes do you think should be revised?

6. Entrapment is a defense when the defendant was entrapped into committing the crime. To what extent should law enforcement personnel induce the commission of an offense?

7. What legal principles can be used to justify self-defense? Given that the law seeks to prevent crime, not promote crime it, are such principles sound?

8. What are the minimum standards of criminal procedure required in the criminal justice system?

Part 2

THE POLICE AND LAW ENFORCEMENT

On a November night in 2006, Sean Bell was holding his bachelor's party at a strip club in the borough of Queens in New York City. The club was under investigation by an NYPD undercover unit for suspicion of prostitution and complaints about guns and drugs. The events of that night are disputed, but when the dust settled, Sean Bell had been shot 50 times by five different undercover officers. His injuries were fatal, and two of his companions were wounded. All three men were unarmed. Three of the five officers were tried for crimes ranging from manslaughter to reckless endangerment. At trial, the officers testified that one of Bell's friends was heard saying, "Yo, get my gun" as they headed to Bell's car. Joseph Guzman, one of the surviving victims, claimed that he and Bell were simply attempting to flee from armed men they could not identify. On April 25, 2008, all three officers were cleared of any wrongdoing. In response to the verdict, on May 7, 2008, the Reverend Al Sharpton led a "slow down" protest in New York City, where groups of people made an effort to block traffic on busy streets. He and about 200 other people were arrested.

Incidents like that involving Sean Bell are particularly difficult for the police. The officers began with the intention of investigating complaints of criminal activity. In the end, an unarmed man was killed in a hail of bullets. Somewhere along the way to this tragedy, something went horribly wrong. In today's complex world, policing is no longer a simple matter of patrolling the streets and protecting the public. It is about solving complex problems by making split-second decisions on a very public stage.

At the same time, events like this are extremely rare. The media gives the impression that police shootings are commonplace. Publicized protests make it seem that the police are racially biased. Indeed, some shootings are inexcusable, but although there is evidence that some officers make racially biased decisions, the vast majority of police officers follow the letter of the law and make decisions objectively. What's more, they are not a trigger-happy group of zealous crime fighters. Most police work is "under the radar" and never appears in the media spotlight.

> The media gives the impression that police shootings are commonplace. Publicized protests make it seem that the police are racially biased.
> Indeed, some shootings are inexcusable, but although there is evidence that some officers make racially biased decisions, the vast majority of police officers follow the letter of the law and make decisions objectively. What's more, they are not a trigger-happy group of zealous crime fighters. Most police work is "under the radar" and never appears in the media spotlight.

Chapter 4
Police in Society: History and Organization

Chapter 5
The Police: Role and Function

Chapter 6
Issues in Policing: Professional, Social, and Legal

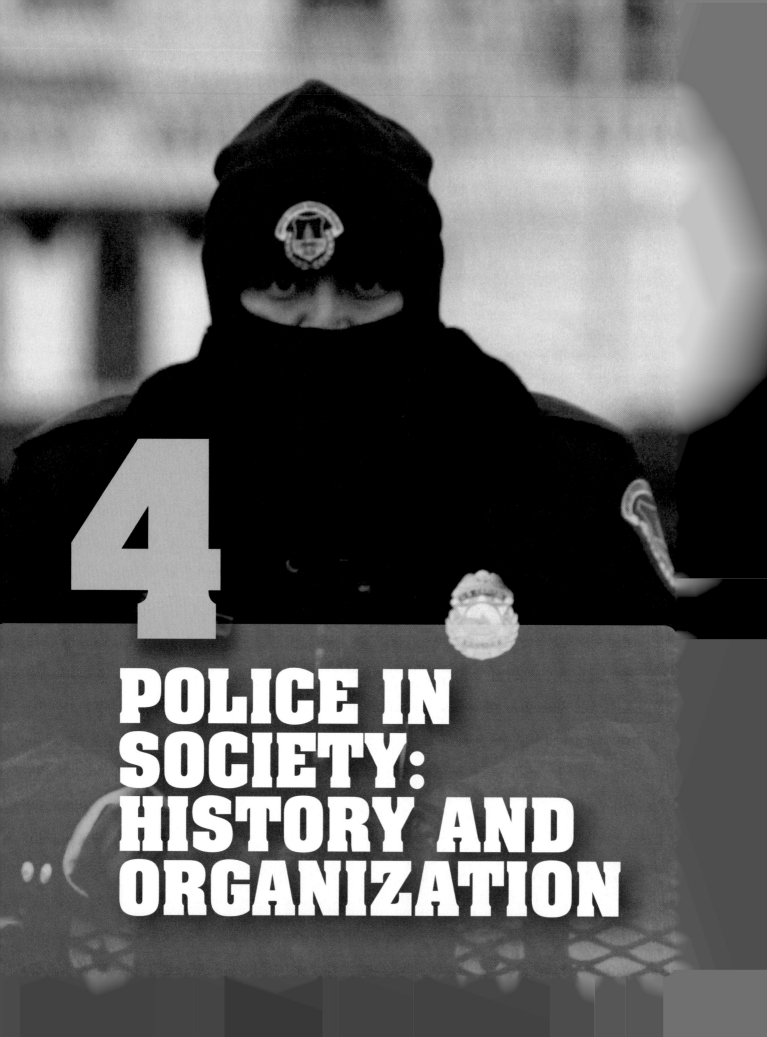

4

POLICE IN SOCIETY: HISTORY AND ORGANIZATION

© Molly Riley/Reuters/Landov

RealityCheck

MYTH or REALITY?

▶ The first modern police force was established in London.

▶ During the nineteenth century, the police were regarded as competent and professional.

▶ Federal law enforcement agencies are housed solely within cabinet-level departments (such as the State Department).

▶ The core mission of the FBI is to enforce the criminal laws of the United States.

▶ Most metropolitan law enforcement agencies employ more than 50 officers.

▶ There are fewer private police than public police.

Learning Objectives

1. Describe how law enforcement developed in feudal England

2. Know what the first police agencies were like

3. Discuss the development of law enforcement in the United States

4. Analyze the problems of early police agencies

5. Discuss how reformers attempted to create professional police agencies

6. Describe the major changes in law enforcement between 1970 and today

7. Be familiar with the major federal law enforcement agencies

8. Know the differences among state, county, and local law enforcement

9. Describe how technology is changing police work

10. Discuss the future of police technology and be familiar with the direction it is taking

Chapter Outline

© Molly Riley/Reuters/Landov

Career Profile

John Sullivan is a Massachusetts state trooper assigned to the substation in Revere, just outside Boston. Before becoming a sworn member of the State Police, he spent 14 years in the United States Merchant Marines and as a commissioned officer in the United States Navy. He thus entered the law enforcement profession in a somewhat unorthodox fashion.

While there is no formal requirement that one must have a college degree to become a Massachusetts state trooper, John believes that people with criminal justice degrees have a distinct advantage in the early part of their careers. He feels it puts them in a more competitive position. He also notes that

most troopers who rise through the ranks have degrees, so having a college education is advantageous from that standpoint as well.

John thinks the greatest challenges on his job are keeping a positive attitude and resisting the temptation to become cynical. Law enforcement officials are often called on to make difficult decisions, and some of these decisions come to the attention of the press. John feels that, unfortunately, reporters often portray the police in a critical light. This sometimes makes it hard for the public to maintain a favorable attitude toward him and his colleagues.

Although it is true that a law enforcement career can be difficult, it also carries with it the potential for great personal fulfillment. John especially prizes his opportunities to turn what could otherwise become a negative encounter with the public into a positive one. Not every interaction with the police has to result in a citation, arrest, or other formal sanction. Part of the job, he says, involves community care-taking.

T he police, John Sullivan among them, are the gatekeepers of the criminal justice process. They initiate contact with violators of the law and decide whether to arrest them formally and start their journey through the criminal justice system, to settle the issue in an informal way (such as by issuing a warning), or to take no action at all. The strategic position of law enforcement officers, their visibility and contact with the public, and their use of weapons and arrest power kept them in the forefront of public thought for most of the twentieth century.

This and the following two chapters evaluate the history, role, organizational issues, and procedures of police agents and agencies and discuss the legal rules that control police behavior.

The History of Police

The origin of U.S. police agencies, like the origins of criminal law, can be traced to early English society.[1] Before the Norman Conquest in 1066 c.e., no regular English police force existed. Every person living in the villages scattered throughout the countryside was responsible for aiding neighbors and protecting the settlement from thieves and marauders. This was known as the "pledge system." People were grouped in collectives of 10 families, called **tithings**, and were entrusted with policing their own minor problems. When trouble occurred, the citizen was expected to make a **hue and cry**. Ten tithings were grouped into what was called a **hundred**, whose affairs were supervised by a **constable** appointed by the local nobleman. The constable, who might be considered the first real police officer, dealt with more serious breaches of the law.[2]

Shires, which resembled the counties of today, were controlled by the **shire reeve**, who was appointed by the Crown or by local landowner to supervise the territory and ensure that order was kept. The shire reeve, a forerunner of today's **sheriff**, soon began to pursue and apprehend law violators as part of his duties.

In the thirteenth century, the **watch system** was created to help protect property in England's larger cities and towns. Watchmen patrolled at night and helped protect the community against robberies, fires, and disturbances. They reported to the area constable, who became the primary metropolitan law enforcement agent. In larger cities, such as London, the watchmen were

tithing
In medieval England, a group of 10 families who collectively dealt with minor disturbances and breaches of the peace.

hue and cry
A call for assistance in medieval England. The policy of self-help that prevailed in villages demanded that everyone respond if a citizen raised a hue and cry to get their aid.

hundred
In medieval England, a group of 100 families responsible for maintaining order and trying minor offenses.

constable
In medieval England, an appointed official who administered and supervised the legal affairs of a small community.

shire reeve
In medieval England, the senior law enforcement figure in a county; the forerunner of today's sheriff.

sheriff
The chief law enforcement officer in a county.

watch system
During the Middle Ages in England, men were organized in church parishes to guard at night against disturbances and breaches of the peace under the direction of the local constable.

organized within church parishes and were usually members of the parish they protected.

justice of the peace
Established in 1326 England, the office was created to help the shire reeve in controlling the county; it later took on judicial functions.

In 1326 the office of **justice of the peace** was created to assist the shire reeve in controlling the county. Eventually, these justices took on judicial functions in addition to their primary role as peacekeepers. The local constable became the operational assistant to the justice of the peace, supervising the night watchmen, investigating offenses, serving summonses, executing warrants, and securing prisoners. This system helped establish the relationship between police and the judiciary, which has continued for more than 670 years.

Private Police and Thief Takers

As the eighteenth century began, rising crime rates encouraged a new form of private, monied police, who profited both legally and criminally from the lack of formal police departments. These private police agents, referred to as "thief takers," were universally corrupt, taking profits not only from catching and informing on criminals but also from receiving stolen property, theft, intimidation, perjury, and blackmail. They often relieved their prisoners of money and stolen goods and made even more income by accepting hush money, giving perjured evidence, swearing false oaths, and operating extortion rackets. Petty debtors were especially easy targets for those who combined thief taking with the keeping of alehouses and taverns. While prisoners were incarcerated, their health and safety was entirely at the whim of the keepers, or thief takers, who were free to charge virtually whatever they wanted for board and other necessities. Court bailiffs who also acted as thief takers were the most passionately detested legal profiteers. They seized debtors and held them in small lockups, where they forced their victims to pay exorbitant prices for food and lodging.

The thief takers' use of violence was notorious. They went armed and were prepared to maim or kill in order to gain their objectives. Before he was hanged in 1725, Jack Wild, the most notorious thief taker, "had two fractures in his skull and his bald head was covered with silver plates. He had seventeen wounds in various parts of his body from swords, daggers, and gunshots, [and] . . . his throat had been cut in the course of his duties."[3]

Henry Fielding (famed author of *Tom Jones*), along with Saunders Welch and his brother John Fielding, sought to clean up the thief-taking system. Appointed a city magistrate in 1748, Henry Fielding operated his own group of monied police out of Bow Street in London, directing and deploying them throughout the city and its environs, deciding which cases to investigate and what streets to protect. His agents were carefully instructed on their legitimate powers and duties. Fielding's Bow Street Runners were a marked improvement over the earlier monied police, because they actually had an administrative structure that improved record keeping and investigative procedures.

Although an improvement, Fielding's forces were not adequate, and by the nineteenth century state police officers were needed. Ironically, almost 200 years later, private policing is now considered essential. Private police forces are burgeoning, and many local police work closely with private security firms and similar entities. In some gated communities and special tax assessment districts, property owners pay a special levy, in addition to their tax dollars, to hire additional private police, who may work in partnership with local law enforcement to investigate criminal activities.[4]

Creating Public Police

In 1829 Sir Robert Peel, England's home secretary, guided through Parliament an "Act for Improving the Police in and near the Metropolis." The Metropolitan Police Act established the first organized police force in London.

Composed of over 1,000 men, the London police force was structured along military lines; its members were known from then on as "bobbies," after its creator. They wore a distinctive uniform and were led by two magistrates, who were later given the title of commissioner. However, the ultimate responsibility for the police fell to the home secretary and consequently to the Parliament.

The early bobbies suffered from many of the same ills as their forebears. Many were corrupt, they were unsuccessful at stopping crime, and they were influenced by the wealthy. Owners of houses of ill repute, who in the past had guaranteed their undisturbed operations by bribing watchmen, now turned their attention to the bobbies. Metropolitan police administrators fought constantly to terminate cowardly, corrupt, and alcoholic officers, dismissing in the beginning about one-third of the bobbies each year.

Despite its recognized shortcomings, the London experiment proved a vast improvement over what had gone before. It was considered so successful that the London Metropolitan Police soon began providing law enforcement assistance to outlying areas that requested it. Another act of Parliament empowered justices of the peace to establish local police forces, and by 1856 every borough and county in England was required to form its own police force.

REALITY CHECK

MYTH OR REALITY? The first modern police force was established in London.

REALITY: Although there were some signs of organized policing as early as the 1600s, the London "Metropolitan Police," formed in 1829, is widely regarded as the first modern organized police force.

What were some of the other early modernized police forces besides the Metropolitan Police?

London Metropolitan Police

To learn more about the history of the **London Metropolitan Police**, and for their contemporary story, visit

www.cengage.com/criminaljustice/siegel

Law Enforcement in Colonial America

Law enforcement in colonial America paralleled the British model. In the colonies, the county sheriff became the most important law enforcement agent. In addition to keeping the peace and fighting crime, sheriffs collected taxes, supervised elections, and handled a great deal of other legal business.

The colonial sheriff did not patrol or seek out crime. Instead, he reacted to citizens' complaints and investigated crimes that had occurred. His salary, related to his effectiveness, was paid on a fee system. Sheriffs received a fixed amount for every arrest made. Unfortunately, their tax-collecting chores were more lucrative than fighting crime, so law enforcement was not one of their primary concerns. In the cities, law enforcement was the province of the town marshal, who was aided, often unwillingly, by a variety of constables, night watchmen, police justices, and city council members. However, local governments had little power of administration, and enforcement of the criminal law was largely an individual or community responsibility. After the American Revolution, larger cities relied on elected or appointed agents to serve warrants and recover stolen property, sometimes in cooperation with the thieves themselves. Night watchmen, who were referred to as "leatherheads" because of the leather helmets they wore, patrolled the streets calling the hour, equipped with a rattle to summon help and a nightstick to ward off lawbreakers. Watchmen were not widely respected: Rowdy young men enjoyed tipping over the watch houses with the leatherhead inside, and a favorite saying in New York was "While the city sleeps the watchmen do too."[5]

In rural areas in the South, slave patrols charged with recapturing escaped slaves were an early—if loathsome—form of law enforcement.[6] When these patrols apprehended runaway slaves, they often administered "justice" on the spot, often with violence. In the western territories, individual initiative was encouraged by the practice of offering rewards for the capture of felons. If

vigilantes

Groups of citizens who tracked down wanted criminals in the Old West.

trouble arose, the town vigilance committee might form a posse to chase offenders. These **vigilantes** were called on to eradicate such social problems as theft of livestock through force or intimidation; the San Francisco Vigilance Committee actively pursued criminals in the mid-nineteenth century.

As cities grew, it became exceedingly difficult for local leaders to organize ad hoc vigilante groups. Moreover, the early nineteenth century was an era of widespread urban unrest and mob violence. Local leaders began to realize that a more structured police function was needed to control demonstrators and keep the peace.

Early Police Agencies

The modern police department was born out of urban mob violence that wracked the nation's cities in the nineteenth century. Boston created the first formal U.S. police department in 1838. New York formed its police department in 1844, Philadelphia in 1854. The new police departments replaced the night-watch system and relegated constables and sheriffs to serving court orders and running jails.

At first, the urban police departments inherited the functions of the institutions they replaced. For example, Boston police were charged with maintaining public health until 1853, and in New York the police were responsible for street sweeping until 1881. Politics dominated the departments and determined the recruitment of new officers and the promotion of supervisors. An individual with the right connections could be hired despite a lack of qualifications. Early police agencies were corrupt, brutal, and inefficient.[7] At first, police were expected to live in the area they patrolled, but as the nineteenth century drew to a close, officers left the most dangerous areas and commuted to work, thereby separating themselves from the people they were being asked to supervise and control.[8]

John X. Beidler, pictured here, was leader of the Montana Vigilantes, a secretive band formed to fight crime in Montana in the 1860s. He later became a stagecoach guard and a deputy U.S. marshal. Vigilante groups like Beidler's were precursors to organized police forces in colonial America.

© Print Collector/HIP/The Image Works

In the late nineteenth century, police work was highly desirable because it paid more than most other blue-collar jobs. By 1880 the average factory worker earned $450 a year, whereas a metropolitan police officer made $900 annually. For immigrant groups, having enough political clout to be appointed to the police department was an important step up the social ladder.[9] However, job security was uncertain because it depended on the local political machine's staying in power.

Police work itself was primitive. There were few of even the simplest technological innovations common today, such as centralized record keeping. Most officers patrolled on foot, without backup or the ability to call for help. Officers were commonly taunted by local toughs and responded with force and brutality. The long-standing conflict between police and the public was born in the difficulty that untrained, unprofessional officers had in patrolling the streets of nineteenth-century U.S. cities and in breaking up and controlling labor disputes. Police were not crime fighters as we know them today. Their main role was maintaining order, and their power was almost unchecked. The average officer had little training, no education in the law, and a minimum of supervision, yet the police became virtual judges of law and fact with the ability to exercise unlimited discretion.[10]

At mid-nineteenth century, the detective bureau was set up as part of the Boston police. Until then, thief taking had been the province of amateur bounty hunters, who hired themselves out to victims for a price. When professional police departments replaced bounty hunters, the close working relationships that developed between police detectives and their underworld informants produced many scandals and, consequently, high personnel turnover.

Police during the nineteenth century were regarded as incompetent and corrupt and were disliked by the people they served. The police role was only minimally directed at law enforcement. Its primary function was serving as the enforcement arm of the reigning political power, protecting private property, and keeping control of the ever-rising numbers of foreign immigrants.

Police agencies evolved slowly through the second half of the nineteenth century. Uniforms were introduced in 1853 in New York. The first technological breakthroughs in police operations came in the area of communications. The linking of precincts to central headquarters by telegraph began in the 1850s. In 1867 the first telegraph police boxes were installed; an officer could turn a key in a box, and his location and number would automatically register at headquarters. Additional technological advances were made in transportation. The Detroit Police Department outfitted some of its patrol officers with bicycles in 1897. By 1913 the motorcycle was being used by departments in the eastern part of the nation. The first police car was used in Akron, Ohio, in 1910, and the police wagon became popular in Cincinnati in 1912.[11] Nonpolice functions, such as care of the streets, had begun to be abandoned by police departments after the Civil War.

The control of police departments by local politicians impeded effective law enforcement and fostered an atmosphere of graft and corruption. In the nineteenth century, big-city police were still not respected by the public, were largely unsuccessful in their role as crime stoppers, and were involved in no progressive activities.

REALITYCHECK

MYTH OR REALITY? During the nineteenth century, the police were regarded as competent and professional.

MYTH: Policing in the 1800s was anything but professional. Competence often was lacking as well.

It would not be until the 1900s that police departments began making major strides toward professionalism. Is policing a profession today? What are the hallmarks of a profession?

Policing in the Twentieth Century

The modern era of policing can be traced from the turn of the nineteenth century to the present. What are the major events that occurred during this period?

The Emergence of Professionalism

In an effort to reduce police corruption, civic leaders in a number of jurisdictions created police administrative boards to reduce local officials' control over the police. These tribunals were responsible for appointing police administrators and controlling police affairs. In many instances, these measures failed because the private citizens appointed to the review boards lacked expertise in the intricacies of police work. Another reform movement was the takeover of some metropolitan police agencies by state legislators. Although police budgets were financed through local taxes, control of police was usurped by rural politicians in the state capitals. New York City temporarily lost authority over its police force in 1857. It was not until the first decades of the twentieth century that cities regained control of their police forces.

The Boston police strike of 1919 heightened interest in police reform. The strike came about basically because police officers were dissatisfied with their status in society. Other professions were unionizing and increasing their standard of living, but police salaries lagged behind. The Boston police officers' organization, the Boston Social Club, voted to become a union affiliated with the American Federation of Labor. The officers went out on strike on September 9, 1919. Rioting and looting broke out, resulting in Governor Calvin Coolidge's mobilization of the state militia to take over the city. Public support turned against the police, and the strike was broken. Eventually, all the striking officers were fired and replaced by new recruits. The Boston police strike ended police unionism for decades and solidified power in the hands of reactionary, autocratic police administrators. In the aftermath of the strike, various local,

© AP Images/Boston Public Library

Great precaution is taken to guard police headquarters in Pemberton Square during the Boston police strike of 1919. Here the cavalrymen of the state guard ride horses previously used by the mounted policemen who went on strike. The Boston police strike ended police unionism for decades and solidified power in the hands of reactionary, autocratic police administrators. In the aftermath of the strike, various local, state, and federal crime commissions began to investigate the extent of crime and the ability of the justice system to deal with it and made recommendations to improve police effectiveness.

state, and federal crime commissions began to investigate the extent of crime and the ability of the justice system to deal with it effectively; they then made recommendations to improve police effectiveness.[12] With the onset of the Depression, however, justice reform became a less important issue than economic revival, and for many years little changed in the nature of policing.

At about the same time, a number of nationally recognized leaders called for measures to help improve and professionalize the police. In 1893 the International Association of Chiefs of Police (IACP), a professional society, was formed. IACP called for creating a civil service police force and for removing political influence and control. The most famous police reformer of the time was August Vollmer. While serving as police chief of Berkeley, California, Vollmer instituted university training for young officers and helped develop the School of Criminology at the University of California at Berkeley. Vollmer's disciples included O. W. Wilson, who pioneered the use of advanced training for officers and was instrumental in applying modern management and administrative techniques to policing. During this period, police professionalism was equated with an incorruptible, tough, highly trained, rule-oriented department organized along militaristic lines. The most respected department was that of Los Angeles, which emphasized the police as incorruptible crime fighters who would not question the authority of the central command.

August Vollmer, Berkeley Police Department

To read more about **August Vollmer** and the history of the **Berkeley Police Department**, visit

www.cengage.com/criminaljustice/siegel

The 1960s and Beyond

Turmoil and crisis were the hallmarks of policing during the 1960s. Throughout this decade, the Supreme Court handed down a number of decisions designed to control police operations and procedures. Police officers were now required to follow strict legal guidelines when questioning suspects, conducting searches, and wiretapping, among other duties. As the civil rights of suspects were significantly expanded, police complained that they were being "handcuffed by the courts."

Also during this time, civil unrest produced a growing tension between police and the public. African Americans, who were battling for recognition and enforcement of their rights and freedoms in the civil rights movement, found themselves confronting police lines. When riots broke out in New York, Detroit, Los Angeles, and other cities between 1964 and 1968, the spark that ignited conflict often involved the police. When students across the nation began marching in anti–Vietnam War demonstrations, local police departments were called on to keep order. Police forces were ill equipped and poorly trained to deal with these social problems; it is not surprising that the 1960s were marked by a number of bloody confrontations between the police and the public.

Confounding these problems was a rapidly growing crime rate. The number of violent and property crimes increased dramatically. Drug addiction and abuse grew to be national concerns, common among all social classes. Urban police departments could not control the crime rate, and police officers resented the demands placed on them by dissatisfied citizens.

The 1970s witnessed many structural changes in police agencies themselves. The end of the Vietnam War significantly reduced tensions between students and police. The relationship between police and minorities was still rocky, however. Local fears and distrust, combined with conservative federal policies, encouraged police departments to control what was perceived as an emerging minority group "threat."[13]

Increased federal government support for criminal justice greatly influenced police operations. During the decade, the Law Enforcement Assistance Administration (LEAA) devoted a significant portion of its funds to police agencies. Although a number of police departments used this money to purchase little-used hardware, such as antiriot gear, most of it went to supporting innovative research on police work and advanced training of police officers. Perhaps most significant, LEAA's Law Enforcement Education Program helped thousands of officers further their college education. Hundreds of criminal justice programs were developed on college campuses around the country, providing a pool of highly educated police recruits. LEAA funds were also used to transfer technology originally developed in other fields into law enforcement. Technological innovations involving computers transformed the way police kept records, investigated crimes, and communicated with one another. State training academies improved the way police learned to deal with such issues as job stress, community conflict, and interpersonal relations. More women and minorities were recruited into police work. Affirmative action programs helped to slowly alter the ethnic, racial, and gender composition of U.S. policing.

As the 1980s began, the police role seemed to be changing significantly. A number of experts acknowledged that the police were not simply crime fighters and called for police to develop a greater awareness of community issues, which resulted in the emergence of the community policing concept.[14]

Police unions, which began to grow in the late 1960s, continued to have a great impact on departmental administration in the 1980s. Unions fought for and won increased salaries and benefits for their members. In many instances, union efforts eroded the power of the police chief to make unquestioned policy and personnel decisions. During the decade, chiefs of police commonly consulted with union leaders before making significant decisions about departmental operations.

Although police operations improved markedly during this time, police departments were also beset by problems that impeded their effectiveness. State and local budgets were cut back during the Reagan administration, and federal support for innovative police programs was severely curtailed with the demise of the LEAA.

Police–community relations continued to be a major problem. Riots and incidents of urban conflict occurred in some of the nation's largest cities.[15] They triggered persistent concern about what the police role should be, especially in inner-city neighborhoods.

The 1990s began on a sour note and ended with an air of optimism. The incident that helped change the face of American policing occurred on March 3, 1991, when Rodney King and his friend Bryant Allen were driving in Los Angeles, California. They refused to stop when signaled by a police car behind them but instead increased their speed; King, the driver, was apparently drunk or on drugs. When police finally stopped the car, they delivered 56 baton blows and 6 kicks to King in a period of two minutes, producing 11 skull fractures, brain damage, and kidney damage. They did not realize that their actions were being videotaped by an observer, who later gave the tape to the media. The officers involved were eventually tried and acquitted in a suburban court by an all-white jury, a decision that set off six days of rioting.[16]

The King case prompted an era of reform. Several police experts decreed that the nation's police forces should be evaluated not on their crime-fighting ability but on their courteousness, deportment, and helpfulness. Interest renewed in reviving an earlier style of police work featuring foot patrols and increased citizen contact. Police departments began to embrace new forms of policing that stressed cooperation with the community and problem solving. Ironically, urban police departments began to shift their focus to becoming community organizers at a time when technological improvements increased their ability to identify suspects. An ongoing effort was made to make departments more diverse, and African Americans began to be hired as chiefs of police, most notably in Los Angeles and Atlanta. The following are some of the most notable achievements of police departments in the 1990s:

- The intellectual caliber of the police rose dramatically.
- Police began to use advanced management techniques and applied empirical data to their decision making.

- Standards of police conduct climbed. Despite well-publicized incidents of brutality, police tended to treat the public more fairly, more equitably, and more civilly than they did in the 1960s.
- Police became more diverse in race and gender.
- The work of the police became intellectually more demanding, requiring an array of new specialized knowledge about technology, forensic analysis, and crime.
- Police gradually accepted civilian review of police discipline.[17]

Policing and Law Enforcement Today

Contemporary law enforcement agencies are still undergoing transformation. There has been an ongoing effort to make police "user friendly" by decentralizing police departments and making them responsive to community needs. Police and law enforcement agencies are also adapting to the changing nature of crime: They must be prepared to handle terrorism, Internet fraud schemes, and identity theft, as well as rape, robbery, and burglary.[18]

Law enforcement duties are distributed across local, county, state, and federal jurisdictions. There are approximately 700,000 sworn law enforcement officers in the United States, employed in almost 20,000 different agencies.[19] Police and law enforcement agencies can be found in a variety of levels of government. There is no real hierarchy, and each branch has its own sphere of operations, though overlap may exist.

Federal Law Enforcement Agencies

The federal government has a number of law enforcement agencies designed to protect the rights and privileges of U.S. citizens; no single agency has unlimited

The police are often called on to help in times of crisis. Here, a Houston police officer helps distribute ice and water at Zion Lutheran Church near downtown Houston on September 15, 2008. Ice, bottled water, and other vital supplies poured into the city as it struggled without electricity to recover from Hurricane Ike's mighty punch. About 2,000 people were plucked from flooded areas by helicopters and boats in the largest rescue effort in Texas history, as searchers scoured hard-hit places such as the devastated island city of Galveston.

© Reuters/Richard Carson/Landov

REALITYCHECK

MYTH OR REALITY?   Federal law enforcement agencies are housed solely within cabinet-level departments (such as the State Department).

MYTH: There are law enforcement agencies all throughout the federal government.

Many federal law enforcement agencies are not associated with a particular cabinet-level department (an example is the Postal Inspection Service). Try to identify some of the lesser-known federal law enforcement agencies.

jurisdiction, and each has been created to enforce specific laws and cope with particular situations. Federal agencies have no particular rank order or hierarchy of command or responsibility, and each reports to a specific department or bureau.

Dozens of federal law enforcement agencies exist both inside and outside the cabinet-level departments. Here we focus on law enforcement agencies in two cabinet-level departments: the U.S. Justice Department and the Department of Homeland Security.

U.S. JUSTICE DEPARTMENT AGENCIES

The U.S. Justice Department houses four of the better-known federal law enforcement agencies.

Federal Bureau of Investigation (FBI)

The arm of the U.S. Justice Department that investigates violations of federal law, seeks to protect America from terrorist attacks, gathers crime statistics, runs a comprehensive crime laboratory, and helps train local law enforcement officers.

Drug Enforcement Administration (DEA)

The federal agency that enforces federal drug control laws.

• **Federal Bureau of Investigation (FBI)** The Federal Bureau of Investigation is an investigative agency with jurisdiction over all matters in which the United States is or may be an interested party. Its jurisdiction is limited, however, to federal laws, including all federal statutes not specifically assigned to other agencies. The FBI has approximately 30,000 employees, including more than 12,000 special agents and 17,000 support personnel who perform professional, administrative, technical, clerical, craft, trade, or maintenance operations. Since 9/11, the FBI has announced a reformulation of its priorities, making protecting the United States from terrorist attack its number one commitment. It is now charged with coordinating intelligence collection with the Border Patrol, the Secret Service, and the CIA. To carry out its newly formulated mission, the FBI is expanding its force of agents. In addition to recruiting candidates with the traditional background in law enforcement, law, and accounting, the Bureau is concentrating on hiring agents with scientific and technological skills, as well as foreign-language proficiency in priority areas such as Arabic, Farsi, Pashtun, Urdu, all dialects of Chinese, Japanese, Korean, Russian, Spanish, and Vietnamese, and with other priority backgrounds such as foreign counterintelligence, counterterrorism, and military intelligence. Among the agency's other activities are gathering crime statistics, running a comprehensive crime laboratory, and training local law enforcement officers.

REALITYCHECK

MYTH OR REALITY?   The core mission of the FBI is to enforce the criminal laws of the United States.

MYTH: Since 9/11, the FBI's priorities have changed. Now protection of the United States from terrorist attacks ranks near the top if its priority list.

To what extent does the FBI's decision to give priority to protection from terrorism affect its ability to fight other types of crime? Has America's law enforcement apparatus overreacted to the threat of terrorism?

• **Drug Enforcement Administration (DEA)** DEA agents assist local and state authorities in investigating illegal drug use and carrying out independent surveillance and enforcement activities to control the importation of narcotics. For example, DEA agents work with foreign governments in cooperative efforts aimed at destroying opium and marijuana crops at their source—hard-to-find fields tucked away in the interiors of Latin America, Asia, Europe, and Africa. Undercover DEA agents infiltrate drug rings and simulate buying narcotics to arrest drug dealers.

- **Bureau of Alcohol, Tobacco, Firearms, and Explosives (ATF)** The ATF helps control sales of untaxed liquor and cigarettes and, through the Gun Control Act of 1968 and the Organized Crime Control Act of 1970, has jurisdiction over the illegal sale, importation, and criminal misuse of firearms and explosives.
- **U.S. Marshals Service** The U.S. Marshals Service is America's oldest federal law enforcement agency and one of the most versatile. Its more than 3,000 deputy marshals and criminal investigators perform a number of functions, including judicial security, fugitive investigations, witness protection, prisoner transportation, prisoner services (the agency houses nearly 60,000 federal detainees each day), and administration of the U.S. Justice Department's Asset Forfeiture Program.

HOMELAND SECURITY AGENCIES ● Soon after the 9/11 attacks on the Pentagon and the World Trade Center towers in New York City, President Bush proposed the creation of a new cabinet-level agency called the **Department of Homeland Security (DHS).** On November 19, 2002, Congress passed legislation authorizing the creation of the DHS and assigned it the mission of providing intelligence analysis and infrastructure protection, strengthening the borders, improving the use of science and technology to counter weapons of mass destruction, and creating a comprehensive response and recovery division. Rather than working from the ground up, the DHS combined a number of existing agencies into a superagency that carries out a variety of missions, from border security to infrastructure protection. Two of the main law enforcement agencies housed within DHS are described in some detail below. We will revisit the work of the DHS in Chapter 14.

- **Customs and Border Protection (CBP)** After 9/11, the U.S. Border Patrol, portions of the U.S. Customs Service, the Immigration and Naturalization Service, and the Animal and Plant Health Inspection Service were combined into one office of Customs and Border Protection. The agency employs more than 40,000 personnel and is primarily responsible for protection of America's borders and ports of entry. The largest and most visible element of CBP is the Border Patrol. Its 10,000 agents combine to form one of the largest uniformed law enforcement agencies in the United States (see the Careers in Criminal Justice feature below).

Bureau of Alcohol, Tobacco, Firearms, and Explosives (ATF)
Federal agency with jurisdiction over the illegal sale, importation, and criminal misuse of firearms and explosives and the distribution of untaxed liquor and cigarettes.

U.S. Marshals Service
Federal agency whose jurisdiction includes protecting federal officials, transporting criminal defendants, and tracking down fugitives.

U.S. Marshals
The **U.S. Marshals** home page can be accessed via
www.cengage.com/ criminaljustice/siegel

Department of Homeland Security (DHS)
Federal agency responsible for preventing terrorist attacks within the United States, reducing America's vulnerability to terrorism, and minimizing the damage and assisting in recovery from attacks that do occur.

Customs and Border Protection (CBP)
Federal agency responsible for the control and protection of America's borders and ports of entry. Its first priority is keeping terrorists and their weapons out of the United States.

Careers in Criminal Justice

BORDER PATROL AGENT

Duties and Characteristics of the Job

- The U.S. Border Patrol is the uniformed law enforcement arm of U.S. Customs and Border Protection (CBP). Its overall mission is to detect and prevent the illegal entry of aliens and terrorists into the United States, so the activities of all agents revolve around this mission.
- One of the key responsibilities of an agent is "line watch," which involves the detection, prevention, and apprehension of terrorists, undocumented aliens, and smugglers of aliens near the border.
- Border Patrol agents are also involved in farm and ranch check, traffic check, traffic observation, city patrol, transportation check, administrative, intelligence, and antismuggling activities.

Careers in Criminal Justice (Continued)

Job Outlook

- Good benefits, a generous retirement policy, and the prestige associated with the position combine to make it highly desirable and thus very competitive.
- An early retirement policy ensures that there will always be job openings. Recruitment is ongoing, and the Border Patrol is always accepting applications.

Salary

- New agents are hired at a salary between $36,658 (GL-5) and $46,542 (GL-9), depending on education and experience. As in most federal government positions, there are excellent benefits.
- Salary varies according to the amount of overtime pay and where the agent is located.
- Agents promoted to supervisory positions earn higher pay, as do those who work in a geographical area where pay is higher in general.

Qualifications

- The Border Patrol wants applicants who are independent thinkers and can work alone, but also team players who work well with others.
- In order to apply to be an agent, it is necessary to be a U.S. citizen, to have no conviction for domestic violence, to have lived in the United States for the past three years, to have a valid driver's license at the time of appointment, and to be under age 40 at the time of appointment.
- Applicants must also pass a medical exam, drug testing, a physical fitness exam, and a background investigation.
- Candidates must be willing to travel wherever their assignments take them and be willing to move, particularly somewhere along the U.S.–Mexico border.

Education and Training

- To qualify for the GL-5 level salary, the applicant must have at least one year of work experience comparable in difficulty and responsibility to GL-4. This requirement is often met through a combination of work and educational experience. There is no degree requirement for joining the Border Patrol.
- If accepted, applicants spend several weeks at a training program in Artesia, New Mexico, where they learn necessary skills.
- After completion of this program at the academy, there is a two-year internship period, during which time formal training continues.

Word to the Wise

- Candidates must be willing to accept an initial assignment along the U.S. Southwest border with Mexico. The first assignment will be at the U.S.–Mexico border.
- It is necessary to work rotating shifts, often at night. Agents also work alone much of the time.
- Nine to ten hours of overtime are mandatory (called Administratively Uncontrolled Overtime). This is also a benefit, however, because it enables agents to make 25 percent over and above their base salary.
- Training and testing in Spanish proficiency are mandatory throughout training. A series of tests must be passed before an applicant can advance to agent status. Students interested in pursuing a Border Patrol career may wish to start taking Spanish courses if they have not already done so.
- Misdemeanor domestic violence and felony convictions are disqualifiers. Other misdemeanor convictions are not necessarily a barrier to employment, but full disclosure is required.
- Problems with bad credit and other background experiences that may imply poor character can lead to disqualification.

- **Secret Service** The U.S. Secret Service performs two main functions. The more visible of these is protection of national leaders, notably the president but also the vice president, the president-elect, the vice president-elect, the immediate families of these individuals, former presidents and their families, visiting heads of state, and other officials. The Secret Service was first established as a law enforcement entity in 1865 and was tasked with investigating the counterfeiting of U.S. currency. It continues this investigative function today. Since 1984, Secret Service investigative activities have been expanded to include the investigation of financial institution fraud, computer and telecommunications fraud, false identification documents, and other criminal activities.

Secret Service
Federal agency responsible for executive protection and for investigation of counterfeiting and various forms of financial fraud.

Secret Service
The **Secret Service** home page can be accessed via
www.cengage.com/ criminaljustice/siegel

State Law Enforcement Agencies

Unlike municipal police departments, state police were legislatively created to deal with the growing incidence of crime in nonurban areas, a consequence of the increase in population mobility and the advent of personalized mass transportation in the form of the automobile. County sheriffs—elected officials with occasionally corrupt or questionable motives—had proved ineffective in dealing with the wide-ranging criminal activities that developed during the latter half of the nineteenth century. In addition, most local police agencies were unable to protect effectively against highly mobile lawbreakers who randomly struck at cities and towns throughout a state. In response to citizens' demands for effective and efficient law enforcement, state governors began to develop plans for police agencies that would be responsible to the state, instead of being tied to local politics and possible corruption.

Texas Rangers
Want to read more about the legendary **Texas Rangers**? Check out their website at
www.cengage.com/ criminaljustice/siegel

The Texas Rangers, created in 1835, was one of the first state police agencies formed. Essentially a military outfit that patrolled the Mexican border, it was followed by the Massachusetts State Constables in 1865 and the Arizona Rangers in 1901. The states of Connecticut (1903) and Pennsylvania (1905) formed the first truly modern state police agencies.[20]

Today about 23 state police agencies have the same general police powers as municipal police and are territorially limited in their exercise of law enforcement regulations only by the state's boundaries. They provide investigative services to smaller communities when the need arises. The remaining state police agencies are primarily responsible for highway patrol and traffic law enforcement.

Some state police direct most of their attention to the enforcement of traffic laws. Others are restricted by legislation from becoming involved in the enforcement of certain areas of the law. For example, in some jurisdictions, state police are prohibited from becoming involved in strikes or other labor disputes, unless violence erupts.

The nation's 90,000 state police employees (about 60,000 officers and 30,000 civilians) carry out a variety of functions besides law enforcement and highway safety, including maintaining a training academy and providing emergency medical services.[21] State police crime laboratories aid local departments in investigating crime scenes and analyzing evidence. State police also provide special services and technical expertise in such areas as bomb-site analysis and homicide investigation. Some state police departments, such as California's, are involved in highly sophisticated traffic and highway safety programs, including the use of helicopters for patrol and rescue, the testing of safety devices for cars, and the conducting of postmortem examinations to determine the causes of fatal accidents.

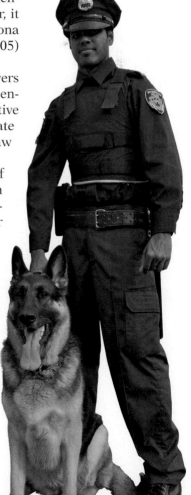

© Radius Images/Alamy

Sheriffs' departments, along with state and metropolitan law enforcement agencies, combine to make up the bulk of America's law enforcement apparatus. Here a sheriff's deputy accompanies accused killer Nicholas Sheley as he arrives at the Knox County Courthouse in Galesburg, Illinois, on July 11, 2008, for a hearing. Sheley was suspected of bludgeoning eight people to death and faced murder charges in Missouri and Illinois.

© AP Images/*The Register-Mail*, Bill Gather

County Law Enforcement Agencies

The county sheriff's role has evolved from that of the early English shire reeve, whose primary duty was to assist the royal judges in trying prisoners and enforcing sentences. From the time of the westward expansion in the United States until municipal departments were developed, the sheriff was often the sole legal authority over vast territories.

Today, sheriffs' offices contain about 330,000 full-time employees, including about 175,000 sworn personnel. Employment has risen an average of about 4 percent per year since 1990.[22] The duties of a sheriff's department vary according to the size and degree of development of the county. In some jurisdictions, sheriffs' offices provide basic law enforcement services such as performing routine patrols, responding to citizen calls for service, and investigating crimes.

Other standard tasks of a typical sheriff's department are serving civil process (summons and court orders), providing court security, and operating the county jail. Less commonly, sheriffs' departments may serve as coroners, tax collectors, overseers of highways and bridges, custodians of the county treasury, and providers of fire, animal control, and emergency medical services. In years past, sheriffs' offices also conducted executions. Typically, the law enforcement functions of a sheriff's department are restricted to unincorporated areas of a county, unless a city or town police department requests its help.

Some sheriffs' departments are exclusively law enforcement oriented; some carry out court-related duties only; some are involved solely in correctional and judicial matters and not in law enforcement. However, a majority are full-service programs that carry out judicial, correctional, and law enforcement activities. As a rule, agencies serving heavily populated areas (over 1 million) are devoted to maintaining county correctional facilities, whereas those in areas of smaller population are focused on law enforcement.

Metropolitan Law Enforcement Agencies

Local police form the majority of the nation's authorized law enforcement personnel. Metropolitan police departments range in size from the New York City Police Department, with almost 40,000 full-time officers and 10,000 civilian employees, to rural police departments, which may consist of a single officer. At last count, the more than 13,000 local police departments nationwide had an estimated 565,000 full-time employees, including about 440,000 sworn personnel.[23] Metropolitan police departments are attracting applicants who value an exciting, well-paid job that also offers them an opportunity to provide valuable community service. Salaries in municipal police agencies are becoming more competitive.

Most TV police shows feature the crime-fighting efforts of big-city police officers, but the overwhelming majority of departments have fewer than 50 officers and serve a population of under 25,000. Recent data indicated that 70 law enforcement agencies employed 1,000 or more full-time sworn personnel, including 46 local police departments with 1,000 or more officers; these agencies accounted for about a third of all local police officers.[24] In contrast, nearly 800 departments employed just one officer.

Municipal police officers' responsibilities are immense, and they are often forced to make split-second decisions on life-and-death matters. At the same time, they must be sensitive to the needs of citizens who are often of diverse racial and ethnic backgrounds. What's more, local police perform multiple roles, including (but not limited to) investigating crimes, identifying suspects, and making arrests (see Exhibit 4.1).

REALITYCHECK

MYTH OR REALITY? Most metropolitan law enforcement agencies employ more than 50 officers.

MYTH: The overwhelming majority of metropolitan law enforcement agencies employ *fewer* than 50 officers.

Big-city police departments are the exception. Why do television shows and the movies seem to favor big-city police? How does this influence people's perceptions of the police in America?

Smaller agencies can have trouble carrying out many of the same functions as their big-city counterparts; the hundreds of small police agencies in each state often provide duplicate services. Whether consolidating smaller police agencies into "superagencies" would improve services is often debated among police experts. Smaller municipal agencies can provide important specialized services that might have to be relinquished if they were combined and incorporated into larger departments. Another approach has been to maintain smaller departments but to link them via computerized information sharing and resource management networks.[25]

Private Policing

Supplementing local police forces has recently been a burgeoning private security industry. Private security service has become a multibillion-dollar industry with 10,000 firms and 1.5 million employees. Even federal police services have been privatized to cut expenses. Today, people employed in private policing outnumber public police by almost three to one.[26]

Some private security firms have become billion-dollar industries. The Wackenhut Corporation is the U.S.-based division of Group 4 Securicor, the

EXHIBIT 4.1

Core Functions of Municipal Police

Law Enforcement Functions
- Identifying criminal suspects
- Investigating crimes
- Apprehending offenders and participating in their trials
- Deterring crime through patrol
- Enhancing public safety by maintaining a visible police presence

Order Maintenance Functions
- Resolving conflict and keeping the peace
- Maintaining a sense of community security and public order (i.e., peacekeeping) within the patrol area.

- Keeping vehicular and pedestrian movement efficient
- Promoting civil order

Service Functions
- Aiding individuals in danger or in need of assistance
- Providing emergency medical services
- Providing public education and outreach
- Maintaining and administering police services
- Recruiting and training new police officers

REALITY CHECK

MYTH OR REALITY? There are fewer private police than public police.

MYTH: Private police outnumber public police by almost three to one.

Not only do private police outnumber public police, but they are not subject to the same legal constraints as public police. Is this beneficial? How so?

www

Technological developments in law enforcement

To read more about **technological developments in law enforcement**, browse back issues of *Law Enforcement Technology* magazine at

www.cengage.com/ criminaljustice/siegel

world's second largest provider of security services. Among its clients are a number of Fortune 500 companies. It has a number of subsidiaries that work for the U.S. government. For example, Wackenhut Services Incorporated (WSI) is a primary contractor to NASA and the Army. Wackenhut also provides security and emergency response services to local governments—for example, helping them guard their public transport systems. Wackenhut helps the U.S. government protect nuclear reactors, guards the Trans-Alaska Pipeline System, and maintains security in secret government laboratories and facilities. It maintains a Custom Protection Officer Division, made up of highly trained uniformed security officers assigned to critical or complex facilities or situations requiring special skills in places such as government buildings and banks.

There will be more legal scrutiny as the private security business blossoms. A number of questions remain to be answered. One important issue is whether security guards are subject to the same search and seizure standards as police officers. For example, the U.S. Supreme Court has repeatedly stated that purely private search activities do not violate the Fourth Amendment's prohibitions. Is this cause for concern, considering that there are more private than public police in America?

Technology and Law Enforcement

Policing relies more and more frequently on modern technology to increase effectiveness, and there is little doubt that the influence of technology on policing will continue to grow. Police officers now trained to prevent burglaries may someday have to learn to create high-tech forensic labs that can identify suspects involved in theft of genetically engineered cultures from biomedical labs.[27] Criminal investigation will be enhanced by the application of sophisticated electronic gadgetry: computers, cell phones, and digital communication devices.

Police are becoming more sophisticated in their use of computer software to identify and convict criminals. Advanced computer software has helped in both the allocation of resources and the investigation of crime. And, as the Criminal Justice and Technology feature on page 132 shows, high-tech solutions are now being applied to crime scene investigations.

A number of other information technology techniques are now being used to increase police effectiveness and efficiency. Some of the more important initiatives are discussed here.

Technology has and will continue to have a significant impact on law enforcement operations. The threat of terrorism, the war on drugs, and the fight against violent crimes have spurred surveillance measures such as security cameras that monitor crime and drug activity 24 hours a day. These cameras, mounted in New York City's Times Square, are part of the city's surveillance system. Officers monitor over 300 camera feeds and 30 mobile license plate readers in lower Manhattan.

© AP Images/Mark Lennihan

Crime Mapping

It is now recognized that there are geographic "hot spots" where a majority of predatory crimes are concentrated.[28] Computer mapping programs that can translate addresses into map coordinates allow departments to identify problem areas for particular crimes, such as drug dealing. Computer maps enable police to identify the location and time of day at which crimes occurred, as well as the linkage among criminal events, and to concentrate their forces accordingly. Figure 4.1 on page 133 shows a typical crime map.

Crime maps offer police administrators graphical representations of where crimes are occurring in their jurisdiction. Computerized crime mapping gives the police the power to analyze and correlate a wide array of data to create immediate, detailed visuals of crime patterns. The simplest maps display crime locations or concentrations and can be used to help direct patrols to the places where they are most needed. More complex maps can be used to chart trends in criminal activity, and some have even proved valuable in solving individual criminal cases. For example, a serial rapist may be caught by observing and understanding the patterns of his crime so that detectives may predict where he will strike next and stake out that area with police decoys.

Crime mapping makes use of new computer technology. Instead of archaic pin maps, computerized crime mappings let the police detect crime patterns and pathologies of related problems. It enables them to work with multiple layers of information and scenarios, and thus to identify

© PhotoLink/Photodisc/Getty Images

emerging hot spots of criminal activity far more successfully and target resources accordingly.

License Plate Recognition Technology

Already in use, but not yet widespread, license plate recognition (LPR) technology employs cameras and computer software to discern the letters and numbers of vehicle license plates and then compares them with records contained

Criminal Justice and Technology

Crime Scene Investigation

Using advanced technology to analyze crime scenes has caught the public interest now that CSI-type programs are routine TV fare. But in truth, CSI technology is undergoing considerable change as cyber capabilities are being added to the investigators' bag of tricks.

Traditionally, to investigate and evaluate a crime scene, detectives relied on photographic evidence and two-dimensional drawings. However, it can be difficult to visualize the positional relationships of evidence with two-dimensional tools. Now, through a combination of laser and computer technology, high-definition surveying (HDS) creates a virtual crime scene that enables investigators to maneuver every piece of evidence.

High-definition surveying gives law enforcement a complete picture of a crime scene. HDS reflects a laser light off objects in the crime scene and back to a digital sensor, creating three-dimensional spatial coordinates that are calculated and stored using algebraic equations. An HDS device projects light in the form of a laser in a 360-degree horizontal circumference, measuring millions of points and thus creating a "point cloud." The data points are bounced back to the receiver, collected, converted, and used to create a virtual image of any location. A personal computer can now take the data file and project that site onto any screen.

Not only does HDS technology make it possible to preserve the crime scene exactly, but the perspective can be manipulated to provide additional clues. For instance, if the crime scene was the front room of an apartment, the three-dimensional image allows the investigator to move around and examine different points of view. Or if a victim was found seated, an investigator could see—and show a jury—what the victim might have seen just before the crime occurred. If witnesses outside said they looked in a living room window, an investigator could zoom around and determine just how much the witnesses could—or could not—have seen through that window.

HDS technology can also limit the crime scene contamination. Investigators may inadvertently touch an object at a crime scene, leaving their fingerprints, or may move evidence or take it from the scene, perhaps by picking up fibers on their shoes. Evidence is compromised if disturbed or moved from its resting place, which may contaminate the scene and undermine the case. HDS technology is a "stand off" device that enables investigators to approach the scene in stages by scanning from the outer perimeter and moving inward, reducing the chances of contamination.

The investigative and prosecutorial value of virtual crime scenes is evident. If an HDS device is used at the scene, detectives, prosecutors, and juries can return to a crime scene in its preserved state. Showing a jury exactly what a witness could or could not have seen can be very valuable.

Critical Thinking

1. What technologies that are now being used in the private sector or on campus can be employed in crime investigations?

2. Are you worried about your personal privacy as police departments become more technologically sophisticated?

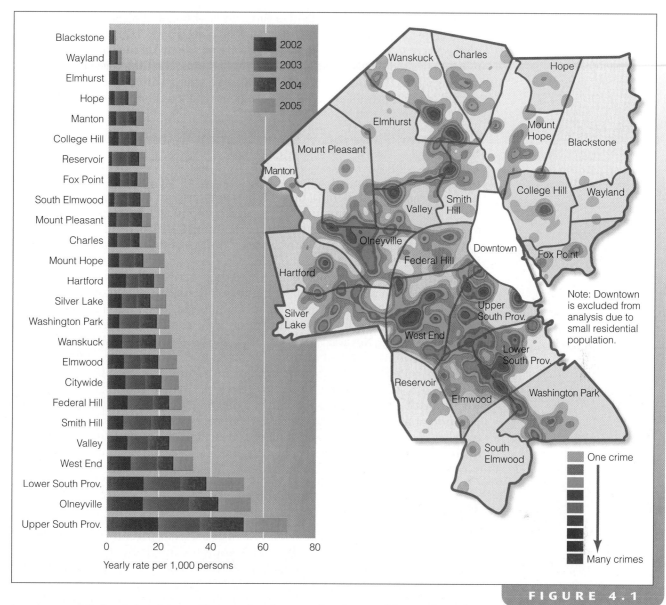

FIGURE 4.1

Violent Crime in Providence, Rhode Island

SOURCE: The Providence Plan, www .provplan.org. Used by permission.

in state and federal databases. New technology makes it possible to place the imaging cameras on the front or roof of a vehicle or in a patrol unit's light bar. Initially designed for use in parking lots (to record the time a vehicle entered), for access control (allowing authorized vehicles into a secure area), and for paying tolls, LPR technology recently has expanded into the realms of border control, identification of stolen vehicles, and traffic-fine enforcement (e.g., issues tickets for running red lights), and vendors are marketing systems specifically for use by the law enforcement community.[29]

Digitizing Criminal Identification

Some police departments are using computerized imaging systems for criminal identification. Several software companies have developed identification programs that help witnesses create a composite picture of the perpetrator. A vast library of photographed or drawn facial features can be stored in computer files and accessed on a terminal screen. Witnesses can scan thousands of noses, eyes, and lips until they find those that match the perpetrator's. Eyeglasses, mustaches, and beards can be added; skin tones can be altered.

Another technique is to digitize thousands of facial images. Police can then easily create a "photo lineup" of all suspects having a particular characteristic described by a witness. New computer software allows two-dimensional mug shots to be re-created on a three-dimensional basis. Effects on the three-dimensional image such as lighting and angles can also be changed to better reproduce the conditions that prevailed in the environment where a crime took place.[30]

Automated Fingerprint Identification Systems

The use of computerized automated fingerprint identification systems (AFIS) is growing in the United States. Using mathematical models, AFIS can classify fingerprints and identify up to 250 characteristics (minutiae) of the print. These automated systems use high-speed computer chips to plot each point of minutiae and count the number of ridge lines between that point and its four nearest neighbors. This substantially improves the speed and accuracy of fingerprint identification.

Some police departments report that computerized fingerprint systems are enabling them to make over 100 identifications a month from fingerprints taken at crime scenes. AFIS files have been regionalized. For example, the Western Identification Network (WIN) consists of eight central site members (Alaska, Idaho, Montana, Nevada, Oregon, Utah, Wyoming, and the Portland Police Bureau), two interface members (California and Washington), multiple local members, and five federal members (DEA, FBI, Immigration and Naturalization Service, IRS, and the Postal Inspection Service).[31] When it began, the system had a centralized automated database of 900,000 fingerprint records; today, with the addition of new jurisdictions (Alaska, California, and Washington), the system's number of searchable fingerprint records has increased to more than 14 million. Technology is constantly improving the effectiveness and reliability of the AFIS system, making it easier to use and more efficient in identifying suspects.[32]

Digital Dental Records

Not only fingerprints but also dental records are being digitized. The National Dental Image Repository (NDIR), which contains supplemental dental images related to the records of missing, unidentified, and wanted persons, is now being operated by the FBI. The NDIR provides law enforcement organizations with an avenue for posting their supplemental dental images in a Web environment that will afford direct access to the digital images of the dental records. This new effort eliminates the need to contact each police agency to retrieve and review physical copies of the records when attempting to make an identification.[33]

DNA Testing

DNA profiling
The identification of criminal suspects by matching DNA samples taken from their person with specimens found at the crime scene.

Advanced technology is also spurring new forensic methods of identification and analysis.[34] The most prominent technique is **DNA profiling**, a procedure that gained national attention because of the O. J. Simpson murder trial. This procedure allows suspects to be identified on the basis of the genetic material found in hair, blood, and other bodily tissues and fluids. When DNA is used as evidence in a rape trial, DNA segments are taken from the victim, the suspect, and blood and semen found on the victim. A DNA match indicates a 4-billion-to-1 likelihood that the suspect is the offender.

Two methods of DNA matching are used. The most popular technique, known as RFLP (restriction fragment length polymorphism), uses radioactive material to produce a DNA image on an X-ray film. The second method, PCR (polymerase chain reaction), amplifies DNA samples through molecular photocopying.[35]

DNA testing has become an invaluable tool for law enforcement. Here Theresa White, a forensic scientist at the New York State Police lab in Albany, New York, processes DNA samples. The Federal Bureau of Investigation and several states now collect DNA samples from those awaiting trial. The intent is to solve more crimes, but critics of the practice raise privacy concerns. Should authorities gather DNA samples from anyone charged (though not necessarily convicted) of a crime?

© AP Images/Mike Groll

© Chris Stein/Getty Images

DNA fingerprinting is now used as evidence in criminal trials in a majority of states.[36] The use of DNA evidence to gain convictions has also been upheld on appeal.[37] Its use in criminal trials received a boost in 1997, when the FBI announced that the evidence has become so precise that experts no longer have to supply a statistical estimate of accuracy while testifying at trial ("The odds are a billion to one that this is the culprit"). They can now simply state in court that there exists "a reasonable degree of scientific certainty" that evidence came from a single suspect.[38]

Leading the way in the development of the most advanced forensic techniques is the Forensic Science Research and Training Center operated by the FBI in Washington, D.C., and Quantico, Virginia. The lab provides information and services to hundreds of crime labs throughout the United States. The National Institute of Justice is also sponsoring research to identify a wider variety of DNA segments for testing and is involved in developing a PCR-based DNA-profiling examination using fluorescent detection that will reduce the time required for DNA profiling. The FBI is now operating the DNA Index System (NDIS), a computerized database that will allow DNA taken at a crime scene to be searched electronically to find matches against samples taken from convicted offenders and from other crime scenes. The first database will allow suspects to be identified, and the second will allow investigators to establish links between crimes, such as those involving serial killers or rapists. In 1999 the FBI announced that the system had made its first "cold hit" by linking evidence taken from crime scenes in Jacksonville, Florida, to ones in Washington, D.C., thereby tying nine crimes to a single offender.[39] When Timothy Spence was executed in Virginia on April 27, 1994, he was the first person tried, convicted, and executed almost entirely on the basis of DNA evidence.[40]

Future Technology

New investigation techniques are constantly being developed. Here are four examples:

- *Genetic algorithms.* Using these mathematical models, investigators will be able to construct a computerized composite image of a suspect's face from relatively little information. Digitization of photographs will make possible the reconstruction of blurred images. Videotapes of bank robbers or blurred photos of license plates—even bite marks—can be digitized using highly advanced mathematical models.

- *Discretionless policing.* Technology may also be used to limit police discretion. In an effort to reduce charges of racial profiling, objective and impersonal technology may be employed to assess which cars present the greatest hazard to motorists or which have the greatest potential to be involved in a crime.[41]

- *Augmented reality (AR) technology.* Now in the development stage, **augmented reality (AR) technology** will provide wearable components that can project computer-generated virtual information onto individuals' real-world view to improve and enhance their ability to accomplish tasks and missions. AR technology displays information in real time, in a way that enhances the individual abilities of people operating in the real world. (An example of AR technology is the virtual lines drawn by broadcasters on football fields to show the first down marker.) Uniformed patrol officers will have many potential uses for AR, ranging from real-time language translation, to the immediate display of real-time intelligence about crimes, to facial and voice recognition data that will tell them whether a suspect is wanted in connection with another crime.[42]

- *ABIS (Automated Biometric Identification System).* This Web-based facial recognition system is now being designed to sift through millions of images to find duplicates before issuing an ID or clearing a passport. **ABIS** can be used by law enforcement agencies in facial searches or for matching suspects who use false identities to their mug shots from past crimes.[43] ABIS may one day be mated to closed-circuit TV (CCTV) surveillance systems. Today, second-generation CCTV can be positioned to observe environments (such as harbors, airports, or freeways), to link the recorded images to a computer system that can detect unusual behavior, unauthorized traffic, or surprising and unexpected changes, and then to alert a human operator.[44] Closed-circuit surveillance cameras armed with **ABIS** technology will be able to pick out and track wanted felons or terrorists using computer-recorded facial recognition patterns. Big Brother will be watching you!

augmented reality (AR) technology
Wearable components that supply computer-generated virtual information.

ABIS (Automated Biometric Identification System)
Facial recognition system designed to sift through millions of images to find duplicates before issuing an ID or clearing a passport.

ETHICAL CHALLENGES IN CRIMINAL JUSTICE

A Writing Assignment

FBI officials say they have developed surveillance cameras that can instantly compare people's "faceprints" against those of suspected terrorists and known criminals in a computerized database. This biometric facial recognition system uses measurable facial features, such as the distances and angles between geometric points on the face, to recognize a specific individual. This highly automated, computerized process can be installed at airports and train stations in order to constantly monitor people using transportation. Those who match photos can be called out, detained, and questioned.

Write an essay on the ethics of using this system. Is this use of technology cause for alarm? Is it an undesirable invasion of individual privacy, or does it represent a positive advance in security measures that generates benefits for society?

RealityCheck Revisited

If you want to learn a little more about the myths and realities related to law enforcement that we presented in this chapter, you might want to visit the following websites:

- Find links to a number of federal law enforcement agencies at

http://www.officer.com/links/Agency_Search/Federal/

- Get objective state and local law enforcement statistics at

http://www.ojp.usdoj.gov/bjs/sandlle.htm

- Read more about careers in private security at

http://www.asisonline.org/careercenter/index.xml

- Read more about how technology is transforming policing at

http://www.policeone.com/police-technology / http://www.iacptechnology.org/

SUMMARY

© Molly Riley/Reuters/Landov

1. Describe how law enforcement developed in feudal England

- Before the Norman Conquest, every person was responsible for aiding neighbors and protecting the settlement from thieves and marauders. This was known as the pledge system.

- People were grouped in collectives of 10 families, called tithings, and were entrusted with policing their own minor problems. When trouble occurred, citizens were expected to make a hue and cry.

- Ten tithings were grouped into a "hundred," whose affairs were supervised by a constable appointed by the local nobleman.

- The constable, who might be considered the first real police officer, dealt with more serious breaches of the law.

- Shires, which resembled the counties of today, were controlled by the shire reeve.

2. Know what the first police agencies were like

- Early thief takers were private police who apprehended criminals for reward payments.

- The first organized police force was founded by Sir Robert Peel in London.

- This rudimentary beginning was the ancestor of today's police departments.

3. Discuss the development of law enforcement in the United States

- Law enforcement in colonial America paralleled the British model.

- In the colonies, the county sheriff became the most important law enforcement agent.

- The modern police department was born out of urban mob violence that wracked the nation's cities in the nineteenth century.

- The first true U.S. police departments were formed in Boston, New York, and Philadelphia in the early nineteenth century.

(continued)

4. *Analyze the problems of early police agencies*

   - The police were viewed as being dominated by political bosses who controlled their hiring practices and policies.

   - In the nineteenth century, big-city police were still not respected by the public, were unsuccessful in their role as crime stoppers, and were not involved in progressive activities.

5. *Discuss how reformers attempted to create professional police agencies*

   - Reform movements begun in the 1920s culminated in the concept of professionalism.

   - Police professionalism was interpreted to mean tough, rule-oriented police work featuring advanced technology and hardware.

   - The view that these measures would quickly reduce crime proved incorrect.

   - Civic leaders in a number of jurisdictions created police administrative boards to reduce local officials' control over the police.

   - Another reform movement was the takeover of some metropolitan police agencies by state legislators.

   - In 1893 the International Association of Chiefs of Police (IACP), a professional society, was formed.

6. *Describe the major changes in law enforcement between 1970 and today*

   - The police experienced turmoil in the 1960s and 1970s, which led to reforms such as the hiring of women and members of minority groups.

   - Questions about the effectiveness of law enforcement have led to the development of community policing.

   - Police departments began to embrace new forms of policing that stressed cooperation with the community and problem solving.

   - An ongoing effort was made to make departments more diverse.

   - Standards of police conduct climbed.

7. *Be familiar with the major federal law enforcement agencies*

   - There are several major law enforcement agencies.

   - On the federal level, the FBI is the largest federal agency.

   - Other agencies include the Drug Enforcement Administration and the U.S. Marshals Service.

8. *Know the differences among state, county, and local law enforcement*

   - County-level law enforcement is provided by sheriffs' departments, who run jails and patrol rural areas.

   - Most states maintain state police agencies, who investigate crimes and patrol the roadways.

   - Local police agencies engage in patrol, investigative, and traffic functions, as well as many support activities.

9. *Describe how technology is changing police work*

   - Most police departments have begun to rely on advanced computer-based technology to identify suspects and collate evidence.

   - Computer mapping programs translate addresses into map coordinates and enable departments to identify problem areas for particular crimes, such as drug dealing.

   - The use of automated fingerprint systems and computerized identification systems has become widespread.

10. *Discuss the future of police technology and be familiar with the direction it is taking*

   - In the future, police will be employing new and sophisticated technology.

   - Genetic algorithms allow a computerized composite image of a suspect's face to be constructed from relatively little information.

   - Discretionless policing technology may also be used to make some police decision making less subjective.

- Augmented reality (AR) technology will provide wearable components to supplement individuals' real-world view with computer-generated virtual information to improve and enhance their ability to accomplish tasks and missions.

- ABIS (Automated Biometric Identification System) is a Web-based facial recognition system that is being designed to sift through millions of images to find duplicates before issuing an ID or clearing a passport.

Key Terms

tithing, 115
hue and cry, 115
hundred, 115
constable, 115
shire reeve, 115
sheriff, 115
watch system, 115
justice of the peace, 116
vigilantes, 118
Federal Bureau of Investigation (FBI), 124
Drug Enforcement Administration (DEA), 124

Bureau of Alcohol, Tobacco, Firearms, and Explosives (ATF), 125
U.S. Marshals Service, 125
Department of Homeland Security (DHS), 125
Customs and Border Protection (CBP), 125
Secret Service, 127
DNA profiling, 134
augmented reality (AR) technology, 136
ABIS (Automated Biometric Identification System), 136

Review Questions

1. List the problems faced by today's police departments that were also present during the early days of policing.

2. Distinguish between the duties of the state police, sheriffs' departments, and local police departments.

3. Do you believe that the general public has greater respect for the police today than in the past? If so, why? If not, why not?

4. What are some of the technological advances that should help the police solve more crimes? What are the dangers of these advances?

5. Discuss the trends that will influence policing during the coming decade. What other social factors may affect police?

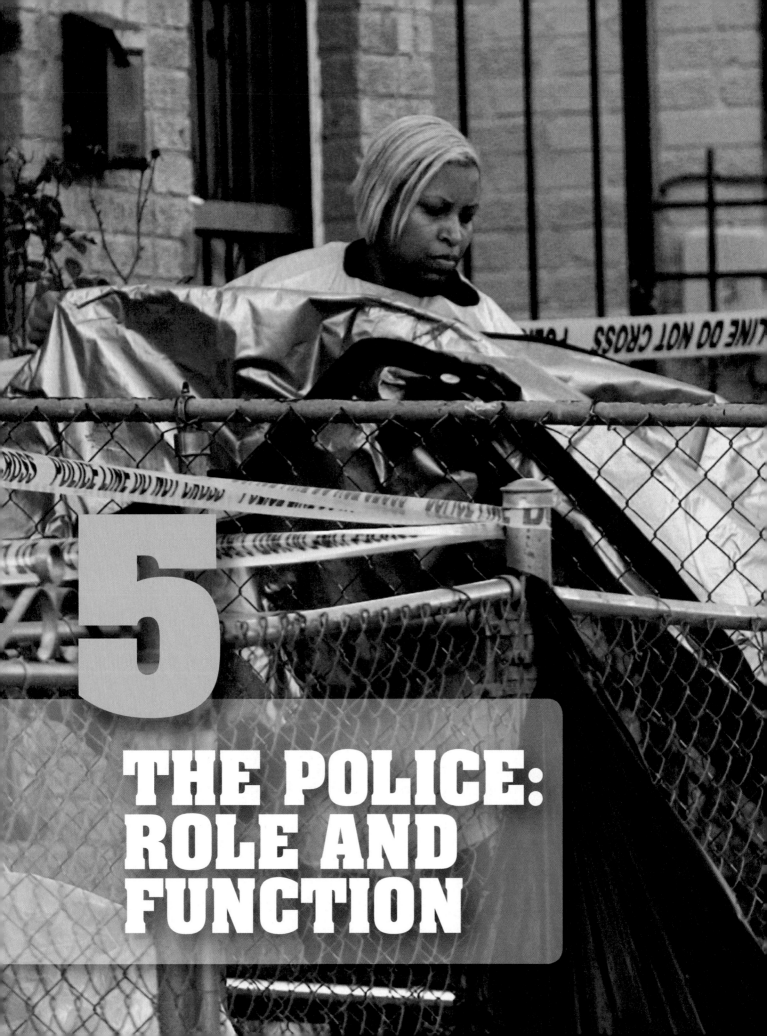

5

THE POLICE: ROLE AND FUNCTION

© AP Images/Jacquelyn Martin

Learning Objectives

1. Understand the organization of police departments

2. Articulate the complexities of the police role

3. Discuss the concept of patrol and its effectiveness

4. Be familiar with methods of improving patrol, including broken windows policing

5. Be able to discuss the organization of police detectives

6. Know what forensics is and what forensics experts do for police agencies

7. Understand the concept of community policing

8. Discuss the concept of problem-oriented policing

9. Be familiar with the various police support functions

Chapter Outline

© AP Images/Jacquelyn Martin

Career Profile

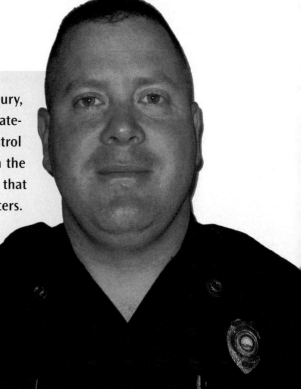

Larry Napolitano is a patrolman with the Shrewsbury, Massachusetts, Police Department. Shrewsbury, a city of approximately 34,000, is located about an hour west of Boston. One of 35 patrol officers in the department, Larry holds a bachelor's degree from the College of the Holy Cross in Worcester, Massachusetts. Larry feels that a criminal justice education can be helpful for aspiring police officers. "A criminal justice degree gives you a necessary level of knowledge which you can rely upon to make certain decisions," he says. "It does not, however, prepare you for some of the things that you will see and experience. There are certain things, as is true with any job, that you cannot learn from school and a textbook."

There was no single event that caused Larry to choose a career in law enforcement, but one thing left a lasting impression. When he was a boy, police officers would stop and talk to him and his friends. Most often they would just say "hi." In hindsight, Larry feels the officers were making sure that he and his friends were staying out of trouble. In any case, the encounters were positive and cast the officers in a favorable light. This contributed to his decision to become a police officer.

The greatest challenge Larry faces on his job is overcoming complacency. Officers must always remain vigilant and prepared during any encounter; otherwise, they might not be ready for the danger that could arise. "When you stop a motor vehicle, you really have no knowledge of who that person is, what kind of day they had, or what they are capable of. You obviously stopped them for a reason, whether it be motor vehicle–related or for another reason, but you really don't know what lies ahead. If you get complacent and treat every stop the same way, it could get you seriously hurt or killed." Another challenge he faces is dealing with a side of life that most people never see. "You start to learn that people are capable of anything when put in certain situations. I think that the only way that you can overcome that is a strong support system around you. I also think that's why police officers tend to 'stay together.'"

One of greatest rewards on the job, according to Larry, is when people offer a simple "Thank you." "You often encounter people in their worst possible moment, whether it be a personal tragedy or something that they did in the heat of the moment. It makes a big difference when people come back and thank you for helping them through their tough times. It's always rewarding when you can help someone resolve a situation."

The police role, while rewarding, is extremely varied and complex. Police officers are called on to deal with increasingly difficult and unpredictable situations. Officers like Larry Napolitano are asked to serve as enforcers of the law in suburban communities, rural towns, and some of the toughest urban streets in America. Whereas rural/suburban police tend to be generalists who focus on social problems ranging from public disorder to family dysfunction, urban police must confront heavily armed drug-dealing gangs on a regular basis.[1] In both instances, the public demands that the police "make them feel safe" and will lose confidence in them if they fear crime in the streets.[2] Yet these same officers who are called upon to allay the public's fears are criticized when their tactics become too aggressive, when they confront angry demonstrators with a show of force, or when they use interrogation tactics that are considered abusive.

This chapter describes the organization of police departments and their various operating branches: patrol, investigation, service, and administration. It discusses the realities and ambiguities of the police role and traces how the concept of the police mission has been changing radically. The chapter concludes with a brief overview of some of the most important administrative issues confronting today's U.S. law enforcement agencies.

The Police Organization

Most municipal police departments in the United States are independent agencies within the executive branch of government, operating without specific administrative control from any higher governmental authority. Although

Los Angeles Police Department

You can view the organizational chart for one of America's largest police departments, the **Los Angeles Police Department**, at

www.cengage.com/criminaljustice/siegel

police chief

The top administrator of the police department, who sets policy and has general control over departmental policies and practices. The chief is typically a political rather than a civil service appointee and serves at the pleasure of the mayor.

they often cooperate and participate in mutually beneficial enterprises, such as a joint task force with state and federal law enforcement agencies, local police agencies are functionally independent organizations with unique sets of rules, policies, procedures, norms, budgets, and so on.

Most local police departments are organized in a hierarchical manner, as illustrated in Figure 5.1. Within this organizational model, each element of the department normally has its own chain of command. In a large municipal department, there may be a number of independent investigation units headed by a captain who serves as the senior administrator, a lieutenant who oversees cases and investigations and acts as liaison with other police agencies, and sergeants and inspectors who carry out fieldwork. Smaller departments may have a captain or lieutenant as head of a particular branch or unit. Department size also affects the number of subunits. A department the size of New York's may contain several specialized investigative units, such as special victims or sex crimes, whereas many smaller departments do not employ detectives at all and rely on county or state police investigators to probe unsolved crimes. Regardless of its size, at the head of the organization is the **police chief**, who sets policy and has general administrative control over all the department's various operating branches.

Pros and Cons of Police Organization

Police administrative organization has both its pros and cons. Because most departments are civil service organizations, administrators must rise through the ranks to get to command positions. To be promoted, they must pass a battery of tests, profiles, interviews, and so on. Most police departments employ

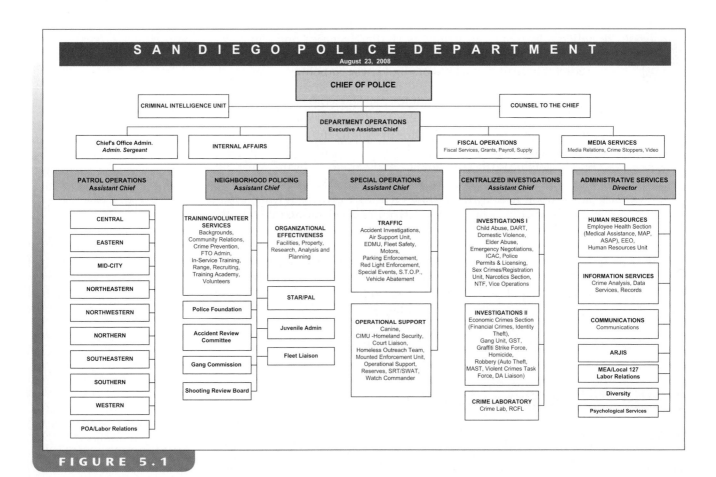

FIGURE 5.1

a **time-in-rank system** for determining promotion eligibility. This means that before moving up the administrative ladder, an officer must spend a certain amount of time in the next lowest rank; a sergeant cannot become a captain without serving an appropriate amount of time as a lieutenant. This system has both benefits and shortcomings: On the plus side, it is designed to promote stability and fairness and to limit favoritism. The chief's favorite cannot be promoted over a more experienced officer who is better qualified. Once earned, a rank can rarely be taken away or changed if new management takes over. The rank system also protects police agencies from losing talented officers trained at public expense to other departments who offer more money or other incentives.

On the downside, the rank system restricts administrative flexibility. Unlike in the private sector, where the promotion of talented people can be accelerated in the best interests of the company, the time-in-rank system prohibits rapid advancement. A police agency would probably not be able to hire a computer systems expert with a Ph.D. and give her a command position in charge of its data-analysis section. The department would be forced to hire the expert as a civilian employee under the command of a ranking senior officer who might not be as technically proficient. Because senior administrators are promoted from within only after years of loyal service, time-in-rank may render some police agencies administratively conservative. Even when police executives adopt new programs, such as CompStat (see later in this chapter for more on CompStat), they are most likely to choose those elements that confer legitimacy on existing organizations, and on implementing them in ways that minimize disruption to existing organizational routines, rather than embracing truly innovative changes.[3]

> **time-in-rank system**
> For police officers to advance in rank, they must spend an appropriate amount of time, usually years, in the preceding rank—for example, to become a captain, an officer must first spend time as a lieutenant.

> **National Association of Police Organizations (NAPO)**
>
> The **National Association of Police Organizations (NAPO)**, a coalition of police unions and associations from across the United States, serves to advance the interests of America's law enforcement officers through legislative and legal advocacy, political action, and education. Visit their site at
>
> **www.cengage.com/criminaljustice/siegel**

The Police Role

In countless books, movies, and TV shows, the public has been presented with a view of policing that romanticizes police officers as fearless crime fighters who think little of their own safety as they engage in daily high-speed chases and shootouts. How close is this portrayal of a crime fighter to real life? Not very close, according to most research. A police officer's crime-fighting efforts are only a small part of his or her overall activities. Studies of police work indicate that a significant portion of an officer's time is spent handling minor disturbances, service calls, and administrative duties. Police work, then, involves much more than catching criminals. The most recent national survey of police contacts with civilians (2005) found that almost 44 million persons had at least one contact with police that year.[4]

More than half of the contacts are for traffic-related matters, and about 30 percent are to report problems or ask for assistance—for example, responding to a neighbor's complaint about music being too loud during a party, or warning kids not to shoot fireworks. This survey indicates that the police role is both varied and complex. These results are not surprising when Uniform Crime Report (UCR) arrest data is considered. Each year, about 700,000 local, county, and state police officers make about 14 million arrests, or

REALITYCHECK

MYTH OR REALITY? Police work primarily involves crime fighting.

MYTH: Crime fighting makes up only a small fraction of what police work usually entails.

Most police work entails relatively mundane tasks, such as responding to service calls and completing administrative tasks. Television programs and movies almost completely ignore this side of police work. Instead, they focus on the crime-fighting role. What are the consequences of this?

about 20 each. Of these, about 2 million (approximately 3 per officer) are for serious Part I crimes. Given an even distribution of arrests, it is evident that the average police officer makes fewer than 2 arrests per month and fewer than a single felony arrest every four months.

These figures should be interpreted with caution because not all police officers are engaged in activities that allow them to make arrests, such as patrol or detective work. About one-third of all sworn officers in the nation's largest police departments are in such units as communications, antiterrorism, administration, and personnel. Even if the number of arrests per officer were adjusted by one-third, it would still amount to only 9 or 10 serious crime arrests per officer per year. So even though police handle thousands of calls each year, relatively few result in an arrest for a serious crime such as a robbery or burglary; in suburban and rural areas, years may go by before a police officer arrests someone for a serious crime.

The evidence, then, shows that unlike their TV and film counterparts, the police engage in many activities that are not related to crime. Police officers function in a variety of roles ranging from dispensers of emergency medical care to keepers of the peace on school grounds. Although officers in large urban departments may be called on to handle more felony cases than those in small towns, they too will probably find that most of their daily activities are not crime related. What are some of the most important functions of police?

The Patrol Function

Regardless of style of policing, uniformed patrol officers are the backbone of the police department, usually accounting for about two-thirds of a department's personnel.[5] Patrol officers are the most highly visible components of the entire criminal justice system. The major purposes of patrol are to

- Deter crime by maintaining a visible police presence
- Maintain public order (peacekeeping) within the patrol area
- Enable the police department to respond quickly to violations of law or other emergencies
- Identify and apprehend law violators
- Aid individuals and care for those who cannot help themselves
- Facilitate the movement of traffic and people
- Create a feeling of security in the community[6]

Patrol Activities

Most experts agree that the great bulk of patrol efforts are devoted to what has been described as **order maintenance**, or **peacekeeping**: maintaining order and civility in their assigned jurisdiction.[7] Order-maintenance functions occupy the border between criminal and noncriminal behavior. The patrol officer's discretion often determines whether a noisy neighborhood dispute involves the crime of disturbing the peace or can be controlled by exercising street-corner diplomacy and sending the combatants on their way. Similarly, teenagers milling around in the shopping center parking lot may be brought in and turned over to the juvenile authorities or dispersed in a less formal and often more efficient manner.

The primary role of police seems to be "handling the situation." Police encounter many troubling incidents that need some sort of "fixing up."[8] Enforcing the law might be one tool a patrol officer uses; threat, coercion, sympathy, and understanding might be others. Most important is keeping things under control so that there are no complaints that the officer is doing nothing at all or doing too much. The real police role, then, may be as a community problem solver.

International Police Association

Want to read more about the police role? Go to the website of the **International Police Association**, a nonprofit, worldwide fraternal organization whose membership consists solely of active and retired law enforcement personnel. You can access it at

www.cengage.com/criminaljustice/siegel

order maintenance (peacekeeping)
The order-maintenance aspect of the police role involves peacekeeping, maintaining order and authority without the need for formal arrest, "handling the situation," and keeping things under control by using threats, persuasion, and understanding.

Despite what the media might lead us to believe, police work does not always involve chasing down criminals and making arrests. The great bulk of patrol efforts are devoted to order maintenance and peacekeeping rather than to shootouts with dangerous criminals. Here Sacramento police officers Sara Butler and Mike Cooper talk with a homeless man as they hand out eviction notices to residents at a homeless tent city. Hundreds of residents living in a tent city along the American River were issued notices of eviction and were told to relocate to a nearby shelter. Their tent city was located on land belonging to the Sacramento Municipal Utility District.

© Justin Sullivan/Getty Images

Police officers actually practice a policy of selective enforcement, concentrating on some crimes but handling the majority in an informal manner. A police officer is supposed to know when to take action and when not to, whom to arrest and whom to deal with by issuing a warning or some other informal action. If a mistake is made, the officer can come under fire from peers and superiors, as well as the media and the general public.

Does Patrol Deter Crime?

A primary goal of police patrol has been to deter criminal behavior. The visible presence of patrol cars on the street and the rapid deployment of police officers to the scene of a crime are viewed as an effective method of crime control. Is this view correct? The most widely heralded attempt at measuring patrol effectiveness was undertaken during the early 1970s in Kansas City, Missouri, where researchers divided 15 separate police districts into three groups: One group retained normal patrol; the second (proactive) set of districts were supplied with two to three times the normal amount of patrol forces; and the third (reactive) group had its preventive patrol eliminated, with police officers responding only when summoned by citizens to the scene of a particular crime.[9] The Kansas City study found that these variations in patrol had little effect on the crime patterns in the 15 districts. The presence or absence of patrol officers did not seem to affect residential or business burglaries, motor vehicle thefts, larceny involving auto accessories, robberies, vandalism, or other criminal behavior, nor did they influence citizens' attitudes toward the police, their satisfaction with police, or their fear of future criminal behavior.

Since the Kansas City study findings were published, dozens of researchers have continued to seek an answer to the question of whether adding more police helps to bring down the crime rate. At one time, reviews of the existing research found that the actual number of law enforcement officers in a jurisdiction seemed to have little effect on area crimes.[10] However, during the past decade, larger cities have expanded their police forces, and crime rates have plummeted—a trend that suggests that adding police may in fact reduce crime rates. The association between number of police personnel and crime rates has also been supported by a number of recent studies. Using a variety of methodologies, these studies have found that police presence may actually reduce crime levels and that adding police may bring crime levels down.[11]

Improving Patrol

Police departments have in recent years initiated a number of programs and policies to try to improve patrol effectiveness. Some have proved more effective than others. Some are also more controversial than others.

PROACTIVE POLICING AND DIRECTED PATROL ● Although the mere presence of police may not be sufficient to deter crime, the manner in which they approach their task may make a difference. Police departments that use a proactive, aggressive law enforcement style may help reduce crime rates. Jurisdictions that encourage patrol officers to stop motor vehicles to issue citations and to aggressively arrest and detain suspicious persons also experience lower crime rates than jurisdictions that do not follow such proactive policies.[12] Departments that more actively enforce minor regulations, such as laws prohibiting disorderly conduct and traffic laws, are also more likely to experience lower felony rates.[13]

Pinpointing why **proactive policing** works so effectively is difficult. Proactive patrol efforts may help improve response time and increase the number of patrol cars that respond per crime.[14] It may have a **deterrent effect**: Aggressive policing increases community perception that police arrest many criminals and that most violators get caught. Criminals may think twice about committing crimes in a town that has such an active police force! Proactive policing may also help control crime because it results in conviction of more criminals. Because aggressive police arrest more suspects, there are fewer left on the street to commit crime; fewer criminals produce lower crime rates.

Evidence also shows that targeting specific crimes through **directed patrol** can be successful. One aggressive patrol program, known as the Kansas City

proactive policing
A police department policy that emphasizes stopping crimes before they occur, rather than reacting to crimes that have already occurred.

deterrent effect
Stopping or reducing crime by convincing would-be criminals that they stand a significant risk of being apprehended and punished for their crimes.

directed patrol
A patrol strategy that involves concentrating police resources in areas where certain crimes are a significant problem.

Police departments around the country continue to improve patrol with strategies that help them adapt to the demands of the situation. Here police on bicycles patrol Judiciary Square (Washington, D.C.) on the lookout for protestors during the annual International Monetary Fund and World Bank spring meetings. Bicycles afford police a tactical advantage in situations like this, because they can get officers close to the action.

© Mandel Ngan/AFP/Getty Images

Gun Experiment, was directed at restricting the carrying of guns in high-risk places at high-risk times. Working with academics from the University of Maryland, the Kansas City Police Department focused extra patrol attention on a "hot spot" high-crime area identified by computer analysis of all gun crimes. Over a 29-week period, the gun patrol officers conducted thousands of car and pedestrian checks and traffic stops and made over 600 arrests. Using frisks and searches, they found 29 guns; an additional 47 weapons were seized by other officers in the experimental area. There were 169 gun crimes in the target beat in the 29 weeks before the gun patrol but only 86 while the experiment was under way, a decrease of 49 percent.[15]

Strategies such as these have been a critical success. The downturn in the violent crime rate over the past decade has been attributed to aggressive police work in large cities such as New York aimed at controlling or eliminating lifestyle crimes: vandalism, panhandling, and graffiti.[16] Some commentators fear that aggressive policing will result in antagonism between proactive cops and the general public. However, recent research indicates that precinct-level efforts to ensure that officers are respectful of citizens helped lower the number of complaints and improved community relations.[17]

MAKING ARRESTS ● Can formal police action, such as an arrest, reduce crime? The evidence is mixed, but some research studies do show that contact with the police may cause some offenders to forgo repeat criminal behavior. Many first offenders will forgo criminal activity after undergoing arrest.[18] For example, an arrest for drunk driving reduces the likelihood of further driving while intoxicated.

Why do arrests deter crime? It is possible that news of increased and aggressive police arrest activity is rapidly diffused through the population and has an immediate impact on crime rates.[19] Arrests may also alter perceptions. An arrest for drunk driving may convince people that they will be rearrested if they drink and drive.[20] Consequently, as the number of arrests per capita increases, crime rates go down.

RAPID RESPONSE ● Improving response time may be one way of increasing police efficiency. Unfortunately, however, the research fails to support such assumptions. A National Institute of Justice study examined police response times in four cities. The authors found that rapid response had virtually no effect on crime.[21] Why? One explanation is that people tend to be slow when it comes to reporting crime. For example, a person may wake up in the morning and find that his or her car was vandalized. By then the trail has gone cold, making it nearly impossible to capture the perpetrator even if the police are summoned immediately upon discovery of the crime.

REALITYCHECK

MYTH OR REALITY? Rapid response to 911 calls reporting a crime in progress increases the likelihood that the offender will be apprehended.

MYTH: Research shows that rapid response has almost no effect on the probability of capturing the offender. This is a fairly general conclusion, however.

Are there certain types of crimes for which rapid response could work?

BROKEN WINDOWS POLICING ● A critical 1982 paper by George Kelling and James Q. Wilson advocated a new approach to improving police relations in the community, an approach that has come to be known as the **broken windows model**.[22] Kelling and Wilson made three points:

1. *Neighborhood disorder creates fear.* Urban areas filled with street people, youth gangs, prostitutes, and the mentally disturbed are the ones most likely to maintain a high degree of crime.[23]

broken windows model
A term used to describe the role of the police as maintainers of community order and safety.

2. *Neighborhoods give out crime-promoting signals.* A neighborhood filled with deteriorated housing, broken windows, and disorderly behavior gives out crime-promoting signals. Honest citizens live in fear in these areas, and predatory criminals are attracted to them.

3. *Police need citizen cooperation.* If police are to reduce fear and successfully combat crime in these urban areas, they must have the cooperation, support, and assistance of the citizens.

According to the broken windows concept, a deteriorated neighborhood, whose residents are fearful, pessimistic, and despondent, is a magnet for crime. In contrast, neighborhoods where residents are civil to one another and where disorder is not tolerated send a different message: Criminals are not wanted here, and criminal behavior will not be allowed. The broken windows approach holds that police administrators would be well advised to deploy their forces where they can encourage public confidence, strengthen feelings of safety, and elicit cooperation from citizens. Community preservation, public safety, and order maintenance—not crime fighting—should become the primary focus of patrol. Put another way, just as physicians and dentists practice preventive medicine and dentistry, police should help maintain an intact community structure rather than simply fighting crime. Does it work? In one of the most rigorous tests of broken windows theory in recent years, researchers identified 34 crime-ridden areas in Lowell, Massachusetts. Half (the treatment group) received broken windows policing; the other half (the control group) received the same levels of patrol as before. Results revealed substantial reductions in crime, disorder, and calls for service in the treatment areas, but not in the control areas.[24]

CompStat

A program originated by the New York City police that used carefully collected and analyzed crime data to shape policy and evaluate police effectiveness.

USING TECHNOLOGY • Police departments have also relied on technology to help guide patrol efforts. The best-known program, **CompStat**, was begun in New York City as a means of directing police efforts in a more productive way.[25] William Bratton, who had been appointed NYC police chief, wanted to revitalize the department and break through its antiquated bureaucratic structures. He installed CompStat, a computerized system that gave local precinct commanders up-to-date information about where and when crime was occurring in their jurisdictions. Part of the CompStat program, twice-weekly "crime control strategy meetings," brought precinct commanders together with the department's top administrators, who asked them to report on crime problems in their precincts and tell what they were doing to turn things around. Those involved in the strategy sessions had both detailed data and electronic pin maps that showed how crime clustered geographically in the precinct and how patrol officers were being deployed. The CompStat program required local commanders to demonstrate their intimate knowledge of crime trends and develop strategies to address them effectively. When ideas were presented by the assembled police administrators, the local commanders were required to demonstrate, in follow-up sessions, how they had incorporated the new strategies in their patrol plan. CompStat proved extremely successful and is generally credited with making a major contribution to the dramatic drop in New York City's crime rate during the past decade.

The Investigation Function

Since the first independent detective bureau was established by the London Metropolitan Police in 1841, criminal investigators have been romantic figures vividly portrayed in novels and in movies. Consider Clint Eastwood's

Dirty Harry series and Mel Gibson's four *Lethal Weapon* films, in which he plays the slightly mad Martin Riggs, who always seems to be shooting down helicopters with a handgun.[26] These fictional detectives shoot first and ask questions later and, when they do conduct an interrogation, think nothing of beating a confession out of the suspect. How accurate are these portrayals? Not very. The modern criminal investigator is likely to be an experienced civil servant, trained in investigatory techniques, knowledgeable about legal rules of evidence and procedure, and at least somewhat cautious about the legal and administrative consequences of his or her actions.[27] The character of Gil Grissom, head of television's *Crime Scene Investigation* team in Las Vegas, may be a more realistic portrayal of the modern investigator than Dirty Harry. Although detectives are often handicapped by limited time, money, and resources, they are certainly aware of how their actions will one day be interpreted in a court of law.

Investigative services can be organized in a variety of ways. In New York, each borough or district has its own detective division that supervises investigators assigned to neighborhood police precincts (stations). Local squad detectives work closely with patrol officers to provide an immediate investigative response to crimes and incidents. (In some TV shows and movies, New York City detectives are shown barking commands at patrol officers and even snapping orders at uniformed sergeants and lieutenants; in reality, both branches are considered equal, so that would never happen. A patrol sergeant is the superior officer of a junior grade detective.) New York City also maintains specialized borough squads—homicide, robbery, and special victims—to give aid to local squads and help identify suspects whose crimes may have occurred in multiple locations. There are also specialty squads that help in areas such as forensics. In smaller cities, detective divisions may be organized into sections or bureaus, such as homicide, robbery, or rape (see Exhibit 5.1).

How Do Detectives Detect?

Detectives investigate the causes of crime and attempt to identify the individuals or groups responsible for committing particular offenses. They may enter a case after patrol officers have made the initial contact, such as when a patrol car interrupts a crime in progress and the offenders flee before they can be apprehended. Detectives can investigate a case entirely on their own, sometimes by following up on leads provided by informants. Sometimes detectives go undercover in order to investigate crime: A lone agent can infiltrate a criminal group or organization to gather information on future criminal activity. Undercover officers can also pose as victims to capture predatory criminals who have been conducting street robberies and muggings.[28]

In his recent study of investigation techniques, Martin Innes found that police detectives rely heavily on interviews and forensic evidence to create or manufacture a narrative of the crime, creating in a sense the "story" that sets out how, where, and why the incident took place.[29] To create their story, contemporary detectives typically use a three-pronged approach:[30]

- **Specific focus.** Interview witnesses, gather evidence, record events, and collect facts at the immediate crime scene.
- **General coverage.** (1) Canvass the neighborhood and make observations; (2) conduct interviews with friends, families, and associates;

Philadelphia Police

To see how the **Philadelphia Police** organizes its detective branch, visit

www.cengage.com/ criminaljustice/siegel

© Darryl Estrine/UpperCut Images/Getty Images

(3) contact coworkers or employers for information about victims and suspects; (4) construct victim/suspect timelines to outline their whereabouts prior to incident.

- **Informative.** Use modern technology to collect records of cell phones and pagers, computer hard drives (palm pilots, laptops, notebooks, desktops,

EXHIBIT 5.1

Baton Rouge Police Detectives

Division I: Crimes against Persons
Homicide, Armed Robbery, Juvenile/Sex Crimes, Major Assaults/Missing Persons, Computer Crimes

- The **Homicide** division is responsible for investigating all criminal calls where a death or life-threatening injury has occurred, any officer-involved shooting, or the attempted murder of a police officer.
- The **Armed Robbery** division is responsible for investigating all criminal calls involving all degrees of robbery.
- The **Juvenile/Sex Crimes** division is responsible for maintaining juvenile investigation records, cases of child abuse, and all types of sex crimes.
- The **Major Assaults** division is responsible for investigating a wide range of non-life-threatening felony personal crimes and missing person cases.
- The **Computer Crimes** division investigates crimes committed against persons or computer systems using the Internet, email, or other electronic means.

Division II: Property Crimes
Burglary, Auto/Impound, Forgery, Felony Theft

- The **Burglary** division is responsible for coordinating all follow-up investigations of burglaries, as well as the recovery of stolen property from local pawn shops.
- The Auto **Theft/Impound** division is responsible for conducting follow-up investigations of auto thefts and unauthorized use of movables. The unit also coordinates all records and information relating to vehicles stored and impounded by the department and monitoring local towing services to insure compliance with applicable standards and ordinances.
- The **Forgery** division is responsible for investigating all crimes involving thefts by fraudulent use of access cards, and forgeries of negotiable documents.

- The **Felony Theft** unit is responsible for all felony theft investigations that do not fall under the Auto Theft, Burglary, or Forgery divisions. The office is also responsible for felony damage to property cases. Priority is placed on business embezzlement incidents.

Division III: Investigative Support
Evidence, Crime Scene, Polygraph, Crime Stoppers

- The **Evidence** division is responsible for the collection, storage, cataloguing, and disposition of all evidence and property seized by, or turned in to, the department.
- The **Crime Scene** division is responsible for assisting in investigations by taking photographs, sketching major crime scenes, collecting and tagging evidence, and performing various scientific tests on suspects and/or evidence as needed.
- The **Polygraph** division conducts all polygraph, or lie detector, tests given to recruits, employees, or criminal suspects.
- The **Crime Stoppers** office coordinates all facets of the Crime Stoppers program with local news media, businesses, and the public.

Division IV: Special Operations
Narcotics, School Drug Task Force, State and Federal Liaisons

- The **Narcotics** division is responsible for investigating crimes involving illegal drugs as well as related vice crimes. This division administers the HIDTA and LSP Task Forces.
- The **School Drug Task Force** investigates crimes involving narcotics, explosives, and weapons in schools, school buses, and at school-sponsored events within the parish.
- Liaison Detectives assigned to outside state and federal agencies work jointly with these agencies to participate in multijurisdictional investigations.

Source: Baton Rouge, Louisiana, Police Department, http://brgov.com/dept/brpd/criminal.htm (accessed August 27, 2009).

and servers), diaries, notes, and documents. This approach includes data that persons of interest in the investigation use, which, in turn, tell about their lives, interactions with others, and geographic connections. (See Concept Summary 5.1.)

Detective work is an art as well as a science, based on experience and knowledge of human behavior gained on the job. As sociologist Robert Jackall found when he studied detectives in New York, the investigative branch has a unique culture and operating style. His observations are described in the Policies, Programs, and Issues in Criminal Justice feature on pages 156–157.

Sting Operations

Another approach to investigation, commonly referred to as a **sting operation**, involves organized groups of detectives or patrol officers working in plain clothes who deceive criminals into openly committing illegal acts or conspiring to engage in criminal activity.

To sting criminals, some jurisdictions maintain **vice squads**, patrol officers working in plain clothes who focus on crimes of public morals such as prostitution or gambling. For example, female police officers may pose as prostitutes and arrest men who solicit their services.

Sting operations can be highly successful, but they are also open to criticism.[31] Covert police activities have often been criticized as violating the personal rights of citizens, while forcing officers into demeaning roles. Ironically, Mary Dodge and her associates found that rather than considering it demeaning, female officers find their sting work as make-believe prostitutes exciting; they also consider it a stepping-stone for promotion.[32]

By its very nature, a sting involves deceit by police agents that often comes close to entrapment. Sting operations may encourage criminals to commit new crimes because they have a new source for fencing stolen goods. Innocent people may damage their reputations by buying merchandise from a

sting operation
An undercover police operation in which police pose as criminals to trap law violators.

vice squad
Police officers assigned to enforce morality-based laws, such as those on prostitution, gambling, and pornography.

Investigative Techniques

Specific Focus	General Coverage	Informative
Specific witnesses	Neighborhood canvass	Cell phone records
Specific evidence	Friends, family, and associates	Computer hard drives
Specific events	Coworkers	Other records
Specific facts	Victim/suspect timelines	Private papers

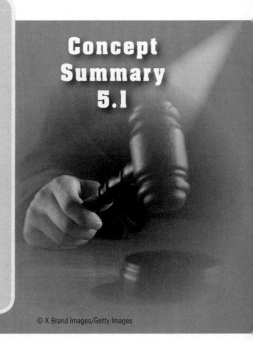

Concept Summary 5.1

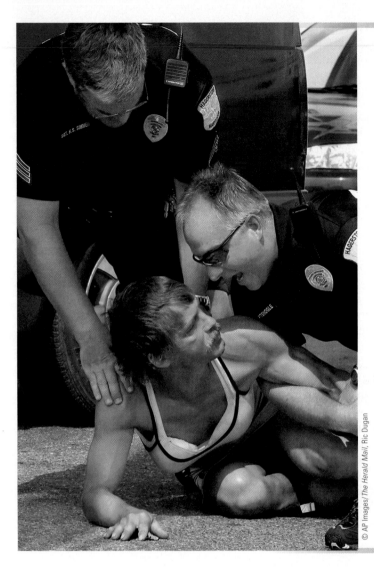

Sting operations are often helpful in combating drug and vice crimes. Here Martin Joe McDaniel is brought down by Hagerstown (Maryland) Police Department Sgt. Kevin Simmers, left, and Officer Martin Pitsnogle, right, during one of many prostitution stings. McDaniel was one of three men arrested in this particular operation. The department's frequent use of undercover sting operations won praise from the pastors of nearby churches, who had long complained about open solicitation in the area.

© AP Images/*The Herald Mail*, Ric Dugan

sting operation when they had no idea the items had been stolen. By putting the government into the fencing business, such operations blur the line between law enforcement and criminal activity.

Evaluating Investigations

Serious criticism has been leveled at the nation's detective forces for being bogged down in paperwork and relatively inefficient in clearing cases. One famous study of 153 detective bureaus by the RAND Corporation, a well-known think tank, found that a great deal of a detective's time was spent in unproductive work and that investigative expertise did little to solve cases; half of all detectives could be replaced without negatively influencing crime clearance rates.[33]

Although some question remains about the effectiveness of investigations, police detectives do make a valuable contribution to police work because their skilled interrogation and case-processing techniques are essential to eventual criminal conviction.[34] Detective work may be improved if investigators are able to spend more time on each case, allowing them to carefully collect physical evidence at the scene of the crime, identify witnesses, check departmental records, and use informants. Research shows that in more serious cases, especially homicide investigations, where detectives devote a lot of attention to a single crime, the likelihood increases that they will eventually identify and arrest the culprit.[35]

Nonetheless, a majority of cases that are solved are done so when the perpetrator is identified at the scene of the crime by patrol officers. Research shows that if a crime is reported while in progress, the police have about a 33 percent chance of making an arrest; the arrest probability declines to about 10 percent if the crime is reported 1 minute later, and to 5 percent if more than 15 minutes have elapsed. As the time between the crime and the arrest grows, the chances of a conviction are also reduced, probably because the ability to recover evidence is lost. Put another way, once a crime has been completed and the investigation is put in the hands of detectives, the chances of identifying and arresting the perpetrator diminish rapidly.[36]

One reason for investigation ineffectiveness is that detectives often lack sufficient resources to carry out a lengthy ongoing probe of any but the most serious cases. Research shows the following:

- *Unsolved cases.* Almost 50 percent of burglary cases are screened out by supervisors before assignment to a detective for a follow-up investigation. Of those assigned, 75 percent are dropped after the first day of the follow-up investigation. Although robbery cases are more likely to be assigned to detectives, 75 percent of them are also dropped after one day of investigation.

- *Length of investigation.* The vast majority of cases are investigated for no more than four hours stretching over three days. An average of 11 days elapses between the initial report of a crime and suspension of the investigation.

- *Sources of information.* Early in an investigation, the focus is on the victim; as the investigation is pursued, emphasis shifts to the suspect. The most critical information for determining case outcome is the name and description of the suspect and related crime information. Victims are most often the source of information; unfortunately, witnesses, informants, and members of the police department are consulted far less often. However, when these sources are tapped, they are likely to produce useful information.

- *Effectiveness.* Preliminary investigations by patrol officers are critical. In situations where the suspect's identity is not known immediately after the crime is committed, detectives make an arrest in less than 10 percent of all cases.[37]

REALITY CHECK

MYTH OR REALITY? The more serious the crime, the more likely it is that detectives will solve it.

REALITY: Investigations of serious criminal incidents receive more attention. Consequently, they are solved at a higher rate.

Are there any unintended side effects of concentrating resources on serious crimes at the expense of less serious ones? Or are serious crimes solved for other reasons than just prioritizing them?

REALITY CHECK

MYTH OR REALITY? Most crimes are solved when the perpetrator is identified at the crime scene.

REALITY: The majority of cases are solved when the perpetrator is identified early.

This is contrary to the view portrayed in the fictional media, wherein the investigators always apprehend criminals by examining trace evidence and following up on questionable leads. What other misconceptions are conveyed by programs such as *CSI* and *Cold Case*?

Policies, Programs, and Issues in Criminal Justice

Street Stories: The World of Police Detectives

In his book *Street Stories*, sociologist Robert Jackall narrates the stories and insights he gathered while interviewing and hanging with New York City detectives. Jackall formed close associations with veteran detectives and observed them in action as they controlled a crime scene, canvassed for witnesses, interviewed suspects, gathered evidence, and honed their interrogation techniques.

He found that detectives get great satisfaction from solving crimes and putting criminals behind bars. But they also see themselves caught in a bureaucratic and moral dilemma: They are outsiders because they must play the game of the streets and work amidst the mayhem caused by the city's most dangerous criminals and then bring the case to the organized and controlled processing unit that is the criminal court. Detectives believe that the court rules victimize them and all too often neutralize their hard work. They get to know the suspect and the criminals' entire recorded criminal histories. Talking with them for hours on end, they form iron-clad beliefs based on their assessment of the criminal's character and record. Because the reliability of these assessments may be questionable, even the best detectives are sometimes dead wrong. Partly to guard against such errors of judgment, the law deliberately ignores individuals' criminal histories and allows no consideration at trial of the police detective's assessment of the suspect's moral character. Of course, these rules conflict with the detective's views of the case and the culpability of the suspect.

To reach the truth and assign blame, the detectives develop a slew of investigative skills, including the "rules" for conducting a proper interview:

- Know the case from beginning to end, down to the smallest detail. Specific knowledge is the key to successful interrogation.
- Listen patiently to suspects. Never confront them in an accusatory way.
- At first, write nothing, taking in everything a suspect says without challenge. Then go back over the suspect's statement, writing it out carefully.
- Read it back to the suspect and have him sign it. Lock suspects into their statements, whether true or false.
- Then key in on inconsistencies in the statements or on aspects of the statements one knows independently to be false.
- Make careful notes of casual conversations with suspects. Sometimes suspects blurt out damning statements spontaneously at off-guard moments.
- If one has no tangible evidence on hand, use dodges, ruses, or tricks to elicit statements from suspects.
- At a certain point, offer the suspect an out—a plausible explanation, justification, or excuse for his depredation, suppressing all personal moral revulsion and clearly indicating that one understands and indeed empathizes with such a motive or account.
- In short, let suspects convict themselves with their own words. Denials of guilt are as useful legally as admissions or

Improving Investigation with Technology

In Chapter 4, the technological breakthroughs that have aided crime investigation were discussed in some detail. Information technology (IT) has revolutionized police work in many areas, including communications, criminal identification, and record storage. A number of tasks that used to involve painstaking labor by individuals are now being conducted with IT. Take, for instance, searching criminal histories. Police agencies are now using a program called CopLink to facilitate this time-consuming task. CopLink integrates information from different jurisdictions into a single database that detectives can access when working on investigations.[38] The CopLink program enables investigators to search the entire database of past criminal records and computes a list of possible suspects even if only limited data is available, such as first or last name, partial license plate numbers, vehicle type, vehicle color, location of crime, and/or weapon used.

confessions if one has independent evidence to undermine the denials and thus the suspect's credibility before a jury.

Detectives also find themselves regularly competing with other agencies such as the FBI and with other detective branches for cases. They resent the federal agencies for their large budgets, their agents' lack of understanding of how the city works, and especially agents' unwillingness to share information about criminal groups. Some detective squads regularly hide important information from other units, even within their own departments, so that they won't steal the case or get credit for its solution. Boroughwide homicide squads steal good cases from precinct detectives, and bosses regularly appropriate credit for their subordinates' work on the streets.

Detectives have the privilege of seeing the underside of life, even the lives of the rich and famous. As Jackall puts it:

> Detectives' work regularly takes them behind respectable public faces, where they glimpse messy, sometimes tumultuous, sometimes sad, sometimes

ironic, sometimes tragic, sometimes comic, sometimes despairing, sometimes vice-filled private lives. (343)

They watch as a man walks into the squad room clad only in his underwear, claiming that he and a friend were just having a quiet conversation in his parked car when a robber reached through the window and snatched their clothes. They come across otherwise respectable professionals addicted to narcotics. In one case, while investigating the murder of a man dressed up in women's clothes, they uncover a genteel "butterfly society" of established professional men who cross-dress for Friday evening cocktails. These journeys behind respectable public façades stir prurient interests in some detectives, but profound class resentments in most. Police officers come overwhelmingly from the working class. They are the sons and daughters of policemen and firemen, they are appalled at the antics of the rich and their ability to get away with crimes for which the poor would be sent to prison.

Critical Thinking

Jackall finds that because detectives are agents of the state, symbols of authority, ultimate insiders with privileged access to hidden social arenas and forbidden knowledge, they become objects of fear, anger, and resentment. This double-sided role, Jackall concludes, shapes the meanings of detectives' work, their images of the world, and their own self-images. Is this status an inevitable part of policing, or can something be done to reduce the tension between police and the public they serve, and whose secrets they are privy to?

© Mike Kemp/Rubberball Productions/Getty

Another technique that is improving investigation success is the use of DNA profiling. Using DNA in support of criminal investigations has increased both in the United States and around the world. The first national DNA database—the National DNA Database of England & Wales—is regarded by many police experts as the most important development in investigative technology since the adoption of fingerprint comparison early in the last century.[39]

Improving Investigations with Forensic Science

Investigations have improved along with advances in **forensic science**. The *CSI* television series has drawn attention to the developing field of forensics in police work, which uses a variety of sciences, mathematical principles, and problem-solving methods to identify perpetrators. Forensic means "pertaining to the law," and forensic scientists perform comprehensive chemical

forensic science
The use of scientific techniques to investigate questions of interest to the justice system and solve crimes.

Advances in forensic science continue to help police apprehend offenders—even in crimes that took place years ago. This picture features a police forensics officer who, along with several other officials, exhumed the body of a man who was killed 18 years ago. The body was exhumed from the Haywards Heath Cemetery in Sussex, New York, in the hope that recent scientific advances could enable police to determine the dead man's identity and the cause of his death.

and physical analyses on evidence submitted by law enforcement agencies. Although most forensic scientists focus on criminal cases (they are sometimes referred to as criminalists), others work in the civil justice system—for example, performing handwriting comparisons to determine the validity of a signature on a will. Today, forensic specialists can examine blood and other body fluids and tissues for the presence of alcohol, drugs, and poisons and can compare body fluids and hair for typing factors, including DNA analysis. Forensic scientists analyze trace physical evidence such as blood spatters, paint, soil, and glass to help reconstruct a crime scene and interpret how the crime was committed. In addition to forensics, investigation is being improved by information technology, which allows investigators to compare evidence found at the crime scene with material collected from similar crimes by other police agencies.

See the Policies, Programs, and Issues in Criminal Justice feature on page 159 for a somewhat different perspective on forensics.

Forensic analyses involve the use of complex instruments and of chemical, physical, and microscopic examining techniques. In addition to analyzing crime scene investigations, forensic scientists provide testimony in a court of law when the case is brought to trial. Some forensic scientists are generalists, and others specialize in a particular scientific area, including toxicology,

Policies, Programs, and Issues in Criminal Justice

"Forensics under the Microscope"

The *Chicago Tribune's* "Forensics under the Microscope" series suggests that all is not well in the world of forensic sciences. Such concerns were echoed in a more recent National Academy of Sciences (NAS) report entitled *Strengthening Forensic Science in the United States: A Path Forward*. The authors of the report highlighted a series of problems with the forensic sciences, many of which are not well known to people on the outside—and particularly not to those who owe their knowledge of forensics and investigations to fictional television programs. Here are some of those problems.

- *Case Backlog* The NAS called attention to another report in which it was learned that federal, state, and local laboratories reported a backlog of nearly 500,000 requests for forensic analysis. This backlog has been made even more serious by requests for quick test results. Labs are having a difficult time keeping up.

- *DNA Demands* The ascendancy of DNA evidence and the opportunities to use it during investigations has further burdened crime labs. And even though the NAS, along with other experts and commissions, has heralded the advent of DNA testing as valuable for criminal investigation, there is only so much it can do. According to the NAS report, "DNA evidence comprises only about 10 percent of case work and is not always relevant to a particular case. Even if DNA evidence is available, it will assist in solving a crime only if it supports an evidential hypothesis that makes guilt or innocence more likely. For example, the fact that DNA evidence of a victim's husband is found in the house in which the couple lived and where the murder took place proves nothing. The fact that the husband's DNA is found under the fingernails of the victim who put up a struggle may have very different significance" (pp. 1–5 and 1–6).

- *Questionable Evidence* Now that DNA evidence is regarded as a gold standard in criminal investigations, this has started to cast doubt on convictions secured through other, more traditional types of evidence. According to the report, "The fact is that many forensic tests—such as those used to infer the source of toolmarks or bite marks—have

never been exposed to stringent scientific scrutiny. ... Even fingerprint analysis has been called into question" (p. 1–6)

- *Errors* The NAS also called attention to several disturbing examples of errors and fraud in the forensic sciences. In one case, a state-mandated examination of the West Virginia State Police laboratory revealed that the convictions of more than 100 people were in doubt. Another scandal involving the Houston Crime Laboratory came to light in 2003. An investigation revealed "routine failure to run essential scientific controls, failure to take adequate measures to prevent contamination of samples, failure to adequately document work performed and results obtained, and routine failure to follow correct procedures for computing statistical frequencies" (p. 1–8).

- *Incompatible Fingerprint Identification Systems* Law enforcement agencies around the country have developed and put in place automated fingerprint identification systems in an effort to solve crimes. The problem, according to the NAS, is that there is inadequate integration of these systems.

- *Lack of Preparation for Mass Disasters* According to the NAS, "Threats to food and transportation, concerns about nuclear and cyber security, and the need to develop rapid responses to chemical, nuclear, radiological, and biological threats underlie the need to ensure that there is a sufficient supply of adequately trained forensic specialists ... [but] public crime laboratories are insufficiently prepared to handle mass disasters" (p. 1–13).

- *The CSI Effect* The so-called "*CSI* effect," named for the popular television program, is concerned with the real-world implications of Hollywood's fictional spin on the forensic sciences and criminal investigations. The NAS found that some prosecutors believe they must make their in-court presentations as visually appealing as possible in an effort to please jurors who think they understand forensic work from having watched their favorite television programs. Attempts to satisfy such unrealistic expectations may possibly compromise the pursuit of justice. More attention will be given to the *CSI* effect in Chapter 8.

Critical Thinking

Clearly there is room for improvement in the rapidly evolving forensic sciences. To what extent has the recent attention paid to wrongful convictions fueled calls for improvement, such as those in the NAS report? At the other extreme, what *improvements* have been made in recent years? The news cannot be all doom and gloom. Find out more on the National Academies website at www.nap.edu.

Chicago Tribune's "Forensics under the Microscope" series

Read all the articles in the *Chicago Tribune*'s **"Forensics under the Microscope" series** here:

www.cengage.com/ criminaljustice/siegel

blood pattern analysis, crime scene investigation, impression evidence (e.g., footprints), trace evidence (e.g., hair left at a crime scene), and questioned documents. There is a forensics expert for nearly every conceivable type of evidence and criminal activity.

Are you interested in a career as a forensics expert? Read the Careers in Criminal Justice feature on page 161.

Community Policing

For more than 30 years, police agencies have been trying to gain the cooperation and respect of the communities they serve. At first, efforts at improving the relationships between police departments and the public involved programs with the general title of police–community relations (PCR). Developed at the station house and departmental levels, these initial PCR programs were designed to make citizens more aware of police activities, alert them to methods of self-protection, and improve general attitudes toward policing.

Although PCR efforts demonstrated the willingness of police agencies to cooperate with the public, some experts believed that law enforcement agencies needed to undergo a significant transformation to create meaningful partnerships with the public. In their view, community relations and crime control effectiveness cannot be the province of a few specialized units housed within a traditional police department. Instead, the core police role must be altered if community involvement is to be won and maintained. This led to the development of **community policing**, a set of programs and strategies designed to bring police and the public closer together and create a more cooperative working environment between them.

community policing
Programs and strategies designed to bring police and the public closer together and create a more cooperative working environment between them.

Community police officers routinely meet with the public to become personally familiar with their problems. Here, Andy Gonzalez, commander of the Third District in Cleveland, Ohio, listens to Sandra Fruits talk about her concern for safety of her daughter, Amira, 10. Police, residents, and the mayor had met at a local recreation center to discuss mutual concerns about public safety.

© AP Images/*The Plain Dealer*, Lynn Ischay

Careers in Criminal Justice

FORENSIC SCIENTIST

Duties and Characteristics of the Job

- Forensic scientists perform comprehensive chemical and physical analyses on evidence submitted by law enforcement agencies.
- Forensic scientists analyze the physical evidence they receive from police and then prepare reports describing the results of their analysis. Those documents, along with forensic scientists' expert testimony, can be important prosecutorial tools for convicting the accused. Therefore, their work is often instrumental in apprehending and convicting criminals.
- Although most forensic scientists focus on criminal cases and are sometimes called criminalists, others work in the civil justice system—performing duties such as comparing handwriting to determine the validity of a signature on a will.
- Forensic scientists perform two roles in their work. One is to analyze physical evidence found on a victim, at the scene. The other is to provide expert testimony in a court of law.
- Most forensic scientists work in crime laboratories run by city, county, or state governments; the next largest group work for federal agencies, including the justice department (FBI, DEA, and Secret Service) and the treasury department; a smaller number work in private labs and colleges and universities.
- Forensic scientists usually work a regular 40-hour week. Sometimes they have to travel and work long, irregular hours.
- They spend much time in laboratories analyzing evidence, but they also work in offices to record and draft reports on the results of their analyses.

Job Outlook

- Job opportunities are expected to increase as a result of the judicial system's continuing need for corroborating evidence in prosecutions.
- Forensic scientists can expect competition for jobs at the Departments of Justice, Treasury, and other federal law enforcement agencies.
- Job opportunities will be best for crime lab professionals who have an advanced degree or certification.

Salary

- About 13,000 forensic scientists are now employed, with starting salaries in the $45,000 range.
- Experienced crime lab professionals can earn upwards of $100,000 a year.
- Lab directors earn in the low to mid-$100,000 range.

Opportunities

- Job opportunities will be best for crime lab professionals who have an advanced degree or certification.
- The Bureau of Labor Statistics projects that there may be 17,000 positions for forensic scientists in 1016, so growth is anticipated.

Qualifications

- Employment of most crime lab professionals is contingent upon satisfactory completion of a background investigation and random drug testing.
- Those who work in large labs may use technologically advanced equipment such as chromatographs to analyze drugs, alcohol, arson evidence, and fibers; spectrographs to identify chemicals; and computerized laboratory equipment.
- Crime lab professionals may be exposed to health or safety hazards when working in the lab or handling certain chemicals, but there is little risk if procedures are followed.

(continued)

Careers in Criminal Justice (Continued)

Education and Training

- Beginning forensic scientists usually must have at least a bachelor's degree in forensic science, chemistry, biology, physics, or physical anthropology.
- Several colleges and universities offer a bachelor's degree in forensic science; most also offer advanced degrees in specialized areas of forensic science.
- Whatever the major, required college courses include sciences such as biology, physics, chemistry, and pharmacology.
- A course in quantitative analysis and statistics is frequently required.
- Laboratory experience involving analytical instruments or blood sample analysis is helpful.
- Computer courses are also recommended, because employers prefer job applicants with computer skills to perform modeling and simulation tasks and to operate computerized laboratory equipment.

Word to the Wise

- A career in forensics is not what it is made out to be on television, in such programs as *CSI*, *Cold Case*, *Bones*, and *Criminal Minds*. Much time is spent in a laboratory, and little (if any at all) on the streets chasing down criminals.
- Forensics experts are often employed in criminal justice agencies, so certain criminal activities and convictions in one's past can serve as a bar to employment.
- A degree in the social sciences is generally not enough for success as a forensic scientist. The very term "scientist" calls for training, and generally a degree, in the natural sciences.
- Compared to the nearly 700,000 sworn law enforcement personnel in the United States, there are very few forensic scientists (around 13,000).
- Most job opportunities will be found in and around large cities.

Implementing Community Policing

foot patrol
Police patrols that take officers out of cars and put them on a walking beat in order to strengthen ties with the community.

The community policing concept was originally implemented through a number of innovative demonstration projects.[40] Among the most publicized were experiments in **foot patrol**, which took officers out of cars and set them to walking beats in the neighborhood. Foot patrol efforts were aimed at forming a bond with community residents by acquainting them with the individual officers who patrolled their neighborhood and letting them know that police were caring and available. The first foot patrol experiments were conducted in cities in Michigan and New Jersey. An evaluation of foot patrol indicated that although it did not bring down the crime rate, residents in areas where foot patrol was added perceived greater safety and were less afraid of crime.[41]

Since the advent of these programs, hundreds of communities have adopted innovative forms of decentralized, neighborhood-based community policing models. The federal government has encouraged the growth of community policing by providing billions of dollars to hire and train officers through its Office of Community Oriented Policing Services (COPS) program, which has given local departments more than $10 billion in aid since its inception.[42] Recent surveys indicate that there has been a significant increase in community policing activities and that certain core programs, such as crime prevention, have become embedded in the police role.[43] Community-oriented policing (COP) programs have been implemented in large cities, suburban areas, and rural communities.[44]

Changing the Police Role

Community policing also emphasizes sharing power with local groups and individuals. A key element of the community policing philosophy is that citizens must actively participate with police to fight crime. Such participation is essential because community climate is influenced by the informal social control created by a concerned citizenry coupled with effective policing.[45] Participation might involve providing information in areawide crime investigations or helping police reach out to troubled youths. The following are some other changes that have been linked to community policing initiatives.

- *Neighborhood orientation.* To achieve the goals of COP, some police agencies have tried to decentralize, an approach sometimes referred to as **neighborhood-oriented policing (NOP)**.[46] According to this view, problem solving is best done at the neighborhood level where issues originate, not at a far-off central headquarters. Because each neighborhood has its own particular needs, police decision making must be flexible and adaptive. For example, neighborhoods undergoing change in racial composition may experience high levels of racially motivated violence and require special police initiatives to reduce tensions.[47]

- *Changing management styles.* Community policing also means the redesign of police departments' administration and management. Management's role must be reinterpreted to focus on the problems of the community, not on the needs of the police department. The traditional vertical police organizational chart must be altered so that top-down management gives way to bottom-up decision making. The patrol officer becomes the manager of his beat and a key decision maker.

- *Changing recruitment and training.* Community policing means that police departments must alter their recruitment and training requirements. Future officers must develop community-organizing and problem-solving skills, along with traditional police skills. Their training must prepare them to succeed less on their ability to make arrests or issue citations and more on their ability to solve problems effectively.

Challenges of Community Policing

The core concepts of police work are changing as administrators recognize the limitations and realities of police work in modern society. If they are to be successful, community policing strategies must be able to react effectively to some significant administrative problems.

DEFINING COMMUNITY ● Critics believe that community policing works best in stable, affluent areas that are

COPS office
Go to the **COPS office** website to see its current programs. You can access the site via

www.cengage.com/ criminaljustice/siegel

neighborhood-oriented policing (NOP)
Community policing efforts aimed at individual neighborhoods.

© imac/Alamy

already characterized by a strong sense of community. The challenge of community is to reach out to all people in all neighborhoods, including young people and minorities, who may previously have been left out of the process.

REALITY CHECK

MYTH OR REALITY? Community policing can succeed in any community if the police try hard enough.

MYTH: Community policing is a two-way street. It requires both police efforts and community participation.

Research shows that areas already defined by a clear sense of community benefit from community policing initiatives more than those that are not. Is community policing thus biased toward more affluent or cohesive areas? Can community policing really solve the historical problems it is intended to address?

DEFINING ROLES • Police administrators must also establish the exact role of community police agents. How should they integrate their activities with those of regular patrol forces? For example, should foot patrols have primary responsibility for policing in an area, or should they coordinate their activities with officers assigned to patrol cars?

CHANGING SUPERVISOR ATTITUDES • Some supervisors are wary of community policing because it supports a decentralized command structure. Supervisors who learn to actively embrace community policing concepts are the ones best able to encourage patrol officers to follow suit.[48]

REORIENTING POLICE VALUES • Research shows that police officers who have a traditional crime control orientation are less satisfied with community policing efforts than those who are public service–oriented.[49] In some instances, officers holding traditional values may go as far as stigmatizing their own comrades assigned to community policing; their targets feel penalized by a lack of administrative support.[50] It is thus unlikely that community policing activities can be successful unless police line officers make a firm commitment to the values of community policing.[51]

REVISE TRAINING • Because the community policing model calls for an expansion of the police role from law enforcer to community organizer, police training must be revised to reflect this new mandate. If community policing is to be adopted on a wide scale, a whole new type of police officer must be recruited and trained in a whole new way. Training must prepare officers to succeed less on their ability to make arrests or issue citations and more on their ability to solve problems, prevent crime effectively, and deal with neighborhood diversity and cultural values.[52]

REORIENT RECRUITMENT • To make community policing successful, midlevel managers must be recruited and trained who are receptive to and can implement community-change strategies.[53] The selection of new recruits must be guided by a desire to find individuals with the skills and attitudes that support community policing.

© Robert W. Ginn/Alamy

Community Policing Effectiveness

There is empirical evidence that *some* community policing efforts can reduce disorder and impact the crime rate.[54] The most successful programs give officers time to meet with local residents to talk about crime in the neighborhood and to use personal initiative to solve problems. Although not all programs work (police–community newsletters and cleanup campaigns do not seem to do much good), the overall impression has been that patrol officers can actually reduce the level of fear in the community. Where it is used, citizens seem to like community policing, and those who volunteer and get involved in community crime prevention programs report higher confidence in the police force and its ability to create a secure environment.[55]

On the other hand, there is no clear-cut evidence that community policing is highly successful at reducing crime across the board. Crime rate reductions in cities that have used COP may be the result of an overall downturn in the nation's crime rate, rather than a result of community policing efforts. Researchers have also found that it is difficult to change the traditional values and attitudes of police officers involved in the programs.[56]

Problem-Oriented Policing

Closely associated with, yet independent from, the community policing concept are **problem-oriented policing** strategies. Traditional police models focus on responding to calls for help in the shortest possible time, dealing with the situation, and then getting on the street again as soon as possible. In contrast, problem-oriented policing is proactive.

Problem-oriented policing (POP) strategies require police agencies to identify particular long-term community problems—street-level drug dealers, prostitution rings, gang hangouts—and develop strategies to eliminate them.[57] As with community policing, police departments must rely on local residents and private resources in order to be problem solvers. This means that police managers must learn how to develop community resources, design efficient and cost-effective solutions to problems, and become advocates as well as agents of reform.[58]

A significant portion of police departments are now using special units to confront specific social problems. Problem-oriented policing models are supported by ample evidence that a great deal of urban crime is concentrated in a few hot spots.[59] A significant portion of all police calls in metropolitan areas typically radiate from a relatively few locations: bars, malls, the bus depot, hotels, and certain apartment buildings.[60] By implication, concentrating police resources on these **hot spots of crime** could reduce crime appreciably.[61]

Problem-oriented strategies are being developed that focus on specific problem areas and/or specific criminal acts. For example, a POP effort in Sarasota, Florida, which was aimed at reducing prostitution, involved intensive, focused, high-visibility patrols to discourage prostitutes and their customers, undercover work to arrest prostitutes and drug dealers, and collaboration with hotel and motel owners to identify and arrest pimps and drug dealers.[62]

Another well-known program, Operation Ceasefire, is a problem-oriented policing intervention aimed at reducing youth homicide and youth firearms violence in Boston. According to evaluations of the program, Ceasefire produced significant reductions in youth homicide victimization and gun assault incidents in Boston that were not experienced in other communities in New England or elsewhere in the nation.[63]

Although programs such as these seem successful, the effectiveness of any street-level problem-solving effort must be interpreted with caution.[64] It is possible that the criminals will be displaced to other, "safer" areas of the

Center for Problem-Oriented Policing

Visit the website of the **Center for Problem-Oriented Policing** for the latest on problem-solving policing. You can access it via

www.cengage.com/criminaljustice/siegel

problem-oriented policing
A style of police operations that stresses proactive problem solving, rather than reactive crime fighting.

hot spots of crime
Places from which a significant portion of all police calls originate. These hot spots include taverns and housing projects.

city and will return shortly after the program is declared a success and the additional police forces have been pulled from the area.[65] Nonetheless, evidence shows that whereas merely saturating an area with police may not deter crime, focusing efforts on a particular problem may indeed have a crime-reducing effect.

Support Functions

As the model of a typical police department indicates (see again Figure 5.1), not all members of a department engage in what the general public regards as "real police work"—patrol, detection, and traffic control. Even in departments that are embracing community- and problem-oriented policing, a great deal of police resources are actually devoted to support and administrative functions. There are too many tasks to mention in detail, but the most important include those discussed next.

Many police departments maintain their own personnel service, which carries out such functions as recruiting new police officers, creating exams to determine the most qualified applicants, and handling promotions and transfers. Innovative selection techniques are constantly being developed and tested. For example, the Behavioral-Personnel Assessment Device (B-PAD) requires police applicants to view videotaped scenarios and respond as though they were officers handling the situation; reviews indicate that this procedure may be a reliable and unbiased method of choosing new recruits.[66]

internal affairs

The branch of the police department that investigates charges of corruption or misconduct on the part of police officers.

Larger police departments often maintain an **internal affairs** branch charged with policing the police. Internal affairs units process citizen complaints of police corruption, investigate what may be the unnecessary use of force by police officers, and probe police participation in actual criminal activity, such as burglaries or narcotics violations. In addition, internal affairs divisions may assist police managers when disciplinary action is brought against individual officers. Internal affairs is a controversial function since

The traffic patrol function is becoming ever more important as police departments struggle with budget cuts in cash-strapped cities across the country. Here, a Fairfax, Virginia, motorcycle officer aims his ProLaser III toward drivers who may be speeding.

© Paul J. Richards/AFP/Getty Images

investigators are feared and distrusted by fellow police officers. Nonetheless, rigorous self-scrutiny is the only way police departments can earn the respect of citizens. Because of these concerns, it has become commonplace for police departments to institute citizen oversight over police practices and to establish civilian review boards that have the power to listen to complaints and conduct investigations.

Most police departments are responsible for the administration and control of their own budgets. This task includes administering payroll, purchasing equipment and services, planning budgets for future expenditures, and auditing departmental financial records.

Police departments include separate units charged with maintaining and disseminating information on wanted offenders, stolen merchandise, traffic violators, and so on. Modern data management systems enable police to use their records in a highly sophisticated fashion. For example, officers in a patrol car who spot a suspicious-looking vehicle can instantly receive a computerized rundown on whether it has been stolen. And if stolen property is recovered during an arrest, police using this sort of system can determine who reported the loss of the merchandise and arrange for its return.

Another important function of police communication is the effective and efficient dispatching of patrol cars. Again, modern computer technologies have been used to make the most of available resources.[67]

In many departments, training is continuous throughout an officer's career. Training usually begins at a police academy, which may be run exclusively for larger departments or may be part of a regional training center serving smaller and varied governmental units. More than 90 percent of all police departments require preservice training, including nearly all departments in larger cities (population over 100,000). The average officer receives more than 500 hours of preservice training, including 400 hours in the classroom and the rest in field training. Police in large cities receive over 1,000 hours of instruction divided almost evenly between classroom and field instruction.[68] Among the topics usually covered are law and civil rights, firearms handling, emergency medical care, and restraint techniques.[69]

After assuming their police duties, new recruits are assigned to field-training officers who break them in on the job. However, training does not stop here. On-the-job training is a continuous process in the modern police department and covers such areas as weapons skills, first aid, crowd control, and community relations. Some departments use roll call training, in which superior officers or outside experts address police officers at the beginning of the workday. Other departments allow police officers time off to attend annual training sessions to sharpen their skills and learn new policing techniques.

Police departments provide emergency aid to the ill, counsel youngsters, speak to school and community agencies on safety and drug abuse, and provide countless other services designed to improve citizen–police interactions.

Larger police departments maintain specialized units that help citizens protect themselves from criminal activity. They advise citizens on effective home security techniques or conduct Project ID campaigns—engraving valuables with an identifying number so that they can be returned if recovered after a burglary; police also work in schools teaching kids how to avoid drug use.[70] Police agencies maintain (or have access to) forensic laboratories that enable them to identify substances to be used as evidence and to classify fingerprints.

Planning and research functions include designing programs to increase police efficiency and strategies to test program effectiveness. Police planners monitor recent technological developments and institute programs to adapt them to police services.

ETHICAL CHALLENGES IN CRIMINAL JUSTICE

A WRITING ASSIGNMENT

The Middle City police force has created Crime Control Teams—decentralized units relieved of routine, non-crime-related duties and given responsibility for controlling serious crime, apprehending offenders, conducting investigations, and increasing clearance rates on a neighborhood basis. Two team members, Officers Donald Libby and Karen Johnson, each of whom has more than 15 years on the force, were part of a team assigned to displace gangs of local teenagers who were constantly causing problems in the neighborhood. After a few months on the job, Libby and Johnson were the target of numerous complaints related to their treatment of neighborhood youths. They were charged with roughing up neighborhood kids, slapping some of them around, and being disrespectful. In the most serious incident, they used a nightstick on the head of a 15-year-old who they claim had resisted arrest after they found him smoking marijuana in the park. The youth suffered a broken arm and concussion and required hospitalization. When interviewed by the Internal Affairs Bureau, the officers admitted they scuffled with the boy but claimed they were "only doing their job." Besides, they argued, community leaders had demanded results, and their aggressive style had helped lower the crime rate in the area by more than 20 percent. The boy and his parents have also filed suit, claiming that the amount of force used was unnecessary and violated his civil rights. As their defense attorney, you are asked to write an essay outlining their defense. Don't worry about legal rules. How would you defend the two officers?

RealityCheck Revisited

If you want to learn a little more about the myths and realities checks related to the police that were presented in this chapter, you might want to visit the following websites:

• Read about what policing is really like and listen to some interviews with police officers the world over at

http://policeinsights.com/about.html

• Read more about the relationship between policing and crime in this report by the Government Accountability Office:

http://www.gao.gov/new.items/d06104.pdf

• Read more about criminal investigations, particularly the role of forensics, at the website for the American Academy of Forensic Sciences:

http://www.aafs.org/

• For more on the relationship between community policing and problem solving, see the discussion at

http://www.cops.usdoj.gov/default.asp?item=36

SUMMARY

© AP Images/Jacquelyn Martin

1. Understand the organization of police departments

- The public demands that the police "make them feel safe" and lose confidence in them if they fear crime in the streets.
- Most municipal police departments in the United States are independent agencies within the executive branch of government. Most local police departments are organized in a hierarchical manner.
- Most police departments employ a time-in-rank system for determining promotion eligibility.

2. Articulate the complexities of the police role

- A police officer's crime-fighting efforts are only a small part of his or her overall activities.
- Studies of police work indicate that a significant portion of an officer's time is spent handling minor disturbances, service calls, and administrative duties. The police role involves many activities that are not crime related. The primary role of police seems to be "handling the situation."

3. Discuss the concept of patrol and its effectiveness

- Uniformed patrol officers are the backbone of the police department, usually accounting for about two-thirds of a department's personnel.

- Most experts agree that the great bulk of patrol efforts are devoted to what has been described as order maintenance, or peace-keeping: maintaining order and civility in their assigned jurisdiction.
- One of the primary goals of police patrol has been to deter criminal behavior.
- The visible presence of patrol cars on the street and the rapid deployment of police officers to the scene of a crime are viewed as an effective method of crime control.

4. Be familiar with methods of improving patrol, including broken windows policing

- Police departments that use proactive policing and directed patrol may help reduce crime rates.
- There is evidence that certain arrest strategies can deter crime.
- Research studies show that contact with the police may cause some offenders not to repeat criminal behavior.
- Rapid response to 911 calls does not appear to increase the chances that the perpetrator will be apprehended.
- According to the broken windows concept, a deteriorated neighborhood, whose residents are fearful, pessimistic, and despondent, is a magnet for crime. There is evidence that broken windows policing is effective.
- Police departments have also relied on technology to help guide patrol efforts.
- The CompStat program required local commanders to demonstrate their intimate knowledge of crime trends and develop strategies to address them effectively.

5. Be able to discuss the organization of police detectives

- The first independent detective bureau was established by the London Metropolitan Police in 1841.
- Investigative services can be organized in a variety of ways.
- Detectives investigate the causes of crime and attempt to identify the individuals or groups responsible for committing particular offenses.

(continued)

- A sting operation involves organized groups of detectives or patrol officers working in plain clothes who deceive criminals into openly committing illegal acts or conspiring to engage in criminal activity.

- Police detectives make a valuable contribution to police work because their skilled interrogation and case-processing techniques are essential to eventual criminal conviction.

6. Know what forensics is and what forensics experts do for police agencies

- Investigations have improved along with advances in forensic science.

- Forensic scientists perform comprehensive chemical and physical analyses on evidence submitted by law enforcement agencies.

7. Understand the concept of community policing

- Hundreds of communities have adopted innovative forms of decentralized, neighborhood-based community policing models.

- There is empirical evidence that some community policing efforts can reduce disorder and impact the crime rate.

8. Discuss the concept of problem-oriented policing

- Closely associated with, yet independent from, the community policing concept are problem-oriented policing strategies. Problem-oriented policing is proactive.

- Problem-oriented policing strategies require police agencies to identify particular long-term community problems (such as street-level drug dealers, prostitution rings, and gang hangouts) and to develop strategies to eliminate them.

- The core concepts of police work are changing as administrators recognize the limitations and realities of police work in modern society. If they are to be successful, community policing strategies must react effectively to some significant administrative problems.

9. Be familiar with the various police support functions

- A great deal of police resources are actually devoted to support and administrative functions.

- Many police departments maintain their own personnel service, which carries out such functions as recruiting new police officers, creating exams to determine the most qualified applicants, and handling promotions and transfers.

- Larger police departments often maintain an internal affairs branch charged with "policing the police."

- Another important function of police communication is the effective and efficient dispatching of patrol cars. Again, modern computer technologies have been used to make the most of available resources.

Key Terms

police chief, 144
time-in-rank system, 145
order maintenance (peacekeeping), 146
proactive policing, 148
deterrent effect, 148
directed patrol, 148
broken windows model, 149
CompStat, 150
sting operation, 153

vice squad, 153
forensic science, 157
community policing, 160
foot patrol, 162
neighborhood-oriented policing (NOP), 163
problem-oriented policing, 165
hot spots of crime, 165
internal affairs, 166

Review Questions

1. Should the primary police role be law enforcement or community service? Explain.

2. Should a police chief be permitted to promote an officer with special skills to a supervisory position, or should all officers be forced to spend "time in rank"? Explain your answer.

3. Do the advantages of proactive policing outweigh the disadvantages? Explain.

4. Explain the concept of broken windows policing. Why might it be successful?

5. What are the problems facing investigators and forensics experts these days?

6. Can the police and the community ever form a partnership to fight crime? Why or why not? Does the community policing model remind you of early forms of policing? Explain.

6

ISSUES IN POLICING: PROFESSIONAL, SOCIAL, AND LEGAL

© AP Images/Tyler Morning Telegraph, Tom Worner

RealityCheck

MYTH or REALITY?

▶ Male police officers believe that female police officers can perform the job as well as they can.

▶ Police officers feel that no one else understands what they do for a living.

▶ Veteran police officers receive the most citizen complaints.

▶ Thousands of people are fatally shot by police each year.

▶ The police are required to advise all arrested persons of their *Miranda* rights.

▶ Warrantless searches are permissible as long as the police have probable cause.

▶ There are legal loopholes that enable guilty criminals to go free in alarming numbers.

Learning Objectives

1. Discuss some of the problems of minority and female police officers
2. Know the issues involving education and police
3. Be able to discuss police culture and styles
4. Be able to identify distinct policing styles
5. Be familiar with how police use discretion
6. Be able to discuss four major problems of policing
7. Discuss the use of force and the factors related to police shootings
8. Know various methods of controlling police force
9. Define less-lethal weapons and provide examples
10. Be familiar with the Supreme Court's involvement with the police through its effort to control search and seizure and interrogation, and through establishment of the exclusionary rule

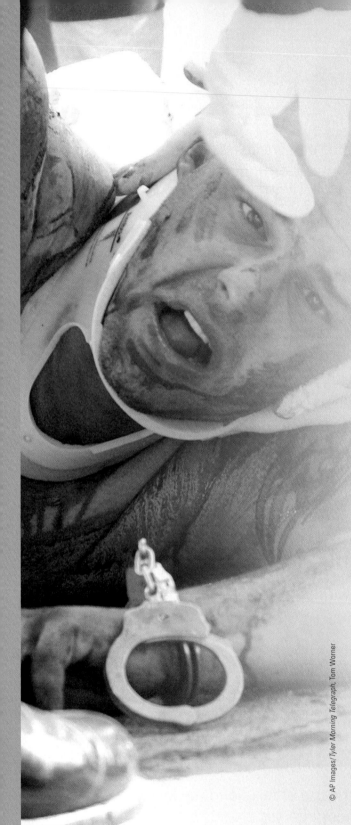

© AP Images/*Tyler Morning Telegraph*, Tom Worner

Chapter Outline

Career Profile

Stephen Bishopp is a sergeant in the Dallas Police Department and a patrol division training coordinator. He has worked for the department since 1990 and has been a sergeant since 2000. A typical day for him entails planning and coordinating training for sworn officers, as well as running the field training program for the recruits at the patrol division. Most days are spent at a computer, but he also meets with recruits to guide their training and occasionally goes out on the street to observe them in the field.

His undergraduate degree was in psychology, but he took many criminal justice classes and was a security policeman in the Air National Guard while in college. He is also currently enrolled in the Criminology Ph.D. program at the University of Texas at Dallas. Steve feels that having a criminal justice education helps prepare officers for the dynamics among officers, offenders, and law-abiding citizens. Nothing, he says, "can ever really prepare you for what you will encounter and see. However, a criminal justice education can put some of those encounters in perspective with an understanding of crime theory and etiology. It can also shape a more realistic idea of what to expect out of the criminal justice system as a whole."

Steve feels that many people do not understand the very basics of law enforcement. "Many people allow television to shape their perception of law enforcement," he says. "However, the biggest and most dangerous misperception is of why officers are called in the first place. Citizens don't realize that officers are often called when things are completely out of hand. Officers may have 30 seconds to a minute to make a decision over a situation that may have been years in the making. This leads to bitterness on both sides; the officer is berated by those who called him because they feel he made the wrong choice. This can cause many of us to become cynical, and many citizens feel they were unjustly dealt with."

Another challenge is dealing with family and friends who are not cops. "People don't understand how we can describe a gruesome and violent crime scene and joke about it, but that is sometimes how we deal with the difficult situations we face," Steve explains. "I also don't care much to be introduced everywhere I go as Steve Bishopp, 'the cop.' It bothers me when the conversation turns to, 'Hey why do you cops always…?'"

Steve feels that the most rewarding aspect of his job is putting truly bad people in jail. "I've come across some truly violent, vicious people who should never be out in society. I have worked many bloody and violent murders and sexual assaults, and putting those people in jail (particularly after assisting the prosecution in getting a conviction) gives me a huge sense of accomplishment and pride." Steve also enjoys being a role model for his four kids. These positives tend to outweigh the difficulties that can go along with constantly being in the spotlight and interacting with a public that doesn't always understand the nuances of the job.

Police behavior is now more visible than ever before, because it is commonly captured on video; when police make the local news, these accounts of the use of force can have an extremely negative impact on public perceptions of police behavior, especially in the minority community.[1] And the effects of this exposure are not lost on police officers, many of whom feel significant amounts of job-related stress, a condition that may lead them to develop negative attitudes and to lose enthusiasm for and commitment to the job.[2] This chapter focuses on these and other problems facing police officers in contemporary society. It looks at issues police face on the job, in court, and in society. We begin with a discussion of the makeup of the police and the police profession.

Websites of various police departments

To access the **websites of various police departments** via a clickable map, go to

www.cengage.com/criminaljustice/siegel

Careers in Criminal Justice

POSTAL INSPECTOR

Duties and Characteristics of the Job

- The Postal Inspection Service is a law enforcement body of the United States Postal Service (USPS).
- Postal inspectors investigate crimes that involve violations of postal laws and ensure the security of the U.S. Postal Service.
- The duties of postal inspectors include general law enforcement tasks such as executing warrants, arresting offenders, and testifying in court.
- A large part of a postal inspector's job is investigating crimes such as mail theft, mail fraud, drug trafficking, child pornography, and identity theft.
- Postal inspectors conduct investigations using a combination of advanced technology and forensic skills.

Job Outlook

- Opportunities for employment as a postal inspector open up at irregular intervals. When hiring, the Postal Inspection Service looks for a diversity of skills and backgrounds in potential postal inspectors.
- Because of the good pay, benefits, prestige, and opportunities these positions offer, applicants should expect competition.

Salary

- Salaries are based on the Inspection Service Law Enforcement (ISLE) pay scale, which corresponds to the GS pay scale for federal law enforcement officials. The average salary for a postal inspector is between $48,295 and $88,105.

Opportunities

- Accounting experience, computer skills, and a law degree are helpful when applying for a position.
- Law enforcement experience as a detective or even a patrol officer will also be helpful.
- Students who earned a bachelor's or an advanced degree with a 3.0 average or higher can qualify for the academic achievement track with or without full-time job experience.

Qualifications

- Candidates must be American citizens at least 21 years old but younger than 36½, must have a four-year degree, must have no felonies or domestic violence convictions, and must have a driver's license.
- A candidate must be in sound mental and physical health, including passing a hearing test.

Who Are The Police?

The composition of the nation's police forces is changing. Less than 50 years ago, police agencies were composed primarily of white males with a high school education who viewed policing as a secure position that brought them the respect of family and friends and took them a step up the social ladder. It was not uncommon to see police families in which one member of each new generation would enter the force. This picture has been changing and will continue to change. As criminal justice programs turn out thousands of graduates every year, an increasing number of police officers have at least some college education. In addition, affirmative action programs have slowly helped change the racial and gender composition of police departments to reflect community makeup. The following sections explore these changes in detail.

- Qualities such as good communication skills (written and oral), sound decision-making skills, and the ability to follow instruction are highly valued.
- Once she or he has satisfied the general requirements, a candidate must qualify for training under one of several tracks offered: language skills, postal experience, specialized nonpostal experience (includes those with law degrees, certification in auditing or computer systems, law enforcement experience, and others), or academic achievement.
- Additionally, applicants must undergo a background check, pass a polygraph, and be interviewed. After completing the proper training, a postal inspector may be relocated, so willingness to move is necessary.

Education and Training

- To apply for a position, a potential candidate must have a four-year degree.
- After successfully moving through the application process and being hired, new employees will be sent to Basic Inspector Training in Potomac, Maryland, where they learn about the responsibilities of their organization, investigative techniques, firearms proficiency, and physical defense.
- Those with no postal experience will then enter a six-month probation period before becoming a full-time employee.

Word to the Wise

- Postal inspectors are exempt from the Fair Labor Standards Act and do not qualify for overtime pay.
- Candidates who have used any illegal drug (besides *cannabis*) in the past 10 years are not eligible for employment. *Cannabis* use within the past 3 years is considered a bar to employment.
- Candidates without "special knowledge" in certain areas will be considered only minimally qualified. Special knowledge areas include certain language skills, past postal experience, specialized nonpostal experience (such as auditing skills, a law degree, or computer skills), and academic achievement (such as a four-year degree with work experience).
- It is often necessary for new inspectors to relocate to their first duty station. Certain moving expenses are reimbursed.
- Postal inspectors no longer investigate crimes committed by postal employees. The USPS Office of the Inspector General now performs this function.
- Computer and/or business skills, particularly accounting skills, are in high demand.

Demographic Makeup

With few exceptions, the personnel in most early police departments were white and male, a condition that persisted through most of the twentieth century. However, in most regions, the image of the police department as a bastion of white male dominance is either obsolete or rapidly changing. For more than 30 years, U.S. police departments have made a concerted effort to attract women and minority police officers, and there have been some impressive gains.[3] Today, about 11 percent of all officers are female, and about 23 percent are members of minority groups.[4]

The reasons behind this effort are varied. Viewed in its most positive light, diversity initiatives by police departments are intended to field a more balanced force that truly represents the communities they serve. A heterogeneous police force can be instrumental in gaining the confidence of the community by helping dispel the view that police departments are generally bigoted or biased organizations.[5] Furthermore, women and minority police officers possess special qualities that can serve to improve police performance. Spanish-speaking officers can facilitate investigations in Hispanic neighborhoods, and Asian officers are essential for undercover or surveillance work with Asian gangs and drug importers.

Minority Police Officers

The earliest known date of when an African American was hired as a police officer was 1861 in Washington, D.C.; Chicago hired its first African American officer in 1872.[6] By 1890 an estimated 2,000 minority police officers were employed in the United States. At first, African American officers suffered a great deal of discrimination. Their work assignments were restricted, as were their chances for promotion. Minority officers were often assigned solely to patrolling African American neighborhoods, and in some cities they were required to call a white officer to make an arrest. Racial prejudice was common among white officers, and as late as the 1950s some refused to ride with African Americans in patrol cars.[7]

The experience of African American police officers has not been an easy one. In his classic 1969 book *Black in Blue*, Nicholas Alex pointed out that African American officers of the time suffered from what he called **double marginality**.[8] On the one hand, African American officers had to deal with the expectation that they would give members of their own race preferential treatment. On the other hand, black officers were the target of institutional racism. Alex found that African American officers adapted to these pressures in a range of ways, from denying that African American suspects should be treated differently from whites, to treating African American offenders more harshly than white offenders in order to prove their lack of bias. Alex offered several reasons why some African American officers are tougher on African American offenders: they desire acceptance from their white colleagues; they are particularly sensitive to any disrespect shown them by African American teenagers; and they view themselves as protectors of the African American

double marginality

The social burden African American police officers carry by virtue of being both minority group members and law enforcement officers.

Today there are more minority officers than ever before, but progress has not always come easy. Minority officers face difficulties even today. Here five Hoboken, New Jersey, police officers, Sgt. Edwin Pantoja (right), Detective Mario Novo, Detective George Fonseca, Detective James Perez, and Detective Cesar Olavarria (left) attend a news conference in Newark on October 24, 2007, as their attorney announces a discrimination lawsuit filed on their behalf against the Hoboken police department. The five officers charged that they endured constant racial slurs and intimidation because they are Hispanic and that superiors fabricated charges against them.

© AP Images/Mike Derer

community. Ironically, minority citizens may actually be more likely to accuse a minority officer of misconduct than to accuse white officers—a circumstance that underscores the difficult position the minority officer occupies in contemporary society.[9]

Today, 40 years after Alex's pioneering work was published, the minority community is still concerned that local police are racially and ethnically biased and use racial profiling to routinely stop young African American males and search their cars. Some cynics suggest that police have created a new form of crime: DWB, "driving while black."[10] Recent research by Stephen Rice and Alex Piquero revealed that African Americans living in New York City were three times more likely than Caucasians to perceive that police are racially biased, to believe that discrimination is still widespread, and to report that they had personally experienced police bias.[11] And this despite evidence that racial profiling has subsided or ended in many jurisdictions. (Racial profiling will be discussed again later in this chapter.)

There are also some positive developments. Minority police officers now seem as self-assured as white officers.[12] They may even be more willing than white officers to use their authority to take official action: The higher the percentage of black officers on the force, the higher the arrest rate for crimes such as assault.[13] However, minority officers appear to be experiencing some of the same problems and issues encountered by white officers.[14] They report feeling similar rates of job-related stress and strain stemming from the same types of stressors, such as family conflict.[15] Minority officers do report more stress when they consider themselves "tokens" or marginalized within the department.[16] They may also deal with stress in a somewhat different way than white officers: They are more likely to seek aid from fellow minority officers, whereas white officers are more likely to try to express their feelings to others, form social bonds, and try to get others to like them more.[17]

Women in Policing

In 1910, Alice Stebbins Wells became the first woman to hold the title of police officer (in Los Angeles) and to have arrest powers.[18] For more than half a century, female officers endured separate criteria for selection, were assigned menial tasks, and were denied the opportunity for advancement.[19] Some relief was gained with the passage of the 1964 Civil Rights Act and its subsequent amendments. Courts have consistently supported the addition of women to police forces by striking down entrance requirements that eliminated almost all female candidates but could not be proved to predict job performance, such as criteria involving height and upper-body strength.[20] (Women do not do as well as men on strength tests and are much more likely to fail the entrance physical than male recruits; critics contend that many of these tests do not reflect the actual tasks of police on the job.[21]) Nonetheless, the role of women in police work is still restricted by social and administrative barriers that have been difficult to remove. Today, as we have noted, women make up more than 11 percent of officers, up from 7.6 percent in 1987.[22]

Studies of policewomen indicate that they are still struggling for acceptance, believe that they do not receive equal credit for their job performance, and report that it is common for them to be sexually harassed by their coworkers.[23] One reason for this may be that many male police officers tend to view policing as an overtly masculine profession that is not appropriate for women. Surveys of male officers show that many do not think women can handle the physical requirements of the job as well as men can.[24] Female police officers may also be targeted for more disciplinary action by administrators and, if

National Organization of Black Law Enforcement Executives (NOBLE)

The **National Organization of Black Law Enforcement Executives (NOBLE)** has a website; you can access it at www.cengage.com/criminaljustice/siegel

© AP Images/Matt Rourke

Women have made great strides in their representation among the ranks of America's law enforcement agencies. Here a Philadelphia police officer draws her weapon during the search for a man police say shot a rookie officer in the face with a shotgun.

REALITY CHECK

MYTH OR REALITY? Male police officers believe that female police officers can perform the job as well as they can.

MYTH: Although there are certainly exceptions, survey research reveals that male officers tend to view policing as mainly a masculine profession.

Are these perceptions changing? What positive traits and characteristics do female officers bring to the job that male officers may not?

cited, are more likely to receive harsher punishments than male officers—that is, a greater percentage receive punishments more severe than a reprimand.[25] Considering the sometimes hostile reception they get from male colleagues and supervisors, it may not come as a surprise that female officers report significantly higher levels of job-related stress than male officers.[26]

Gender bias is certainly not supported by research on job performance, which indicates that female officers are highly successful police officers.[27] The evidence also shows that women are more likely than their male colleagues to receive support from the community and less likely to be charged with improper conduct.[28] Because female officers seem to have the ability to avoid violent encounters with citizens and to defuse potentially violent arrest situations, they are typically the target of fewer citizen complaints.[29]

MINORITY WOMEN • African American women, who account for less than 5 percent of police officers, occupy a unique status. In a study of African American policewomen serving in five large municipal departments, Susan Martin found that they perceive significantly more discrimination than both other female officers and African American male officers.[30] However, white policewomen were significantly more likely to perceive sexual discrimination than African American policewomen were.

African American policewomen often incur the hostility of both white women and African American men, who feel that their jobs may be threatened. On patrol, African American policewomen are treated differently than are white policewomen by male officers. The women in neither group are viewed as equals: White policewomen are more likely to be seen as protected and coddled, whereas African American policewomen are more likely to be viewed as passive, lazy, and unequal. In the station house, male officers show little respect for African American women, who face "widespread racial stereotypes as well as outright racial harassment."[31] African American women also report having difficult relationships with African American male officers; their relationships are strained by tensions and dilemmas "associated with sexuality and competition for desirable assignments and promotions."[32] Surprisingly, there was little unity among the female officers. Susan Martin summarizes the situation: "Despite changes in the past two decades, the idealized image of the representative of the forces of 'law and order' and protector who maintains 'the thin blue line' between 'them' and 'us' remains white and male."[33]

Despite these problems, the future of women in policing grows brighter every year.[34] Female officers want to remain in policing because it pays a good salary, offers job security, and is a challenging and exciting occupation.[35] These factors should continue to bring women to policing for years to come.

Educational Characteristics

Even though most law enforcement agencies still do not require recruits to have a college degree, the number that require advanced education in the hiring and promotion process is growing. Today about one-third of all police departments require at least some type of college for new recruits, more than three times the number in 1990.[36]

At one time, police administrators feared that educated cops might become frustrated with the time-in-rank system and leave policing to look for opportunities in the private sector. Yet research shows that officers holding college degrees are just as likely to remain police officers as those lacking an advanced degree.[37]

What type of major are police departments looking for? About half the surveyed departments expressed a preference for criminal justice majors, most often because of their enhanced knowledge of the entire criminal justice system and of issues that arise in policing.

What are the benefits of higher education for police officers? Better communication with the public, especially minority and ethnic groups, is believed to be one benefit. Educated officers write better and more clearly and are more likely to be promoted. Police administrators believe that education enables officers to perform more effectively, generate fewer citizen complaints, show more initiative in performing police tasks, and generally act more professionally.[38] In addition, educated officers are less likely to have disciplinary problems and are viewed as better decision makers.[39] Higher education is also associated with greater self-confidence.[40]

The Police Profession

All professions have unique characteristics that distinguish them from other occupations and institutions. Policing is no exception. Police experts have long sought to understand the unique nature of the police experience and to determine how the challenges of police work shape the field and its employees. In this section, some of the factors that make policing unique are discussed in detail.

Police Culture

cynicism
The belief that most people's actions are motivated solely by personal needs and selfishness.

blue curtain
The secretive, insulated police culture that isolates officers from the rest of society.

Police experts have found that the experience of becoming a police officer and the nature of the job itself cause most officers to band together in a police subculture, characterized by **cynicism**, clannishness, secrecy, and insulation from others in society—the so-called **blue curtain**. Police officers tend to socialize with one another and believe that their occupation cuts them off from relationships with civilians. Joining the police subculture means always having to stick up for fellow officers against outsiders; maintaining a tough, macho exterior; and distrusting the motives and behavior of outsiders.[41] The code of silence demands that officers never turn in their peers, even if they engage in corrupt or illegal practices.[42]

Some police experts have described the following core beliefs as the heart of the police culture today:

- **Police are the only real crime fighters.** The public wants the police officer to fight crime; other agencies, both public and private, only play at crime fighting.

- **No one else understands the real nature of police work.** Lawyers, academics, politicians, and the public in general have little concept of what it means to be a police officer.

REALITY CHECK

MYTH OR REALITY? Police officers feel that no one else understands what they do for a living.

REALITY: Many officers feel that the public neither understands nor fully appreciates what they do. There are exceptions to this view, but it remains a fairly common characteristic of police culture.

Police officers tend to move in the same circles. What are the implications of this for relations between police and the public and for policing effectiveness?

- **Loyalty to colleagues counts above everything else.** Police officers have to stick together, because everyone is out to get the police and make the job more difficult.

- **It is impossible to win the war against crime without bending the rules.** Courts have awarded criminal defendants too many civil rights.

- **Members of the public are basically unsupportive and unreasonably demanding.** People are quick to criticize police unless they themselves need police help.

- **Patrol work is the pits.** Detective work is glamorous and exciting.[43]

The forces that support a police culture are generally believed to develop out of on-the-job experiences. Most officers, both male and female, originally join police forces because they want to help people, fight crime, and have an interesting, exciting, prestigious career with a high degree of job security.[44] Recruits often find that the social reality of police work does not mesh with their original career goals. They are unprepared for the emotional turmoil and conflict that accompany police work today.

Some experts fear that the police culture divides officers from the people they serve and creates an "us against the world" mentality, an independent police culture in which violations of the law may result in stigmatization of offenders and lead to a leveling of sanctions against those who occupy the "other" status.[45] Criminals are referred to as "terrorists" and "predators," terms that suggest they are evil individuals eager to prey upon the poor and vulnerable. This vision may encourage and promote violence and brutality.

At first glance the existence of an independent police subculture seems damaging, but it may also have some benefits. Membership in the police culture helps recruits adjust to the rigors of police work and provides the emotional support needed for survival.[46] The culture encourages decisiveness in the face

© UpperCut Images/Getty Images

of uncertainty and the ability to make split-second judgments that may later be subject to extreme criticism. Officers who view themselves as crime fighters are the ones most likely to value solidarity and depend on the support and camaraderie of their fellow officers.[47] The police subculture encourages its members to draw a sharp distinction between good and evil. Officers, more than mere enforcers of the law, are warriors in the age-old battle between right and wrong.[48] Police officers perceive their working environment to be rife with danger, an outlook that reinforces cohesion among officers.[49] And because criminals—"predators"—represent a real danger, the police culture demands that its members be both competent and concerned with the safety of their peers and partners.[50]

In sum, the police culture has developed in response to the insulated, dangerous lifestyle of police officers. Policing is a dangerous occupation, and the unquestioned support and loyalty of their peers is not something officers could readily do without.[51] Although it is feared that an independent police culture may isolate police officers from the community and make them suspicious and mistrustful of the public they serve, it may also unify the police and improve the camaraderie and solidarity among fellow officers.

The Police Personality

To some commentators, the typical police personality can be described as dogmatic, authoritarian, and suspicious.[52] Cynicism has been found at all levels of policing (including chiefs of police) and throughout all stages of a police career.[53] These negative values and attitudes are believed to cause police officers to be secretive and isolated from the rest of society, weaving the blue curtain.[54]

How does cynicism develop? The police officer's working personality is shaped by constant exposure to danger and the need to use force and authority to defuse and control threatening situations.[55] Police feel suspicious of the public they serve and defensive about the actions of their fellow officers. There are two opposing viewpoints on the cause of this phenomenon. One is that police departments attract recruits who are by nature cynical, authoritarian, secretive, and so on.[56] Other experts maintain that socialization and experience on the police force itself cause these character traits to develop in officers. According to this view, as their experiences in the separate police culture develops, officers eventually embrace a unique set of personality traits that distinguishes them from the average citizen.[57]

Despite popular belief and some research support, efforts to find and identify a classic "police personality" have had mixed results. Although some research concludes that police values are different from those of the general adult population, other efforts reach an opposite conclusion: Some have found that police officers are actually more psychologically healthy than the general population, less depressed and anxious, and more social and assertive.[58] Police officers have been found to value such personality traits as warmth, flexibility, and emotion; these qualities are far removed from rigidity and cynicism.[59] Because research has found evidence supportive of both viewpoints, it is not possible to determine how the police personality develops—or even whether one actually exists.

Policing Style

Part of the socialization of a police officer is developing a working attitude, or style, through which to approach policing. For example, some police officers may view the job as a well-paid civil service position that emphasizes careful compliance with written departmental rules and procedures. Other officers may see themselves as part of the "thin blue line" that protects the public from wrongdoers. They will use any means to get the culprit, even if it involves planting evidence on an obviously guilty person who has so far escaped arrest.

Several studies have attempted to define and classify police styles into behavioral clusters. An examination of this literature suggests that four styles of police work seem to fit the current behavior patterns of most police agents: the crime fighter, the social agent, the law enforcer, and the watchman. These are described in Exhibit 6.1. Although officers who embrace a particular style of policing may emphasize one area of law enforcement over another, their daily activities are likely to require them to engage in some police duties they consider trivial or unimportant.

EXHIBIT 6.1

The Four Basic Styles of Policing

The Crime Fighter To the crime fighter, the most important aspects of police work are investigating serious crimes and apprehending criminals. Crime fighters focus on the victim and view effective police work as the only force that can keep society's "dangerous classes" in check. They are the thin blue line protecting society from murderers and rapists. They consider property crimes to be less significant and believe that such matters as misdemeanors, traffic control, and social service functions would be better handled by other agencies of government. The ability to investigate criminal behavior that poses a serious threat to life and safety, combined with the power to arrest criminals, separates a police department from other municipal agencies. Crime fighters see diluting these functions with minor social service and nonenforcement duties as harmful to police efforts to create a secure society.

The Social Agent The social agent believes that police should be involved in a wide range of activities without regard for their connection to law enforcement. Rather than viewing themselves as "criminal catchers," the social agents consider themselves as community problem solvers. They are troubleshooters who patch the holes that appear where the social fabric wears thin. They are happy to work with special-needs populations, such as the homeless, school kids, and those in need of emergency services. The social agent fits well in a community policing unit.

The Law Enforcer According to this view, duty is clearly set out in law. Law enforcers stress playing it "by the book." Since the police are specifically charged with apprehending all types of lawbreakers, they see themselves as generalized law enforcement agents. Although law enforcers may prefer working on serious crimes—because they are more intriguing and rewarding in terms of achievement, prestige, and status—they see the police role as one of enforcing all statutes and ordinances. They perceive themselves neither as community social workers nor as vengeance-seeking vigilantes: quite simply, they are professional law enforcement officers who perform the functions of detecting violations, identifying culprits, and taking the lawbreakers before a court. The law enforcer is devoted to the profession of police work and is the officer most likely to aspire to command rank.

The Watchman The watchman style is characterized by an emphasis on maintaining public order as the police goal, rather than law enforcement or general service. Watchmen choose to ignore many infractions and requests for service unless they believe that the social or political order is jeopardized. Juveniles are "expected" to misbehave and are best ignored or treated informally. Motorists will often be left alone if their driving does not endanger or annoy others. Vice and gambling are problems only when the currently accepted standards of public order are violated. Like the watchman of old, this officer takes action only when and if a problem arises. The watchman is the most passive officer, more concerned with retirement benefits than crime rates.

Sources: William Muir, *Police: Streetcorner Politicians* (Chicago; University of Chicago Press, 1977); James Q. Wilson, *Varieties of Police Behavior* (Cambridge, Mass.: Harvard University Press, 1968).

Police Discretion

Police have the ability to deprive people of their liberty, arrest them and take them away in handcuffs, and even use deadly force to subdue them. A critical aspect of this professional responsibility is the personal **discretion** each officer has in carrying out his or her responsibilities. Discretion can involve selective enforcement of the law—as occurs, for instance, when a vice squad plainclothes officer decides not to take action against a tavern that is serving drinks after hours. Patrol officers use discretion when they decide to arrest one suspect for disorderly conduct but to escort another home.

The majority of police officers use a high degree of personal discretion in carrying out daily tasks, sometimes referred to as "low-visibility decision making" in criminal justice.[60] This terminology suggests that, unlike members of almost every other criminal justice agency, police are neither regulated in their daily procedures by administrative scrutiny nor subject to judicial review (except when their behavior clearly violates an offender's constitutional rights). The public recognizes the right of police to exercise discretion, even if it means using force to control an unruly suspect while treating a more cooperative one with deference and respect.[61]

The concept of **emotional intelligence** has important implications for the study of police discretion. Defined as the "ability to monitor one's own and others' feelings and emotions, to discriminate among them and to use this information to guide one's thinking and actions,"[62] emotional intelligence is critically important for police officers. Being in tune with one's emotions, being able to act in an emotionally "mature fashion," and managing one's own mental state during difficult encounters can make all the difference in responding to the many situations that make policing a unique profession. Only recently has emotional intelligence training begun working its way into police training curricula.[63]

Researchers have identified a number of factors that affect police decision making.[64] The following sections describe the factors that influence police discretion and review suggestions for its control.

discretion
The use of personal decision making and choice in carrying out operations in the criminal justice system. For example, police discretion can involve deciding whether to make an arrest; prosecutorial discretion can involve deciding whether to accept a plea bargain.

emotional intelligence
"The ability to monitor one's own and others' feelings and emotions, to discriminate among them and to use this information to guide one's thinking and actions."

Whether a police officer makes an arrest may depend on how the individual officer views offense severity. Here officer Deon Joseph waits for a squad car to transport Marco Rodriguez to a detox center in the Skid Row area of downtown Los Angeles, rather than to jail.

© AP Images/Tracy Gitnick

Legal Factors

Police discretion is inversely related to the severity of the offense. This means police have far less personal discretion when they confront a suspect in a case involving murder or rape than when the offense is a simple assault or trespass.[65] For example, if a weapon is brandished or used, police are much more likely to respond with a formal arrest.[66] The likelihood of a police officer taking legal action, then, partly depends on how the individual officer views the severity of the offense.

Environmental Factors

The degree of discretion an officer will exercise is at least partially defined by the officer's living and working environment.[67] Police officers may work or dwell in a community culture that either tolerates eccentricities and personal freedoms or expects extremely conservative, professional, no-nonsense behavior on the part of its civil servants. Communities that are proactive and include progressive governmental institutions also may influence a police officer's discretion. Police officers in communities that provide training in domestic violence prevention and maintain local shelters for battered women are more likely to take action in cases involving spousal abuse.[68]

Departmental Factors

Where and how the department operates also shapes police practices. For example, officers are more likely to be proactive and use their arrest powers when they work in departments that are located in high-crime areas but have relatively few personnel.[69] In these departments, individual officers may believe they have to be proactive to compensate for the lack of resources. Departments also issue directives intended to influence police conduct, such as mandatory arrest policies for certain crimes.

Peer Factors

Police discretion is also subject to peer influence.[70] Police officers turn to their peers for both on-the-job advice and off-the-job companionship, essentially forming a subculture to provide a source of status, prestige, and reward. The peer group affects how police officers exercise discretion on two distinct levels. In an obvious, direct manner, other police officers dictate acceptable responses to street-level problems by providing or withholding approval in office discussions. Second, officers who take their job seriously and desire the respect and friendship of others will take their advice, abide by their norms, and seek out the most experienced and influential patrol officers on the force to adopt as behavior models.

Situational Factors

demeanor
The way in which a person outwardly manifests his or her personality.

Some research efforts find that police officers rely on **demeanor** (the attitude and appearance of the offender) in making decisions.[71] That is, if an offender is surly, talks back, or otherwise challenges the officer's authority, formal action is more likely to be taken.[72] Not everyone agrees, however. David Klinger, a police officer turned criminologist, maintains that demeanor may not be as much of a factor in shaping discretion as most others believe. Klinger believes that the average officer becomes used to surly demeanor and uncivil behavior, so it takes more than that to influence discretion.[73]

The way a crime or situation is encountered may also influence discretion. When a police officer stumbles on an altercation or break-in, the discretionary response may be different from the response when the officer is summoned by police radio. If an act has received official police recognition, such as the dispatch of a patrol car, police action must be taken or an explanation made as to why it was not. If a matter is brought to an officer's attention by a citizen observer, the officer can ignore the request and risk a complaint or take discretionary action.

Extralegal Factors

One oft-debated issue is whether police take race, class, and gender into account when making arrest decisions. Research results are mixed: Some studies show that the offender's age, gender, and racial characteristics are key determinants that shape the arrest process.[74] Others find that this unequal treatment is not a serious problem. For example, the gender gap in police arrests is closing; women are getting arrested for certain offenses (such as drunk driving) more than they ever have been in the past.[75]

Victim characteristics also appear to influence police action. For example, police are more willing to make an arrest when the *victim* is older, white, affluent, and so on.[76] Neighborhood factors matter, as well. Related to this is the relationship between the parties. If the victim and the offender know one another, there is less of a chance that an arrest will be made.[77]

One significant issue is whether race plays a role in the decision to stop, question, and search motorists, a practice referred to as **racial profiling**. Table 6.1 shows data from the most recent survey on police–citizen contacts. Although this data shows that the police stop Hispanic, African American, and Caucasian motorists at similar rates, some researchers have found that police officers routinely stop minority motorists at a rate far greater than their representation in the driving pool.[78] There is also evidence that minorities are searched more often than whites.[79] Yet a number of researchers have found little to no evidence of racial profiling.[80] Some argue that it can even be beneficial. How could profiling be beneficial? Two Harvard scholars, Mathias Risse and Richard Zeckhauser, have argued that there is a significant correlation between membership in certain racial groups and the propensity to commit certain crimes.[81]

racial profiling
The practice of police targeting minority groups because of a belief that they are more likely to be engaged in criminal activity.

TABLE 6.1

Drivers Stopped and Searched by Police, by Race

Race/Hispanic origin of resident	Percentage of drivers stopped by police		Percentage of drivers searched by police	
	2002	**2005**	**2002**	**2005**
Total	8.8%	8.8%	5.0%	4.8%
White	8.8	8.9	3.5	3.6
Black/African American	9.2	8.1	10.2	9.5
Hispanic/Latino	8.6	8.9	11.4	8.8

SOURCE: Matthew Durose, Erica Smith, and Patrick Langan, *Contacts Between Police and the Public, 2005* (Washington, D.C.: Bureau of Justice Statistics, 2007), www.ojp.usdoj.gov/bjs/pub/pdf/cpp05.pdf.

Problems of Policing

Law enforcement is not an easy job. The role ambiguity, social isolation, and threat of danger present in "working the street" are the police officer's constant companions. What effects do these strains have on police? This section discusses four of the most significant problems: job stress, fatigue, violence, and corruption.

Stress

The complexity of their role, the need to exercise prudent discretion, the threat of having to use violence and of having violence used against them, and isolation from the rest of society all take a toll on law enforcement officers. It is not surprising, then, that police officers experience tremendous stress, a factor that leads some to alcoholism, depression, and even suicide. There is evidence that police officers are all too often involved in marital disputes and even incidents of domestic violence that may be linked to stress.[82] These developments are not lost on police officers, many of whom feel significant amounts of job-related stress, a condition that may undermine their enthusiasm and commitment.[83] Stress and burnout become part of the job. Stress may not be constant, but at some time during their career (usually the middle years) most officers will feel the effects of stress.[84]

CAUSES OF STRESS ● A number of factors have been associated with job stress.[85] The pressure of being on duty 24 hours a day leads to stress and emotional detachment from both work and public needs. Policing is a dangerous profession, and officers are at risk for many forms of job-related accidental deaths. Stress has been related to internal conflict with administrative policies that deny officers support and a meaningful role in decision making. Some

Terrance Hough Jr. awaits statements from victims' families on May 22, 2008, in Cleveland, after he was sentenced to life in prison without chance of parole for killing three people over late-night Fourth of July fireworks. Officials and experts say some police officers and firefighters can be susceptible to the high stress inherent in putting one's life on the line to protect others and constantly dealing with human tragedy.

© AP Images/*The Plain Dealer,* Peggy Turbett

officers may become stressed when they are forced to adapt to the demands of community-oriented policing but are skeptical about the utility or effectiveness of this change in policy.[86] In addition, police suffer stress in their personal lives when they "bring the job home" or when their work hours are shifted, causing family disruptions.[87] Those who feel alienated from family and friends at home are more likely to feel stress on the job.[88]

Other stressors include poor training, substandard equipment, inadequate pay, lack of opportunity, job dissatisfaction, role conflict, exposure to brutality, and fears about competence, success, and safety.[89] Some officers may feel stress because they believe that the court system favors the rights of the criminal and handcuffs the police; others may be sensitive to a perceived lack of support from governmental officials and the general public.[90] Some officers even believe that their superiors care little about their welfare.[91]

The effects of stress can be shocking. Police work has been related to both physical and psychological ailments.[92] Police have a high rate of premature death caused by such conditions as heart disease and diabetes. They also experience a disproportionate number of divorces and other marital problems. Research indicates that police officers in some departments, but not all, have higher suicide rates than the general public.[93] Police who feel stress may not be open to adopting new ideas and programs such as community policing.[94]

COMBATING STRESS ● Research efforts have shown that the more support police officers get in the workplace, the lower their feelings of stress and anxiety.[95] Consequently, departments have attempted to fight job-related stress by training officers to cope with its effects. Today stress training includes diet information, biofeedback, relaxation and meditation, and exercise. Many departments include stress management as part of an overall wellness program also designed to promote physical and mental health, fitness, and good nutrition.[96] Some programs have included family members: They may be better able to help the officer cope if they fully understand the difficulties of police work. Total wellness programming enhances the physical and emotional well-being of officers by emphasizing preventive physical and psychological measures.[97] And because police are aware of the many benefits of their job and enjoy the quality of life it provides, stress reduction programs can help officers focus on the positive aspects of police work.[98]

Fatigue

© UpperCut Images/Getty Images

Nearly everyone has been tired at work from time to time. But whereas on-the-job sleepiness is inconsequential for many workers, it can lead to disaster for others. No one wants airline pilots to fall asleep, and the prospect of a truck driver sleeping behind the wheel is equally disturbing. What about a police officer? A police officer who is overly tired may be at a higher risk of acting inappropriately or being injured on the job.[99]

The problem of "tired cops"[100] has largely been overlooked, but it should not be.[101] Police officers often work lengthy shifts with unpredictable hours. The *Boston Globe* investigated one agency and found that 16 officers worked more than 80 hours in a week.[102] One even worked 130 hours! Although it is difficult to fault anyone for seeking overtime pay, too much work can lead to disaster. Here are some examples:

● A Michigan police officer working nearly 24 hours straight crashes his cruiser while chasing a fleeing motorist. He is critically injured.

- In California, a sheriff's deputy working alone drifts off a deserted highway and is killed instantly when his patrol car crashes into a tree.
- An officer in Florida, who has had trouble staying awake, runs a red light in her patrol car and crashes into a van driven by a deputy sheriff, injuring him severely.
- A police officer driving home from working in Ohio nods off at the wheel, begins swerving in and out of traffic, and runs off the road, striking and killing a man jogging down the sidewalk.[103]

CONTROLLING FATIGUE • What can be done to control police fatigue? One option is for administrators to make special efforts, during scheduling, to ensure that officers do not work too much overtime. Another is for administrators to adopt policies that place limitations on second jobs. Many officer moonlight as security guards, which may affect their on-the-job performance. A recent government report offered several other recommendations for limiting fatigue.

Violence and Brutality

There is evidence that only a small proportion of officers are continually involved in use-of-force incidents. Why do these cops continually get involved in violent confrontations? Aggressive cops may overreact to the stress of police work and at the same time feel socially isolated. They believe that the true source of their frustration is beyond their reach, so they take their frustrations out on readily available targets: vulnerable people in their immediate environment.[104]

What kind of police officer gets involved in problem behavior? Are some officers "chronic offenders"? Research seems to show that a few officers are in fact chronic offenders who account for a significant portion of all citizen complaints. The officers receiving the bulk of complaints tend to be young and less experienced.[105] Efforts to deal with these "problem cops" are now being undertaken in police departments around the nation.

REALITYCHECK

MYTH OR REALITY? Veteran police officers receive the most citizen complaints.

MYTH: Younger and less-experienced officers receive the most complaints.

Why do younger and less-experienced officers receive the most complaints? Can training solve the problem? If so, what kind of training, academy or on-the-job?

CURBING VIOLENCE • Because incidents of brutality undermine efforts to build a bridge between police and the public, police departments around the United States have instituted specialized training programs to reduce them. A number of larger departments are instituting early warning systems to change the behavior of individual officers who have been identified as having performance problems. In most systems, problem officers are identified by their behavior profiles: citizen complaints, firearm discharge and use-of-force reports, civil litigation, incidents of resisting arrest, and high-speed pursuits and vehicular damage. The initial intervention generally consists of a review by the officer's immediate supervisor, who advises the officer of the sanctions he faces if problems continue; some cases are referred to counseling, training, or police psychologists. Evaluations of early warning programs indicate that they are quite successful.[106]

Some departments have developed administrative policies that emphasize limiting the use of force and containing armed offenders until specially trained backup teams are sent to take charge of the situation. Administrative policies have been found to be an effective control on use of deadly force, and their influence can be enhanced if they are clearly supported by the chief of police.[107]

Some cities are taking an aggressive, proactive stance to curb violent cops. Since 1977 the New York Police Department has been operating a Force-Related Integrity Testing program in which undercover officers pose as angry citizens in elaborate sting operations intended to weed out officers with a propensity for violence. In a typical encounter, officers responding to a radio call on a domestic dispute confront an aggressive husband who spews hatred at everyone around, including the police. The "husband" is actually an undercover officer from the Internal Affairs Bureau, who is testing whether the officers, some of whom have a history of civilian complaints, will respond to verbal abuse with threats or violence. The NYPD conducts about 600 sting operations each year to test the integrity of its officers; several dozen are devoted to evaluating the conduct of officers with a history of abuse complaints.[108]

Perhaps the greatest factors in controlling the use of **police brutality** are the threat of civil judgments against individual officers who use excessive force, police chiefs who ignore or condone violent behavior, and the expectations that prevail in the cities and towns in which they are employed.

Corruption

Ever since their creation, U.S. police departments have wrestled with the problem of controlling illegal and unprofessional behavior by their officers. **Corruption** pervaded the American police when the early departments were first formed. In the nineteenth century, police officers systematically ignored violations of laws related to drinking, gambling, and prostitution in return for regular payoffs. Some actually entered into relationships with professional criminals, especially pickpockets. Illegal behavior was tolerated in return for goods or information. Police officers helped politicians gain office by allowing electoral fraud to flourish; some senior officers sold promotions to higher rank in the department.[109] Although most police officers are not corrupt, the few who are dishonest bring discredit to the entire profession.

VARIETIES OF CORRUPTION ● Police deviance can include a number of activities. In a general sense, it involves misuse of authority by police officers in a manner designed to yield personal gain for themselves or others.[110] However, debate continues over whether a desire for personal gain is an essential part of corruption. Some experts argue that police misconduct also involves such issues as the unnecessary use of force, unreasonable searches, or an immoral personal life and that these should be considered just as serious as corruption motivated by economic gain.

Scholars have attempted to create typologies categorizing the forms that the abuse of police powers can take. When investigating corruption among police officers in New York City, the **Knapp Commission** classified abusers into two categories: **meat eaters** and **grass eaters**. Meat eaters aggressively misuse police power for personal gain by demanding bribes, threatening legal action, or cooperating with criminals. In contrast, grass eaters accept payoffs when their everyday duties place them in a position to "look the other way."

Other police experts have attempted to create models to better understand police corruption. It may be possible to divide police corruption into four major categories:[111]

- *Internal corruption.* This corruption takes place among police officers themselves, involving both the bending of departmental rules and the outright performance of illegal acts.

---

police brutality
Usually involves such actions as the use of abusive language, the unnecessary use of force or coercion, threats, prodding with nightsticks, stopping and searching people to harass them, and so on.

corruption
Exercising legitimate discretion for improper reasons or using illegal means to achieve approved goals.

Knapp Commission
A public body that led an investigation into police corruption in New York and uncovered a widespread network of payoffs and bribes.

meat eaters
A term for police officers who actively solicit bribes and vigorously engage in corrupt practices.

grass eaters
A term for police officers who accept payoffs when everyday duties place them in a position to "look the other way."

Bernard Kerik, former NYPD commissioner, is escorted away from a federal courthouse in White Plains, New York, in 2007. He appeared in court after being indicted on conspiracy, corruption, and tax evasion charges.

© AP Images/Craig Ruttle

- *Selective enforcement or nonenforcement.* This occurs when police abuse or exploit their discretion. If an officer frees a drug dealer in return for valuable information, *that is considered a legitimate use of discretion*; if the officer does so for money, that is an abuse of police power.
- *Active criminality.* This is participation by police in serious criminal behavior. Police may use their positions of trust and power to commit the very crimes they are entrusted with controlling.
- *Bribery and extortion.* This includes practices in which law enforcement roles are exploited specifically to raise money. Bribery is initiated by the citizen; extortion is initiated by the officer.

CAUSES OF CORRUPTION ● No single explanation satisfactorily accounts for the various forms the abuse of power takes. One view holds that policing tends to attract individuals who do not have the financial means to maintain a coveted middle-class lifestyle. As they develop the cynical, authoritarian police personality, accepting graft seems an all-too-easy method of achieving financial security. A second view is that the wide discretion police enjoy, coupled with low visibility among the public and their own supervisors, makes them likely candidates for corruption. A third perspective holds that corruption is a function of society's ambivalence toward many forms of vice-related criminal behavior that police officers are sworn to control. Unenforceable laws governing moral standards promote corruption because they create large groups with an interest in undermining law enforcement. These include consumers who do not want to be deprived of their chosen form of recreation—people who gamble, wish to drink after the legal closing hour, or patronize prostitutes.

CONTROL OF CORRUPTION ● How can police misconduct be controlled? One approach is to strengthen the internal administrative review process in police departments. A strong and well-supported internal affairs division

---

EXHIBIT 6.2

Models of Police Review Boards

Class I agencies are responsible for receiving and investigating citizen complaints.

Class II agencies review complaint investigations conducted by the police department.

Class III agencies hear appeals of complaint investigations and dispositions made by the police department.

Class IV agencies audit or monitor the police department's complaint process.

Class V is a new form of oversight. It involves non-sworn persons employed by the police department who have some input into or control over the complaint process.

Source: Based on Samuel Walker, *The New World of Police Accountability* (Thousand Oaks, Calif.: Sage Publishing, 2005).

---

has been linked to lowered corruption rates.[112] Another approach, instituted by then New York Commissioner Patrick Murphy in the wake of the Knapp Commission, is the *accountability system*. This holds that supervisors at each level are directly accountable for the illegal behaviors of the officers under them. Consequently, a commander can be demoted or forced to resign if someone under his or her command is found guilty of corruption.[113] Close scrutiny by a department, however, can lower officer morale and create the impression that the officers' own supervisors distrust them.

Another approach is to create outside review boards or special prosecutors, such as the Mollen Commission in New York and the Christopher Commission in Los Angeles, to investigate reported incidents of corruption. However, outside investigators and special prosecutors are often limited by their lack of intimate knowledge of day-to-day operations. As a result, they depend on the testimony of a few officers who are willing to cooperate, either to save themselves from prosecution or because they have a compelling moral commitment. Outside evaluators also face the problem of the blue curtain, which is quickly drawn when police officers feel their department is under scrutiny.

Some jurisdictions have even developed review boards that monitor police behavior and tactics and investigate civilian complaints (see Exhibit 6.2). Although police agencies in some communities have embraced citizen reviews, others find them troublesome. Departmental opposition is most likely when oversight procedures represent outside interference, oversight staff lack experience with and understanding of police work, and/or oversight processes are unfair. Despite serious reservations about citizen oversight, many law enforcement administrators have identified positive outcomes from having a review board in place. These include improving community relations, enhancing an agency's ability to police itself, and (most important) improving an agency's policies and procedures. Citizen oversight bodies can recommend changes in the way the department conducts its internal investigations into alleged misconduct and can also suggest ways to improve department policies governing officer behavior.[114]

Use of Force

How much force is being used by the police in the United States today?[115]
Despite some highly publicized incidents that get a lot of media attention, the research data shows that the use of force is not very common. The most recent national (2005) survey on police contacts with civilians, sponsored by the federal government, sheds some light on this issue.[116] Among the survey's most important findings:

REALITY CHECK

MYTH OR REALITY? Thousands of people are fatally shot by police each year.

MYTH: Fatal police shootings are very rare. On the order of 250–300 people are fatally shot each year.

Media portrayals, in the news and television, make it seem that police shootings are more common. Why? What are the implications for police work of a view that police shootings are more common than they really are?

- An estimated 19 percent of U.S. residents age 16 or older had a face-to-face contact with a police officer.
- Contact between police and the public was more common among males, whites, and younger residents.
- Overall, about 9 out of 10 persons who had contact with police in 2005 felt the police acted properly.
- An estimated 2 percent of people stopped by police had force used or threatened against them during their most recent contact.
- Blacks and Hispanics experienced police use of force at higher rates than whites.

The data indicates that (a) relatively few contacts with police and the public involve physical force, but (b) there seem to be race and ethnic differences in the rate at which force is applied. As Table 6.2 shows, half of the force incidents involved more than scuffling or shouting. And even though African Americans (82%) were less likely than whites (91%) to feel that the police acted properly during a contact, the great majority of citizens of all races considered police behavior to be appropriate given the circumstances of the contact.

RACE AND FORCE ● The routine use of force may be diminishing, but debate continues over whether police are more likely to get rough with minority suspects.

TABLE 6.2

Police Response in Encounters with Citizens in which Use of Force was Reported

Type of force used or threatened by police	Percent
Pushed or grabbed	43
Kicked or hit	9
Sprayed chemical/Pepper spray	3
Pointed gun	15
Used other force	10
Police threatened to use force	27
Shouted or cursed at by police	10
Type of force used or threatened was not reported	7

Source: Matthew Durose, Erica Smith, and Patrick Langan, *Contacts Between Police and the Public: Findings from the 2005 National Survey* (Washington, D.C.: Bureau of Justice Statistics, 2007), www.ojp.usdoj.gov/bjs/pub/pdf/cpp05.pdf. Percentages do not sum to 100 because some people reported, in cases where force was used, that officers used more than one type of force.

The national survey on police contacts with civilians found that African Americans and Hispanics were more likely than whites to experience police threat or use of force as a consequence of police contact, to be handcuffed, and/or to be searched (Table 6.3). Cities with large black populations also experience the highest amount of lethal violence by police.[117] Considering this evidence, it is not surprising that surveys of minority group members show they are more likely than majority group members to disapprove of the police use of force.[118] Minority citizens are much more likely to claim that police "hassle them"—stop them or watch them closely when they have done nothing wrong.[119]

As troubling as *any* evidence of racial disparity is, such national data must be interpreted with caution. Race may be one among many factors that affect the outcome of police–citizen encounters. In some research efforts, it was found that race actually played an insignificant role in the decision to use force and that a suspect's immediate behavior was much more important.[120] William Terrill studied 3,544 police–suspect encounters and found that situational factors often influence the extent to which force is applied. Use of force seems to escalate when a police officer gives a suspect a second chance (i.e., "dump the beer out of your car and I'll let you go") but the suspect hesitates or defies the order. People who resist police orders or actually grapple with officers are much more likely to be the target of force than those who are respectful, passive, and noncombative. Members of certain subpopulations, such as intravenous drug users, may be more likely than the general population to perceive or experience police coercion and violence.[121] Moreover, the general public seems to understand the situational use of force: Even people who condemn police violence are more supportive of its use if the officer is in danger or a suspect is confrontational.[122] So the evidence suggests that suspect behavior may be a more important determinant of force than race or ethnicity.

Deadly Force

As it is commonly used, the term **deadly force** refers to the actions of a police officer who shoots and kills a suspect who flees from arrest, assaults a victim, or attacks an officer.[123] The justification for the use of deadly force can be traced to English common law, in which almost every criminal offense was a felony and bore the death penalty. The use of deadly force in the course of arresting a felon was considered expedient, saving the state the trouble of conducting a trial (the "fleeing-felon rule").[124]

deadly force
Force that is likely to cause death or serious bodily harm.

TABLE 6.3

Characteristics of Contacts with Police in Which Force Was Used, by Race/Hispanic Origin

Characteristic of contact involving force	Total	White	Black/ African American	Hispanic/ Latino
Searched the resident	54%	48%	53%	72%
Handcuffed the resident	41	37	41	50
Arrested the resident	32	31	27	38
Actions of resident may have caused police to use force	17	19	12	17
Estimated number	707,520	401,610	186,060	97,190

SOURCE: Matthew Durose, Erica Smith, and Patrick Langan, *Contacts Between Police and the Public: Findings from the 2005 National Survey* (Washington, D.C.: Bureau of Justice Statistics, 2007), www.ojp.usdoj.gov/bjs/pub/pdf/cpp05.pdf.

The term "deadly force" refers to the actions of a police officer who shoots and kills a suspect who is fleeing from arrest, assaults a victim, or attacks an officer. Here police assist a victim of an attempted robbery in Kokomo, Indiana. One man was wounded by police, and another was arrested following a four-hour standoff at a home, authorities said. Police said the standoff began about 3:30 P.M., when an officer on patrol was flagged down by a person reporting an armed robbery.

© AP Images/Kokomo Tribune, Tim Bath

suicide by cop

A form of suicide in which a person acts in an aggressive manner with police officers in order to induce them to shoot to kill.

suicide by cop

Want to read more about **suicide by cop**? Go to www.cengage.com/criminaljustice/siegel

Although the media depict hero cops in a constant stream of deadly shoot-outs in which scores of bad guys are killed, the actual number of people killed by the police each year is usually between 250 and 300.[125] And some of these shootings may even be precipitated by the target as a form of suicide.[126] This tragic event has become so common that the term **suicide by cop** has been coined to denote victim-precipitated killings by police.[127]

Although the police use of deadly force may not be as common as previously believed, it remains a central part of the police role. It is difficult to get an accurate figure, but at least 6,600 civilians have been killed by the police since 1976, and the true number is probably much higher.[128]

Factors Related to Police Shootings

Is police use of deadly force a random occurrence, or are social, legal, and environmental factors associated with it? The following patterns have been related to police shootings:

- *Exposure to violence.* The community violence hypothesis maintains that areas with high violence levels will also have higher numbers of police killings of citizens. A strong association has been found between police use of force and "gun density" (the proportion of suicides and murders committed with a gun).[129] Most police shootings involve armed suspects who either attack the officer or are engaged in violent crimes.

- *National crime rates.* A number of studies have found that fatal police shootings are closely related to reported violent crime rates and criminal homicide rates; police officers kill civilians at a higher rate in years when the general level of violence in the nation is higher.[130] The perception of danger may contribute to the use of violent means for self-protection.[131]

- *Community threat levels.* According to the threat hypothesis, more police are killed in cities with a large underclass.[132] David Jacobs and Jason Carmichael found that cities with the greatest economic and political subordination of minority group members are also the location of the highest number of officers killed and wounded.[133] Police violence rates are highest in cities where members of the minority community experience a distinct economic disadvantage compared to the white majority.

- *Administrative factors.* The philosophy, policies, and practices of individual police chiefs and departments significantly influence the police use of deadly force.[134] Departments that emphasize restrictive policies on the use of force and exert more control over officer behavior generally have lower shooting rates than those that favor tough law enforcement and encourage officers to shoot when necessary. In this vein, officers who have not been adequately trained to deal with emergency situations may respond with unnecessary violence; training can help reduce these incidents by teaching proper preparations.[135]

Controlling Deadly Force

Because the police use of deadly force is such a serious issue, ongoing efforts have been made to control it. One of the most difficult issues in controlling the problem was the continued use of the fleeing-felon rule in a number of states. In 1985 the Supreme Court outlawed the indiscriminate use of deadly force with its decision in *Tennessee v. Garner*. In this case, the Court ruled that the use of deadly force against apparently unarmed and nondangerous fleeing felons is an illegal seizure of their person under the Fourth Amendment. Deadly force may not be used unless it is necessary to prevent the escape and the officer has probable cause to believe that the suspect poses a significant threat of death or serious injury to the officer or others. The majority opinion stated that where the suspect poses no immediate threat to the officer and no threat to others, the harm resulting from failing to apprehend the suspect does not justify the use of deadly force to do so: "A police officer may not seize an unarmed, nondangerous suspect by shooting him dead."[136]

Garner applied to deadly force. What about nondeadly force? In *Graham v. Connor*, the Supreme Court ruled that issues related to nondeadly force must be judged from the standpoint of a reasonable officer.[137] For example, say an officer is approached in a threatening manner by someone wielding a knife. The assailant fails to stop when warned and is killed by the officer, but it turns out later that the shooting victim was deaf and could not hear the officer's command. The officer would not be held liable if, at the time of the incident, he had no way of knowing the person's disability.

Individual state jurisdictions still control police shooting policy. Some states have adopted statutory policies that restrict the police use of violence. Others have upgraded training in the use of force. The Federal Law Enforcement Training Center has developed the FLETC use-of-force model, illustrated in Figure 6.1, to teach officers the proper method to escalate force in response

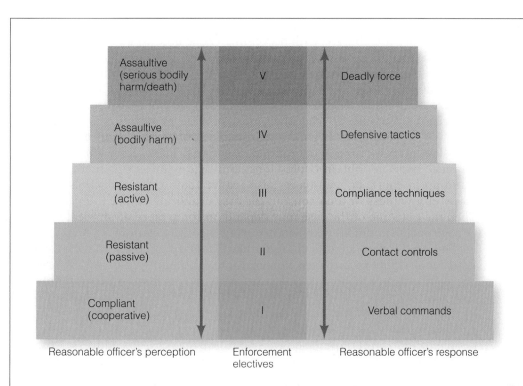

The Federal Law Enforcement Center's Use-of-Force Model

Source: Franklin Graves and Gregory Connor, Federal Law Enforcement Training Center, Glynco, Georgia.

Assaultive (serious bodily harm/death)	V	Deadly force
Assaultive (bodily harm)	IV	Defensive tactics
Resistant (active)	III	Compliance techniques
Resistant (passive)	II	Contact controls
Compliant (cooperative)	I	Verbal commands

Reasonable officer's perception   Enforcement electives   Reasonable officer's response

FIGURE   6 . 1

to the threat they face. As the figure shows, resistance ranges from compliant and cooperative to assaultive with the threat of serious bodily harm or death. Officers are taught via lecture, demonstration, computer-based instruction, and training scenarios to assess the suspect's behavior and apply an appropriate and corresponding amount of force.[138]

Another way to control police shootings is through internal review and policymaking by police administrative review boards. For example, since 1972, the New York City Police Department has conducted an internal investigation any time an officer's weapon is discharged (within the exception of training situations). Several dispositions are possible. These can range from a conclusion that the shooting was in accordance with law and policy, all the way to termination and even criminal prosecution (if the prosecutor feels criminal charges are merited). The review board approach is controversial because it can mean that the department recommends that one of its own officers be turned over for criminal prosecution.[139]

Less-Lethal Weapons

In the last few years, about a thousand local police forces have started using so-called **less-lethal weapons** to subdue certain suspects. Some of the most widely used nonlethal weapons are wood, rubber, or polyurethane bullets shot out of modified 37-mm pistols or 12-gauge shotguns. At short distances, officers use pepper spray and Tasers, which deliver electric shocks with long wire tentacles, producing intense muscle spasms. Other technologies still in development include guns that shoot giant nets, guns that squirt sticky glue, and lights that can temporarily blind a suspect, among many others.

Recent research efforts indicate that nonlethal weapons may help reduce police use of force.[140] Greater effort must be made to regulate these nonlethal weapons and create effective policies for their use.[141]

Police and the Rule of Law

The police are charged with preventing crime and, when crime does occur, with investigating the case, identifying the culprit, and making an arrest, all the while gathering sufficient evidence to convict the culprit at trial. To carry out these tasks, police officers need to be able to search for evidence, to seize items such as guns and drugs, and to question suspects, witnesses, and victims, because at trial, they must provide prosecutors with sufficient evidence to prove guilt "beyond a reasonable doubt." This requirement means that soon after a crime is committed, they must make every effort to gather physical evidence, obtain confessions, and take witness statements that will stand up in court. Police officers also realize that evidence such as the testimony of a witness or a co-conspirator may evaporate before the trial begins. Then the outcome of the case may depend on some piece of physical evidence or a suspect's statement taken early during the investigation.

The need for police officers to gather evidence can conflict with the constitutional rights of citizens. For example, although police might prefer a free hand to search homes and cars for evidence, the Fourth Amendment restricts police activities by limiting searches and seizures to those deemed "reasonable." Likewise, when police wish to vigorously interrogate a suspect, they must honor the Fifth Amendment's prohibition against forcing people to incriminate themselves. The following sections address some key areas in which police operations have been restricted or curtailed by the courts.

Lectric Law Library's stacks site

The **'Lectric Law Library's stacks site** contains an informative essay on deadly force; access it via

www.cengage.com/criminaljustice/siegel

---

less-lethal weapons
Weapons designed to disable or immobilize rather than kill criminal suspects.

Interrogation and Confessions

After an arrest is made, police want to interrogate suspects, hoping they will confess to a crime, name co-conspirators, or make incriminating statements that can be used against them in court. But the Fifth Amendment guarantees people the right to be free from self-incrimination. The courts have used this phrase to prohibit law enforcement agents from using physical or psychological coercion while interrogating suspects to get them to confess or give information. Confessions obtained from defendants through coercion, force, trickery, or promises of leniency are inadmissible because their trustworthiness is questionable.

THE *MIRANDA* RULE ● In 1966, in the case of *Miranda v. Arizona*, the Supreme Court created objective standards for questioning by police after a defendant has been taken into custody.[142] Custody occurs when a person is not free to walk away, such as when an individual is arrested. The Court maintained that before the police can question a person who has been arrested or is in custody, they must inform the individual of her or his Fifth Amendment right to be free from self-incrimination. This is accomplished by the police issuing what is known as the ***Miranda* warning**, which informs the suspect that

- He has the right to remain silent.
- If he makes a statement, it can be used against him in court.
- He has the right to consult an attorney and to have the attorney present at the time of the interrogation.
- If he cannot afford an attorney, one will be appointed by the state.

If the defendant is not given the *Miranda* warning before the investigation, the evidence obtained from the interrogation cannot be admitted at trial. An accused person can waive his or her *Miranda* rights at any time. For the waiver to be effective, however, the state must first show that the defendant was aware of all the *Miranda* rights and must then prove that the waiver was made with the full knowledge of constitutional rights. People who cannot understand the *Miranda* warning because of their age, mental handicaps, or language problems cannot be legally questioned without their attorney present; if they *can* understand their rights, they may be questioned.[143]

Once the suspect asks for an attorney, all questioning must stop unless the attorney is present. And if the criminal suspect has invoked his or her *Miranda* rights, police officials cannot reinitiate interrogation in the absence of counsel, even if the accused has consulted with an attorney in the meantime.[144]

***Miranda* warning**
The requirement that police officers inform suspects subjected to custodial interrogation that they have a constitutional right to remain silent, that their statements can later be used against them in court, that they can have an attorney present to help them, and that the state will pay for an attorney if they cannot afford to hire one.

MYTH OR REALITY? The police are required to advise all arrested persons of their *Miranda* rights.

MYTH: *Miranda* rights need be read only when custody (such as arrest) is coupled with interrogation.

Police departments may adopt more restrictive policies, however, requiring *Miranda* warnings any time a person is arrested. Should the *Miranda* warnings be read every time a person is arrested?

THE *MIRANDA* RULE TODAY ● The Supreme Court has used case law to define the boundaries of the *Miranda* warning since its inception. Although statements made by suspects who were not given the *Miranda* warning, or who received it improperly, cannot be used against them in a court of law, it is possible to use statements and the evidence they produce in some well-defined instances. Here are the rules resulting from several important *Miranda*-related Supreme Court decisions:

- Evidence obtained in violation of the *Miranda* warning can be used by the government to impeach defendants' testimony during trial, if they perjure themselves.[145]

- It is permissible to use information provided by a suspect who has not been given the *Miranda* warning that leads to the seizure of incriminating evidence if the evidence would have been obtained anyway by other means or sources.[146]
- Initial errors by police in getting statements do not make subsequent statements inadmissible; a subsequent *Miranda* warning that is properly given can "cure the condition" that made the initial statements inadmissible.[147]
- The admissions of mentally impaired defendants can be admitted in evidence as long as the police acted properly and there is a "preponderance of the evidence" that the defendants understood the meaning of *Miranda*.[148]
- A suspect can be questioned in the field without a *Miranda* warning if the information the police seek is needed to protect public safety; in an emergency, suspects can be asked where they hid their weapons.[149] This is known as the public safety doctrine.
- Suspects need not be aware of all the possible outcomes of waiving their rights for the *Miranda* warning to be considered properly given.[150]
- An attorney's request to see the defendant does not affect the validity of the defendant's waiver of the right to counsel; police misinformation to an attorney does not affect waiver of *Miranda* rights.[151]
- A suspect who makes an ambiguous reference to an attorney during questioning, such as "Maybe I should talk to an attorney," is not protected under *Miranda;* the police may continue their questioning.[152]
- If police intentionally mislead suspects by questioning them before giving them a *Miranda* warning, their statements made after the warning is given are inadmissible in court. The "*Miranda* rule would be frustrated were the police permitted to undermine its meaning and effect."[153]
- A voluntary statement given in the absence of the *Miranda* warning can be used to obtain evidence that can be used at trial. Failure to give the warning does not make seizure of evidence illegal per se.[154]
- Failure to give a suspect a *Miranda* warning is not illegal unless the case actually becomes a criminal matter.[155] A "criminal case" at the very least requires the initiation of legal proceedings, and police questioning by itself does not constitute such a case.

Miranda is now a police (and a prime-time television) institution. It is not surprising that today police administrators who in the past might have been wary of the restrictions forced by *Miranda* now actually favor its use.[156] Yet in spite of its acceptance, critics have called the *Miranda* decision incomprehensible and difficult to administer. How can one tell when a confession is truly voluntary or when it has been produced by pressure and coercion? Aren't all police interrogations essentially coercive?[157] To ensure that *Miranda* rules are being followed, many departments now routinely videotape interrogations.[158] Nonetheless, the *Miranda* decision continues to be a source of debate. For some comparative perspective on this subject, see the International Justice feature on page 201.

Search and Seizure

When conducting investigations, police officers want to collect evidence, seize it, and carry it away. They may wish to enter a suspect's home; look for evidence of a crime, such as bloody clothes, drugs, the missing money, or a weapon; seize the evidence; and store it in the evidence room so it can later be used at trial. The manner in which police may seize evidence is governed by the search-and-seizure requirements of the Fourth Amendment of the U.S. Constitution, which was designed by the framers to protect a criminal suspect from unreasonable searches and seizures. Under normal circumstances, no search or seizure undertaken without a search warrant is lawful.

ℐnternational ℐustice

Interrogation Law in Three Other Countries

The Fifth Amendment states that those suspected of criminal activity cannot be forced to incriminate themselves and that they have the right to counsel. The Supreme Court's *Miranda* decision requires the police to advise certain criminal suspects of these important protections. In no other area of criminal procedure are the police required to advise suspects of their rights.

Miranda and the Fifth Amendment's self-incrimination clause are controversial. On the one hand, they help protect the innocent accused from being forced to confess. On the other hand, is justice served when the one person who may know most about a particular crime is under no obligation to talk?

To gain an appreciation for the significance of the right to counsel in the United States—and for the *Miranda* decision—it is helpful to take a look at interrogation laws in some other countries. Neither *Miranda*-like warnings nor the right to counsel are uniquely American creations. Several other countries adopt similar procedures, but to varying degrees. Here we look at three of them: the United Kingdom, France, and China.

The United Kingdom

The United Kingdom has no single constitutional document as the United States does. Police interrogation is instead governed by the Police and Criminal Evidence Act and the Code of Practice for the Detention, Treatment, and Questioning of Persons by Police Officers.

In the UK, if a suspect is taken into custody and the police intend to question the suspect, they are required to advise him or her that there is no obligation to talk. The British approach is somewhat stricter than that employed in the United States, because police are required to advise the suspect of the right to silence as soon as there are reasonable grounds to believe he or she has committed an offense. The *Miranda* rule in the United States applies only when both custody and interrogation occur.

There is also a right to counsel in the UK, but the suspect generally receives assistance only when he or she asks for it. If a suspect exercises his or her rights and refuses to answer police questions, the court is later permitted to draw adverse inferences from this action. For example, the prosecutor can comment at trial that the suspect failed to answer questions. This can work against him or her at trial.

In the United States, the prosecutor *cannot* comment on a defendant's pretrial silence.

France

In contrast to both the United States and the United Kingdom, France is known for long having put society's interest in crime control ahead of individual rights and liberties. France's interrogation law provides evidence of this. First, there is no clear requirement that a suspect be advised that he or she is not required to answer police questions. Second, the right to counsel is also limited. Suspects do not have the right to counsel immediately following their detention. This right does not apply until 20 hours after the person has been detained for ordinary offenses. For more serious cases, such as those involving drug rings or terrorism, the right to counsel does not attach for up to 72 hours from the detention. Finally, the accused has the right to consult with counsel only for a limited time; there is no right to have counsel present during police interrogations.

China

In its earlier days, the "People's Republic" operated without much regard for individual rights. To this day there are criticisms that the Chinese government curtails citizens' freedoms, but legal reforms have brought China's criminal justice system somewhat in line with that of other modernized nations. The 1979 Criminal Procedure Law (CPL), which was significantly amended in 1996, has led to considerable progress in terms of protections afforded to those accused of criminal activity.

The CPL requires that prior to an interrogation, the police must give the suspect an opportunity to make a statement concerning his or her involvement (or lack of involvement) in the crime. This presumably protects the suspect from having the police proceed under the assumption that he or she is guilty. Critics have argued that the police routinely ignore this requirement and use psychological pressures to extract confessions. In any case, there is no recognized right to freedom from self-incrimination in China. The CPL prohibits the use of torture, but this does not protect a suspect from incriminating himself or herself. There *is* a right to counsel, but it attaches only after the police have completed their first interrogation.

© Li-Hua Lan/*Syracuse Newspapers*/The Image Works

Arizona v. Gant (2009)
A police officer searches a car for evidence after arresting the driver. How much freedom do police have to search people, their cars, or their possessions after a traffic stop? In an important 2009 case, Arizona v. Gant, *the Supreme Court limited a police officer's ability to search a car for evidence. After Rodney Gant was arrested for driving with a suspended license, he was handcuffed and locked in the back of a patrol car. A police officer then noticed a jacket on Rodney's back seat, searched the jacket, and found cocaine. Police are typically allowed to search people in custody to protect themselves from hidden weapons. But Gant could not have accessed his car to retrieve weapons or evidence at the time of the search, because he was handcuffed away from the vehicle. Was the search of the jacket justified? The Court ruled that police may search a vehicle in connection with a recent occupant's arrest only if the arrestee is within reaching distance of the passenger compartment at the time of the search or if it is reasonable to believe that the vehicle contains evidence of the offense that led to the arrest. The search of Gant's jacket was unreasonable because he could not gain access to it, and the cocaine was therefore inadmissible at trial. The Gant case is important because controlling a suspect after arrest is critical to police safety. Some officers may now be tempted to compromise their own safety, by minimally restraining suspects, in order to legally search them or their vehicles.*

search warrant
An order issued by a judge, directing officers to conduct a search of specified premises for specified objects or persons and bring them before the court.

probable cause
The evidentiary criterion necessary to sustain an arrest or the issuance of an arrest or search warrant; less than absolute certainty or "beyond a reasonable doubt," but greater than mere suspicion or "hunch."

A **search warrant** is a court order authorizing and directing the police to search a designated place for evidence of a crime. To obtain a search warrant, the following procedural requirements must be met: (1) the police officer must request the warrant from the court; (2) the officer must submit an affidavit establishing the proper grounds for the warrant; and (3) the affidavit must state the place to be searched and the property to be seized. A warrant cannot be issued unless the presiding magistrate is presented with sufficient evidence to conclude that an offense has been or is being committed and that the suspect is the one who committed the offense; this is referred to as the **probable cause** requirement. In other words, the presiding judge must conclude from the facts presented by the police that there is probable cause a crime has been committed and that the person or place to be searched is materially involved in that crime; there must be solid evidence of criminal involvement.

Searches must also be reasonable under the circumstances of the crime. Police would not be able to get a warrant to search a suspect's desk drawer for a missing piano! Nor could police obtain a warrant that allows them to tear down the walls of a person's house because it is suspected that they contain drugs. A search is considered unreasonable when it exceeds the scope of police authority or is highly invasive of personal privacy, even if it reveals incriminating evidence.

WARRANTLESS SEARCHES • To make it easier for police to conduct investigations and to protect public safety, the Court has ruled that under certain circumstances, a valid search may be conducted without a search warrant. The six major exceptions are search incident to a valid arrest, stop and frisk, automobile search, consent search, plain-view search, and exigent circumstances.

1. *Search incident to a valid arrest.* A warrantless search is valid if it is made incident to a lawful arrest. The reason for this exception is that

the arresting officer must have the power to disarm the accused, protect himself or herself, preserve the evidence of the crime, and prevent the accused from escaping from custody. Because the search is lawful, the officer retains what he or she finds if it is connected with a crime. The officer is permitted to search only the defendant's person and the areas in the defendant's immediate physical surroundings that are under his or her control.[159]

2. ***Stop and frisk.*** In the landmark *Terry v. Ohio* decision, the Supreme Court held that police officers can perform a **stop and frisk** when they have reasonable suspicion to believe criminal activity is afoot. For example, say the individual is found lurking behind a closed store. In such a case, the officer has a right to stop and question the individual and, if she or he has reason to believe that the person is carrying a concealed weapon, may frisk the subject—that is, pat down the person's outer clothing for the purpose of finding a concealed weapon. If an illegal weapon is found, then an arrest can be made and a search incident to the arrest performed.[160] Would it be legal to pat down a person merely because that person is standing in a high-crime neighborhood? Probably not. The Supreme Court suggests that an officer would need more suspicion—for example, if the person ran away when he spotted the police approaching.[161]

3. ***Automobile search.*** An automobile may be searched without a warrant if there is probable cause to believe the car was involved in a crime.[162] Because automobiles are inherently mobile, there is a significant chance that evidence will be lost if the search is not conducted immediately; also, people should not expect as much privacy in their cars as in their homes.[163] Police officers who have legitimately stopped an automobile and who have probable cause to believe that contraband is concealed somewhere inside it may conduct a warrantless search of the vehicle that is as thorough as a magistrate could authorize by warrant. The Supreme Court has also ruled that police who have stopped a motorist for a routine traffic violation can conduct a search if they find probable cause that the vehicle has been involved in a crime—as in stopping a car for an illegal U-turn and spotting drug paraphernalia in the front seat.[164]

Because traffic stops can be dangerous, the Court has ruled that if a police officer perceives danger during a routine traffic stop, he can order the driver and passengers from the car without suspicion and conduct a limited search of their persons to ensure police officer safety.[165] Police officers can search the car and passengers after a traffic stop, as long as the search is reasonable and related to officer safety.[166] Usually, the search must be limited to the area under the driver's control or reach. If a person was arrested for drunk driving, the police can search under the driver's seat but not the trunk of the car. In *Thornton v. United States*, the Court ruled that an automobile search is permissible even when an officer does not make contact until the person has left the vehicle and starts walking down the street.[167]

4. ***Consent search.*** In a consent search, individuals waive their constitutional rights; therefore, neither a warrant nor probable cause need exist. For a

stop and frisk
The situation when police officers who are suspicious of an individual run their hands lightly over the suspect's outer garments to determine whether the person is carrying a concealed weapon. Also called a patdown or threshold inquiry, a stop and frisk is intended to stop short of any activity that could be considered a violation of Fourth Amendment rights.

REALITYCHECK

MYTH OR REALITY? Warrantless searches are permissible as long as the police have probable cause.

MYTH: Only certain types of warrantless searches are permissible, even if officers have probable cause. For example, it is never permissible for an officer, with probable cause and no warrant, to enter a private residence in the absence of exigent circumstances.

Has the Supreme Court created enough exceptions to the Fourth Amendment warrant requirement? Why or why not?

exclusionary rule

The principle that prohibits the use, in a trial, of evidence illegally obtained. Based on the Fourth Amendment "right of the people to be secure in their persons, houses, papers, and effects, against unreasonable searches and seizures," the rule is not a bar to prosecution, because legally obtained evidence may be available that may be used in a trial.

consent search to be legal, the consent must be given voluntarily; threat or compulsion invalidates the search.[168] Although it has been held that voluntary consent is required, it has also been maintained that the police are under no obligation to inform individuals of their right to refuse the search.[169]

5. *Plain-view search.* Even when an object is in a house or other areas involving an expectation of privacy, the object can be freely inspected if it can be seen by the general public. If a police officer looks through a fence and sees marijuana growing in a suspect's fields, no search warrant is needed for the property to be seized. The articles are considered to be in plain view, and therefore a search warrant need not be obtained to seize them.[170]

6. *Exigent circumstances.* The Supreme Court has identified a number of exigent, or emergency, circumstances in which a search warrant might normally have been required but, because of some immediate emergency, police officers can search suspects and places without benefit of a warrant. These circumstances include hot pursuit, danger of escape, threats to evidence, and threats to others. In each situation, officers must have probable cause.[171]

REALITY CHECK

MYTH OR REALITY? There are legal loopholes that enable guilty criminals to go free in alarming numbers.

MYTH: One of the supposed loopholes is the exclusionary rule, discussed in this section. Although it *can* result in the guilty going free, it is rarely invoked. Police mistakes and misconduct that lead to the exclusion of evidence are extremely rare.

Despite the evidence, many people still feel that the exclusionary rule is a loophole. Why do such perceptions persist?

The Exclusionary Rule

The **exclusionary rule** provides that all evidence obtained by unreasonable searches and seizures is inadmissible in criminal trials. Similarly, it excludes the use of illegal confessions under Fifth Amendment prohibitions.

After police agencies were created in the mid-nineteenth century, evidence obtained by unreasonable searches and seizures was admitted by state and federal governments in criminal trials. The only criteria for admissibility were whether the evidence was incriminating and whether it would help the judge or jury reach a verdict. Then, in 1914, the U.S. Supreme Court established the exclusionary rule in the case of *Weeks v. United States*, when it ruled that evidence obtained by unreasonable search and seizure must be excluded from a federal criminal trial.[172] In 1961, the Supreme Court made the exclusionary rule applicable to state courts in the landmark decision of *Mapp v. Ohio.*[173]

exclusionary rule

Want to read more about the debate over the **exclusionary rule**? Read Timothy Lynch's defense of it at

www.cengage.com/ criminaljustice/siegel

CONTROVERSY AND CURRENT STATUS ● When the exclusionary rule applies, valuable evidence may not be usable at trial because the police made an error or failed to obtain a proper warrant. This means that guilty defendants can go free when the police make mistakes, intentional or otherwise. What's more, because courts frequently decide in many types of cases (particularly those involving victimless offenses, such as gambling and drug use) that certain evidence should be excluded, the rule is believed to result in excessive court delays and to affect plea-bargaining negotiations negatively. In fact, however, the rule appears to result in relatively few case dismissals. Research efforts show that prosecutions are lost because of suppression rulings less than 1 percent of the time.[174]

Over time the Supreme Court has been diminishing the scope of the exclusionary rule. For example, evidence is admissible in court if the police officers acted in good faith by first obtaining court approval for their search, even if the warrant they received was deficient or faulty.[175] This has come to be known as the **good faith exception.**

good faith exception
The principle that evidence may be used in a criminal trial, even though the search warrant used to obtain it is technically faulty, if the police acted in good faith and to the best of their ability when they sought to obtain it from a judge.

ETHICAL CHALLENGES IN CRIMINAL JUSTICE

A Writing Assignment

Sgt. Jennifer Dorety is an eight-year veteran of the Midcity police force. On the morning of November 5, 2007, Paul C. Bessey, a city councilman, spots Dorety leaving a local restaurant without paying. When he queries the restaurant owner, she laughingly states that "Officer Jen" had been coming there for breakfast for two years and it's "always on the house." It is a mutual understanding they have because Dorety has been very helpful in keeping "riffraff" out of the place. In fact, she tells the councilman that she once called for her at the station house, and Officer Jen drove all the way across town to tell a troublemaker to leave.

The town has a strict policy prohibiting police officers from accepting or soliciting bribes or gratuities, so Councilman Bessey files a complaint against Dorety with the city's Civilian Review Board. There will be a hearing on the matter, and, if found liable, Dorety faces three possible penalties: suspension, suspension and loss of rank, or dismissal. Dorety asks you to act as her representative at the meeting.

Write an essay on how you would defend her actions before the board and what you believe is a fair outcome in the case.

RealityCheck Revisited

To learn more about the myths and realities related to policing that were raised in this chapter, visit the following websites:

- To get details on the race, ethnicity, and gender of full-time sworn police officers in the United States, see

http://www.albany.edu/sourcebook/pdf/t1372003.pdf

- To read more about police corruption and the methods some departments have used to address it, see the following sites:

http://www.nyc.gov/html/ccpc/html/home/home.shtml

http://www.lapdonline.org/consent_decree

- For a detailed report on citizen complaints about the police, see

http://www.ojp.gov/bjs/pub/pdf/ccpuf.pdf

- For a series of objective reports on police use of force, see these sites:

http://www.cops.usdoj.gov/Default.asp?Item=1375

http://www.ncjrs.gov/pdffiles1/nij/176330-1.pdf

You can read about recent court cases involving the police and criminal procedure (by topic) at the following sites:

http://aele.org/

http://www.law.cornell.edu/supct/cases/topic.htm

SUMMARY

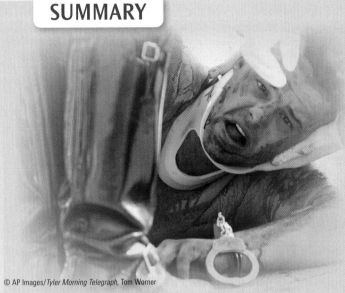

© AP Images/*Tyler Morning Telegraph*, Tom Worner

1. Discuss some of the problems of minority and female police officers

- U.S. police departments have made a concerted effort to attract women and minority police officers, and today about 11 percent of all officers are female and about 23 percent are racial minorities.

- Minority police officers now seem as self-assured as white officers. They may even be more willing to use their authority to take official action than white officers.

- In 1910, Alice Stebbins Wells became the first woman to hold the title of police officer (in Los Angeles) and to have arrest powers.

- Studies of policewomen indicate that they are still struggling for acceptance, believe that they do not receive equal credit for their job performance, and report that it is common for them to be sexually harassed by their coworkers.

- African American women, who account for less than 5 percent of police officers, occupy a unique status. They often incur the hostility of both white women and African American men, who feel threatened that these officers will take their place.

2. Know the issues involving education and police

- Although most law enforcement agencies still do not require recruits to have a college degree, the number requiring advanced education in the hiring and promotion process is growing.

- Police administrators believe that education enables officers to perform more effectively, generate fewer citizen complaints, show more initiative in performing police tasks, and generally act more professionally.

3. Be able to discuss police culture and personality

- Police experts have found that the experience of becoming a police officer and the nature of the job itself cause most officers to band together in a police subculture characterized by cynicism, clannishness, secrecy, and insulation from others in society—the blue curtain.

- The police officer's working personality is shaped by constant exposure to danger and the need to use force and authority to defuse and control threatening situations.

- Despite popular belief and some research support, efforts to find and identify a classic "police personality" have been inconclusive.

4. Be able to identify distinct policing styles

- Four styles of police work seem to fit the current behavior patterns of most police agents: the crime fighter, the social agent, the law enforcer, and the watchman.

- Style and role orientation may influence how police officers carry out their duties and the way they use their discretion.

5. Be familiar with how police use discretion

- The majority of police officers use a high degree of personal discretion in carrying out daily tasks, a phenomenon sometimes referred to as "low-visibility decision making" in criminal justice.

- An officer's "emotional intelligence" can help dictate how discretion will be invoked.

- Several factors contribute to discretionary decision making: legal factors, environmental factors, departmental factors, peer factors, situational factors, and extralegal factors.

6. Be able to discuss four major problems of policing

- The complexity of their role, the need to exercise prudent discretion, the threat of having to use violence and of having violence used against them, and isolation from the rest of society mean that police officers experience tremendous stress.

- Fatigue is a problem in modern police agencies. Officers often work long hours and can become overly tired from performance of their duties.

- Because incidents of brutality undermine efforts to build a bridge between police and the public, police departments around the United States have instituted specialized training programs to reduce it.

- Ever since their creation, U.S. police departments have wrestled with the problem of controlling illegal and unprofessional behavior by their officers.

- No single explanation satisfactorily accounts for the various forms that the abuse of power takes.

- A strong and well-supported internal affairs division has been linked to lowered corruption rates.

7. Discuss the use of force and the factors related to police shootings

- Police officers are empowered to use force in the pursuit of their daily tasks.

- There is evidence that only a small proportion of officers are continually involved in use-of-force incidents.

- The term "deadly force" refers to the actions of a police officer who shoots and kills a suspect who flees from arrest, assaults a victim, or attacks an officer.

- A number of critics have claimed that police are more likely to shoot and kill minority offenders than whites.

8. Know various methods of controlling police force

- Because the police use of deadly force is such a serious problem, ongoing efforts have been made to control its use.

- Methods used to control police force include adhering to important court decisions and formulating appropriate policies.

- Another way to control police shootings is through internal review and policymaking by police administrative review boards.

9. Define less-lethal weapons and provide examples

- Less-lethal weapons give police officers an opportunity to subdue certain suspects without the need for lethal force.

- Examples of less-lethal weapons include Tasers, pepper spray, and guns that shoot wood, rubber, or polyurethane bullets.

10. Be familiar with the Supreme Court's involvement with the police through its effort to control search and seizure and interrogation, and through establishment of the exclusionary rule

- The need for police officers to gather evidence can conflict with the constitutional rights of citizens.

- In the 1966 case of *Miranda v. Arizona*, the Supreme Court created objective standards for questioning by police after a defendant has been taken into custody.

- The Court has used case law to define the boundaries of the *Miranda* warning since its inception.

- Under normal circumstances, no search or seizure undertaken without a search warrant is lawful.

- The Supreme Court has ruled that under certain circumstances, a valid search may be conducted without a search warrant.

- The exclusionary rule provides that all evidence obtained by unreasonable searches and seizures is inadmissible in criminal trials.

Key Terms

double marginality, 178
cynicism, 182
blue curtain, 182
discretion, 185
emotional intelligence, 185
demeanor, 186
racial profiling, 187
police brutality, 191
corruption, 191
Knapp Commission, 191
meat eaters, 191

grass eaters, 191
deadly force, 195
suicide by cop, 196
less-lethal weapons, 198
Miranda warning, 199
search warrant, 202
probable cause, 202
stop and frisk, 203
exclusionary rule, 204
good faith exception, 205

Review Questions

1. Should male and female officers have the same duties in a police department? Explain your reasoning.

2. How can education enhance the effectiveness of police officers?

3. Do you think that an officer's working the street will eventually produce a cynical personality and distrust for civilians? Explain.

4. Should a police officer who accepts a free meal from a restaurant owner be dismissed from the force? Why or why not?

5. A police officer orders an unarmed person running away from a burglary to stop; the suspect keeps running and is shot and killed by the officer. Has the officer committed murder? Explain.

6. Would you like to live in a society that abolished police discretion and used a full enforcement policy? Why or why not?

7. Should illegally seized evidence be excluded from trial, even though it is conclusive proof of a person's criminal acts? Might there be another way to deal with police violation of the Fourth Amendment—for example, making them pay a fine?

8. Have criminals been given too many rights by the courts? Should courts be more concerned with the rights of victims or the rights of offenders? Have the police been "handcuffed" and prevented from doing their job in the most efficient manner?

Part 3 | COURTS AND ADJUDICATION

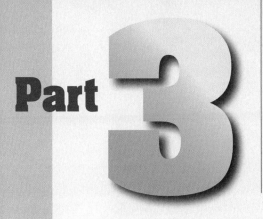

Joshua Mauldin admitted severely burning his infant daughter by putting her in a hotel microwave for several seconds. Following Joshua's arrest, Eva Marie Mauldin, the mother, claimed Satan compelled her husband to do what he did because the devil disapproved of Joshua's decision to become a preacher. "Satan saw my husband as a threat. Satan attacked him because he saw (Joshua) as a threat," she told a Houston television station.[1] "He would never do anything to hurt her. He loves her," she went on.

During a videotaped interview after his arrest, Joshua Mauldin used a teddy bear to show officers how he punched and threw his daughter before putting her into the microwave and turning it on.[2] He even reportedly put the girl in the hotel safe and the refrigerator before microwaving her. Mauldin confessed and was charged with injury to a child causing serious bodily harm, a crime that carried a possible prison term of 99 years. Even though Mauldin confessed, he pled not guilty by reason of insanity. On March 26, 2008, a jury sentenced Mauldin to 25 years in prison and fined him $10,000.

The girl survived and is under the care of relatives. Joshua and Eva Marie have been understandably barred from contacting their daughter or the relatives who have her in their care.

> Most cases don't involve graphic murders, violent assaults, or stranger-on-stranger rapes. In fact, most criminal cases don't involve violence at all. And very few of them even go to trial. Cases such as Mauldin's give the impression that every defendant gets his or her "day in court," but reality works differently.

The Joshua Mauldin case is but one of many cases that the U.S. court system handled that year, but it was also an exceptional and heinous case. It is not the *typical* case. Most cases don't involve graphic murders, violent assaults, or stranger-on-stranger rapes. In fact, most criminal cases don't involve violence at all. And very few of them even go to trial. Cases such as Mauldin's give the impression that every defendant gets his or her "day in court," but reality works differently. For example, as a consequence of plea bargaining, the vast majority of cases are resolved without a trial. Others, even if they do go to court, are disposed of relatively quickly. The drawn-out criminal trial involving the deranged sociopath, complete with daily press coverage, is most unusual.

Chapter 7
Courts, Prosecution, and the Defense

Chapter 8
Pretrial and Trial Procedures

Chapter 9
Punishment and Sentencing

7

COURTS, PROSECUTION, AND THE DEFENSE

RealityCheck

MYTH or REALITY?

▶ Every state has just one court of last resort.

▶ There are almost no formal qualifications for federal judges.

▶ Elected state judges can be affiliated with a political party.

▶ Prosecutors base their charging decisions solely on legal factors, such as the seriousness of the offense.

▶ Privately retained defense attorneys are more effective than court-appointed defense attorneys.

Learning Objectives

1. Be familiar with the role of the court in the justice process

2. Recognize the varying structures of state and federal court systems

3. Describe the selection and duties of the trial judge

4. Discuss the role and duties of prosecutors

5. Be familiar with the pros and cons of prosecutorial discretion

6. Understand the role of the defense attorney in the justice process

7. Discuss the different forms of indigent defense

8. Debate the pros and cons of private attorneys

9. Be familiar with the expanding role of technology in the court process

© AP Images/Galveston Daily News, Jennifer Reynolds

Chapter Outline

Career Profile

Carlos Martinez is an official court reporter who works for the Sonoma County (California) superior courts. Before assuming his current position, Carlos was a deposition firm owner for seven years. He has been a court reporter for 15 years. Two events shaped his career path. First, a friend's father was a court reporter, and Carlos found the job very intriguing. Second, when he was 19, Carlos was called to jury duty. He spoke with the court reporter during a break and asked questions about career opportunities. Realizing the career prospects were favorable, he enrolled in and completed court reporting school at the College of the Redwoods in Eureka, California. He received a certificate as a certified shorthand reporter from the State of California.

Carlos's typical day includes making a verbatim record of the morning court proceedings, which consist of pretrial conferences, pleas, prison sentencing hearings, preliminary hearings, and motions. Afternoons, he says, are reserved for jury trials. His spare time during the workday is used to prepare transcripts (the detailed word-for-word record of the proceedings) as mandated by the law and as requested by the parties to each case.

Court reporters use a shorthand system to create a verbatim record of the proceedings. In order to gain the necessary skills, each reporter completes a six-month theory course. What a lot of people do not realize is that after the theory course, it is up to the student to develop a personal dictionary using key strokes that are unique to him or her. This enables the reporter to prepare transcripts as quickly and accurately as possible.

The greatest technical challenges Carlos faces in a typical day are dealing with rapid speakers and technical jargon. He sometimes has to interrupt the proceedings and ask fast speakers to slow down so that the record can reflect their statements accurately. Also, he finds that he has to read back the record and ask many questions of expert witnesses in order to ensure that he makes no mistakes. On a more personal level, Carlos finds some cases, especially those involving murders, molestations, rapes, and abuse, difficult to listen to. "You never get used to it and you never really forget," he says. "You just learn to live with it."

Carlos Martinez's career illustrates the variety of options open to people who choose legal careers. Some choose to go to law school and become prosecutors, defense attorneys, and even judges. Others join the ranks of the court staff and become clerks, administrators, security officials, court reporters, and other professionals. The range of career paths in the court system is extensive.

The criminal court is the setting in which many of the most important decisions in the criminal justice system are made. Eyewitness identification, bail, trial, plea negotiations, and sentencing all involve court decisions. The criminal court is a complex social agency with many independent but interrelated subsystems: administrator, prosecutor, defense attorney, judge, and probation department. The entire process—from filing of the initial complaint to final sentencing of the defendant—is governed by precise rules of law designed to ensure fairness. However, in today's crowded court system, such abstract goals are often impossible to achieve. The nation's court system is chronically underfunded, and recent economic downturns have not helped matters.

These constraints have a significant impact on the way courts carry out justice. Quite often, the U.S. court system is the scene of accommodation and "working things out," rather than an arena for a vigorous criminal defense. Plea negotiations and other nonjudicial alternatives, such as diversion, are far more common than the formal trial process. Consequently, U.S. criminal justice can be selective. Discretion accompanies defendants through every step of the process, determining what will happen to them and how their cases will be resolved. "Discretion" means that two people committing similar crimes may receive highly dissimilar treatment; most people convicted of homicide receive a prison sentence, but about 5 percent receive probation as a sole sentence; indeed, more murderers get probation than the death penalty.[1]

In this chapter, we examine the structure and function of the court system. The U.S. court system has evolved over the years into an intricately balanced legal process. To carry out this complex process, each state maintains its own state court organization and structure, and the federal court has an independent trial court system. These are described next.

State Courts

Every state maintains its own court system. States are free to create as many courts as they wish, to name courts what they like (in New York, felony courts are known as supreme courts!), and to establish specialized courts that handle a single type of legal matter, such as drug courts and domestic courts. Consequently, no two court organizations are exactly alike. State courts handle a wide variety of cases and regulate numerous personal behaviors ranging from homicide to property maintenance.

Courts of Limited Jurisdiction

state courts of limited jurisdiction

Courts that have jurisdiction over misdemeanors and conduct preliminary investigations of felony charges.

Depending on the jurisdiction in which they are located, **state courts of limited jurisdiction** are known by a variety of names—municipal courts, county courts, district courts, and metropolitan courts, to mention just a few. They are known as courts of limited jurisdiction because they are restricted to hearing minor or less serious civil and criminal cases.

Usually, courts of limited jurisdiction handle misdemeanor criminal infractions, violations of municipal ordinances, traffic violations, and civil suits where the damages involve less than a certain amount of money (usually $1,000 or less). In criminal matters, they hear cases involving misdemeanors such as shoplifting, disorderly conduct, and simple assault. Their sanctioning power is also limited. In criminal matters, punishments may be limited to fines, community sentencing, or incarceration in the county jail for up to a year. In addition to their trial work, limited jurisdiction courts conduct arraignments,

Limited jurisdiction courts include a variety of so-called specialized courts. Among the most popular specialized courts are drug courts. Here Program Supervisor Jeff Schultz (left) presents Brad Zeroni with his diploma after Zeroni completed the Polk County Adult Drug Court program in Des Moines, Iowa. Drug courts are now commonplace in the criminal justice system and appear to be an effective alternative to the traditional court model.

© AP Images/Steve Pope

preliminary, and bail hearings in felony cases (before they are transferred to superior courts).

Some states separate limited courts into those that handle civil cases and those that settle criminal cases. Included in the category of courts of limited jurisdiction are special courts, such as juvenile, family, and probate courts (which handle custody, divorce, and estate issues, respectively). State lawmakers may respond to a particular social problem, such as drug use, by creating specialized courts that focus on treatment and care for these offenders. One of the most common is the family or juvenile court, which handles custody cases, delinquency, and other issues involving children (juvenile courts will be discussed further in Chapter 13).

The nation's approximately 13,500 independent courts of limited jurisdiction are the ones most often accused of providing assembly-line justice. Because the matters they decide involve minor personal confrontations and conflicts—family disputes, divorces, landlord–tenant conflicts, barroom brawls—the rule of the day is "handling the situation" and resolving the dispute.

SPECIALIZED COURTS • A growing phenomenon in the United States is the creation of specialty courts that focus on one type of criminal act, such as drug courts and mental health courts.[2] All cases within the jurisdiction that involve this particular type of crime are funneled to the specialty court, where presumably they will be resolved promptly.

- **Drug Courts** The drug court movement began in Florida to address the growing problem of prison overcrowding due in large part to an influx of drug-involved offenders. Drug courts were created to have primary jurisdiction over cases involving substance abuse and trafficking. The aim is to channel nonviolent first offenders into intensive treatment programs rather than into jail or prison. Today there are more than 2,000 drug courts throughout the United States and its territories.[3] Drug courts address the overlap between the public health threats of drug abuse and crime: Crimes are often drug related; drug abusers are frequently involved with the criminal justice system. Drug courts provide an ideal setting to address these problems by linking the justice system with health services and drug treatment providers, while easing the burden on the already overtaxed correctional system.

- **Mental Health Courts** Based largely on the organization of drug courts, mental health courts focus their attention on mental health treatment to help people with emotional problems reduce their chances of reoffending.[4] By focusing on the need for treatment, along with providing supervision and support from the community, mental health courts provide a venue for those dealing with mental health issues to avoid the trauma of jail or prison, where they will have little if any access to treatment.

There are now specialized courts for nearly every difficult problem confronting the criminal justice system. There are domestic violence courts, gang courts, gun courts, sex offender courts, homeless courts, parole reentry courts, community courts, and so on.

Courts of General Jurisdiction

Approximately 2,000 **courts of general jurisdiction** exist in the United States; they are variously called felony, superior, supreme, county, and circuit courts. Courts of general jurisdiction handle the more serious felony cases, such as murder, rape,

courts of general jurisdiction
State or federal courts that have jurisdiction over felony offenses and more serious civil cases (that is, cases involving more than a dollar amount set by the legislature).

© Tim Pannell/Corbis

and robbery, and civil cases where damages are over a specified amount, such as $10,000. Courts of general jurisdiction may also be responsible for reviewing cases on appeal from courts of limited jurisdiction. In some instances they base their decision on a review of the transcript of the case, whereas in others they can actually grant a new trial; this latter procedure is known as the "trial de novo process."

Courts of general jurisdiction are typically organized in judicial districts or circuits, based on a political division such as a county or a group of counties ("Superior Court for the Southern Tier"). They then receive cases from the various limited courts located within the county or jurisdiction. Some general courts separate criminal and civil cases so that some specialize in civil matters while others maintain a caseload that is exclusively criminal.

State court systems now handle about 100 million new cases each year, a number that has increased more than 10 percent in the past decade. The great majority of these cases are traffic related, and about 20 million of these cases involve some form of criminal conduct.[5]

Appellate Courts

appellate court
A court that reconsiders a case that has already been tried in order to determine whether the measures used complied with accepted rules of criminal procedure and were in accordance with constitutional doctrines.

If defendants believe that the procedures used were in violation of their constitutional rights, they may ask an **appellate court** to review the trial process. Appellate courts do not try cases; they review the procedures of the case to determine whether an error was made by judicial authorities. In some instances, defendants can file an appeal if they believe that the law they were tried under was in violation of constitutional standards (for example, the crime they were charged with—say, "being a public nuisance"—was vague and ill defined) or if the procedures used in the case contravened principles of due process and equal protection or were in direct opposition to a constitutional guarantee (for example, they were denied the right to have competent legal representation).

It is the role of the appellate court to decide whether the trial judge made a legal error that influenced the outcome of the case, thereby denying the defendant a fair trial. Judicial error can include admitting into evidence illegally seized material, improperly charging a jury, allowing a prosecutor to ask witnesses improper questions, and so on. If, upon review, the appellate court decides that an error has been made, it can order a new trial or even allow the defendant to go free.

court of last resort
A court that handles the final appeal on a matter. The U.S. Supreme Court is the official court of last resort for criminal matters.

State criminal appeals are heard in one of the appellate courts in the 50 states and the District of Columbia. Each state has at least one **court of last resort**, usually called a state supreme court, which reviews issues of law and fact appealed from the trial courts; a few states have two high courts, one for civil appeals and the other for criminal cases. In addition, many states have established intermediate appellate courts (IACs) to review decisions by trial courts and administrative agencies before they reach the supreme court stage. Currently, 39 states have at least one permanent IAC. The most recently created IAC is in Mississippi; it began operations in 1995.

Many people believe that criminal appeals clog the nation's court system because so many convicted criminals try to "beat the rap" on a technicality. Actually, criminal appeals represent a small percentage of the total number of cases

REALITYCHECK

MYTH OR REALITY? Every state has just one court of last resort.

MYTH: Most states have just one, but Oklahoma and Texas have two courts of last resort.

In Texas, the Court of Criminal Appeals is the highest court for criminal cases. The Texas Supreme Court is the court of last resort for juvenile and civil cases. Is this a favorable arrangement? Why do Texas's and Oklahoma's courts of last resort differ in their structure from the rest of the nation?

processed by the nation's appellate courts. All types of appeals, including criminal ones, continue to inundate the courts, so most courts are having problems processing cases expeditiously.

State courts have experienced an increase in the number of appellate cases each year. In the meantime, the number of judges and support staff has not kept pace. The resulting imbalance has led to the increased use of intermediate courts to screen cases.

Figure 7.1 illustrates the interrelationship of appellate and trial courts in a model state court structure. Each state's court organization, of course,

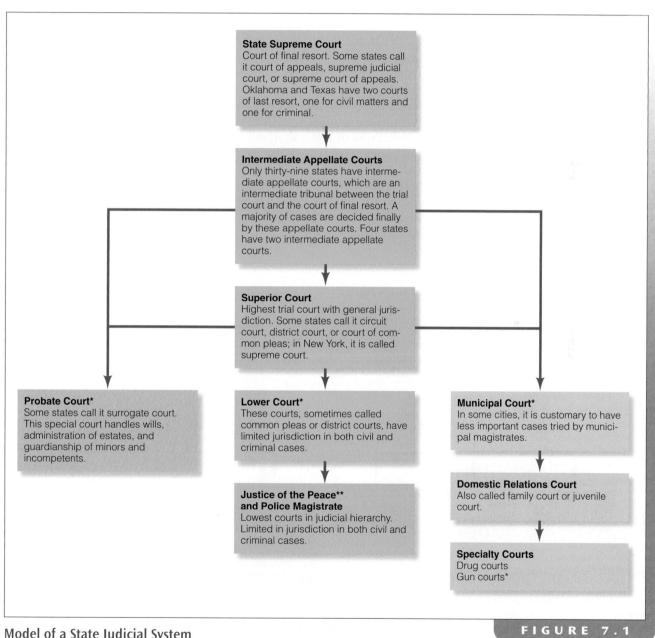

Model of a State Judicial System

FIGURE 7.1

*Courts of special jurisdiction, such as probate, family, and juvenile courts, and the so-called inferior courts, such as common pleas and municipal courts, may be separate courts or part of the trial court of general jurisdiction.
**Justices of the peace do not exist in all states. Where they do exist, their jurisdictions vary greatly from state to state.

SOURCES: American Bar Association, *Law and the Courts* (Chicago: ABA, 1974), 20; Bureau of Justice Statistics, State Court Organization–1998 (Washington, D.C.: Department of Justice, 2000).

may vary from this standard pattern. Though most states have a tiered court organization (lower, upper, and appellate courts), all vary in the way they delegate responsibility to a particular court system, and some have consolidated their courts into a single, unified system.

Federal Courts

The legal basis for an independent federal court system is contained in Article 3, Section 1, of the U.S. Constitution, which provides that "the judicial power of the United States shall be vested in one Supreme Court, and in such inferior courts as Congress may from time to time ordain and establish." The important clauses in Article 3 indicate that the federal courts have jurisdiction over the laws of the United States and over treaties and cases involving admiralty and maritime jurisdiction, as well as over controversies between two or more states and citizens of different states.[6] This complex language generally means that state courts have jurisdiction over most common-law crimes but that the federal system maintains jurisdiction over violations of federal criminal statutes, civil suits between citizens of different states, and suits between a citizen and an agency of the federal government.

Within this authority, the federal government has established a three-tiered hierarchy of court jurisdiction that, in order of ascendancy, consists of the (1) U.S. district courts, (2) U.S. courts of appeals (circuit courts), and (3) the U.S. Supreme Court (see Figure 7.2).

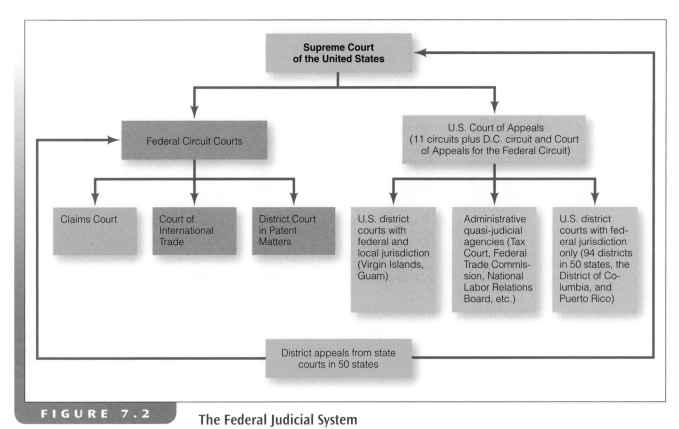

FIGURE 7.2

The Federal Judicial System

Source: American Bar Association, *Law and the Courts* (Chicago: ABA, 1974), 21; updated information provided by the Federal Courts Improvement Act of 1982 and West Publishing Company, St. Paul, Minnesota.

U.S. District Courts

The trial courts of the federal system, U.S. district courts were organized by Congress in the Judicial Act of 1789. Today, 94 independent courts are in operation. Originally, each state was allowed one court; as the population grew, however, so did the need for courts, so now some states have multiple jurisdictions.

U.S. district courts have jurisdiction over cases involving violations of federal laws, including civil rights abuses, interstate transportation of stolen vehicles, and kidnappings. They may also hear cases on questions involving citizenship and the rights of aliens. The jurisdiction of the U.S. district court will occasionally overlap that of state courts. Citizens who reside in separate states and are involved in litigation of an amount in excess of $10,000 may choose to have their cases heard in either of the states or in the federal district court. Finally, federal district courts hear cases where one state sues a resident (or firm) in another state, where one state sues another, or where the federal government is a party in a suit. For an overview of the cases most commonly heard in federal district courts, see Figure 7.3.

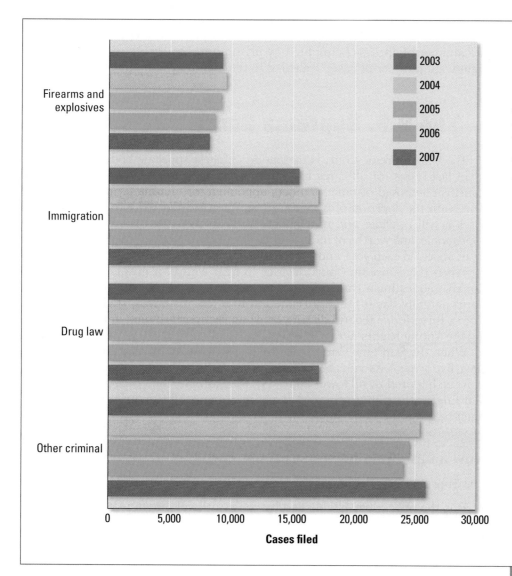

Criminal Cases Filed in U.S. District Courts

Source: Administrative Office of the United States Courts, *Annual Report of the Director, 2007* (Washington, D.C.: Administrative Office of the United States Courts, 2008), p. 25. www.uscourts.gov/judbus2007/JudicialBusinesspdfversion.pdf (accessed May 23, 2008).

FIGURE 7.3

U.S. Courts of Appeals

There are 13 judicial circuits, each with a court of appeals. The smallest court is the First Circuit, with 6 judgeships, and the largest court is the Ninth Circuit, with 28 judgeships. Approximately 40,000 appeals are heard in these "U.S. circuit courts." This name is derived from the historical practice of having judges ride the circuit and regularly hear cases in the judicial seats of their various jurisdictions. Today, appellate judges are not required to travel (although some may sit in more than one court), and each federal appellate court jurisdiction contains a number of associate justices who share the caseload. Circuit court offices are usually located in major cities, such as San Francisco and New York, and cases to be heard must be brought to these locations by attorneys.

The circuit court is empowered to review federal and state appellate court cases on substantive and procedural issues involving rights guaranteed by the Constitution. Circuit courts do not actually retry cases, nor do they determine whether the facts brought out during trial support conviction or dismissal. Instead, they analyze judicial interpretations of the law, such as the charge (or instructions) to the jury, and reflect on the constitutional issues involved in each case they hear.

Although federal court criminal cases make up only a small percentage of appellate cases, they are still of concern to the judiciary. Steps have been taken to make appealing more difficult. The U.S. Supreme Court has tried to limit the number of appeals being filed by prison inmates, which often represent a significant number of cases appealed in the federal criminal justice system.

The U.S. Supreme Court

The U.S. Supreme Court is the nation's highest appellate body and the court of last resort for all cases tried in the various federal and state courts. The Court is composed of nine members appointed for lifetime terms by the president, with the approval of Congress. The Court has discretion over most of the cases it will consider and may choose to hear only those it deems important, appropriate, and worthy of its attention. The Court chooses some 300 of the 5,000 cases appealed each year, and only about 100 of these receive full opinions.

writ of certiorari
An order of a superior court requesting that the record of an inferior court (or administrative body) be brought forward for review or inspection.

landmark decision
A decision handed down by the U.S. Supreme Court that becomes the law of the land and serves as a precedent for resolving similar legal issues.

When the Supreme Court decides to hear a case, it grants a **writ of certiorari**, requesting a transcript of the proceedings of the case for review. The Court actually has original jurisdiction in a few instances, such as decisions from a three-judge federal district court on reapportionment and cases involving the Voting Rights Act.

When the Supreme Court rules on a case, usually by majority decision (at least five votes), its rule becomes a precedent, or **landmark decision**, that must be honored by all lower courts. If, for example, the Court grants a particular litigant the right to counsel at a police lineup, all similarly situated clients must be given the same right.

How a Case Gets to the Supreme Court

The Supreme Court is unique in several ways:

- It is the only court established by constitutional mandate rather than federal legislation.
- It decides basic social and political issues of grave consequence and importance to the nation, such as the outcome of the 2000 presidential election.
- The Court shapes the future meaning of the U.S. Constitution by identifying a citizen's rights and liberties.

The Supreme Court hears a select number of cases appealed from the lower courts. Often it lets the lower-court decision stand because there are simply too many cases. Here members of the Narragansett Indian Tribe sit in Washington County District Court in South Kingstown, Rhode Island, where they pleaded not guilty to criminal charges stemming from a 2003 Rhode Island State Police raid on a smoke shop on tribal land in 2007. The raid was challenged, but the U.S. Supreme Court let a lower-court ruling stand, thus allowing the criminal proceeding to get under way.

© AP Images/Joe Giblin

The device the Court uses to choose cases is the writ of certiorari. *Certiorari,* from the Latin term "to be informed of," refers to an order a court issues so that it can review the decision and proceedings that occurred in a lower court. Under this procedure, an appellant requests a writ to be issued so that his or her case may be reviewed. If the writ is denied, the Supreme Court refuses to hear the appeal, and the judgment in the lower court stands unchanged. If the writ is granted, the Supreme Court hears the appeal. For the appellant to be successful, at least four of the nine justices sitting on the Court must vote to grant the writ of certiorari even before the case can be considered for review. Generally, these votes are cast in a secret meeting attended only by the justices. More than 90 percent of the cases heard by the Court are brought by petition for a writ of certiorari.

After the Supreme Court decides to hear a case, it reviews written arguments referred to as legal briefs outlining the case and the points of law to be considered.

After the written material is reviewed, attorneys for each side in the case are allowed 30 minutes to present an oral argument before the court members. Then the justices normally meet in what is known as a "case conference" to discuss the case and vote to reach a decision. This procedure is outlined in Figure 7.4.

In reaching a decision, the Supreme Court reevaluates and reinterprets state statutes, the U.S. Constitution, and previous case decisions. On the basis of its review of the case, the Court either affirms or reverses the decision of the lower court. When the justices reach a decision, and in the event that the Court's decision is split, the chief justice of the Court assigns a member of the majority group to write the opinion. Another justice normally writes a dissent, or minority, opinion; a single opinion may be written if the decision is unanimous. When the case is finished, it is submitted to the public and becomes the law of the land. The decision represents the legal precedents that add to the existing body of law on a given subject, change it, and guide its future development.

Tracing the Course of a Case to the Supreme Court

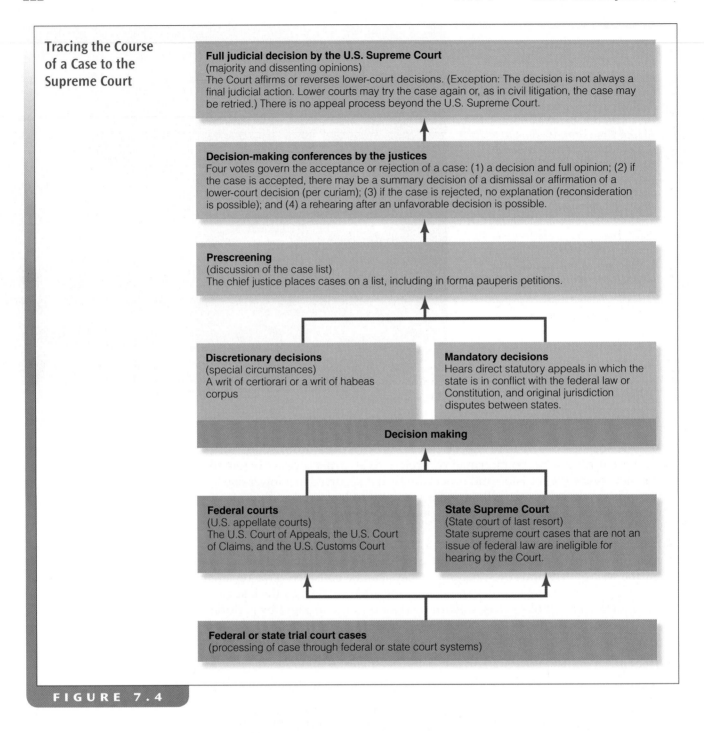

Full judicial decision by the U.S. Supreme Court
(majority and dissenting opinions)
The Court affirms or reverses lower-court decisions. (Exception: The decision is not always a final judicial action. Lower courts may try the case again or, as in civil litigation, the case may be retried.) There is no appeal process beyond the U.S. Supreme Court.

Decision-making conferences by the justices
Four votes govern the acceptance or rejection of a case: (1) a decision and full opinion; (2) if the case is accepted, there may be a summary decision of a dismissal or affirmation of a lower-court decision (per curiam); (3) if the case is rejected, no explanation (reconsideration is possible); and (4) a rehearing after an unfavorable decision is possible.

Prescreening
(discussion of the case list)
The chief justice places cases on a list, including in forma pauperis petitions.

Discretionary decisions
(special circumstances)
A writ of certiorari or a writ of habeas corpus

Mandatory decisions
Hears direct statutory appeals in which the state is in conflict with the federal law or Constitution, and original jurisdiction disputes between states.

Decision making

Federal courts
(U.S. appellate courts)
The U.S. Court of Appeals, the U.S. Court of Claims, and the U.S. Customs Court

State Supreme Court
(State court of last resort)
State supreme court cases that are not an issue of federal law are ineligible for hearing by the Court.

Federal or state trial court cases
(processing of case through federal or state court systems)

FIGURE 7.4

The Judiciary

The judge is the senior officer in a court of criminal law. Judges' duties are quite varied and far more extensive than might be expected.

- Their primary duty is to oversee the trial process. This means that during trials, judges control the appropriateness of conduct, settle questions of evidence and procedure, and guide the questioning of witnesses.
- In a **jury trial** the judge must instruct jurors on which evidence it is proper to examine and which should be ignored. The judge also formally charges the jury by instructing its members on what points of law and evidence they must consider to reach a decision of either guilty or not guilty.

jury trial
The process of deciding a case by a group of persons selected and sworn in to serve as jurors at a criminal trial, often as a 6- or 12-person jury.

Judge Lael Montgomery, center, talks with attorneys at the bench during a trial at the Boulder County Justice Center in Boulder, Colorado. Colorado and other states are increasingly using performance reviews to hold judges more accountable without resorting to term limits or taking other measures that some fear would threaten the judiciary's independence.

© AP Images/*The Daily Camera*, Mark Leffingwell

- When a jury trial is waived, in a bench trial, the judge must decide whether the defendant is guilty as charged. If a defendant is found guilty, the judge must decide on the sentence (in some cases, this is legislatively determined), which includes choosing the type of sentence, its length, and, in the case of probation, the conditions under which it may be revoked.
- The judge controls and influences court agencies: probation, the court clerk, the police, and the district attorney's office. Probation and the clerk may be under the judge's explicit control. In some courts, the operations, philosophy, and procedures of these agencies are within the magistrate's administrative domain. In others—where a state agency controls the probation department—the attitudes of the county or district court judge greatly influence the way a probation department is run and how its decisions are made.

While carrying out their duties, judges must be wary of the legal controls placed on the trial process by the appellate court system. If an error is made, the judge's decision may be reversed, causing (at the very least) personal embarrassment. Some experts believe that fear of reversal may shape judicial decision making, but research shows that judges may be more independent than previously believed. Judges relish using their judicial power as a policy-making tool to influence important social policies such as affirmative action or privacy.[7]

Of course, judges do not wield their power in isolation. They work together with prosecutors and defense attorneys, whose work is featured shortly. They are also assisted by a number of courtroom personnel, including clerks, court administrators, security personnel, court reporters, and other support staff. See Exhibit 7.1 for additional details.

The Judge and the Justice System

Judicial attitudes and philosophy have a major impact on how the justice system operates. Judicial attitudes may extend way beyond the courtroom. Police policies may be directly influenced by the judge, whose sentencing discretion affects the arrest process. If a local judge usually imposes minimal sentences—such as a fine—for a particular offense, the police may be reluctant to arrest offenders for that crime, knowing that doing so will basically be a waste of

EXHIBIT 10.1

Court Staff

The most visible courtroom personnel include the judge, the prosecutor, and the defense attorney. But there are many other important court personnel and staff persons. The typical large jurisdiction probably has a mix of the following personnel working in the courtroom or courthouse at any given time.

Clerk Court clerks are responsible for a wide range of duties. Their main responsibilities include maintaining court records; receiving, processing, and maintaining judgments; issuing process, such as summonses, subpoenas, and wage garnishments; preserving the court seal; swearing in witnesses, jurors, and grand jurors; collecting fees and fines; handling inquiries from attorneys and other parties; and printing and distributing opinions of the court.

Court Administrator There are two general types of court administrators. The first is a state employee. In each state, these individuals are part of the state administrative office of the court, which is usually under the direction of the state supreme court. Court administrators help develop and implement policies and services for the judicial branch throughout the state. They also conduct research and determine whether judicial needs are identified and incorporated into long-term plans. They establish priorities for the courts, address financial problems and budgeting issues, and manage the use of technology within a state's judicial branch.

The second type of court administrator is a local court administrator. These individuals manage the daily operations of the court, usually under the direction of the presiding judge. They provide administrative support for court programs, help the court establish new programs and evaluate them, and manage purchasing and accounts payable, among other responsibilities.

Court Security The marshal or bailiff for the court is responsible for courthouse security. In some states, such as California, court security is provided by sheriff's deputies who screen people entering the building, provide security during trials, and transport suspects to court from jail. Depending on the jurisdiction, court security personnel may take on additional responsibilities, including some investigation, bond supervising, community service monitoring, and making arrests as needed.

Legal Staff The larger and more powerful the court, the more likely it will have a variety of legal staff. These personnel can include legal counsel (prosecutors and defense attorneys), staff attorneys, research attorneys, and law clerks. Law clerks are not to be confused with court clerks. Unlike court clerks, law clerks are often recent law school graduates who assist judges with researching issues before the courts and writing opinions. U.S. Supreme Court law clerks are the cream of the crop, having graduated from many of the nation's top law schools.

Judicial Support Staff A judge's support staff may include executive assistants, administrative assistants, secretaries, or a mix of all three. Support staff edit and type judicial opinions, create and arrange files, coordinate meetings, coordinate travel arrangements, answer telephone and e-mail inquiries, mail correspondence, and serve as an intermediary between the judge and other outside parties.

Court Reporter The court reporter records judicial proceedings word for word. See the Careers in Criminal Justice box in Chapter 8 for more on court reporters.

Jury Staff Many courts have dedicated jury personnel who maintain and review lists of prospective jurors. They may also determine who is eligible to serve, determine the number of jurors needed, issue summonses for jury service, and handle requests by jurors for dismissal, exemption, or disqualification. These individuals may also meet with prospective jurors to explain the process, tell them where to go, and dismiss them from service at the end of the day.

Other Officers Many courts have representatives on site from other criminal justice agencies. There may be juvenile officers who are vested with the authority to take charge of children who come under the jurisdiction of the juvenile or family court. Representatives from probation may assist judges by performing pre-sentence investigations that can be used during sentencing. In some states, the probation department is part of the judiciary and is thus more closely connected with the court than probation departments in other states.

time. Similarly, if a judge is known to have a liberal attitude toward police discretion, the local department may be more inclined to engage in practices that border on entrapment or to pursue cases through easily obtained wiretaps. However, a magistrate oriented toward strict use of due process guarantees would stifle such activities by dismissing all cases involving apparent police abuses of personal freedoms.

The district attorney's office may also be sensitive to judicial attitudes. The district attorney might forgo indictments in cases that the presiding magistrate expressly considers trivial or quasi-criminal and in which the judge has been known to take only token action, such as the prosecution of pornographers.

Finally, the judge considers requests by prosecutors for leniency (or severity) in sentencing. The judge's reaction to these requests is important if the police and the district attorney are to honor the bargains they may have made with defendants to secure information, cooperation, or guilty pleas. When police tell informers that they will try to convince the judge to go easy on them to secure required information, they will often discuss the terms of the promised leniency with representatives of the court. If a judge ignores police demands, the department's bargaining power is severely diminished, and communication within the criminal justice system is impaired.

Judicial Qualifications and Selection

Judicial qualifications and selection vary between the federal and state levels. In general, there are fewer formal qualifications and more *informal* qualifications at the federal level. The opposite is often true at the state level.

FEDERAL LEVEL • Federal judges are appointed by the president with the advice and consent of the Senate. Senate confirmation of federal judiciary appointees, especially those chosen to serve on the U.S. Supreme Court, can be a contentious process. One exception to this process exists for the appointment of a **U.S. magistrate judge**. Magistrate judges are federal trial judges appointed by district court judges who preside over various civil cases with the consent of the parties and over certain misdemeanor cases.

Interestingly, there are almost no formal qualifications for federal judges. The Constitution and federal law are silent on judicial qualifications. There are no exams that must be passed, and there is not even a requirement that a federal judge be a lawyer. Even so, positions in the federal judiciary are very prestigious and sought-after. They thus attract highly qualified, seasoned attorneys.

STATE LEVEL • The qualifications for appointment to one of the existing 30,000 judgeships vary from state to state and court to court. Most often, the potential judge must be a resident of the state, licensed to practice law, a member of the state bar association, and at least 25 years and less than 70 years of age. However, a significant degree of diversity exists in the basic qualifications, depending on the level of court jurisdiction. Although almost every state requires judges to have a law degree if they are to serve on appellate courts or courts of general jurisdiction, it is not uncommon for municipal or town court judges to lack a legal background, even though they

Federal Magistrate Judges Association

Interested in learning more about federal magistrate judges? Check out the site for the **Federal Magistrate Judges Association** here:

www.cengage.com/ criminaljustice/siegel

U.S. magistrate judge
A federal trial judge who is appointed by a district court judge and who presides over various civil cases with the consent of the parties and over certain misdemeanor cases.

REALITY CHECK

MYTH OR REALITY? There are almost no formal qualifications for federal judges.

REALITY: It is true that there are almost no formal qualifications for federal judges.

There are no exams, no age requirements, and no requirements that a federal judge be a U.S. citizen. There is not even a law degree requirement! Even so, the federal judiciary attracts highly qualified people. Why do you suppose there are almost no formal qualifications for federal judges?

have the power to incarcerate criminal defendants for petty crimes such as vandalism.

Many methods are used to select judges, depending on the level of court jurisdiction. In some jurisdictions, judges are appointed officials, most often appointed by the state governor. In some states, in an effort to remove politics from judicial appointments, the governor's recommendations must be confirmed by the state senate, the governor's council, a special confirmation committee, an executive council elected by the state assembly, or an elected review board. Some states employ a judicial nominating commission that submits names to the governor for approval.

Another form of judicial selection is popular election. Judges may run as members of the Republican, Democratic, or other parties, or without party affiliation. Although this practice is used in a majority of states, each state sets its own terms of appointment. In some states judges are elected to 15-year terms, in others to 4-year terms.[8] See Figure 7.5 for a map of judicial selection methods by state.

The state of Missouri pioneered a nonpartisan method of selecting judges. This **Missouri Plan** is now used in some manner in the majority of states. The plan consists of three parts:

1. A judicial nominating commission selects and nominates potential candidates for the bench. In Missouri, the judicial commission is composed of the chief justice of the state supreme court, three lawyers elected by the Missouri bar (the organization of all lawyers licensed in this state), and three citizens selected by the governor.

2. An elected official (usually from the executive branch, such as the governor) makes appointments from the list submitted by the commission.

3. Subsequent nonpartisan and noncompetitive elections take place, in which incumbent judges run on their records and voters can choose either to retain or to dismiss them.[9]

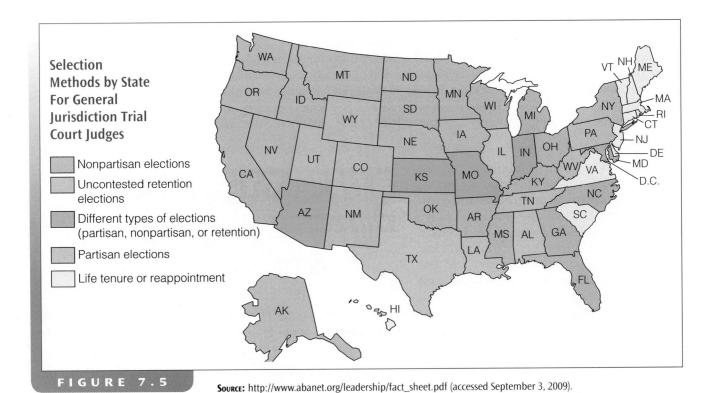

FIGURE 7.5

Source: http://www.abanet.org/leadership/fact_sheet.pdf (accessed September 3, 2009).

The quality of the judiciary is a concern. Although merit plans, screening committees, and popular elections are designed to ensure a competent judiciary, it has often been charged that many judicial appointments are made to pay off political debts or to reward cronies and loyal friends. Also not uncommon are charges that those who wish to be nominated for judgeships are required to make significant political contributions.

JUDICIAL OVERLOAD ● There has been great concern about stress placed on judges by the size of their assigned caseloads. In most states, people appointed to the bench have had little or no training in the role of judge. Others may have held administrative posts and may not have appeared before a court in years. Once they are appointed to the bench, judges confront an overwhelming amount of work. The number of civil and criminal filings per state court judge has increased significantly. State court judges deal with far more cases, but federal cases may be more complex and demand more judicial time. In any event, the number of civil and criminal cases, especially in state courts, seems to be outstripping the ability of states to create new judgeships.

REALITYCHECK

MYTH OR REALITY? Elected state judges can be affiliated with a political party.

REALITY: This is not true in all states, but some states permit partisan judicial elections. This means a judge can run as a Democrat, a Republican, an independent, or a member of any other political party.

Should judges be allowed to run on political platforms? Why or why not?

The Prosecutor

Depending on the level of government and the jurisdiction in which he or she functions, the prosecutor may be known as a district attorney, county attorney, state's attorney, or U.S. attorney. Whatever the title, the **prosecutor** is the people's attorney, who is responsible for representing the public in criminal matters.

Because they are the chief law enforcement officers of a particular jurisdiction, their jurisdiction spans the entire justice system process from the time when search and arrest warrants are issued or a grand jury is impaneled to the final sentencing decision and appeal. These are some of the general duties of a prosecutor:

- Provides advice to law enforcement officers during investigation to determine whether criminal charges should be filed
- During the pretrial stage, represents the state in plea negotiations, pretrial motions, and bail hearings
- Represents the state at hearings, criminal trials, and appeals
- Acts as legal advisor to county commissioners and other elected officials

In addition to these duties, local jurisdictions may create specific programs directed by local prosecutors. One example is career-criminal prosecution programs, which involve identifying dangerous adult and juvenile offenders who commit a high number of crimes, so that prosecutors can target them for swift prosecution. Many jurisdictions have developed protection programs so that victims of domestic violence can obtain temporary court orders (and, after a hearing, more long-term court orders) protecting them from an abusive spouse; research indicates that protection orders can reduce the incidence of repeat violence.[10]

prosecutor
Representative of the state (executive branch) in criminal proceedings; advocate for the state's case—the charge—in the adversary trial. Examples include the attorney general of the United States, U.S. attorneys, the attorneys general of the states, district attorneys, and police prosecutors. The prosecutor participates in investigations both before and after arrest, prepares legal documents, participates in obtaining arrest or search warrants, and decides whether to charge a suspect and, if so, with which offense. The prosecutor argues the state's case at trial, advises the police, participates in plea negotiations, and makes sentencing recommendations.

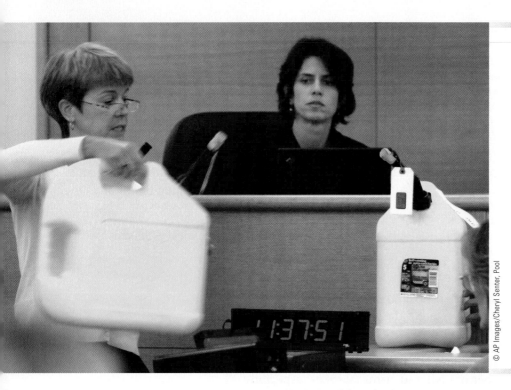

Prosecuting attorney Ann Rice, left, displays gas cans found at the farm of Sheila LaBarre, who was charged with the murder of her boyfriend, Kenneth Countie, 24, of Wilmington, Massachusetts. Police discovered that LaBarre had killed a previous boyfriend months earlier on her horse farm.

© AP Images/Cheryl Senter, Pool

Types of Prosecutors

National District
Attorneys Association

To learn more about prosecutors, go to the **National District Attorneys Association** website,

www.cengage.com/ criminaljustice/siegel

In the federal system, prosecutors are known as U.S. attorneys and are appointed by the president. They are responsible for representing the government in federal district courts. The chief prosecutor is usually an administrator, and assistants normally handle the actual preparation and trial work. Federal prosecutors are professional civil service employees with reasonable salaries and job security.

On the state and county levels, the attorney general and the district attorney, respectively, are the chief prosecutorial officers. Again, the bulk of the criminal prosecution and staff work is performed by scores of full- and part-time attorneys, police investigators, and clerical personnel. Most attorneys who work for prosecutors at the state and county levels are political appointees who earn low salaries, handle many cases, and (in some jurisdictions) maintain private law practices. Many young lawyers take these staff positions to gain the trial experience that will qualify them for better opportunities.

In urban jurisdictions, the structure of the district attorney's office is often specialized, with separate divisions for felonies, misdemeanors, and trial and appeal assignments. In rural offices, chief prosecutors handle many of the criminal cases themselves. Where assistant prosecutors are employed, they often work part time, have limited professional opportunities, and depend on the political patronage of chief prosecutors for their positions.

The personnel practices, organizational structures, and political atmosphere of many prosecutors' offices often restrict their effectiveness in investigating and prosecuting criminal offenses. For many years, prosecutors have been criticized for bargaining justice away, using their positions as stepping stones to higher political office, and often failing to investigate or simply dismissing criminal cases. Lately, however, the prosecutor's public image has improved. Violations of federal laws, such as white-collar crime, drug peddling, and corruption, are being more aggressively investigated by the 94 U.S. attorneys and the nearly 2,000 assistant U.S. attorneys. Aggressive federal prosecutors have also made extraordinary progress in the war against insider trading and securities fraud on Wall Street. There have been a number of highly publicized indictments alleging that some corporate managers abused their power to loot company assets.

State crimes ranging from murder to larceny are prosecuted in state courts by district attorneys, who are stepping up their efforts against career criminals, shortening the time it takes to bring serious cases to trial, and addressing the long-neglected problems of victims and witnesses. With such actions, the prosecutor will continue to be one of the most powerful and visible professionals in the justice system.

Today, there are about 2,400 state court prosecutors' offices, which employ about 79,000 attorneys, investigators, and support staff to handle felony cases in the state trial courts. Usually, the most active prosecutors are employed in larger counties with populations of over 500,000.

Prosecutors, like other justice system professionals, are now confronting issues related to cyber crime and terrorism and the use of technology both to commit crimes and to solve them once they occur. According to the most recent federal survey of prosecutors,

- At least two-thirds of state court prosecutors had litigated a computer-related crime such as credit card fraud (80%), identity theft (69%), or transmission of child pornography (67%).
- One-quarter (24%) of the offices participated in a state or local task force for homeland security; one-third reported that an office member attended training on homeland security issues.
- Most prosecutors (95%) relied on state-operated forensic laboratories to perform DNA analysis, with about a third (34%) also using privately operated DNA labs.[11]

The Careers in Criminal Justice feature on page 230 examines the job of the prosecutor more closely.

Prosecutorial Discretion

One might expect that after the police arrested and brought a suspect to court, the entire criminal court process would be mobilized. This is often not what happens, however. For a variety of reasons, a substantial percentage of defendants are never brought to trial. The prosecutor decides whether to bring a case to trial or to dismiss it outright. Even if the prosecutor decides to pursue a case, the charges may later be dropped if conditions are not favorable for a conviction; this is referred to as *nolle prosequi*. The courts have protected the prosecutor's right to exercise discretion over processing of legal cases, maintaining that prosecutorial decision making can be controlled or overturned only if a defendant can prove that the prosecutor let discrimination guide his or her decision making.[12]

Even in felony cases, the prosecutor ordinarily exercises much discretion in deciding whether to charge the accused with a crime.[13] After a police investigation, the prosecutor may be asked to review the sufficiency of the evidence to determine whether a criminal complaint should be filed. In some jurisdictions, this may involve presenting the evidence at a preliminary hearing. In other cases, the prosecutor may decide to seek a criminal complaint through the grand jury or other information procedure.

There is little question that prosecutors exercise a great deal of discretion in even the most serious cases. In a now classic study, Barbara Boland examined the flow of felony cases through three jurisdictions in the United States: Golden, Colorado; the borough of Manhattan in New York City; and Salt Lake City, Utah.[14] Although procedures were different in the three districts, prosecutors used their discretion to dismiss a high percentage of the cases before

Careers in Criminal Justice

PROSECUTOR

Duties and Characteristics of the Job

- Prosecutors represent the public in criminal trials and are responsible for proving in court that the accused is guilty of the charges brought against him or her.
- Prosecutors work at the municipal, state, and federal levels of government. During a trial, a prosecutor is opposed by a defense attorney, who represents the interests of the accused offender.
- To convince the judge or jury of the defendant's guilt, the prosecutor questions witnesses and gives statements, using evidence collected during the investigative phase of the case.
- Prosecutors also decide which cases to bring to trial and have the authority to settle cases out of court. Even though they represent the people, prosecutors often meet with victims of crime and present the case from their point of view when in court.
- Victims of crime and their families, community members, and law enforcement depend on the prosecutor to prove the guilt of an alleged offender to a jury or judge and achieve a conviction.
- Prosecutors may work long hours, especially during trials. In general, prosecutors tend to be paid less than their counterparts in private practice, but many report high personal satisfaction from seeing that justice is served.

Job Outlook

- Crime rates and budgets dictate the number of job openings. In light of recent budget crises, prosecutors offices have scaled back on hiring.
- Opportunities should open up on a regular basis, because the position has a high turnover rate.

Salary

- Prosecutors working at federal and state offices tend to earn more than those working at county and municipal levels.
- In larger cities, pay will be higher. Entering prosecutors earn an average of $42,500. Senior prosecutors often earn in excess of $100,000 per year.

Opportunities

- There are opportunities for advancement in larger offices, especially in urban areas. A state prosecutor may also wish to seek a position as a federal prosecutor.
- After leaving their position, former prosecutors might open up their own private practice, possibly with the intent of running a lucrative defense attorney business.
- Prosecutors can also seek appointments to prestigious and well-paying judge positions or choose to leave the practice of law for a political career.

Qualifications

- Like other lawyers, prosecutors need to be comfortable and practiced at public speaking, and they also need well-developed analytical skills.
- There is something of a political aspect to gaining this position, because in some areas one must be elected or appointed to it.

Education and Training

- A bachelor's degree with an emphasis on writing, analytical, and research skills is necessary.
- A law degree is also required.
- Law school graduates must pass the state bar exam in order to practice law.

Word to the Wise

- Entry into law school is very competitive, and the educational requirements are challenging.
- Prosecutors are government employees. As such, they do not earn as much as some attorneys in the private sector.

- Most criminal cases never make it to trial, so prosecutors with ambitions of doing nothing but argue jury trials may be disappointed.
- For cases that *do* go to trial, there is a great deal of behind-the-scenes preparation. A successful prosecutor is a detail-oriented person, not just a skilled orator.
- There is high turnover, partly as a result of prosecutors "burning out" after a few years. This can be attributed to the relatively low-pay, high-volume work, and to dealing with unpleasant criminal cases.

trial. When cases were forwarded for trial, very few defendants were actually acquitted, indicating that the prosecutorial discretion was exercised to screen out the weakest cases. In addition, of those cases accepted for prosecution, a high percentage ended with the defendant pleading guilty. All the evidence here points to the conclusion that prosecutorial discretion is used to reduce potential trial cases to a minimum.

The prosecutor may also play a limited role in exercising discretion in minor offenses. This role may consist of simply consulting with the police after their investigation results in a complaint being filed against the accused. In such instances, the decision to charge a person with a crime may be left primarily to the discretion of the law enforcement agency. The prosecutor may decide to enter this type of case after an arrest has been made and a complaint filed with the court, and she may subsequently determine whether to adjust the matter or proceed to trial.

The power to institute formal charges against the defendant is the key to the prosecutorial function, and it gives the prosecutor significant control over the liberty of the accused. More than 70 years ago, Newman Baker commented on the problems of prosecutorial decision making:

"To prosecute or not to prosecute?" is a question which comes to mind of this official scores of times each day. A law has been contravened and the statute says he is bound to commence proceedings. His legal duty is clear. But what will be the result? Will it be a waste of time? Will it be expensive to the state? Will it be unfair to the defendant (the prosecutor applying his own ideas of justice)? Will it serve any good purpose to society in general? Will it have good publicity value? Will it cause a political squabble? Will it prevent the prosecutor from carrying the offender's home precinct when he, the prosecutor, runs for Congress after his term as prosecutor? Was the law violated a foolish piece of legislation? If the offender is a friend, is it the square thing to do to reward friendship by initiating criminal proceedings? These and many similar considerations are bound to come to the mind of the man responsible for setting the wheels of criminal justice in motion.[15]

Factors Influencing Prosecutorial Discretion

Research indicates that a wide variety of factors influence prosecutorial discretion in invoking criminal sanction. These include legal issues, victim issues, extralegal issues, and resource issues.

LEGAL ISSUES ● Legal issues can include the characteristics of the justice system, the crime, the criminal, and the victim. The quality of police work and the amount and relevance of the evidence the police gather are critical legal variables that a prosecutor considers in deciding whether to bring a case forward to trial.[16] A defendant who is a known drug user, has a long history of criminal offending, and caused the victim extensive physical injuries is more likely to be prosecuted than one who is a first offender, does not use drugs, and did not seriously injure a victim.[17] Crime seriousness certainly influences discretion. As might be expected, prosecutors are much more likely to use their discretion in minor incidents than in more serious ones.[18]

VICTIM ISSUES • In some instances, the victim's behavior may influence charging decisions. Some victims may become reluctant to press charges, especially if the offender is a parent or spouse. Domestic violence cases are often difficult to prosecute. Some victims are unlikely to encourage or work with prosecutors even after the police get involved. African American women are less likely to support prosecution than Caucasian women, perhaps because they have had disappointing experiences with the justice system or lack the resources—such as money to pay babysitters—to vigorously pursue a legal solution to their problems.[19] Thus victim cooperation is a key factor in the decision to prosecute cases: The odds of a case being prosecuted are seven times greater when victims are considered "cooperative."[20]

EXTRALEGAL ISSUES • Extralegal factors include the offender's race, gender, and ethnic background. Of course, due process considerations demand that these personal characteristics have no bearing on the use of prosecutorial discretion. Nonetheless, some research efforts have found that the race of the offender or victim influences prosecutorial discretion, but others show that decisions are relatively unbiased.[21] Proving racial influence is difficult. In order to establish bias, a defendant must produce credible evidence that similarly situated defendants of other races could have been prosecuted but were not.

RESOURCE ISSUES • Resource issues that influence prosecutorial discretion include the availability of treatment and detention facilities, the size of caseloads, and the number of prosecutors available. In some drug cases, prosecutors may decline to bring the case to trial because preparing it for prosecution would demand costly forensic analysis, expert witnesses, and forensic accountants.[22] Some research efforts have concluded that the availability of resources may be a more critical factor in shaping prosecutorial discretion than either legal or extralegal factors. In a world of tight government budgets, a prosecutor's office may be forced to accept plea bargains simply because it lacks the resources and personnel to bring many cases to trial.[23]

REALITY CHECK

MYTH OR REALITY? Prosecutors base their charging decisions solely on legal factors, such as the seriousness of the offense.

MYTH: Limited resources, along with several other extralegal factors, shape prosecutorial decision making.

Resource concerns are all the more important in this day and age. News accounts of courts strapped for money and prosecutors dropping charges against some suspects in order to save precious resources seem all too common. In what other ways are resource constraints likely to affect the administration of justice?

The Role of Prosecutorial Discretion

Regardless of its source, the proper exercise of prosecutorial discretion can improve the criminal justice process by preventing the rigid implementation of criminal law. Discretion allows the prosecutor to consider alternative decisions and humanize the operation of the criminal justice system. If prosecutors had little or no discretion, they would be forced to prosecute all cases brought to their attention. As Judge Charles Breitel put it, "If every policeman, every prosecutor, every court, and every postsentence agency performed his or its responsibility in strict accordance with rules of law, precisely and narrowly laid down, the criminal law would be ordered but intolerable."[24]

On the other side, too much discretion can lead to abuses that result in the abandonment of law. Prosecutors are political creatures. Although they are charged with serving the people, they also must keep their reputations in mind; losing too many high-profile cases may jeopardize their chances of re-election. They therefore may be unwilling to prosecute cases where the odds of conviction are low; they are worried about convictability.[25]

Prosecutorial Ethics

Although the prosecutor's primary duty is to enforce criminal law, his fundamental obligation as an attorney is to seek justice, as well as to convict those who are guilty. If the prosecutor discovers facts suggesting that the accused is innocent, he must bring this information to the attention of the court.

In carrying out their stated duties, prosecutors are sometimes caught in an ethical conundrum. They are compelled by their supervisors to do everything possible to obtain a guilty verdict, all the while acting as public officials concerned to ensure that justice is done. Sometimes this conflict can lead to prosecutorial misconduct. According to some legal authorities, unethical prosecutorial behavior is often motivated by the desire to obtain a conviction and by the fact that such misbehavior is rarely punished by the courts.[26] Some prosecutors may conceal evidence, or misrepresent it, or influence juries by impugning the character of opposing witnesses. Even where a court may instruct a jury to ignore certain evidence, a prosecutor may attempt to sway the jury or the judge by simply mentioning the tainted evidence. Because appellate courts generally uphold convictions in cases where such misconduct is not considered serious (the "harmless error doctrine"), prosecutors are not penalized for their misbehavior, nor are they personally liable for their conduct. Overzealous, excessive, and even cruel prosecutors, motivated by a desire for political gain or notoriety, may produce wrongful convictions, thereby abusing their office and the public trust.[27] According to legal expert Stanley Fisher, prosecutorial excesses appear when the government always seeks the highest charges, interprets the criminal law expansively, wins as many convictions as possible, and obtains the severest penalties.[28]

PROSECUTORIAL MISCONDUCT ● Because prosecutorial misconduct is a serious matter, the courts have reviewed such prosecutorial behavior as making disruptive statements in court, failing to adhere to sentence recommendations pursuant to a plea bargain, making public statements harmful to the state's case that are not constitutionally protected under the First Amendment, and withholding evidence that might exonerate a defendant.

Courts have also been more concerned about prosecutors who use their discretion in a vindictive manner to punish defendants who exercise their legal rights. Three cases illustrate controls placed on "vindictive" prosecutors:

- ***North Carolina v. Pearce.*** In this case, the U.S. Supreme Court held that a judge in a retrial cannot impose a sentence more severe than that originally imposed. In other words, a prosecutor cannot seek a stricter sentence for a defendant who succeeds in getting her first conviction set aside.[29]
- ***Blackledge v. Perry.*** The U.S. Supreme Court found that imposing a penalty on a defendant for having successfully pursued a statutory right of appeal is a violation of due process of law and amounts to prosecutorial vindictiveness.[30]
- ***Bordenkircher v. Hayes.*** In this case, the Court allowed the prosecutor to carry out threats of increased charges made during plea negotiations when the defendant refused to plead guilty to the original charge.[31]

These decisions provide the framework for the "prosecutorial vindictiveness" doctrine: Due process of law may be violated if the prosecutor retaliates against a defendant and there is proof of actual vindictiveness. The prosecutor's legitimate exercise of discretion must be balanced against the defendant's legal rights.

The Defense Attorney

The defense attorney is the counterpart of the prosecuting attorney in the criminal process. The accused has a constitutional right to counsel, and when the defendant cannot afford an attorney, the state must provide one. The accused may obtain counsel from the private bar if he can afford to do so; if the defendant is indigent, private counsel or a **public defender** may be assigned by the court (see the discussion on the defense of the indigent later in this chapter).

public defender

An attorney usually employed (at no cost to the accused) by the government to represent poor persons accused of a crime.

The Role of the Criminal Defense Attorney

The defense counsel is an attorney as well as an officer of the court. As an attorney, the defense counsel is obligated to uphold the integrity of the legal profession and to observe the requirements of the American Bar Association's Code of Professional Responsibility in the defense of a client. In the code, the duties of a lawyer to the adversary system of justice are stated as follows:

> Our legal system provides for the adjudication of disputes governed by the rules of substantive, evidentiary, and procedural law. An adversary presentation counters the natural human tendency to judge too swiftly in terms of the familiar that which is not yet fully known; the advocate, by his zealous preparation of facts and law, enables the tribunal to come to the hearing with an open and neutral mind and to render impartial judgments. The duty of a lawyer to his client and his duty to the legal system are the same: to represent his client zealously within the boundaries of the law.[32]

Defense attorneys are viewed as the prime movers in what is essentially an **adversarial procedure**: the procedure used to determine truth in the adjudication of guilt or innocence, in which the defense (advocate for the accused) is pitted against the prosecution (advocate for the state), with the judge acting as arbiter of the legal rules. Under the adversary system, the burden is on the state to prove the charges beyond a reasonable doubt. The defense uses all

adversarial procedure

The process of publicly pitting the prosecution and the defense against one another in pursuit of the truth.

Michelle Harris, a former Georgia Tech employee, rests her head on her hand as her lawyer, Clay Thompson, right, makes a plea to the judge on March 16, 2009, in Atlanta. Fulton County Superior Court Judge John Goger sentenced Harris to 20 years, voicing disdain for the defendant and calling the prosecution's suggested sentence too lenient. Citing the "obscene amount of money she stole" and her violation of the public trust, the judge sentenced Michelle Harris to 10 years in prison and 10 years on probation for stealing more than $173,000 from the university by running up fraudulent charges on her university credit card.

© AP Images/Atlanta-Journal Constitution, Joey Ivansco

means at its disposal to refute the state's case. This system of having the two parties publicly debate, though imperfect, is thought to be the most effective method of arriving at the truth in a criminal case.

As a member of the legal profession, however, the defense counsel must be aware of her role as an officer of the court. The defense counsel is obligated to uphold the integrity of the legal profession and to rely on constitutional ideals of fair play and professional ethics to provide adequate representation for a client.

The Right to Counsel

The **Sixth Amendment** to the U.S. Constitution allows for provision of counsel at trial. But what about the **indigent** criminal defendant who cannot afford to retain an attorney?

In the 1963 landmark case of **Gideon v. Wainwright**, the U.S. Supreme Court took the first major step on the issue of right to counsel by holding that state courts must provide counsel to indigent defendants in felony prosecutions.[33] Almost 10 years later, in the 1972 case of *Argersinger v. Hamlin*, the Court extended the obligation to provide counsel to all criminal cases where the penalty includes imprisonment—regardless of whether the offense is a felony or a misdemeanor.[34] These two major decisions are related to the Sixth Amendment right to counsel as it applies to the presentation of a defense at the trial stages of the criminal justice system.

In numerous Supreme Court decisions since *Gideon v. Wainwright*, the states have been required to provide counsel for indigent defendants at virtually all other stages of the criminal process, beginning with arrest and concluding with the defendant's release from the system. Today, the Sixth Amendment right to counsel and the Fifth and Fourteenth Amendments' guarantee of due process of law have been judicially interpreted together to provide the defendant with counsel by the state in all types of criminal proceedings. The Supreme Court generally requires the states to provide counsel in proceedings that involve the

National Association of Criminal Defense Lawyers (NACDL)

The **National Association of Criminal Defense Lawyers (NACDL)** is the largest U.S. organization of defense attorneys. Check out this association at

www.cengage.com/ criminaljustice/siegel

Sixth Amendment
The U.S. constitutional amendment containing various criminal trial rights, such as the right to public trial, the right to trial by jury, and the right to confrontation of witnesses.

indigent
Without the means to hire an attorney.

Gideon v. Wainwright
The 1963 U.S. Supreme Court case that granted counsel to indigent defendants in felony prosecutions.

loss of personal liberty, such as criminal trials, juvenile court hearings, and mental health commitments.

Areas remain in the criminal justice system where the courts have not required that the assistance of counsel be provided for the accused. These include preindictment lineups; booking procedures, including the taking of fingerprints and other forms of identification; grand jury investigations; appeals beyond the first review; disciplinary proceedings in correctional institutions; and revocation hearings after release. Nevertheless, the general rule of thumb is that no person can be deprived of freedom or lose a "liberty interest" without representation by counsel.

Legal Services for the Indigent

To satisfy the constitutional requirements that indigent defendants be provided with the assistance of counsel at various stages of the criminal process, the federal government and the states have had to evaluate and expand criminal defense services. Today, about 3,000 state and local agencies are providing indigent legal services in the United States.

Providing legal services for the indigent offender is a huge and costly undertaking. And although most states have a formal set of rules to signify who is an indigent, and many require indigents to repay the state for at least part of their legal services (known as "recoupment"), indigent legal services still cost over $1.5 billion annually.

assigned counsel

A lawyer appointed by the court to represent a defendant in a criminal case because the person is too poor to hire counsel.

contract system (attorney)

Providing counsel to indigent offenders by having attorneys under contract to the county handle all (or some) such cases.

Programs providing counsel assistance to indigent defendants can be divided into three major categories: public defender systems, **assigned counsel** systems, and **contract systems** (see Exhibit 7.2). Other approaches to the delivery of legal services include the use of mixed systems, such as representation by both the public defender and the private bar, law school clinical programs, and prepaid legal services. Although many jurisdictions have a combination of these programs, statewide public defender programs seem to be on the increase.[35]

These three systems can be used independently or in combination. The majority of Maine's indigent criminal defense services are provided through an assigned counsel program; Oregon primarily uses a system of awarded contracts; Minnesota and New Mexico do not have assigned counsel programs but instead rely on statewide public defender programs and contract attorney programs.[36]

In general, the attorney list/assigned counsel system is used in less populated areas, where case flow is minimal and a full-time public defender is not needed. Public defenders are usually found in larger urban areas with high case flow rates. So although a proportionately larger area of the country is served by the assigned counsel system, a significant proportion of criminal defendants are represented by public defenders.

The Private Bar

Although most criminal defendants are represented by publicly supported lawyers, there are also private attorneys who specialize in criminal practice. Because most lawyers are not prepared in law school for criminal work, their skill often results from their experience in the trial courts. Some nationally known criminal defense attorneys represent defendants for large fees in celebrated and widely publicized cases, these are actually relatively few in number.

Besides this limited group of well-known criminal lawyers, some lawyers and law firms serve as house counsel for such professional criminals as narcotics dealers, gamblers, prostitutes, and even big-time burglars. These lawyers, however, constitute a very small percentage of the private bar practicing criminal law.

EXHIBIT 7.2

The Forms of Indigent Defense

- *Public defender.* A salaried staff of full-time or part-time attorneys who render indigent criminal defense services through a public or private nonprofit organization, or as direct government-paid employees. The first public defender program in the United States opened in 1913 in Los Angeles. Public defenders can be part of a statewide agency, county government, the judiciary, or an independent nonprofit organization or other institution.

- *Assigned counsel.* The appointment is from a list of private bar members who accept cases on a judge-by-judge, court-by-court, or case-by-case basis. This may include an administrative component and a set of rules and guidelines governing the appointment and processing of cases handled by the private bar members. There are two main types of assigned counsel systems. In the first, which makes up about 75 percent of all assigned counsel systems, the presiding judge appoints attorneys on a case-by-case basis; this is referred to as an ad hoc assigned counsel system. The second type is referred to as a coordinated assigned counsel system, in which an administrator oversees the appointment of counsel and sets up guidelines for the administration of indigent legal services. The fees awarded to assigned counsels can vary widely, ranging from a low of $10 per hour for handling a misdemeanor out of court to over $100 per hour for a serious felony handled in court. Some jurisdictions may establish a maximum allowance per case of $750 for a misdemeanor and $1,500 for a felony. Average rates seem to be between $40 and $80 per hour, depending on the nature of the case. Restructuring the attorney fee system is undoubtedly needed to maintain fair standards for the payment of such legal services.

- *Contract.* Nonsalaried private attorneys, bar associations, law firms, consortiums or groups of attorneys, or nonprofit corporations contract with a funding source to provide court-appointed representation in a jurisdiction. In some instances, an attorney is given a set amount of money and is required to handle all cases assigned. In other jurisdictions, contract lawyers agree to provide legal representation for a set number of cases at a fixed fee. A third system involves representation at an estimated cost per case until the dollar amount of the contract is reached. At that point, the contract may be renegotiated, but the lawyers are not obligated to take new cases.

SOURCE: Carol J. DeFrances, *State-Funded Indigent Defense Services, 1999* (Washington, D.C.: Bureau of Justice Statistics, 2001).

A large number of criminal defendants are represented by lawyers who often accept many cases for small fees. These lawyers may belong to small law firms or work alone, but a sizable portion of their practice involves representing those accused of crime. Other private practitioners occasionally take on criminal matters as part of their general practice. A lawyer whose practice involves a substantial proportion of criminal cases is often considered a specialist in the field. And there is little question that having a preeminent private attorney can help clients prove their innocence. Just ask O. J. Simpson, who was represented in his murder trial by the late Johnny Cochran, one of the nation's best-known attorneys. Recent research by Talia Roitberg Harmon and William Lofquist found that having a competent private attorney who puts on a rigorous defense is the single most important factor separating those exonerated in murder cases from those who are executed.[37]

Does the Type of Lawyer Matter?

Do criminal defendants who hire their own private lawyers do better in court than those who depend on legal representatives provided by the state? Is one type of defense attorney for the indigent better than another?

PUBLIC VS. PRIVATE ATTORNEYS ● Although there are some advantages to private counsel, national surveys indicate that state-appointed attorneys do quite well in court. According to data compiled by the federal government:

- Conviction rates for indigent defendants and for those with their own lawyers were about the same in federal and state courts. About 90 percent of the federal defendants and 75 percent of the defendants in the most populous counties were found guilty regardless of which type of attorneys represented them.
- Of those found guilty, however, those represented by publicly financed attorneys were incarcerated at a higher rate than those defendants who paid for their own legal representation.
- On average, sentence lengths for defendants sent to jail or prison were shorter for those with publicly financed attorneys than for those who hired counsel. In federal district court, those with publicly financed attorneys were given just under five years on average, and those with private attorneys just over five years. In large state courts, those with publicly financed attorneys were sentenced to an average of two and a half years, and those with private attorneys to three years.[38]

REALITYCHECK

MYTH OR REALITY? Privately retained defense attorneys are more effective than court-appointed defense attorneys.

MYTH: Research reveals that public defenders and court-appointed attorneys perform similarly on average.

There is no clear evidence that having an expensive, privately retained attorney markedly increases one's chance of acquittal. What does this say about privately retained defense attorneys? What about court-appointed attorneys?

PUBLIC VS. PUBLIC ATTORNEYS ● Are there also differences between types of public defense attorneys for the indigent? Some recent research by Radha Iyengar indicates that differences do in fact exist. Iyengar analyzed the performance of defense counsel for the indigent working in the federal court system. Her research is unique because judges randomly assign cases to court-appointed attorneys and to federal public defenders. After ensuring that the cases were in fact assigned randomly, Iyengar found that defendants assigned to salaried public defenders fared much better than those who were assigned to the lawyers retained by the hour. Defendants with assigned attorneys are on average more likely to be found guilty and on average to receive longer sentences. Overall, the expected sentence for defendants with assigned counsel was nearly eight months longer than for those with public defenders.[39]

How can this discrepancy be explained? It is possible that full-time public defenders generally handle more cases and have more interactions with prosecutors, so they may have better plea bargaining skills. Salaried lawyers also tend to have superior credentials and more legal experience. The court-appointed lawyers tend to be quite young, from small practices, and from lower-ranked law schools. They have a smaller client base and fewer interactions with prosecutors.

Are you better off with a public defender than with an assigned counsel? Iyengar's findings indicate that if you want to avoid prison or at least get a shorter sentence, ask for a public defender!

The Competence of Defense Attorneys

Does the Sixth Amendment guarantee of counsel for virtually all defendants require that a "competent" attorney be appointed, and if so, how is competency defined?

People can be wrongfully convicted for a variety of reasons, including inadequate representation of counsel. Here Karen Richey, in Edinburgh, Scotland, holds a picture of her partner, Kenneth Richey, who was on death row in the United States for 18 years. A federal appeals court threw out the conviction and death sentence of the dual U.S.-British citizen, who was found guilty of killing a 2-year-old girl in Ohio in 1986, saying he received incompetent counsel at trial.

© AP Images/PA

HAPPY BIRTHDAY KENNY

LIFE BEGINS AT 40 !!

Inadequacy of counsel may occur in a variety of instances. The attorney may refuse to meet regularly with the client, fail to cross-examine key government witnesses, or fail to investigate the case properly. A defendant's plea of guilty may be based on poor advice, where the attorney may misjudge the admissibility of evidence. When co-defendants have separate counsel, conflicts of interest between the defense attorneys may arise. On an appellate level, the lawyer may decline to file a brief, instead relying on a brief submitted for one of the co-appellants.

The U.S. Supreme Court defined the concept of attorney competence in the 1984 case of *Strickland v. Washington*.[40] Strickland had been arrested for committing a string of extremely serious crimes, including murder, torture, and kidnapping. Against his lawyer's advice, he pleaded guilty and threw himself on the mercy of the trial judge at a capital sentencing hearing. He also ignored his attorney's recommendation that he exercise his right to have an advisory jury at his sentencing hearing.

In preparing for the hearing, the lawyer spoke with Strickland's wife and mother but did not otherwise seek character witnesses. Nor was a psychiatric examination requested because, in the attorney's opinion, Strickland did not have psychological problems. The attorney also did not ask for a pre-sentence investigation because he felt such a report would contain information damaging to his client.

Although the presiding judge had a reputation for leniency in cases where the defendant confessed, he sentenced Strickland to death. Strickland appealed on the grounds that his attorney had rendered ineffective counsel, citing his failure to seek psychiatric testimony and present character witnesses.

© Guy Cali/Corbis

The case eventually went to the Supreme Court, which upheld Strickland's sentence. The Strickland case established the two-pronged test for determining effectiveness of counsel:

1. The defendant must show that the counsel's performance was deficient and that such serious errors were made as to essentially eliminate the presence of counsel guaranteed by the Sixth Amendment.

2. The defendant must also show that the deficient performance prejudiced the case to such an extent that the defendant was deprived of a fair trial.

In the case at hand, the Court found insufficient evidence that the attorney had acted beyond the boundaries of professional competence and thus upheld Strickland's sentence.

Determining whether defense counsel is ineffective is a subjective decision. The Supreme Court has ruled that an attorney can be effective even when he admits a client's guilt before the trial is over, as long as doing so is part of a reasonable defense strategy, such as gaining sympathy from the jury.[41] For a defense attorney to be considered incompetent, he or she would have to miss filings, fail to follow normal trial procedure, and/or fail to use defense tactics that the average attorney would be sure to follow, such as using expert witnesses or mentioning past behaviors that might mitigate guilt.

Court Administration

In addition to qualified personnel, there is a need for efficient management of the judiciary system. The need for efficient management techniques in an ever-expanding criminal court system has led to the recognition that improving court administration is one way to relieve court congestion. Management goals include improving the organization and scheduling of cases, devising methods to allocate court resources efficiently, administering fines and monies due the court, preparing budgets, and overseeing personnel.

The federal courts have led the way in creating and organizing court administration. In 1939, Congress passed the Administrative Office Act, which established the Administrative Office of the United States Courts. Its director

© AP Images/Gary C. Knapp

Technology will become ever more present in the courtrooms of the future. The courtroom featured here contains flat-screen televisions throughout, including one in front of each juror. Courts like this one rely on computer technology and the Internet to bring together witnesses, lawyers, judges, and the jury.

was charged with gathering statistics on the work of the federal courts and preparing the judicial budget for approval by the Conference of Senior Circuit Judges. One clause of the act created a judicial council with general supervisory responsibilities for the district and circuit courts.

Unlike the federal government, the states have experienced slow and uneven growth in the development and application of court management principles. The first state to establish an administrative office was North Dakota in 1927. Today, all states employ some form of central administration.

The federal government has encouraged the development of state court management through funding assistance to court managers. In addition, the federal judiciary has provided the philosophical impetus for better and more effective court management.

Using Technology in Court Management

In most jurisdictions today, centralized court administrative services perform numerous functions with the help of sophisticated computers that free the judiciary to fulfill their roles as arbiters of justice. Rapid retrieval and organization of data are now being used for such functions as these:

- Maintaining case histories and statistical reporting
- Monitoring and scheduling cases
- Preparing documents
- Indexing cases
- Issuing summonses
- Notifying witnesses, attorneys, and others of required appearances
- Selecting and notifying jurors
- Preparing and administering budgets and payrolls

The federal government has encouraged the states to experiment with computerized information systems. Federal funds were used to begin a 50-state consortium for the purpose of establishing a standardized crime-reporting system called SEARCH (Systems for the Electronic Analysis and Retrieval of Criminal Histories).

Computer technology is also being applied in the courts in such areas as videotaped testimonies, new court reporting devices, information systems, and data processing systems to handle such functions as court docketing and jury management. In 1968, only 10 states had state-level automated information systems; today all states employ such systems for a variety of tasks and duties. A survey of Georgia courts found that 84 percent used computers for three or more court administration applications.

Other developing areas of court technology include the following:[42]

COMMUNICATIONS ● Court jurisdictions are also cooperating with police departments in the installation of communications gear that makes it possible to arraign defendants over closed-circuit television while they are in police custody. Closed-circuit television has been used for judicial conferences and scheduling meetings. Some courts are using voice-activated cameras to record all testimony during trials; these are the sole means of keeping trial records.

VIDEOCONFERENCING ● About 400 courts across the country have videoconferencing capability. It is now being employed for juvenile detention hearings, expert witness testimony at trial, oral arguments on appeal, and parole hearings. More than 150 courts use two-way live, televised remote linkups for first appearance and arraignment. In the usual arrangement, defendants appear from a special location in the jail where they can see and hear, and be seen and heard by, the presiding magistrate.

EVIDENCE PRESENTATION • High-tech courtrooms are now equipped for real-time transcription and translation, audio-video preservation of the court record, remote witness participation, computer graphics displays, television monitors for jurors, and computers for counsel and judge.

CASE MANAGEMENT • Case management will soon be upgraded. In the 1970s, municipal courts installed tracking systems, which used databases to manage court data. These older systems were limited and could not process the complex interrelationships that pervade information about persons, cases, time, and financial matters in court cases. Contemporary relational databases now provide the flexibility to handle complex case management. The Criminal Justice and Technology feature below explores this issue in more depth.

INTERNET UTILIZATION • The Internet has begun finding its way into the court system. In the federal system, "J-Net" is the judiciary's intranet website. J-Net makes it easier for judges and court personnel to find important information in a timely fashion. The federal court's Administrative Office has

Criminal Justice and Technology

Improving Court Functions with Technology

Can technology help courts to function more effectively? One important contribution that information technology (IT) can make is to allocate resources and court time in a more efficient manner. For example, in most jurisdictions today, there is often a logjam of people in the morning and nearly empty courthouses at 4:00 P.M. How can IT improve this unsatisfactory situation? A number of strategies are now possible.

Time-Certain Scheduling

Many services (from beauty parlors to physicians' offices) commonly give customers a specific time to show up for an appointment. With all of the data collected in court case management and court record systems, courts use existing data to project when a hearing is likely to take place. Although many proceedings, particularly those scheduled for the judge's chambers, already have an arranged schedule, other court business requires that defendants show up "in the morning" or "in the afternoon" of the court day. IT can now be used to analyze existing data and create statistical models directing people to show up in a particular half-hour period. For example, five hearings are normally held from 9:00 to 9:30 A.M. and another five from 9:30 to 10:00 A.M., so that is the time period provided on the schedule given to

the participants. This would allow cycling of persons using the parking spaces, security, and the outcome services in the clerk's office.

Reminders

Doctors, dentists, and even hotels send reminders to their customers automatically, via computer, to an email address or to a landline or mobile telephone, based on customer preference. A few courts are very good at sending original scheduling documents via the communication medium of the past, the U.S. Postal Service, but most have not adopted methods used by general commerce. It is now possible for courts to apply computer-driven telephone calling systems or automatic email systems authorized by the user, or both. This means that the case management system will need to have telephone number and email data recording, plus automated connections to the telephone and email systems. Although these reminder systems are intrusive, they can help solve the problem of defendants and litigants not appearing and then claiming they were never notified.

Check-in Systems

Upon arrival at an airport, a traveler can use a touch-screen automated kiosk to sign in and receive a boarding pass.

begun sending official correspondence by email, which provides instantaneous communication of important information. In 2002, 11 federal courts announced that they would allow Internet access to criminal case files as part of a pilot program adopted by the Judicial Conference of the United States (a panel of 27 federal judges responsible for crafting policy in the federal court system). This was the first time the public could gain access to criminal case files.

INFORMATION SHARING ● Technology has been harnessed to make it easier for courts to share information within and between states. This helps cut down on costs and accelerates the criminal justice process.

The computer cannot replace the judge, but it can be used to help speed up the trial process by identifying backlogs and bottlenecks that can be eradicated with intelligent managerial techniques. Just as a manager must know the type and quantity of goods on hand in a warehouse, so an administrative judge must have available information about those entering the judge's domain, what happens to them once they are in it, and how they fare after judgment has been rendered.

court technology

Interested in the latest on **court technology**? The National Center for State Courts maintains a site devoted to the subject at

www.cengage.com/ criminaljustice/siegel

Many people wish to use these to save time. Once the court knows that a person has arrived and is available, couldn't that person be rewarded by going to the head of the line for a hearing? Under present conditions, if a group of people are required for the procedure, they have to wait for everyone to arrive. But if they all arrived early, couldn't they again be rewarded? In technology circles, this behavior is sometimes known as the "smart mob." A smart mob self-regulates using technology. Therefore, some people or groups might elect to arrive later or in the middle of a time period to get a parking space or a shorter wait time. The check-in system would also benefit the court's operations by eliminating calls or the need to search for people who are either not in the courthouse/courtroom or not ready to proceed because not everyone involved has arrived. The check-in system could be enhanced by allowing an individual to enter her cell phone number so that the computer system could call her into the courtroom when there were, say, three or four cases ahead of her in the queue. The courts of Finland use such an automated system to call their law enforcement officers, which enables the latter to use their waiting time more productively.

Visible Queuing

The correlating technology to the "check-in" system is some type of visible queue that can be viewed from screens in the courthouse and courtroom or online. Amusement parks provide an excellent example. When one is standing in line at an amusement park, there are signs at the entrance to the ride, and often again along the line, indicating how long a wait remains. The new "Law Enforcement Center" courthouse in Ramsey County (St. Paul), Minnesota, uses flat panel video screens in the courtroom and hallways to display the "batting order" of defendants who have been interviewed by their attorneys and are ready to go before the judge for an initial appearance or similar proceeding. This allows the guards in the holding area, as well as the attorneys, to gauge the timing of their activities to the defendant's appearance. If the queue can be shown on displays in the courthouse, the same output can be sent to the Internet for display on computers and cell phones with browser capabilities.

Critical Thinking

Does the use of technology undermine the personal nature of the trial? Would you be comfortable in a virtual trial in which the jury was watching via CCTV and the judge was located in another state? Or can technology improve the trial process by removing emotion and bias and replacing it with more objective decision making?

ETHICAL CHALLENGES IN CRIMINAL JUSTICE

A WRITING ASSIGNMENT

You are a defense attorney whose newest client is on trial for a burglary. During an interview held in confidence, your client admits to killing three people and burying their bodies near where he lives. He takes you to the gravesites to prove his claims. The police and prosecutor seem totally unaware of these crimes.

Write an essay describing how you would or should handle this disclosure: keep it confidential, call the cops, send an anonymous tip, or whatever. Consider the legal, moral, and practical issues associated with your decision. Would it make a difference if your client told you that if he were set free, he might kill again?

RealityCheck Revisited

To learn more about the myths and realities related to the court system that were raised in this chapter, visit the following websites.

● For more on state court structures and for links to each state's court-related websites, see

http://www.ojp.usdoj.gov/bjs/pub/pdf/sco04.pdf

http://www.ncsconline.org/D_kis/info_court_web _sites.html

● For more on the federal judiciary, including biographies of every federal judge, see

http://www.fjc.gov/public/home.nsf/hisj

● Interested in reading more about judicial selection methods? The American Judicature Society's websites on the subject have extensive information:

http://www.judicialselection.us

http://www.ajs.org/selection/sel_stateselect.asp

SUMMARY

© AP Images/*Galveston Daily News*, Jennifer Reynolds

1. Be familiar with the role of the court in the justice process

● The criminal court is the setting in which many of the most important decisions in the criminal justice system are made.

● The criminal court is a complex social agency with many independent but interrelated subsystems: administrator, prosecutor, defense attorney, judge, and probation department.

● The entire process is designed to ensure fairness.

● The U.S. court system is the scene of accommodation and "working things out." Plea negotiations and other nonjudicial alternatives, such as diversion, are far more common than the formal trial process.

2. *Recognize the varying structures of state and federal court systems*

- Every state maintains its own court system; no two court organizations are exactly alike.

- State courts handle a wide variety of cases and regulate numerous personal behaviors ranging from homicide to property maintenance.

- Courts of limited jurisdiction are restricted in the types of cases they may hear. This is particularly true for specialized courts, such as drug courts and mental health courts.

- The nation's approximately 13,500 independent courts of limited jurisdiction are the ones most often accused of providing assembly-line justice.

- Approximately 2,000 courts of general jurisdiction exist in the United States; they may be called felony, superior, supreme, county, or circuit courts.

- Courts of general jurisdiction handle the more serious felony cases (such as murder, rape, and robbery) and civil cases in which damages are over a specified amount, such as $10,000.

- Appellate courts do not try cases; they review the procedures of the case to determine whether an error was made by judicial authorities.

- The federal government has established a three-tiered hierarchy of court jurisdiction that, in order of ascendancy, consists of the U.S. district courts, the U.S. courts of appeals (circuit courts), and the U.S. Supreme Court.

3. *Describe the selection and duties of the trial judge*

- The judge is the senior officer in a court of criminal law. His or her duties are varied and far more extensive than might be expected.

- Judicial attitudes and philosophy have a major impact on how the justice system operates. Judicial attitudes may extend way beyond the courtroom.

- The qualifications for appointment to one of the existing 30,000 judgeships vary between the federal and state level—and from state to state.

- Most typically, the potential judge must be a resident of the state, must be licensed to practice law, must be a member of the state bar association, and must be at least 25 years of age and less than 70 years of age.

- The state of Missouri pioneered a nonpartisan method of selecting judges; this so-called Missouri Plan is now used in some manner in more than 30 states.

4. *Discuss the role and duties of prosecutors*

- In the federal system, prosecutors are known as U.S. attorneys and are appointed by the president. On the state and county levels, the attorney general and the district attorney, respectively, are the chief prosecutorial officers.

- Whatever the title, the prosecutor is the people's attorney, who is responsible for representing the public in criminal matters.

- Even if the prosecutor decides to pursue a case, the charges may later be dropped, if conditions are not favorable for a conviction, in a process called nolle prosequi.

- Even in felony cases, the prosecutor ordinarily exercises much discretion in deciding whether to charge the accused with a crime.

5. *Be familiar with the pros and cons of prosecutorial discretion*

- Regardless of its source, the proper exercise of prosecutorial discretion can improve the criminal justice process by preventing the rigid implementation of criminal law.

- Although the prosecutor's primary duty is to enforce criminal law, his or her fundamental obligation as an attorney is to seek justice, as well as to convict those who are guilty.

6. Understand the role of the defense attorney in the justice process

- The defense attorney is the counterpart of the prosecuting attorney in the criminal justice process.
- The accused may obtain counsel from the private bar if he or she can afford to do so.
- The Sixth Amendment to the Constitution allows for provision of counsel at trial. But what about the indigent criminal defendant who cannot afford to retain an attorney?
- In the 1963 landmark case of *Gideon v. Wainwright*, the Supreme Court took the first major step on the issue of right to counsel by holding that state courts must provide indigent defendants in felony prosecutions with private counsel or a public defender.

7. Discuss the different forms of indigent defense

- To satisfy the constitutional requirements that indigent defendants be provided with the assistance of counsel at various stages of the criminal process, the federal government and the states have had to evaluate and expand indigent defense services.
- Most criminal defendants are represented by publicly supported lawyers, but there are also private attorneys who specialize in criminal practice.

8. Debate the pros and cons of private attorneys

- Even though there are some advantages to private counsel, national surveys indicate that state-appointed attorneys do quite well in court.
- The *Strickland v. Washington* case established the two-pronged test for determining effectiveness of counsel.

9. Be familiar with the expanding role of technology in the court process

- Technology is important to the administration and management of courts.
- Court jurisdictions are also cooperating with police departments in the installation of communications gear that makes it possible to arraign defendants over closed-circuit television while they are in police custody.
- About 400 courts across the country have videoconferencing capability.
- High-tech courtrooms are now equipped for real-time transcription and translation, audio-video preservation of the court record, remote witness participation, computer graphics displays, television monitors for jurors, and computers for counsel and judge.
- Contemporary relational databases now provide the flexibility to handle complex case management.

Key Terms

state courts of limited jurisdiction, 214

courts of general jurisdiction, 215

appellate court, 216

court of last resort, 216

writ of certiorari, 220

landmark decision, 220

jury trial, 222

U.S. magistrate judge, 225

Missouri Plan, 226

prosecutor, 227

public defender, 234

adversarial procedure, 234

Sixth Amendment, 235

indigent, 235

Gideon v. Wainwright, 235

assigned counsel, 236

contract system (attorney), 236

Review Questions

1. Should attorneys disclose information given them by their clients about participation in an earlier unsolved crime?

2. Should defense attorneys cooperate with a prosecutor if it means their clients will go to jail?

3. Should a prosecutor have absolute discretion over which cases to proceed on and which to drop?

4. Should clients be made aware of an attorney's track record in court?

5. Does the assigned counsel system present an inherent conflict of interest, inasmuch as attorneys are hired and paid by the institution they are to oppose?

6. Should victims play a role in the application of prosecutorial discretion? Before you answer, consider how that system might harm some defendants and benefit others.

8

PRETRIAL AND TRIAL PROCEDURES

RealityCheck

MYTH or REALITY?

▶ There is a constitutional right to bail.

▶ A significant percentage of those released on bail never show up for their scheduled court dates.

▶ A person arraigned on criminal charges must plead either guilty or innocent.

▶ The Sixth Amendment right to a jury trial extends to defendants in all criminal trials.

▶ Trials are closed to the public.

▶ There is nothing inherently wrong with a black jury deciding the fate of a white defendant.

▶ Appellate court judges are partially responsible for the number of appeals filed by convicted individuals.

Learning Objectives

1. Identify why the pretrial stage of justice is so critical to the entire process

2. Understand the bail process

3. Discuss the history of, the direction of, and the reasons behind bail reform

4. Differentiate between the two main mechanisms for charging defendants (grand jury indictment and prosecutor's information)

5. Know about pleas and plea negotiation

6. Discuss the pros and cons of plea bargaining

7. Contrast and compare the roles of judge, prosecutor, defense counsel, and victim in the plea bargaining process

8. Know what is meant by the term "pretrial diversion"

9. Describe the goals and purpose of the trial process

10. Discuss the legal rights of the accused at trial

11. Explain the trial process

Chapter Outline

© AP Images/Hector Mata

Career Profile

Patricia Sullivan is a social worker with the Commonwealth of Massachusetts's Department of Children and Family Services. She works mainly with adolescents who are having difficulty at home, in the community, or at school. She is required to work with the youths and their families, to meet with them at least once a month, and to arrange for and coordinate services for them. She also represents the department at meetings and during court proceedings.

Because she works with adolescents, many whom have been adjudicated by the juvenile court as in need of services, Patricia feels that a criminal justice education is of tremendous value. She spends many days in court, working with attorneys, assistant district attorneys, magistrates, probation officers, police officers, and court clinicians. She is also called on frequently to present to a judge her beliefs regarding the best course of treatment for youths in her care. Having knowledge about procedures, expectations, and protocol is a great help to her in these tasks. What's more, having some understanding of the environmental, social, and psychological theories of crime makes her more empathic, compassionate, and effective in her work with youths and their families.

According to Patricia, the greatest challenge in her career is learning to balance her personal life with the emotional challenges she faces on a regular basis in her professional life. "There are so many children who have no family to connect to, and many of them see their social worker as their parental figure. Trying to find a way to put it aside and be a mother to my own children, to leave work at the office, and to put some of the horrible things I see and know may happen out of my mind, at times can be difficult." Patricia feels, however, that family support and her active lifestyle help her overcome the emotional challenges of the job.

Even though Patricia's work is demanding, it also carries with it rewards that keep her motivated. "Seeing a child complete high school and go on to college, which is often difficult for the children in our care since we lack enough foster homes and they frequently are moved to homes in different communities and school districts, is satisfying." Over the years, she has had several of the youths she once worked with come back to see her and talk about their accomplishments. "It is most rewarding to see youths grow into productive adults and overcome the obstacles they faced."

atricia Sullivan is one of the many different kinds of professionals whose work and activities have an impact on the courts during the pretrial and trial phases of the criminal justice process. She is not an officer of the court, but her involvement and input are invaluable—and help ensure that justice is done.

This chapter reviews the pretrial and trial process, beginning with the pretrial procedures. **Pretrial procedures** are important components of the justice process because the vast majority of criminal cases are resolved informally at this stage and never come before the courts. Although the media like to focus on the elaborate jury trial with its dramatic elements and impressive setting, formal criminal trials are relatively infrequent. Consequently, understanding the events that take place during the pretrial period is essential to grasping the reality of the criminal justice process.

pretrial procedures
Critical pretrial processes and decisions, including bail, arraignment, and plea negotiation.

Bail

A cash bond or some other security provided to the court to ensure the appearance of the defendant at every subsequent stage of the criminal justice process, especially trial, is known as **bail**. Its purpose is to obtain the release from custody of a person charged with a crime. Once the amount of bail is set by the court, the defendant is required to deposit all or a percentage of the entire amount in cash or security (or to pay a professional bonding agent to submit a bond). If the defendant is released on bail but fails to appear in court at the stipulated time, the bail deposit is forfeited. A defendant who fails to make bail is confined in jail until the court appearance.

bail
The monetary amount for or condition of pretrial release, normally set by a judge at the initial appearance. The purpose of bail is to ensure the return of the accused at subsequent proceedings.

Right to Bail

The Eighth Amendment to the U.S. Constitution does not guarantee a right to bail but rather prohibits "excessive bail." Because many state statutes place no

It is common practice to release on bail defendants who pose a low flight risk. Here Bernard Madoff leaves a federal court building in New York after a hearing regarding his bail on January 14, 2009. A judge ruled that he would remain free on bail pending trial. Later, in March, he was denied bail after pleading guilty to an 11-count criminal complaint that included perpetrating a $50 billion investment fraud, the largest Ponzi scheme in history. Still later, on June 29, Madoff was sentenced to 150 years in prison.

© Timothy A. Clary/AFP/Getty Images

precise limit on the amount of bail a judge may impose, many defendants who cannot make bail are placed in detention while awaiting trial. It has become apparent over the years that the bail system is discriminatory because defendants who are financially well off can make bail, whereas indigent defendants languish in **pretrial detention** in the county jail. In addition, keeping a person in jail imposes serious financial burdens on local and state governments—and, in turn, on taxpayers—who must pay for the cost of confinement. These factors have given rise to bail reform programs that depend on the defendant's personal promise ("recognizance") to appear in court for trial, rather than on her or his financial ability to make bail.

pretrial detention
Holding an offender in secure confinement before trial.

The Eighth Amendment restriction on excessive bail may also be interpreted to mean that the sole purpose of bail is to ensure that the defendant returns for trial; bail may not be used as a form of punishment, nor may it be used to coerce or threaten a defendant. In most cases, a defendant has the right to be released on reasonable bail. Many jurisdictions also require a bail review hearing by a higher court when the initial judge has set what might be considered excessive bail.

In *Stack v. Boyle*, the Supreme Court found bail to be a traditional right to freedom before trial that permits unhampered preparation of a defense and prevents the criminal defendant from being punished

REALITYCHECK

MYTH OR REALITY? There is a constitutional right to bail.

MYTH: The Eighth Amendment only prohibits excessive bail (and cruel and unusual punishment).

The prohibition against excessive bail does not extend to everyone, because the Supreme Court has not required that the states honor this part of the Eighth Amendment. Nearly every state constitution has some sort of prohibition against excessive bail, but there can still be considerable variability in what is considered "excessive."

prior to conviction.[1] The Court held that bail is excessive when it exceeds an amount reasonably calculated to ensure that the defendant will return for trial. To meet this criterion, bail should be in the amount that is generally set for similar offenses. Higher bail can be imposed when evidence supporting the increase is presented at a hearing at which the defendant's constitutional rights can be protected. Although *Stack* did not mandate an absolute right to bail, it did set guidelines for state courts to follow: If a crime is bailable, the amount set should not be frivolous, unusual, or beyond a person's ability to pay.

Bail Release Mechanisms

When and how are bail decisions made? Bail in a felony case is typically considered at a court hearing conducted shortly after a person has been taken into custody. At the hearing, such issues as type of crime, flight risk, and dangerousness are considered before a bail amount is set. In jurisdictions with pretrial release programs, program staff often interview arrestees detained at the jail before the first hearing, verify their background information, and present recommendations to the court at arraignment. Prior record is an important factor: Less than half of defendants with an active criminal justice status (such as parole or probation) at the time of arrest are released, compared to more than two-thirds of those with no active status. Some jurisdictions have developed bail schedules to make amounts uniform based on crime and criminal history.

Bail is typically granted during a court hearing in felony cases, but in less serious cases, bail may be handled in a variety of ways:

- *Police field citation release.* An arresting officer releases the arrestee on a written promise to appear in court, at or near the actual time and location of the arrest. This procedure is commonly used for misdemeanor charges and is similar to the issuance of a traffic ticket.

- *Police station house citation release.* The determination of an arrestee's eligibility and suitability for release and the actual release of the arrestee are deferred until after he or she has been removed from the scene of an arrest and brought to the station house or police headquarters.

- *Police/pretrial jail citation release.* The determination of an arrestee's eligibility and suitability for citation release and the actual release of the arrestee are deferred until after he or she has been delivered by the arresting department to a jail or other pretrial detention facility for screening, booking, and admission.

- *Direct release programs.* To streamline release processes and reduce the length of stay in detention, pretrial program courts may authorize pretrial programs to release defendants without direct judicial involvement.

- *Police/court bail schedule.* An arrestee can post bail at the station house or jail according to amounts specified in a bail schedule. The schedule is a list of all bailable charges and a corresponding dollar amount for each. Schedules vary widely from jurisdiction to jurisdiction.

In practice, a significant majority of criminal defendants are released on bail prior to trial.[2] The most recent surveys of pretrial release practices show that about two-thirds of felony defendants were released before the final disposition of their case. As might be expected, defendants charged with the most serious violent offenses were less likely to be released than those charged with less serious public-order or drug offenses. Nonetheless, more than half of all violent criminals are released before trial. As might be expected, defendants charged with murder are the least likely to be released prior to case disposition (about 8% are released on pretrial bail), followed by defendants whose most serious arrest charge was robbery (about 42% are released on bail), motor vehicle theft (44% bail release rate), burglary (49%), or rape (55%).

Types of Bail

There are a variety of ways or mechanisms to secure bail, depending on the jurisdiction, the crime, and the defendant.

- *Full cash bail.* The defendant pays the full bail amount out of pocket. In some jurisdictions, property can be pledged instead of cash.
- *Deposit bail.* The defendant deposits a percentage of the bail amount, typically 10 percent, with the court. When the defendant appears in court, the deposit is returned, sometimes minus an administrative fee. If the defendant fails to appear, he or she is liable for the full amount of the bail.
- *Surety bail.* The defendant pays a percentage of the bond, usually 10 percent, to a bonding agent who posts the full bail. The fee paid to the bonding agent is not returned to the defendant if he or she appears in court. The bonding agent is liable for the full amount of the bond should the defendant fail to appear. Bonding agents often require posting collateral to cover the full bail amount.
- *Conditional bail.* The defendant is released after promising to obey some specified conditions in lieu of cash, such as attending a treatment program before trial.
- *Unsecured bond.* The defendant is released with no immediate requirement of payment. However, if the defendant fails to appear, he or she is liable for the full amount.
- *Release on recognizance.* According to the **release on recognizance (ROR)** concept, eligible defendants are released without bail upon their promise to return for trial.

As Figure 8.1 shows, surety bond is now the most common type of bail used with felony defendants, followed by release on recognizance and conditional bail. Relatively few defendants pay full cash bail out of pocket.

Bail Issues

Whether a defendant can be expected to appear for his or her trial is a key issue in determining bail.[3] Bail cannot be used to punish an accused, nor can

release on recognizance (ROR)

A nonmonetary condition for the pretrial release of an accused individual; an alternative to monetary bail that is granted after the court determines that the accused has ties in the community, has no prior record of default, and is likely to appear at subsequent proceedings.

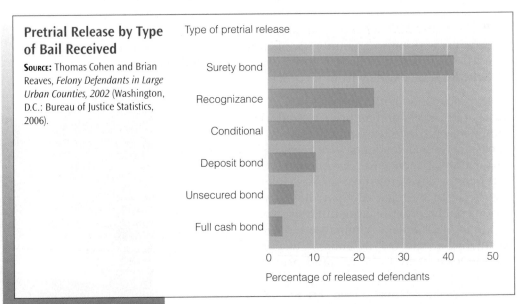

Pretrial Release by Type of Bail Received

Source: Thomas Cohen and Brian Reaves, *Felony Defendants in Large Urban Counties, 2002* (Washington, D.C.: Bureau of Justice Statistics, 2006).

FIGURE 8.1

it be denied or revoked at the whim of the court. Nonetheless, for the following reasons, critics argue that money bail is one of the most objectionable aspects of the criminal justice system.

- It is discriminatory because it works against the poor.
- It is costly because the government must pay to detain those offenders who cannot make bail but who would otherwise remain in the community.
- It is unfair because a higher proportion of detainees receive longer sentences than people released on bail.
- It is dehumanizing because innocent people who cannot make bail suffer in the nation's deteriorated jail system.

There is also the problem of racial and ethnic disparity in the bail process. Some research efforts show that the decision whether to grant bail may be racially or ethnically biased; black and Latino defendants receive less favorable treatment than whites charged with similar offenses.[4] Although these results are troubling, it is often difficult to gauge racial/ethnic disparity in the bail process because differences in income, community ties, family support, and criminal record, rather than judicial bias, may account for any observed differences in the bail process.

Despite these drawbacks, the bail system remains in place to ensure that defendants return for trial and that the truly dangerous can be kept in secure confinement pending their court proceedings.

BONDSMEN AND BOUNTY HUNTERS ● When bailees abscond before trial, bondsmen routinely hire skip tracers, enforcement agents, or bounty hunters to track them down. Each year an estimated 400 full-time bail enforcement agents catch some 25,000 fugitives in the United States.[5] Although organizations such as the National Institute of Bail Enforcement attempt to provide training, some untrained and/or unprofessional bounty hunters may use brutal tactics that can end in tragedy. Consequently, efforts have been made to reform and even eliminate money bail and reduce the importance of bonding agents.

PRETRIAL DETENTION CONDITIONS ● The criminal defendant who is not eligible for bail or ROR is subject to pretrial detention in the local county jail. The jail has long been a trouble spot for the criminal justice system. Conditions tend to be poor, and rehabilitation is a low priority.

In terms of the number of persons affected each year, pretrial custody accounts for more incarceration in the United States than does imprisonment after sentencing. On any given day in the United States, more than 600,000 people were held in more than 3,500 local jails. Over the course of a year, many times that number pass through the jailhouse door. More than 50 percent of those held in local jails have been accused of crimes but not convicted; they are pretrial detainees. In the United States, people are detained at a rate twice that of neighboring Canada and three times that of Great Britain. Hundreds of jails are overcrowded, and many are under court orders to reduce their populations and improve conditions. The national jail-crowding crisis has worsened over the years.

Jails are often considered the weakest link in the criminal justice process. They are frequently dangerous, harmful, decrepit, and filled with the poor and friendless. The costs of holding a person in jail range up to more than $100 per day and $36,000 per year. In addition, detainees are often confined with those convicted of crimes and those who have been transferred from other institutions because of overcrowding. Many felons are transferred to jails from state prisons to ease crowding there. It is possible to have in close quarters a convicted rapist, a father jailed for nonpayment of child support, and a person awaiting trial for a crime he did not commit. Thus jails contain a mix of inmates, which can lead to violence, brutality, and suicide.

National Institute of Bail Enforcement

The **National Institute of Bail Enforcement**, headquartered in Chicago, provides training and education in the field of bail enforcement. To read more about it, go to

www.cengage.com/ criminaljustice/siegel.

What happens to people who do not get bail or who cannot afford to put up bail money? Traditionally, these individuals are more likely to be convicted and then to get longer prison sentences than those who commit similar crimes but who were released on bail. A federally sponsored study of case processing in the nation's largest counties found that about 63 percent of all defendants granted bail were convicted; in contrast, 78 percent of detainees were convicted.[6] Detainees are also more likely than releasees to be convicted of a felony offense and, therefore, are eligible for a long prison sentence instead of the much shorter term of incarceration given misdemeanants. People being held in jails are in a less attractive bargaining position than those released on bail, and prosecutors, knowing their predicament, may be less generous in their negotiations. It is for these reasons that bail reform advocates have tried so hard to eliminate, whenever possible, the detention of nondangerous criminal defendants.

BAIL REFORM ● Critics believe that the bail system is discriminatory because defendants who are financially well off can make bail, whereas indigent defendants languish in pretrial detention in the county jail. Another problem is the legal effect of detention. About 60 percent of released offenders are eventually convicted, compared to more than 80 percent of detainees. Once they are convicted, detainees receive somewhat longer sentences than people released before trial. These factors, along with high costs of confinement, have given rise to bail reform programs that depend on the personal promise of the defendant (who is said to have been released on her or his own recognizance) to appear in court for trial, instead of on financial ability to meet bail. These reforms have enabled many deserving but indigent offenders to go free; but another trend has been to deny people bail on the grounds that they are a danger to themselves or to others in the community.

The first bail reform program was pioneered by the Vera Institute of Justice in an experiment called the **Manhattan Bail Project**, which began in 1961 with the cooperation of the New York City criminal courts and local law students.[7] The project found that if the court had sufficient background information about the defendant, it could make a reasonably good judgment about whether the accused would return to court. When release decisions were based on such information as the nature of the offense, family ties, and employment record, most defendants who were released on their own recognizance returned to court. The results of the Vera Institute's initial operation showed a default rate of less than 0.7 percent. The bail project's experience suggested that releasing a person on the basis of verified information more effectively guaranteed appearance in court than did money bail. Highly successful ROR projects were set up in major cities around the country, including Philadelphia and San Francisco. By 1980, more than 120 formal programs were in operation, and today they exist in almost every major jurisdiction.[8]

The success of ROR programs in the early 1960s resulted in bail reforms that culminated with the enactment of the federal Bail Reform Act of 1966, the first change in federal bail laws since 1789.[9] This legislation sought to ensure that release would be granted in all noncapital cases in which there was sufficient reason to believe that the defendant would return to court. The law clearly established the presumption of ROR that must be overcome before money

Manhattan Bail Project
The innovative experiment in bail reform that introduced and successfully tested the concept of release on recognizance.

REALITY CHECK

MYTH OR REALITY? A significant percentage of those released on bail never show up for their scheduled court dates.

MYTH: Research suggests otherwise. The Manhattan Bail Project found that less than 1 percent of those released default.

Official statistics tell a similar story; relatively few people released before their trial dates reoffend, get arrested, or fail to show up when they are required to do so. Could the same be expected with release on recognizance programs?

bail is required, authorized 10 percent **deposit bail**, introduced the concept of conditional release, and stressed the philosophy that release should be under the least restrictive conditions necessary to ensure court appearance.

During the 1970s and early 1980s, the pretrial release movement was hampered by public pressure over pretrial increases in crime. As a result, the more recent federal legislation, the **Bail Reform Act of 1984**, mandated that no defendants shall be kept in pretrial detention simply because they cannot afford money bail, established the presumption for ROR in all cases in which a person is bailable, and formalized restrictive preventive detention provisions (these are explained later in this chapter). The 1984 act required that community safety, as well as the risk of flight, be considered in the release decision. Consequently, such criminal justice factors as the seriousness of the charged offense, the weight of the evidence, the sentence that may be imposed upon conviction, court appearance history, and prior convictions are likely to influence the release decisions of the federal court.

PREVENTIVE DETENTION • Bail reform acts have made it easier for some people to secure pretrial release, but they have also helped keep defendants who are considered dangerous behind bars before trial without the possibility of bail—a practice known as preventive detention. These laws require that certain dangerous defendants be confined before trial for their own protection and that of the community. **Preventive detention** is an important manifestation of the crime control perspective on justice, because it favors the use of incapacitation to control the future behavior of suspected criminals. Critics, however, are concerned that preventive detention amounts to punishment before trial.

The most striking use of preventive detention can be found in the federal Bail Reform Act of 1984.[10] Although the act does contain provisions for ROR, it also allows judges to order preventive detention if they determine "that no condition or combination of conditions will reasonably assure the appearance of the person as required and the safety of any other person and the community."[11]

A number of state jurisdictions have incorporated elements of preventive detention into their bail systems. Although most of the restrictions do not constitute outright preventive detention, they serve to narrow the scope of bail eligibility. These provisions include three main features: (1) exclusion of certain crimes from bail eligibility, (2) definition of bail to include appearance in court and community safety, and (3) the limitations on right to bail for those previously convicted.

Preventive detention has also been a source of concern for civil libertarians, who believe it violates the due process clause of the U.S. Constitution because it means that a person will be held in custody before being proven guilty. In two important cases, the U.S. Supreme Court disagreed with this analysis. In *Schall v. Martin*, the Court upheld the application of preventive detention statutes to juvenile defendants on the grounds that such detention is useful to protect the welfare of the minor and of society as a whole.[12] In 1987, the Court upheld the Bail Reform Act's provision on preventive detention as it applied to adults in the case of *United States v. Salerno*. Here, the Supreme Court held that the preventive detention provision had a legitimate and compelling regulatory purpose and did not violate the Constitution's due process clause. Preventive detention was not designed to punish dangerous individuals but to find a solution for the social problem of people committing crimes while on bail, and preventing danger to the community is a legitimate societal goal. In 2003, the Court applied the preventive detention concept to deportable aliens who commit crime, reasoning that their status makes them a special risk and that detention has the legitimate purpose of preventing the aliens from fleeing before or during such proceedings.[13]

PRETRIAL SERVICES • In our overburdened court system, it is critical to determine which defendants can safely be released on bail pending trial.[14] In many jurisdictions specialized pretrial services help courts deal with this problem.

deposit bail
The monetary amount set by a judge at a hearing as a condition of pretrial release; the percentage of the total bond required to be paid by the defendant.

Bail Reform Act of 1984
Federal legislation that provides for both greater emphasis on release on recognizance for nondangerous offenders and preventive detention for those who present a menace to the community.

preventive detention
The practice of holding dangerous suspects before trial without bail.

Hundreds of pretrial bail programs have been established in rural, suburban, and urban jurisdictions; they are typically operated in probation departments, court offices, and local jails and through independent county contractors.

When first created in the 1960s, pretrial services were part of the effort to improve the release/detention decision-making process by improving the breadth and quality of information available to judges at the point of initial decision making. Personnel gathered information on such factors as the defendant's housing arrangements, family ties, and employment. When the federal government passed the Federal Bail Reform Act of 1966, it encouraged judges to consider factors other than the seriousness of the charge in setting conditions of release and to use conditions other than the setting of a money bond amount, further encouraging the development of pretrial service programs. A "second generation" of pretrial service programs that developed during the 1980s and 1990s focused primarily on trying to identify defendants who were unable to make bail but who would be acceptable risks for release either on their own recognizance or under supervision.

These programs provide a number of critical services:

- Gathering and verifying information about arrestees—including criminal history, current status in the criminal justice system, address, employment, and drug and alcohol use history—that judicial officers can then take into account in making release/detention decisions.
- Assessing each arrestee's likelihood of failure to appear and chances of being rearrested.
- Monitoring released defendants' compliance with conditions of release designed to minimize pretrial crime, including curfews, orders restricting contact with alleged victims and possible witnesses, home confinement, and drug and alcohol testing.
- Providing direct "intensive" supervision for some categories of defendants by using program staff and collaborating with the police, other agencies, and community organizations.

Virtually all larger jurisdictions in the United States have pretrial release in one form or another. Court-administered programs make up the greatest percentage of pretrial programs, although most newer programs are located within probation departments. The general criteria used to assess eligibility for release center on the defendant's community ties and prior criminal justice involvement. Many jurisdictions have conditional and supervised release and third-party custody release, in addition to release on a person's own recognizance.

Some pretrial services programs are now being aimed at special needs. One type focuses on defendants suffering from mental illness; almost three-quarters of pretrial services programs now inquire about mental health status and treatment as a regular part of their interview, and about one-quarter report having implemented special supervision procedures for defendants with mental illness. Another area of concern is domestic violence. About one-quarter of all pretrial programs have developed special risk-assessment procedures for defendants charged with domestic violence offenses, and about one-third have implemented special procedures to supervise defendants charged with domestic violence offenses.

Pretrial Justice Institute

The **Pretrial Justice Institute** is an independent, nonprofit clearinghouse for information on pretrial issues and a technical assistance provider for pretrial practitioners, criminal justice officials, academicians, and community leaders nationwide. You can access it at

www.cengage.com/ criminaljustice/siegel.

Charging the Defendant

Charging a defendant with a crime is a process that varies somewhat, depending on whether it occurs via a grand jury or a preliminary hearing.

The Indictment Process and the Grand Jury

The grand jury was an early development of the English common law. Under the Magna Carta (1215), no freeman could be seized and imprisoned unless he had been judged by his peers. To determine fairly who was eligible to be tried, a group of freemen from the district where the crime was committed would be brought together to examine the facts of the case and determine whether the charges had merit. Thus, the grand jury was created as a check against arbitrary prosecution by a judge who might be a puppet of the government.

The concept of the grand jury was brought to the American colonies by early settlers and later incorporated into the Fifth Amendment of the U.S. Constitution, which states that "no person shall be held to answer for a capital, or otherwise infamous crime, unless on presentment or indictment of a grand jury." What is the role of the grand jury today? First, the grand jury has the power to act as an independent investigating body. In this capacity, it examines the possibility of criminal activity within its jurisdiction. These investigative efforts may be directed toward general rather than individual criminal conduct—for example, organized crime or insider trading. After an investigation is completed, a report called a **presentment** is issued. The presentment contains not only information concerning the findings of the grand jury but also, usually, a recommendation of indictment.

The grand jury's second and better-known role is to act as the community's conscience in determining whether the accusation of the state (the prosecution) justifies a trial. The grand jury relies on the testimony of witnesses called by the prosecution through its subpoena power. After examining the evidence and the testimony of witnesses, the grand jury decides whether probable cause exists for prosecution. If it does, an **indictment**, or true bill, is affirmed. If the grand jury fails to find probable cause, a **no bill** (meaning that the indictment is ignored) is passed. In some states, a prosecutor can present evidence to a different grand jury if a no bill is returned; in other states, this action is prohibited by statute.

CRITIQUING THE GRAND JURY ● The grand jury usually meets at the request of the prosecution, and hearings are closed and secret. Neither the defense attorney nor the defendant is allowed to attend, and grand jury hearings are not open to the public. The prosecuting attorney presents the charges and calls witnesses who testify under oath to support the indictment. This process

presentment
The report of a grand jury investigation, which usually includes a recommendation of indictment.

indictment
The action by a grand jury when it finds that probable cause exists for prosecution of an accused suspect.

no bill
The action by a grand jury when it votes not to indict an accused suspect.

Former Boston University student Philip Markoff, center, stands with his attorney John Salsberg, right, during his arraignment at Suffolk Superior Court on June 22, 2009, in Boston. Markoff, the suspected Craigslist killer, was charged with first-degree murder in the fatal shooting of one woman and the gunpoint robbery of another woman in downtown Boston hotels.

© AP Images/Bizuayehu Tesfaye, Pool

has been criticized as being a "rubber stamp" for the prosecution, because the presentation of evidence is shaped by the district attorney, who is not required by law to reveal information that might exonerate the accused.[15] An alternative is to open the grand jury room to the defense and hold the government to the same types of constitutional safeguards to protect defendants that are now used at trial.[16]

The Information Process and the Preliminary Hearing

information

A written accusation submitted to the court by a prosecutor, alleging that a particular individual committed the offense in question.

preliminary hearing

A hearing that occurs in lieu of a grand jury hearing, when the prosecutor charges via information. Three issues are decided: whether a crime was committed, whether the court has jurisdiction over the case, and whether there is sufficient probable cause to believe the defendant committed the alleged crime.

In about half the states, a prosecutor's **information** is the charging mechanism of choice. When a person is charged in this fashion, a **preliminary hearing** is necessary. The purposes of the preliminary hearing and the grand jury hearing are the same—to establish whether probable cause is sufficient to merit a trial. The procedures differ between the two, however.

The preliminary hearing is conducted before a magistrate or lower-court judge and, unlike the grand jury hearing, is open to the public unless the defendant requests otherwise. Present at the preliminary hearing are the prosecuting attorney, the defendant, and the defendant's counsel, if one has already been retained. The prosecution presents its evidence and witnesses to the judge. The defendant or the defense counsel then has the right to cross-examine witnesses and to challenge the prosecutor's evidence.

After hearing the evidence, the judge decides whether there is sufficient probable cause to believe that the defendant committed the alleged crime. If so, the defendant is bound over for trial, and the prosecuting attorney's information (described earlier; it is similar to an indictment) is filed with the superior court, usually within 15 days. When the judge does not find sufficient probable cause, the charges are dismissed and the defendant is released from custody.

A unique aspect of the preliminary hearing is the defendant's right to waive the proceeding, a procedure that has advantages (and disadvantages) for both the prosecutor and the defendant. For the prosecutor, waiver helps avoid the need to reveal evidence to the defense before trial. Defense attorneys may waive the preliminary hearing for three possible reasons: (1) when the defendant has already decided to plead guilty, (2) in order to speed the criminal justice process, and/or (3) to avoid the negative publicity that might result from the hearing. On the other hand, a preliminary hearing may have some advantage to the defendant who believes that it will result in a dismissal of the charges. In addition, the preliminary hearing gives the defense an opportunity to learn what evidence the prosecution has.

Figure 8.2 outlines the significant differences between the grand jury and the preliminary hearing processes.

Arraignment

After an indictment or information is filed following a grand jury or preliminary hearing, an arraignment takes place before the court that will try the case. At the arraignment, the judge informs the defendant of the charges against her and appoints counsel if one has not yet been retained. According to the Sixth Amendment of the U.S. Constitution, the accused has the right to be informed of the nature and cause of the accusation; thus, the judge at the arraignment must make sure that the defendant clearly understands the charges.

After the charges are read and explained, the defendant is asked to enter a plea. If a plea of not guilty or not guilty by reason of insanity is entered, a trial date is set. When the defendant pleads guilty or nolo contendere, a date for sentencing is arranged. The magistrate then either sets bail or releases the defendant on personal recognizance.

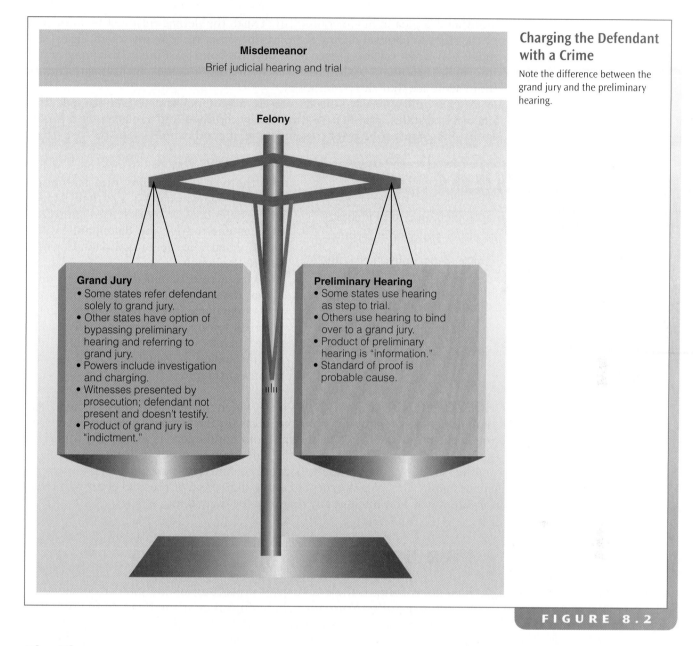

Misdemeanor
Brief judicial hearing and trial

Felony

Grand Jury
- Some states refer defendant solely to grand jury.
- Other states have option of bypassing preliminary hearing and referring to grand jury.
- Powers include investigation and charging.
- Witnesses presented by prosecution; defendant not present and doesn't testify.
- Product of grand jury is "indictment."

Preliminary Hearing
- Some states use hearing as step to trial.
- Others use hearing to bind over to a grand jury.
- Product of preliminary hearing is "information."
- Standard of proof is probable cause.

Charging the Defendant with a Crime

Note the difference between the grand jury and the preliminary hearing.

FIGURE 8.2

The Plea

Ordinarily, a defendant in a criminal trial will enter one of three pleas: guilty, not guilty, or nolo contendere.

GUILTY • Most defendants appearing before the courts plead guilty prior to the trial stage. A guilty plea has several consequences. It functions not only as an admission of guilt but also as a surrender of the entire array of constitutional rights designed to protect a criminal defendant against unjustified conviction, including the right to remain silent, the right to confront witnesses against him or her, the right to a trial by jury, and the right to have an alleged offense proven beyond a reasonable doubt. Once a plea is made, it cannot be rescinded or withdrawn after sentencing, even if there is a change in the law that might have made conviction more problematic.[17]

As a result, judges must follow certain procedures when accepting a plea of guilty. First, the judge must clearly state to the defendant the constitutional guarantees that he or she automatically waives by entering this plea. Second, the judge must believe that the facts of the case establish a basis for the plea and that the plea is made voluntarily. Third, the defendant must be informed of the right to counsel during the pleading process. In many felony cases, the judge will insist on the presence of defense counsel. Finally, the judge must inform the defendant of the possible sentencing outcomes, including the maximum sentence that can be imposed.

After a guilty plea has been entered, a sentencing date is arranged. In a majority of states, a guilty plea may be withdrawn and replaced with a not-guilty plea at any time prior to sentencing, if good cause is shown.

REALITYCHECK

MYTH OR REALITY? A person arraigned on criminal charges must plead either guilty or innocent.

MYTH: There are three pleas: guilty, not guilty, and nolo contendere.

The media routinely get it wrong, claiming that so-and-so pled innocent. There is no such plea! What is the difference between "not guilty" and "innocent"?

NOT GUILTY ● At the arraignment or before the trial, a not-guilty plea is entered in one of two ways: (1) it is verbally stated by the defendant or the defense counsel, or (2) it is entered for the defendant by the court when the defendant stands mute before the bench.

Once a plea of not guilty is recorded, a trial date is set. In misdemeanor cases, trials take place in the lower-court system, whereas felony cases are normally transferred to the superior court. At this time, a continuance or issuance of bail is once again considered.

NOLO CONTENDERE ● With this plea (which means "no contest"), the defendant does not accept or deny responsibility for the crime(s) charged but agrees to accept punishment. Even though nolo contendere is essentially a plea of guilty, it may not be held against the defendant as proof in a subsequent legal matter, such as a civil lawsuit, because technically there has been no admission of guilt. This plea is accepted at the discretion of the trial court and must be voluntarily and intelligently made by the defendant.

Plea Bargaining

plea bargaining
Nonjudicial settlement of a case in which the defendant exchanges a guilty plea for some consideration, such as a reduced sentence.

Plea bargaining is the exchange of prosecutorial and judicial concessions for pleas of guilty. Normally, a bargain can be made between the prosecutor and the defense attorney in one of four ways: (1) The initial charges may be reduced to those of a lesser offense, thus automatically reducing the sentence imposed. (2) In cases where many counts are charged, the prosecutor may reduce the number of counts. (3) The prosecutor may promise to recommend a lenient sentence, such as probation. (4) When the charge imposed has a negative label attached (e.g., child molester), the prosecutor may alter the charge to a more "socially acceptable" one (such as assault) in exchange for a plea of guilty. There is little question that these methods result in lesser sentences, especially when defendants are in states whose sentencing policies limit judicial discretion. Pleading guilty to reduced charges may help replace the absence of judicial leniency.[18]

Plea bargaining is one of the most common practices in the criminal justice system and a cornerstone of the informal justice system. Today more than 90 percent of criminal convictions are the result of negotiated pleas of guilty. Even in serious felony cases, plea bargaining can be an option.

Plea bargaining is actually a relatively recent development, which took hold late in the nineteenth century. During the first 150 years after the nation's birth, the trial by jury was viewed as the fairest and most reliable method of determining the truth in a criminal matter. However, plea bargaining became more attrac-

Plea bargaining allows prosecutors to earn a sure conviction and defendants to receive a lighter sentence in return for their cooperation. Celebrity Nicole Richie did just that when she worked out a deal to avoid a long incarceration sentence stemming from her arrest on DUI charges. Richie was sentenced to four days in jail, ordered to undergo drug and alcohol treatment, fined $2,048, and put on three years' probation.

© Fred Prouser/Reuters/Landov

tive at the turn of the twentieth century, when the mechanization of manufacture and transportation prompted a flood of complex civil cases; this event persuaded judges that criminal cases had to be settled quickly lest the court system break down.[19]

Pros and Cons of Plea Negotiation

Because of excessive criminal court caseloads and the personal and professional needs of the prosecution and the defense (to reach disposition of the case in the least possible time), plea bargaining has become an essential yet controversial part of the administration of justice. Proponents contend that plea bargaining actually benefits both the state and the defendant in the following ways:

- The overall costs of the criminal prosecution are reduced.
- The administrative efficiency of the courts is greatly improved.
- The prosecution can devote more time to more serious cases.
- The defendant avoids possible detention and an extended trial and may receive a reduced sentence.
- Resources can be devoted more efficiently to cases that need greater attention.[20]

Those who favor plea bargaining believe it is appropriate to enter into plea discussions when the interests of the state in the effective administration of justice will be served.

Opponents of the plea bargaining process believe that the negotiated plea should be eliminated for the following reasons:

- It encourages defendants to waive their constitutional right to trial.
- Plea bargains allow dangerous offenders to receive lenient sentences. Jesse Timmendequas, a previously convicted sex offender, was given a 10-year plea-bargained sentence for child rape. Upon his release, he raped and killed seven-year-old Megan Kanka in one of the nation's most notorious crimes.[21]
- Plea bargaining also raises the danger that an innocent person will be convicted of a crime if he or she is convinced that the lighter treatment ensured by a guilty plea is preferable to the risk of conviction and a harsher sentence following a formal trial.

- Prosecutors are given a free hand to induce or compel defendants to plea bargain, thus circumventing law.[22]
- It is possible that innocent persons will admit guilt if they believe that the system is biased and that they have little chance of being acquitted.
- A guilty-plea culture has developed among defense lawyers. Elements of this attitude include the belief that most of their clients are dishonest people who committed the crime with which they have been charged and that getting a "sentence discount" for them is the best and only way to go.[23]

Despite these issues, it is unlikely that plea negotiations will be eliminated or severely curtailed in the near future. Supporters of the total abolition of plea bargaining are in the minority. As a result of abuses, however, efforts are being made to improve plea bargaining operations. Such reforms include development of uniform plea practices, representation of counsel during plea negotiations, and establishment of time limits on plea negotiations.

Legal Issues in Plea Bargaining

The U.S. Supreme Court has reviewed the propriety of plea bargaining in several decisions and, while imposing limits on the practice, has upheld its continued use. The Court has ruled in several key cases that

- Defendants are entitled to the effective assistance of counsel to protect them from pressure and influence.[24]
- Pleas must be made voluntarily and without pressure. However, a prosecutor can tell defendants that they may be facing the death penalty if they go to trial.[25]
- Any promise made by the prosecutor during the plea negotiations must be kept after the defendant admits guilt in open court. A prosecutor who promises leniency in private negotiations must stick to that position in court.[26]
- Defendants must also keep their side of the bargain to receive the promised offer of leniency.[27] For example, if they agree to testify against a co-defendant, they must give evidence at trial or forfeit the bargain.
- A defendant's due process rights are not violated when a prosecutor threatens to reindict the accused on more serious charges—for example, as a habitual offender—if the defendant does not plead guilty to a lesser offense.[28]
- Accepting a guilty plea from a defendant who maintains his or her innocence is valid.[29]
- Statements made during a plea bargain may be used under some circumstances at trial if the negotiations break down. Statements made during a plea negotiation can be used if the defendant (a) admits to a crime during the bargaining process but then (b) later testifies in open court that he or she did not do the act and (c) is innocent of the charges.[30]

Plea Bargaining Decision Making

The plea bargaining process is largely informal, lacking in guidelines, and discretionary. Research shows that prosecutorial discretion rather than defendant characteristics controls plea negotiations.[31] Yet studies also show that plea bargaining reflects a degree of cooperation between prosecutors and defense attorneys; in the vast majority of cases, they work together to achieve a favorable outcome.[32]

Despite its discretionary nature, some effort has been made to determine what kinds of information and how much information is used by the prosecutor to make plea bargaining decisions. It is possible to view plea bargaining as a form of cost-benefit analysis: Defendants compare the pain of punishment guaranteed by the bargain—for instance, 2 years in prison—with the punishment associated with a conviction at trial—for instance, 20 years. If they conclude that conviction is inevitable, they will be inclined to accept the guaranteed punishment rather than risk trial and harsher treatment. The district attorney uses much the same reasoning process and therefore is less willing to make concessions as the strength of the evidence and the likelihood of conviction increase.

Research on plea negotiation indicates that the process is actually much more complex. Offender, case, and community characteristics weigh heavily on the negotiation process.[33] Such factors as the offense, the defendant's prior record and age, and the type, strength, and admissibility of evidence are important in the plea bargaining decision. The attitude of the complainant is also an important factor in the decision-making process. In victimless cases, such as heroin possession, the attitude of the police is most often considered, whereas in victim-related crimes, such as rape, the victim's attitude is a primary concern.

Several intangible factors also affect the bargaining decision:

- The prosecutor's ego and need for self-esteem may shape the negotiations.
- Because they want to win every case, some prosecutors may offer deals the defendant simply cannot refuse.
- Prosecutors seeking publicity for a political run may refuse to bargain so that they may preside over a trial that will be closely covered by the media, such as the Michael Jackson case.
- A bargain may be offered when a prosecutor realizes that a criminal trial could expose sloppy police work and investigation.
- The prosecutor's offices may simply not have sufficient funds to engage in complex and costly trials. An appointed defense counsel may find that his or her fees are capped by the courts and a plea bargain becomes an economic necessity.[34]
- The defendant's retaining a highly respected private attorney with a strong trial reputation may encourage prosecutors to offer a favorable bargain: Who wants to look bad at trial and lose the case?
- Court-appointed lawyers may want to gain trial experience. They may convince their clients not to accept favorable bargains because they fear that the case will be settled out of court and they will lose the opportunity to try it.
- Both the prosecution and the defense may be overly optimistic about their abilities and skills. Overconfidence in their abilities may cloud attorneys' judgment, causing them either to refuse to offer a bargain, in the case of the prosecution, or to refuse to accept one, in the case of the defense.
- Some defendants mistakenly assume they are so charismatic and appealing that a jury will never reach a conviction.[35] Their inflated ego and sense of entitlement inhibit their accepting their own guilt.

THE ROLE OF THE DEFENSE COUNSEL • Although the prosecutor formulates and offers the deal, the defense counsel—a public defender or a private attorney—is required to play an advisory role in plea negotiations. The defendant's counsel is expected to be aware of the facts of the case and familiar with the law and to advise the defendant of the alternatives available. The defense attorney is basically responsible for making certain that the accused understands the nature of the plea bargaining process and the guilty plea. This means that the defense counsel should explain to the defendant that by pleading guilty, he is waiving certain rights that would be available if he were to go to trial. In addition, the defense attorney has the duty to keep the defendant informed of

Plea bargains are used in some of the most notorious violent cases. Here, on November 5, 2003, Gary Leon Ridgway initials his plea agreement in the King County Courthouse in Seattle, where he pleaded guilty to 48 murders. Ridgway added a confession read out by the prosecutor in open court: "I killed so many women I have a hard time keeping them straight." The plea agreement spared Ridgway his life, but he was sentenced to 48 life sentences with no possibility of parole.

© Elaine Thompson/Reuters/Landov

developments and discussions with the prosecutor regarding plea bargaining. While doing so, the attorney for the accused cannot misrepresent evidence or mislead the client into making a detrimental agreement. The defense counsel is not just ethically but also constitutionally required to communicate all plea bargaining offers to a client, even if counsel believes the offers to be unacceptable.[36]

THE ROLE OF THE JUDGE • One of the most confusing issues in the plea bargaining process has been the proper role of the judge. Should the judge act only in a supervisory capacity or actually enter into the negotiation process? The leading national legal organization, the ABA, is opposed to judicial participation in plea negotiations.[37] According to ABA standards, judges should not be a party to arrangements for the determination of a sentence, whether as a result of a guilty plea or a finding of guilty based on proof. According to this view, judicial participation in plea negotiations (a) creates the impression in the mind of defendants that they cannot receive a fair trial, (b) lessens the ability of the judge to make an objective determination of the voluntary nature of the plea, (c) is inconsistent with the theory behind the use of pre-sentence investigation reports, and (d) may induce innocent defendants to plead guilty because they are afraid to reject the disposition desired by the judge.[38] How, then, are judges involved in plea bargaining? Judges must approve plea agreements.

THE ROLE OF THE VICTIM • What role should victims play in plea bargaining? Some suggest that the system today is too "victim driven" and that prosecutors too often seek approval for the plea from a victim or family member. Others maintain that the victim plays an almost secondary role in the process. In reality, the victim is not "empowered" at the pretrial stage of the criminal process. Statutes do not require that the prosecutor defer to the victim's wishes, and there are no legal consequences of ignoring the victim in a plea bargaining decision. Even the ABA's Model Uniform Victims of Crime Act only suggests that the prosecutor "confer" with the victim.[39] Despite these limitations, there is no question that the prosecutor should consider the impact that a plea bargain may have on the victim or the victim's family. Some victims' groups even suggest that the victim's family have statutory authority to approve or disapprove any plea bargain between the prosecutor and defense attorney in criminal homicide cases. Given the volume of plea bargains, it appears that the victim should have greater control and participation.

Plea Bargaining Reform

Plea bargaining is an inevitable result of the criminal justice process and is essential to its continued functioning.[40] Yet despite its prevalence, its merits are still hotly debated. Those opposed to the widespread use of plea bargaining assert that it is coercive in its inducement of guilty pleas, that it encourages the unequal exercise of prosecutorial discretion, and that it complicates sentencing as well as the job of correctional authorities. Others argue that it is unconstitutional and results in cynicism and disrespect for the entire system. Its proponents, however, contend that the practice ensures the flow of guilty pleas essential to administration efficiency. It gives the system the flexibility to individualize justice and inspires respect for the system because it is associated with certain and prompt punishment.[41]

In recent years, efforts have been made to convert plea bargaining into a more visible, understandable, and fair dispositional process. Safeguards and guidelines have been developed to ensure that innocent defendants do not plead guilty under coercion. For example, the judge questions the defendant about the facts of the guilty plea before accepting the plea; the defense counsel is present and can advise the defendant of his or her rights; the prosecutor and the defense attorney openly discuss the plea; and full and frank information about the defendant and the offenses is made available at this stage of the process. In addition, judicial supervision ensures that plea bargaining is conducted in a fair manner.

NEGOTIATION OVERSIGHT ● Some jurisdictions have established guidelines to provide consistency in plea bargaining cases. Guidelines define the kinds and types of cases and offenders that may be suitable for plea bargaining. Guidelines cover such aspects as avoiding overindictment and controlling unprovable indictments, reducing felonies to misdemeanors, and bargaining with defendants. Other controls might include procedures for internally reviewing decisions by the chief prosecutor and the use of written memoranda to document the need for and acceptability of a plea bargain in a given case. Pleas may also be offered on a "take it or leave it" basis. Under this system, a special prosecutor, whose job it is to screen cases, sets the bargaining terms. If the defense counsel cannot accept the agreement, there is no negotiation, and the case must go to trial. Only if complications arise in the case, such as witnesses changing their testimony, can negotiations be reopened.[42]

BANNING PLEA BARGAINING ● What would happen if plea bargaining were banned outright, as its critics advocate? Numerous jurisdictions throughout the United States have experimented with bans on plea bargaining. In 1975, Alaska eliminated the practice. Honolulu has also attempted to abolish plea bargaining. Other jurisdictions, including Iowa, Arizona, Delaware, and the District of Columbia, have sought to limit the use of plea bargaining.[43] In theory, eliminating plea bargains means that prosecutors in these jurisdictions make no concessions to a defendant in exchange for a guilty plea.

In reality, however, in these and most jurisdictions, sentence-related concessions, charge-reduction concessions, and alternative methods for prosecution continue to be used in one way or another.[44] Where plea bargaining is limited or abolished, the number of trials may increase, the sentence severity may change, and more questions about the right to a speedy trial may arise. Discretion may also be shifted further up the system. Instead of spending countless hours preparing for and conducting a trial, prosecutors may dismiss more cases outright or decide not to prosecute them after initial action has been taken.

Reform can be difficult. Candace McCoy's study of plea reform in California investigated legislative efforts to eliminate the state's plea bargaining process. Instead of achieving a ban on plea bargaining, the process shifted from the superior to the municipal courts. McCoy found that the majority of defendants pled guilty after some negotiations and that the new law actually accelerated the guilty plea process. McCoy's alternative model of plea bargaining reform includes emphasizing public scrutiny of plea bargaining, adhering to standards of professionalism, and making a greater commitment to due process procedures.[45]

In sum, plea bargaining is a complex process. It involves such issues as trial costs; attorney competence, compensation, and workloads; sentencing and bail rules; witness availability; and estimations of trial outcomes, among a myriad of other factors.[46] Though heavily criticized, it remains a mainstay of the justice process.

Pretrial Diversion

diversion
A noncriminal alternative to trial, usually featuring counseling, job training, and educational opportunities.

Another important feature in the early court process is placing offenders into noncriminal **diversion** programs before their formal trial or conviction. The first pretrial diversion programs were established more than 40 years ago to reduce the stigma created by the formal trial process. To avoid stigma and labeling, diversion programs suspend criminal proceedings so that the accused can participate in a community treatment program under court supervision. Diversion programs give the client an opportunity to

- Avoid the stigma of a criminal record
- Continue to work and support his or her family
- Continue pursuing educational goals
- Access rehabilitation services, such as anger management, while remaining in the community
- When needed, make restitution to the victim of crime or pay back the community through volunteer services

Diversion also enables the justice system to reduce costs and alleviate prison crowding.

Diversion programs can take many forms. Some are run by separate, independent agencies that were originally set up with federal funds but are now being continued with county or state assistance. Others are organized as part of a police, prosecutor, or probation department's internal structure. Still others represent a joint venture between the county government and a private, nonprofit organization that carries out the treatment process.

First viewed as a panacea that could reduce court congestion and help treat minor offenders, diversion programs soon came under fire when national evaluations concluded that they are no more successful at avoiding stigma and reducing recidivism than traditional justice processing.[47] There was also the suspicion that diversion might *widen the net of the justice system*. By this, critics meant that the people placed in diversion programs were the ones most likely to have otherwise been dismissed after a brief hearing with a warning or small fine.[48] Now they were receiving more treatment than they would have if the program had not been in place. Those who would ordinarily have received a more serious sentence were not eligible for diversion anyway. Thus, rather than limiting contact with the system, the diversion programs actually increase its grasp.

Diversion programs
To read more about **diversion programs** in the state of Florida, go to
www.cengage.com/ criminaljustice/siegel.

Diversion is a popular option in lieu of criminal prosecution for certain offenders. Here Middlebury College professor Jay Parini presents a class on poet Robert Frost to students in a court diversion program in Middlebury, Vermont, on May 28, 2008. More than two dozen young people were convicted of charges that, in a rampage fueled by beer and marijuana, they vandalized a farmhouse where poet Robert Frost spent 20 of his summers. The home is owned by Middlebury College.

© AP Images/Toby Talbot

Of course, not all justice experts agree with this charge, and some programs have shown great promise. Recent evaluations indicate that given the proper treatment, some types of offenders, such as drug offenders, who are offered a place in pretrial programs can significantly lower their rates of recidivism.[49]

The Trial

The criminal trial is an open and public hearing designed to examine the facts of the case brought by the state against the accused. Criminal trials are relatively rare events (most cases are settled by a plea bargain during the pretrial stage), but they are an important and enduring fixture in the criminal justice system. By its very nature, the criminal trial is a symbol of the moral authority of the state. It is the symbol of the administration of objective and impartial justice. Regardless of the issues involved, the defendant's presence in a courtroom is designed to guarantee that she will have a hearing conducted under rules of procedure in an atmosphere of fair play and objectivity and that the outcome of the hearing will be clear and definitive. If the defendant believes that her constitutional rights and privileges have been violated, she may appeal the case to a higher court, where the procedures of the original trial will be examined. If, after examining the trial transcript, the appellate court rules that the original trial employed improper and unconstitutional procedures, it may order that a new hearing be held or even that the charges against the defendant be dismissed.

Most formal trials are heard by a jury, although some defendants waive their constitutional right to a jury trial and request a **bench trial**, in which the judge alone renders a **verdict**. In this situation, which occurs daily in the lower criminal courts, the judge may initiate a number of formal or informal dispositions, including dismissing the case, finding the defendant not guilty, finding the defendant guilty and imposing a sentence, or even continuing the case indefinitely. The decision the judge makes often depends on the seriousness of the offense, the background and previous record of the defendant, and the judgment of the court about whether the case can be properly dealt with in the criminal process. The judge may simply continue the case

bench trial
The trial of a criminal matter by a judge only. The accused waives any constitutional right to trial by jury.

verdict
A finding of a jury or a judge on questions of fact at a trial.

Policies, Programs, and Issues in Criminal Justice

The *CSI* Effect

When *CSI: Crime Scene Investigation,* debuted, it was a surprise television hit. At one point, it was labeled the most popular show in the world. Its spinoff programs, *CSI: Miami* and *CSI: New York,* were also popular. *CSI* spawned an entire genre of similar programs, including *Cold Case, Bones,* and *NUMBERS.* In 2006, five of the top 10 television programs involved criminal investigations.

The criminal investigations genre is but the latest to evolve in the long history of television programming that has featured (and sensationalized) criminal investigations and courtroom proceedings. More than most other shows, though, *CSI* and its progeny may have started to blur the lines between reality and fiction. And this effect may be enhanced by the popularity of crime magazine shows such as *48 Hours Mystery, American Justice,* and (sometimes) *Dateline NBC,* which feature real cases. But it's *not* that these entertainment programs portray the criminal justice system so accurately that they seem more realistic than fictional. Read on.

Many attorneys, judges, and journalists have started to claim that *CSI*-like programs have influenced jurors' expectations. Some have alleged that jurors sometimes acquit defendants when no scientific evidence is presented. Others have alleged that jurors have developed unrealistic expectations about just what information scientific investigations can bring to bear on a case. As one prosecutor put it, "Jurors now expect us to have a DNA test for just about every case. They expect us to have the most advanced technology possible, and they expect it to look like it does on television."

Does a *CSI* Effect Really Exist?

Donald Shelton, a judge, and his colleagues, criminology professors at Eastern Michigan University, surveyed 1,000 prospective jurors in an effort to determine whether there is a real "*CSI* effect." They asked questions concerning expectations and demands for scientific evidence and the television programs that the respondents regularly watched. The respondents were asked about several crime types and then asked to report what scientific evidence they would expect to see presented at trial. Choices for the latter ranged from eyewitness testimony and circumstantial evidence to DNA, ballistics, and fingerprint evidence. They were even asked how likely they would be to find the defendant guilty or not guilty based on the evidence presented by the prosecution. What did the researchers find?

- 46 percent expected to see scientific evidence presented in *every* criminal case.
- 22 percent expected to see DNA evidence in *every* criminal case.
- 36 percent expected to see fingerprint evidence in *every* criminal case.
- 32 percent expected to see ballistic or other firearms evidence in *every* criminal case.

What do the percentages mean? Are expectations unrealistic? In one-third of all criminal cases, it is virtually impossible to gather fingerprint evidence. It appears, indeed, that the respondents' expectations were driven somewhat by their television-watching habits. For all the categories of evidence, *CSI* viewers tended to have higher expectations for being presented with scientific evidence. This suggests there is evidence of a *CSI* effect, but Shelton and his colleagues also found that respondents were only somewhat likely to alter their verdicts based on the presence or absence of scientific evidence in a trial. They found, for example, that

- *CSI* viewers were more likely than their non-*CSI*-viewing counterparts to convict without scientific evidence if eyewitness testimony was available.
- In rape cases, *CSI* viewers were less likely to convict if DNA evidence was not presented.
- In breaking-and-entering and theft scenarios, victim or other testimony was sufficient to convict.

Shelton and his colleagues concluded, in short, that there *is* a *CSI* effect, but it may not be as influential as was previously thought. Not everyone agrees, however. The National Academy of Sciences report presented in the Policies, Programs, and Issues feature "*Forensics under the Microscope*" in Chapter 5 revealed that a number of prosecutors are concerned about a supposedly real *CSI*-like effect.

Critical Thinking

It is said that life imitates art. As the popularity of the crime scene investigator profession grows, more students will probably be drawn into forensics, and more police and law enforcement agencies are likely to use forensic specialists in their daily operations. Do you think that crime is better solved in the lab or on the beat?

without a finding, in which case the verdict is withheld without a finding of guilt to induce the accused to improve her behavior in the community; if the defendant's behavior does improve, the case is ordinarily closed within a specific amount of time.

This section reviews some of the institutions and processes involved in **adjudication** and trial. We begin with a discussion of the legal rights that structure the trial process.

Legal Rights during Trial

Underlying every trial are constitutional principles, complex legal procedures, rules of court, and interpretations of statutes—all designed to ensure that the accused will receive a fair trial.

THE RIGHT TO AN IMPARTIAL JUDGE ● Even though the Constitution does not say so, every criminal defendant enjoys the right to a trial by an impartial judge. The Supreme Court ruled as much way back in the 1927 case of *Tumey v. Ohio*. In that case, a municipal court judge was also the mayor, an executive official. What's more, he received fines and fees that he ordered against defendants who were convicted in his courtroom. The Supreme Court held that it is a violation of due process when a judge "has a direct, personal, substantial pecuniary interest in reaching a conclusion against [a defendant] in his case."[50]

What if a judge is not impartial? How can such a judge be removed? Generally, the judge will excuse him or herself if there is a conflict of interest. Judicial codes of ethics provide the guidelines judges need to make such decisions. Some jurisdictions, however, permit peremptory removal of judges.[51] These are like the peremptory challenges used in jury selection (covered later in this chapter). When this occurs, one of the attorneys can move to have the judge removed, and another judge will come on board. Usually the peremptory removal can occur only once.

THE RIGHT TO BE COMPETENT AT TRIAL ● To stand trial, a criminal defendant must be considered mentally competent to understand the nature and extent of the legal proceedings. If a defendant is considered mentally incompetent, his trial must be postponed until treatment renders him capable of participating in his own defense.

Can state authorities force a mentally unfit defendant to be treated so that he can be tried? In *Riggins v. Nevada* (1992), the U.S. Supreme Court ruled that forced treatment does not violate a defendant's due process rights if it was medically appropriate and, considering less intrusive alternatives, was essential for the defendant's own safety or the safety of others.[52]

THE RIGHT TO CONFRONT WITNESSES ● The Sixth Amendment states that "In all criminal prosecutions, the accused shall enjoy the right…to be confronted with the witnesses against him." The accused enjoys this right not just by being able to confront witnesses in person, but by being allowed to participate in his or her trial. That is, trials cannot be conducted without the accused being afforded the right to appear in person. This right can be waived or forfeited through misconduct. The accused may choose not to show up,[53] which is constitutionally permissible, and he or she may forfeit the right to appear by acting out and causing a significant distraction in the courtroom.[54] There are also some exceptions, such as in child abuse cases, where it is felt that child victims would suffer irreparable harm be being forced to appear before their abusers.[55]

adjudication
The determination of guilt or innocence; a judgment concerning criminal charges. The majority of offenders charged plead guilty; of the remainder, some cases are adjudicated by a judge and a jury, some are adjudicated by a judge without a jury, and others are dismissed.

confrontation clause
A part of the Sixth Amendment that establishes the right of a criminal defendant to see and cross-examine all the witnesses against him or her.

hearsay evidence
Testimony that is not firsthand but, rather, relates information told by a second party.

compulsory process
Compelling the production of witnesses via a subpoena.

The **confrontation clause** is essential to a fair criminal trial because it restricts and controls the admissibility of **hearsay evidence**. Hearsay evidence is akin to secondhand evidence; rather than being told firsthand, it consists of information related by a second party (it is what one person hears and then says—hence the term "hearsay"). The Framers of the Constitution sought face-to-face accusations in which the defendant has a right to see and cross-examine all witnesses. The idea is that it is always more difficult to tell lies about people to their face than behind their back underlies the confrontation clause.

THE RIGHT TO COMPULSORY PROCESS • The Sixth Amendment says, in part, that the accused shall "have compulsory process for obtaining witnesses in his favor." **Compulsory process** means to compel the production of witnesses via a subpoena. A subpoena is an order requiring a witness to appear in court at a specified time and place. The Supreme Court decided that compulsory process is a fundamental right in the case of *Washington v. Texas* (1967).[56]

THE RIGHT TO AN IMPARTIAL JURY • It is no accident that of all the rights guaranteed to the people by the Constitution, only the right to a jury trial in criminal cases appears in both the original Constitution (Article III, Section 2) and the Bill of Rights (the Sixth Amendment). Although they may have disagreed on many points, the Framers did not question the wisdom of the jury trial.

Today, the criminal defendant has the right to choose whether the trial will be before a judge or a jury. Although the Sixth Amendment guarantees the defendant the right to a jury trial, the defendant can and often does waive this right. A substantial proportion of defendants, particularly those charged with misdemeanors, are tried before the court without a jury.

The major legal issue surrounding jury trial has been whether all defendants—those accused of misdemeanors as well as those accused of felonies—have an absolute right to a jury trial. Although the Constitution says that the right to a jury trial exists in *"all criminal prosecutions,"* the U.S. Supreme Court has restricted this right. In *Baldwin v. New York* (1970), the Supreme Court decided that a defendant has a constitutional right to a jury trial when facing a possible prison sentence of six months or more, regardless of whether the crime committed was a felony or a misdemeanor.[57] When the possible sentence is six months or less, the accused is not entitled to a jury trial unless it is authorized by state statute. In most jurisdictions, the more serious the charge, the greater likelihood of trial—and of a trial by jury.

THE RIGHT TO COUNSEL AT TRIAL • Recall from previous chapters that the defendant has a right to counsel at numerous points in the criminal justice process. Today, state courts must provide counsel at trial to indigent defendants who face even the possibility of incarceration.[58] The threat of incarceration need not be immediate. Even if the defendant might be sentenced to probation in which a prison or jail term is suspended, or might receive

REALITY CHECK

MYTH OR REALITY? The Sixth Amendment right to a jury trial extends to defendants in all criminal trials.

MYTH: Although the Sixth Amendment says otherwise, the Supreme Court has restricted this right to cases where the possible sentence exceeds imprisonment for six months.

There are some exceptions to the general rule that jury trials are offered when the possible punishment exceeds six months, but the fact remains that those accused of minor crimes are rarely tried before juries. Is this fair? Is it just? Before answering, consider that serious crimes (those that would merit jury trials) are the exception rather than the rule.

any other type of sentence containing a threat of future incarceration, he is afforded the right to counsel at trial.[59]

What if a defendant wants to serve as his or her own attorney? As a result of a 1975 Supreme Court decision, defendants are now permitted to proceed **pro se**, or for themselves.[60] Today, when defendants ask to be permitted to represent themselves and are found competent to do so, the court normally approves their requests. However, these defendants are nearly always cautioned by the court against self-representation. When pro se defendants' actions are disorderly and disruptive, the court can terminate their right to represent themselves.

pro se
Literally "for oneself"; presenting one's own defense in a criminal trial; self-representation.

THE RIGHT TO A SPEEDY TRIAL ● The tactics employed by wary defense attorneys (pretrial motions, complex plea negotiations, delay tactics during trial), along with inefficiencies in the court process (such as the frequent granting of continuances, poor scheduling procedures, and the abuse of time by court personnel), have made delay in criminal cases a serious and constitutional issue. As the American Bar Association states in the *Standards Relating to Speedy Trial*, "Congestion in the trial courts of this country, particularly in urban centers, is currently one of the major problems of judicial administration."[61] Delays in the trial process conflict with the Sixth Amendment's guarantee of a right to a speedy trial.[62]

The Supreme Court has called the right to a speedy trial "as fundamental as any of the rights secured by the Sixth Amendment."[63] Its primary purposes are to

- Improve the credibility of the trial by having witnesses available for testimony as early as possible.
- Help criminal defendants avoid lengthy pretrial detention.
- Avoid extensive pretrial publicity and questionable conduct of public officials that may influence the defendant's right to a fair trial.
- Avoid any delay that could affect the defendant's ability to defend himself or herself against charges.

Defense attorney Peter Persaud, left, and defendant Curtis Fry listen to the prosecution's final remarks during Fry's trial on March 13, 2009, at the Johnson County Courthouse in Iowa City, Iowa. Fry faced second-degree murder charges in the death of Jerome "Patrick" McEwen. Police say 22-year-old Fry broke into the Iowa City home of 75-year-old McEwen and beat him to death on February 7, 2008.

© AP Images/Dan Williamson, Pool

There is no set time that defines a speedy trial. In *Doggett v. United States*, the Court found that a delay of eight and a half years between indictment and arrest was prejudicial to the defendant and required a dismissal of the charges against the defendant.[64] But this is an extreme case. Typically, when a defendant invokes the speedy trial clause, the appellate court will evaluate the length of delay, the reason for the delay, when the defendant made the claim, and what damage the delay caused. If the prosecution deliberately slows the case down, that may have a greater effect on the appeal process than if the case was delayed because a witness could not be located. And if the defendant agreed to the delay or caused the delay, the speedy-trial right may be lost.

THE RIGHT TO A PUBLIC TRIAL • The Sixth Amendment refers to a "public trial." This simply means that all trials must be open to the public. The right to a public trial is generally unrestricted. Anyone who wants to see a criminal trial can do so.

Sometimes having a trial open to the public can cause problems. In the 1966 case of *Sheppard v. Maxwell*, the courtroom was packed with people, including members of the media, for all nine weeks of the trial. Reporters handled evidence and took pictures throughout the trial. The Supreme Court eventually reversed the defendant's conviction, citing the "carnival atmosphere." The case did not lead to the exclusion of cameras from the courtroom, but some judges require that they be kept out. This is why one sometimes sees sketches of a case instead of actual photos.

Adverse pretrial publicity can prevent a defendant from getting a fair trial. The release of premature evidence by the prosecutor, extensive and critical reporting by the news media, and vivid and uncalled-for details in indictments can all prejudice a defendant's case. Press coverage can begin early in a criminal case and can even affect the outcome.

Judges involved in newsworthy criminal cases have attempted to place restraints on pretrial media coverage to preserve the defendant's right to a fair trial. The Supreme Court has shaped pretrial publicity in three significant cases:

* *Nebraska Press Association v. Stuart* (1976). It is unconstitutional for a trial judge to prohibit the press from reporting on details of the crime.[65] "Prior restraints on speech and publication," the justices state, "are the most serious and least tolerable infringement on First Amendment rights."[66]

* *Gannett Co. v. DePasquale* (1979). The press corps's right to attend pretrial judicial hearings can be outweighed by the defendant's right to due process.[67] The interest of justice requires that the defendant's case not be jeopardized by press coverage.

* *Press-Enterprise Co. v. Superior Court* (1986). Closing a hearing is permissible under the First Amendment only if there is substantial probability that the defendant's right to a fair trial would be prejudiced by publicity[68]

Thus, as a general rule, pretrial publicity and reporting cannot be controlled. However, judges may bar the press from some pretrial legal proceedings and hearings, such as preliminary hearings, when police officers make an arrest, or when a warrant is being served, if their presence

REALITY CHECK

MYTH OR REALITY? Trials are closed to the public.

MYTH: Nearly every trial, civil or criminal, is open to the public.

Seeing artists' sketches of high-profile trials on the evening news gives the impression that trials are closed to the public, but the fact that restrictions are placed on the press in most trials (for example, cameras are generally not allowed) does not mean trials are closed to the public. What are some advantages of having trials open to the public? What are some disadvantages?

will infringe on the defendant's right to a fair trial.[69] Other steps can be taken as well. These include changes of venue (moving the trial to another jurisdiction, where there is less press coverage and hence less contamination of the pool of potential jurors) and gag orders (restrictions on what the parties or the media can report), among others.

What about press coverage *during* trial? In the landmark case *Richmond Newspapers, Inc. v. Virginia* (1980), the Supreme Court clearly established that criminal trials must remain open to the press.[70] The Court extended the right of the press to attend trials involving even highly sensitive, sexually related matters in which the victim is under 18 years of age.[71]

More recently, the issue of press coverage has focused on bringing TV cameras into the courtroom. Because of the public interest in high-profile criminal cases, whether jury trials should be televised is one of the most controversial questions in the criminal justice system. The legal community is divided over the use of TV cameras in the courtroom. Today, many state courts permit such coverage, often at the judge's discretion, but federal courts prohibit TV coverage altogether. In 1981, the U.S. Supreme Court in *Chandler v. Florida* removed any constitutional obstacles to the use of electronic media coverage and still photography of public criminal proceedings over the objections of a criminal defendant.[72] Certainly, the defendant has a constitutional right to a public trial, but it is equally imperative that the media be allowed to exercise their **First Amendment** rights, which include making that public trial truly public.

THE RIGHT TO BE CONVICTED BY PROOF BEYOND A REASONABLE DOUBT •

The standard required to convict a defendant charged with a crime at the adjudicatory stage of the criminal process **is proof beyond a reasonable doubt**. This requirement dates back to early American history and over the years has become the accepted measure of persuasion needed by the prosecutor to convince the judge or jury of the defendant's guilt. Many twentieth-century U.S. Supreme Court decisions have reinforced this standard by making "beyond a reasonable doubt a due process and constitutional requirement."[73] In *Brinegar v. United States* (1949), for instance, the Supreme Court stated:

> Guilt in a criminal case must be proven beyond a reasonable doubt and by evidence confined to that which long experience in the common-law tradition, to some extent embodied in the Constitution, has crystallized into rules of evidence consistent with that standard. These rules are historically grounded rights of our system, developed to safeguard men from dubious and unjust convictions with resulting forfeitures of life, liberty, and property.[74]

The reasonable doubt standard is an essential ingredient of the criminal justice process. It is the prime instrument for reducing the risk of convictions based on factual errors.[75] The underlying premise of this standard is that it is better to release a guilty person than to convict someone who is innocent. Because the defendant is presumed innocent until proven guilty, this standard forces the prosecution to overcome this presumption with the highest standard of proof. Unlike the civil law, where a mere **preponderance of the evidence** is the standard, the criminal process requires proof beyond a reasonable doubt for each element of the offense.[76] The various evidentiary standards of proof are analyzed and compared in Exhibit 8.1.

First Amendment
The amendment to the U.S. Constitution that guarantees freedom of speech, religion, press, and assembly, and the right of the people to petition the government for redress of grievances.

proof beyond a reasonable doubt
The standard of proof needed to convict in a criminal case. The evidence offered in court does not have to amount to absolute certainty, but it should leave no reasonable doubt that the defendant committed the alleged crime.

preponderance of the evidence
The level of proof in civil cases; more than half the evidence supports the allegations of one side.

© Image Source/Corbis

EXHIBIT 8.1

Evidentiary Standards of Proof: Degrees of Certainty

Standard	Definition	Ruling
Absolute certainty	No possibility of error; 100% certainty	Not used in civil or criminal law
Beyond reasonable doubt; moral certainty	Conclusive and complete proof, without leaving any reasonable doubt about the innocence or guilt of the defendant; allows the defendant the benefit of any possibility of innocence	Criminal trial
Clear and convincing	Prevailing and persuasive to the trier of fact	Civil commitments, insanity defense evidence
Preponderance of the evidence	Greater weight of evidence in terms of credibility; more convincing than an opposite point of view	Civil trial
Probable cause	U.S. constitutional standard for arrest and search warrants, requiring existence of facts sufficient to warrant that a crime has been committed	Arrest, preliminary hearing, motions
Sufficient evidence	Adequate evidence to reverse a trial court	Appellate review
Reasonable suspicion	Rational, reasonable belief that facts warrant investigation of a crime on less than probable cause	Police investigations
Less than probable cause	Mere suspicion; less than reasonable belief to conclude criminal activity exists	Prudent police investigation where safety of an officer or others is endangered

The Trial Process

The trial of a criminal case is a formal process conducted in a specific and orderly fashion in accordance with rules of criminal law, procedure, and evidence. Unlike what transpires in popular TV programs involving lawyers—where witnesses are often asked leading and prejudicial questions and where judges go far beyond their supervisory role—the modern criminal trial is a complicated and often time-consuming, technical affair. It is a structured adversarial proceeding in which both prosecution and defense follow specific procedures and argue the merits of their cases before the judge and jury. Each side seeks to present its case in the most favorable light. When possible, the prosecutor and the defense attorney object to evidence they consider damaging to their positions. The prosecutor uses direct testimony, physical evidence, and a confession, if available, to convince the jury that the accused is guilty beyond a reasonable doubt. The defense attorney will rebut the government's case with her own evidence, make certain that the rights of the criminal defendant under the federal and state constitutions are considered during all phases of the trial, and determine whether an appeal is appropriate if the client is found guilty.

Although each jurisdiction in the United States has its own trial procedures, all jurisdictions conduct criminal trials in a generally similar fashion. The basic steps of the criminal trial, which proceed in an established order, are described in this section and outlined in Figure 8.3.

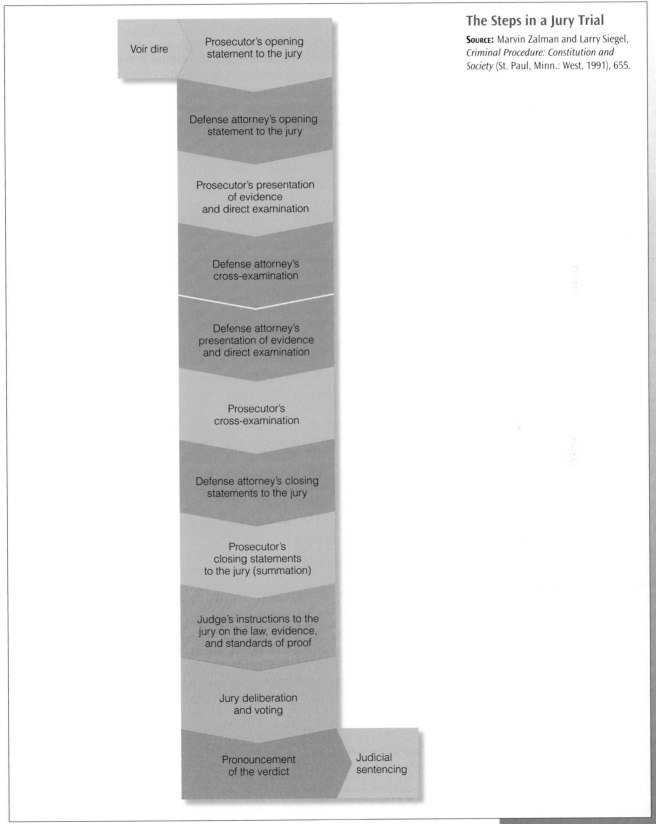

The Steps in a Jury Trial

Source: Marvin Zalman and Larry Siegel, *Criminal Procedure: Constitution and Society* (St. Paul, Minn.: West, 1991), 655.

Voir dire

Prosecutor's opening statement to the jury

Defense attorney's opening statement to the jury

Prosecutor's presentation of evidence and direct examination

Defense attorney's cross-examination

Defense attorney's presentation of evidence and direct examination

Prosecutor's cross-examination

Defense attorney's closing statements to the jury

Prosecutor's closing statements to the jury (summation)

Judge's instructions to the jury on the law, evidence, and standards of proof

Jury deliberation and voting

Pronouncement of the verdict

Judicial sentencing

FIGURE 8.3

JURY SELECTION • In both civil and criminal cases, jurors are selected randomly from licensing or voter registration lists within each court's jurisdiction. Few states impose qualifications on those called for jury service, although most mandate a residency requirement.[77] There is also little uniformity in the amount of time served by jurors; the term ranges from one day to months, depending on the nature of the trial. In addition, most jurisdictions prohibit convicted felons from serving on juries, as well as others exempted by statute, such as public officials, physicians, and attorneys.

The initial list of persons chosen, which is called a **venire**, or jury array, provides the state with a group of potentially capable citizens able to serve on a jury. Many states, by rule of law, review the venire to eliminate unqualified persons and to exempt those who, by reason of their professions, are not allowed to be jurors. The actual jury selection process begins with those remaining on the list.

The court clerk, who handles the administrative affairs of the court—including the processing of the complaint and other documents—randomly selects what he or she believes will be enough names to fill the required number of places on the jury. After reporting to a courtroom, the prospective jurors are first required to swear that they will truthfully answer all questions asked about their qualifications to serve. A group of 12 will be asked to sit in the jury box while the remaining group stands by.

Once prospective jurors are chosen, the lengthy process of **voir dire** (from the French for "to tell the truth") starts. To determine their appropriateness to sit on the jury, prospective jurors are examined under oath by the government, the defense, and sometimes the judge about their backgrounds, occupations, residences, and possible knowledge of or interest in the case. A juror who acknowledges any bias for or prejudice against the defendant—if the defendant is a friend or relative, or if the juror has already formed an opinion about the case—may be removed by either the prosecution or the defense with a **challenge for cause** asking the judge to dismiss the biased juror. If the judge accepts the challenge, the juror is removed for cause and replaced with another juror from the remaining panel. Because normally no limit is placed on the number of challenges for cause that can be exercised, it often takes considerable time to select a jury, especially for controversial and highly publicized criminal cases.

Besides challenges for cause, both the prosecution and the defense are allowed **peremptory challenges**, which enable the attorneys to excuse jurors for no particular reason or for undisclosed reasons. A prosecutor might not want a bartender as a juror in a drunk-driving case, believing that a person with that occupation would be sympathetic to the accused. Or the defense attorney might excuse a male prospective juror because the attorney prefers to have a predominantly female jury. The number of peremptory challenges given to the prosecution and defense is limited by state statute and often varies by case and jurisdiction.

The peremptory challenge has been criticized by legal experts who question the fairness and propriety with which it has been used.[78] Historically, the most significant criticism was that it was used by the prosecution to exclude African Americans from serving on juries in which the defendant was also African American—a policy that seemed to allow legally condoned

---

venire
The group called for jury duty from which jury panels are selected.

voir dire
The process in which a potential jury panel is questioned by the prosecution and the defense in order to select jurors who are unbiased and objective.

challenge for cause
A request that a prospective juror be removed because he or she is biased or has prior knowledge about a case, or for other reasons that demonstrate the individual's inability to render a fair and impartial judgment in a particular case.

peremptory challenge
The dismissal of a potential juror by either the prosecution or the defense for unexplained, discretionary reasons.

REALITYCHECK

MYTH OR REALITY? There is nothing inherently wrong with a black jury deciding the fate of a white defendant.

REALITY: The Sixth Amendment requires an "impartial jury of the state." If a black jury can be impartial with respect to a white defendant, there is no problem. The reverse is also true.

The problem is one of appearances. Also, and very important, if it can be shown that prospective jurors were excluded because of race, then the resulting jury will not conform to Sixth Amendment requirements.

discrimination against minority group members. In the landmark 1986 case *Batson v. Kentucky,* the Supreme Court held that the use of peremptory challenges against potential jurors by prosecutors in criminal cases violated the U.S. Constitution if the challenges were based solely on race.[79] Since that decision, the issue of race discrimination in the use of peremptory challenges has been raised by defendants in numerous cases. Exhibit 8.2 summarizes these decisions.

It is becoming increasingly difficult to find impartial jurors, especially in this technological age. Heinous crimes have always been broadcast all over the news, and the result has sometimes been to contaminate the pool of prospective jurors. This still happens, of course, but such crimes are the exception rather than the rule. But now jurors are able to turn to their BlackBerrys and iPhones to seek information about *any* case. By searching the Internet and sharing information (such as on Facebook), they often learn more about cases than is presented in court, which they are expressly forbidden to do. As one article recently noted, this practice is "wreaking havoc on trials around the country, upending deliberations and infuriating judges."[80] Although there is no official tally of the number of cases compromised by jurors' Internet research, the number is certainly growing. For example, a Florida case involving a man accused of illegally selling prescription drugs was upended because one juror researched the case on her own and was able to discover information not presented at trial. After her actions came to light, the judge had no choice but to declare a mistrial.

OPENING STATEMENTS • Once the jury has been selected and the criminal complaint has been read to the jurors by the court clerk, the prosecutor and

EXHIBIT 8.2

Evolution of *Batson v. Kentucky* and Its Progeny

Case	Ruling
Batson v. Kentucky (1986)	Under the Fourteenth Amendment, the Supreme Court ruled that prosecutors were barred from using peremptory challenges to remove black jurors because of their race.
Powers v. Ohio (1991)	The Court concluded that defendants have the standing to object to the race-based exclusion by the use of peremptory challenges of jurors on the grounds of equal protection, even if they were not of the same race as the challenged jurors.
Edmonson v. Leesville Concrete Co. (1991)	The *Batson* ruling applies to attorneys in civil lawsuits. In other words, a private party in a civil action may not raise peremptory challenges to exclude jurors on the basis of race.
Georgia v. McCollum (1992)	On the basis of *Batson,* the *McCollum* decision prohibited the exercise of peremptory challenges on the basis of race by defense attorneys in criminal cases.
J.E.B. v. Alabama (1994)	The Court held that the equal protection clause of the Fourteenth Amendment bars discrimination in jury selection on the basis of sex. Discrimination in jury selection, whether based on race or gender, causes harm to the litigants, the community, and the individual jurors who are wrongfully excluded from participation in the judicial process.

the defense attorney may each make an opening statement about the case. The purpose of the prosecutor's statement is to acquaint the judge and jury with the particular criminal charges, to outline the facts, and to describe how the government will prove the defendant guilty beyond a reasonable doubt. The defense attorney reviews the case and indicates how the defense intends to show that the accused is not guilty.

Typically, the prosecutor is entitled to offer an opening statement, which is followed by the defense's opening statement. Both sides use the statement to give the jury a concise overview of the evidence that is to follow. Neither attorney is allowed to make prejudicial remarks or inflammatory statements or to mention irrelevant facts. Both are free, however, to identify what they will eventually prove by way of evidence, which includes witnesses, physical evidence, and the use of expert testimony. The opening statements are important because they give both sides an opportunity to sway the jury before the trial begins.

direct examination

The questioning of one's own (prosecution or defense) witness during a trial.

cross-examination

The process in which the defense and the prosecution interrogate witnesses for the other side during a trial.

directed verdict

The right of a judge to direct a jury to acquit a defendant because the state has not proved the elements of the crime or otherwise has not established guilt according to law.

PROSECUTION'S CASE • Following the opening statements, the government begins its case by presenting evidence to the court through its witnesses. Numerous types of evidence are presented at trial (see Exhibit 8.3). Those called as witnesses—such as police officers, victims, or experts—provide testimony via **direct examination**. During direct examination, the prosecutor questions the witness to reveal the facts believed pertinent to the government's case. Testimony involves what the witness actually saw, heard, or touched; it does not include opinions. However, a witness's opinion can be given in certain situations, such as when describing the motion of a vehicle or indicating whether a defendant appeared to act intoxicated or insane. Witnesses may also qualify to give opinions because they are experts on a particular subject relevant to the case. For example, a psychiatrist may testify about a defendant's mental capacity at the time of the crime.

Upon completion of the prosecutor's questioning, the defense usually conducts a **cross-examination** of the witness. During this exchange, the defense attorney may challenge elements of the testimony, such as the witness's accuracy in reporting what was seen or heard. The right to cross-examine witnesses is an essential part of a trial, and unless extremely unusual circumstances exist (such as a person's being hospitalized), witness statements will not be considered unless they are made in court and are open for question. If desired, the prosecutor may seek a second direct examination after the defense attorney has completed cross-examination; this allows the prosecutor to ask additional questions about information brought out during cross-examination. Finally, the defense attorney may then question, or re-cross-examine, the witness once again. All witnesses for the trial are sworn in and questioned in the same basic manner.

THE CRIMINAL DEFENSE • Once the prosecutor has provided all the government's evidence against a defendant, he will inform the court that he rests the people's case. The defense attorney at this point may enter a motion for a **directed verdict**. This is a procedural device in which the defense attorney asks the judge to order the jury to return a verdict of not guilty. Depending on the weight of the prosecution's case, the judge

© moodboard/Corbis

EXHIBIT 8.3

Types of Evidence Presented at Trial

In general, the primary test for the admissibility of evidence in a criminal proceeding is its relevance; that is, the court must consider whether the gun, tool, or bottle has relevant evidentiary value in determining the issues in the case. Ordinarily, evidence that establishes an element of the crime is acceptable to the court. In a prosecution for possession of drugs, evidence that shows the defendant to be a known drug user might be relevant. In a prosecution for bribery, photos of the defendant receiving a package from a co-conspirator would clearly be found relevant to the case. There are four main types of evidence:

- *Testimonial evidence.* Given by police officers, citizens, and experts, this is the most basic form of evidence. The witness must state, under oath, what he or she heard, saw, or experienced.
- *Real evidence.* Exhibits that can be taken into the jury room for review by the jury constitute real evidence. A revolver that may have been in the defendant's control at the time of a murder, tools in the possession of a suspect charged with a burglary, and a bottle allegedly holding narcotics are examples of real, or physical, evidence. Photographs, maps, diagrams, and crime scene displays are other types of real evidence.
- *Documentary evidence.* This type of evidence includes writings, government reports, public records, business or hospital records, fingerprint identification, and DNA profiling.
- *Circumstantial evidence.* In trial proceedings, circumstantial (indirect) evidence is often inferred or indirectly used to prove a fact in question. For example, in a murder case, evidence that carpet fibers found on the body match the carpet in the defendant's home may be used at trial to link the two, even though they do not provide direct evidence that the suspect actually killed the victim.

may either sustain or overrule this motion. In essence, the defense attorney argues in the directed verdict that the prosecutor's case against the defendant is insufficient to support the legal elements needed to prove the defendant guilty beyond a reasonable doubt. If the court sustains the motion, the trial is terminated. If it rejects the motion, the defense begins to legally rebut the prosecution's case.

The defense attorney has the option of presenting many, some, or no witnesses on behalf of the defendant. The burden of proving guilt is on the prosecution, and if the defense team believes that the burden has not been met, they may feel there is no need to present witnesses of their own. In addition, the defense attorney must decide whether the defendant should take the stand and testify in his own behalf. In a criminal trial, the defendant is protected by the Fifth Amendment right to be free from self-incrimination, which means that a person cannot be forced by the state to testify against himself. However, defendants who choose voluntarily to tell their side of the story can be subject to cross-examination by the prosecutor.

The defense attorney is charged with putting on a vigorous defense in the adversary system of justice. She presents her own witnesses and introduces evidence to refute the prosecution's allegations. After the defense concludes its case, the government may then present rebuttal evidence. If the judge grants permission, this involves bringing forward evidence to refute, counteract, or disprove evidence introduced by the defense. A prosecutor may not go into new matters or present evidence that further supports or reinforces his own case. At the end of rebuttal, the defense may be allowed so-called surrebuttal—presenting witnesses to respond to issues that were raised for the first time in the prosecutor's rebuttal case. The defense cannot restate its case or introduce new issues during surrebuttal evidence.

CLOSING ARGUMENTS ● In closing arguments the attorneys review the facts and evidence of the case in a manner favorable to their respective positions. At this stage of the trial, both prosecution and defense are permitted to draw reasonable inferences and to show how the facts prove or refute the defendant's guilt. Often both attorneys have a free hand in arguing about the facts, issues, and evidence, including the applicable law. They cannot comment on matters not in evidence, however, or on the defendant's failure to testify in a criminal case. Normally, the prosecutor makes a closing statement first, followed by the defense, and many jurisdictions allow the prosecution an opportunity for rebuttal. Either party can elect to forgo the right to make a final summation to the jury.

INSTRUCTIONS TO THE JURY ● In a criminal trial, the judge will instruct, or charge, the jury members on the principles of law that ought to guide and control their decision on the defendant's innocence or guilt. Included in the charge will be information about the elements of the alleged offense, the type of evidence needed to prove each element, and the burden of proof that must be met to obtain a guilty verdict. Although the judge commonly provides this instruction, he or she may ask the prosecutor and the defense attorney to submit instructions for consideration; the judge will then exercise discretion in determining whether to use any of their instructions. The instructions that cover the law applicable to the case are extremely important because they may serve as the basis for a subsequent appeal. (The Policies, Programs, and Issues in Criminal Justice feature on page 270 discusses the CSI Effect, a relatively recent phenomenon that judges need to be aware of as they instruct the jury on how to go about its business.)

DELIBERATION AND VERDICT ● Once the charge is given to the jury members, they retire to deliberate on a verdict. In highly publicized and celebrated cases, the judge may sequester the jury, preventing them from having contact with the outside world. This process is discretionary, and most judges believe that sequestering or "locking up a jury" is needed only in sensational cases.

A judge's instructions to the jury are among the most important parts of the trial process. Flawed instructions can form the basis of an appeal. Here, Gage County District Court judge Paul Korslund briefs members of the jury during the trial of Richard Griswold at the Gage County Court, in Beatrice, Nebraska, on May 19, 2008. Griswold, 43, of Beatrice, was charged with first-degree murder and use of a weapon to commit a felony in the death of 49-year-old Connie Eacret. In what is believed to have been a first for the state, media cameras were being allowed in the courtroom for a criminal trial.

A review of the case by the jury may take hours or even days. The jurors always meet privately during their deliberations, and in certain lengthy and highly publicized cases, they are kept overnight in a hotel until the verdict is reached. In less sensational cases, the jurors may be allowed to go home, but they are cautioned not to discuss the case with anyone.

If a verdict cannot be reached, the trial may result in a hung jury, after which the prosecutor must bring the defendant to trial again if the prosecution desires a conviction. If found not guilty, the defendant is released from the criminal process. If the defendant is convicted, the judge will normally order a pre-sentence investigation by the probation department before imposing a sentence. Before sentencing, the defense attorney will probably submit a motion for a new trial, alleging that legal errors occurred in the trial proceedings. The judge may deny the motion and impose a sentence immediately, a practice quite common in most misdemeanor offenses. In felony cases, however, the judge will set a date for sentencing, and the defendant will either be placed on bail or held in custody until that time.

Although jurors are required by law to base their decision on the facts of the case and on the judge's legal instructions, they are sometimes asked by the defense to ignore both and render decisions based on emotion and personal preference.[81] This strategy, called **jury nullification**, has been in practice since 1735 when John Peter Zenger, editor of the *New York Weekly Journal*, was charged with printing libelous statements about the governor of the Colony of New York, William Cosby. Despite the fact that Zenger clearly printed the alleged libels and the trial judge gave the jury clear instructions for a finding of guilt, the jury found Zenger not guilty on all charges. The Zenger case remains one of the most famous examples of jury nullification in the nation's history.

Supporters of jury nullification argue that it is an important safeguard against government oppression and that the function of the jury is to serve as a safety valve against the unjust application of the law. Critics, however, see jury nullification as an abuse of power. Would it be fair if jurors, motivated

jury nullification
A defense tactic that consists of suggesting that the jury acquit a defendant, despite evidence that he actually violated the law, by maintaining that the law was unjust or not applicable to the case.

O. J. Simpson appears in court before a verdict of guilty on all counts is read following his trial at the Clark County Regional Justice Center in Las Vegas on October 3, 2008. The verdict came 13 years to the day after Simpson was acquitted of murdering his ex-wife Nicole Brown Simpson and Ron Goldman.

REALITY CHECK

by racial bias, found a person accused of a hate crime not guilty despite overwhelming evidence of guilt?[82]

THE SENTENCE ● Imposing the criminal sentence is normally the responsibility of the trial judge. In some jurisdictions, the jury may determine the sentence or make recommendations involving leniency for certain offenses. Often, the sentencing decision is based on information and recommendations given to the court by the probation department after a pre-sentence investigation of the defendant. The sentence itself is determined by the statutory requirements for the particular crime as established by the legislature; in addition, the judge ordinarily has a great deal of discretion in reaching a sentencing decision. The different criminal sanctions available include fines, probation, imprisonment, and even commitment to a state hospital. The sentence may be a combination of all these.

The most critical trial stages are reviewed in Concept Summary 8.1.

APPEALS ● Once a verdict has been rendered and a defendant found guilty, the defense may petition an appellate court to review the procedures used during trial. Defendants have two main avenues to challenge such procedures: appeals and habeas corpus. These both give the convicted person an opportunity to appeal to a higher state or federal court on the basis of an error that affected the conviction in the trial court. Extraordinary trial court errors, such as denial of the right to counsel or inability to provide a fair trial, are subject to the plain error rule of the federal courts.[83] Harmless errors, such as the use of innocuous identification procedures or the denial of counsel at a noncritical stage of the proceeding, would not necessarily result in the overturning of a criminal conviction.

appeal
A request for an appellate court to examine a lower court's decision in order to determine whether proper procedures were followed.

A postconviction **appeal** is request for an appellate court to examine a lower court's decision in order to determine whether proper procedures were followed. It is important to note that appeals do not give the convicted an opportunity to try the case a second time, only to challenge procedural matters (such as a judge's decision to exclude a witness's testimony). Most defendants benefit from at least one so-called "direct appeal." Direct appeals are guaranteed by law; the result is that most defendants get to appeal at least once, even if they cannot afford it.[84] "Discretionary appeals" are also possible. It is up to the appellate court to decide whether it will hear a discretionary appeal. There is no restriction on the number of discretionary appeals that can be filed.

Through objections made at the pretrial and trial stages of the criminal process, the defense counsel will reserve specific legal issues on the record as the basis for appeal. A copy of the transcript of these proceedings will serve as the basis on which the appellate court will review any errors that may have occurred during the lower-court proceedings. The Careers in Criminal Justice feature on pages 286-87 describes the work of the court reporter, the person who prepares these transcripts.

writ of habeas corpus
A judicial order requesting that a person who detains another person produce the body of the prisoner and give reasons for his or her capture and detention. Habeas corpus is a legal device used to request that a judicial body review the reasons for a person's confinement and the conditions of confinement. Habeas corpus is known as "the great writ."

A **writ of habeas corpus** is the primary means by which state prisoners have their convictions or sentences reviewed in the federal court. A writ of habeas corpus (which means "you have the body") seeks to determine the validity of a detention by asking the court to release the person or give legal reasons for the incarceration.

Stages of the Jury Trial

Stage 1

Jury Selection

The judge and attorneys question potential jurors until a panel of 12 is agreed upon by all sides. The voir dire process is designed to excuse jurors who might have difficulty in rendering a fair and impartial verdict in that particular case.

Stage 2

Opening Statements

Brief statements are made by prosecution and defense that outline their view of the facts of the case and what they hope to prove. The prosecutor in a criminal case gives the first statement and the defense attorney follows.

Stage 3

Presentation of Evidence

Witnesses for the prosecution in a criminal case testify first, witnesses for the defense testify next, and any rebuttal witnesses testify last. The attorney who calls the witness asks questions in direct examination. The attorney for the opposing side then questions the witness in cross-examination.

Stage 4

Closing Arguments

The prosecutor in a criminal case first attempts to convince the jury to decide in favor of her side of the case. The defense attorney follows with his argument, attempting to do the same. The prosecutor has the opportunity to present a rebuttal to the defense attorney's argument.

Stage 5

Jury Deliberations

After the judge instructs the jury on the law they must apply in the particular case, they retire from the courtroom to deliberate in secret. When the jurors reach a verdict, they return to the courtroom and the verdict is read aloud to the parties.

Stage 6

Sentencing

If a guilty verdict is reached, the judge will impose a sentence, choosing the most appropriate sanction from those legislatively available.

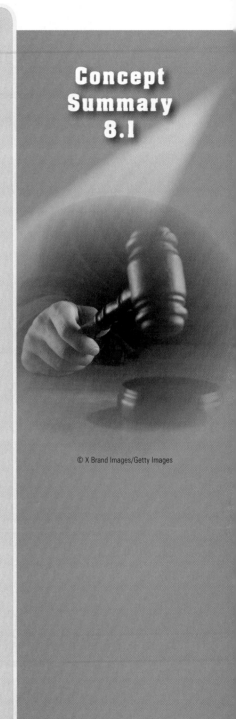

© X Brand Images/Getty Images

Careers in Criminal Justice

COURT REPORTER

Duties and Characteristics of the Job

- Court reporters create the official transcripts of legal proceedings such as trials and depositions.
- These transcripts include all the dialogue as well as other important details, such as emotional reactions.
- Court reporters use voice writers that make an audio record of the proceedings.
- Some use audio equipment to tape an event and then supplement this recording later with notes taken during the proceedings.
- The commonly used recording method in legal and courtroom settings is stenographic machines that transcribe spoken words. A court reporter can press multiple keys simultaneously to represent words, sounds, or even phrases.
- Although the primary responsibility of court reporters is to record courtroom legal proceedings, when requested they also provide this information from the official record.
- Court reporters can advise lawyers on legal procedure when necessary.

Job Outlook

- The number of jobs available for court reporters is greater than the number of trained professionals entering the field.
- The job outlook is favorable for entry-level court reporters, especially those who are certified.
- Court reporters are always needed in courtrooms and lawyers' offices across the country, although jobs may be more plentiful in urban areas.
- They often freelance for extra income at attorneys' offices or as closed captioners and/or real-time translators.
- Other court reporters work for court reporting agencies or freelance full time.
- Agency workers and freelancers enjoy the flexibility of setting their own schedules.

Salary

- Pay will depend on several factors, including method of transcription, region of the United States, type of employer, amount of previous work experience, and level of certification.
- The median annual salary for court reporters is around $45,000. The majority of court reporters earn between $33,000 and $62,000. At the extremes, a small percentage of court reporters earn $23,690, and the highest paid earn $80,000 or more.

Qualifications

- The qualifications one must have to be a practicing court reporter vary by state.
- In some states, court reporters are required to be notary publics; in others, an individual must become a certified court reporter (CCR) by passing a state certification test.
- Court reporters must continually study and practice their skills.

Education and Training

- At the minimum, a court reporter needs an associate's degree, although requiring a bachelor's degree is more common.
- In addition to general education, training programs are available at vocational or technical schools.
- There are 70 programs approved by the National Court Reporters Association in the United States and Canada.

Word to the Wise

- Because a court reporter must create a record of events as they occur, the ability to listen carefully and work quickly is key. Familiarity with legal terms and practices is necessary, as is a thorough knowledge of grammar, spelling, and vocabulary.

- Court reporters must become intimately familiar with stenotype machines. As one reporter said, "Your wrists will become your worst enemy if you don't show them some love."
- Despite the seemingly simple training requirements, many people drop out, partly as a consequence of the high speed required (around 225 words per minute, far in excess of the speed at which skilled typists can type).
- There can be considerable stress in the job because of the constant pressure to be fast and accurate.
- The future is somewhat uncertain; digital audio recorders could well replace court reporters some day.

ETHICAL CHALLENGES IN CRIMINAL JUSTICE

A WRITING ASSIGNMENT

Critics argue that the holding of terrorist suspects at Guantánamo in Cuba is the ultimate use of preventive detention. As of this writing, about 400 terrorism suspects are detained as enemy combatants, as material witnesses, or for immigration violations. In June 2006, three prisoners at the Guantánamo Bay detention center committed suicide, sparking renewed calls for closure of the facility. The Obama administration is now trying to make good on its promise to close Guantánamo.

Write an essay on the practice of detaining terror suspects without trial. Is it justified, or does it violate age-old concepts of due process and equal protection?

RealityCheck Revisited

To learn more about the myths and realities related to pretrial and court procedures that were raised in this chapter, visit the following websites.

- For official statistics relating to bail, including crimes committed on bail, see

http://www.ojp.usdoj.gov/bjs/pub/pdf/prfdsc.pdf

- For detailed data on the disposition of criminal cases by offense type (including guilty pleas and convictions), see

http://www.albany.edu/sourcebook/pdf/t5172004.pdf

- For further information on jury trials, including jury sizes and voting requirements by state, see Tables 40–42 here:

http://www.ojp.usdoj.gov/bjs/pub/pdf/sco04.pdf

- To read more about jury selection and decision making, see these sites:

http://www.albany.edu/scj/CJPhome.htm

http://www.njp.com/

http://www.abanet.org/juryprojectstandards/home.html

http://www.nyjuryinnovations.org/

SUMMARY

© AP Images/Hector Mata

1. Identify why the pretrial stage of justice is so critical to the entire process

- The great majority of all criminal cases are resolved informally at the pretrial stage and never come before the courts.
- The prosecution and the defense meet to try to arrange a nonjudicial settlement for most cases.

2. Understand the bail process

- The purpose of bail is to obtain the release from custody of a person charged with a crime.
- The Eighth Amendment to the U.S. Constitution does not guarantee a right to bail but, rather, prohibits "excessive bail."
- Bail is typically granted during a court hearing, but there are other stages in the system in which bail may be granted, depending on the jurisdiction, the crime, and the defendant.
- In practice, a majority of criminal defendants are released on bail prior to trial.
- Bail in a felony case is typically considered at a court hearing conducted shortly after a person has been taken into custody.

3. Discuss the history of, the direction of, and the reasons behind, bail reform

- Bail reform programs depend on the defendant's personal promise to appear in court for trial (recognizance), instead of on her or his financial ability to make bail.

- Critics argue that money bail is one of the most objectionable aspects of the criminal justice system because it discriminates against the poor.
- The first bail reform program was pioneered by the Vera Institute of Justice in an experiment called the Manhattan Bail Project.
- The Bail Reform Act of 1984 mandated that no defendants shall be kept in pretrial detention simply because they cannot afford money bail; it also formalized restrictive preventive detention provisions.
- Preventive detention laws require that certain dangerous defendants be confined before trial for their own protection and that of the community.
- Hundreds of pretrial bail programs have been established

4. Differentiate between the two main mechanisms for charging defendants (grand jury indictment and prosecutor's information)

- The grand jury's role is to act as the community's conscience in determining whether the accusation of the state (the prosecution) justifies a trial.
- If the grand jury believes charges are merited, an indictment will be issued. If not, a "no bill" is passed.
- The charging mechanism used in about half the states, as an alternative to the grand jury, is a prosecutor's information.
- An information is a written accusation submitted to the court by a prosecutor, alleging that a particular individual committed the offense in question
- The preliminary hearing is conducted before a magistrate or lower-court judge and is open to the public unless the defendant requests otherwise.

5. Know about pleas and plea negotiation

- The defendant in a criminal trial will enter one of three pleas: guilty, not guilty, or nolo contendere.

- Plea bargaining is one of the most common practices in the criminal justice system today and is a cornerstone of the informal justice system.

- Today more than 90 percent of criminal convictions are estimated to result from negotiated pleas of guilty.

6. *Discuss the pros and cons of plea bargaining*

- Because of excessive criminal court caseloads and the personal and professional needs of the prosecution and the defense, plea bargaining has become an essential part of the administration of justice.

- The Supreme Court has upheld plea bargaining in several decisions and, though it has imposed limits on the practice, has upheld the continued use of plea bargaining.

- Some critics of plea bargaining believe that defendants are treated with leniency as a result of the practice.

7. *Contrast and compare the roles of judge, prosecutor, defense counsel, and victim in the plea bargaining process*

- The plea bargaining process is largely informal, lacking in guidelines, and discretionary; research shows that prosecutorial discretion, rather than defendant characteristics, controls plea negotiations.

- Defense counsel—a public defender or a private attorney—is required to play an advisory role in plea negotiations.

- Judges should not be a party to arrangements for the determination of a sentence, whether as a result of a guilty plea or as a result of a finding of guilty based on proof.

- The victim is not empowered at the pretrial stage of the criminal process to influence a plea bargaining decision.

- Efforts have been made to convert plea bargaining into a more visible, understandable, and fair dispositional process.

8. *Know what is meant by the term "pretrial diversion"*

- Another important feature in the early court process is placing offenders into noncriminal diversion programs before their formal trial or conviction.

9. *Describe the goals and purpose of the trial process*

- The criminal trial is an open and public hearing designed to examine the facts of the case brought by the state against the accused.

- The trial is an important and enduring fixture in the criminal justice system. By its very nature, it is a symbol of the moral authority of the state and impartial justice.

- Most formal trials are heard by a jury, although some defendants waive their constitutional right to a jury trial and request a bench trial, in which the judge alone renders a verdict.

- Underlying every trial are constitutional principles, complex legal procedures, rules of court, and interpretations of statutes—all designed to ensure that the accused will receive a fair trial.

10. *Discuss the legal rights of the accused at trial*

- Legal rights at trial include the right to an impartial judge, the right to be competent at trial, the right to confront witnesses, the right to compulsory process, the right to an impartial jury, the right to counsel, the right to a speedy trial, the right to a public trial, and the right to be convicted by proof beyond a reasonable doubt.

11. *Explain the trial process*

- The trial of a criminal case is a formal process conducted in a specific and orderly fashion in accordance with rules of criminal law, procedure, and evidence.

- In both civil and criminal cases, jurors are selected randomly from licensing or voter registration lists within each court's jurisdiction.

- Once prospective jurors are chosen, the lengthy process of voir dire (from the French for "to tell the truth") starts.

- During voir dire, a juror who acknowledges any bias in favor of or prejudice against the defendant may be removed by either the prosecution or the defense with a challenge for cause.

- During voir dire, both the prosecution and the defense are allowed peremptory challenges, which enables them to excuse jurors for no particular reason or for undisclosed reasons.

- Once the jury has been selected, the prosecutor and the defense attorney may each make an opening statement about the case.

- Following the opening statements, the government begins its case by presenting evidence to the court through its witnesses.

- The central purpose of the direct examination process is to introduce evidence upon which the jury can decide the case.

- Once the prosecution has provided all the government's evidence against a defendant, it will inform the court that it rests the people's case. The defense attorney at this point may enter a motion for a directed verdict.

- Closing arguments are used by the attorneys to review the facts and evidence of the case in a manner favorable to their respective positions.

- According to a strategy called jury nullification, jurors are sometimes asked by the defense to ignore the facts of the case and the judge's legal instructions and instead to render decisions based on emotion and personal preference.

- In a criminal trial, the judge will instruct, or charge, the jury members on the principles of law that ought to guide and control their decision on the defendant's innocence or guilt.

- Once the charge is given to the jury members, they retire to deliberate on a verdict.

- Imposing the criminal sentence is normally the responsibility of the trial judge.

- Once a verdict has been rendered and a defendant found guilty, that individual may petition an appellate court to review the procedures used during trial.

Key Terms

Review Questions

1. Should those accused of violent acts be subjected to preventive detention instead of bail, even though they have not been convicted of a crime? Is it fair to the victim to have the alleged attacker running around loose?

2. Should criminal defendants be allowed to bargain for a reduced sentence in exchange for a guilty plea? Should the victim always be included in the plea bargaining process?

3. What purpose does a grand jury or preliminary hearing serve in adjudicating felony offenses? Should one of these methods be abandoned, and if so, which one?

4. Do criminal defendants enjoy too many rights at trial? Why or why not?

5. Should people be denied the right to serve as jurors without explanation or cause? In other words, should the peremptory challenge be maintained?

6. "In the adversary system of criminal justice, the burden of proof in a criminal trial to show that the defendant is guilty beyond a reasonable doubt is on the government." Explain the meaning of this statement.

9

PUNISHMENT AND SENTENCING

Imposing the Sentence

In most felony cases, except where the law provides for mandatory prison terms, sentencing is usually based on a variety of information available to the judge. Some jurisdictions allow victims to make impact statements that are considered at sentencing hearings. Most judges also consider a pre-sentence investigation report by the probation department as they make a sentencing decision. This report is a social and personal history, as well as an evaluation of the defendant's chances for rehabilitation within the community. Judges may also issue credit for time already served, such as during pretrial detention.

Concurrent vs. Consecutive Sentences

In some instances, when an accused is convicted of two or more charges, the judge must decide whether to impose consecutive or **concurrent sentences**. If the sentences are concurrent, they begin the same day and are completed when the longest term has been served. For example, say a defendant is convicted of burglarizing an apartment and assaulting its occupant. He is sentenced to 3 years on a charge of assault and 10 years for burglary, with the sentences to be served concurrently. After 10 years in prison, the sentences would be completed.

concurrent sentences
Prison sentences for two or more criminal acts, served simultaneously and run together.

In contrast, receiving a **consecutive sentence** means that upon completion of the sentence for one crime, the offender begins serving time for the second of multiple crimes. If the defendant in the previous example had been sentenced consecutively, he would serve 3 years on the assault charge and then 10 years for the burglary. Therefore, the total term on the two charges would be 13 years. Concurrent sentences are the norm; consecutive sentences are requested for the most serious criminals and for those who are unwilling to cooperate with authorities. Figure 9.3 shows the difference between a consecutive and a concurrent sentence.

consecutive sentences
Prison sentences for two or more criminal acts, served one after the other.

The Effect of Good Time

When judges impose an incarceration sentence, they know and take into account the fact that the amount of time spent in prison is reduced by the implementation of "time off for good behavior." This concept was first used in 1817 in New York, and it was quickly adopted in most other jurisdictions.

Consecutive vs. Concurrent Sentences

Example: In state X
1. Rape is punishable by 10 years in prison
2. Possession of a handgun by 3 years
3. Possession of heroin by 4 years

Consecutive sentence
Rape + possession of a handgun + possession of heroin

10 + 3 + 4 = 17 years

(each sentence must be served individually)

Concurrent sentence
Rape + possession of a handgun + possession of heroin

10 years

(all sentences served simultaneously)

FIGURE 9.3

Many prison sentences carry with them a provision for the possibility of good time, which takes time off the sentence for good behavior. Here Nick Hogan, son of the famous wrestler Hulk Hogan, hugs his sister, Brooke Hogan, as he leaves the Pinellas County Jail after serving five months behind bars for being involved in the car crash that seriously injured Marine John Graziano. He had been sentenced to serve eight months but was released early for good behavior.

© Tim Boyles/Getty Images

Good time is still in use today; inmates can accrue standard good time at a rate ranging from 10 to 15 days per month. In addition, some correctional authorities grant earned sentence reductions to inmates who participate in treatment programs, such as educational and vocational training, or who volunteer for experimental medical testing programs. In some jurisdictions more than half of a determinate sentence can be erased by accumulating both standard and earned good time.

Good-time laws enable inmates to calculate their release date at the time they enter prison by subtracting the expected good time from their sentence. However, good time can be lost if inmates break prison rules, get into fights, or disobey correctional officers. In some jurisdictions, former inmates can be returned to prison to serve the balance of their unexpired sentence when their good time is revoked for failing to conform to conditions set down for their release (for example, by not reporting to a postrelease supervisor or by abusing drugs).

How People Are Sentenced

The federal government conducts surveys on sentencing practices in state and federal courts.[35] The most recent survey found that more than 1 million adults are convicted of felonies in a single year. What happens after convictions? About 70 percent of all felons convicted in state courts were sentenced to a period of confinement—40 percent to state prisons and 30 percent to local jails.[36] The remaining 30 percent were sentenced to straight probation with no

TABLE 9.1

Lengths of Felony Sentences Imposed by State Courts

Most serious conviction offense	Mean sentence length in state courts for felons sentenced to incarceration or probation			
	Total	Prison	Jail	Straight probation
All offenses	37 mo.	57 mo.	6 mo.	33 mo.
Violent offenses	68	92	7	44
Property offenses	29	45	6	38
Drug offenses	31	51	6	38
Weapon offenses	32	47	7	34
Other offenses	24	41	6	38

NOTE: Means exclude life sentences and death sentences.

SOURCE: Matthew Durose and Patrick Langan, *Felony Sentences in State Courts, 2004* (Washington, D.C.: Bureau of Justice Statistics, 2007); www.ojp.usdoj.gov/bjs/pub/pdf/fssc04.pdf.

jail or prison time to serve. Felons sentenced to a state prison had an average sentence of four and a half years but were likely to serve only half of that sentence before release. Besides being sentenced to incarceration or probation, about one-third of all sentenced offenders are typically expected to pay a fine, pay victim restitution, receive treatment, perform community service, or comply with some other additional penalty. As Table 9.1 shows, violent offenders who are given a prison sentence average about eight years, whereas property offenders are typically sentenced to about four years. If they receive a jail sentence, their period of confinement is considerably less.

As you may recall (Figure 9.1), the number of convicted offenders being sent to prison today is actually lower than a decade ago, illustrating the increasing popularity of cost-effective community sentencing. However, because of tough sentencing laws requiring people to spend more time behind bars, the average time served per offense has not decreased substantially.

What Factors Affect Sentencing?

What factors influence judges when they decide on criminal sentences? As already mentioned, crime seriousness and the offender's prior record are certainly considered. State sentencing codes usually include various factors that can legitimately influence the length of prison sentences, including the following:

- The severity of the offense
- The offender's prior criminal record
- Whether the offender used violence
- Whether the offender used weapons
- Whether the crime was committed for money

Research does in fact show a strong correlation between these legal variables and the type and length of sentence received. Judges sentence more severely in cases involving the most serious criminal charges, such as terrorism, while tempering the severity of sentencing in less egregious offenses.[37] As

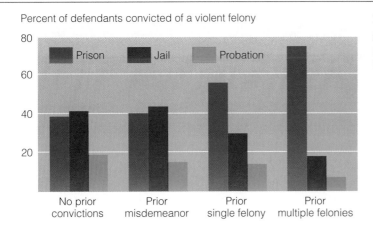

Percent of defendants convicted of a violent felony

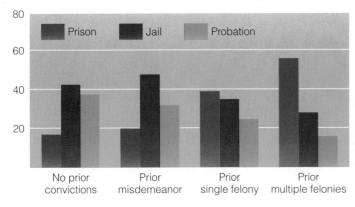

Percent of defendants convicted of a nonviolent felony

Sentence by Prior Record

Source: Tracey Kyckelhahn and Thomas H. Cohen, *Felony Defendants in Large Urban Counties, 2004* (Washington, D.C.: Bureau of Justice Statistics, 2008).

FIGURE 9.4

REALITYCHECK

MYTH OR REALITY? When it comes to sentencing, there is one standard rule: If you commit a serious crime, you serve a lot of time.

MYTH: It would be ideal if justice were blind, but judges are human and, whether consciously or unconsciously, base their decisions in part on other factors, many of which are not related to the crime in question. Scores of studies bear this out.

Factors such as class, race, gender, and age have been shown to influence sentencing. What are the consequences of this? Can anything be done to limit the influence of such extralegal factors on sentencing?

Figure 9.4 shows, people with prior felony convictions are much more likely to receive prison time than those convicted of misdemeanors and those who have no prior convictions.

Besides these legally appropriate factors, sentencing experts suspect that judges may also be influenced by the defendant's social class, gender, age, and race—and even by victim characteristics. Consideration of such variables would be a direct violation of constitutional due process and equal protection, as well as of federal statutes, such as the Civil Rights Act. Limiting judicial bias is one reason why states have adopted determinate and mandatory sentencing statutes. Do extralegal factors actually influence judges when they make sentencing decisions?

SOCIAL CLASS ● Evidence supports an association between social class and sentencing outcomes: Members of the lower class may expect to get longer prison

sentences than more affluent defendants. Not all research efforts have found a consistent relationship between social class and sentence length. The relationship may be more robust for some crime patterns than for others. Nonetheless, the consensus is that affluent defendants are more likely than the indigent to receive lenient sentences.[38]

GENDER ● Does a defendant's gender influence how he or she is sentenced? Some theorists believe that women benefit from sentence disparity because the criminal justice system is dominated by men who have a paternalistic or protective attitude toward women; this is referred to as the **chivalry hypothesis**. In contrast, others argue that female criminals can be the victim of bias because their law breaking violates what men view as "proper" female behavior.[39]

Which position is true? Most research indicates that women receive more favorable outcomes the further they go in the criminal justice system: They are more likely to receive preferential treatment from a judge at sentencing than they are from the police officer making the arrest or the prosecutor seeking the indictment.[40] This favoritism crosses both racial and ethnic lines, benefiting African American, white, and Hispanic women.[41] Gender bias may be present because judges perceive women as better risks than men. Women have been granted more lenient pretrial release conditions and lower bail amounts than men; women are also more likely to spend less time in pretrial detention.[42] Ironically, mandatory and structured sentences, designed originally to limit bias and discretion, have resulted in harsher sentences for women. Because these methods are "gender neutral," they reverse any advantage women may have had in sentencing decisions. Some women who were peripherally involved in drug trafficking through association with boyfriends and husbands have received very long sentences.[43]

chivalry hypothesis
The view that the low rates of female crime and delinquency are a reflection of the leniency with which police and judges treat female offenders.

AGE ● Another extralegal factor that may play a role in sentencing is age. It should be expected that older people will be punished more harshly than younger ones, because they have had a greater opportunity to accumulate a criminal record and most state laws increase penalties for multiple offenders. Of course, this creates a dilemma: Because of crimes he might have committed years ago, an older offender may be punished more severely than a younger offender who is actually more dangerous or is committing more crimes in the present.[44] This association of more severe punishment with older offenders does not always hold, however. Some judges may instead be more lenient with older defendants and more punitive toward younger ones.[45] Although sentencing leniency may be a result of judges' perception that the elderly pose little risk to society, such practices are a violation of the civil rights of younger defendants.[46] On the other hand, some judges may wish to protect the youngest defendants, sparing them the pains of a prison experience.[47]

RACE ● No issue concerning personal factors in sentencing is more important than the suspicion that race influences sentencing outcomes. Racial disparity in sentencing has been suspected because a disproportionate number of African American inmates are in state prisons and on death row. Minorities—especially those who are indigent or unemployed—seem to receive longer sentences than Caucasians.[48] In one recent study, Shawn Bushway and Anne Morrison Piehl studied sentencing outcomes in Maryland and found that, on average, African Americans have 20 percent longer sentences than whites, even when age, gender, and recommended sentence length are held constant.[49] Young black men are more likely to be imprisoned for drug offenses, a practice (says sentencing expert Michael Tonry) that places the entire cohort of young African American males in jeopardy.[50]

Although some research does indicate that a defendant's race has a direct effect on sentencing outcomes, other efforts show that the influence of race

Careers in Criminal Justice

FORENSIC PSYCHOLOGIST

Duties and Characteristics of the Job

- Forensic psychologists apply the knowledge and scientific methods drawn from the field of psychology in legal settings.
- They evaluate the mental health of parolees, run inmate mental health programs, and provide counseling to victims.
- In the court system, forensic psychologists consult with attorneys to assess individuals' mental health to determine whether their mental state makes them capable of standing trial. These specialists may also help in crafting sentences based on the clinical needs of the criminal defendant.
- They consult with law enforcement at all levels in order to apprehend criminals. They might create a psychological model of a suspect to predict her behavior.

Job Outlook

- Employment outlook is good.
- Recognition of the importance of psychological factors in behavior and functioning is increasing.

Salary

- Like other psychologists, a forensic psychologist's mean annual salary is $74,250.
- The majority of these psychologists make between $51,520 and $93,870 a year.
- Some will earn around $33,150 a year, whereas others will earn as much as or more than $111,620 a year.

Opportunities

- The number of educational institutions that offer graduate programs in forensic science is relatively small, so entry into a program is competitive.

Qualifications

- The primary qualifier for a position as a forensic psychologist is educational.
- A forensic psychologist will have to gain entrance into a select number of master's or doctoral programs.
- A master's degree will prepare future forensic psychologists for entry-level work in places such as police departments, prisons and jails, and mental health centers.
- The two most advanced programs confer a Ph.D. in psychology and a Psy.D. in forensic psychology, respectively.
- Some states require certification.

Education and Training

- A forensic psychologist can earn either a Ph.D. or a Psy.D.
- The differences are quite clear; the two programs have two different focuses, depending on the career goals of a future forensic psychologist.
- A program that leads to a doctorate prepares students primarily to fill administrative or management positions at law enforcement and health organizations, and to provide services such as mediation and research for organizations.
- Psy.D. training prepares students for an applied focus in jobs, such as providing mental health treatment and being an expert court witness.

Word to the Wise

- Five to seven years of graduate study are necessary, so the time commitment is extensive.
- The salary is relatively low when compared to the amount of training required.
- Many clients are experiencing problems that are not easily fixed. Forensic psychologists need patience and commitment, and they must enjoy working with others.
- Stress and burnout are not uncommon.

on sentencing is less clear-cut than anticipated, and, as John Wooldredge has found recently, in some contexts minority group members actually get lesser sentences than whites.[51] It is possible, the counterargument goes, that the disproportionate number of minority group members in prison is not a function of racial bias by judges but, rather, reflects actual racial and ethnic differences in the crime rate: Minority group members go to prison more often simply because they commit more crime.

Why does the critical issue of racial disparity remain so murky? One reason is that it may involve multiple factors that lie outside judicial sentencing practices:

- African Americans are more likely to be detained before trial than whites.
- Prosecutors are less likely to divert minorities from the legal system than they are whites.
- Members of minority groups have less money for bail and private attorneys.
- Disproportionate numbers of minorities live in poor communities, and people living in poor areas get harsher sentences, regardless of their race.
- African Americans receive longer sentences for drug crimes than whites because (a) they are more likely than whites to be arrested for crack possession and sales, and (b) crack dealing is more severely punished by state and federal laws than other drug crimes.

Race may also affect sentencing in other ways. Research indicates that it is the victim's race, rather than the offender's, that structures sentencing outcomes.[52] Minority defendants are sanctioned more severely if their victim is white than if their target is a fellow minority group member; minority defendants who kill whites are more likely to get the death penalty than are those who kill other minorities.[53]

In sum, although the true association between race and sentencing is complex, there is little question that the defendant's race helps shape the contours of justice. Whatever the cause, the effects can be devastating. As Bruce Western warns, whole communities are being destabilized by the marginalizing and incarcerating of so many African American men. And doing prison time, Western warns, can turn minor offenders into hardened criminals, which removes any chance of rehabilitation. The prison boom, Western writes, "may be a self-defeating strategy for crime control."[54]

VICTIM CHARACTERISTICS ● Victim characteristics may also influence sentencing. Victims may be asked or allowed to make a **victim impact statement** before the sentencing judge, which gives them the opportunity to tell of their experiences and describe their ordeal. In a murder case, the surviving family can recount the effect the crime has had on their lives and well-being.[55] The effect of victim and witness statements on sentencing has been the subject of some debate. Some research suggests that victim statements result in a higher rate of incarceration, but other efforts find that the effects of victim and witness statements are insignificant.[56]

A victim's personal characteristics may influence sentencing. Sentences may be reduced when victims have "negative" personal characteristics or qualities. For example, people convicted of raping prostitutes or substance abusers receive much shorter sentences than those who assault women without these negative characteristics.[57]

Sentences may also be tailored to the needs of offenders, especially when they have severe psychological deficits. In making their decision, judges may rely on the opinion of a forensic psychologist, who may be asked to clinically evaluate the defendant before sentencing. The Careers in Criminal Justice feature on page 312 discusses forensic psychologists.

victim impact statement
A postconviction statement by the victim of crime that may be used to guide sentencing decisions.

Historically, victims had little to no involvement in the criminal process. Today, they often make victim impact statements, which gives the judge an opportunity to hear their side of the story. Here Sandra Burke, oldest daughter of murder victim Lloyd Ford, reads a victim impact statement to Fourth District Court judge Darla Williamson on March 20, 2009, during the sentence hearing for Judy Gough, far right, in Boise, Idaho. Gough, who admitted to killing her husband in 1980 with a deer rifle and burying his body in the backyard of her Boise home, was sentenced to 10 years in prison.

© AP Photo/The Idaho Statesman, Darin Oswald

Capital Punishment

The most severe sentence used in the United States is capital punishment, or execution. More than 14,500 confirmed executions have been carried out in America under civil authority, starting with the execution of Captain George Kendall in 1608. Most of these executions have been for murder and rape. However, federal, state, and military laws have conferred the death penalty for other crimes, including robbery, kidnapping, treason (offenses against the federal government), espionage, and desertion from military service.

In recent years, the Supreme Court has limited the death penalty to first-degree murder and only then when aggravating circumstances, such as murder for profit or murder using extreme cruelty, are present.[58] The federal

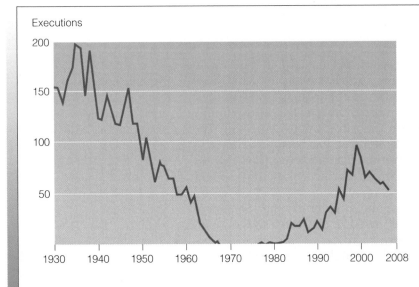

Executions

Executions, 1930–Present
- In 2008, 37 inmates were executed, 7 fewer than in 2007.
- Of the 37 executions that took place in 2008, 18 were in Texas, 4 in Virginia, and 3 each in Georgia and South Carolina, 2 each in Florida, Mississippi, Ohio, and Oklahoma, and 1 in Kentucky.
- Of all persons executed in 2008, 20 were white and 17 were black.
- All 37 inmates executed in 2008 were men.
- Lethal injection was used for 36 of the executions in 2008, electrocution for one.
- At the end of 2007, 37 states and the federal government had capital statutes.

Capital Punishment Statistics, http://www.ojp.usdoj.gov/bjs/cp.htm.

FIGURE 9.5

government still has provisions for imposing the death penalty for espionage by a member of the armed forces, treason, and killing during a criminal conspiracy, such as drug trafficking. Some states have laws permitting capital punishment for such crimes as aircraft piracy, ransom kidnapping, and the aggravated rape of a child, but it remains to be seen whether the courts will allow criminals to be executed today for any crime less heinous than aggravated first-degree murder. Figure 9.5 provides a perspective on executions from 1930 to the present. Figure 9.6 presents a map of the death penalty states and non-death-penalty states. Although the death penalty is generally approved of in the United States, it fares less well abroad; see the International Justice feature on page 316.

No issue in the criminal justice system is more controversial or emotional than implementation of the death penalty. Opponents and proponents have formulated a number of powerful arguments in support of their positions; these arguments are reviewed in the following sections.

Arguments for the Death Penalty

The death penalty has long been one of the most controversial aspects of the justice system, and it will probably continue to be a source of significant debate.[59] Let's first consider the views supporting availability of the death penalty.

INCAPACITATION ● Supporters argue that death is the "ultimate incapacitation" and the only one that can ensure that convicted killers can never be pardoned, be paroled, or escape. Most states that do not have capital punishment provide the sentence of "life in prison without the chance of parole." However, 48 states endow their chief executive with the power to grant clemency and commute a life sentence and may give "lifers" eligibility for various furlough and release programs.

Death penalty advocates believe that the potential for recidivism is a serious enough threat to require that murderers be denied further access to the public.[60] More than 250 inmates on death row today had prior homicide convictions; if they had been executed for their first offense, at least 250 innocent people would still be alive.[61]

DETERRENCE ● Proponents of capital punishment argue that executions serve as a strong deterrent for serious crimes. Although capital punishment would probably not deter the few mentally unstable criminals, it could have an effect on the cold, calculating murderer, such as the hired killer or someone who kills for profit. The fear of death may also convince felons not to risk using handguns during armed robberies.

Proponents maintain that the deterrent effect of an execution can produce a substantial decline in the murder rate.[62] They argue, for example, that homicide rates *increased* dramatically in the 1960s and 1970s, when executions were halted by the courts and death penalty laws were subsequently abolished. It is not a coincidence that murder rates have dropped since the death penalty was reinstated; murder rates would actually be much higher if capital punishment were not being used.[63] The death penalty scares would-be criminals, and not surprisingly, homicide rates drop after a well-publicized execution.[64]

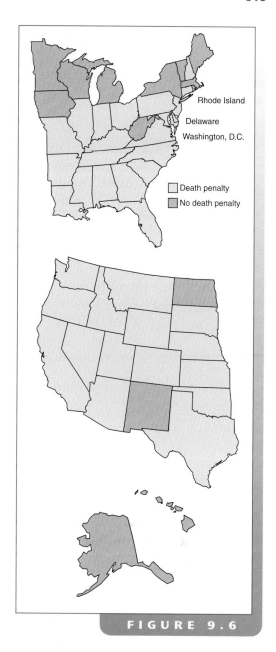

Rhode Island
Delaware
Washington, D.C.

☐ Death penalty
■ No death penalty

FIGURE 9.6

Death Penalty and Non-Death Penalty States with Executions Since 1976

Source: Death Penalty Information Center: http://www.deathpenaltyinfo.org/states-and-without-death-penalty.

REALITYCHECK

MYTH OR REALITY? The United States is one of the few countries that still retains the death penalty.

REALITY: According to Amnesty International, 135 countries have abolished the death penalty in law or practice, or for certain crimes, leaving 62 "retentionist countries."

Few of the retentionist countries are what we would call industrialized, advanced, or close allies of the United States. Why does the United States retain the death penalty when the majority of the industrialized countries in the world have abolished it?

MORALLY CORRECT ● This argument contends that the death penalty is morally correct: It is mentioned in the Bible and other religious works. Although the U.S. Constitution forbids "cruel and unusual punishments," this prohibition does not include the death penalty because capital punishment was widely used at the time the Constitution was drafted. The "original intent" of the founding fathers was to allow the states to use the death penalty; capital punishment may be cruel, but it is not unusual.

The death penalty is morally correct because it provides the greatest justice for the victim and helps alleviate the psychic pain of the victim's family and friends. The death penalty makes a moral statement: There is behavior that is so unacceptable to a community of human beings that one who engages in such behavior forfeits his right to live.[65]

PROPORTIONAL TO THE CRIME ● Putting dangerous criminals to death also conforms to the requirement that the punishment must be proportional to the seriousness of the crime. We use a system of escalating punishments, so it follows that the most serious punishment should be used to sanction the most

International Justice

International Use of the Death Penalty

The United States is not alone in using the death penalty, although the trend has been to abolish its usage. According to the latest data from the Death Penalty Information Center, over half the countries in the world have now abolished the death penalty in law or practice. Its information shows that

- 91 countries and territories have abolished the death penalty for all crimes.
- 11 countries have abolished the death penalty for all but exceptional crimes such as wartime crimes.
- 33 countries can be considered abolitionist in practice: They retain the death penalty in law but have not carried out any executions for the past 10 years or more and are believed to have a policy or established practice of not carrying out executions. This makes a total of 135 countries that have abolished the death penalty in law or practice.
- 62 other countries and territories retain and use the death penalty, but the number of countries that actually execute prisoners in any one year is much smaller.

Progress toward Worldwide Abolition

Since 1990, more than 45 countries have abolished the death penalty for all crimes, bringing the total number of countries to well over half the countries in the world. They include countries in Africa (recent examples: Liberia, Côte d'Ivoire), the Americas (Canada, Paraguay, Mexico), Asia and the Pacific (Bhutan, Samoa), and Europe and Central Asia (Armenia, Bosnia-Herzegovina, Cyprus, Serbia and Montenegro, Turkey, Turkmenistan).

Reinstating the Death Penalty

Once abolished, the death penalty is seldom reintroduced. Since 1985, over 50 countries have abolished the death penalty in law or, having previously abolished it for ordinary crimes, have gone on to abolish it for all crimes. During the same period only four abolitionist countries reinstated the death penalty. One of them, Nepal, has since abolished serious crime. Before the brutality of the death penalty is considered, the cruelty with which the victim was treated should not be forgotten.

REFLECTS PUBLIC OPINION • The death penalty is justified because it represents the will of the people. A majority of the general public believe that criminals who kill innocent victims should forfeit their own lives. Public opinion polls show that Americans favor the use of the death penalty by a wide majority.[66] Public approval rests on the belief that the death penalty is an important instrument of social control, can deter crime, and is less costly than maintaining a murderer in prison for life.[67] Research by Alexis Durham and his associates found that almost everyone (95%) would give criminals the death penalty under some circumstances, and the most heinous crimes are those for which the public is most likely to approve capital punishment.[68]

UNLIKELY CHANCE OF ERROR • The many legal controls and appeals currently in use make it almost impossible for an innocent person to be executed or for the death penalty to be used in a racist or capricious manner. Although some unfortunate mistakes may have been made in the past, the current system makes it virtually impossible to execute an innocent person. Federal courts closely scrutinize all death penalty cases and rule for the defendant in an estimated 60 to 70 percent of the appeals. Such judicial care should ensure that only those who are both unquestionably guilty and deserving of death are executed.

In sum, those who favor the death penalty find it to be traditional punishment for serious crimes and one that can help prevent criminality; in keeping with the traditional moral values of fairness and equity; and highly favored by the public.

---

the death penalty again; one, the Philippines, resumed executions but later stopped. There have been no executions in the other two (Gambia, Papua New Guinea).

Death Sentences and Executions

During 2008, at least 2,390 prisoners were executed in 25 countries, and 8,864 people were sentenced to death in 52 countries. In 2008, 72 percent of all known executions took place in China. There were 508 executions in the Middle East and North Africa, followed distantly by the Americas and some other countries. Unfortunately, many of these figures represent the tip of the iceberg. The official statistics in certain countries (e.g., China) remain state secrets, making monitoring and analysis problematic.

Executions of Juveniles

International human rights treaties prohibit anyone under 18 years old at the time of the crime from being sentenced to death. The International Covenant on Civil and Political Rights, the American Convention on Human Rights, and the UN Convention on the Rights of the Child all have provisions to this effect. More than 100 countries have laws specifically excluding the execution of juvenile offenders or may be presumed to exclude such executions by being parties to one or another of the above treaties. A small number of countries continue to execute juvenile offenders. Nine countries since 1990 are known to have executed prisoners under 18 years old at the time of the crime—China, Iran, Nigeria, Pakistan, Congo, Saudi Arabia, Sudan, the United States, and Yemen. Since 1990 there have been 73 executions of juvenile offenders, including 18 in the United States (before the practice was prohibited).

Critical Thinking

1. The movement toward abolition in the United States is encouraged by the fact that so many nations have abandoned the death penalty. Should we model our own system of punishments after other nations, or is our crime problem so unique that it requires the use of capital punishment?

2. Do you believe that those who join terrorist groups and train to kill Americans deserve the death penalty, even if they have never actually killed anyone?

Arguments against the Death Penalty

Arguments for the death penalty are countered as follows by those who support its abolition.

POSSIBILITY OF ERROR ● On January 11, 2003, Illinois Governor George Ryan announced a decision to commute all Illinois death sentences—a gesture that spared the lives of 163 men and 4 women who have served a collective 2,000 years for the murders of more than 250 people. Ryan and other critics of the death penalty believe capital punishment has no place in a mature democratic society.[69] They point to the finality of the act and the real possibility that innocent persons can be executed.

Examples of people wrongfully convicted of murder abound. According to classic research by Michael Radelet and Hugo Bedau, there have been about 350 wrongful murder convictions since 1900, of which 23 led to executions. They estimate that about three death sentences are returned every two years in cases where the defendant has been falsely accused. In addition to the 23 who were executed, 128 of the falsely convicted served more than 6 years in prison, 39 served more than 16 years in confinement, and 8 died while serving their sentence.[70] An important congressional report cited 48 cases in which people who served time on death row were released because of new evidence proving their innocence; one Maryland man served nine years on death row before DNA testing proved that he could not have committed the crime.[71]

The recent use of scientific evidence based on DNA has also resulted in numerous exonerations of wrongfully convicted death row inmates. One study found that an average of 42 exonerations of death row inmates occurred each year between 1989 and 2003.[72] Such research reveals that even today, there is grave risk of an innocent person's being executed.[73]

The recent attention to exonerations has both prompted and been influenced by an "innocence movement." In the early 1990s only two organizations existed to take on cases of prisoners claiming to be factually innocent—that is, they claimed they played no role in the crime of which they were convicted. Today more than 50 of these innocence projects exist. Collectively, they screen claims of innocence, work to exonerate the factually innocent, promote policies to reduce errors of justice, and provide support for exonerees.

Why so many errors? There are several reasons. As many as 25 percent of all eyewitness identifications may be wrong; many of these errors are caused by suggestive police lineups. Once a person is misidentified, police may develop "tunnel vision"—an unshakeable belief that the suspect is the real criminal. Tunnel vision can lead police to become overly aggressive during interrogations, causing innocent persons to confess simply in order to escape the enormous psychological strain of high-pressure interrogation. This is a special problem with suspects who are more easily manipulated, such as teenagers and mentally challenged suspects. Police often rely on informants, especially jailhouse snitches claiming that a suspect confessed. These snitches may be pathological liars willing to say anything to get a break in their cases.

Police are also not required to include exculpatory evidence—evidence that favors innocence—in their investigative reports. Even if they do, many prosecutors fail to turn over exculpatory evidence to defense lawyers, although they are required to do so by law. Overworked or incompetent defense attorneys often fail to provide a thorough defense. Judges and appellate courts tend to favor the prosecution and in a large proportion of cases simply overlook serious errors. In a number of cases, junk science, substandard forensic laboratories, or fraudulent forensic scientists have presented juries with completely erroneous conclusions.

In the last few years, a number of reform efforts have begun to percolate through several cities and states in response to the crisis of convicting the innocent. In 2006 North Carolina became the first state to establish an Innocence Inquiry Commission to review and investigate prisoners' claims that they were wrongly convicted. Several states and a large number of police departments have started videotaping the entire interrogation of suspects, not just the confession. This reform is well liked by police because confessions by guilty suspects provide strong proof at trial, and the videotape can be used to confirm that they used proper procedures.

A number of lineup reforms are shown by psychological experiments to reduce eyewitness errors. The most important include "double-blind" lineup administration, where even the officer running the lineup does not know the identity of the suspect. Other procedures to ensure lineup accuracy include carefully documenting the identification, telling eyewitnesses that the perpetrator may or may not be included in the lineup, and picking "fillers" from witnesses' verbal descriptions and not the likeness of the suspect (who might be innocent). Somewhat more controversial is the recommendation that the traditional side-by-side, live or photographic simultaneous lineups be replaced with a one-at-a-time or sequential lineup.

In addition to these and many other suggested reforms, there has been a call for all states to allow for monetary compensation and psychological and other support for the wrongly convicted, many of whom suffer serious psychological damage from their ordeals.

The conviction of a factually innocent person creates multiple victims: the wrongly convicted person who does time for another person's crime; the original crime victims, who later learn that instead of offering closure, the criminal justice system compounded their woes; and those people victimized by the real criminal who was not caught in the first place. Knowledge about wrongful convictions should be viewed as an important topic in criminal justice and an opportunity to create a more professional criminal justice system.

Because of the chances of error, a number of states have even placed a moratorium on executions until the issue of errors in the process can be adequately addressed.[74] Because errors may occur, some commentators have called for a new evidentiary standard of "absolute certainty" to replace "beyond a reasonable doubt" in death penalty cases (others argue that this standard would put an end to guilty verdicts because at least one juror would always have some uncertainty).[75]

UNFAIR USE OF DISCRETION ● Critics also frown on the tremendous discretion used in seeking the death penalty and the arbitrary manner in which it is imposed. Of the approximately 10,000 persons convicted each year on homicide charges, only 250 to 300 are sentenced to death, while an equal number receive a sentence of probation or community supervision only. It is true that many convicted murderers do not commit first-degree murder and therefore are ineligible for execution, but it is also likely that many serious criminals who could have received the death penalty are not sentenced to death because of prosecutorial discretion. Some escape death by cooperating or giving testimony against their partners in the crime. A person who commits a particularly heinous crime and knows full

© moorboard/Corbis

well that he will receive the death penalty if convicted may be the one most likely to plea bargain to avoid capital punishment. Is it fair to spare the life of a dangerous killer who cooperates with the prosecutor, while executing another who does not?

Abolitionists also argue that juries use inappropriate discretion when they make capital punishment recommendations. The ongoing Capital Jury Project has been interviewing members of juries involved in making death penalty decisions and finds that many are motivated by ignorance and error.

Those who abhor the use of discretion in capital cases also point to instances where offenders who kill on the spur of the moment are executed but truly vicious criminals who grievously injure victims during murder attempts are spared the death penalty. Some particularly heinous crimes are not punished with death simply because a physician's skill saved the victim. Some notable cases come to mind. Lawrence Singleton used an axe to cut off the arms of a woman he raped, yet he served only eight years in prison because the victim's life was saved by prompt medical care. (After being released from prison, Singleton killed a female companion in 1997.) "David," a boy severely burned in a murder attempt, lives in fear because his assailant—his father, Charles Rothenberg—was paroled from prison after serving a short sentence.[76] Although these horrific crimes received national attention and the intent to kill the victim was present, the death penalty could not be applied because of the availability of effective medical treatment. Areas that have superior medical resources actually have lower murder rates than less well-equipped areas; for example, ambulance response time can reduce the death rate by expeditiously transporting victims to an appropriate treatment center.[77] It makes little sense to punish someone for an impulsive murder while sparing the lives of those who intentionally maim and torture victims who survive only because of prompt medical care.

MISPLACED VENGEANCE • Although critics acknowledge that the general public approves of the death penalty, they maintain that prevailing attitudes reflect a primitive desire for revenge and not "just desert." Public acceptance of capital punishment has been compared to the approval of human sacrifices practiced by the Aztecs in Mexico 500 years ago.[78] Just because the public approves does not make it morally correct. It is ironic, they suggest, that many death penalty advocates oppose abortion on the grounds that it is the taking of human life.[79] The desire to be vengeful and punitive outweighs their scruples about taking life.

At least 30 states now have a sentence of life in prison without the possibility of parole, and many argue that this sentence can be as harsh as execution. Being locked up in prison without any chance of release (barring a rare executive reprieve) may be a worse punishment than a painless death by lethal injection. If vengeance is the goal, life without parole may eliminate the need for capital punishment.

WEAK PUBLIC SUPPORT • Politicians favor the death penalty in the mistaken belief that the public is uniformly in favor of capital punishment.[80] Approval ratings have been in decline for the past decade.[81] When surveys give respondents a choice of punishments, such as life without parole, support for the death penalty declines to the 50 percent level.[82] Well-publicized cases of innocent people being sentenced to death have helped erode support for capital punishment.[83] So although a majority of the public still support the death penalty in principle, a substantial proportion lack confidence in its use and believe that executions should be halted until the justice system can be made foolproof.[84]

Death Penalty Information System

To read more about capital punishment, go to **Death Penalty Information System** at

www.cengage.com/criminaljustice/siegel

Public opinion for the death penalty is not solid and may be influenced by such factors as the personal characteristics of the offender and the circumstances of the offense.[85] People who generally support the death penalty may not want to see it used with juveniles, the mentally challenged, or the mentally ill.[86] And even if a majority support capital punishment, their motives must be closely examined: Is it possible that support for the death penalty is a function of racist attitudes and the belief that capital punishment helps control and restrain the minority population?[87]

LITTLE DETERRENT EFFECT • Considerable empirical research has been carried out on the effectiveness of capital punishment as a deterrent. In particular, studies have tried to determine whether the death sentence serves as a more effective deterrent than life imprisonment for capital crimes such as homicide. Three methods have been used:

- *Immediate-impact studies*, which calculate the effect that a well-publicized execution has on the short-term murder rate
- *Time-series analysis*, which compares long-term trends in murder and capital punishment rates
- *Contiguous-state analysis*, which compares murder rates in states that have the death penalty with murder rates in a similar state that has abolished capital punishment

Using these three methods over a 60-year period, most researchers have failed to show any deterrent effect of capital punishment.[88] Most of the studies show that murder rates do not seem to rise when a state abolishes capital punishment, nor do they decrease when the death penalty is adopted. The murder rates are also quite similar in states that use the death penalty and in neighboring states that have abolished capital punishment. Finally, little evidence shows that executions can lower the murder rate. One test of the deterrent effect of the death penalty in Texas found no association between the frequency of execution during the years 1984–1997 and murder rates.[89]

A few studies have found that the long-term application of capital punishment may actually reduce the murder rate.[90] However, these have been disputed by researchers who questioned the methodology used and maintain that the deterrent effects the studies uncovered are an artifact of the statistical techniques used in the research.[91]

The general consensus among death penalty researchers today is that the threat of capital punishment has little effect on murder rates. It is still not known why capital punishment fails as a deterrent, but the cause may lie in the nature of homicide. As noted earlier, murder is often a crime of passion involving people who know each other, and many murders are committed by people under the influence of drugs and alcohol—more than 50 percent of all people arrested for murder test positive for drug use. People caught up in intense conflict with friends, acquaintances, and family members and people under the influence of drugs and alcohol are not likely to take into account the threat of the death penalty.

Despite the less-than-conclusive empirical evidence, many people still insist on the efficacy of the death penalty as a crime deterrent, and recent U.S. Supreme Court

REALITYCHECK

MYTH OR REALITY? The death penalty deters homicide.

MYTH: The vast majority of the research on this subject has shown that the death penalty does little, if anything, to deter homicide.

Why are most researchers convinced the death penalty fails to deter homicide? Clearly it is effective from a specific deterrent standpoint, but why might would-be killers not be deterred by the threat of capital punishment?

decisions seem to justify its use. And some researchers still continue to find that the death penalty can deter crime, although their findings are the exception.[92] Of course, even if the death penalty were no greater a deterrent than a life sentence, some people would still advocate its use on the grounds that it is the only way to permanently rid society of particular dangerous criminals who deserve to die.

NO HOPE OF REHABILITATION ● The death sentence rules out any hope of offender rehabilitation. There is evidence that convicted killers frequently make good parole risks; convicted murderers are often model inmates and, once released, commit fewer crimes than other parolees. It is possible that the general public, including people who sit on juries, overestimate the dangerousness of people who commit murder. In reality, those people given a life sentence for capital murder have *much less than a 1 percent* (0.2%) chance of committing another homicide over a 40-year term; the risk of their committing an assault is about 16 percent.[93]

Many serious criminals who could have received the death penalty are not sentenced to death because of discretion. Some escape death by cooperating or giving testimony against their partners in the crime. Here Lori Lister gives her son Blake, 16, and daughter Shara, 13, a hug after speaking at a rally in Houston, Texas. Lister survived a murder attempt by Coral Eugene Watts and aided in his capture 20 years ago. Watts, a Texas inmate known to have killed 13 women and suspected of more than 80 slayings, could have been paroled in 2006 because of a plea bargain. In exchange for being allowed to plead guilty only to a charge of "burglary with the intent to commit murder" and receiving a 60-year prison sentence, Watts offered to confess to 12 unsolved homicides if he were given immunity for them. Everyone assumed Watts would die in prison an old man, but a series of court rulings changed that. As a first-time offender, Watts was granted time off for good behavior—three days off his sentence for every day served. So instead of serving a 60-year sentence, under Texas law Watts would automatically be released after just 24 years. To make matters worse, Watts made it clear he would kill again if he ever got out of prison. To prevent this from happening, authorities appealed to possible witnesses in order to try and convict Watts of murder to ensure he was never released. Joseph Foy of Westland, Michigan, came forward to say that he had seen a man fitting Watts's description murder Helen Dutcher, a 36-year-old woman who died after being stabbed 12 times in December 1979. Foy identified Watts by his eyes, which he described as being evil and devoid of all emotion. Watts was promptly charged with the murder of Helen Dutcher, and on November 17, 2004, a Michigan jury convicted him. On December 7, he was sentenced to life imprisonment, virtually ensuring that he would never get out of prison. He died of prostate cancer in 2007.

RACE, GENDER, AND OTHER BIAS ● Capital punishment may be tarnished by gender, racial, and ethnic and other biases. More people are sentenced to death, and the death penalty is used more often, in nations with a large minority population. This phenomenon has led to formulation of what is referred to as the "minority-group-threat hypothesis"—that the use of extreme punishment is related to the regulation of groups that are racially, culturally, or ethnically different).[94] Let's look at some of the evidence:

- There is evidence that homicides with male offenders and female victims are more likely to result in a death sentence than homicides involving female offenders and male victims.[95]
- Homicides involving strangers are more likely to result in a death sentence than homicides involving nonstrangers or acquaintances.
- Prosecutors are more likely to recommend the death sentence for people who kill white victims than they are in any other racial combination of victim and criminal.[96] Prosecutors are less likely to seek the death penalty if the victim is a minority group member.[97] A male minority group member killing a white female is more likely to result in the death penalty than any other race/gender combination.[98]

Ever since the death penalty was first instituted in the United States, disproportionate numbers of minorities have been executed. Charges of racial bias are supported by the disproportionate numbers of African Americans who have received the death sentence, who are currently on death row, and who have been executed (53.5% of all executions). Racism was particularly blatant when the death penalty was invoked in rape cases: Of those receiving the death penalty for rape, 90 percent in the South and 63 percent in the North and West were African American.[99] Today, about 40 percent of the inmates on death row are African American, a number disproportionate to the minority representation in the population. When a black criminal kills a white victim, the likelihood of the death penalty being invoked is far greater than when a white criminal kills a black victim.[100] In contrast, since 1976 only two white criminals have been executed for murdering a black victim, the most recent being Kermit Smith, who was executed on January 24, 1995, in North Carolina for the kidnapping, rape, and murder of a 20-year-old college cheerleader.[101] Considering these patterns, it is not surprising that support for the death penalty is significantly lower in the minority community than among European Americans.[102]

CAUSES MORE CRIME THAN IT DETERS ● Some critics fear that the introduction of capital punishment will encourage criminals to escalate their violent behavior, consequently putting police officers at risk. A suspect who kills someone during a botched robbery may be inclined to "fire away" upon encountering police rather than to surrender peacefully. The killer faces the death penalty already, so what does he have to lose? Geoffrey Rapp studied the effect of capital punishment on the killings of police and found that, all other things being equal, the greater the number of new inmates on death row, the greater the number of police officers killed by citizens.[103] Rapp concluded that what the death penalty seems to do is create an extremely dangerous environment for law enforcement officers, because it does not deter criminals and may lull officers into a false sense of security, leading them to believe that the death penalty will deter violence directed against them and causing them to let their guard down.

brutalization effect
An outcome of capital punishment that enhances, rather than deters, the level of violence in society. The death penalty reinforces the view that violence is an appropriate response to provocation.

The death penalty may also produce more violence than it prevents—the so-called **brutalization effect**.[104] Executions may increase murder rates because they raise the general violence level in society and because people prone to violence actually identify with the executioner, not with the target of the death penalty. When someone gets in a conflict with such violence-prone individuals or challenges their authority, these individuals may "execute" them, just as the state executes people who violate its rules.[105] There is evidence that the brutalization effect does influence murder rates: Stranger homicides increase after an execution.[106] People may be more inclined to settle conflicts with violence after a state executes a criminal—"If they can do it, why can't I?"[107]

IT IS CRUEL AND INHUMAN ● Abolitionists believe that executions are unnecessarily cruel and inhuman and come at a high moral and social cost. Even death by lethal injection, which is considered relatively humane by advocates, has been challenged because it may cause extreme pain and can take much longer to cause death than was originally believed.[108] Our society does not punish criminals by subjecting them to the same acts they themselves committed. Rapists are not sexually assaulted, and arsonists do not have their houses burned down. Why, then, should murderers be killed?

Robert Johnson has described the execution process as a form of torture in which the condemned are first tormented psychologically by being made to feel powerless and alone while on death row; suicide is a constant problem among those awaiting death.[109] The execution itself is a barbaric affair marked by the smell of burning flesh and stiffened bodies. The executioners suffer from delayed stress reactions, including anxiety and a dehumanized personal identity.

Because of its brutality, many countries, including Denmark and Sweden, have long since abandoned the death penalty, and 40 percent of the countries with a death penalty have active abolitionist movements.[110] It is ironic that citizens of countries that have eliminated the death penalty sometimes find themselves on death row in the United States.

IT IS EXPENSIVE ● Some people complain that they do not want to support "some killer in prison for 30 years." Abolitionists counter that legal appeals drive the cost of executions far higher than the cost of years of incarceration. If the money spent on the judicial process were invested, the interest would more than pay for the lifetime upkeep of death row inmates. Because of numerous appeals, the median time between conviction by a jury, sentencing by a judge, and execution recently averaged 14 years in California; the state spends more than $5 million per year on death row appeals.[111] Several states have begun to explore abolishing the death penalty to save money in light of the recession.

MORALLY WRONG ● The death penalty is brutal and demeaning. Abolitionists argue that even if the general public voices approval of the death penalty, "social vengeance by death is a primitive way of revenge which stands in the way of moral progress."[112] And although early religious leaders accepted the death penalty, today many (such as the Catholic Church) condemn the practice of execution.[113] In his recent book *The Contradictions of American Capital Punishment*, Franklin Zimring links America's obsession with the death penalty—unique among developed nations—with its vigilante tradition, in which people on the frontier took justice in their own hands, assuming that their targets were always guilty as charged.[114] The death penalty was widely practiced against slaves, and at one time mass executions were a brutal and common practice to stifle any thought of escapes and/or revolts.[115]

While the debate continues, there seems to be little question that the public's support for the death penalty has weakened, and concomitantly, the number of death sentences being handed down is in sharp decline (see Figure 9.7).[116] Whether these developments portend the demise of capital punishment remains to be seen.

Legal Issues in Capital Punishment

The constitutionality of the death penalty has been a major concern to both the nation's courts and its social scientists. In 1972 the U.S. Supreme Court in *Furman v. Georgia*, decided that the discretionary imposition of the death penalty was cruel and unusual punishment under the Eighth and Fourteenth Amendments of the U.S. Constitution.[117] The Supreme Court did not completely rule out the use of capital punishment as a penalty; rather, it objected to the arbitrary and capricious manner in which it was imposed. After *Furman*, many states changed statutes that had allowed jury discretion in imposing the death penalty. Then, in July 1976, the Supreme Court ruled on the constitutionality of five state death penalty statutes. In the first case, *Gregg v. Georgia*, the Court found valid the Georgia statute holding that a finding by the jury of at least 1 "aggravating circumstance" out of 10 is required in pronouncing the death penalty in murder cases.[118] In the *Gregg* case, the jury imposed the death penalty after finding beyond a reasonable doubt two aggravating circumstances: (1) the offender was engaged in the commission of two other capital felonies, and (2) the offender committed the offense of murder for the purpose of receiving money and other financial gains (specifically, an automobile).[119] The *Gregg* decision signaled the return of capital punishment as a sentencing option.

Although the Court has supported the legality of the death penalty, it has also placed significant limitations on its use. Rulings have promoted procedural fairness in the capital sentencing process. In *Ring v. Arizona*, the Court found that juries, not judges, must make the critical findings that send convicted killers to death row. The Court reasoned that the Sixth Amendment's right to a jury trial would be "senselessly diminished" if it did not allow jurors to decide whether a person deserves the death penalty.[120] The Court has also limited who may be eligible for death:

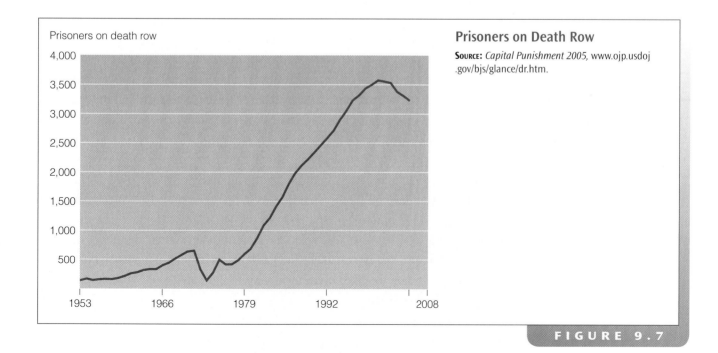

Prisoners on death row

Prisoners on Death Row

Source: *Capital Punishment 2005*, www.ojp.usdoj.gov/bjs/glance/dr.htm.

FIGURE 9.7

- The Court has limited the crimes for which the death penalty can be employed by ruling that it is not permissible to punish rapists, even those who rape children, with death.[121] Only people who commit intentional or felony murder may be executed.
- The mentally ill may not be executed.[122] In a 2002 case, *Atkins v. Virginia*, the Court also ruled that execution of mentally challenged criminals is "cruel and unusual punishment" prohibited by the Eighth Amendment.[123]
- In *Roper v. Simmons* (2005), the Court set a limit of 18 years as the age of defendants who could be sentenced to death.[124] The Court said that executing young teens violates "the evolving standards of decency that mark the progress of a maturing society" and that American society regards juveniles as less responsible than adult criminals. Prior to *Simmons*, nineteen states had laws allowing the execution of teenagers under 18 years old.

ETHICAL CHALLENGES IN CRIMINAL JUSTICE

A WRITING ASSIGNMENT

Carla B. is a 36-year-old white female convicted of killing her husband of 12 years, Jack B., a wealthy and prominent attorney. The police report shows that in order to inherit his substantial trust fund, Carla gave her husband a large dose of a sleeping sedative and, when he felt uncomfortable and dizzy, offered to take him to the emergency room at the local hospital. After he passed out in the car, she slid the comatose man into the driver's seat and then rolled the vehicle down an embankment. After watching the car burst into flames, she walked to her own car, which she had hidden earlier, and drove home. When police came to report the accident, she told the officers that Jack had gone to get some groceries and she was wondering why he had taken so long. At first she expressed shock over his death and burst into tears. Later, forensic evidence and an eyewitness to the event helped investigators unravel her plot.

The investigators found that Carla suspected her husband was going to divorce her because he had discovered that she was having an extramarital affair with her tennis instructor. Carla had incurred large debts and bank loans, which she kept secret from her husband because she had been buying gifts for her young paramour. These included leasing a new car and putting a down payment on a condo. Carla had a taste for luxury and travel and few occupational skills, which made divorce out of the question.

This is Carla B.'s first conviction. She is a highly educated woman with a degree in French literature from an Ivy League university. She comes from a loving and devoted family. Her parents and sisters, though in shock, are willing to stand beside her. She has two young children who are currently living with relatives; they also seem devoted to their mother. She has done charitable work and is well liked. She has no prior history of violence, mental instability, or the like. Psychiatric reports show that she is unlikely to commit further crimes.

At the sentencing hearing, Carla is filled with remorse and states that her greed overcame her reasoning. She is currently on a suicide watch at the county jail because she has told her counselor that she "does not deserve to live"; her anguish seems genuine.

As a member of the jury during the capital sentencing stage, you hold her fate in your hands. You can recommend death, life in prison, a prison sentence, or even probation. State law requires that each jury member provide a written document stating the reasons for his or her sentencing decision. Please state them here.

RealityCheck Revisited

To learn more about the myths and realities related to punishment and sentencing that were raised in this chapter, visit the following websites.

- For more on "three strikes," especially California's controversial law, see

http://www.threestrikes.org/

http://www.lao.ca.gov/2005/3_strikes/3_strikes_102005.htm

http://www.rand.org/pubs/research_briefs/RB4009/index1.html

- For more on how sentencing is affected by extralegal factors, particularly race, see

http://www.ncjrs.gov/criminal_justice2000/vol_3/03i.pdf

- Read more on the international use of the death penalty and view a map of abolitionist and retentionist countries here:

http://www.deathpenaltyinfo.org/abolitionist-and-retentionist-countries

- For a detailed review of the literature concerned with the deterrent effect of the death penalty, see

http://www.deathpenaltyinfo.org/FaganTestimony.pdf

SUMMARY

© Reuters/Issac Brekken/Pool

1. Outline the historical development of punishment

- Historically, people who violated the law were considered morally corrupt and in need of strong discipline.
- In early Greece and Rome, the most common state-administered punishment was banishment, or exile.
- During the Middle Ages, people found guilty of crime faced a wide range of punishments, including physical torture, branding, whipping, and for most felony offenses, death.

- During this period the main emphasis of criminal law and punishment was on maintaining public order.

- *Wergild* was used to repay the injured party and ensure that a personal crime would not develop into a blood feud and anarchy.

- The development of the common law in the eleventh century brought some standardization to penal practices.

- By the end of the sixteenth century, many offenders were made to do hard labor for their crimes.

- In England, transporting convicts to the colonies became popular.

- By 1820, long periods of incarceration in walled institutions called reformatories or penitentiaries began to replace physical punishment in England and the United States.

2. List the major goals of contemporary sentencing

- The goals of criminal sentencing today can be grouped into six distinct areas: general deterrence, incapacitation, specific deterrence, retribution/just desert, rehabilitation, and equity/restitution.

3. Distinguish among general and specific deterrence, incapacitation, and retribution

- According to the concept of general deterrence, people will be too afraid to break the law if they believe that they will be caught and punished severely.

- The purpose of specific deterrence, another goal of punishment, is to convince offenders that the pains of punishment are greater than the potential benefits of crime.

- Because criminals will not be able to repeat their criminal acts while they are under state control, incapacitation of criminals is another goal of sentencing.

- According to the retributive goal of sentencing, the essential purpose of the criminal process is to punish offenders—fairly and justly—in a manner that is proportionate to the gravity of their crimes.

4. Compare rehabilitation with just deserts

- Some sentences are based on the need to treat and/or rehabilitate criminal offenders.

- Because criminals gain from their misdeeds, it seems both fair and just to demand that they reimburse society for losses it has sustained because of their crimes.

5. Identify the various types of sentencing structures

- Indeterminate sentences are tailored to fit individual needs. Convicted offenders are typically given a "light" minimum sentence that must be served and a lengthy maximum sentence that is the outer boundary of the time that can be served.

- Determinate sentences offer a fixed term of years, the maximum set in law by the legislature, to be served by the offender sentenced to prison for a particular crime.

- Sentencing guidelines have been implemented to provide judges with a recommended sentence based on the seriousness of a crime and the background of an offender.

- Some states have passed mandatory sentence legislation prohibiting people convicted of certain offenses, such as violent crimes or drug trafficking, from being placed on probation; they must serve at least some time in prison.

- Three-strikes (and-you're-out) laws provide lengthy terms for any person convicted of three felony offenses, even if the third crime is relatively trivial.

- Truth-in-sentencing laws require offenders to serve a substantial portion of their prison sentence behind bars.

6. Know how sentences are imposed

- In some instances, when an accused is convicted of two or more charges, the judge must decide whether to impose consecutive or concurrent sentences.

- When judges impose an incarceration sentence, they know and take into account the fact that the amount of time spent in prison is reduced by the implementation of "time off for good behavior."

7. Discuss how people are sentenced today

- About two-thirds (69%) of all felons convicted in state courts were sentenced to a period of confinement— 41 percent to state prisons and 28 percent to local jails. The remaining third were sentenced to straight probation with no jail or prison time to serve.

- State sentencing codes usually include various factors that can legitimately influence the length of prison sentences, including the severity of the offense, the offender's prior criminal record, whether the offender used violence, whether the offender used weapons, and whether the crime was committed for money.

- Evidence supports an association between social class and sentencing outcomes: Members of the lower class may expect to get longer prison sentences than more affluent defendants.

- Most research indicates that women receive more favorable outcomes the further they go in the criminal justice system.

- It should be expected that older people will be punished more harshly than younger ones, because they have had a greater opportunity to accumulate a criminal record and most state laws increase penalties for multiple offenders.

- Minorities seem to receive longer sentences than Caucasians, especially those who are indigent or unemployed.

8. Demonstrate your knowledge of the law, practice, and impact of capital punishment

- The most severe sentence used in the United States is capital punishment, or execution.

- The United States is not alone in using the death penalty, but over half the countries in the world have now abolished the death penalty in law or practice.

- Despite its continued use and public acceptance, there seems to be growing unease with administration of the death penalty, and the recent use of scientific evidence based on DNA has resulted in numerous exonerations of death row inmates.

9. Be familiar with the arguments for and against capital punishment

- Supporters argue that death is the "ultimate incapacitation" and the only one that can ensure that convicted killers can never be pardoned, be paroled, or escape.

- Proponents of capital punishment argue that executions serve as a strong deterrent for serious crimes.

- Putting dangerous criminals to death also conforms to the requirement that the punishment be proportional to the seriousness of the crime.

- The death penalty is justified because it represents the will of the people.

- The many legal controls and appeals currently in use make it almost impossible for an innocent person to be executed or for the death penalty to be used in a racist or capricious manner.

- Critics of the death penalty believe capital punishment has no place in a mature democratic society.

- Because of the chances of error, a number of states have placed a moratorium on executions until the issue of errors in the process can be adequately addressed.

- The pressure to ensure convictions in homicide cases may lead to a higher rate of wrongful convictions in murder cases.

- Critics frown on the tremendous discretion used in seeking the death penalty and on the arbitrary manner in which it is imposed.

- Politicians favor the death penalty in the mistaken belief that the public overwhelmingly favors such harsh punishment for criminal offenders.

- Capital punishment may be tarnished by gender, racial, and ethnic and other biases.

- Abolitionists believe that executions are unnecessarily cruel and inhuman and come at a high moral and social cost.

10. Discuss the legal issues associated with capital punishment

- The constitutionality of the death penalty has been a major concern to both the nation's courts and its social scientists.

- In *Gregg v. Georgia*, the Court found valid the Georgia statute holding that a finding by the jury of at least 1 "aggravating circumstance" out of 10 is required for pronouncing the death penalty in murder cases.

- The Court has limited the crimes for which the death penalty can be employed by ruling that it is not permissible to punish rapists, even child rapists, with death.

- People who are mentally ill may not be executed.

- In *Roper v. Simmons* (2005), the Court set a limit of 18 years as the youngest age at which a defendant could be sentenced to death.

Key Terms

penitentiary, 298

general deterrence, 299

specific deterrence, 300

incapacitation, 300

blameworthy, 300

just desert, 300

rehabilitation, 301

equity, 302

indeterminate sentence, 302

determinate sentence, 303

sentencing guidelines, 303

mandatory sentence, 304

concurrent sentences, 307

consecutive sentences, 307

chivalry hypothesis, 311

victim impact statement, 313

brutalization effect, 324

Review Questions

1. Discuss the sentencing dispositions in your jurisdiction. What are the pros and cons of each?

2. Compare the various types of incarceration sentences. What are the similarities and differences? Why are many jurisdictions considering the passage of mandatory sentencing laws?

3. Discuss the issue of capital punishment. In your opinion, does it serve as a deterrent? What new rulings has the Supreme Court made on the legality of the death penalty?

4. Why does the problem of sentencing disparity exist? Do programs exist that can reduce the disparity of sentences? If so, what are they? Should all people who commit the same crime receive the same sentence? Explain.

5. Should convicted criminals be released from prison when correctional authorities are convinced they are rehabilitated? Why or why not?

Part 4

CORRECTIONS AND ALTERNATIVE SANCTIONS

On July 18, 2009, a jury indicted star quarterback Michael Vick and three other men on charges related to their operation of a dogfighting ring based at a property that Vick used as the main area for housing and training the pit bulls involved in the dogfighting and for staging dogfights.[1] In December 2007, he was sentenced to serve a 23-month federal prison term.[2] Vick was released from custody on May 20, 2009 and permitted to serve the remainder of his sentence in home confinement in his Hampton, Virginia, home with his fiancée and two of his children, while working a 40-hour-per-week job at a construction company.

What should have been the proper punishment for a famous athlete such as Michael Vick? Should he have been incarcerated? Does he present a danger to society requiring that he be locked up? Or did his punishment merely serve a symbolic purpose, letting

> Although the myth persists that most serious felony offenders serve time in prison, in reality, a significant portion of violent offenders—even repeaters—are treated in the community and never spend a day behind bars.

people know that no one is above the law? That is, was he incarcerated to set an example for others contemplating crime? And is it fair to punish someone to send other people "a message"?

Throughout history people have struggled to determine the proper punishment for crime, hoping to find a formula that results in penalties that are neither too harsh nor too lenient. In this section we will review the various forms of correctional punishment and treatment now being used with criminal offenders such as Vick. Although the myth persists that most serious felony offenders serve time in prison, in reality, a significant portion of violent offenders—even repeaters—are treated in the community and never spend a day behind bars. If a rapist can get community treatment, why was Michael Vick forced to serve time in prison?

Chapter 10
Community Sentences: Probation, Intermediate Sanctions, and Restorative Justice

Chapter 11
Corrections: History, Institutions, and Populations

Chapter 12
Prison Life: Living In and Leaving Prison

10

COMMUNITY SENTENCES: PROBATION, INTERMEDIATE SANCTIONS, AND RESTORATIVE JUSTICE

RealityCheck

MYTH or REALITY?

▶ The number of people being put on probation is way down because the crime rate is falling.

▶ Probation is reserved for nonviolent first offenders.

▶ Probation rules cannot force sex offenders to register with state authorities and/or require them to take periodic polygraph tests to determine whether they have engaged in illegal behavior; this would be a violation of their privacy rights.

▶ Probation officers can search a probationer's home without a warrant if they suspect foul play or criminal activity.

▶ Convicted criminals can be forced to surrender their homes and cars.

▶ It is permissible to force people to remain in their homes under "house arrest."

▶ Some jurisdictions encourage face-to-face meetings between offenders and victims and allow victims to participate in justice decision making.

Learning Objectives

1. Be familiar with concept of community sentencing

2. Know the history of community sentences

3. Recognize the different types of probation sentences

4. Be familiar with the rules of probation

5. Discuss the organization and administration of probation services

6. Define and discuss the term "risk classification"

7. Be familiar with the legal issues of probation

8. Debate the effectiveness of probation

9. Know what is meant by intermediate sanctions

10. Define restorative justice and discuss its merits

Chapter Outline

© AP Images/Matt York

Career Profile

Probation officer **Ann Beranis** first got interested in the justice system while in the Clinical Psychology master's program at the Illinois School of Professional Psychology. She started an internship at a counseling agency that specialized in batterers' intervention groups for domestic violence offenders. She found her work enjoyable and rewarding, because she was helping to protect victims of domestic violence. After receiving a master's degree, she applied for a job with the Probation Department, and she has worked as a probation officer for more than eight years.

She finds the job both challenging and rewarding. Most people, she explains, do not understand that community corrections is not about punishing offenders but about helping them change their thinking and behavior. Although the job does involve monitoring compliance and holding offenders accountable if they violate the rules, most of a probation officer's time is spent diagnosing the cause of an individual's antisocial behavior and then devising strategies for behavior change. The job is most challenging when clients are resistant to change and it becomes a matter of finding the resources necessary to convince them to make positive changes—and then help them to do so. Though it is difficult, accurate assessments can be made and techniques applied to increase the client's motivation to make positive changes. Probation officers must learn to tap into community resources, such as employment opportunities, and create strong partnerships with service providers. Ann's greatest reward on the job is seeing some clients turn their lives around and leave probation with confidence in themselves and hope for the future. It is also rewarding, she says, knowing that the hard work she puts into a case helps crime victims and protects the community from further victimization.

Probation officer Ann Beranis's career is in many ways exemplary of the qualities and goals found in the people who are most satisfied and effective as part of the contemporary correctional system. Her ideals reflect the core values of community corrections: probation, alternative sanctions, and restorative justice. These values include recognition of the following:

- Most convicted criminals are neither dangerous nor a menace to society and can be reformed within the community.

- Imprisonment can be harmful. It forces younger criminals to interact with hardened offenders, and the "ex-con" label makes it much more difficult for people to adjust successfully to society upon their release.

- Community sentencing provides offenders with the opportunity to prove themselves and gives them a second chance.

- Community sentences enable nondangerous offenders to be closely supervised in the community by trained personnel who can help them reestablish proper forms of behavior in the community.

- Even felony offenders can be successfully rehabilitated in the community if given the proper balance of supervision, treatment, and control.

- Community sentences are a cost-effective alternative to incarceration; they are just as effective as imprisonment but cost taxpayers less than 10 percent of the cost of imprisonment.

- The overwhelming majority of convicted offenders appreciate getting a "second chance" and view probation both as a deterrent to future crime and as a means of receiving treatment that can lead them to resume a more productive lifestyle.[1]

According to this correctional view, it is foolish to incarcerate nondangerous offenders in our overcrowded prison system, an experience that only exposes them to hardened criminals and results in long-term psychological stress and damage. It is more effective and efficient to treat them in the community under the supervision of a trained court officer, where they can receive therapy that will help them turn their lives around.

In a tight economic environment, cost-effective programming such as probation makes economic sense. It is not surprising that a growing number of convicted offenders are being offered community sentences ranging from traditional probation to house arrest and placement in community correctional centers.

This chapter reviews these criminal sanctions. It begins with a brief history of community sentencing. It then discusses the role of traditional probation as a community-based correctional practice. Next it focuses on so-called alternative or intermediate sanctions such as intensive supervision, house arrest, and electronic monitoring. Finally, the chapter turns to a discussion of the concept of restorative justice and programs based on its principles.

The History of Community Sentencing

Where did the idea of community supervision and control begin? During medieval times the practice of **judicial reprieve** allowed judges to suspend punishment so that convicted offenders could seek a pardon, gather new evidence, or demonstrate that they had reformed their behavior. Another practice, called **recognizance**, enabled convicted offenders to go unpunished if they agreed to refrain from further criminal behavior. Sometimes **sureties** were required—these were people who made themselves responsible for the behavior of an offender after the offender's release.

John Augustus and the Creation of Probation

John Augustus of Boston is usually credited with originating community sentencing.[2] As a private citizen, Augustus began in 1841 to supervise offenders released to his custody by a Boston judge. Over an 18-year period, Augustus supervised close to 2,000 convicted offenders and helped them get jobs and establish themselves in the community. Augustus had an amazingly high success rate, and few of his charges became involved in crime again.

In 1878, Augustus's work inspired the Massachusetts legislature to pass a law authorizing the appointment of a paid probation officer for the city of Boston. In 1880, probation was extended to other jurisdictions in Massachusetts, and by 1898 the probation movement had spread to the superior (felony) courts.[3] The Massachusetts experience was copied by Missouri (1887) and Vermont (1898) and, soon after, by most other states. In 1925, the federal government established a probation system for the U.S. district courts. The probation concept soon became the most widely used correctional mechanism in the United States.[4]

Probation Today

Probation is a criminal sentence that suspends or delays a correctional term in a prison or jail so that, instead of being incarcerated, offenders are returned to the community for a period in which they must (a) abide by certain conditions set forth by the court and (b) be supervised by a probation officer.

Probation has taken hold, and there are now approximately 2,000 adult probation agencies in the United States. Slightly more than half are associated with a state-level agency, whereas the remainder are organized at the county or municipal level of government. About 30 states combine probation and parole supervision into a single agency.

More than 4 million people are currently on probation. As Figure 10.1 shows, the adult probation population has grown about 2 percent per year since 1995, although increases have slowed in the past few years. Without probation, the

Annual Probation Population and Entries to Population

Source: Lauren Glaze and Thomas Bonczar, *Probation and Parole in the United States, 2007 Statistical Tables* (Washington, D.C.: Bureau of Justice Statistics, 2008), http://www.ojp.usdoj.gov/bjs/pub/pdf/ppus07st.pdf (accessed February 17, 2009).

Annual probation population and entries to probation, 1995–2008
Number of probationers (millions)

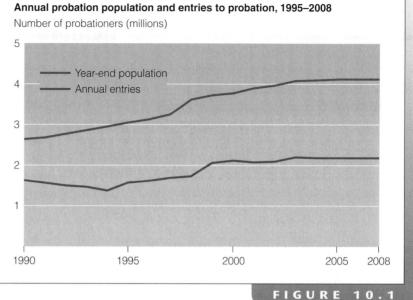

FIGURE 10.1

correctional system would rapidly become even more overcrowded, prohibitively expensive, and unmanageable.

Although the term today has many meanings, "probation" usually indicates a nonpunitive form of sentencing for convicted criminal offenders and delinquent youths, emphasizing maintenance in the community and treatment without institutionalization or other forms of punishment.[5] Once on probation, the offender is subject to certain rules and conditions that she or he must follow in order to remain in the community.

Most probation orders involve a contract between the court and the offender in which a prison or jail term is suspended and the probationer promises to obey a set of **probation rules**, or conditions mandated by the court. If the rules are violated, or if the probationer commits another criminal offense, probation may be revoked. **Revocation** means that the community sentence is terminated and the original sentence of incarceration is enforced. If an offender on probation commits a second offense that is more serious than the first, he or she may also be indicted, tried, and sentenced to prison on the second offense. However, probation may be revoked when the rules and conditions of probation have not been met; it is not necessary for an offender to commit another crime.

Awarding Probation

Probationary sentences may be granted by state and federal district courts and state superior (felony) courts. In some states, juries may recommend probation if the case meets certain legally regulated criteria (e.g., if it falls within a certain class of offenses as determined by statute). Even in those jurisdictions that allow juries to recommend probation, judges have the final say in the matter and may grant probation at their discretion. In nonjury trials, probation is granted solely by judicial mandate. Some states have attempted to shape judicial discretion by creating guidelines for granting probation. California's probation statute directs judges to use the criteria set out in Exhibit 10.1 in making the decision to award probation.

probation rules
Conditions or restrictions mandated by the court that must be obeyed by a probationer.

revocation
An administrative act performed by a parole authority that removes a person from parole, or a judicial order by a court removing a person from parole or probation, in response to a violation on the part of the parolee or probationer.

Bureau of Justice Statistics
For up-to-date data on probation, go to the **Bureau of Justice Statistics** website at **www.cengage.com/ criminaljustice/siegel**

REALITY CHECK

MYTH OR REALITY? The number of people being put on probation is way down because the crime rate is falling.

MYTH: The number of people on probation is at an all-time high and growing.

Do you suppose it's because community sentencing is less expensive than prisons, which are overcrowded anyway?

EXHIBIT 10.1

California Rules of Court: Probation

Rule 4.414. Criteria affecting probation

Criteria affecting the decision to grant or deny probation include:

(a) Facts relating to the crime, including:

(1) The nature, seriousness, and circumstances of the crime as compared to other instances of the same crime.

(2) Whether the defendant was armed with or used a weapon.

(3) The vulnerability of the victim.

(4) Whether the defendant inflicted physical or emotional injury.

(5) The degree of monetary loss to the victim.

(6) Whether the defendant was an active or passive participant.

(7) Whether the crime was committed because of an unusual circumstance, such as great provocation, which is unlikely to recur.

(8) Whether the manner in which the crime was carried out demonstrated criminal sophistication or professionalism on the part of the defendant.

(9) Whether the defendant took advantage of a position of trust or confidence to commit the crime.

Rule 4.413. Probation eligibility when probation is limited

In cases where probation is limited by statute, a judge may grant community supervision if the following circumstances exist:

(2) A fact or circumstance not amounting to a defense, but reducing the defendant's culpability for the offense, including:

(i) The defendant participated in the crime under circumstances of great provocation, coercion, or duress not amounting to a defense, and the defendant has no recent record of committing crimes of violence.

(ii) The crime was committed because of a mental condition not amounting to a defense, and there is a high likelihood that the defendant would respond favorably to mental health care and treatment that would be required as a condition of probation.

(iii) The defendant is youthful or aged, and has no significant record of prior criminal offenses.

---

suspended sentence

A prison term that is delayed while the defendant undergoes a period of community treatment. If the treatment is successful, the prison sentence is terminated.

More than half of all cases involve a direct sentence to probation without a prison term being suspended or delayed. In about 27 percent of probation sentences, judges will formulate a prison sentence and then suspend it if the offender agrees to obey the rules of probation while living in the community (a **suspended sentence**).[6] Some offenders (about 10 percent) receive some form of split sentence in which they must first serve a jail term before being released on probation; in about 8 percent of cases, the imposition of the sentence is suspended and the case continued without a finding until further notice.

The term of a probationary sentence may simply extend to the limit of the suspended prison term, but in most cases the judge will devise a specific probationary period. For misdemeanors, probation usually extends for the entire period of the jail sentence, whereas felonies are more likely to warrant probationary periods that are actually shorter than the suspended prison sentences. The typical probation sentence is about 40 months for violent offenses, 37 months for property offenses, and 36 months for drugs.[7]

Probation Eligibility

Although originally conceived as a way to provide a second chance for young offenders who committed nonserious crimes, probation today is also a means of reducing the population overload in an overcrowded and underfunded correctional system. Many serious criminal offenders are therefore given probation sentences, including people with prior felony convictions.

Most people convicted of felonies do receive some form of incarceration, in either prison or jail, but more than 30 percent of first-time felons are sentenced to probation, and about 15 percent of repeat felony offenders are given community sentences![8] This means that 15 percent of criminal defendants receive probation even though the current offense was at least their second conviction for a felony offense. Nor are violent criminals exempt from receiving a community sentence: About 20 percent of all people convicted of violent felonies receive probation. So there are two distinct sides to probation: (1) the treatment and rehabilitation of nondangerous offenders deserving of a "second chance" and (2) the supervision and control of criminals who might otherwise be incarcerated if probation were not available.

REALITY CHECK

MYTH OR REALITY? Probation is reserved for nonviolent first offenders.

MYTH: Many repeat violent offenders receive a probationary sentence.

Does this practice undermine the deterrent power of the justice system?

Conditions of Probation

When granting probation, the court sets down certain conditions or rules of behavior that the probationer is bound to obey. Although probation officers themselves can later set some conditions, courts have typically ruled that the most restrictive ones must be approved by the sentencing judge and that probation officers cannot require the defendant to adhere to new requirements of supervision about which he or she did not have reasonable notice.[9]

Conditions of probation can include warrantless searches of the probationer and his or her residence. Here Actor Ryan O'Neal, left, and his son Redmond O'Neal appear for an arraignment on methamphetamine possession charges at the courthouse in Malibu, California, on November 11, 2008. Redmond O'Neal, 23, also faced misdemeanor charges for possession of drug paraphernalia and possession of pepper spray. These were found when his probation officer searched the men's Malibu home, a condition of Redmond's probation for previous convictions. As a result of the seizures, Redmond was forced to serve a jail sentence. He was still in jail when his mother, Farrah Fawcett, died of cancer on June 30, 2009.

© Reed Saxton/UPI photo/Landov

REALITYCHECK

MYTH OR REALITY?   Probation rules cannot force sex offenders to register with state authorities and/or require them to take periodic polygraph tests to determine whether they have engaged in illegal behavior; this would be a violation of their privacy rights.

MYTH: Convicted sex offenders can be required to register as part of their probation orders.

Comment on this statement: Probation is a privilege, not a right.

Some conditions are standard and are applied in every probation case (e.g., "Do not leave the jurisdiction"), but the sentencing judge usually has broad discretion to set specific conditions on a case-by-case basis. Sometimes an individual probationer is given specific rules related to his or her particular circumstances, such as the requirement to enroll in an anger management or drug treatment program, make a personal apology to the victim, or have no contact with his or her ex-spouse.[10] A presiding judge may not impose capricious or cruel conditions, of course, such as requiring an offender to make restitution out of proportion to the seriousness of the criminal act.[11] Judges may, however, legally impose restrictions tailored to fit the probationer's individual needs and/or to protect society from additional harm. For example, they can force sex offenders to register with state authorities and require probationers to take periodic polygraph tests to determine whether they have engaged in illegal behavior.[12] Community supervision may be revoked if probationers fail to comply with the conditions of their probation and do not obey the reasonable requests of the probation staff to meet their treatment obligations.[13]

Administration of Probation Services

Probation services are organized in a variety of ways, depending on the state and the jurisdiction in which they are located. Some states have an independent statewide probation service, and in others, probation is controlled by local courts. Thirty-five states combine probation and parole supervision services in a single unit situated within the department of corrections or organized as an independent agency; about one-quarter of probationers are supervised in these joint operations. Some departments combine juvenile and adult probation departments, whereas others maintain these departments separately.

© Thinkstock/Getty Images

Regardless of how probation services are organized, probation officers (POs) are typically assigned to a department situated in a single court district, such as a juvenile, superior, district, or municipal court. The relationship between the department and court personnel (especially the judge) is extremely close.

In the typical department, the chief probation officer (CPO) sets policy, supervises hiring, determines training needs, and may personally discuss with or recommend sentencing to the judge. The probation staff carries out the actual monitoring and treatment of offenders. The duties of the chief are set out in Exhibit 10.2, and the duties of the line staff are set out in Exhibit 10.3.

An officer's working style is influenced by both personal values and the department's general policies and orientation toward the goals of probation.[14] Some POs view themselves as "social workers" and maintain a treatment orientation; their goal is to help offenders adjust in the community. Others are "law enforcers" who are more concerned with supervision, control, and public safety. New York City probation officers are authorized to carry handguns under a departmental policy intended to enhance the supervision of their clients, the majority of whom are felons. Arming the officers became necessary when the department began to require officers to spend more time visiting

EXHIBIT 10.2

Duties of the Chief Probation Officer

- Plans, directs, coordinates, and supervises probation officers and clerical support staff engaged in intake, casework, and probation activities
- Oversees personnel selection, evaluation, training, and disciplinary practices and policies of the department
- Administers the department's budget
- Provides oversight of and direction to the various divisions and organizational units of the department
- Provides oversight on the department's compliance with county, state, and federal legal requirements and regulations, as well as ordinances, policies, and procedural guidelines
- Supervises special programs such as drug monitoring and home incarceration

- Directs work routines, procedures, and methods for efficient division operation; formulates and writes policies and procedures affecting the probation and intake programs
- Explores the community for resources available for treatment and rehabilitative services for offenders and develops rehabilitative programs to provide alternative sentences to imprisonment
- Serves as liaison between probation and other public agencies, other departments, and the general public
- Analyzes, prepares, and distributes division statistical reports

EXHIBIT 10.3

Duties of a Probation Officer

- Investigates the lives of convicted offenders to enable the court to make intelligent sentencing decisions
- Investigates clients' personal or criminal histories
- Schedules meetings, appointments, or interviews with clients
- Monitors the location of clients
- Compiles records or other written materials
- Determines the status of criminal complaints and prepares investigative fact-finding reports
- Advises judges on case issues and prepares cases for hearing
- Provides guidance to clients or customers with personal problems or specific needs (e.g., substance abuse)
- Provides guidance to the families or guardians of clients, including recommendation

of treatment programs and counseling alternatives
- Conducts intake interviews to determine whether criminal action should be taken, whether cases can be decided informally, whether diversion should be advocated, and so on
- Provides testimony as an officer of the courts; collects samples or specimens to test for alcohol or substance abuse; performs related work as required
- Supervises or monitors cases assigned to ensure that the rules of probation are followed
- Recommends treatment programs for clients or customers; recommends therapeutic or rehabilitative placements; determines that clients are attending treatment programs

their clients in the latters' neighborhoods and homes. Other departments have armed their officers as the number of probationers has increased and the officers' duties have become more dangerous.[15] For more on a career as a probation officer, see the Careers in Criminal Justice feature on pages 342–43.

Elements of Probation

Probation departments engage in five primary tasks: pre-sentence investigation, intake, diagnosis, treatment supervision, and risk classification.

Careers in Criminal Justice

PROBATION OFFICER

Duties and Characteristics of the Job

- Probation officers monitor offenders' behavior through personal contact with the offenders and their families.
- Another part of the probation officer's job involves working in the courts.
- The number of cases a probation officer has depends on both the counseling needs of offenders and the risks they pose to society.
- Probation officers may find their jobs stressful because they work with convicted criminals and interact with many other individuals, including family members and friends of their clients, who may be angry, upset, or uncooperative.
- Although stress makes these jobs difficult at times, the work also can be rewarding. Many probation officers gain personal satisfaction from counseling members of their community and helping them become productive citizens.

Job Outlook

- Jobs for probation officers are more plentiful in urban areas.
- There are also more jobs in states that have numerous men and women on probation.

Salary

- Median annual earnings of probation officers is about $36,130. The middle 50 percent earned between $29,260 and $44,890.
- The lowest 10 percent earned less than $24,310, and the highest 10 percent earned more than $54,810.
- Officers and specialists who work in urban areas usually have higher earnings than those working in rural areas.

Opportunities

- Employment of probation officers is projected to grow during the next few years.
- Overcrowding in prisons also has swelled the probation population as judges and prosecutors search for alternative forms of punishment, such as electronic monitoring and day reporting centers.
- Other openings will result from the need to replace workers who leave the occupation permanently—including the large number expected to retire over the next several years.

Qualifications

- Prospective probation officers must be in good physical condition and must be emotionally stable.
- Most agencies require applicants to be at least 21 years old and, for federal employment, not older than 37. Those convicted of felonies may not be eligible for employment in these occupations.
- Probation officers need strong writing skills because of the large number of reports they must prepare.
- Familiarity with computers is often required.
- Job candidates also should be knowledgeable about laws and regulations pertaining to corrections.

Education and Training

- Educational requirements for probation officers vary by state, but a bachelor's degree in social work or criminal justice is usually required.
- Some states require probation officers to have one year of work experience in a related field or one year of graduate study in criminal justice, social work, or psychology.
- Most probation officers must complete a training program and work as trainees for about six months.
- Candidates who successfully complete the training period obtain a permanent position.

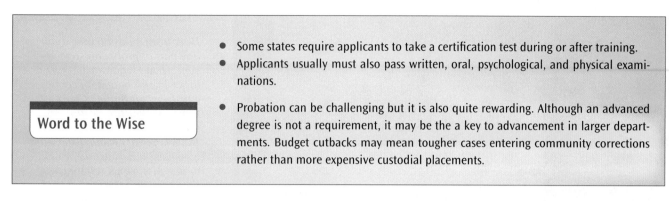

Word to the Wise

- Some states require applicants to take a certification test during or after training.
- Applicants usually must also pass written, oral, psychological, and physical examinations.
- Probation can be challenging but it is also quite rewarding. Although an advanced degree is not a requirement, it may be the a key to advancement in larger departments. Budget cutbacks may mean tougher cases entering community corrections rather than more expensive custodial placements.

PRE-SENTENCE INVESTIGATION ● In the investigative stage, the supervising probation officer accumulates important information on the background and activities of the offender being considered for probation. This **pre-sentence investigation** serves as the basis for sentencing and controls whether the convicted defendant will be granted community release or sentenced to secure confinement. In the event that the offender is placed on probation, the investigation becomes useful as a tool to shape treatment and supervision efforts.

The style and content of pre-sentence investigations may vary among jurisdictions and also among individual POs within the same jurisdiction. Some departments require voluminous reports covering every aspect of the defendant's life. Other departments require that officers stick to the basic facts, such as the defendant's age, race, sex, and previous offense record.

At the conclusion of most pre-sentence investigations, a recommendation is made to the presiding judge that reflects the department's sentencing posture on the case at hand. This is a crucial aspect of the report, because the sentencing judge usually follows the probation department's recommendation. Numerous factors may contribute to a recommendation of community treatment; among the most critical are the investigator's conclusion that the defendant is someone whom probation officers can work with and effectively treat. Equally important is the belief that the perspective probationer will be able to abide by both legal and institutional rules.[16]

INTAKE ● Probation officers who conduct **intake** interviews may be looking to settle the case without the necessity of a court hearing. The probation officer will work with all parties involved in the case—offender, victim, police officer, and so on—to design an equitable resolution of the case. If the intake process is successful, the probation officer may settle the case without further court action, recommend restitution or other compensation, or recommend unofficial or informal probation. If an equitable solution cannot be found, the case would be filed for a court hearing.

DIAGNOSIS ● In order to select appropriate treatment modes, probation officers—using their training in counseling, social work, or psychology—analyze the probationer's character, attitudes, and behavior. The goal of diagnosis is to develop a personality profile that may be helpful in treating the offender. An effective diagnosis integrates all that has been learned about the individual, organized in such a way as to facilitate the establishment of future treatment goals. The emergence of standardized diagnostic tools and tests (see later in this chapter) has diminished the probationer officer's individual role in diagnosis. To some commentators, this is problematic because it removes the human element from diagnosis and treatment.[17]

TREATMENT SUPERVISION ● After the diagnosis has been completed, the probation staff is asked to carry out the treatment supervision, a program of therapy designed to help the client deal with the problems that resulted in her or his

pre-sentence investigation
An investigation performed by a probation officer attached to a trial court after the conviction of a defendant. The report contains information about the defendant's background, education, previous employment, and family; his or her own statement concerning the offense; any prior criminal record; interviews with neighbors or acquaintances; and his or her mental and physical condition (that is, information that would not be made public record in the case of a guilty plea or that would be inadmissible as evidence at a trial but could be influential and important at the sentencing stage).

intake
The process in which a probation officer settles cases at the initial appearance before the onset of formal criminal proceedings; also, the process in which a juvenile referral is received and a decision is made to file a petition in the juvenile court, release the juvenile, or refer the juvenile elsewhere.

Drug testing has become a routine part of probation supervision. Here Fred Daniels waits to see his probation officer for a drug test at Suffolk County Superior Court in Boston, Massachusetts, on May 30, 2008. His test results would determine whether Daniels would be able to attend his high school prom that evening or be sent to jail for violating his conditions of probation. In the end, the probation officer chose to administer the test the following week, allowing Fred to go to the prom!

© Yoon S. Byun/*Boston Globe*/Landov

antisocial behavior. In years past, the probation staff had primary responsibility for supervision and treatment, but today's large caseloads limit opportunities for hands-on treatment; most probation treatment efforts rely on community resources.

Treatment protocols may vary according to client needs. Some of those who have a drinking problem may be asked to participate in a community-based 12-step program; others might spend time in a residential detoxification center. A spousal abuser may be required to enroll in an anger management program, make a personal apology to the victim, or have no contact with his or her ex-spouse.[18] A probation officer may work with teachers and other school officials to help a young probationer reduce his or her truancy and avoid becoming a "dropout."

In addition to meeting the organizational goal of client rehabilitation, effective supervision is critical for another reason: It protects the probation department from civil liability. Failure to supervise probationers adequately and determine whether they are obeying the rules of probation can result in the officer and the department being held legally liable for civil damages. For example, if a probationer with a history of child molestation attacked a child while working as a school custodian, the probationer's case supervisor could be held legally responsible for failing to check on the probationer's employment activities.[19] The Criminal Justice and Technology feature on page 345 describes how probation officers use technology to monitor clients in the community.

RISK CLASSIFICATION ● As part of clients' entry into probation, an assessment is made about the "risk level" they pose to the community and themselves. On the basis of this assessment, offenders are assigned to specific supervision levels, where a variety of "tools and techniques" will be applied in an attempt to manage the risk they pose to the community and to themselves. Developing effective risk assessment has taken on greater importance because probation is now routinely employed with felons who have been convicted of violent crimes such as rape and murder. Data shows that many of these clients have a significant likelihood of killing or being killed and that most murders in the United States are committed by people who are current community corrections clients.[20] Because more than 4 million people must now be managed,

Criminal Justice and Technology

Monitoring Probationers with Technology

It is a myth that supervising people on probation is merely a form of social work and that probation officers spend all their time dispensing counseling to clients. The fact is that monitoring and control are also a significant aspect of the probation officer's job. Many probationers have substance abuse problems that can interfere with their community sentence. Several newly developed technologies may help uncover and curb these behaviors and provide probation officers with tools to better manage their caseloads by doing their jobs more effectively and efficiently.

Sleep Pattern Analysis

Sleep pattern analysis technology, already used by some jurisdictions, can provide preliminary indications of substance abuse and help community corrections officials determine whether more testing is warranted. Sleep disruption due to substance abuse can occur in several ways, including altering the sequence and duration of various stages of sleep, total sleep time, and the amount of time needed to fall asleep. The technology consists of a small device, secured to an offender's wrist with a tamper-evident band, that measures sleep quality by recording gross motor activity. Analysis of the data collected may indicate sleep disorders, which might be caused by substance abuse. The device passively collects and records body movement information, and when the offender reports to the probation office or drug court, data can be downloaded and analyzed in a matter of minutes. If data analysis indicates possible substance abuse, the offender can be required to immediately provide a urine specimen for further testing.

Infrared Spectroscopy

Currently in field tests, this technology seeks to modify a glucose-monitoring device into an alcohol-testing product. The device uses a light source, an optical detector, and spectrometers to conduct chemical analysis of tissue and measure alcohol levels. Results, available within just 1 minute, have accuracy comparable to that of breathalyzers and blood tests. The technology uses infrared spectroscopy to make a nonintrusive examination of a subject's inner forearm; the device also could be modified to examine other parts of the body. The analysis process incorporates a biometric component that identifies an individual's unique tissue structure and tissue chemistry, thus ensuring accurate identification of the person being tested.

Driver Monitoring and Surveillance

This surveillance technology consists of a pair of ankle bracelets that collect data on the unique patterns of movement associated with foot-to-brake, foot-to-gas pedal, and acceleration and deceleration of a motor vehicle. Data analysis can then indicate whether and when a subject has been driving. In the case of an individual whose license is restricted rather than suspended, it can also indicate whether the driving took place during a prohibited time (such as outside the normal workday). The bracelets can store and process data for up to 30 days, allowing a community corrections officer to upload data during a scheduled monthly visit. This technology would help community corrections professionals deal with a widespread and long-standing problem; research indicates that up to 75 percent of all drivers with suspended or restricted licenses continue to drive.

Critical Thinking

1. Does this type of monitoring interfere with the treatment aspects of probation? Is it possible to help people who believe they are regarded as untrustworthy and must be monitored 24/7?

2. Even though it might pay to closely monitor probationers soon after their community sentence begins, does it pay to continue close control two, three, or even five years after they have been in the community? If they haven't violated probation in years, aren't they a safe bet?

experts argue that risk assessment is the single most important decision being made by probation officers today.[21]

risk classification
Classifying probationers so that they may receive an appropriate level of treatment and control.

Probationers typically receive a **risk classification** that assigns them to a specific level and type of supervision on the basis of their particular needs and the risks they present to the community. Some clients may receive frequent (intensive) supervision in which they are contacted by their supervising probation officer almost every day, whereas other, minor offenders are assigned to minimum monitoring by a PO. A number of risk assessment classification approaches are used, but most employ such objective measures as the offender's age, employment status, drug abuse history, prior felony convictions, and number of address changes in the year prior to sentencing. Some departments are using standardized tests to predict failure and assign treatment. The most widely advertised system is the Level of Service Inventory—Revised (or LSI-R), which was developed in Canada and has been adopted by a number of U.S. correctional agencies. The LSI-R consists of 54 items that are sorted into the following 10 substantive areas believed to be related to future criminal behavior:

1. Criminal history (10 items)
2. Education and employment (10 items)
3. Financial (2 items)
4. Family and marital (4 items)
5. Accommodations (3 items)
6. Leisure and recreation (2 items)
7. Companions (5 items)
8. Alcohol and drugs (9 items)
9. Emotional and personal (5 items)
10. Attitude and orientation (4 items)[22]

Evaluations of the LSI-R and of several other risk assessment instruments show that when used properly, they can be highly valid and effective.[23]

Legal Rights of Probationers

What are the legal rights of probationers? How has the U.S. Supreme Court set limits on the probation process? A number of important legal issues surround probation, one set involving the civil rights of probationers and another involving the rights of probationers during the revocation process.

CIVIL RIGHTS ● The Court has ruled that probationers have a unique status and therefore are entitled to fewer constitutional protections than other citizens.

- *Minnesota v. Murphy (1984)*.[24] The probation officer–client relationship is not confidential, as are physician–patient and or attorney–client relationships. If a probationer admits to committing a crime to his or her probation supervisor, the information can be passed on to the police or district attorney. The *Murphy* decision held that a probation officer could even use trickery or psychological pressure to get information and turn it over to the police.
- *Griffin v. Wisconsin (1987)*.[25] *Griffin* held that a probationer's home may be searched without a warrant because probation departments "have in mind the welfare of the probationer" and must "respond quickly to evidence of misconduct."
- *United States v. Knights (2001)*.[26] The warrantless search of a probationer's home for the purposes of gathering criminal evidence is legal under some circumstances—for example if (a) the search was based on a reasonable suspicion that the probationer had committed another crime while on probation and (b) submitting to searches was part of the probation order.

The government's interest in preventing crime, combined with Knights's diminished expectation of privacy, required only a *reasonable suspicion* to make the search fit within the protections of the Fourth Amendment.

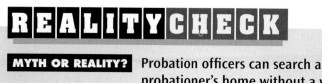

REVOCATION RIGHTS ● During the course of a probationary term, violating the rules or terms of probation or committing a new crime can result in probation being revoked, at which time the offender may be placed in an institution. Revocation is not often an easy decision, because it conflicts with the treatment philosophy of many probation departments.

MYTH OR REALITY? Probation officers can search a probationer's home without a warrant if they suspect foul play or criminal activity.

REALITY: Probationers have less expectations of privacy than the average citizen and their home can be searched without a warrant if there is cause.

Do you think that's fair?

If revocation is a possibility, the offender is notified, and a formal hearing is scheduled to look into the matter. If the charges against the probationer are upheld, the offender can either be maintained on probation or have his probation revoked and be forced to serve the remainder of his sentence behind bars.

In some significant decisions, the U.S. Supreme Court provided procedural safeguards to apply at proceedings to revoke probation (and parole):

- *Mempa v. Rhay (1967)*. A probationer is constitutionally entitled to counsel in a revocation-of-probation proceeding where the imposition of sentence had been suspended.[27]

- *Morrissey v. Brewer (1972)*. *Morrissey*, a parole case, established that an informal inquiry must be held to determine whether there is probable cause that a parolee has violated the conditions of parole. If so, a formal revocation hearing is required before parole can be revoked. Because the revocation of probation and that of parole are similar, the standards in the *Morrissey* case are applied to probation process as well.[28]

- *Gagnon v. Scarpelli (1973)*. *Gagnon* established that both probationers and parolees have a constitutionally limited right to legal counsel in revocation proceedings.[29] A judge may deny counsel under some circumstances, such as when probation will be continued despite the violation.

- *Beardon v. Georgia (1983)* In *Beardon*, the U.S. Supreme Court ruled that a judge cannot revoke a defendant's probation for failure to pay a fine and/or make restitution. The state may not thereafter imprison a defendant solely because he or she lacks the resources to pay, because this would be a violation of a probationer's right to equal protection.[30]

- *United States v. Granderson (1994)*. The *Granderson* ruling helped clarify what can happen to a probationer whose community sentence is revoked. Granderson was eligible for a 6-month prison sentence but instead was given 60 months of probation. When he tested positive for drugs, his probation was revoked. The statute he was sentenced under required that he serve one-third of his original sentence in prison. When the trial court sentenced him to 20 months, he appealed. Was his original sentence 6 months or 60 months? The Supreme Court found that it would be unfair to force a probationer to serve more time in prison than he would have served if originally incarcerated and ruled that the proper term should have been one-third of the 6 months, or 2 months.[31]

How Successful Is Probation?

Probation is the most commonly used alternative sentence for a number of reasons: It is humane, it helps offenders maintain community and family ties, and it is cost-effective. Incarcerating an inmate typically costs over $25,000 per year, whereas probation costs about $2,000 per year.

Although unquestionably inexpensive, is probation successful? If most probation orders fail, the costs of repeated criminality would certainly outweigh the cost savings of a probation sentence. National data indicates that about 60 percent of probationers successfully complete their probationary sentence, whereas about 40 percent are rearrested, violate probation rules, or abscond; about 18 percent find themselves behind bars.[32]

Most revocations occur for technical violations during the first three months of the probation sentence.[33] Ironically, many revocations stem from failure to attend required treatment programs that were originally created to help probationers kick their drug habits, stay out of trouble, and succeed on probation.[34]

Studies of federal probationers show even better results (30 percent failure rate).[35] Although a 30–40 percent failure rate may seem high, even the most serious criminals who receive probation are less likely to recidivate than those who are sent to prison or jail for committing similar crimes.[36]

How Successful Is Felony Probation?

Are probationers convicted of serious felonies more likely to recidivate than minor offenders who receive probation? Does their lenient sentence present a threat to the community? Tracking the outcome of felony probation was the goal of Joan Petersilia and her colleagues at the RAND Corporation, a private think tank, when they traced 1,672 men convicted of felonies who had been granted probation in Los Angeles and Alameda counties in California.[37] In this now-classic study, Petersilia found that 1,087 (65 percent) were rearrested; of those rearrested, 853 (51 percent) were convicted; and of those convicted, 568 (34 percent) were sentenced to jail or prison. Of the probationers who had new charges filed against them, 75 percent were charged with burglary, theft, robbery, and other predatory crimes; 18 percent were convicted of serious, violent crimes.

The RAND researchers found that probation is by far the most common sentencing alternative to prison; it is used in about 60 to 80 percent of all criminal convictions. However, the crimes and criminal records of about 25 percent of all probationers are indistinguishable from those of offenders who go to prison. This data indicates that many people given prison sentences could have been granted community sentences, and vice versa. This is a disturbing finding when so many felons granted community sentences fail to complete their probationary period.

Although the failure rate found by Petersilia seems disturbingly high, her findings still support the continued use of probation, given the fact that felons who receive probation are less likely to recidivate than felons who are sent to prison for committing similar crimes.[38]

Who Fails on Probation and Who Succeeds?

Who is most likely to fail on probation? Many probationers have grown up in troubled households in which family members are or have been incarcerated and/or are drug abusers. Others have lived part of their lives in foster homes or state institutions and have suffered high rates of physical and sexual abuse. This sort of deprived background often makes it difficult for probationers to comply with the rules of probation and forgo criminal activity. Surveys indicate that almost 20 percent of probationers suffer from mental illness and that those with a history of instability are most likely to be rearrested.[39]

Prior record is also related to probation success: Clients who have a history of criminal behavior, prior probation, and previous incarceration are the most likely to fail.[40] Also, as probation sentences have become more common, caseloads now contain significant numbers of serious repeat offenders, a group that is difficult to treat and control.[41]

In contrast, probationers who are married with children, have lived in the area for two or more years, and are adequately employed are the most likely to be successful on probation.[42] Among female probationers, those who have stable marriages, are better educated, and are employed are more likely to complete probation orders successfully than male or female probationers who are single, less educated, and unemployed.

The Future of Probation

Some critics are worried that probation is now undergoing a shift from traditional casework methods that featured diagnosis and treatment to an emphasis on risk assessment and control.[43] To improve the effectivenesss of probation even more, in a process that leading expert Joan Petersilia calls "reforming, reinvesting, and restructuring," several steps appear to be necessary, including providing more financial resources and implementing quality programming for appropriate probation target groups.[44] A number of initiatives that are now ongoing or being suggested may help shape the future of probation:

- *Making probationers pay*. At least 25 states now impose some form of fee on probationers to defray the cost of community corrections. Massachusetts initiated **day fees**, which are based on the probationer's wages (the usual fee is between one and three days' wages each month).[45] Texas requires judges to impose supervision fees unless the offender is truly unable to pay; fees make up more than half the probation department's annual budget.[46]

- *Making probation more effective*. Legislatures are instituting policies that reward the most effective and efficient local departments. In 2008, the Arizona legislature established an incentive system that rewards departments with up to 40 percent of any cost savings in each county resulting from a reduction in probation revocations. The money can then be used to fund substance abuse treatment, community supervision services, and victim services.[47]

- *HotSpot probation*. HotSpot probation initiatives involve police officers, probation agents, neighbors, and social service professionals in community supervision teams. Using a team approach, they provide increased monitoring of offenders through home visits and drug testing. They also work with the offenders to ease reentry through offender creation of work crews that participate in community cleanups, work on vacant houses, and participate in other projects.[48]

- *Area needs*. Some experts suggest that probation caseloads be organized around area needs rather than client needs. Research shows that probationers' residences are concentrated in certain locations. In the future, probation officers may be assigned cases on the basis of where they live so that they can acquire a working knowledge of community issues and develop expertise on how best to serve their clients' interests and needs.[49]

- *Specialized probation*. Some probation departments are experimenting with focused or specialized probation, in which teams of probation officers take on clients convicted of one specific type of crime, such as drug offenses or domestic violence, rather than treating a mixed bag of offenders. Focusing on specialized caseloads enables probation officers to develop specific treatment and control skills.[50]

- *Private probation*. Used in at least 10 states, including Colorado and Missouri, private probation involves contracting with companies that, for a fee, engage in many typical probation activities from supervision to giving periodic breathalyzer tests.[51] By utilizing private probation for low-risk offenders, state probation departments can commit more resources to high-risk offenders.[52]

- *Swift and sure punishment*. The threat of swift and sure punishment that is somewhat less than a full revocation may help reduce rule violations.

day fees
A program requiring probationers to pay some of the costs of their treatment.

Hawaii has been experimenting with a system that provides immediate punishment for any probationers found in violation of their court orders. Probations are warned during a court hearing that if they violate the conditions of probation, they will be immediately arrested, will appear in court within hours, and will have the terms of their supervision modified to include a short stay in jail. The jail terms imposed are usually only a few days, but sentence length increases for successive violations. The program appears to be highly successful in reducing violations.[53]

Probation is unquestionably undergoing dramatic changes. In many jurisdictions, traditional probation is being supplemented by **intermediate sanctions**, which are penalties that fall between traditional community supervision and confinement in jail or prison. These new correctional services are discussed in the following section.

intermediate sanctions
Punishments that fall between probation and prison ("probation plus"). Community-based sanctions, including house arrest and intensive supervision, serve as alternatives to incarceration.

Intermediate Sanctions

In 2005, Jennifer Wilbanks became notorious for running away just before her wedding and claiming to have been abducted. When the truth was revealed, she pled guilty to charges of filing a false police report. At her hearing she told the court, "I'm truly sorry for my actions and I just want to thank Gwinnett County and the city of Duluth." The judge, Ronnie Batchelor, then sentenced "The Runaway Bride" to two years of probation and 120 hours of community service. He also ordered her to continue mental health treatment and pay the sheriff's office $2,550 in addition to the $13,250 she had previously agreed to pay the city of Duluth, Georgia, to help cover the overtime costs incurred in searching for her.[54]

Wilbanks's sentence reflects the growing trend to add sanctions to traditional probation sentences; in her case, the sanctions were monetary fines and community service. These programs can be viewed as "probation plus," because they add restrictive penalties and conditions to traditional community service orders, which feature treatment and rehabilitation over control and restraint.[55] These newer forms of community sentences have the potential to become reasonable alternatives to treatment and rehabilitation alone, and thus to help address many of the economic and social problems faced by correctional administrators. Here are some of the advantages of intermediate sanctions:

- They are less costly than jail or prison sentences.
- They help the offender maintain family and community ties.
- They can be structured to maximize security and maintain public safety.
- They can be scaled in severity to correspond to the seriousness of the crime.
- They can feature restoration and reintegration rather than punishment and ostracism.
- By siphoning off offenders from the secure correctional system, they reduce the need for future prison and jail construction.
- Intermediate sanctions help meet the need to develop community sentences that are fair, equitable, and proportional.[56]
- They can be designed to increase control over probationers whose serious or repeat crimes make a straight probation sentence inappropriate, yet for whom a prison sentence would be unduly harsh and counterproductive.[57]
- Intermediate sanctions can potentially be used as halfway-back strategies for offenders who violate the conditions of their community release. Rule violators can be placed under increasingly more intensive supervision before actual incarceration is required.

Intermediate sanctions include programs that are usually administered by probation departments: intensive probation supervision, house arrest, electronic

Intermediate sanctions can include house arrest, electronic monitoring, community service restitution, and the like. Here Rapper T.I., whose real name is Clifford Harris Jr., speaks to a group of students in Atlanta, Georgia, on February, 20, 2009. T.I. was convicted on federal weapons charges. Instead of being incarcerated, he was allowed to make community service restitution. He was sentenced to complete 1,000 hours of community service warning youths about the pitfalls of living a hustler's life.

©AP Images/John Bazemore

monitoring, restitution orders, shock probation or split sentences, and residential community corrections.[58] Some experts also include high-impact shock incarceration, or boot camp experiences, within the definition of intermediate sanctions, but these programs are usually operated by correctional departments and are therefore discussed separately in Chapter 11. Intermediate sanctions also involve sentences administered independently of probation staffs: fines and forfeiture, pretrial programs, and pretrial and posttrial residential programs. Intermediate sanctions therefore range from the barely intrusive, such as restitution orders, to the highly restrictive, such as house arrest accompanied by electronic monitoring and a stay in a community correctional center.

As Figure 10.2 illustrates, intermediate sanctions can form the successive steps of a meaningful "ladder" of scaled punishments outside of prison, thereby restoring fairness and equity to nonincarceration sentences.[59] Forgers may be ordered to make restitution to their victims, and rapists can be placed in a community facility and receive counseling at a local clinic. This feature of intermediate sanctions enables judges to fit the punishment to the crime without resorting to a prison sentence.

The forms of intermediate sanctions currently in use are more thoroughly discussed in the following sections.

Fines

Monetary payments, or **fines**, can be imposed on offenders as an intermediate punishment for their criminal acts. They are a direct offshoot of the early common-law practice of requiring that compensation be paid to the victim and the state (*wergild*) for criminal acts. Fines are still commonly used in Europe, where they are often the sole penalty, even in cases involving chronic offenders who commit fairly serious crimes.[60]

In the United States, fines are most commonly used in cases involving misdemeanors and lesser offenses. Fines are also frequently used in felony cases where the offender benefited financially.

Fines may be used as a sole sanction but are typically combined with other punishments, such as probation. Judges commonly levy other monetary sanctions along with fines, such as court costs, public defender fees, probation and treatment fees, and victim restitution, to increase the force of the financial

fine
A money payment levied on offenders to compensate society for their misdeeds.

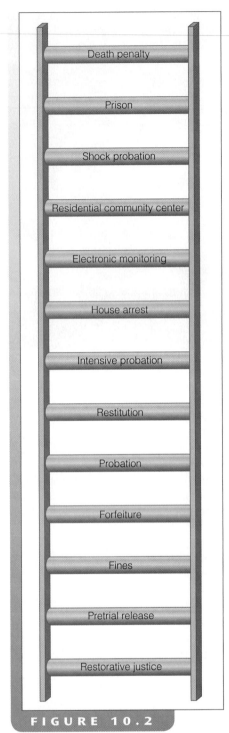

FIGURE 10.2

Punishment Ladder

day fine
A fine geared to the average daily income of the convicted offender in an effort to bring equity to the sentencing process.

forfeiture
The seizure of personal property by the state as a civil or criminal penalty.

punishment. However, there is evidence that many offenders fail to pay fines and that courts are negligent in their efforts to collect unpaid fees.[61]

In most jurisdictions, little guidance is given to the sentencing judge directing the imposition of the fine. Judges often have inadequate information on the offender's ability to pay, and this results in defaults and contempt charges. Because the standard sanction for nonpayment is incarceration, many offenders held in local jails are confined for nonpayment of criminal fines. Even though the U.S. Supreme Court in *Tate v. Short* (1971) recognized that incarcerating a person who is financially unable to pay a fine discriminates against the poor, many judges continue to incarcerate offenders for noncompliance with financial orders.[62]

DAY FINES ● Because judges rely so heavily on offense seriousness to fix the level of fines, financial penalties may have a negative impact on success rates. The more serious the offense and the higher the fine, the greater the chances that the offender will fail to pay the fine and risk revocation of probation. To overcome this sort of problem, some jurisdictions began experimenting with **day fines**. The first day fines pilot program in the United States was designed and operated by the Vera Institute of Justice in Staten Island, New York, between 1987 and 1989. Since then, similar structured-fine systems have been tried experimentally in Arizona, Connecticut, Iowa, and Oregon.[63]

A concept that originated in Europe, day fines are geared to an offender's net daily income. In an effort to make them equitable and fairly distributed, fines are based on the severity of the crime, weighted by a daily-income value taken from a chart similar to an income tax table; the number of the offender's dependents is also taken into account. The day fine concept means that the severity of punishment is geared to the offender's ability to pay.

Day fines hold the promise of becoming an equitable solution to the problem of setting the amount of a fine according to the offender's ability to pay. However, there is little conclusive evidence on whether the day fine program actually works as intended.[64]

Forfeiture

Another intermediate sanction with a financial basis is criminal (in personam) and civil (in rem) **forfeiture**. Both involve the seizure of goods and instrumentalities related to the commission or outcome of a criminal act. The difference is that criminal forfeiture proceedings target criminal defendants and can only follow a criminal conviction. In contrast, civil forfeiture proceedings target property used in a crime and do not require that formal criminal proceedings be initiated against a person or that the person be proved guilty of a crime.[65] For example, federal law provides that after arresting drug traffickers, the government may seize the boats they used to import the narcotics, the cars they used to carry the drugs overland, the warehouses in which the drugs were stored, and the homes paid for with the drug profits; on conviction, the drug dealers lose permanent ownership of these "instrumentalities" of crime.

Forfeiture is not a new sanction. During the Middle Ages, "forfeiture of estate" was a mandatory result of most felony convictions. The Crown could seize all of a felon's real and personal property. Forfeiture derived from the common-law concept of "corruption of blood," or "attaint," which prohibited a felon's family from inheriting or receiving his property or estate. The common law mandated that descendants could not inherit property from a relative who might have obtained the property illegally: "[T]he Corruption of Blood stops the Course of Regular Descent, as to Estates, over which the Criminal could have no Power, because he never enjoyed them."[66]

Forfeiture was reintroduced to U.S. law with the passage of the Racketeer Influenced and Corrupt Organization (RICO) Act and the Continuing Criminal Enterprises Act, both of which allow the seizure of any property derived from illegal enterprises or conspiracies. Although these acts were designed to apply to ongoing criminal conspiracies, such as drug or pornography rings, they are now being applied to a far-ranging series of criminal acts, including white-collar crimes. More than 100 federal statutes use forfeiture of property as a punishment.

Although law enforcement officials at first applauded the use of forfeiture as a hard-hitting way of seizing the illegal profits of drug law violators, the practice has been criticized because the government has often been overzealous in its application. For example, million-dollar yachts have been seized because someone aboard possessed a small amount of marijuana; this confiscatory practice is referred to as **zero tolerance**. This strict interpretation of the forfeiture statutes has come under fire because it is often used capriciously, the penalty is sometimes disproportionate to the crime involved, and it makes the government a "partner in crime."[67] It is also alleged that forfeiture unfairly targets a narrow range of offenders. For example, it is common for government employees involved in corruption to forfeit their pensions, but employees of public companies are exempt from such punishment.[68] There is also the issue of conflict of interest: Because law enforcement agencies can use forfeited assets to supplement their budgets, they may direct their efforts to cases that promise the greatest "payoff" rather than to cases that have the highest law enforcement priority.[69]

Restitution

Another popular intermediate sanction is **restitution**, which can take the form of requiring offenders either to pay back the victims of crime (**monetary restitution**) or to serve the community to compensate for their criminal acts

REALITYCHECK

MYTH OR REALITY? Convicted criminals can be forced to surrender their homes and cars.

REALITY: Under forfeiture programs, people can be forced to surrender the instrumentalities of their criminal behavior.

Should someone convicted of DWI for the third time forfeit her vehicle?

zero tolerance
The practice of seizing all instrumentalities of a crime, including homes, boats, and cars. It is an extreme example of the law of forfeiture.

restitution
A condition of probation in which the offender repays society or the victim of crime for the trouble and expense the offender caused.

monetary restitution
A sanction requiring that convicted offenders compensate crime victims by reimbursing them for out-of-pocket losses caused by the crime. Losses can include property damage, lost wages, and medical costs.

Restitution can either be community service or financial, depending on the crime and the defendant. Here bailiff Dave Matson, left, puts handcuffs on Mauricio Celis on March 26, 2009, before escorting him to jail following Celis's sentencing at the Nueces County Courthouse in Corpus Christi, Texas. Celis was the owner of CGT Law Group International, a once-prestigious law firm in Corpus Christi that regularly referred big-money cases to other lawyers. A rival denounced Celis as a fraud who did not have a law degree. Celis responded that he had never represented himself as a lawyer, but only as a manager. However, in Texas it is illegal for lawyers to share fees with nonlawyers, and it is illegal for nonlawyers to own an interest in a law firm. Celis was not a member of the bar but had been identified as a lawyer in local papers and magazines. A state judge sentenced Celis to more than 10 years of probation and ordered him to pay $1.35 million in restitution.

© AP Images/Corpus Christi Caller-Times/Michael Zamora

community service restitution

An alternative sanction that requires an offender to work in the community at such tasks as cleaning public parks or working with disabled children in lieu of an incarceration sentence.

(**community service restitution**).[70] Restitution programs offer offenders a chance to avoid a jail or prison sentence or a lengthier probation period. The programs may help them develop a sense of allegiance to society, better work habits, and some degree of gratitude for being given a second chance. Restitution serves many other purposes, including giving the community something of value without asking it to foot the bill for an incarceration, and helping victims regain lost property and income.

If a defendant is sentenced to pay monetary restitution as part of her probation order, a determination of victim loss is made and a plan for paying fair compensation developed. To avoid the situation in which a wealthy offender can fill a restitution order by merely writing a check, judges will sometimes order that compensation be paid out of income derived from a low-paid social service or public works job.

Community service orders usually require duty in a public nursing home, shelter, hospital, drug treatment unit, or works program; some young vandals may find that they must clean up the damage they caused to a school or park. Judges and probation officers have embraced the concept of restitution because it appears to benefit the victim, the offender, the criminal justice system, and society.[71] Financial restitution is inexpensive to administer, helps avoid stigma, and provides some compensation for victims of crime. Offenders ordered to do community service work have been placed in schools, hospitals, and nursing homes. Helping them avoid a jail sentence can mean saving the public thousands of dollars that would have gone to maintaining them in a secure institution, frees up needed resources, and gives the community the feeling that equity has been restored to the justice system.

Does restitution work? Most reviews rate it as a qualified success. One recent evaluation of community service in Texas found that nearly three-fourths of offenders with community service orders met their obligations and completed community service work.[72] The Texas experience is not atypical; most restitution clients successfully complete their orders and have no subsequent contact with the justice system.[73]

Shock Probation and Split Sentencing

shock probation

A sentence in which offenders serve a short prison term before they begin probation, to impress them with the pains of imprisonment.

split sentence

A practice that requires convicted criminals to spend a portion of their sentence behind bars and the remainder in the community.

Shock probation and **split sentences** are alternative sanctions designed to allow judges to grant offenders community release only after they have sampled prison life. These sanctions are based on the premise that if offenders get a taste of incarceration sufficient to shock them into law-abiding behavior, they will be reluctant to violate the rules of probation or commit another crime.

In a number of states and in the Federal Criminal Code, a jail term can actually be a condition of probation, an arrangement known as split sentencing. About 10 percent of probationers are now given split sentences. The shock probation approach involves resentencing an offender to probation after a short prison stay. The shock comes because the offender originally received a long maximum sentence but is then eligible for release to community supervision at the discretion of the judge (usually within 90 days of incarceration).

Some states have linked the short prison stay with a boot camp experience, referred to as shock incarceration, in which young inmates undergo a brief but intense period of military-like training and hard labor designed to impress them with the rigors of prison life.[74] (Boot camp programs are discussed in greater detail in Chapter 11.) Shock probation and split sentencing have been praised as ways to limit prison time, reintegrate the client quickly into the community, maintain family ties, and reduce prison populations and the costs of corrections.[75] An initial jail sentence probably makes offenders more receptive to the conditions of probation, because it amply illustrates the problems they will face if probation is violated.

But split sentences and shock probation programs have been criticized by those who believe that even a brief period of incarceration can interfere with the purpose of probation, which is to provide the offender with nonstigmatizing, community-based treatment. Even a short-term commitment subjects probationers to the destructive effects of institutionalization, disrupts their life in the community, and stigmatizes them for having been in jail.

Intensive Probation Supervision

Intensive probation supervision (IPS) programs, also referred to as intensive supervision programs, have been implemented in some form in about 40 states and today include about 100,000 clients. IPS programs involve small caseloads of 15 to 40 clients who are kept under close watch by probation officers.[76] IPS programs typically have three primary goals:

- *Decarceration*. Without intensive supervision, clients would normally be sent to already overcrowded prisons or jails.
- *Control*. High-risk offenders can be maintained in the community under much closer security than traditional probation efforts can provide.
- *Reintegration*. Offenders can maintain community ties and be reoriented toward a more productive life, while avoiding the pains of imprisonment.

In general, IPS programs rely on a great degree of client contact to achieve the goals of decarceration, control, and reintegration. Most programs have admissions criteria based on the nature of the offense and the offender's criminal background. Some programs exclude violent offenders; others will not take substance abusers. In contrast, some jurisdictions do not exclude offenders based on their prior criminal history.

IPS programs are used in several ways. In some states, IPS is a direct sentence imposed by a judge; in others, it is a postsentencing alternative used to divert offenders from the correctional system. A third practice is to use IPS as a case management tool to give the local probation staff flexibility in dealing with clients. Other jurisdictions use IPS in all three ways, in addition to applying it to probation violators to bring them halfway back into the community without resorting to a prison term.

THE EFFECTIVENESS OF IPS ● There are indications that the failure rate in IPS caseloads is high, in some cases approaching 50 percent. Some studies have found that IPS clients have a higher rearrest rate than other probationers, and others suggest that these failure rates are about equal.[77] More encouraging is evidence that IPS clients have better records than similar offenders who suffer incarceration. Evaluation of a Minnesota IPS program aimed at DWI offenders found that although 13 percent of the IPS group were arrested after completion of the program, 23 percent of a similar group of offenders who had been sent to jail or prison were arrested after their incarceration ended.[78]

It should come as no surprise that IPS clients have a high failure rate because, after all, they are more serious criminals who might otherwise have been incarcerated. Probation officers may also be more willing to revoke the probation of IPS clients because they believe these clients pose a greater risk to the community. Why risk the program to save a few "bad apples"?

Although national evaluations of the program have not been encouraging, IPS seems to work better for some offenders than for others. Those with good employment records seem to do better than the underemployed or unemployed.[79] Younger offenders who commit petty crimes are the most likely to fail on IPS; ironically, people with these characteristics are the ones most likely to be included in IPS programs.[80]

IPS may also be more effective when it is combined with particular treatment modalities such as cognitive-behavioral treatment, which stresses such

intensive probation supervision (IPS)
A type of intermediate sanction involving small probation caseloads and strict monitoring on a daily or weekly basis.

life skills as problem solving, social skills, negotiation skills, management of emotion, and values enhancement.[81]

House Arrest

When Martha Stewart was released from prison in 2005, she was required to serve a five-month term of house arrest in which she could not leave home for more than 48 hours at a time and had to wear an electronic tracking device. Her sentence was not unique—except for the fact that her estate is so big that walking to the edges of the property put her out of range of her tracking device.

House arrest requires convicted offenders to spend extended periods of time in their own home as an alternative to an incarceration sentence. For example, persons convicted on a drunk-driving charge might be sentenced to spend between 6:00 P.M. Friday and 8:00 A.M. Monday and every weekday after 5:30 P.M. in their home for six months. According to current estimates, more than 10,000 people are under house arrest.

As with IPS programs, there is a great deal of variation in house arrest initiatives. Some are administered by probation departments, and others are simply judicial sentences monitored by surveillance officers. Some check clients 20 or more times a month, whereas others do only a few curfew checks. Some use 24-hour confinement; others allow offenders to attend work or school.

house arrest
A form of intermediate sanction that requires the convicted offender to spend a designated amount of time per week in his or her own home—such as from 5:00 P.M. Friday until 8:00 A.M. Monday.

No definitive data indicates that house arrest is an effective crime deterrent, nor is there sufficient evidence to conclude that it has utility as a device to lower the recidivism rate. One evaluation found that nearly 10 percent of the house arrest sample had their probation revoked for technical violations within 18 months of their sentencing.[82] Another found that recidivism rates were almost identical to a those of a matched sample of inmates released from secure correctional facilities; four out of five offenders in both forms of correction recidivated within five years.[83] Although

REALITY CHECK

MYTH OR REALITY?   It is permissible to force people to remain in their homes under "house arrest."

REALITY: House arrest is a widely used alternative sanction.

Is it punishment to be forced to stay at home with a 60-inch plasma TV, a high-speed Internet connection, good food, and a Jacuzzi?

House arrest allows convicted defendants to remain in the community with their families rather than being locked away in a distant prison. Magdalana Domingo Ramirez Lopez, 29, of Guatemala, shown here with one of her sons, Issias, tearfully talks about her ordeal a day after being arrested by federal agents at The House of Raeford's Columbia Farms chicken plant on October 8, 2008, in Greenville, South Carolina. Lopez was released for humanitarian reasons and put under house arrest for the sake of her three young sons, whom she cares for.

© AP Images/Mary Ann Chastain

these findings are troublesome, the advantages of house arrest in reducing costs and overcrowding in the correctional system probably make further experimentation inevitable.

Electronic Monitoring

For house arrest to work, sentencing authorities must be assured that arrestees are actually at home during their assigned times. Random calls and visits are one way to check on compliance with house arrest orders. However, one of the more interesting developments in the criminal justice system has been the introduction of **electronic monitoring (EM)** devices to manage offender obedience to home confinement orders.[84]

The most commonly used EM devices are described in Exhibit 10.4. Newer electronic monitoring systems now feature automatic tracking devices that limit offenders' movements to acceptable areas. Some rely on global positioning satellite (GPS) technology that enables authorities to monitor geographic locale and conditions of release. For example, the system can be programmed to indicate a violation whenever a known sex offender approaches a school or a day care center. Omnilink Systems of Alpharetta, Georgia, has developed an EM system that employs a cellular technology to locate a tracking device even when it's indoors. A single-unit ankle monitoring device is paired with monitoring software that gives law enforcement administrators the ability to set up offender profiles and then configure inclusion and exclusion zones for each one. If an offender violates a zone, an alert is immediately sent to appropriate individuals. In addition, a wireless tracking device alerts potential victims when a monitored offender is in the victim's vicinity in violation of a court restraining or protection order.[85] This is done by linking the wireless device to the victim's cell phone; if the offender comes within a certain distance of the cell phone, the victim is notified via phone and can seek safety until the police arrive. The Omnilink monitoring device can be programmed to various types

electronic monitoring (EM)
Requiring convicted offenders to wear a monitoring device as part of their community sentence. Typically part of a house arrest order, this enables the probation department to ensure that offenders are complying with court-ordered limitations on their freedom.

Electronic monitoring allows offenders to remain in the community where they can rehabilitate themselves and start a new life. This May 6, 2009, photo shows Deputy Larry LeJeune removing the ankle bracelet from Georgette Dietz in Opelousas, Louisiana, after she has been confined to the mechanism for one year. Dietz was the first person to receive an electronic ankle bracelet rather than jail time as part of an experimental program by the St. Landry Parish Sheriff's Office. After her release, Dietz said, "This program throws you a rope. You are either going to hang yourself or climb out of the hole you are in. It is a good opportunity if you want it to work." Dietz was convicted of distribution of Lortab, a prescription pain killer, and in February 2008 was fitted with one of the tracking bracelets. Today she is a cook at Kelly's Meat Block and Diner in Opelousas. "I run the grill. I make hamburgers, I grill chicken, fish, shrimp—whatever you want, I'll grill it," Dietz said. Owner Kelly Cormier admits he was not sure about the program at first but is now a strong supporter. He has so far hired three other former offenders.

© AP Images/*The Daily World*/Freddie Herpin

EXHIBIT 10.4

Available Electronic Monitoring Systems

- **Identity verification devices** range from personal identification numbers to biometric verification that recognizes different parts of the human body to ensure that the reporting person is the intended offender.

- **Remote alcohol detection devices** require users to blow into the device, which is usually in the offender's home, to measure blood alcohol content. The results are recorded by a computer to determine compliance with conditions of alcohol consumption.

- **Ignition interlock devices** are linked to the electrical systems of automobiles. The driver must expel deep lung air into the device to operate the vehicle. If the driver's blood alcohol content registers above a predetermined level deemed unsafe to drive, the vehicle will not start.

- **Programmed contact systems** are used to contact and verify the location of offenders in their homes or elsewhere. They use a central computer that either receives telephone calls from or makes calls to offenders in one or more locations.

- **Continuous signaling devices** are battery-powered and transmit a radio signal two or more times per minute. They are placed on the offender's wrist or ankle with a tamper-resistant strap and must be worn at all times. A receiver detects the transmitter's signals and conveys a message via telephone report to a central computer when either it stops receiving the radio frequency or the signal resumes. When installed in a typical home environment, receivers can detect transmitter signals from a distance of 150 feet or more.

- **Victim notification systems** alert the victim when the offender is approaching that person's residence. A transmitter is worn by both the offender and the victim, and a receiver is placed at both residences.

- **Field monitoring devices**, or "drive-by" units, are another type of continuous signaling technology. Probation or parole officers or other authorities use a portable device that can be handheld or used in a vehicle with a roof-mounted antenna. When within 200 to 800 feet of an offender's ankle or wrist transmitter, the portable device can detect the radio signals of the offender's transmitter.

- **Group monitoring units** allow supervisors to monitor several offenders in the same location, such as for verifying attendance of multiple offenders in a day-reporting program or monitoring offenders confined in a residential group setting.

- **Location tracking systems**, also known as global positioning systems, offer yet another way to monitor offenders. Receivers detect satellite signals that include the exact time the signal is sent and the identity of the satellite sending the signal. This information is processed to determine the person's location. This more expensive technology generally is used for high-risk offenders. It can determine when offenders leave an area where they are supposed to be (inclusion zone) or enter an area where they are not allowed to be (exclusion zone).

SOURCE: William Burrell and Robert Gable, "From B. F. Skinner to Spiderman to Martha Stewart: The Past, Present and Future of Electronic Monitoring of Offenders," *Journal of Offender Rehabilitation* 46 (2008): 101–118; Hugh Downing, "Emergence of Global Positioning Satellite (GPS) Systems in Correctional Applications," *Corrections Today* 68 (2006): 42–45.

of monitoring, including time-related curfews, enforcing prohibitions against monitored offenders being in certain areas (e.g., pedophiles being in specified areas frequented by children), and continuous tracking no matter where the offender is located.[86] These services are particularly important in domestic violence cases, where victims may not feel safe in their own home and are forced to flee to shelters.[87]

Electronic monitoring supporters claim EM has the benefits of relatively low cost and high security, while helping offenders avoid the pains of imprisonment in overcrowded, dangerous state facilities. Because offenders are monitored by computers, an initial investment in hardware eliminates the need for hiring many more supervisory officers to handle large numbers of clients. Because of its low cost and assumed effectiveness, EM is now being used with a wide variety of offenders, even those who have committed serious felony sex offenses.[88]

There is some evidence that EM can be effective. When Kathy Padget and her associates evaluated data on more than 75,000 offenders placed on home confinement in Florida, they found that EM significantly reduces the likelihood of technical violations, reoffending, and absconding.[89] However, some critics argue that the evidence that EM can lower recidivism rates is thin and that it may not work well as a stand-alone program. Instead, EM can improve public safety when it is combined with some other treatment modality, such as social interventions and counseling.[90]

Residential Community Corrections

The most secure intermediate sanction is a sentence to a **residential community corrections (RCC)** facility. Such a facility has been defined as "a freestanding nonsecure building that is not part of a prison or jail and houses pretrial and adjudicated adults. The residents regularly depart to work, to attend school, and/or [to] participate in treatment activities and programs."[91]

Traditionally, the role of community corrections was played by the nonsecure halfway house, which was designed to reintegrate soon-to-be-paroled prison inmates into the community. Inmates spend the last few months of their sentence in the halfway house, acquiring suitable employment, building up cash reserves, obtaining an apartment, and developing a job-related wardrobe.

The traditional concept of community corrections has expanded. Today, the community correctional facility is a vehicle to provide intermediate sanctions as well as a prerelease center for those about to be paroled from the prison system. RCC has been used as a direct sentencing option for judges who believe particular offenders need a correctional alternative halfway between traditional probation and a stay in prison. Placement in an RCC center can be used as a condition of probation for offenders who need a nonsecure community facility that provides a more structured treatment environment than traditional probation. It is commonly used in the juvenile justice system for youths who need a more secure environment than can be provided by traditional probation yet are not deemed a threat to the community and do not require a secure placement.

Probation departments and other correctional authorities have been given the responsibility of running RCC centers that serve as a pre-prison sentencing alternative. In addition, some RCC centers are operated by private, nonprofit groups that receive referrals from the county or district courts and from probation or parole departments. Portland House, a private residential center in Minneapolis, operates as an alternative to incarceration for young adult offenders. The 25 residents regularly receive group therapy and financial, vocational, educational, family, and personal counseling. Residents may work to earn a high school equivalency degree. With funds withheld from their earnings at work-release employment, residents pay room and board, family and self-support, and income taxes. Portland House appears to be successful. It is significantly cheaper to run than a state institution, and the recidivism rate of clients is much lower than that of those who have gone through traditional correctional programs.[92]

More than 2,000 state-run community-based facilities are in use today. In addition, up to 2,500 private, nonprofit RCC programs operate in the United States. About half also house inmates who have been released from prison and use the RCC placement as a way to ease back into society. The remainder are true intermediate sanctions, including about 400 federally sponsored programs.

residential community corrections (RCC)
A nonsecure facility, located in the community, that houses probationers who need a more secure environment. Typically, residents are free during the day to go to work, school, or treatment, and they return in the evening for counseling sessions and meals.

© VisionsofAmerica/Joe Sohm /Getty Images

day reporting center (DRC)

A nonresidential community-based treatment program.

DAY REPORTING CENTERS ● One recent development in community corrections has been the use of RCC facilities as **day reporting centers (DRCs)**.[93] These provide a single location to which a variety of clients can report for supervision and treatment. Used in New Jersey, Georgia, Delaware, Utah, and other jurisdictions, DRCs serve nonresidential clients in existing RCC facilities. They can be used as a step up in security for probationers who have failed in the community and as a step down in security for jail or prison inmates.[94] The Atlanta Day Reporting Center, which opened in June 2001, was developed as a joint project by the Georgia Parole Board and the Department of Corrections. It provides 125 probationers and parolees with structured daily programs in GED preparation, recovery from substance abuse, and cognitive skills training. Although offenders return to their homes at night, the center intensifies training and support and thus offers many of the well-documented benefits of traditional halfway houses.[95]

Evaluations show that DRCs can be successful at reducing recivism.[96] DRCs seem to work better with certain types of offenders, such as those who are older and more experienced, than with others, such as younger offenders.[97] DRC participants with alcohol problems, criminal companions, and poor living situations are also more likely to fail. In contrast, those who receive counseling seem to do better.[98]

Concept Summary 10.1 sets out the goals and problems of the various forms of intermediate sanctions.

© X Brand Images/Getty Images

Concept Summary 10.1

Intermediate Sanctions

Sanction	Goal	Problems
Fines	Monetary sanction	Overburdens the poor
Forfeiture	Monetary sanction, equity	Can be overreaching
Restitution	Pay back victim	Does not reduce recidivism
Shock incarceration and split sentence	"Taste of bars" as a deterrent	Can cause labeling and stigma
Intensive probation	Small caseloads, more supervision	High failure rate
House arrest	Avoids jail	Lacks treatment possibility
Electronic monitoring	Supervision by computer	Technology-dependent, no treatment
Residential community	Less secure than prison	Expensive, high failure rate

Restorative Justice

Some critics and specialists in criminal justice believe that the new alternative and intermediate sanctions add a punitive aspect to community sentencing that can hinder rehabilitation efforts. Instead, the advocates of **restorative justice** suggest a policy based on restoring the damage caused by crime and creating a system of justice that includes all the parties harmed by the criminal act: the victim, the offender, the community, and society.[99]

Restorative justice models are consistent with the thought of Australian justice expert John Braithwaite, who argues that crime control today involves shaming and stigmatizing offenders. This helps set them apart from normative society and undermines their potential for change. Instead he calls for a policy of "reintegrative shaming." Here disapproval is limited to the offender's evil deeds. Law violators must be brought to realize that although their actions have caused harm, they are still valuable people—people who can be reaccepted by society. A critical element of reintegrative shaming occurs when the offenders themselves begin to understand and recognize their wrongdoing and shame. To be reintegrative, shaming must be brief and controlled, and it must be followed by ceremonies of forgiveness, apology, and repentance.[100] Braithwaite's work is at the core of the restorative justice movement.

restorative justice
A view of criminal justice that focuses on crime as an act against the community rather than the state. Justice should involve all parties affected by crime—victims, criminals, law enforcement, and the community.

Restorative Justice Online

Restorative Justice Online is a clearing house of information, including research tools, bibliographies, training, tutorials, and articles on restoration. It is available at **www.cengage.com/criminaljustice/siegel**

A Florida Parishes Juvenile Detention Center detainee works in the center's garden in Goodbee, Louisiana. Detainees give back to the community by harvesting the produce and donating it to a local food pantry. Juvenile detainees are learning restorative justice with programs like these that teach new skills and encourage them to give back to the community.

© AP Images/Daily Star/Keri Wheeler

The Concept of Restoration

According to the restorative view, crimes bring harm to the community in which they occur. The traditional justice system has done little to involve the community in the justice process. What has developed is a system of coercive punishments administered by bureaucrats that is inherently harmful to offenders and reduces the likelihood that they will ever again become productive members of society. This system relies on punishment, stigma, and disgrace. What is needed instead is a justice policy that repairs the harm caused by crime and involves all parties that have suffered from that harm, including the victim, the community, and the offender. Exhibit 10.5 sets out the principles of the restorative justice approach.

An important aspect of achieving these goals is that offenders must accept accountability for their actions and responsibility for the harm their actions caused. Only then can they be restored as productive members of their community. Restoration involves turning the justice system into a "healing" process rather than a distributor of retribution and revenge.

Most people involved in offender–victim relationships actually know one another or were related in some way before the criminal incident took place. Instead of treating one of the involved parties as a victim deserving sympathy and the other as a criminal deserving punishment, it is more productive to address the issues that produced the conflict between these people. Rather than taking sides and choosing whom to isolate and punish, society should try to reconcile the parties involved in conflict.[101] The effectiveness of justice ultimately depends on the stake a person has in the community (or a particular social group). If a person does not value her membership in the group, she will be unlikely to accept responsibility, show remorse, or repair the injuries caused by her actions.

Restoration Programs

Restoration programs try to include all the parties involved in a criminal act: the victim, the offender, and the community. Although processes differ in structure and style, they generally include the following:

- Recognition by offenders that they have caused injury to personal and social relations, and a determination and acceptance of responsibility (ideally accompanied by a statement of remorse)

EXHIBIT 10.5

Basic Principles of Restorative Justice

- Crime is an offense against human relationships.
- Victims and the community are central to justice processes.
- The first priority of justice processes is to assist victims.
- The second priority is to restore the community, to the greatest degree possible.
- The offender has a personal responsibility to victims and to the community for crimes committed.
- The offender will develop improved competency and understanding as a result of the restorative justice experience.
- Stakeholders share responsibilities for restorative justice through partnerships for action.

Source: Anne Seymour, "Restorative Justice/Community Justice," in the *National Victim Assistance Academy Textbook* (Washington, D.C.: National Victim Assistance Academy, 2001); updated June 2008.

- A commitment to both material reparation (e.g., monetary restitution) and symbolic reparation (e.g., an apology)
- A determination of community support and assistance for both victim and offender

The intended result of the process is to repair injuries suffered by the victim and the community, while ensuring reintegration of the offender.

Negotiation, mediation, consensus building, and peacemaking have been part of the dispute resolution process in European and Asian communities for centuries.[102] Native American people and members of Canada's First Nations have long used the type of community participation in the adjudication process (in sentencing circles, sentencing panels, and panels of elders) that restorative justice advocates are now embracing.[103]

In some Native American communities, people accused of breaking the law meet with community members, victims (if any), village elders, and agents of the justice system in a **sentencing circle**. All members of the circle express their feelings about the act that was committed and raise questions or concerns. The accused can express regret about his or her actions and a desire to change the harmful behavior. People may suggest ways in which the offender can make things up to the community and those who were harmed. A treatment program, such as Alcoholics Anonymous, may be suggested, if appropriate.

Restoration in Practice

Restorative justice policies and practices are now being adapted around the world. Legislation in 19 states includes reference to the use of victim–offender mediation. There are more than 1,400 victim–offender mediation programs in North America and Europe.[104] Restorative justice is being embraced on many levels in the justice system.

SCHOOLS ● Some schools have employed restorative justice practices to avoid more punitive measures such as expulsion in dealing with students involved in drug and alcohol abuse. Schools in Minnesota, Colorado, and elsewhere are now trying to involve students in "relational rehabilitation" programs, which strive to improve offenders' relationships with key figures in the community who may have been harmed by their actions.[105]

POLICE PROGRAMS ● Restorative justice has also been implemented when police first encounter crime. The new community policing models can be viewed as an attempt to incorporate restorative concepts into law enforcement. Restorative justice relies on criminal justice policymakers listening to and responding to the needs of those who will be affected by their actions, and community policing relies on policies established with input and exchanges between officers and citizens.[106] The technique is also being used by police around the world. In England, police are using a format called restorative cautioning. After an arrest is made, police in England and Wales traditionally had four alternative procedures they could follow: (1) take no further action; (2) give an informal warning; (3) administer a formal police caution; or (4) decide to prosecute by sending the case to the Crown Prosecution Service. English police forces are now experimenting with a form of restorative cautioning. In this approach, a trained police facilitator uses a script to encourage an offender to take responsibility for repairing the harm caused by the offense. Sometimes the victim is present, in which case the meeting is called a restorative conference; usually, however, the victim is not present. Traditional cautioning, by contrast, lasts only a few minutes, requires no special training, and focuses on the officer explaining the possible consequences of future offending. Even

sentencing circles
A type of sentencing in which victims, family members, community members, and the offender participate in an effort to devise fair and reasonable sanctions that are ultimately aimed at reintegrating the offender into the community.

though the police report that the new system seems to be working quite well (crime rates are down as much as 30 percent), some experts have questioned whether restorative cautioning can produce the results being claimed.[107]

PRETRIAL PROGRAMS • Some jurisdictions have instituted restorative justice programs as a form of diversion from the court process. One program is called conferencing; its aim is to divert offenders from the justice system by offering them the opportunity to attend a conference to discuss and resolve the offense instead of being charged and appearing in court.[108] Conferencing is not offered when offenders wish to contest their guilt. Those who do not are referred to the conference, which normally lasts one to two hours and is attended by the victims and their supporters, the offenders and their supporters, and other relevant parties. The conference coordinator focuses the discussion on condemning the act without condemning the character of the actor. Offenders are asked to explain what happened, how they have felt about the crime, and what they think should be done. The victims and others are asked to describe the physical, financial, and emotional consequences of the crime. This discussion may lead the offenders, their families, and their friends to experience the shame of the act, prompting an apology to the victim. A plan of action is developed and signed by key participants. The plan may include the offender paying compensation to the victim, doing work for the victim or the community, or any other undertaking the participants may agree on. It is the responsibility of the conference participants to determine the outcomes that are most appropriate for these particular victims and these particular offenders.

COURT PROGRAMS • In the court system, restorative programs usually involve diverting the offender from the formal court process. Instead, these programs encourage meeting and reconciling the conflicts between offenders and victims via victim advocacy, mediation programs, and sentencing circles, in which crime victims and their families are brought together with offenders and their families in an effort to formulate a sanction that addresses the needs of each party. Victims are given a chance to tell their stories, and offenders can help compensate them financially or provide some service (such as repairing damaged property).[109] Again, the goal is to enable offenders to appreciate the damage they have caused, to make amends, and to be reintegrated into society. Restorative justice has found a niche all over the world. It is even being used to resolve cases in the Middle East involving Arabs and Israelis![110]

REALITY CHECK

MYTH OR REALITY? Some jurisdictions encourage face-to-face meetings between offenders and victims and allow victims to participate in justice decision making

REALITY: Restorative justice programs encourage offender–victim reconciliation.

What do you think of this type of program?

The Challenge of Restorative Justice

Although restorative justice holds great promise, there are also some concerns.[111] One issue is whether programs reach out to all members of the community. Research indicates that entry into these programs may be tilted toward white offenders and more restrictive to minorities, a condition that negates the purpose of the restorative movement.[112]

Restorative justice programs must be especially aware of cultural and social differences, which can be found throughout America's heterogeneous society.[113] What may be considered restorative in one subculture may be considered insulting and damaging in another.[114] Similarly, so many diverse programs call themselves restorative that evaluating them is difficult. Each one may be pursuing a unique objective. In other words, no single definition of restorative justice has been arrived at.[115]

Possibly the greatest challenge to restorative justice is the difficult task of balancing the needs of offenders with those of their victims. If programs focus solely on responding to the victim's needs, they may risk ignoring the offender's needs and increasing the likelihood of reoffending. Sharon Levrant and her colleagues suggest that restorative justice programs featuring short-term interactions with victims fail to help offenders learn prosocial ways of behaving. Advocates of restorative justice may falsely assume that relatively brief interludes of public shaming will change deeply rooted criminal predispositions.[116] But is it reasonable to include any form of punishment or sanction in a "restorative"-based program?[117]

In contrast, programs focusing on the offender may turn off victims and their advocates. Some victim advocacy groups have voiced concerns about the focus of restorative justice programs. Some believe that victims' rights are threatened by features of the restorative justice process, such as respectful listening to the offender's story and consensual dispositions. These features seem affronts to a victim's claim of the right to be seen as a victim, to insist on the offender being branded a criminal, to blame the offender, and not to be "victimized all over again by the process." Many victims do want apology, if it is heartfelt and easy to get. But some want, even more urgently, to put the traumatic incident behind them, to retrieve stolen property being held for use at trial, and to be assured that the offender will receive treatment he is thought to need if he is not to victimize someone else. For victims such as these, restorative justice processes can seem unnecessary at best.[118]

These are a few of the obstacles that restorative justice programs must overcome in order to be successful and productive. Yet because the method holds so much promise, criminologists are conducting numerous demonstration projects to find the most effective means of returning the ownership of justice to the people and the community.

ETHICAL CHALLENGES IN CRIMINAL JUSTICE

A WRITING ASSIGNMENT

You are a district court judge. Before you is the case of a famous 26-year-old party-girl-model-hotel-heiress who was arrested for reckless driving at 2:00 A.M., even though she was under a probation order forbidding any misbehavior and imposing an 11:00 P.M. curfew. The sentencing judge had warned her against any further violations and made it clear that violating the conditions of probation would not be tolerated. How would you deal with the case? Should she be jailed for her behavior, or are alternative sanctions available? How do you justify your decision, and on what theory or view of justice is it based?

RealityCheck Revisited

To learn more about the myths and realities related to community sentences that were raised in this chapter, visit the following websites.

- You can learn more about victim/offender reconciliation at

http://www.restorativejustice.org/

http://www.vorp.com/

- Worried about forfeiting your house or car? Go to

http://www.expertlaw.com/library/criminal/forfeiture.html

http://www.drugwarfacts.org/cms/?q=node/42

SUMMARY

© AP Images/Matt York

1. Be familiar with the concept of community sentencing

- Many of those convicted in criminal courts can be reintegrated into the community, and, given the proper treatment, they are unlikely to recidivate.

- There are now a great variety of community sentences, ranging from traditional probation to house arrest and placement in community correctional centers.

- Community sentences can be structured to maximize security and maintain public safety.

2. Know the history of community sentences

- The roots of probation can be traced to the traditions of the English common law.

During the Middle Ages, judges who wanted to spare deserving offenders the pains of punishment granted clemency and stays of execution.

- The common-law practice of judicial reprieve allowed judges to suspend punishment so that convicted offenders could seek a pardon, gather new evidence, or demonstrate that they had reformed their behavior.

- John Augustus of Boston is usually credited with originating the modern probation concept.

3. Recognize the different types of probation sentences

- Probation today is a nonpunitive form of sentencing for convicted criminal offenders and delinquent youths, emphasizing maintenance in the community and treatment without institutionalization or other forms of punishment.

- Offenders who are on probation have been convicted of a crime, but instead of being incarcerated, they are returned to the community for a period in which they must abide by certain conditions set forth by the court under the supervision of a probation officer.

- Probationary sentences may be granted by state and federal district courts and state superior (felony) courts.

- Probation is also a means of reducing the population overload in an overcrowded and underfunded correctional system.

- About 4 million people are currently on probation.

4. Be familiar with the rules of probation

- When granting probation, the court sets down certain conditions or rules of behavior that the probationer is bound to obey.

- Rules can set curfews, prohibit behaviors such as drinking and owning a gun, and/or mandate that the probationer hold a job and not leave the jurisdiction without permission.

- Probation may be revoked if clients fail to comply with rules and disobey reasonable requests to meet their treatment obligations.

5. Discuss the organization and administration of probation services

- Some states have a statewide probation service, but each court jurisdiction controls its local department. Other states maintain a strong statewide authority with centralized control and administration.

- Staff officers in probation departments are usually charged with five primary tasks: investigation, intake, diagnosis, treatment supervision, and risk classification.

6. Define and discuss the term "risk classification"

- As part of clients' entry into probation, an assessment is made about how much risk they pose to the community and themselves.

- On the basis of this assessment, offenders are assigned to a specific supervision level.

7. Be familiar with the legal issues of probation

- The U.S. Supreme Court has ruled that probationers have a unique status and therefore are entitled to fewer constitutional protections than other citizens.

- During the course of a probationary term, violating the rules or terms of probation or committing a new crime can result in probation being revoked.

8. Debate the effectiveness of probation

- Probation is cost-effective. Incarcerating an inmate typically costs over $25,000 per year, whereas probation costs about $2,000 per year.

- National data indicates that about 60 percent of probationers successfully complete their probationary sentence, whereas about 40 percent are rearrested, violate probation rules, or abscond.

- Although the failure rate seems disturbingly high, even the most serious criminals who receive probation are less likely to recidivate than those who are sent to prison for committing similar crimes.

- Young males who are unemployed or who have a very low income, a prior criminal record, and a history of instability are most likely to be rearrested.

9. Know what is meant by intermediate sanctions

- Intermediate sanctions offer effective alternatives to prisons and jails.

- They also have the potential to save money; although they are more expensive than traditional probation, they are far less costly than incarceration.

- Fines are monetary payments imposed on offenders as an intermediate punishment for their criminal acts.

- In the United States, fines are most commonly used in cases involving misdemeanors and lesser offenses.

- Day fines are geared to an offender's net daily income.

- Criminal (in personam) and civil (in rem) forfeiture involve the seizure of goods and instrumentalities related to the commission or outcome of a criminal act.

- Restitution, which can take the form of requiring offenders either to pay back the victims of crime (monetary restitution) or to serve the community to compensate for their criminal acts (community service restitution), is a popular intermediate sanction.

(continued)

- Shock probation and split sentences are alternative sanctions designed to allow judges to grant offenders community release only after they have sampled prison life.

- Intensive probation supervision (IPS) programs involve small caseloads of 15 to 40 clients who are kept under close watch by probation officers.

- The house arrest concept requires convicted offenders to spend extended periods of time in their own home as an alternative to an incarceration sentence.

- Electronically monitored offenders wear devices that send signals to a control office; the devices are worn around their ankles, wrists, or necks.

- The most secure intermediate sanction is a sentence to a residential community corrections (RCC) facility.

- Day reporting centers provide a single location to which a variety of clients can report for supervision and treatment.

10. *Define restorative justice and discuss its merits*

- Restorative justice advocates suggest a policy based on restoring the damage caused by crime and creating a system of justice that includes all the parties harmed by the criminal act: the victim, the offender, the community, and society.

- Restorative programs stress healing and redemption rather than punishment and deterrence.

- Restoration means that offenders accept accountability for their actions and responsibility for the harm their actions caused.

- Restoration programs are now being used around the nation and involve mediation, sentencing circles, and the like.

- Although restorative justice holds great promise, there are also some concerns.

Key Terms

Review Questions

1. What is the purpose of probation? Identify some conditions of probation and discuss the responsibilities of the probation officer.

2. Discuss the procedures involved in probation revocation. What are the rights of the probationer? Is probation a privilege or a right? Explain.

3. Should a convicted criminal make restitution to the victim? Why or why not? When is restitution inappropriate?

4. Should offenders be fined on the basis of the seriousness of what they did or in terms of their ability to pay? Is it fair to base day fines on wages? Why or why not? Should offenders be punished more severely because they are financially successful? Explain.

5. Does house arrest involve a violation of personal freedom? Does wearing an ankle bracelet smack of "Big Brother"? Would you want the government monitoring your daily activities? Could this be expanded, for example, to monitor the whereabouts of AIDS patients? Explain.

6. Do you agree that criminals can be restored through community interaction? Considering the fact that recidivism rates are so high, are traditional sanctions a waste of time and restorative ones the wave of the future?

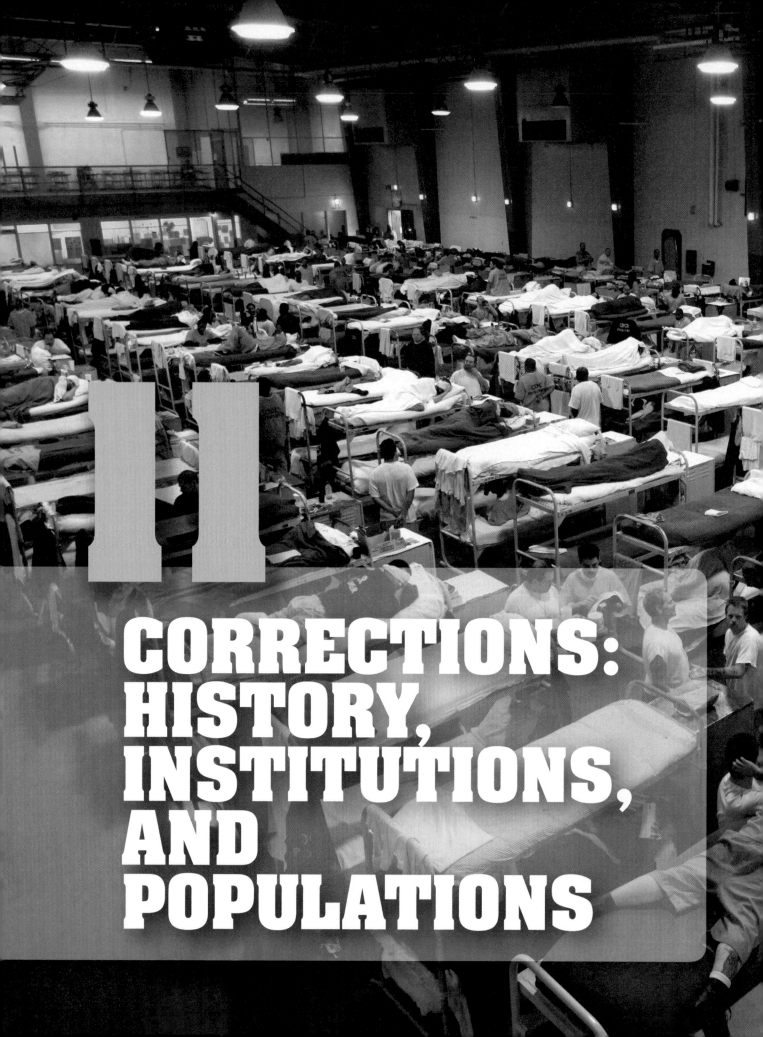

II

CORRECTIONS: HISTORY, INSTITUTIONS, AND POPULATIONS

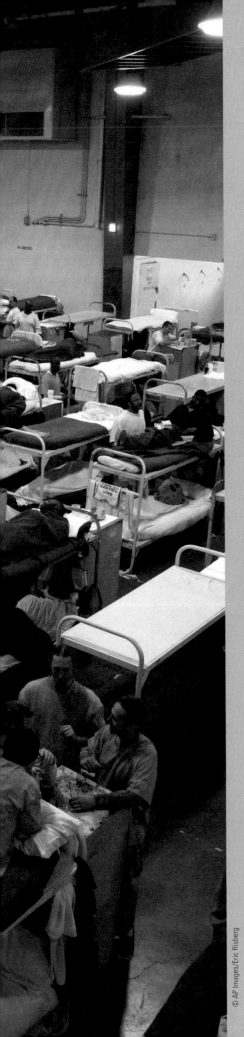

© AP Images/Eric Risberg

RealityCheck

MYTH or REALITY?

▶ The correctional system is not as effective as was hoped: Recidivism rates remain unacceptably high.

▶ The first correctional institutions were actually considered a "liberal" reform.

▶ Educating inmates began in the 1960s during the Kennedy administration.

▶ Many jail inmates suffer from social and mental problems.

▶ Super-maximum-security prisons are highly effective.

▶ The inmate population is now decreasing because the crime rate is down.

Learning Objectives

1. Identify the various components of the correctional institution system

2. Discuss some of the most significant problems facing the correctional system

3. Be able to explain how the first penal institutions developed in Europe

4. Explain how William Penn revolutionized corrections

5. Compare the New York and Pennsylvania prison models

6. Chart the development of penal reform

7. List the purposes of jails and be familiar with the makeup of jail populations

8. Be familiar with the term "new-generation jail"

9. Classify the different types of federal and state penal institutions

10. Discuss prison population trends

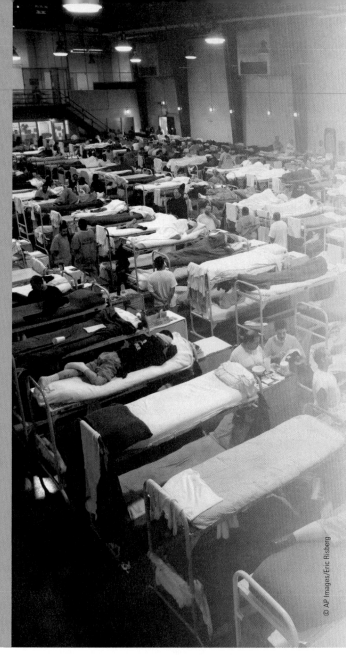

Chapter Outline

© AP Images/Eric Risberg

Career Profile

Gina Curcio is a correctional officer at the Essex County House of Corrections in Middleton, Massachusetts. Her many duties include supervising inmates; conducting random and timed rounds to ensure inmate census and safety; updating the daily unit logs that record unit activities; documenting all incidents/altercations (fights, medical emergencies, inmates harming themselves, and the like); enforcing unit rules and regulations, as well as department policies and procedures; developing working relationships with offenders in order to connect them with appropriate programs and services; and conducting cell searches and pat searches for contraband.

Gina finds that her job can be a mystery to people and that most civilians have no idea what a correctional facility is like or what kinds of programs and services it offers. Her friends think that jails (which are called "houses of correction" in Massachusetts) hold only offenders who commit minor offenses, such as DUI or failure to pay child support. But Essex County also holds pretrial detainees, many of whom are federal inmates charged with very serious offenses, including murder, drug trafficking, and rape. Why are they being held in a local jail? The corrections department is paid a daily fee to detain and house federal inmates until they can be tried and sentenced.

Another common misconception, Gina finds, is that people think guards are armed to the teeth inside the facility in order to be able to protect themselves from inmates. People are dumbfounded when she tells them that because the Essex County House of Corrections is a direct-supervision facility (meaning that officers are on the housing units with all the inmates), correctional officers are not permitted to carry weapons inside the facility. Only when transporting inmates or doing a hospital detail are correctional officers allowed to carry a gun, a baton, and/or pepper spray.

Gina holds a bachelor's degree in Criminal Justice with a minor in Spanish; she is enrolled in a masters degree program in criminal justice. She really likes her job and finds the greatest rewards are the sense of camaraderie and teamwork, the experience in criminal justice, and some great job-related benefits, such as health insurance, all kinds of incentives (including opportunities to enhance physical fitness, education, and so on), and tuition reimbursement. She works hard to gain respect, which, as a young female officer, is something she feels she has to do. She hopes someday to teach criminal justice and use the experience and knowledge she has gained on the job in the classroom.

Correctional officers such as Gina Curcio are the backbone of a vast organization of corrections that has branches in the federal, state, and county levels of government. Felons may be placed in state or federal penitentiaries (prisons), which are usually isolated, high-security structures. Misdemeanants are housed in local county jails, reformatories, or houses of correction. Juvenile offenders have their own institutions called schools, camps, ranches, or homes; these are typically nonsecure facilities that provide both confinement and rehabilitative services for young offenders. However, not all juveniles are confined in separate institutions. Some who commit serious crimes can be transferred to the adult court and serve their sentence in an adult prison with older, more experienced criminals.

The contemporary correctional system, then, encompasses a wide range of institutions ranging from nonsecure camps that house white-collar criminals to super-maximum-security institutions, such as the federal prison in Florence, Colorado, where the nation's most dangerous felons are confined.

One of the great tragedies of our time is that "correctional" institutions—whatever form they may take—do not seem to "correct," and many former inmates recidivate soon after reentering society. It can be reasonably estimated that more than half of all inmates will be back in prison within six years of their release; this means that each year about 250,000 former inmates return to prison because they failed on parole.[1]

REALITYCHECK

MYTH OR REALITY? The correctional system is not as effective as was hoped: Recidivism rates remain unacceptably high.

REALITY: More than half of all released inmates return to prison.

What is it about the prison experience that causes people to fail on parole?

prison

A state or federal correctional institution for incarceration of felony offenders for terms of one year or more.

jail

A place to detain people awaiting trial, to serve as a lockup for drunks and disorderly individuals, and to confine convicted misdemeanants serving sentences of less than one year.

There has been an on-going debate over the true role of secure corrections. Some penal experts maintain that **prisons** and **jails** should be used to keep dangerous offenders apart from society, dispensing "just deserts" for their crimes.[2] Under this model, correctional effectiveness is measured in terms of such outcomes as physical security, length of incapacitation, and inmates who return to society fearing criminal sanctions. An opposing view is that the purpose of corrections is treatment and that, when properly funded and effectively directed, correctional facilities can provide successful offender rehabilitation.[3] Numerous examples of successful treatment programs flourish in prisons: Educational programs enable inmates to get college credits, vocational training has become more sophisticated, counseling and substance abuse programs are almost universal, and every state maintains early-release and community correctional programs of some sort.

Today the desert/incapacitation model, sometimes called the *new penology*, holds sway. Rather than administer individualized treatment, decision makers rely of actuarial tables and tests to make decisions; indeed, they seem more concerned with security and "managing" large inmate populations than with treating individual offenders.[4] Critics charge that this policy has resulted in a rapidly increasing prison population that is bereft of the human touch; defenders counter that it is effective because the crime rate has declined as the number of people under lock and key has risen. The connection between a declining crime rate and a rising prison population is not lost on politicians who are eager to energize their political campaigns by advocating a "get tough" policy toward crime.[5] Nonetheless, even though the new penology dominates, correctional rehabilitation is still an important element of the justice system, and there are numerous opportunities for careers in such positions as corrections counselor (see the Careers in Criminal Justice feature on page 375).

In this chapter, we explore the correctional system, beginning with the history and nature of correctional institutions. Then, in Chapter 12, we will examine institutional life in some detail.

The History of Correctional Institutions

The original legal punishments were typically banishment or slavery, restitution, corporal punishment, and execution. The concept of incarcerating convicted offenders for long periods of time as a punishment for their misdeeds did not become the norm of corrections until the nineteenth century.[6]

Although the use of incarceration as a routine punishment began much later, some early European institutions were created specifically to detain and punish criminal offenders. Penal institutions were constructed in England during the tenth century to hold pretrial detainees and those waiting for their sentence to be carried out.[7] During the twelfth century, King Henry II constructed a series of county jails to hold thieves and vagrants before the disposition of their sentence. In 1557 the workhouse in Brideswell was built to hold people convicted of relatively minor offenses who would work to pay off their debt to society. Those who had committed more serious offenses were held there pending execution.

Le Stinche, a prison in Florence, Italy, was used to punish offenders as early as 1301.[8] Prisoners were enclosed in separate cells, classified on the basis of gender, age, mental state, and seriousness of their crime. Furloughs and conditional release were permitted, and—perhaps for the first time—a period of incarceration replaced corporal punishment for some offenses. Although Le Stinche existed for 500 years, relatively little is known about its administration or whether this early example of incarceration was unique to Florence.

Careers in Criminal Justice

CORRECTIONS COUNSELOR

Duties and Characteristics of the Job

- Corrections counselors' responsibility is to review the situation of individual offenders and determine the most effective method of rehabilitation.
- They create, enact, manage, and sometimes evaluate programs designed to improve the psychosocial functioning of offenders.
- Correctional counselors also provide counseling and educational sessions, survey the needs of offenders, and prepare reports for court.
- Counselors can choose a specialization, such as substance abuse or juvenile rehabbilitation.
- Corrections counselors most often work in an office setting.
- Counseling can be a stressful job, considering the population being served, the often serious nature of their problems, and the pressure for immediate results.

Job Outlook

- The employment of counselors is expected to grow at a faster than average rate in the near future.
- The expansion of the prison system means that opportunities for employment as a corrections counselor are good.

Salary

- Counselors' median salary is $47,350.
- Positions at the federal level will generally pay a higher salary. Those with graduate-level education are also more likely to have higher salaries and greater opportunities for advancement.

Opportunities

- The need for correctional counselors should remain strong, especially if violent crime rates trend upward and courts mandate treatment for all inmates.

Qualifications

- Future corrections counselors should have a bachelor's degree in a field such as social work, criminal justice, or psychology.
- Additional education at the master's level in these fields may be necessary to advance in the field or to achieve certain positions. Qualifications for higher-paid positions are more demanding.
- Special qualifications such as expertise working with drug addicts or violent offenders can lead to a higher-paying position.
- In addition to educational requirements, for many entry-level jobs some previous work experience will be necessary, such as substance abuse counseling or corrections casework.
- The ability to speak a second language is also an advantage.
- Personality characteristics and skills such as the desire to help others and the ability to communicate effectively are important.
- Due to the settings and populations that counselors work with, a future counselor will need to pass a background check and gain security clearance of the appropriate level. Additionally, certain states require certification before a corrections counselor can work in that state.

Education and Training

- Counselors' education and work experience should familiarize them with the criminal justice system and prepare them for determining how to reduce a client's chances of recidivism as well as how to deal with unwilling clients.
- For some positions, clinical training can take the place of experience.

World to the Wise

- Counselors should be prepared to work with needy, troubled people. Burnout can be a problem. It is important not to personalize the work or "take it home."

Jail conditions were deplorable because jailers ran them for personal gain. The fewer the services provided, the greater their profit. Early jails were catch-all institutions that held not only criminal offenders awaiting trial but also vagabonds, debtors, the mentally ill, and assorted others.

From 1776 to 1785, a growing inmate population that could no longer be transported to North America forced the English to house prisoners on **hulks**—abandoned ships anchored in harbors.

hulks

Abandoned ships, anchored in harbors, that were used in eighteenth-century England to house prisoners.

The hulks became infamous for their degrading conditions and brutal punishments but were not abandoned until 1858. The writings of John Howard, the reform-oriented sheriff of Bedfordshire, drew attention to the squalid conditions in British penal institutions. His famous book *The State of the Prisons* (1777), condemned the lack of basic care given English inmates awaiting trial or serving sentences.[9] Howard's efforts to create humane standards in the British penal system resulted in the Penitentiary Act, by which Parliament established a more orderly penal system, with periodic inspections, elimination of the fee system, and greater consideration for inmates.

The Origin of Corrections in the United States

Although Europe had jails and a variety of other penal facilities, correctional reform was first instituted in the United States. The first American jail was built in James City in the Virginia colony in the early seventeenth century. However, the modern American correctional system had its origin in Pennsylvania under the leadership of William Penn.

At the end of the seventeenth century, Penn revised Pennsylvania's criminal code to forbid torture and the capricious use of mutilation and physical punishment. These penalties were replaced with imprisonment at hard labor, flogging, fines, and forfeiture of property. All lands and goods belonging to felons were to be used to make restitution to the victims of their crimes, with restitution being limited to twice the value of the damages. Felons who owned no property were assigned by law to the prison workhouse until the victim was compensated.

Penn ordered that a new type of institution be built to replace the widely used public forms of punishment—stocks, pillories, gallows, and branding irons. Each county was instructed to build a house of corrections similar to today's jails. County trustees or commissioners were responsible for raising money to build the jails and providing for their maintenance, although they were operated by the local sheriff. Penn's reforms remained in effect until his death in 1718, at which time the criminal penal code was changed back to open public punishment and harsh brutality.

Two of the first American penal institutions were Newgate Prison, which opened in 1773 in Connecticut on the site of an abandoned copper mine and was in use until the 1820s.[10] In 1785, Castle Island prison was opened in Massachusetts and operated for about 15 years. However, the origin of the modern correctional system is usually traced to eighteenth-century developments.

The Development of Prisons

Why did prisons develop at this time? One reason was that during this period of enlightenment, a concerted effort was made to alleviate the harsh punishments and torture that had been the norm. The interest of religious groups, such as the Quakers, in prison reform was prompted in part by humanitarian ideals. Another factor was the economic potential of prison industry, which was viewed as a valuable economic asset in times of short labor supply.[11]

In 1776 these trends led Pennsylvania once again to adopt William Penn's code, and in 1787 a group of Quakers led by Benjamin Rush formed the Philadelphia

Society for Alleviating the Miseries of Public Prisons. The aim of the society was to bring some degree of humane and orderly treatment to the growing penal system. The Quakers' influence on the legislature resulted in limiting the use of the death penalty to cases involving treason, murder, rape, or arson. Their next step was to reform the institutional system so that the prison could serve as a suitable alternative to physical punishment.

The only models of custodial institutions at that time were the local county jails that Penn had established. These facilities were designed to detain offenders, to securely incarcerate convicts awaiting other punishment, or to hold offenders who were working off their crimes. The Pennsylvania jails placed men, women, and children of all ages indiscriminately in one room. Liquor was often freely sold.

Under pressure from the Quakers to improve these conditions, the Pennsylvania legislature in 1790 called for the renovation of the prison system. The eventual result was the creation of a separate wing of Philadelphia's **Walnut Street Jail** to house convicted felons (except those sentenced to death). Prisoners were placed in solitary cells, where they remained in isolation and did not have the right to work.[12] Quarters that contained the solitary or separate cells were called the **penitentiary house**, as was already the custom in England.

The new Pennsylvania prison system took credit for a rapid decrease in the crime rate—from 131 convictions in 1789 to 45 in 1793.[13] The prison became known as a school for reform and a place for public labor. However, the Walnut Street Jail was not a total success. Isolation had a terrible psychological effect on inmates, and eventually inmates were given in-cell piecework on which they worked for up to eight hours a day. Overcrowding undermined the goal of solitary confinement of serious offenders, and soon more than one inmate was placed in each cell. Despite these difficulties, similar institutions were erected in New York (Newgate in 1791) and New Jersey (Trenton in 1798).

The New York and Pennsylvania Systems

As the nineteenth century got under way, both the Pennsylvania and the New York prison systems were experiencing difficulties maintaining the ever-increasing numbers of convicted criminals. Initially, administrators dealt

Walnut Street Jail
An eighteenth-century institution that housed convicted criminals in Philadelphia.

penitentiary houses
Early prisons, so named because inmates were supposed to be penitent for their sins.

"Prisoners Exercising," by Vincent van Gogh. Painted in 1890, this work captures the despair of the nineteenth-century penal institution. The face of the prisoner near the center of the picture looking at the viewer is van Gogh's.

van Gogh, Vincent: *Prisoners Round* (detail), 1890. Pushkin Museum of Art, Moscow. Scala/Art Resource, New York

with the problem by increasing the use of pardons, relaxing prison discipline, and limiting supervision.

In 1816, New York built a new prison at Auburn, hoping to alleviate some of the overcrowding at Newgate. The Auburn Prison design became known as the **congregate system** because most prisoners ate and worked in groups. In 1819, construction began on a wing of solitary cells to house unruly prisoners. Three classes of prisoners were then created. One group remained continually in solitary confinement as a result of breaches of prison discipline, the second group was allowed labor as an occasional form of recreation, and the third and largest class worked together during the day and was separated only at night.

The philosophy of the Auburn prison system was crime prevention through fear of punishment and silent confinement. The worst felons were to be cut off from all contact with other prisoners, and although they were treated and fed relatively well, they had no hope of pardon to relieve their solitude or isolation. For a time, some of the worst convicts were forced to remain alone and silent during the entire day. This practice, which led to mental breakdowns, suicides, and self-mutilations, was abolished in 1823. The solution adopted at Auburn was to keep convicts in separate cells at night but allow them to work together during the day under enforced silence.

Regimentation became the standard mode of prison life. Convicts did not simply walk from place to place; instead, they went in close order and single file, each looking over the shoulder of the preceding person, faces inclined to the right, feet moving in unison. The lockstep prison shuffle was developed at Auburn and is still used in some institutions today.[14] The inmates' time was regulated by bells telling them when to wake up, sleep, and work. The system was so like the military that many of its early administrators were recruited from the armed services.

When discipline was breached in the Auburn system, punishment was applied in the form of a rawhide whip on the inmate's back. Immediate and effective, Auburn discipline was so successful that when 100 inmates were used to build the famous Sing Sing Prison in 1825, not one dared try to escape, even though they were housed in an open field with only minimal supervision.[15]

In 1818, Pennsylvania took the radical step of establishing a prison that placed each inmate in a single cell for the duration of his sentence. Classifications were abolished because each cell was intended as a miniature prison that would prevent the inmates from contaminating one another. The new Pennsylvania state prison, called the Western Penitentiary, had an unusual architectural design. It was built in a semicircle, with the cells positioned along its circumference. Built back to back, some cells faced the boundary wall, and others faced the internal area of the circle. Its inmates were kept in solitary confinement almost constantly, being allowed out for about an hour a day for exercise. In 1829 a second, similar penitentiary using the isolate system was built in Philadelphia and was called the Eastern Penitentiary.

congregate system
Prison design, first used in New York, that allowed inmates to engage in group activities such as work, meals, and recreation.

REALITYCHECK

MYTH OR REALITY? The first correctional institutions were actually considered a "liberal" reform.

REALITY: Although they might be considered a harsh form of punishment today, prisons were originally considered a humanitarian reform sponsored by religious groups.

Considering that recidivism rates are so high, should we embrace the treatment and rehabilitation elements of incarceration rather than focusing on prison as a means of dispensing punishment?

© ShutterStock RF/ShutterStock

Supporters of the **Pennsylvania system** believed that the penitentiary was truly a place to do penance. By removing the sinner from society and allowing the prisoner a period of isolation in which to consider the evils of crime, the Pennsylvania system reflected the influence of religion and religious philosophy on corrections. Its supporters believed that solitary confinement with in-cell labor would make work so attractive that upon release, the inmate would be well suited to resume a productive existence in society.

The Pennsylvania system eliminated the need for large numbers of guards or disciplinary measures. Isolated from one another, inmates could not plan escapes or collectively break rules. When discipline was a problem, however, the whip and the iron gag were used.

Advocates of the Auburn system believed that theirs was the cheapest and most productive way to reform prisoners and that solitary confinement as practiced in Pennsylvania was cruel and inhumane. In contrast, advocates of Pennsylvania's isolation model argued that their system was quiet, efficient, humane, and well ordered, yielding the ultimate correctional facility.[16] They considered the Auburn system a breeding place for criminal associations, because it allowed inmates to get to know one another.

New York's congregate model eventually prevailed and spread throughout the United States. Many of its features are still used today. Its innovations included congregate working conditions, the use of solitary confinement to punish unruly inmates, military regimentation, and discipline. Concept Summary 11.1 describes the differences between these two prison systems.

Corrections in the Nineteenth Century

The prison of the nineteenth century was remarkably similar to that of today. The congregate system was adopted in all states except Pennsylvania. Prisons were overcrowded, and the single-cell principle was often ignored. Although the prison was viewed as an improvement over capital and corporal punishment, it quickly became the scene of depressed conditions. Inmates were treated harshly and routinely whipped and tortured. Prison brutality flourished in these institutions, which had originally been devised as a more humane

Pennsylvania system
Correctional model, used in Pennsylvania, that isolated inmates from one another to prevent them from planning escapes, make them easy to manage, and give them time to do penitence.

Early Correctional Systems

Prison	Structure	Living Conditions	Activities	Discipline
Auburn system	Tiered cells	Congregate	Group work	Silence, harsh punishment
Pennsylvania system	Single cells set in semicircle	Isolated	In-cell work, Bible study	Silence, harsh punishment

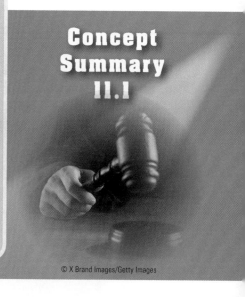

Concept Summary 11.1

correctional alternative. In these early penal institutions, brutal corporal punishment was doled out indoors where, hidden from public view, it could become even more savage.[17]

Prison industry developed and became the predominant theme around which institutions were organized. Some prisons used the **contract system**, in which officials sold the labor of inmates to private businesses. Sometimes the contractor supervised the inmates inside the prison itself. Under the **convict-lease system**, the state leased its prisoners to a business for a fixed annual fee and gave up supervision and control. Finally, some institutions had prisoners produce goods for the prison's own use.[18]

The development of prison industry quickly led to the abuse of inmates, who were forced to work for almost no wages, and to profiteering by dishonest administrators and business owners. During the Civil War era, prisons were major manufacturers of clothes, shoes, boots, furniture, and the like. Beginning in the 1870s, opposition by trade unions sparked restrictions on interstate commerce in prison goods. The prison, like the police department, became the scene of political intrigue and of efforts by political administrators to control the hiring of personnel and dispensing of patronage.

REFORM EFFORTS • The National Congress of Penitentiary and Reformatory Discipline, held in Cincinnati in 1870, heralded a new era of prison reform. Organized by penologists Enoch Wines and Theodore Dwight, the congress provided a forum for corrections experts from around the nation to call for the treatment, education, and training of inmates. By 1870, Zebulon Brockway, warden of the

contract system
The practice of correctional officials selling the labor of inmates to private businesses.

convict-lease system
The practice of the state leasing inmates to businesses for a fixed annual fee.

Prison in the late nineteenth century was a brutal place. This line engraving from 1869 shows an inmate undergoing a water torture in New York's Sing Sing Prison.

The Granger Collection, New York

Elmira Reformatory in New York, advocated individualized treatment, the indeterminate sentence, and parole. The reformatory program initiated by Brockway included elementary education for illiterates, designated library hours, lectures by faculty members of the local Elmira College, and a group of vocational training shops. From 1888 to 1920, Elmira administrators used military-like training to discipline the inmates and organize the institution. The military organization could be seen in every aspect of the institution: schooling, manual training, sports, supervision of inmates, and even parole decisions.[19] The cost to the state of the institution's operations was to be held to a minimum.

THE DEVELOPMENT OF PAROLE • Another innovation, parole, was a concept that developed overseas and was later brought to the United States. The term "parole" itself comes from the French word for "promise," referring to the practice of releasing captured enemy soldiers if they promised not to fight again and adding the threat that they would be executed if recaptured.

In the early seventeenth century, English judges began to spare the lives of offenders by banishing them to the newly formed overseas colonies. In 1617, the Privy Counsel of the British Parliament standardized this practice by passing an order granting reprieves and stays of execution to convicts willing to be transported to the colonies. Transportation was viewed as an answer to labor shortages caused by war, disease, and the opening of new commercial markets.

In 1717, the British Parliament passed legislation embodying the concept of *property in service*, which transferred control of prisoners to a contractor or shipmaster until the expiration of their sentences. When the prisoners arrived in the colonies, their services could be resold to the highest bidder. After sale, an offender's status changed from convict to indentured servant.

REALITY CHECK

MYTH OR REALITY? Educating inmates began in the 1960s during the Kennedy administration.

MYTH: The first attempts to educate inmates actually were developed during the nineteenth century.

Is it fair to provide inmates with college courses, while many non-offenders struggle to pay tuition?

Transportation quickly became the most common sentence for theft offenders. In the American colonies, property in service had to be abandoned after the revolution. Thereafter, Australia, claimed as a British colony in 1770, became the destination for most transported felons. From 1815 to 1850, large numbers of inmates were shipped to Australia to serve as indentured servants working for plantation owners, in mines, or on sheep stations.

The English Penal Servitude Act of 1853 all but ended transportation and substituted imprisonment as a punishment. Part of this act made it possible to grant a *ticket-of-leave* to those who had served a sufficient portion of their prison sentence. This form of conditional release permitted former prisoners to be at large in specified areas. The conditions of their release were written on a license that the former inmates were required to carry with them at all times. Conditions usually included sobriety, lawful behavior, and hard work. Many releasees violated these provisions, prompting criticism of the system. Eventually, members of prisoner aid societies helped supervise and care for releasees.

The concept of parole spread to the United States. As early as 1822, volunteers from the Philadelphia-based Society for Alleviating the Miseries of Public Prisons began to help offenders once they were released from prison. In 1851, the society appointed two agents to work with inmates discharged from Pennsylvania penal institutions. Massachusetts appointed an agent in 1845 to help released inmates obtain jobs, clothing, and transportation.

In the 1870s, using a carefully weighted screening procedure, Zebulon Brockway selected rehabilitated offenders from Elmira Reformatory for early release under the supervision of citizen volunteers known as *guardians*. The guardians met with the parolees at least once a month and submitted written reports on their progress. The parole concept spread rapidly. Ohio created the first parole agency in 1884. By 1901, as many as 20 states had created some type of parole agency. By 1927 only three states (Florida, Mississippi, and Virginia) had not established some sort of parole release. Parole had become institutionalized as the primary method of release for prison inmates, and half of all inmates released in the United States were paroled.[20]

Prisons in the Twentieth Century

The early twentieth century was a time of contrasts in the U.S. prison system.[21] At one extreme were those who advocated reform, such as the Mutual Welfare League, led by Thomas Mott Osborne. Prison reform groups proposed better treatment for inmates, an end to harsh corporal punishment, the creation of meaningful prison industries, and educational programs. Reformers argued that prisoners should not be isolated from society and that the best elements of society—education, religion, meaningful work, and self-governance—should be brought to the prison. Osborne went so far as to spend a week in New York's notorious Sing Sing Prison to learn firsthand about its conditions.

In time, some of the more rigid prison rules gave way to liberal reform. By the mid-1930s, few prisons required inmates to wear the red-and-white-striped convict suit; nondescript gray uniforms were substituted. The code of silence ended, as did the lockstep shuffle. Prisoners were allowed "the freedom of the yard" to mingle and exercise an hour or two each day.[22] Movies and radio appeared in the 1930s. Visiting policies and mail privileges were liberalized.

A more important trend was the development of specialized prisons designed to treat particular types of offenders. In New York, for example, the prisons at Clinton and Auburn were viewed as industrial facilities for hard-core inmates, Great Meadow was an agricultural center for nondangerous offenders, and Dannemora was a facility for the criminally insane. In California, San Quentin housed inmates considered salvageable by correctional authorities, and Folsom was reserved for hard-core offenders.[23]

Prison industry also evolved. Opposition by organized labor helped put an end to the convict-lease system and forced inmate labor. By 1900, a number of states had restricted the sale of prisoner-made goods on the open market. The worldwide Great Depression, which began in 1929, prompted industry and union leaders to further pressure state legislators to reduce competition from prison industries. A series of ever more restrictive federal legislative initiatives led to the Sumners-Ashurst Act (1940), which made it a federal offense to transport interstate commerce goods made in prison for private use, regardless of the laws of the state receiving the goods.[24] The restrictions imposed by the federal government helped to severely curtail prison industry for 40 years. Private entrepreneurs shunned prison investments because they were no longer profitable. The result was inmate idleness and make-work jobs.[25]

Despite some changes and reforms, the prison in the mid-twentieth century remained a destructive penal institution. Although some aspects of inmate life improved, severe discipline, harsh rules, and solitary confinement were the way of life in prison.

Contemporary Correctional Institutions

The modern era has been a period of change and turmoil in the nation's correctional system. Three trends stand out. First, between 1960 and 1980, came the prisoners' rights movement. After many years of indifference (the so-called hands-off doctrine), state and federal courts ruled in case after case that institutionalized inmates had rights to freedom of religion and speech, medical care, procedural due process, and proper living conditions. Inmates won rights unheard of in the nineteenth and early twentieth centuries. Since 1980, however, an increasingly conservative judiciary has curtailed the growth of inmate rights.

Second, violence within the correctional system became a national concern. Well-publicized riots at New York's Attica Prison and the New Mexico State Penitentiary drew attention to the potential for death and destruction that lurks in every prison. Prison rapes and killings have become commonplace. The locus of control in many prisons has shifted from the correctional staff to violent inmate gangs. In reaction, some administrators have tried to improve conditions and provide innovative programs that give inmates a voice in running the institution. Another reaction has been to tighten discipline and build new super-maximum-security prisons to control the most dangerous offenders. The problem of prison overcrowding has made efforts to improve conditions extremely difficult.

Third, the view that traditional correctional rehabilitation efforts have failed prompted many penologists to reconsider the purpose of incarcerating criminals. Between 1960 and 1980, it was common for correctional administrators to cling to the **medical model**, which viewed inmates as sick people who were suffering from some social malady that prevented them from adjusting to society. Correctional treatment could help cure them and enable them to live productive lives once they returned to the community. In the 1970s, efforts were also made to help offenders become reintegrated into society by providing them with new career opportunities that relied on work-release programs. Inmates were allowed to work outside the institution during the day and return in the evening. Some were given extended furloughs in the community. Work-release became a political issue when, in a famous incident, Willie Horton, a furloughed inmate from Massachusetts, raped a young woman. Criticism of the state's "liberal" furlough program helped Vice President George Bush defeat Massachusetts Governor Michael S. Dukakis for the U.S. presidency in 1988. In the aftermath of the Horton case, a number of states, including Massachusetts, restricted their furlough policies.

medical model
A correctional philosophy based on the belief that inmates are sick people who need treatment, rather than punishment, to help them reform.

One of the most dramatic incidents in corrections history took place at the Attica State Prison in Attica, New York, in September 1971, when inmates rioted and seized control of the prison. During the following four days of negotiations, authorities agreed to 28 of the prisoners' demands, but they would not agree to demands for complete amnesty from criminal prosecution for those involved in the prison takeover, or to demands for the removal of Attica's superintendent. Under orders from Governor Nelson Rockefeller, state police took back control of the prison, using shotguns and tear gas. By the time the uprising was put down, more than 43 people had been killed, including 10 correctional officers and civilian employees, some of whom died from "friendly fire."

© AP Images/Associated Press

Prisons have come to be viewed as places for control, incapacitation, and punishment, instead of sites for rehabilitation and reform. Advocates of the "no-frills," or penal harm, movement believe that if prison is a punishing experience, would-be criminals will be deterred from committing crimes and current inmates will be encouraged to go straight. Nonetheless, efforts to use correctional institutions as treatment facilities have not ended, and such innovations as the development of private industries on prison grounds have kept the rehabilitative ideal alive.

The pressure on correctional institutions caused by overpopulation and the burden of constantly increasing correctional costs have prompted the development of alternatives to incarceration, such as intensive probation supervision, house arrest, and electronic monitoring (see Chapter 10). What has developed is a dual correctional policy: Keep as many nonviolent offenders out of the correctional system as possible by means of community-based programs; incarcerate dangerous, violent offenders for long periods of time.[26] These efforts have been compromised by a growing get-tough stance in judicial and legislative sentencing policy, accented by mandatory minimum sentences for gun crimes and drug trafficking. Despite the development of alternatives to incarceration, the number of people under lock and key has skyrocketed.

The following sections review the most prominent types of correctional facilities in operation today.

Jails

The nation's jails are institutional facilities with five primary purposes:

- They detain accused offenders who cannot make, or are not eligible for, bail prior to trial.
- They hold convicted offenders who are awaiting sentence.
- They serve as the principal institution of secure confinement for offenders convicted of misdemeanors.
- They hold probationers and parolees picked up for violations and waiting for a hearing.
- They house felons when state prisons are overcrowded.

A number of formats are used to jail offenders. About 15,000 local jurisdictions maintain short-term police or municipal lockups that house offenders for no more than 48 hours before a bail hearing can be held; thereafter, detainees are kept in the county jail. Today, jails are multipurpose correctional institutions; Exhibit 11.1 sets out their main functions.

Jail Populations and Trends

The number of people being held in jails today has been rising for over a decade, and there are now more than 780,000 jail inmates. This is more than 250 inmates for every 100,000 U.S. residents. Many jails are operating at or near capacity, and the national average is a 96 percent occupancy rate.

Almost 9 out of every 10 jail inmates are adult males, and although whites make up more than 40 percent of the jail population, minority overrepresentation is still a significant problem (Figure 11.1). Members of ethnic and racial minorities make up a disproportionate number of the jail population, presumably reflecting such factors as overrepresentation in the arrest statistics, failure to secure bail, inferior legal representation, and racial/ethnic bias in the justice system.

Between 1990 and 2008, the number of Hispanic jail inmates increased at a higher average annual rate of growth (4.5%) than the numbers of white (3.8%)

EXHIBIT 11.1

Jail Functions and Services

- Receive individuals pending arraignment and hold them awaiting trial, conviction, or sentencing
- Readmit probation, parole, and bail-bond violators and absconders
- Temporarily detain juveniles pending transfer to juvenile authorities
- Hold mentally ill persons pending their movement to appropriate health facilities
- Hold individuals for the military, for protective custody, for contempt, and for the courts as witnesses

- Release convicted inmates to the community upon completion of sentence
- Transfer inmates to federal, state, or other authorities
- House inmates for federal, state, or other authorities because of crowding of their facilities
- Sometimes operate community-based programs as alternatives to incarceration
- Hold inmates who are sentenced to short terms (generally under one year)

Source: Paige M. Harrison and Allen J. Beck, *Prison and Jail Inmates at Midyear 2004* (Washington, D.C.: Bureau of Justice Statistics, 2005).

and black inmates (3.3%). At one time many thousands of minor children were held in jails as runaways, truants, and so on. The number of juveniles held in adult jails has been in decline since 1995, a result of ongoing government initiatives to remove juveniles from adult facilities; nonetheless, about 7,500 minors are still being held in adult jails each day (down from a high of 9,100).

FEMALE JAIL INMATES ● As Figure 11.2 shows, about 10 percent of jail inmates are women. Almost 9 out of every 10 jail inmates are adult males. While most jail inmates are still male, over the past two decades the percentage increase of female inmates (up 250%) is higher than the increase of male inmates (up 170%).

Female jail inmates face many challenges. Most come from significantly disadvantaged backgrounds and have suffered abuse and severe economic disadvantage. One recent study of 100 female inmates found extremely high rates of lifetime trauma exposure (98%), current mental disorders (36%), and drug/alcohol problems (74%).[27]

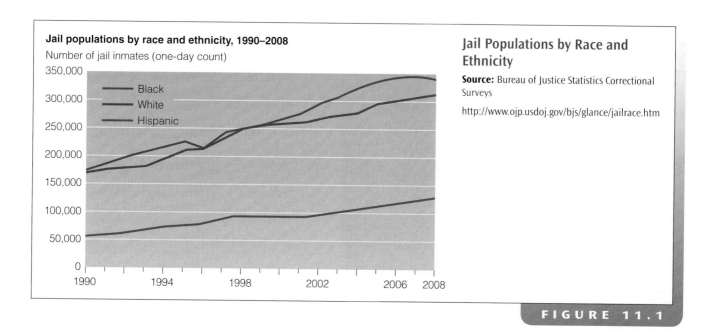

Jail populations by race and ethnicity, 1990–2008

Number of jail inmates (one-day count)

— Black
— White
— Hispanic

Jail Populations by Race and Ethnicity

Source: Bureau of Justice Statistics Correctional Surveys

http://www.ojp.usdoj.gov/bjs/glance/jailrace.htm

FIGURE 11.1

Jail Populations by Gender

Source: Bureau of Justice Statistics Correctional Surveys

http://www.ojp.usdoj.gov/bjs/glance/jailag.htm

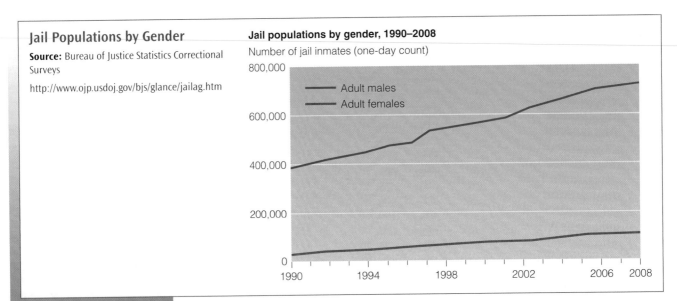

Jail populations by gender, 1990–2008

Number of jail inmates (one-day count)

- Adult males
- Adult females

FIGURE 11.2

Given this background, how can female inmates make a successful reentry into society? Employment seems to be a key issue. Those who have worked recently before their incarceration are most likely to have other survival skills and assets: They are more likely to have a high school education, to have a skill, and to have a driver's license and access to a car.[28] One recent interview study of female inmates at the Baltimore City Detention Center found that their median income in the 30 days before arrest was $145. Those who earned as little as $400–$799 were much more likely to find stable housing after their release and thus have a better chance of making it on the outside.[29]

JAIL POPULATION TRENDS • As you may recall, there has been a national movement to help criminal defendants remain in the community through the adoption of both bail reform measures and pretrial diversion. Nonetheless, as Table 11.1 shows, not only has the number of people in jail been increasing, but so has the jail incarceration rate—the percentage of the population in jail. During a period when the crime rate has been in decline (1995–2008), the incarceration rate has increased almost 30 percent.

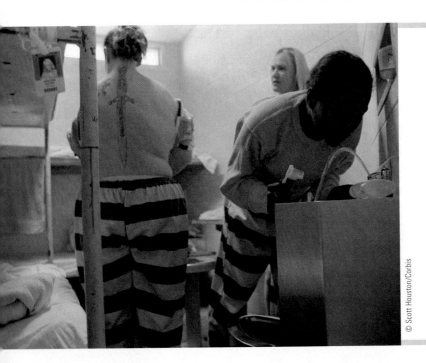

© Scott Houston/Corbis

The Estrella Jail in Phoenix, Arizona, was built in 1991, is podular/dormitory in design, and holds approximately 1,000 inmates, predominantly female. The inmates have committed petty theft, credit card fraud, prostitution, assault, drug use and drug dealing, and other crimes of similar nonserious ilk. The Estrella Jail is also home to the only female chain gang in America. Inmates stay in their tiny 8 × 12-foot cells 23 hours of the day during "lock down," unless they are out on assigned chain gang duty. The inmates must memorize ten rules of conduct that address grooming, behavior, and attitude. Chain gang and other privileged duties can be suspended for infractions such as swearing. The chain gangs work six days a week, contributing thousands of dollars' worth of free labor to the community. Jail administrators view the tough regimen as a means of rehabilitating the inmates through hard work.

TABLE 11.1		
Number of People in Jail and Jail Incarceration Rate		
Year	**Number held in jail**	**Jail incarceration rate***
2008	785,556	258
2007	780,582	259
2006	766,010	256
2005	747,529	252
2004	713,990	243
2003	691,301	238
2002	665,475	231
2001	631,240	222
2000	621,149	220
1995	507,044	193

*Number of jail inmates per 100,000 U.S. residents on July 1 of each year.

SOURCE: Paige M. Harrison and Allen J. Beck, *Prison and Jail Inmates at Midyear 2005* (Washington, D.C.: Bureau of Justice Statistics, 2006); William Sabol, Heather West, Todd Minton, and William J. Sabol, *Prison and Jail Inmates at Midyear 2008* (Washington, D.C.: Bureau of Justice Statistics, 2009).

Considering these measures and the declining crime rate, why do jail populations continue to increase? There are a number of reasons for this phenomenon. As prisons become more overcrowded, prison correctional officials use local jails to house inmates for whom there is no room in state prisons. Jail populations also respond to the efforts being made to reduce or control particular crime problems, including substance abuse, spousal abuse, and driving while intoxicated (DWI). Some jurisdictions have passed legislation requiring that people arrested on suspicion of domestic violence be held in confinement for a number of hours to "cool off" before becoming eligible for bail. Other jurisdictions have attempted to deter drunk driving by passing mandatory jail sentences for people convicted of DWI; such legislation can quickly result in overcrowded jails.[30]

However, the rate of increase in the jail population has been slowing, reflecting a declining U.S. crime rate and greater reliance on alternatives to incarceration such as probation, electronic monitoring, and house arrest. It is possible that in the future, jail populations may stabilize or begin to decline.

Jail Conditions

Jails are usually a low-priority item in the criminal justice system. Because they are often administered on a county level, jail services have not been sufficiently regulated, nor has a unified national policy been developed to mandate what constitutes adequate jail conditions. Consequently, jails in some counties are physically deteriorated, holding dangerous and troubled people, many of whom suffer emotional problems that remain untreated. Not atypical was a recent (2009) review of the Dallas, Texas, jail system by federal inspectors who found the following, among many other problems.

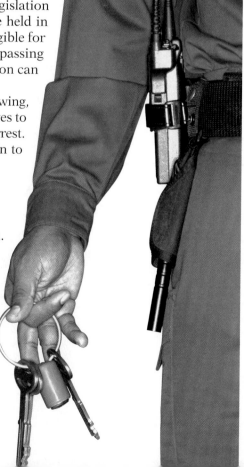

© Thinkstock/Getty Images

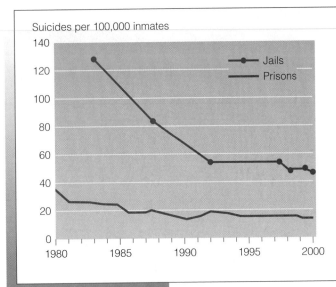

Jail Suicide Trends

Source: Allen J. Beck, Paige Harrison, and Devon B. Adams, *Prison Rape Elimination Act of 2003: Sexual Violence Reported by Correctional Authorities, 2006* (Washington, D.C.: Bureau of Justice Statistics, 2007)

http://www.ojp.usdoj.gov/bjs/pub/pdf/svrca06.pdf

FIGURE 11.3

- The inspectors noted delays in issuing medications, a lack of medical evaluations, inconsistent care, and a lack of medical care for mental health patients.
- The jail kitchen was found to have moldy ceilings that dripped water, live wires next to standing water, and condensation so thick it was almost impossible to see across the room.
- Maintenance and sanitation problems still exist, including broken intercoms, inadequate shower temperatures, sinks without hot water, clogged sinks and shower drains, and broken toilets.[31]

Jail inmates have been victims of prior physical and sexual abuse, including more than 10 percent of male inmates and nearly half of women.[32] About two-thirds of all jail inmates report having a mental health problem, including more than 15 percent who display psychotic symptoms. That means more than 100,000 people in jail today are suffering from severe psychosis, and more than 400,000 have some form of mental disorder.[33] It is not surprising, then, that some counties report that inmate suicides are their biggest concern.[34] And although Figure 11.3 shows that the suicide rate has declined significantly, the percentage of jail inmates who take their own lives is still higher than that of the general population. Why have jail suicides declined? The answer may be found in the development of new-generation jails, discussed below.

New-Generation Jails

To relieve overcrowding and improve effectiveness, a jail-building boom has been under way. Many of the new jails are using modern designs to improve effectiveness; these are referred to as "new-generation jails."[35] Traditional jails are constructed and use what is referred to as the linear/intermittent surveillance model. Jails using this design are rectangular, with corridors leading to either single- or multiple-occupancy cells arranged at right angles to the corridor. Correctional officers must patrol to see into cells or housing areas, and when they are in a position to observe one cell they cannot observe others; unobserved inmates are essentially unsupervised.

In contrast, new-generation jails allow for continuous observation of residents. There are two types: direct-supervision and indirect supervision jails. Direct-supervision jails, like the one where Gina Curcio works, contain a cluster of cells surrounding a living area or "pod," which contains tables, chairs, televisions, and other material. A correctional officer is stationed within the pod. The officer can observe the inmates continuously and is able to relate to them on a personal level. Placing the officer in the pod achieves an increased awareness of the behaviors and needs of the inmates. This results in a safer environment for both staff and inmates. Because interaction between inmates is constantly and closely monitored, dissension can be quickly detected before it escalates. During the day, inmates stay in the open area (dayroom) and typically are not permitted to go into their rooms except with permission of the officer in charge. The officer controls door locks to cells from the control panel. In case of trouble or if the officer leaves the station for an extended period of time, command of this panel can be switched to a panel at a remote location, known as central control. The officer usually wears a device that permits immediate communication with central control, and the area is also covered by a video camera monitored by an officer in the central control room. Indirect-supervision jails are similar in construction, but the correctional officer's station is located inside a secure room. Microphones and speakers inside the living unit permit the officer to hear and communicate with inmates. Although these institutions have not yet undergone extensive evaluation, research shows that they may help reduce postrelease offending in some situations.[36] However, some critics suggest that new-generation jails have failed to live up to their promise because they lack important components, such as a normalized living environment, in their facilities.[37]

REALITY CHECK

MYTH OR REALITY? Many jail inmates suffer from social and mental problems.

REALITY: Jail inmates suffer from severe social and psychological problems, including mental illness.

What can be done to address this problem, or can nothing be accomplished?

Alexandria Detention Center

The **Alexandria Detention Center**, in Virginia, is based on the "new-generation" jail philosophy, a more modern and humane approach than that found in traditional jails. See the center's website at **www.cengage.com/criminaljustice/siegel**

Prisons

The federal Bureau of Prisons and every state government maintain closed correctional facilities, also called prisons, penitentiaries, or reformatories. The most recent government figures show that state prisons cost taxpayers about $40 billion each year, up from about $12 billion in 1986; this amounts to an annual cost of about $125 per year for every American citizen.[38]

The prison is the final repository for the most troubled criminal offenders. Many come from distressed backgrounds and have little hope or opportunity; all too many have emotional problems and grew up in abusive households. A majority are alcohol and drug dependent at the time of their arrest. Those considered both dangerous and incorrigible may find themselves in super-maximum-security prisons, where they spend most of their days confined to their cells.

Types of Prisons

There are more than 1,500 public and private adult correctional facilities housing state prisoners. In addition, there are 84 federal facilities and 26 private facilities that house federal inmates. Usually, prisons are organized or classified on three levels—maximum, medium, and minimum security—and each has distinct characteristics.

Criminal Justice and Technology

Technocorrections: Contemporary Correctional Technology

Technical experts have identified numerous areas of correctional management that can be aided by information technology (IT), including reception and commitment; sentence and time accounting; classification; caseload management; security; discipline; housing/bed management; medical services; grievances; programs; scheduling; investigations/gang management; property; trust accounting; visitation; release and discharge; and community supervision. Because there are so many areas where IT can be applied within correctional establishments, prison administrators have begun to take advantage of the potential offered by the new technologies. How has IT been applied within prison walls? A few examples follow.

Ground-Penetrating Radar

Ground-penetrating radar (GPR) can locate tunnels that inmates use to escape. GPR works almost like an old-fashioned Geiger counter, but instead of detecting metal, the system detects changes in ground composition, including voids such as those created by a tunnel.

Heartbeat Monitoring

Now it is possible to prevent escapes by monitoring inmates' heartbeats! The Advanced Vehicle Interrogation and Notification System (AVIAN) detects the presence of persons trying to escape by hiding in vehicles. Using the data from seismic sensors that are placed on the vehicle, the AVIAN reads the shock wave generated by the beating heart, which couples to any surface or object with which the body is in contact. It collects the data and analyzes it using advanced signal-processing algorithms to detect a person hiding in a vehicle such as a large truck in less than two minutes. The system works by accounting for all the frequencies of movement in the vehicle, such as the expansion and contraction of an engine or rain hitting the roof.

Nonlethal Electrified Fences

Nonlethal electrified containment fences stop inmates without causing severe harm or death. If an inmate tries to climb or cut through the perimeter fence, he or she will receive a nonlethal jolt of electricity, which causes temporary immobilization. At the same time, the system alerts prison staff that an attempt has occurred and identifies its location.

Backscatter Imaging System for Concealed Weapons

This system uses a backscatter imager to detect weapons and contraband. The primary advantage of this device over current walk-through portals is that it can detect nonmetallic as well as metallic weapons. It uses low-power X-rays equal to about five minutes of exposure to the sun at sea level. Although these X-rays penetrate clothing, they do not penetrate the body.

Body-Scanning Screening System

This is a stationary screening system to detect nonmetallic weapons and contraband in the lower body cavities. It uses simplified magnetic resonance imaging (MRI) as a noninvasive alternative to X-ray and physical body cavity searches. The stationary screening system makes use of first-generation medical MRI.

Transmitter Wristbands

These wristbands broadcast a unique serial number via radio frequency every two seconds so that antennas throughout the prison can pick up the signals and pass the data, via a local area network, to a central monitoring station PC. The wristbands can sound an alert when a prisoner gets close to the perimeter fence or when an inmate doesn't return from a furlough on time; they can even tag gang members and notify guards when rivals come in contact with each other.

Personal Health Status Monitor

The personal health status monitor uses acoustics to track the heartbeat and respiration of a person in a cell. More advanced health status monitors are now being developed that can monitor five or more vital signs at once and then, on the basis of these findings, produce an assessment of an inmate's state of health. This more advanced version of the personal health status monitor may take another decade to develop, but the current version may already help save lives that would otherwise be lost to suicide.

All-in-One Drug Detection Spray

Drug detection sprays detect whether someone possesses marijuana, methamphetamines, heroin, or cocaine. A specially made piece of paper is wiped on a surface; when sprayed with one of the aerosol sprays, it changes color within 15 seconds if as little as 4 to 20 micrograms of the drug is present. A new detection device is now being developed that uses a single spray to test for all drugs at once. The test paper will turn different colors depending on which drugs the spray contacts, and several positive results will be possible with a single use of the spray.

Radar Vital Signs Monitor/Radar Flashlight

The handheld radar flashlight can detect the respiration of a human in a cell from behind a 20-centimeter hollow-core concrete wall or an eight-inch cinder block wall. It instantly gives the user a bar-graph readout that is viewed on the apparatus itself. Other miniature radar detectors give users heartbeat and respiration readings. The equipment is expected to be a useful tool in searches for people who are hiding, because the only thing that successfully blocks its functioning is a wall made of metal or conductive material.

Personal Alarm Location System

It is now possible for prison employees to carry a tiny transmitter linking them with a computer in a central control room. In an emergency, they can hit an alarm button and transmit to a computer that automatically records whose distress button has been pushed. An architectural map of the facility instantly appears on screen, showing the exact location of the staff member in need of assistance.

Under-Vehicle Surveillance System

An under-vehicle surveillance system uses a drive-over camera that records a video image of the license plate and the underside of any vehicle entering or leaving the secure perimeter of the prison. This system enables prison staff to check each vehicle for possible escape attempts and keeps a digital recording of every vehicle that enters or exits the prison.

Biometric Recognition

A new biometric system uses facial recognition by matching more than 200 individual points on the human face with a digitally stored image. The system is used to control access in buildings and rooms inside buildings. It is now available and will become much more common in the near future.

Risk Prediction

By employing existing crime-mapping tools to develop a Web-based trend analysis system, the Florida Department of Corrections is creating a correctional crime-mapping and information management system to monitor daily operations and identify trends, patterns, hotspots, and areas of concern for correctional managers. Called COTAS (Correctional Operational Trend Analysis System), the project uses archived data to look for patterns in such areas as inmate health and conduct. The creation of analytical tools using statistics, data-modeling techniques, and mapping will help identify key indicators of disruption, violence, and institutional risk, which in turn will help administrators proactively minimize negative impacts. The implementation of COTAS will place Florida in the forefront of the development and application of technology in correctional operations.

Cell Phone Detection and Defeat

As cell phones become smaller, smuggling them inside correctional facilities becomes easier. In turn, inmates find it easier to continue their criminal activities, harass victims, or transmit photographs. A new government-sponsored project will draw on input from representatives of the cell phone industry, law enforcement, and corrections. On completion of the needs assessment, the project will move on to a technical survey and gap analysis of existing cell phone detection technology. This project will provide guidance on the technology needs and operational requirements related to the field of corrections.

Contraband detection

This technology will consist of a single transportable device that will detect a broad spectrum of all types of contraband, including weapons and cell phones.

Data analysis and integration

Primarily a software package that will analyze datasets of information such as inmate telephone call records and

(continued)

(continued)

financial data, this program will extract information and identify trends that might be related to criminal activity. Secondarily, it will be able to be integrated with other systems so that information can be shared among several facilities.

Duress alarm system

Corrections professionals specifically need a personal alarm system that is cost-effective, accurate, and reliable and works both indoors and outside. A modification of existing technology to meet these requirements could satisfy this need.

Traffic identification system

This technology will provide continuous real-time tracking of both staff and inmates in indoor and outdoor environments.

It must be able to resist tampering by inmates and must be small and unobtrusive.

Surveillance and monitoring

Such a system will need to provide automatic alerts to correctional officials if an inmate is detected trying to escape or act violently. A "smart" camera is an example of this type of technology.

Multithreat biohazard protective apparel

In the future an entire uniform—shirt, pants, gloves, and so on—may be developed that can be worn at all times and protect officers from contact with blood, body fluids, and chemical hazards. Such a suit will need to be lightweight, comfortable, and durable.

Critical Thinking

1. Some elements of technocorrections intrude on the privacy of inmates. Should the need for security outweigh an inmate's right to privacy?

2. Should probationers and parolees be monitored with modern technology? Do they deserve more privacy than incarcerated inmates?

---

maximum-security prison
A correctional institution that houses dangerous felons and maintains strict security measures, high walls, and limited contact with the outside world.

MAXIMUM-SECURITY PRISONS ● Housing the most notorious criminals, and often the subject of films and stories, **maximum-security prisons** are probably the institutions most familiar to the public. Famous "max prisons" have included Sing Sing, Joliet, Attica, Walpole, and the most fearsome prison of all, the now-closed federal facility on Alcatraz Island known as The Rock.

A typical maximum-security facility is fortress-like, surrounded by stone walls with guard towers at strategic places. These walls may be 25 feet high, and sometimes inner and outer walls divide the prison into courtyards. Barbed wire or electrified fences are used to discourage escape. High security, armed guards, and stone walls give the inmate the sense that the facility is impregnable and reassure the citizens outside that convicts will be completely incapacitated. Because they fear that violence may flair up at any minute, prison administrators have been quick to adapt the latest high-tech security measures. Today, prison administrators rely on technology to help them maintain security, a topic covered in the Criminal Justice and Technology feature on pages 390–392.

Inmates live in interior, metal-barred cells that contain their own plumbing and sanitary facilities and are locked securely either by key or by electronic device. Cells are organized in sections called blocks, and in large prisons, a number of cell blocks make up a wing. During the day, the inmates engage in closely controlled activities: meals, workshops, education, and so on. Rule violators may be confined to their cells, and working and other shared recreational activities are viewed as privileges.

The byword of the maximum-security prison is "security." Correctional workers are made aware that each inmate may be a dangerous criminal or violent, and as a result, the utmost security must be maintained. These prisons are designed to eliminate hidden corners where people can congregate, and passages are constructed so that they can be easily blocked off to quell disturbances.

SUPER-MAXIMUM-SECURITY PRISONS • Some states have constructed **super-maximum-security prisons** (supermax prisons) to house the most predatory criminals. These high-security institutions can be independent correctional centers or locked wings of existing prisons.[39] Some supermax prisons lock inmates in their cells 22 to 24 hours a day, never allowing them out unless they are shackled.[40]

The 484-bed facility in Florence, Colorado, has the most sophisticated security measures in the United States, including 168 video cameras and 1,400 electronically controlled gates. Inside the cells, all furniture is unmovable; the desk, bed, and TV stand are made of cement. All potential weapons, including soap dishes, toilet seats, and toilet handles, have been removed. The cement walls are 5,000-pound quality, and steel bars crisscross every eight inches inside the walls. Cells are angled so that inmates can see neither each other nor the outside. This cuts down on communication and denies inmates a sense of location, to prevent escapes.

A number of experts have given supermax prisons mixed reviews. Although they can achieve correctional benefits by enhancing security and quality of life, critics believe that they infringe directly on the right of inmates to due process because they deprive them of such basic rights such as human contact; they also eliminate any opportunity for rehabilitation.[41]

Some recent research by Daniel Mears and his colleagues on supermax prisons yielded mixed results. Mears, along with Jamie Watson, conducted surveys of correctional officials and found that, on the one hand, supermax prisons may actually enhance the quality of life of inmates and consequently improve their mental health. They increase privacy, reduce danger, and even provide creature comforts (such as TV sets) that are unavailable in general-population prisons. Staff report less stress and fear because they have to contend with fewer disruptive inmates.

On the other hand, Mears and Watson found that supermax prisons also have some unintended negative consequences. Staff may have too much control over inmates—a condition that damages staff–inmate relationships. Long hours of isolation may be associated with mental illness and psychological disturbances. Supermax inmates seem to have a more difficult time readjusting upon release. A stay in a supermax prison inhibits reintegration into other prisons, communities, and families. In another study, Mears and Jennifer Castro surveyed wardens and found that even though they seem to favor supermax prisons, they also expressed concern that the general public consider supermax institutions inhumane, that they drain limited funds from state budgets, and that they produce increases in litigation and court interventions, as well as increased recidivism and reentry failure among released inmates.[42]

super-maximum-security prison
The newest form of a maximum-security prison that uses high-level security measures to incapacitate the nation's most dangerous criminals. Most inmates are in lockdown 23 hours a day.

MYTH OR REALITY? Super-maximum-security prisons are highly effective.

MYTH: Although supermax prisons provide high security, they also produce maladjusted residents who have high failure rates upon release.

Would you use them if you were the head of the state corrections department?

MEDIUM-SECURITY PRISONS • Although they are similar in appearance to maximum-security prisons, in **medium-security prisons** the security and atmosphere are neither so tense nor so vigilant. Medium-security prisons are also surrounded by walls, but there may be fewer guard towers or other security precautions; visitations with personal contact may be allowed. Although most prisoners are housed in cells, individual honor rooms in medium-security prisons are used to reward those who make exemplary rehabilitation efforts. Finally, medium-security prisons promote greater treatment efforts, and the relaxed atmosphere allows freedom of movement for rehabilitation workers and other therapeutic personnel.

medium-security prison
A less secure institution that houses nonviolent offenders and provides more opportunities for contact with the outside world.

There are many different types of prisons, and some cater to special populations. The Eloy Detention Center in Eloy, Arizona, is used for undocumented aliens only. Any undocumented alien from the southern United States who is found, after apprehension, to have a criminal record is brought to this prison. People from over 50 countries have been incarcerated at Eloy, and at least 30 countries are usually represented in the inmate population at any given time. Inmates are allowed outdoor recreation every day.

© Scott Goldsmith/Aurora

minimum-security prison
The least secure institution, which houses white-collar and nonviolent offenders, maintains few security measures, and has liberal furlough and visitation policies.

MINIMUM-SECURITY PRISONS ● Operating without armed guards or perimeter walls, **minimum-security prisons** usually house the most trustworthy and least violent offenders; white-collar criminals may be their most common occupants. Inmates are allowed a great deal of personal freedom. Instead of being marched to activities by guards, they are summoned by bells or loudspeaker announcements, and they assemble on their own. Work furloughs and educational releases are encouraged, and vocational training is of the highest level. Dress codes are lax, and inmates are allowed to grow beards or mustaches and to demonstrate other individual characteristics.

Minimum-security facilities may have dormitories or small private rooms for inmates. Prisoners are allowed to own personal possessions that might be deemed dangerous in a maximum-security prison, such as radios.

Minimum-security prisons have been criticized for being like "country clubs"; some federal facilities for white-collar criminals even have tennis courts and pools (they are derisively called "Club Fed"). Yet they remain prisons, and the isolation and loneliness of prison life deeply affect the inmates.

Alternative Correctional Institutions

In addition to prisons and jails, a number of other correctional institutions are operating within the United States. Some have been in use for quite some time, whereas others have been developed more recently as part of innovative or experimental programs.

Prison Farms and Camps

Prison farms and camps are used to detain offenders. These types of facilities are found primarily in the South and the West and have been in operation since the nineteenth century. Today, about 40 farms, 40 forest camps, 80 road camps, and more than 60 similar facilities (vocational training centers, ranches, and so on) exist in the nation. Prisoners on farms produce dairy products, grain, and vegetable crops that are used in the state correctional system and other governmental facilities, such as hospitals and schools. Forestry camp inmates maintain state parks, fight forest fires, and do reforestation work. Ranches, primarily a western phenomenon, employ inmates in cattle raising and horse breeding, among other activities. Road gangs repair roads and state highways.

Shock Incarceration in Boot Camps

Another correctional innovation that gained popularity in the 1980s and 1990s, the **boot camp**, involves youthful, first-time offenders in military discipline and physical training. The concept is that short periods (90 to 180 days) of high-intensity exercise and work will "shock" the inmate into going straight. Tough physical training is designed to promote responsibility and improve decision-making skills, build self-confidence, and teach socialization skills. Inmates are treated with rough intensity by drillmasters who may call them names and punish the entire group for the failure of one member.[43]

Some programs also include educational and training components, counseling sessions, and treatment for special-needs populations, whereas others devote little or no time to therapeutic activities. Some receive program participants directly from court sentencing; others choose potential candidates from the general inmate population. Some allow voluntary participation and others voluntary termination.[44]

Is **shock incarceration** a correctional panacea or another fad doomed to failure? Those who advocate shock incarceration portray it as a lower-cost alternative to overcrowded prisons. Both staff and inmates report benefiting from the experience.[45] The costs of boot camps are no lower than those of traditional prisons on a daily basis, but because sentences are shorter, they provide long-term savings. A number of states, including Georgia and New York, make extensive use of shock incarceration facilities.

Despite such support, empirical research (the majority of it contributed by Doris Layton Mackenzie, a criminologist who has been involved in many evaluations of boot camp), has yielded disappointing results. She finds that clients leaving boot camps often have higher rates of technical violations and revocations than traditional probationers and parolees.[46] Mackenzie's extensive evaluations of the boot camp experience generate little evidence that boot camps can significantly lower recidivism rates. Those few programs that seem to work best stress treatment and therapeutic activities, are voluntary, and are longer in duration.[47] Because of these sketchy results, the future of the boot camp approach is uncertain. For example the federal government, and some state programs, including Florida, have announced the closing of their boot camp programs.[48]

boot camp
A short-term militaristic correctional facility in which inmates undergo intensive physical conditioning and discipline.

shock incarceration
A short prison sentence served in boot camp–type facilities.

Community Correctional Facilities

One goal of correctional treatment is to help reintegrate the offender into society. Placing offenders in a prison makes them more likely to adapt an inmate lifestyle than to reassimilate conventional social norms. As a result, the **community treatment** concept began to take off in the 1960s. State and federal correctional systems created community-based correctional models as an alternative to closed institutions. Many are **halfway houses** to which inmates are transferred just before their release into the community. These facilities are designed to bridge the gap between institutional living and the community. Specialized treatment may be offered, and the residents use the experience to cushion the shock of reentering society.

As you may recall, commitment to a community correctional center may also be used as an intermediate sanction and sole mode of treatment. An offender may be assigned to a community treatment center operated by the state department of corrections or to probation. Alternatively, the corrections department can contract with a private community center. This practice is common in the treatment of drug abusers and other nonviolent offenders whose special needs can be met in a self-contained community setting that specializes in specific types of treatment.

community treatment
The attempt by correctional agencies to maintain convicted offenders in the community instead of in a secure facility; it includes probation, parole, and residential programs.

halfway house
A community-based correctional facility that houses inmates before their outright release so that they can become gradually acclimated to conventional society.

Inside the Ordnance Road Correctional Center in Glen Burnie, Maryland, 19-year-old inmate Kenneth Lee puts sheets on his plastic covered mattress. He serves his prison sentence one weekend at a time, living in a dormitory-style room housing a dozen men. Alternative correctional institutions have been used around the nation as a response to overcrowding and high recidivism rates.

© AP Images/*The Maryland Gazette*/Andy Carruthers

Halfway houses and community correctional centers can look like residential homes and in many instances were originally residences; in urban centers, older apartment buildings can be adapted for the purpose. Usually, these facilities have a central treatment theme—such as group therapy or reality therapy—that is used to rehabilitate and reintegrate clients.

Despite the encouraging philosophical concept presented by the halfway house, evaluation of specific programs has not led to a definite endorsement of this type of treatment.[49] One significant problem has been a lack of support from community residents, who fear the establishment of an institution housing "dangerous offenders" in their neighborhood. Court actions have been brought, and zoning restrictions imposed, in some areas to foil efforts to create halfway houses.[50] As a result, many halfway houses are located in decrepit neighborhoods in the worst areas of town—certainly a condition that must influence the attitudes and behavior of the inmates. Furthermore, the climate of control exercised in most halfway houses, where rule violation can be met with a quick return to the institution, may not be one that the average inmate can distinguish from his former high-security penal institution.

Despite these problems, the promise held by community correctional centers, coupled with their low cost of operations, has led to their continued use into the new millennium.

Private Prisons

Correctional facilities are now being run by private firms as business enterprises. In some instances, a private corporation will finance and build an institution and then contract with correctional authorities to provide services for convicted criminals. Sometimes the private concern will finance and build the institution and then lease it outright to the government. This model has the advantage of allowing the government to circumvent the usually difficult process of getting voters to approve a bond issue and raising funds for prison construction. Another common form of private involvement is specific service contracts; for example, a private concern might be hired to manage the prison health-care system, food services, or staff training.

On January 6, 1986, the U.S. Corrections Corporation opened the first private state prison in Marion, Kentucky—a 300-bed minimum-security facility for inmates who are within three years of parole. Today, more than 20 companies are trying to enter the private prison market, 5 states are contracting with private companies to operate facilities, and more than 10 others—including Oregon, New Mexico, and Florida—have recently passed laws authorizing or expanding the use of private prison contractors.[51]

Private prisons now play a significant role in management of the inmate population. The industry leader, Corrections Corporation of America (CCA), houses approximately 75,000 offenders and detainees in 65 facilities, more than 40 of which are company-owned, with a total bed capacity of nearly 78,000. CCA currently partners with all three federal corrections agencies (the Federal Bureau of Prisons, the U.S. Marshals Service, and Immigration and Customs Enforcement), nearly half of all states and more than a dozen local municipalities.[52] A competitor, The Geo Group, runs facilities in Australia, New Zealand, and South Africa as well as the United States. For example, Geo runs the Arizona State Prison at Florence West, an institution specifically designed for return to custody (RTC) and driving under the influence (DUI) inmates. The Geo Group offers training in employability skills and parenting, substance abuse education and counseling, nutrition/diet education, GED classes, case management, individual/group counseling, stress management, facility work programs, job placement, and prison works/prison labor.[53]

As a result of this expansion, the number of inmates held has increased substantially, and the private prisons now hold almost 120,000 people.[54] Private prisons play an important correctional role in the United States, Australia, and the United Kingdom.[55]

DO PRIVATE PRISONS WORK? ●
The most thorough evaluations of differences in recidivism rates between private and public facilities find little difference between the recidivism rates of inmates released from the two different types of insititutions.[56] There is some evidence that inmates released from private prisons who do reoffend may commit less serious offenses than those released from public institutions, and although private and state institutions cost about the same to operate, private prisons seem cheaper to construct.[57]

Although these findings help support the concept of the private correctional institution, some experts question reliance on private prisons, believing that their use raises a number of vexing problems. Will private providers be able to evaluate programs effectively, knowing that a negative evaluation might cause them to lose their contract? Will they skimp on services and programs in order to reduce costs? Might they not skim off the "easy" cases and leave hardcore inmates to the state's care? And will the need to keep business booming require widening the net to fill empty cells? Must private providers maintain state-mandated liability insurance to cover inmate claims?[58] Some private service providers have been sued because their services were inadequate, causing harm to inmates.[59]

Private corrections firms also run into opposition from existing state correctional staff and management, who fear the loss of jobs and autonomy. Moreover, the public may be skeptical about an untested private concern's ability

Corrections Corporation of America (CCA)

The **Corrections Corporation of America (CCA)** designs, builds, and manages prisons, jails, and detention facilities. You can catch up on what CCA is doing at

www.cengage.com/ criminaljustice/siegel

to provide security and protection. Private corrections also faces administrative problems. How will program quality be controlled? To compete on price, a private facility may have to cut corners to beat the competition. Determining accountability for problems and mishaps will be difficult when dealing with a corporation whose managers and officers are protected legally from personal responsibility for their actions.

LEGAL ISSUES ● There are also unresolved legal problems: Can privately employed guards patrol the perimeter and use deadly force to stop escape attempts? Do private correctional officers have less immunity from lawsuits than state employees? In *Richardson v. McKnight* the Supreme Court held that prison guards employed by a private firm are not entitled to a qualified immunity from suit by prisoners charging a section 1983 violation. Emphasizing that a private firm was systematically organized to manage the prison, the majority said, "[o]ur examination of history and purpose...reveals nothing special enough about the job or about its organizational structure that would warrant providing these private prison guards with a governmental immunity."[60] The case of *Correctional Services Corp. v. Malesko* helps define the rights and protections of inmates in private correctional facilities. Malesko had a heart condition but was forced to walk up stairs rather than take an elevator. When he suffered a heart attack he sued the Correctional Services Corp. (CSC), which was operating the prison, under the federal Civil Rights Act, alleging that the denial of proper medical care violated his civil rights. Citizens are generally allowed to seek damages against federal agents who violate their civil rights. However, the Court ruled that although Malesko could sue an individual employee of the private correctional corporation for allegedly violating his constitutional rights, he could not sue the correctional corporation itself. This decision shields the private prison corporation from suits brought under the federal civil rights statute. The *Malesko* decision bears out the concerns of some critics, who view the private prison as an insidious expansion of state control over citizens: a state-supported entity that actually has more freedom to exert control than the state itself.[61]

In the abstract, a private correctional enterprise may be an attractive alternative to a costly correctional system, but these legal, administrative, and cost issues need to be resolved before private prisons can become widespread.[62] A balance must be reached between the need for a private business to make a profit and the integrity of a prison administration that must be concerned with such complex issues as security, rehabilitation, and dealing with highly dangerous people in a closed environment.[63] And unlike state institutions, private prisons, like all private enterprise systems, must conform to the whims of the marketplace. The private prison industry expanded rapidly during a time when mushrooming inmate populations strained the capacities of existing public institutions to house the inmate population. Now that demand has leveled off, so too has the need for private prisons. In addition, government regulation of the industry has produced conditions in which private prisons have been molded into mirror images of their public sector counterparts. There has also been an anti-privatization movement spearheaded by faith-based groups competing for funding, which has further limited the growth of prisons.[64]

Inmate Populations

This vast correctional system, with more than 1,600 institutions, now contains about 1.5 million inmates. The imprisonment rate—the number of sentenced prisoners per 100,000 residents—is now 506 per 100,000, up from

475 per 100,000 U.S. residents in 2000.[65] During Ronald Reagan's first term as president, 1 in every 77 adults was under the control of the correctional system in the United States. Now, 25 years later, it is 1 in 31, or 3.2 percent of all adults. And the costs of this incarceration binge is high: 1 day in prison costs more than 10 days on parole or 22 days on probation[66]

Who makes up this population? Prison inmates are disproportionately young, male (90%), minority, and poor. Today, there are more than 3,000 black male sentenced prison inmates per 100,000 black males in the United States, 6.5 times the imprisonment rate of white males and 2.5 times that of Hispanic males. Similarly, the black female imprisonment rate (150 prisoners per 100,000 U.S. residents) was almost double the imprisonment rates for Hispanic females (79 prisoners per 100,000) and 3 times the rate for white females (50 per 100,000).[67]

Many inmates suffer from multiple social problems: They are undereducated, underemployed, and come from abusive homes.[68] Recent research found that a significant number, about 9 percent, had experienced homelessness (living on the street or in a homeless shelter) and other, related social problems including mental illness, substance abuse, and unemployment; this is 4–6 times the estimated rate in the general U.S. adult population.[69]

It is not surprising, then, that surveys show that inmates suffer from serious psychological and emotional problems, including psychosis and major depression (Table 11.2).[70]

TABLE 11.2

Mental Health Problems of Prison Inmates

Symptoms in past 12 months or since admission	Percentage of inmates in state prison	Percentage of inmates in federal prison
Major depressive or mania symptoms		
Persistent sad, numb, or empty mood	33	24
Loss of interest or pleasure in activities	35	31
Increased or decreased appetite	32	25
Insomnia or hypersomnia	40	33
Psychomotor agitation or retardation	40	31
Feelings of worthlessness or excessive guilt	35	25
Diminished ability to concentrate or think	28	21
Ever attempted suicide	13	6
Persistent anger or irritability	38	30
Increased/decreased interest in sexual activities	34	29
Psychotic disorder symptoms		
Delusions	12	8
Hallucinations	8	5

Source: Doris James and Lauren Glaze, *Mental Health Problems of Prison and Jail Inmates* (Washington, D.C.: Bureau of Justice Statistics, 2006).

Growth Trends

The inmate population has continued to increase despite a decade-long crime drop, but the rate of increase has slowed (see Figure 11.4). Why has the prison population grown even though the crime rate has fallen? There are a number of reasons for this trend.

- Many people who are released from prison soon return after failing on parole and other forms of early release. Hence, a significant portion of the prison population are re-entries. About 250,000 new inmates, or one-third of the people now entering prison, are parole violators. [71]
- Tough new criminal legislation, including guideline-based mandatory-minimum sentencing laws, increase the chances that a convicted offender will be incarcerated and limit the availability of early release via parole.[72]
- The amount of time served in prison has increased because of such developments as truth-in-sentencing laws that require inmates to serve at least 85 percent of their sentences behind bars.[73]
- There is a significant association among drug use, drug arrests, and prison overcrowding.[74] The drug epidemic in the 1980s and 1990s helped swell prison populations.

As a consequence of these trends, so many people are now going to prison that the federal government estimates that a significant portion of the nation's population will at one time or another be behind prison gates. About 5 percent of the population, or more than 13 million people, will serve a prison sentence sometime during their lives. Men are over eight times more likely than women to be incarcerated in prison at least once. Among men, African Americans (28%) are about twice as likely as Hispanics (16%) and six times as likely as whites (4%) to be admitted to prison during their lives. Among women, about 4 percent of African Americans, 2 percent of Hispanics, and 1 percent of whites will enter prison at least once.[75]

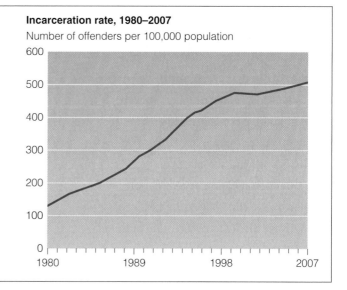

Incarceration Rates

After sharp increases in the 1980s and 1990s, the incarceration rate has recently grown at a slower pace.

Source: Bureau of Justice Statistics, *Correctional Populations in the United States, 1997 and Prisoners in 2007*

http://www.ojp.usdoj.gov/bjs/glance/incrt.htm

Incarceration rate, 1980–2007

Number of offenders per 100,000 population

FIGURE 11.4

Despite the crime drop, the inmate population has not declined, and this has resulted in overcrowding in some institutions. Here, inmates in the reception housing area of the California State Prison in Los Angeles County are jammed into a building that has been turned into a dormitory. California prison officials, grappling with severe overcrowding, are considering moving more long-term inmates to the only state prison in Los Angeles County at Lancaster. State officials, overseen by a federal court judge, are juggling 171,000 prisoners within a prison system built for fewer than half that many inmates. Lancaster residents are worried that additional permanent inmates would mean that their relatives would flock to the area, bringing gang members and a criminal element to a region already hard hit by the recession.

© Ted Soqui/Corbis

Future Trends

The nation's prison population may be "maxing out." Budget cutbacks and belt tightening may halt the expansion of prison construction and the housing of ever more prisoners in already crowded prison facilities. Although new modular construction techniques and double- and triple-bunking of inmates make existing prisons expandable, the secure population probably cannot expand endlessly. As costs skyrocket, some states are now spending more on prisons than on higher education. The public may begin to question the wisdom of a strict incarceration policy. There may also be fewer criminals to incarcerate. The waning of the crack cocaine epidemic in large cities may hasten this decline, because street crimes will decline and fewer offenders will be eligible for the long penalties associated with the possession of crack.[76] As noted earlier, people are now receiving shorter prison sentences than five years ago (even though the time they serve is increasing), and if this trend holds, the prison population may eventually stabilize or even decline.

In the final analysis, change in the correctional population may depend on the faith judges and legislators place in incarceration as a crime control policy. As long as policymakers believe that incarcerating predatory criminals can bring down crime rates, the likelihood of a significant decrease in the institutional population seems remote. But if there is little evidence that this costly system does lower crime rates, then less costly and more effective alternatives may be sought.

REALITY CHECK

MYTH OR REALITY? The inmate population is now decreasing because the crime rate is down.

MYTH: The prison population has continued to grow, even though the crime rate is down.

Tougher prison sentences, coupled with longer stays before release, have resulted in a growing prison population. Nonetheless, the rate of growth seems to be slowing. Why?

ETHICAL CHALLENGES IN CRIMINAL JUSTICE

A Writing Assignment

The governor of your state is running for reelection and wants to build a supermax prison to showcase her willingness to crack down on crime. She also wants to increase the use of mandatory sentences for drug and violent offenders and to put the worst ones in the supermax prison. She has asked you, as a criminal justice expert, to write a paper outlining the pros and cons (no pun intended) of this correctional policy and to come up with alternative models if you disapprove of her plan. What would you say to her?

RealityCheck Revisited

To learn more about the myths and realities related to correctional institutions that were raised in this chapter, visit the following websites.

To read more about supermax prisons, go to

http://www.supermaxed.com/

http://www.nicic.org/pubs/1999/014937.pdf

We noted some myths about the history of corrections. Find out more at

http://www.correctionhistory.org/

http://www.cor.state.pa.us/portal/lib/portal/ overview_updated_july_2008.pdf

http://www.bop.gov/about/history.jsp

SUMMARY

© AP Images/Eric Risberg

1. Identify the various components of the correctional institution system

- The contemporary correctional system has branches in the federal, state, and county levels of government.

- Felons may be placed in state or federal penitentiaries (prisons), which are usually isolated, high-security structures.

- Misdemeanants are housed in county jails, which are sometimes called reformatories or houses of correction.

- Other types of correctional institutions include ranches and farms for adult offenders and community correctional settings, such as halfway houses, for inmates who are about to return to society.

2. Discuss some of the most significant problems facing the correctional system

- The system has problems, and many former inmates recidivate soon after reentering society.

- There is still earnest debate over the true role of secure corrections.

3. Be able to explain how the first penal institutions developed in Europe

- Although the routine use of incarceration as a criminal punishment began in the later eighteenth and early nineteenth centuries, some early European institutions were created specifically to detain and punish criminal offenders.

- The first penal institutions were foul places devoid of proper care, food, and medical treatment.

- From 1776 to 1785, a growing inmate population forced the English to house prisoners on hulks—abandoned ships anchored in harbors.

4. Explain how William Penn revolutionized corrections

- The "modern" American correctional system had its origins in Pennsylvania under the leadership of William Penn.

- Philadelphia's Walnut Street Jail was used to house convicted felons, except those sentenced to death.

5. Compare the New York and Pennsylvania prison models

- In 1816, New York built a new prison at Auburn.

- The Auburn Prison is referred to as the congregate system, because most prisoners ate and worked in groups.

- Pennsylvania established a prison that placed each inmate in a single cell for the duration of his sentence.

- By the late nineteenth century, the congregate system was adopted in all states except Pennsylvania.

6. Chart the development of penal reform

- The National Congress of Penitentiary and Reformatory Discipline, held in Cincinnati in 1870, heralded a new era of prison reform.

- The forerunner of parole began in Ireland in the 1850s, when penitentiary inmates spent the last portion of their sentences living in an intermediate institution and working in the outside community.

- Another important trend was the development of specialized prisons designed to treat particular types of offenders.

- During the past 50 years, the correctional system has undergone a long period of change and turmoil.

- During the prisoners' rights movement, inmates demanded and received civil rights through the court process.

7. List the purposes of jails and be familiar with the makeup of jail populations

- The nation's jails are institutional facilities used to detain accused offenders who cannot make, or are not eligible for, bail prior to trial and to hold convicted offenders awaiting sentence; they serve as the principal institution of secure confinement for offenders convicted of misdemeanors.

- Almost 9 out of every 10 jail inmates are adult males, but the number of adult females in jail has been increasing faster than the number of males.

- Characteristics of jail inmates tend to reflect arrest data: Men, the poor, and racial and ethnic minorities are overrepresented.

8. Be familiar with the term "new-generation jail"

- New-generation jails allow for continuous observation of residents.

9. Classify the different types of federal and state penal institutions

- Maximum-security prisons housing the most notorious criminals are fortress-like, surrounded by stone walls with guard towers at strategic places.

(continued)

- Some states have constructed super-maximum-security prisons (supermax prisons) to house the most predatory criminals.

- Similar in appearance to maximum-security prisons, medium-security prisons are characterized by less vigilant security provisions and a less tense atmosphere.

- Operating without armed guards or perimeter walls, minimum-security prisons usually house the most trustworthy and least violent offenders.

- Prison farms and camps are used to detain offenders.

- Boot camp involves youthful, first-time offenders in military discipline and physical training.

- State and federal correctional systems created community-based correctional models as an alternative to closed institutions.

- Halfway houses are designed to bridge the gap between institutional living and living in the community.

- Correctional facilities are now being run by private firms as business enterprises.

- The most thorough evaluations of recidivism rate differences between private and public facilities find little difference between the recidivism rates of inmates released from the two different types of insititutions.

10. Discuss prison population trends

- The inmate population has continued to increase despite a decade-long crime drop.

- One reason for the increase is that tough new criminal legislation, including mandatory sentencing laws, increases the chances that a convicted offender will be incarcerated and limits the availability for early release via parole.

- The nation's prison population may be "maxing out."

Key Terms

prison, 374
jail, 374
hulks, 376
Walnut Street Jail, 377
penitentiary houses, 377
congregate system, 378
Pennsylvania system, 379
contract system, 380
convict-lease system, 380

medical model, 383
maximum-security prison, 392
super-maximum-security prison, 393
medium-security prison, 393
minimum-security prison, 394
boot camp, 395
shock incarceration, 395
community treatment, 395
halfway house, 395

Review Questions

1. Would you allow a community correctional center to be built in your neighborhood? Why or why not?

2. Should pretrial detainees and convicted offenders be kept in the same institution? Explain.

3. What can be done to reduce overcrowding in correctional facilities?

4. Should private companies be allowed to run correctional institutions? Why or why not?

5. What are the drawbacks to shock incarceration?

12

PRISON LIFE: LIVING IN AND LEAVING PRISON

© John Smierciak, Chicago Tribune/MCT/Landov

RealityCheck

MYTH or REALITY?

▶ The correctional system has failed to live up to its promise because so many inmates recidivate.

▶ Prison rapes are common, and most inmates are sexually assaulted soon after they arrive in prison.

▶ Prisons are total institutions with unique social codes and value systems.

▶ There are significant gender-based differences between the prison experiences of men and women.

▶ Despite negative publicity that "nothing works," many prison rehabilitation efforts are actually effective.

▶ Inmates lose all civil rights once they enter a high-security correctional facility.

▶ Most released inmates fail on parole.

Learning Objectives

1. Discuss the problems of the adult correctional system

2. Know what is meant by the term "total institution"

3. Be familiar with the problem of sexual coercion in prison and with what is being done to help

4. Chart the prisonization process and the development of the inmate social code

5. Compare the lives and cultures of male and female inmates

6. Be familiar with the different forms of correctional treatment

7. Discuss the world of correctional officers

8. Understand the causes of prison violence

9. Know what is meant by prisoners' rights, and discuss some key privileges that have been granted to inmates

10. Be knowledgeable about the parole process and the problems of prisoner reentry

© John Smierciak, *Chicago Tribune*/MCT/Landov

Chapter Outline

Career Profile

Rachel Anita Jung is an executive development program manager in the Arizona Department of Corrections. After receiving her B.A. in Criminal Justice from California State University, San Bernardino, she went on to earn an M.S. in Criminal Justice from the University of Alabama, Tuscaloosa.

Jung always knew she would enter a helping/public service profession. She has a basic curiosity about human behavior, which is why she took courses in both law enforcement and psychology in college. She joined professional associations before taking her first job in the criminal justice field to stay current on issues related to corrections and law enforcement. Jung has held a variety of positions, including jail screener, case manager for a treatment and referral program for substance abusers, and adult probation officer. She is particularly interested in applying restorative justice to corrections.

As program manager, her position has evolved from coordinating training programs for all institutional personnel (officers, support staff, administration, maintenance, health services, and criminal investigations) to developing statewide curricula. Jung delivers training programs periodically in the preservice academy, as well as at various institutions throughout the state. Most recently, she has managed executive development for the corrections staff. She relishes the opportunity to develop in-service programming that influences not only leadership practices with staff specifically, but also the way staff interact with inmates throughout the entire state system. Such a role necessitates continuing professional development and research to ensure inclusion of the field's "best practices" in staff training, while at the same time helping staff to develop the field's "next practices" to meet evolving challenges.

Although the job has challenges, Jung is highly motivated. The restorative justice movement that she favors seems to be having a major impact on corrections. Jung believes her job can help her influence some of the key players in the correctional system—correctional staff, the public, victims, and offenders.

Even though people like Rachel Jung are highly motivated and effective, the sad truth is that a majority of inmates return to prison soon after their release, which contributes to the burgeoning numbers of people behind bars. As the prison population has increased in size, corrections officials have responded by constructing new facilities at a record pace. During the past 25 years, the number of state facilities increased from just under 600 to over 1,000, an increase of about 70 percent. In other words, more than 40 percent of state prisons in operation today were opened in the last 25 years.[1] These facilities take on a variety of forms, including prisons, prison hospitals, prison farms, and boot camps; centers for reception, classification, or alcohol and drug treatment; and work release centers.[2] Although many facilities have a recent pedigree, a significant number are old, decrepit, archaic structures: Of the prisons in this country, 25 were built before 1875, 79 between 1875 and 1924, and 141 between 1925 and 1949. In fact, some of the first prisons ever constructed, such as the Concord Reformatory in Massachusetts, are still in operation.

More than half of all inmates are held in large, fortress-like maximum-security institutions; prison overcrowding is a significant problem. The prison system now holds about 1.5 million people, and many institutions are operating above stated capacity. Recreation and workshop space has been turned into dormitories housing 30 or more inmates in a single room. Most prison experts agree that a minimum of 60 square feet is needed for each inmate, but many prisons fail to reach this standard.

This giant system designed to reform and rehabilitate offenders is instead undergoing a crisis of massive proportions: Meaningful treatment efforts are often wishful thinking, and recidivism rates are shockingly high; about 60 percent return within three years of being released on parole.[3] It is not surprising that many inmates are resentful of the deteriorated conditions or that correctional officers fear the consequences of inmate unrest. Rather than deterring people from future criminality, a prison stay may actually reinforce and/or encourage their criminal offending.[4] The typical prison has been decribed as a "school for crime" in which young offenders are taught by older cons to become sophisticated criminals.

This chapter presents a brief review of some of the most important issues confronting the nation's correctional system and reviews such issues as inmate life, treatment strategies, inmate legal rights, and release from prison.

REALITY CHECK

MYTH OR REALITY? The correctional system has failed to live up to its promise because so many inmates recidivate.

REALITY: Most inmates return to prison, either by committing new crimes or by violating the terms of their parole release.

Do you think this situation reflects the types of people who go to prison or the prison experience itself?

Men Imprisoned

total institution

A regimented, dehumanizing institution such as a prison, in which inmates are kept in social isolation, cut off from the world at large.

Prisons in the United States are **total institutions**. This means that inmates locked within their walls are segregated from the outside world, kept under constant surveillance, and forced to obey strict official rules to avoid facing formal sanctions. Their personal possessions are taken from them, and they must conform to institutional norms of dress and personal appearance. Many human functions are strictly curtailed; heterosexual sex, friendships, family relationships, education, and participation in group activities become privileges of the past.

An inmate's first experience occurs in a classification or reception center, where inmates are given a series of psychological and other tests and evaluated on the basis of their personality, background, offense history, and treatment needs. On the basis of the classification they are given, they are assigned to a permanent facility. Hard-core, repeat, and violent offenders will go to the maximum-security unit; offenders with learning disabilities may be assigned to an institution that specializes in educational services; mentally disordered offenders will be held in a facility that can provide psychiatric care; and so on. Some states have instituted rigorous classification instruments designed to maximize the effectiveness of placements, thereby cutting down on the cost of incarceration. If classification can be conducted in an efficient and effective manner, nondangerous offenders will not needlessly be kept in expensive high-security facilities.[5]

When they arrive at prison, inmates are stripped, searched, shorn, and assigned living quarters. They quickly learn what the term "total institution" really means. Inmate turned author James A. Paluch Jr., calls his cell a "cold coffin . . . leaving a chilling effect on anyone forced to live inside them."[6]

Newcomers swiftly discover that although criminal law applies to inmates just as to any other citizen, it is rarely enforced within prison walls.[7] All previous concepts of personal privacy and dignity are soon forgotten. Inmates in large, inaccessible prisons may find themselves physically cut off from families, friends, and associates. Visitors may find it difficult to travel great distances to see them; mail is censored and sometimes destroyed. And while incarcerated, inmates are instead forced to associate with a peer group afflicted with a disproportionate share of mental and physical problems. Various communicable diseases are commonly found, such as hepatitis C virus, HIV, and syphilis. Not surprisingly, inmate health is significantly worse than that of the general population.[8] Personal losses include the deprivation of liberty, goods and services, heterosexual relationships, autonomy, and security.[9] Inmates may be subject to verbal and physical attack and threats, with little chance of legal redress. Overcrowded prisons are filled with young, aggressive men who are responsible for the majority of inmate-on-inmate assaults.[10]

Prisonerlife.com

Prisonerlife.com is an "Internet magazine" that offers visitors an opportunity to better understand the American justice and prison systems. Visit it at

www.cengage.com/ criminaljustice/siegel

Sexual Coercion

One of the most common aspects of prison life is the threat of sexual coercion, long considered routine in penal insitutions. What factors lead to sexual coercion? Studies show that institutions with the highest sexual coercion rates shared certain characteristics, including barrack-style housing, large prison populations, and lenient security.[11] In these institutions, sexual harassment leads to fights, social isolation, fear, anxiety, and crisis.

Young males may be raped and kept as sexual slaves by older, more aggressive inmates. Some inmates will demand regular sexual access in exchange for protection from even more violent rape and beatings. Younger inmates, gay men, and bisexual men are selected most often to be targets of sexual assaults.[12] In his shocking memoir *Fish*, T. J. Parsell writes about how he was sent to prison at age 17 for a robbery (with a toy gun). Parsell was raped on his first night by four older inmates, who then flipped a coin to decide who would "own" him for the rest of his sentence.[13]

Responding to the threat of prison rape, Congress enacted the Prison Rape Reduction Act of 2003, which established three programs in the Department of Justice:

- A program dedicated to collecting national prison rape statistics, interpreting data, and conducting research
- A program dedicated to the dissemination of information and procedures for combating prison rape
- A program to assist in funding state programs[14]

Even though exposés such as *Fish* indicate that prison rape is an everyday occurrence, it is very difficult to get an accurate reading of the true incidence of prison rape. This is because many inmates refuse to report rape and others may misunderstand what constitutes a "rape"; that is, they don't consider verbally coercing someone to have sex a form of sexual assault.

Surveys show that prison administrators deny or downplay the occurrence of rape.[15] Some research efforts indicate that rape is very rare, whereas others find that nearly half of all inmates experience some form of sexual coercion.[16] For example, a study by the Bureau of Justice Statistics (BJS) examined administrative records from adult and juvenile facilities at state and local levels and found that slightly more than 8,000 male, female, and juvenile inmates—or 0.005 percent of the total incarcerated population—reported being victims of sexual violence; an even smaller percentage of these claims were substantiated.[17] However, it is possible that many inmates do not report sexual attacks and/ or rapes, because they fear retaliation, are embarrassed, or believe nothing can

REALITYCHECK

MYTH OR REALITY? Prison rapes are common, and most inmates are sexually assaulted soon after they arrive in prison.

MYTH: It is difficult to get an accurate measure, but national studies indicate that many inmates are able to avoid sexual coercion and abuse.

Do you think only certain types of inmates are targeted? If so, who is most at risk?

be done. Another federal effort, in which inmates themselves were surveyed, found evidence that 60,000 attacks occur each year. That amounts to an estimated 123 incidents of sexual victimization per 1,000 inmates or the involvement of about 12 percent of all inmates. Surprisingly, inmates report that they are more likely to be sexually abused by prison staff members than by other inmates.[18] In sum, it is difficult to calculate, because many acts are not reported to authorities and because inmates may be reluctant to admit that they were rape victims. However, it is clear that thousands of inmates are sexually assaulted each year.

Adjusting to Prison

Inmates go through a variety of attitude and behavior changes, or cycles, as their sentence unfolds. During the early part of their prison stay, inmates may become easily depressed as they ponder the long duration of their sentence and the loneliness and dangers of prison life. They must learn the ins and outs of survival in the institution: Which persons can be befriended, and which are best avoided? Who will grant favors and for what repayment? To avoid victimization, inmates must learn to adopt a defensive lifestyle.[19] They must discover which areas are relatively safe and which are especially dangerous. Sex offenders in particular often find it difficult to adjust to prison, and some try to create new identities and seek out secure niches that enable them to survive in the prison's general population. Ironically, these new identities and protective niches are undermined when they enter a sex offender treatment program that, by its very efforts to help them, gives them away to the other inmates.[20]

Some learn how to fight back to prove they are not people who can be bullied. Older, more experienced men are better able to cope with the prison experience; younger inmates, especially juveniles sent to adult prisons, are more likely to participate in violent episodes.[21]

Men who viewed violence as an acceptable method of settling disputes before entering prison are the ones most likely to use violence while they are inmates.[22] Inmates who have a history of pre-arrest drug use and have been incarcerated for violent crimes are the ones most likely to get involved in assaults and drug/alcohol offenses while they are incarcerated.[23] Survival in prison may depend on one's ability to identify troubled inmates and avoid contact.

Inmates may find that some prisoners have formed cliques, or groups, based on ethnic backgrounds or personal interests; they are also likely to encounter Mafia-like or racial terror groups that must be dealt with. Inmates may find that power in the prison is shared by correctional officers and inmate gangs; the only way to avoid being beaten and raped may be to learn how to beat and rape. If they are weak and unable to defend themselves, new inmates may find that they are considered "punks"; if they ask a guard for help, they are labeled a "snitch." Those most likely to be targets of sexual assaults may spend their sentence in protective custody, sacrificing the "freedom of the yard" and rehabilitation services for personal protection.[24]

As the prison population expands, the violence and danger of the streets are imported into the prison culture. A recent report funded by New York's Vera Foundation found that violence, medical problems, and segregation of inmates still plague the nation's prisons (see Exhibit 12.1).[25]

EXHIBIT 12.1

Report of the Commission on Safety and Abuse in America's Prisons

Violence There is disturbing evidence of individual assaults and patterns of violence in some U.S. prisons and jails. Corrections officers told the commission about a near-constant fear of being assaulted. Former prisoners recounted gang violence, rape, beatings by officers, and (in one large jail) a pattern of illegal and humiliating strip searches. Former Florida Warden Ron McAndrew described small groups of officers operating as "goon squads" to abuse prisoners and intimidate other staff. Inmate-on-inmate violence is common, even if the prison death rate has been in sharp decline.

Medical Problems High rates of disease and illness among prisoners, coupled with inadequate funding for correctional health care, endanger prisoners, staff, and the public. Much of the public dismiss jails and prisons as sealed institutions, where what happens inside remains inside. In the context of disease and illness, which travel naturally from one environment to another, that view is clearly wrong. Left untreated, staph infections and diseases such as tuberculosis, hepatitis C, and HIV directly affect our families, neighborhoods, and communities. As a result of poverty, substance abuse, and years of poor health care, prisoners as a group are much less healthy than average Americans. Every year, more than 1.5 million people are released from jail and prison carrying a life-threatening contagious disease. At least 350,000 prisoners have a serious mental illness.

Segregation Separating dangerous or vulnerable individuals from the general prison population is now commonplace. In some systems, prisoners who should be housed at safe distances from particular individuals or groups of prisoners end up locked in their cells 23 hours a day, every day, with little opportunity to be productive or prepare for release. People who pose no real threat to anyone and also those who are mentally ill are placed for months or years in high-security units and supermax prisons. In some places, the environment is so severe that people end up completely isolated, confined in constantly bright or constantly dim spaces without any meaningful human contact—torturous conditions that have been proved to cause mental deterioration. Prisoners often are released from solitary confinement and other high-security units directly to the streets, despite the clear dangers of this practice.

Source: John Gibbons and Nicholas de B. Katzenbach, *Confronting Confinement: A Report of the Commission on Safety and Abuse in America's Prisons* (New York: Vera Institute of Justice, 2006).

COPING IN PRISON ● Despite all these hardships, many inmates learn to adapt to the prison routine. Each prisoner has his own method of coping. He may stay alone, become friends with another inmate, join a group, or seek the advice of treatment personnel. Inmates soon learn that their lifestyle and activities can contribute to their being victimized by more aggressive inmates. The more time they spend in closely guarded activities, the less likely they are to become the victims of violence. The more they isolate themselves from others who might protect them, the greater their vulnerability to attack. The more visitors they receive, the more likely they are to be attacked by fellow inmates jealous of their relationships with the outside world.[26]

inmate subculture
The loosely defined culture that pervades prisons and has its own norms, rules, and language.

inmate social code
An unwritten code of behavior, passed from older inmates to younger ones, that serves as a guideline to appropriate inmate behavior within the correctional institution.

The Inmate Social Code

For many years, criminal justice experts maintained that inmates formed their own world with a unique set of norms and rules, known as the **inmate subculture**.[27] A significant aspect of the inmate subculture was a unique **inmate social code**—unwritten guidelines that expressed the values, attitudes, and type of behavior that older inmates demanded of young ones. Passed on from one generation of inmates to another, the inmate social code represented the values of interpersonal relations in the prison.

National attention was first drawn to the inmate social code and subculture by Donald Clemmer's classic book *The Prison Community*, in which he presented a detailed sociological study of life in a maximum-security prison.[28] Clemmer was able to identify a unique language, or argot, that prisoners use. He found that prisoners tend to group themselves into cliques on the basis of such personal criteria as sexual preference, political beliefs, and offense history. He found complex sexual relationships in prison and concluded that many heterosexual men turn to homosexual relationships when faced with long sentences and the loneliness of prison life.

Clemmer's most important contribution may have been his identification of the **prisonization** process. This he defined as the inmate's assimilation into the existing prison culture through acceptance of its language, sexual code, and norms of behavior. Those who become the most "prisonized" are the least likely to reform on the outside.

Using Clemmer's work as a jumping-off point, a number of prominent sociologists have set out to explore more fully the various roles in the prison community. The most important principles of the dominant inmate culture are listed in Exhibit 12.2.

Although some inmates violate the code and exploit their peers, the "right guy" is someone who uses the inmate social code as his personal behavior guide. He is always loyal to his fellow prisoners, keeps his promises, is dependable and trustworthy, and never interferes with inmates who are conniving against the officials.[29] The right guy does not go around looking for a fight, but he never runs away from one; he acts "like a man."

The effects of prisonization may be long-term and destructive. Many inmates become hostile to the legal system, learning to use violence as a means of solving problems and to value criminal peers.[30] For some this change may

prisonization

Assimilation into the separate culture in the prison that has its own set of rewards and behaviors, as well as its own norms, rules, and language. The traditional prison culture is now being replaced by a violent gang culture.

EXHIBIT 12.2

Elements of the Inmate Social Code

1. ***Don't interfere with inmates' interests.*** Within this area of the code are maxims related to serving the least amount of time in the greatest possible comfort. For example, inmates are warned never to betray another inmate to authorities; in other words, grievances must be handled personally. Other aspects of the noninterference doctrine include "Don't be nosy," "Don't have a loose lip," "Keep off the other inmates' backs," and "Don't put another inmate on the spot."

2. ***Don't lose your head.*** Inmates are also cautioned to refrain from arguing, quarreling, or engaging in other emotional displays with fellow inmates. The novice may hear such warnings as "Play it cool," and "Do your own time."

3. ***Don't exploit inmates.*** Prisoners are warned not to take advantage of one another: "Don't steal from cons," "Don't welsh on a debt," and "Be right."

4. ***Be tough and don't lose your dignity.*** Although Rule 2 forbids conflict, once it starts, an inmate must be prepared to deal with it effectively and thoroughly. Maxims include "Don't cop out," "Don't weaken," and "Be tough; be a man."

5. ***Don't be a sucker.*** Inmates are cautioned not to make fools of themselves or support the guards or prison administration over the interest of the inmates: "Be sharp."

Source: Gresham Sykes, *The Society of Captives* (Princeton, N.J.: Princeton University Press, 1958).

be permanent; for others it is temporary, and they may revert to their "normal" life after release.

The New Inmate Culture

The importation of outside values into the inmate culture has had a dramatic effect on prison life. Although the "old" inmate subculture may have been harmful because its norms and values insulated the inmate from change efforts, it also helped create order in the institution and prevented violence among the inmates. People who violated the code and victimized others were sanctioned by their peers. An understanding developed between guards and inmate leaders: The guards would let the inmates have things their own way, and the inmates would not let things get out of hand and draw the attention of the administration.

The old system may be dying or already dead in most institutions. The change seems to have been precipitated by the black power movement in the 1960s and 1970s. Black inmates were no longer content to play a subservient role and challenged the power of established white inmates. As the black power movement gained prominence, racial tension in prisons created divisions that severely altered the inmate subculture. Older, respected inmates could no longer cross racial lines to mediate disputes. Predatory inmates could victimize others without fear of retaliation. Consequently, more inmates than ever are now assigned to protective custody for their own safety.

In the new culture, African American and Latino inmates are much more cohesively organized than whites.[31] Their groups sometimes form out of religious or political affiliations, such as the Black Muslims; out of efforts to combat discrimination in prison, such as the Latino group La Nuestra Familia; or from street gangs, such as the Vice Lords or Gangster Disciples in the Illinois prison system and the Crips in California. Where white inmates have successfully organized, it is in the form of a neo-Nazi group such as the Aryan Brotherhood. Racially homogeneous gangs are so cohesive and powerful that they are able to replace the original inmate code with one of their own.

 MYTH OR REALITY? Prisons are total institutions with unique social codes and value systems.

REALITY: Prisons are a world in themselves, with a unique set of values, attitudes, and behaviors.

Can you think of another type of living arrangement that may be comparable? Hint: Do you live in a dorm?

Women Imprisoned

Before 1960, few women were in prison. Women's prisons were relatively rare and were usually an outgrowth of male institutions. Only four institutions for women were built between 1930 and 1950; in comparison, 34 women's prisons were constructed during the 1980s as crime rates soared.

At the turn of the twentieth century, female inmates were viewed as morally depraved people who flouted conventional rules of female behavior. The treatment of white and African American women differed significantly. In some states, white women were placed in female-only reformatories designed to improve their deportment; black women were placed in male prisons, where they were put on chain gangs and were subject to beatings.[32]

Female Institutions

State jurisdictions have been responding to the influx of female offenders into the correctional system by expanding the facilities for housing and treating

Women's Prison Association

The **Women's Prison Association** is a service and advocacy organization committed to helping women with criminal justice histories realize new possibilities for themselves and their families. Access it via

www.cengage.com/ criminaljustice/siegel

them. Women's prisons tend to be smaller than those housing male inmates. Although some female institutions are strictly penal, with steel bars, concrete floors, and other security measures, the majority are nonsecure institutions similar to college dormitories and group homes in the community. Women's facilities, especially those in the community, commonly offer inmates a great deal of autonomy and allow them to make decisions affecting their daily lives.

However, like men's prisons, women's prisons suffer from a lack of adequate training and of health, treatment, and educational facilities. Psychological counseling often takes the form of group sessions conducted by laypeople, such as correctional officers. Many female inmates are parents and had custody of their children before incarceration, but little effort is made to help them develop better parenting skills. Although most female (and male) inmates have at least one child, less than a quarter actually get an annual visit. Who takes care of these children while their mothers are incarcerated? Most children of incarcerated women are placed with their father, a grandparent, another relative, or a family friend. About 10 percent wind up in foster homes or state facilities.[33]

Job-training opportunities are also a problem. Where vocational training exists, it is in areas that offer limited financial reward, which hinders adjustment upon release. Female inmates, many of whom were on the economic margin before their incarceration began, find little opportunity for improvement during their prison experience.[34] Surveys also indicate that the prison experience does little to prepare women to reenter the workforce after they complete their sentence. Gender stereotypes still shape vocational opportunities.[35] Female inmates are still being trained for "women's roles," such as child rearing, and are not given the preparation they need to make successful adjustments in the community.[36]

Female Inmates

Like their male counterparts, female inmates are young (most are under age 30), minority group members, unmarried, undereducated (more than half are high school dropouts), and either unemployed or underemployed. The typical woman behind bars is a poor, unskilled woman of color with small children, has health problems, has a history of abuse, and is incarcerated for low-level drug or property offenses.[37]

Incarcerated women also have had a troubled family life. Significant numbers were at-risk children, products of broken homes and the welfare system; over half have received welfare at some time during their adult lives. Many claim to have been physically or sexually abused at some point in their lives. This pattern continued in adult life: Many female inmates were victims of domestic violence. It is not surprising that many display psychological problems.[38]

A significant number of female inmates report having substance abuse problems. About three-fourths have used drugs at some time in their lives, and almost half were involved with addictive drugs, such as cocaine, heroin, or PCP. The incarceration of so many women who are low criminal risks yet face a high risk of exposure to HIV and other health threats because of their prior history of drug abuse presents a significant problem. One recent study of incarcerated women found that one-third of the sample reported that before their arrest, they had traded sex for money or drugs; 24 percent of the women reported trading sex for money or drugs "weekly or more often."[39] Such risky behavior significantly increases the likelihood of their carrying the AIDS virus or other sexually transmitted diseases.

The picture that emerges of the female inmate is troubling. After a lifetime of emotional turmoil, physical and sexual abuse, and drug use, it seems improbable that overcrowded, underfunded correctional institutions can forge a dramatic turnaround in the behavior of at-risk female inmates. Many have lost custody of their children, a trauma that is more likely to afflict those who are already substance abusers and suffer from depression.[40] It should come as no surprise that many female inmates feel strain and conflict, which are psychological conditions related to violent episodes.[41]

SEXUAL EXPLOITATION ● Lack of opportunity is not the only problem female inmates face. Just as for male inmates, it is not uncommon for female prisoners to be sexually abused and exploited by male correctional workers, who apply either brute force or psychological coercion to gain sexual control over inmates.[42] Staff-on-inmate sexual misconduct covers a wide range of behaviors, from lewd remarks, to voyeurism, to assault and rape. Because male correctional officers now are commonly assigned to women's prisons, there have also been major scandals involving the sexual exploitation and rape of female inmates. Few if any of these incidents are reported, and perpetrators rarely go to trial. Institutional workers cover for each other, and women who file complaints are offered little protection from vengeful guards.[43] Because the situation persists, more than 40 states and the District of Columbia have passed laws criminalizing some types of staff sexual misconduct in prisons.[44]

Adapting to the Female Institution

Daily life in women's prisons differs somewhat from that in male institutions. For one thing, unlike male inmates, women usually do not present an immediate physical danger to staff and fellow inmates. Relatively few engage in violent behavior, and incidents of inmate-initiated sexual aggression, so common in male institutions, are rare in women's prisons.[45] Few female inmates experience the violent atmosphere common in male institutions or suffer the same racial and ethnic conflict and divisiveness.[46] But even though female inmates may

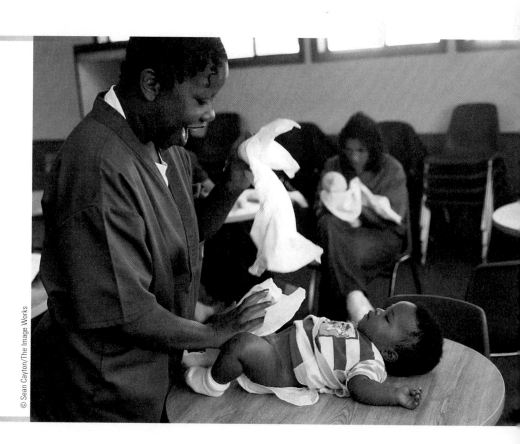

Many female inmates are moms, and keeping them involved with their children can be a challenge. Here a mother changes the diaper on her year-and-a-half-old son, as another mother visits with her newborn baby at the visitor's center inside the Colorado Women's Correctional Facility in Canon City, Colorado. The two incarcerated mothers get to visit with their children for three hours each week through the New Horizon Ministries, a Mennonite prison ministry that cares for the children and, later, reunites them with their parents.

© Sean Cayton/The Image Works

Policies, Programs, and Issues in Criminal Justice

World Apart: Life in a Female Prison

Are women better adjusted in prison than men or is this just another criminal justice–related myth? To find out, Cristina Rathbone has dedicated her journalistic career to both exposing myths about women's prisons and telling the life story of women behind bars. She is appalled at the conditions they are forced to endure, at their exploitation by correctional officers, and at their struggles to maintain ties to family and friends. Rather than being violent and aggressive, the average female inmate she encounters is more likely to be a 35-year-old single mother with three children serving a five-year mandatory sentence for a first-time, nonviolent drug offense.

A great deal of Rathbone's research was conducted in a female prison in Massachusetts, MCI-Framingham. There, after years of battling authorities for entré, she was able to meet and interview female inmates in the visitors' rooms. She finds that, in sharp contrast to the men's prisons in the state, where most inmates are serving time for violent crimes, almost two-thirds of incarcerated women—63 percent—are serving time for nonviolent offenses. Most are drug and alcohol addicts; about a third are seriously mentally ill; more than 70 percent are mothers.

Rathbone finds the female inmates are cut off from their families and provided with little help in maintaining contact with their children. Behind prison walls, they are offered a minimum of education and job-training programs. It is not surprising then that more than 60 percent of the women in Framingham receive some kind of mental health services. The truth, Rathbone finds, is that the air in a female prison reeks more of despair than of depravity.

Rathbone finds that female prisons have not changed as much as we would like to believe since they were instituted more than 100 years ago. When MCI-Framingham first opened its doors in 1877, the prison held just three women convicted of violent acts and more than 240 convicted of nonviolent crimes, including a majority imprisoned for being drunk or promiscuous. Many were sentenced to incarceration for being "lewd," "stubborn," "intemperate," or "idle." At the time, living and sleeping with a man outside marriage was punishable by prison terms of up to five years. The first inmates were almost exclusively poor, first-generation immigrants; apparently, the law applied to some people more than to others. Despite their shortcomings, female prisons such as Framingham were considered an improvement over prior practices, in which women were simply sent to the basements or attics of men's prisons, where they had no opportunities for exercise or education. Rape—at the hands of both guards and male inmates—was common.

© Mike Kemp/Rubberball Productions/Getty Images

experience less discomfort than males, that does not mean their experience is a bed of roses. Many still experience fear and are forced to undergo a process of socialization fraught with danger and volatile situations.[47] However, female inmates seem to receive more social support from both internal sources (e.g., inmate peers, correctional staff) and external sources (e.g., families, peers)—a factor that may lessen the pains of prison life, help them adjust, and improve the social climate within female institutions.[48]

The rigid, anti-authority inmate social code found in many male institutions does not exist in female institutions.[49] Confinement for women, however, may produce severe anxiety and anger because of separation from families and loved ones and the inability to function in normal female roles. Unlike men, who direct their anger outward, female prisoners may turn to more self-destructive acts to cope with their problems. Female inmates are more likely

REALITY CHECK

MYTH OR REALITY?   There are significant gender-based differences between the prison experiences of men and women.

REALITY: Women are less violent than men in prison, and the culture of the female prison has spawned nurturing "make-believe" families and other pseudo-family groups, whereas male institutions are dominated by violent prison gangs.

Do you think this is because women are naturally less violent?

Female prisons had programs that taught inmates how to read, gave them job training, and provided instruction in "domestic skills" such as knitting and sewing.

Rathbone spent more than four years investigating the prison, including the legal fight to gain access to inmates. Even then she was harassed, made to wait hours to enter the visitors' area, and subjected to random searches. She meets Denise, a 32-year-old crack addict serving time for an illegal drug purchase. Denise is terrified when she arrives in prison and is befriended by older, more experienced inmates. She despairs for her 9-year-old son, Pat, who has been left in the care of his abusive father. Denise's fears are well founded; by the time she leaves prison, Pat has been incarcerated for petty theft.

Denise's story is not unique. Framingham inmates are the daughters of abuse and abandonment. Some are given long sentences for acting as drug mules and traffickers for their boyfriends who go free. Others have been ignored by their parents and forced to fend for themselves on the streets. Many of the inmates engage in sexual relationships with correctional officers, even though it is a felony under state law. Some are seeking favors and special treatment, whereas others are simply bored and looking for ways to pass the time. Those who do not wish such intimacies can still be victimized: Inmates are defenseless against sexual abuse and rape, but relatively few cases are prosecuted, and even fewer result in convictions.

Rathbone calls for the reform of women's prisons. Sentences should be geared to the special status of women. Mothers should have better access to their children. Meaningful programming is needed. Women must be protected from predatory guards. Despite the problems, she is convinced that dedicated and sensitive prison administrators can make a meaningful difference. Are female inmates different from their male counterparts? Rathbone's research seems to show that in fact they are!

Critical Thinking

1. What would you suggest might be an effective method of helping imprisoned mothers to have a positive relationship with their children? Should they be given special privileges (such as home visits) that are not available to childless inmates? Or is that unfair and discriminatory?

2. Discuss the concept of a co-ed prison. Would prison life improve if men and women were housed in a single institution? Or might the dangers outweigh any benefit?

© Mike Kemp/Rubberball Productions/Getty Images

than males to mutilate their own bodies and to attempt suicide. For example, one common practice among female inmates is self-mutilation, or "carving." This ranges from simple scratches to carving on their body the name of their boyfriend or even complex statements or sentences ("To mother, with hate").[50]

Another form of adaptation to prison used by women is the **make-believe family**. This group contains masculine and feminine figures acting as fathers and mothers; some even act as children and take on the role of brother or sister. Formalized marriages and divorces may be conducted. Sometimes one inmate plays multiple roles, such that a "sister" in one family may "marry" and become the "wife" of another inmate. It is estimated that about half of all female inmates are members of make-believe families.[51] Life in a female prison is the topic of the Policies, Programs, and Issues feature on page 418.

make-believe family
In female institutions, the substitute family group—including faux father, mother, and siblings—created by some inmates.

Correctional Treatment Methods

Almost every prison facility uses some mode of treatment for inmates. This may come in the form of individual or group therapy programs or educational or vocational training. This section presents a number of therapeutic methods that have been used nationally in correctional settings and identifies some of their more salient features.

Individual and Group Treatment

Prison inmates typically suffer from a variety of cognitive and psychosocial deficits, such as poor emotional control, social skills, and interpersonal problem solving; these deficits are often linked to long-term substance abuse. Modern counseling programs help inmates to control emotions (e.g., understanding why they feel the way they do, dealing with nervousness or anxiety, solving their problems creatively); to communicate with others (e.g., understanding what people tell them, communicating clearly when they write); to deal with legal concerns (e.g., keeping out of legal trouble, avoiding breaking laws); to manage general life issues (e.g., finding a job, dealing with difficult coworkers, being a good parent); and to develop and maintain social relationships (e.g., having good relations with others, making others happy, making others proud).[52]

To achieve these goals, correctional systems use a variety of intensive individual and group techniques, including behavior modification, aversive therapy, milieu therapy, reality therapy, transactional analysis, and responsibility therapy.

anger management programs

Group therapy offered to help participants to control their anger and, in general, to achieve self-control, often through cognitive-behavioral approaches.

ANGER MANAGEMENT • Anger and lack of self-control have been linked to violent criminal behavior both in the institution and, upon release, in the community. As a result, **anger management programs** may be the form of group therapy most frequently offered within prison settings.[53] Anger management is often combined with other group techniques as part of drug treatment and sex offender treatment programs. Cognitive-behavioral approaches are frequently used as a means of helping inmates find ways to control their anger. Anger management or violence management programs have also been implemented in other countries; for example, violence management programs are widely used in Australia.[54]

FAITH-BASED PROGRAMS • Research has shown that inmates involved in religious programs and education do better following release than those in comparison groups but that the differences quickly erode.[55] Nonetheless, under the George W. Bush administration, faith-based rehabilitation efforts flourished.[56] In 2003, then governor Jeb Bush dedicated the first faith-based prison in the United States, a 750-bed medium-security facility for males in Lawtey, Florida. Governor Bush claimed that the only way to achieve the rehabilitation of criminals and to reduce recidivism was to "lead them to God."[57] Missouri and Florida also opened facilities for youthful offenders based on faith-based principles.[58] Faith-based programs seem to work better with some inmates than others, and those who enter such programs with feelings of self-worth are more likely to complete the course than those with less confidence.[59]

therapeutic communities

Institutions that rely on positive peer pressure within a highly structured social environment to create positive inmate change.

DRUG TREATMENT • Most prisons have programs designed to help inmates suffering from alcohol and substance abuse. One approach is to provide abusers with methadone as a substitute for heroin; some evaluations have shown this method to be effective.[60] Because substance abuse is so prevalent among correctional clients, some correctional facilities have been reformulated into **therapeutic communities (TC)** that apply a psychosocial, experiential learning process and rely on positive peer pressure within a highly structured social environment. The community itself, including staff and program participants, becomes the primary method of change. They work together as members of a "family" in order to create a culture where community members confront each other's negative behavior and attitudes and establish an open, trusting, and safe environment. The TC approach, then, relies on mutual self-help. It also encourages personal disclosure rather than the isolation of the general prison culture.[61]

TREATING THE AIDS-INFECTED INMATE ● The AIDS-infected inmate has been the subject of great concern. Two groups of people at high risk of contracting HIV are intravenous drug users who share needles and males who engage in same-sex relations—two behaviors common in prison. Because drug use is common and syringes scarce, many high-risk inmates share drug paraphernalia, increasing the danger of HIV infection.[62]

Although the numbers are constantly changing, the rate of HIV infection among state and federal prisoners has stabilized at around 2 percent, and there are about 25,000 HIV-infected inmates.

Correctional administrators have found it difficult to arrive at effective policies to confront AIDS. Although all state and federal jurisdictions do some AIDS testing, only the federal Bureau of Prisons and relatively few states conduct mass screenings of all inmates. Most states test inmates only if there are significant indications that they are HIV-positive.

Most correctional systems are now training staff about AIDS. Educational programs for inmates are often inadequate because administrators are reluctant to give them information on safe sex and the proper cleaning of drug paraphernalia (both sexual relations and drug use are forbidden in prison).

Educational Programs

Besides programs stressing personal growth through individual analysis or group therapy, inmate rehabilitation is also pursued through vocational and educational training. Although these two kinds of training sometimes differ in style and content, they can also overlap when, for example, education involves practical, job-related study.

The first prison treatment programs were in fact educational. A prison school was opened at the Walnut Street Jail in 1784. Elementary courses were offered in New York's prison system in 1801 and in Pennsylvania's in 1844. An actual school system was established in Detroit's House of Corrections in 1870, and the Elmira Reformatory opened a vocational trade school in 1876. Today, most institutions provide some type of educational program. At some prisons, inmates can obtain a high school diploma or a general educational development (GED) certificate through equivalency exams. Other institutions provide an actual classroom education, usually staffed by certified teachers employed full time at the prison or by part-time teachers who also teach full time at nearby public schools.

© Crime/Alamy

Educational programs vary in quality and intensity. Some are full-time programs employing highly qualified and concerned educators, whereas others are part-time programs without any real goals or objectives. In some institutions, programs have been designed to circumvent the difficulties inherent in the prison structure. They encourage volunteers from the community and local schools to tutor willing and motivated inmates. Some prison administrators have arranged flexible schedules for inmate students and actively encourage their participation in these programs. In several states, statewide school districts serving prisons have been created. Forming such districts can make better-qualified staff available and provide the materials and resources necessary for meaningful educational programs.

Most research indicates that participation in correctional education is related to lower recidivism rates upon release.[63] It may also have benefit for inmates while they are in prison. Karen Lahm found that inmates who take part in GED, high school, vocational, and/or college programs report much fewer rule violations while incarcerated than those who ignore educational opportunities.[64]

Vocational Programs

Every state correctional system also has some job-related services for inmates. Some have elaborate training programs inside the institution, whereas others have instituted prerelease and postrelease employment services. Inmates who hope to obtain parole need to participate in prison industry. Documenting a history of stable employment in prison is essential if parole agents are to convince prospective employers that the ex-offender is a good risk, and postrelease employment is usually required for parole eligibility.[65]

A few of the more important work-related services are discussed in the following sections.

VOCATIONAL TRAINING • Most institutions provide vocational training programs. On the federal level, the Federal Prison Industries, which is more commonly known as UNICOR, teaches inmates to produce goods and services for sale to government agencies only.

- *Clothing and textiles*. This program encompasses about 65 products from mailbag repair to the production of towels.
- *Corporate services*. These contracts include materials, equipment, construction, information technology, lease agreements, partnerships, and joint ventures.
- *Electronics*. This program provides such items as cable assemblies, wiring harnesses, circuit card assemblies, battery boxes, military connectors, power distribution systems, portable light systems, and specialty cables.

© AP Images/Eric Risberg

On June 3, 2009, Michael R. Harris, editor-in-chief of the San Quentin News, *hands out copies of the newspaper to visiting criminal justice students from San Diego State University. Like journalists everywhere, the staff of the* San Quentin News *cover news, sports, and the local arts scene. But these reporters are truly "pen men": The paper is written for and by inmates of the San Quentin State Prison in California. Working on the paper provides inmates with both educational and vocational training.*

- *Fleet management/vehicular components*. These contracts provide items such as retrofit, vehicle components, remanufacturing of engines, and forklifts.
- *Industrial products*. This program provides a diverse array of metal fabrication capabilities. The manufacturing capabilities include stamping, farming, machining, welding, coating-finishing systems, and tool and die operations.
- *Office furniture*. This program comprises a wide variety of furniture products, including Dorm and Quarters furniture, office furniture, office seating, systems furniture, and case goods.

About 25 percent of federal prisoners work in 100 or so factories within federal prisons. The minimum UNICOR wage is 23 cents an hour, and the maximum wage is $1.15. UNICOR sales average about $800 million a year and yield a profit of $120 million a year—making UNICOR the most profitable line of business in the United States.[66]

Despite the promising aspects of such programs, they have also been seriously criticized. Inmates often have trouble finding skill-related, high-paying jobs upon their release. Equipment in prisons is often secondhand, obsolete, and hard to come by. Some programs are thinly disguised excuses for prison upkeep and maintenance, and unions and other groups resent the intrusion of prison labor into their markets.

WORK RELEASE • To supplement programs stressing rehabilitation via in-house job training or education, more than 40 states have attempted to implement **work release** or **furlough** programs. These allow deserving inmates to leave the institution and hold regular jobs in the community.

Inmates enrolled in work release may live at the institutions at night while working in the community during the day. However, security problems (for instance, contraband may be brought in) and the usual remoteness of prisons often make this arrangement difficult. More typical is the extended work release, where prisoners are allowed to remain in the community for significant periods of time. To help inmates adjust, some states operate community-based prerelease centers where inmates live while working. Some inmates may work at their previous jobs, whereas others seek new employment.

Like other programs, work release has its good and bad points. On the one hand, inmates are sometimes reluctantly received in the community and find that certain areas of employment are closed to them. Citizens are often concerned about prisoners "stealing" jobs or working for lower than normal wages; consequently, such practices are prohibited by Public Law 89–176, which controls the federal work release program.

On the other hand, inmates gain many benefits from work release, including the ability to maintain work skills, to maintain community ties, and to make an easier transition from prison to the outside world. For those who have learned a skill in the institution, work release offers an excellent opportunity to try out a new occupation. For others, the job may be a training situation in which new skills are acquired. A number of states have reported that few work release inmates abscond while in the community.

PRIVATE PRISON ENTERPRISE • The federal government helped put private industry into prisons when it approved the Free Venture Program in 1976. Seven states, including Connecticut, South Carolina, and Minnesota, were given grants to implement private industries inside prison walls.

Today, private prison industries have used a number of models. One approach, the state-use model, makes the correctional system a supplier of goods and services that serves state-run institutions. The California Prison Industry

work release

A prison treatment program that allows inmates to be released during the day to work in the community and returned to prison at night.

furlough

A correctional policy that allows inmates to leave the institution for vocational or educational training, for employment, or to maintain family ties.

Authority (PIA) is an inmate work program that provides work assignments for approximately 7,000 inmates and operates 70 service, manufacturing, and agricultural industries in 23 prisons. These industries produce a variety of goods and services, including flags, printing services, signs, binders, eyewear, gloves, office furniture, clothing, and cell equipment. PIA products and services are available to government entities, including federal, state, and local government agencies. Court-ordered restitutions or fines are deducted from the wages earned by PIA inmates and transferred to the Crime Victims' Restitution Fund. PIA inmates receive wages between 30 cents and 95 cents per hour, before deductions.[67]

In another approach, the free-enterprise model, private companies set up manufacturing units on prison grounds or purchase goods made by inmates in shops owned and operated by the corrections department. In the corporate model, a semi-independent business is created on prison grounds, and its profits go to the state government and inmate laborers.[68] Despite widespread publicity, the partnership between private enterprise and the prison community has been limited to a few experimental programs. However, it is likely to grow in the future.

POSTRELEASE PROGRAMS • A final element of job-related programming involves helping inmates obtain jobs before they are released and keep them once they are on the outside. A number of correctional departments have set up employment services designed to ease the transition between institution and community. Employment program staff assess inmates' backgrounds to determine their abilities, interests, goals, and capabilities. They also help them create job plans essential to receiving early release (parole) and successfully reintegrating into the community. Some programs maintain community correctional placements in sheltered environments that help inmates bridge the gap between institutions and the outside world. Services include job placement, skill development, family counseling, and legal and medical assistance.

Can Rehabilitation Work?

Despite the variety and number of treatment programs in operation, questions remain about their effectiveness. In their oft-cited research, Robert Martinson and his associates (1975) found that a majority of treatment programs were failures, giving birth to the cry that "nothing works" in prison rehabiliations.[69] Martinson's work was followed by efforts showing that some high-risk offenders were even more likely to commit crimes after they had been placed in treatment programs than before the onset of rehabilitation efforts.[70] A slew of reviews have claimed that correctional treatment efforts aimed at youthful offenders provide little evidence that rehabilitation can occur within correctional settings. Evidence is scant that treatment efforts—even those that include vocational, educational, and mental health services—can consistently lower recidivism rates.[71]

In the decades since Martinson's work was published, there has been considerable debate over the effectiveness of correctional treatment. Even some of the most carefully crafted treatment efforts, using the most up-to-date rehabilitation modalities (such as cognitive-behavioral therapy), have failed to have a positive impact on inmates returning to the community.[72] In contrast, treatment proponents have dismissed the "nothing works" philosophy as exaggerated and, using sophisticated data analysis techniques, have found evidence that correctional rehabilitation can be effective.[73] When Paul Gendreau and Robert Ross reviewed the published work on correctional rehabilitation programs, they found that many intervention programs reported success.[74] Martinson eventually conceded that "contrary to [his] previous position, some

Connecticut's prison enterprise

To read about **Connecticut's prison enterprise**, go to www.cengage.com/criminaljustice/siegel

treatment programs *do* have an appreciable effect on recidivism. Some programs are indeed beneficial."[75] More recently, Mark Lipsey and Francis Cullen's comprehensive review of the studies of correctional rehabilitation found consistently positive effects on reducing recidivism. However, even these advocates of prison-based rehabilitation recognize that considerable variability exists in those effects, depending on the type of treatment, its implementation, and the nature of the offenders to whom it is applied.[76]

REALITYCHECK

MYTH OR REALITY? Despite negative publicity that "nothing works," many prison rehabilitation efforts are actually effective.

REALITY: Many prison programs have proved effective, and the "nothing works" mantra seems overstated.

How would you treat prison inmates? Should they get a free education and job training, benefits that may not be available to the average American?

Guarding the Institution

Controlling a prison is a complex task. On the one hand, a tough, high-security environment may meet the goals of punishment and control but fail to reinforce positive behavior changes. On the other hand, too liberal an administrative stance can lower staff morale and place inmates in charge of the institution. For many years, prison guards were viewed as ruthless people who enjoyed their power over inmates, fought rehabilitation efforts, were racist, and had a "lock psychosis" developed from years of counting, numbering, and checking on inmates. This view has changed in recent years. Correctional officers are now viewed as public servants who are seeking the security and financial rewards of a civil service position.[77] Most are in favor of rehabilitation efforts and do not harbor any particular animosity toward the inmates.[78] The correctional officer has been characterized as a "people worker" who must be prepared to deal with the problems of inmates on a personal level and also as a member of a complex bureaucracy who must be able to cope with its demands.

Correctional officers play a number of roles in the institution. They supervise cell houses, dining areas, shops, and other facilities, as well as perching up on the walls, armed with rifles, to oversee the yard and prevent escapes. Correctional officers also sit on disciplinary boards and escort inmates to hospitals and court appearances.

The greatest problem faced by correctional officers is the duality of their role: maintainers of order and security *and* advocates of treatment and rehabilitation. Added to this basic dilemma is the changing inmate role. In earlier times, correctional officers could count on inmate leaders to help them maintain order, but now they are faced with a racially charged atmosphere in which violence is a way of life. Today, correctional work in some institutions can be filled with danger, tension, boredom, and little evidence that efforts to help inmates lead to success. Nonetheless, as recent research by Mike Vuolo and Candace Kruttschnitt shows, correctional officers can have a sizable impact on prisoners' ability to adjust to prison life. Correctional staff members who conduct themselves professionally and gain the respect and cooperation of the inmates are able to have a very positive influence on their later readjustment to society. In contrast, those who fail miserably on both counts may be contributing the nation's high recidivism rates.[79]

For more on the work of a correctional officer, read the Careers in Criminal Justice feature on page 426.

Careers in Criminal Justice

CORRECTIONAL OFFICER

Duties and Characteristics of the Job

- The primary job of a correctional officer is to supervise individuals who are serving time in prison after being convicted.
- Their duties include supervising and submitting reports on inmate behavior, maintaining order within the population by enforcing institutional rules and policies, and ensuring order in the institution by searching for contraband or settling disputes between inmates.
- Although correctional officers tend to work a standard five-day, 40-hour work week, odds are they will work overtime on weekends, holidays, and nights as well, because jails and prisons must be staffed at all hours.

Job Outlook

- Opportunities exist for employment at the local level, but a majority of correctional officer positions are at state and federal prisons. A smaller number of jobs are available with private institutions.

Salary

- Median annual salary for a correctional officer is about $36,000.
- Median annual earnings in the public sector were recently $47,750 in the federal government, $36,140 in state government, and $34,820 in local government.
- Correctional officers usually are provided with uniforms or a clothing allowance to purchase their own uniforms. Their retirement coverage entitles correctional officers to retire at age 50 after 20 years of service or at any age with 25 years of service.

Opportunities

- Thanks to a growing demand for correctional officers, combined with high rates of turnover within the field, prospects for employment are very good.
- A good correctional officer with the proper education and training has the potential to be promoted to correctional sergeant and to other administrative and supervisory positions.

Female Correctional Officers

Women now work side by side with male guards in almost every state, performing the same duties. Research indicates that discipline has not suffered because of the inclusion of women in the guard force. Sexual assaults have been rare, and more negative attitudes have been expressed by the female guards' male peers than by inmates. Most commentators believe that the presence of female guards can have an important beneficial effect on the self-image of inmates and can improve the guard–inmate working relationship.

Ironically, female correctional officers may find that an assignment to a male institution can boost their career. Recent restrictions on male staff in female institutions, in the wake of well-publicized sex scandals, have forced administrators to assign women officers to the dormitory areas, the least desirable areas in which to work. Women officers are not similarly restricted in male-only facilities.[80]

Qualifications

- Exact qualifications vary depending on what level of government and what type of setting the position is in.
- A majority of correctional institutions look for several characteristics in potential employees: Correctional officers should be U.S. citizens, be at least 18 to 21 years old, and be able to pass a background check and a drug test.
- Correctional officers must also be in good physical and mental health, meet education requirements, and be able to work in a challenging environment where good judgment and quick thinking are necessary.
- Tests may be administered to judge whether an applicant meets these qualifications.

Education and Training

- Although only a high school diploma may be necessary to become a correctional officer, a bachelor's degree (especially in a field such as Criminology, Sociology, or Criminal Justice) will make career advancement easier and can greatly increase annual salary.
- After hiring and training, there may be a period of on-the-job training with an experienced officer.
- At the federal level, a bachelor's degree or three years of experience in a related occupation is necessary for employment.
- Federal corrections officers will have at least 200 hours of on-the-job training and a period of training at the federal Bureau of Prisons.

Word to the Wise

- Correctional officers are routinely forced to deal with, and sometimes restrain, people who suffer from HIV, hepatitis B and C, tuberculosis, and other contagious diseases.
- Officers are in danger of physical harm from prison-made weapons.
- When conducting body or cell searches, correctional officers are in danger of being jabbed or cut by a piece of contraband.
- Officers must control mentally ill inmates.
- Officers are subject to taunts and verbal harassment

Female correctional workers are routinely employed in male institutions. The danger found in male institutions can create special problems, and female officers must be prepared to handle every situation. Here Texas Department of Criminal Justice Sgt. Louis Garcia works with corrections officer trainee Christy Lawson on her jabs during a training session at the Minnie Houston Training Center in Riverside, Texas, May 3, 2007. Learning self-defense is a critical skill for newly minted corrections officers about to join the nation's second largest prison system.

© AP Images/Pat Sullivan

Prison Violence

Conflict, violence, and brutality are sad but ever-present facts of institutional life. Violence can involve individual conflict: inmate versus inmate, inmate versus staff, staff versus inmate. Nonsexual assaults may stem from an aggressor's desire to shake down the victim for money and personal favors, may be motivated by racial conflict, or may simply be used to establish power within the institution. For example, on March 28, 2008, a riot at the federal penitentiary in Three Rivers, Texas, left one prisoner dead and 22 others injured. Intelligence sources said they believe the riot began when tensions over prison leadership developed between Mexican American inmates who consider themselves Chicanos and inmates who have closer ties to Mexico.[81]

Violence can also involve large groups of inmates, such as the infamous Attica riot in 1971, which claimed 39 lives, or the New Mexico State Penitentiary riot of February 1980, in which the death toll was 33. More than 300 prison riots have occurred since the first one in 1774, 90 percent of them since 1952.[82]

What Causes Violence?

What are the causes of prison violence? There is no single explanation for either collective or individual violence, but theories abound.[83] However, recent research by Benjamin Steiner shows that factors related to prison administration, inmate population characteristics, and the racial makeup of inmates and staff can influence violence levels.[84] Some of the factors related to individual and group inmate violence, respectively, are discussed in some detail below.

Individual Violence

- *History of prior violence*. Before they were incarcerated, many inmates were violence-prone individuals who always used force to get their own way. Some are former gang members who join inmate gangs as soon as

Some prison violence is collective, involving mass riots, vandalism, and arson. Here, on February 5, 2009, plumes of smoke rise from the yard and recreation building of the Reeves County Detention Center unit I in Pecos, Texas. These fires came five days after inmates set fire to other parts of the RCDC units I and II during a riot spurred by complaints about inadequate health care and food. This remote West Texas county secured its finances and kept jobs at home by turning over its sprawling prison to private management, but two inmate riots have led to increased scrutiny of the facility.

© AP Images Pecos Enterprise, Smokey Briggs

they enter the institution.[85] In many instances, street gangs maintain prison branches that unite the inmate with his former violence-prone peers. Having this connection supports and protects gang members while they are in prison, and it assists in supporting gang members' families and associates outside the wall.[86] Gang violence is a significant source of prison conflict.

- *Age.* Younger inmates, those with a record of prior incarceration, and those who have suffered pre-arrest drug use are the ones most likely to engage in disruptive behavior in prison, especially if they are not active participants in institutional treatment programs.[87] Sadly, juvenile offenders who are sentenced to adult institutions have significantly higher violence rates than the adult inmate population.[88]

- *Psychological factors.* Many inmates suffer from personality disorders. Recent research shows that among institutionalized offenders, psychopathy is the strongest predictor of violent recidivism and indifferent response to treatment.[89] In the crowded, dehumanizing world of the prison, it is not surprising that people with extreme psychological distress may resort to violence to dominate others.[90]

- *Prison conditions.* The prison experience itself causes people to become violent. Inhuman conditions, including overcrowding, depersonalization, and the threat of sexual assault, are violence-producing conditions. Aggressive inmates commit more assaults in prisons that are more crowded and have a greater percentage of younger inmates (e.g., younger than age 25).[91] Even in the most humane prisons, life is a constant put-down, and prison conditions are a threat to the inmates' sense of self-worth; violence is an expected consequence of these conditions. Violence levels are not much different between high-security and low-security prisons, suggesting that the prison experience itself, and not the level of control, produces violence.[92] The converse is also true: Effective interventions can help reduce violence in even the most disruptive inmates, especially those who begin to realize that repeat violent incidents are punished by long-term stays in segregation and other negative consequences.[93]

- *Lack of dispute resolution mechanisms.* Many prisons lack effective mechanisms for handling inmate grievances against either prison officials or other inmates fairly and equitably. Prisoners who complain about other inmates are viewed as "rats" or "snitches" and are marked for death by their enemies. Similarly, inmates' complaints or lawsuits filed against the prison administration may result in their being placed in solitary confinement— "the hole."

- *Basic survival.* Inmates resort to violence in order to survive. The lack of physical security. the dearth of adequate mechanisms for resolving complaints, and the code of silence promote individual violence by inmates who might otherwise be effectively controlled.

Collective Violence

- *Inmate-balance theory.* Riots and other forms of collective violence occur when prison officials make an abrupt effort to take control of the prison and limit freedoms. Crackdowns occur when officials perceive that inmate leaders have too much power and take measures to control their illicit privileges, such as gambling or stealing food.[94]

- *Administrative-control theory.* Collective violence is caused by prison mismanagement, lack of strong security, and inadequate control by prison officials. Poor management may inhibit conflict management and set the stage for violence. Repressive administrations give inmates the feeling that nothing will ever change, that they have nothing to lose, and that violence is the only means for change.

- *Overcrowding.* As the prison population continues to climb, unmatched by expanded capacity, prison violence may increase. Overcrowding caused by the rapid increases in the prison population has also been linked to increases in both inmate substance abuse and prison violence.[95]

Despite these problems, both the suicide rate (Figure 12.1) and the homicide rate (Figure 12.2) in prisons have been in sharp decline. Although it is difficult to determine the cause of this drop in violence directed at self and others, more advanced security measures coupled with improved prison administration may be responsible.

Suicide Rate in Prisons, 1980–2003

Source: Bureau of Justice Statistics

http://www.ojp.usdoj.gov/bjs/glance/shipj.htm

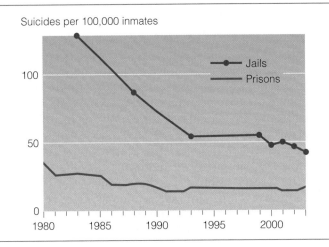

FIGURE 12.1

Homicide Rate in Prisons, 1980–2003

Source: Bureau of Justice Statistics

http://www.ojp.usdoj.gov/bjs/glance/shipj.htm

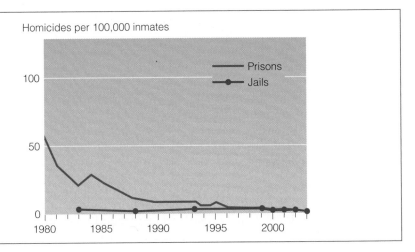

FIGURE 12.2

Prisoners' Rights

Before the early 1960s, it was accepted that upon conviction, an individual forfeited all rights not expressly granted by statutory law or correctional policy; in other words, inmates were civilly dead. The U.S. Supreme Court held that convicted offenders should expect to be penalized for their misdeeds and that part of their punishment was the loss of freedoms that law-abiding citizens take for granted.

One reason why inmates lacked rights was that state and federal courts were reluctant to intervene in the administration of prisons unless the circumstances of a case clearly indicated a serious breach of the Eighth Amendment protection against cruel and unusual punishment. This judicial policy is referred to as the **hands-off doctrine**.

As the 1960s drew to a close, the hands-off doctrine was eroded. Federal district courts began seriously considering prisoners' claims about conditions in the various state and federal institutions and used their power to intervene on behalf of the inmates. In some ways, this concern reflected the spirit of the times, which saw the onset of the civil rights movement, and subsequently emerged in the areas of student rights, public welfare, mental institutions, juvenile court systems, and military justice.

Beginning in the late 1960s, such activist groups as the NAACP Legal Defense Fund and the American Civil Liberties Union's National Prison Project began to search for appropriate legal vehicles to bring prisoners' complaints before state and federal courts. The most widely used device was the federal Civil Rights Act, 42 U.S.C. 1983:

> Every person who, under color of any statute, ordinance, regulation, custom, or usage of any State or Territory subjects, or causes to be subjected, any citizen of the United States or other person within the jurisdiction thereof to the deprivation of any rights, privileges, or immunities secured by the Constitution and laws shall be liable to the party injured in an action at law, suit in equity, or other proper proceeding for redress.

The legal argument went that, as U.S. citizens, prison inmates could sue state officials if their civil rights were violated—for example, if they were the victims of racial or religious discrimination.

The subsequent prisoners' rights crusade, stretching from 1964 to 1980, paralleled the civil rights and women's movements. Battle lines were drawn between prison officials, who hoped to maintain their power and resented interference by the courts, and inmate groups and their sympathizers, who used state and federal courts as a forum for demanding better living conditions and personal rights. Each decision handed down by the courts was viewed as a victory for one side or the other; this battle continues today.

Substantive Rights

Through a slow process of legal review, the courts have granted inmates a number of **substantive rights** that have significantly influenced the entire correctional system. The most important of these rights are discussed in the following sections.

ACCESS TO COURTS, LEGAL SERVICES, AND MATERIALS ●
Courts have held that inmates are entitled to have legal materials available and must be provided with assistance in drawing up and filing complaints. Inmates who help

hands-off doctrine
The legal practice of allowing prison administrators a free hand to run the institution, even if correctional practices violate inmates' constitutional rights; ended with the onset of the prisoners' rights movement in the 1960s.

National Prison Project

The ACLU's **National Prison Project** is the only national litigation program on behalf of prisoners. Access it via

www.cengage.com/ criminaljustice/siegel

substantive rights
A number of civil rights that the courts, through a slow process of legal review, have established for inmates, including the rights to receive mail and medical benefits and to practice their religion.

jailhouse lawyer
An inmate trained in law or otherwise educated who helps other inmates prepare legal briefs and appeals.

others, so-called **jailhouse lawyers**, cannot be interfered with or harassed by prison administrators.

FREEDOM OF THE PRESS AND OF EXPRESSION
● Courts have consistently ruled that only when a compelling state interest exists can prisoners' First Amendment rights be modified; correctional authorities must justify the limiting of free speech by showing that granting it would threaten institutional security. If prison administrators believe that correspondence undermines prison security, the First Amendment rights of inmates can be curtailed.[96]

FREEDOM OF RELIGION
● In general, the courts have ruled that inmates have the right to assemble and pray in the religion of their choice but that religious symbols and practices that interfere with institutional security can be restricted. Administrators can draw the line if responding to religious needs becomes cumbersome or impossible for reasons of cost or security. Special privileges can also be denied on the grounds that they will cause other groups to make similar demands that cannot be met within the institution.

MEDICAL RIGHTS
● In early prisons, inmates' right to medical treatment was restricted through the "exceptional circumstances doctrine." Using this policy, the courts would hear only those cases in which the circumstances revealed utter disregard for human dignity, while denying hearings to less serious cases. The cases that were allowed access to the courts usually entailed total denial of medical care.

To gain their medical rights, prisoners have resorted to class action suits (suits brought on behalf of all individuals affected by similar circumstances—in this case, poor medical attention). In the most significant case, *Newman v. Alabama* (1972), the entire Alabama prison system's medical facilities were declared inadequate.[97] The Supreme Court cited the following factors as contributing to inadequate care: insufficient physician and nurse resources, reliance on untrained inmates for paramedical work, intentional failure in treating the sick and injured, and failure to conform to proper medical standards. The *Newman* case forced corrections departments to upgrade prison medical facilities.

It was not until 1976, in *Estelle v. Gamble*, that the Supreme Court clearly affirmed inmates' right to medical care.[98] Gamble had hurt his back in a Texas prison and filed suit because he contested the type of treatment he had received and questioned the lack of interest that prison guards had shown in his case. The Supreme Court said, "Deliberate indifference to serious medical needs of prisoners constitutes the 'unnecessary and wanton infliction of pain,' proscribed by the Eighth Amendment."[99] The *Gamble* ruling mandated that inmate health care reflect what is available to citizens in the general community. Consequently, correctional administrators must consider access, quality, and cost of health care as part of the prison regime.[100]

cruel and unusual punishment
Physical punishment or punishment that is far in excess of that given to people under similar circumstances and is therefore banned by the Eighth Amendment. The death penalty has so far not been considered cruel and unusual if it is administered in a fair and nondiscriminatory fashion.

CRUEL AND UNUSUAL PUNISHMENT
● The concept of **cruel and unusual punishment** is founded in the Eighth Amendment of the Constitution. The term itself has not been specifically defined by the Supreme Court, but the Court has held that treatment constitutes cruel and unusual punishment when it does the following:

● Degrades the dignity of human beings[101]
● Is more severe than (is disproportional to) the offense for which it has been given[102]
● Shocks the general conscience and is fundamentally unfair[103]
● Is deliberately indifferent to a person's safety and well-being[104]
● Punishes people because of their status, such as race, religion, and mental state[105]

- Is in flagrant disregard of due process of law, such as punishment that is capriciously applied[106]

State and federal courts have placed strict limits on disciplinary methods that may be considered inhumane. Corporal punishment all but ended after the practice was condemned in *Jackson v. Bishop* (1968).[107] Although the solitary confinement of disruptive inmates continues, its prolonged use under barbaric conditions has been held to be in violation of the Eighth Amendment. Courts have found that inmates placed in solitary have the right to adequate personal hygiene, to exercise, mattresses, and ventilation, and to rules specifying how they can earn their release.

In a recent case, *Hope v. Pelzer*, the Supreme Court ruled that correctional officials who knowingly violate the Eighth Amendment rights of inmates can be held liable for damages.[108] Larry Hope, an Alabama prison inmate, was twice handcuffed to a hitching post for disruptive conduct while he was working outside the prison on a chain gang. He was handcuffed above shoulder height, and when he tried moving his arms to improve circulation, the handcuffs cut into his wrists, causing pain and discomfort. He spent seven hours on the hitching post, during which he was given one or two water breaks but no bathroom breaks, and a guard taunted him about his thirst. Hope filed a suit against three guards, charging them with violating his civil rights. The guards argued that they were entitled to **qualified immunity** from lawsuits, a legal doctrine that protects government officials from liability for civil damages if their conduct did not violate clearly established statutory or constitutional rights of which a reasonable person would have known.

The Supreme Court ruled that Hope's allegations established an Eighth Amendment violation. It ruled that among the "'unnecessary and wanton' inflictions of pain [constituting cruel and unusual punishment forbidden by the amendment] are those that are 'totally without penological justification.'" This determination is made in the context of prison conditions by ascertaining whether an official acted with "deliberate indifference" to the inmate's health

qualified immunity
A legal doctrine that shields government officials from liability if their conduct did not violate clearly established civil rights of which a reasonable person would have known.

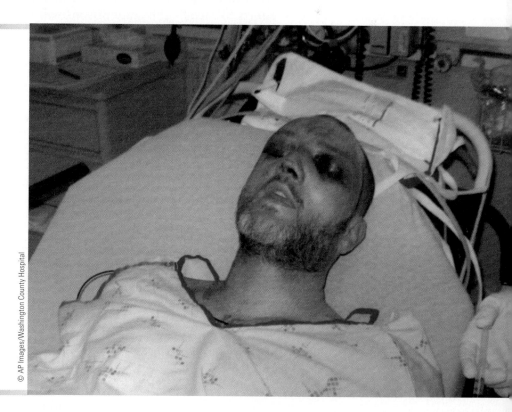

Prisoners may sue correctional authorities for damages if they are subjected to cruel and unusual punishment. This photo shows Kenneth Davis's facial bruises, which he alleges were inflicted by correctional officers at the Roxbury Correctional Institution near Hagerstown, Maryland, on March 8 and 9 of 2008. On May 26, 2009, two former Maryland correctional officers pleaded guilty to assaulting the defenseless inmate at a state prison and agreed to testify against seven coworkers charged with beating the man over a 2-day period.

© AP Images/Washington County Hospital

or safety, a state of mind that can be inferred from the fact that the risk of harm is obvious. The Court reasoned that any safety concerns had long since ended by the time Hope was handcuffed to the hitching post, because he had already been subdued, handcuffed, placed in leg irons, and transported back to prison. The *Hope* case shows that correctional officials can be sued if their behavior violates an inmate's constitutional rights and if they or any reasonable person should have surmised that the behavior was in violation of accepted practices.

RACIAL SEGREGATION   ●   On August 8, 2009, a riot in the California prison at Chino left hundreds injured, buildings burned and property destroyed.[109] The disturbance was sparked by racial tensions between Latino and black inmates, and it later provoked a great deal of controversy over the issue of racial segregation in prison: Should prisons be segregated to prevent violence among gangs such as the Aryan Brotherhood, the Mexican Mafia, and the Black Guerrilla Family? Or are inmates entitled to equal treatment under the law, as in other institutions, and is any form of segregation considered inherently unconstitutional?

In *Johnson v. California* (2005), the Supreme Court ruled that the segregation of prison inmates on the basis of race, in their cells or anywhere on prison grounds, is an inappropriate form of racial classification.[110] However, the ruling left it to lower courts to decide, using a standard of *strict scrutiny*, when segregation is inappropriate and unconstitutional. *Johnson* focused on the policy of segregating inmates upon their arrival at a prison. However, the Court's ruling seemed to suggest that if racial segregation were allowed for incoming inmates, there would be danger that it might also be used "in the dining halls, yards, and general housing areas. . . ." Segregation should be allowed, the judges reasoned, only if a prison administrator could prove that it served a compelling interest to promote prison safety. The Court recognized that "prisons are dangerous places, and the special circumstances they present may justify racial classifications in some contexts." Because the Chino riot occurred after California began to integrate prison entry centers, it is possible that future efforts to racially integrate prisons will be frustrated. It is possible that state courts, even when using a "strict scrutiny" standard, may conclude that racial integration, in some instances, is just too dangerous.

OVERALL PRISON CONDITIONS   ●   Prisoners have long had the right to the minimal conditions necessary for human survival, such as the food, clothing, shelter, and medical care necessary to sustain human life. A number of attempts have been made to articulate reasonable standards of prison care and to make sure that officials adhere to them. Courts have held that although people are sent to prison for punishment, it does not mean that prison should be a punishing experience.[111] In the 1994 case of *Farmer v. Brennan*, the court ruled that prison officials are legally liable if, knowing that an inmate faces a serious risk of harm, they disregard that risk by failing to take measures to avoid or reduce it. Furthermore, prison officials should be able to infer the risk from the evidence at hand; they need not be warned or told.[112]

Although inmates retain the right to reasonable care, if there is a legitimate purpose for the use of governmental restrictions, those restrictions may be considered constitutional. Thus, it might be possible to restrict reading material, allow strip searches, and prohibit inmates from receiving packages from the outside if the restrictions are legitimate security measures. If overcrowded

REALITY CHECK

MYTH OR REALITY? Inmates lose all civil rights once they enter a high-security correctional facility.

MYTH: Inmates retain many civil rights, even behind prison walls.

Do you agree?

conditions require it, inmates may be double-bunked in cells designed for a single inmate.[113]

Leaving Prison

At the expiration of their prison term, most inmates return to society and try to resume their lives. For some inmates, their reintegration into society comes by way of **parole**—the planned community release and supervision of incarcerated offenders before the expiration of their full prison sentences. In states where determinate sentencing statutes have eliminated discretionary parole, offenders are released after having served their determinate sentence, minus time off for good behavior and other credits designed to reduce the term of incarceration. Their release may involve supervision in the community, and rule violations can result in return to prison for the balance of their unexpired sentence.

In a few instances, inmates are released after their sentences have been commuted by a board of pardons or directly by a governor or even the president. About 15 percent of prison inmates are released after serving their entire maximum sentence, without any time excused or forgiven. And despite the efforts of correctional authorities, about 7,000 inmates escape every year from state and federal prisons (the number of escapes is actually declining, thanks in part to better officer training and more sophisticated security measures).[114]

Regardless of how they come to be released, former inmates face the formidable task of readjusting to society. This means regaining legal rights they may have lost when they were convicted, reestablishing community and family ties, and finding employment. After one has been in prison, these goals are often difficult to attain.

parole
The early release of a prisoner from imprisonment, subject to conditions set by a parole board.

Parole

There are more than 800,000 people currently on parole, and each year about 500,000 inmates are released on parole and slightly fewer exit or complete parole, so the total population on parole continues to trend upward.[115]

The format of parole is determined by statutory requirement. In some states parole is granted by a parole board, a duly constituted body of men and women who review inmate cases and determine whether offenders have reached a rehabilitative level sufficient to deal with the outside world. The board also dictates what specific parole rules parolees must obey. In about 16 other jurisdictions, discretionary parole has been abandoned, and the amount of time a person must remain in prison is a predetermined percentage of the sentence, assuming there are no infractions or escape attempts. In this "mandatory parole release" approach, the inmate is released when the unserved portion of the maximum prison term equals his or her earned good time (minus time served in jail awaiting trial). In some states, sentences can be reduced by more than half with a combination of statutory and earned good time. If the conditions of their release are violated, mandatory releasees can have their good time revoked and be returned to the institution to serve the remainder of their unexpired term. The remaining inmates are

© Thinkstock/Getty Images

released for a variety of reasons, including expiration of their term, commutation of their sentence, and court orders to relieve overcrowded prisons. The use of discretionary parole has been in steep decline, while the number of inmates released on mandatory parole has increased significantly.

The Parole Board

In those states that have maintained discretionary parole, the authority to release inmates is usually vested in the parole board. State parole boards have four primary functions:

1. To select and place prisoners on parole
2. To aid, supervise, and provide continuing control of parolees in the community
3. To determine when the parole function is completed and discharge from parole
4. To determine whether parole should be revoked, if violations of conditions occur

Most parole authorities are independent agencies with their own staff and administration, and a few parole boards are part of the state department of corrections. Arguments for keeping the board within a corrections department usually include improved communication and more intimate knowledge about offenders.

The actual (discretionary) parole decision is made at a parole-grant hearing. At this hearing the full board or a selected subcommittee reviews information, may meet with the offender, and then decides whether the parole applicant has a reasonable probability of succeeding outside prison. Each parole board has its own way of reviewing cases.

In a few states, parole board members meet with the applicant before making a decision. Face-to-face meeting can be beneficial because the hearing panel can get feedback from inmates to more thoroughly evaluate their readiness for parole. Parole board officials, many of whom have had varied professional training and experience, can use these meetings to assess an inmate's sincerity and readiness for release.[116]

In addition, parole boards will look at the inmate's crime, institutional record, and willingness to accept responsibility before making the release decision. Some jurisdictions rely on standardized tests that predict whether a potential parolee may recidivate upon release.[117] Inmates who maintain their innocence may find that denying responsibility for their crimes places their release date in jeopardy. The requirement that they admit guilt or culpability is especially vexing for those inmates who are actually innocent and who actively refuse to accept their institutional label of "convicted criminal."[118]

The Parolee in the Community

Upon release into the community, a parolee is given a standard set of rules and conditions that he or she must obey. As with probation, the offender who violates these rules may have parole revoked and be sent back to the institution to serve the remainder of the sentence. Once in the community, the parolee is supervised by a trained staff of parole officers who help him or her search for employment and monitor the parolee's behavior and activities to ensure that the conditions of parole are met.

Parole is generally viewed as a privilege granted to deserving inmates on the basis of their good behavior while in prison. Parole has two conflicting sides, however. On the one hand, the paroled offender is allowed to serve part of the sentence in the community, an obvious benefit for the deserving offender.

On the other hand, because parole is "a privilege and not a right," the parolee is viewed as a dangerous criminal who must be carefully watched and supervised. The conflict between the treatment and enforcement aspects of parole has not been reconciled by the criminal justice system, and the parole process still contains elements of both.

To overcome these roadblocks to success, the parole officer may have to play a much greater role in directing and supervising clients' lives than the probation officer. In some instances, parole programs have become active in creating new postrelease treatment-oriented programs designed to increase the chances of parole success. In other instances, parole agencies have implemented law enforcement–oriented services that work with local police agencies to identify and apprehend parolees who may have been involved in criminal activity.[119]

INTENSIVE SUPERVISION PAROLE ● To achieve effective supervision, some jurisdictions have implemented systems that classify offenders on the basis of their supervision needs. Typically, a point or guideline system (sometimes called a "salient factor score") based on prior record and prison adjustment divides parolees into three groups: (1) those who require intensive surveillance, (2) those who require social service rather than surveillance, and (3) those who require limited supervision.

In some jurisdictions, parolees in need of closer surveillance are placed on **intensive supervision parole (ISP)**. These programs use limited caseload sizes, treatment facilities, the matching of parolee and supervisor by personality, and shock parole (which involves immediate short-term incarceration for parole violators to impress them with the seriousness of a violation). ISP clients are required to attend more office and home visits than routine parolees. ISP may also require frequent drug testing, a term in a community correctional center, and electronic monitoring in the home. More than 17,000 parolees are under intensive supervision; 1,400 of these are monitored electronically by computer.

Evaluations of ISP programs have produced mixed results. Some show that they may actually produce a higher violation rate than traditional parole supervision, because limiting caseload size allows parole officers to supervise their clients more closely and spot infractions more easily.[120] However, some evaluations do show that under some conditions, a properly run ISP program can significantly reduce recidivism upon release. The key factors may be parole officer orientation (a balance between social service and law enforcement seems to work best) and a supportive organizational environment in which the program is being run.[121]

intensive supervision parole (ISP)
A limited-caseload program for those parolees who need intensive surveillance. Parolees are required to meet more often with parole officers than routine parolees and may also have frequent drug testing, serve a term in a community correctional system, and be electronically monitored.

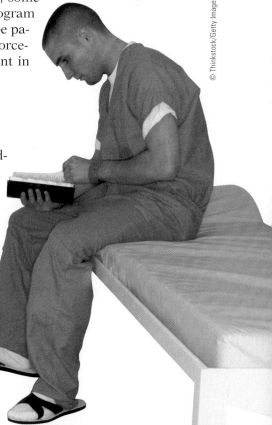

© Thinkstock/Getty Images

The Effectiveness of Parole

Despite all efforts to treat, correct, and rehabilitate incarcerated offenders, more than half return to prison shortly after their release. Persons released from prison face a multitude of difficulties. They remain largely uneducated, unskilled, and usually without solid family support systems—then add to this the burdens of a prison record. Not surprisingly, most parolees fail, and rather quickly; rearrests are most common in the first six months after release.[122] As Figure 12.3 shows, more than 60 percent of parolees return to prison within three years of their release, and the failure rate has actually increased. Moreover, the cost of their recidivism is acute. One federal survey of 156,000 parole violators who had been sent back to prison concluded that these offenders committed at least 6,800 murders, 5,500 rapes, 8,800 assaults, and 22,500 robberies while under supervision in the community for an average of 13 months.[123]

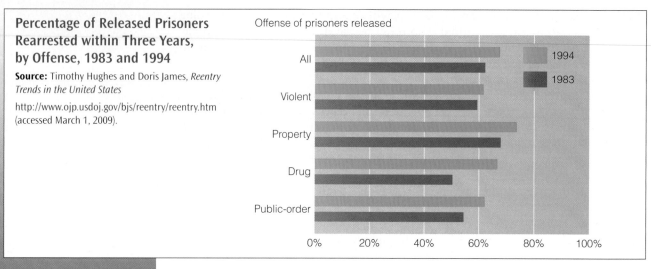

Percentage of Released Prisoners Rearrested within Three Years, by Offense, 1983 and 1994

Source: Timothy Hughes and Doris James, *Reentry Trends in the United States*

http://www.ojp.usdoj.gov/bjs/reentry/reentry.htm (accessed March 1, 2009).

FIGURE 12.3

Why Do People Fail on Parole?

Parole failure is still a significant problem, and a growing portion of the correctional population consists of parolees who failed on the outside. Why has the phenomenon of parole failure remained so stubborn and hard to control?

One reason may be the very nature of the prison experience itself. The psychological and economic problems that lead offenders to recidivism are rarely addressed by a stay in prison. Despite rehabilitation efforts, the typical ex-convict is still the same undereducated, unemployed, substance-abusing, lower-socioeconomic-status male he was when arrested. Being separated from friends and family, not sharing in conventional society, associating with dangerous people, and adapting to a volatile lifestyle probably have done little to improve the offender's personality or behavior. It seems naïve to think that incarceration alone can help someone overcome these lifelong disabilities. By their very nature, prisons seek to impose and maintain order and conformity rather than to help inmates develop skills such as independence and critical thinking—factors that may be essential once the inmate is forced to cope outside the prison walls.[124]

It is also possible that parole failure is tied to the releasee's own lifelong personal deficits. Most research efforts indicate that a long history of criminal behavior, an antisocial personality, and childhood experiences with family dysfunction are all correlated with postrelease recidivism.[125] Many releasees have suffered from a lifetime of substance abuse or dependence disorder.[126] A history of physical and sexual abuse has also been linked to recidivism.[127] It is not surprising that the men who are most likely to return to prison are those who maintain criminal peer associations, carry weapons, abuse alcohol, and harbor aggressive feelings.[128] Another study of youthful ex-offenders trying to make it on the outside found that many experience delayed emotional and cognitive development due to early drug use; most have never learned to use problem-solving or coping skills outside the correctional setting; and most remain drug dependent.[129] In contrast, those who are employed, have stable living arrangements, and are receiving some type of drug and/or alcohol program intervention are far less likely to fail on parole.[130]

Once the parolee is on the outside, these problems do not easily subside. Some ex-inmates may feel compelled to prove that the prison experience has not changed them: Taking drugs or being sexually aggressive may show friends that they have not lost their "heart."[131] In contrast, parolees who have had a

On February 16, 2009, Eugene Nater and Sonya Blevins, who were recently released from prison, prepare salad for customers at Salad Creations at the Westfield Annapolis mall in Annapolis, Maryland. McQucio Moore, a former parole officer in Washington, D.C., and the owner of Salad Creations, hired the two just before Christmas. It is the first time he has ever hired offenders. Having a job is one key step toward successful rehabilitation after reentry into society.

© AP Images / The Annapolis Capital, Joshua McKerrow

good employment record in the past and who maintain jobs after their release are the most likely to avoid recidivating.[132]

MARRIAGE AND FAMILY ISSUES • Recidivism may be a by-product of the disruptive effect a prison experience has on personal relationships. Ex-inmates may find their home life torn and disrupted when they are finally released. Recent research by Beth Heubner shows that incarceration significantly reduces the chances of marriage for all men. Although whites were most likely to be married overall, incarceration was associated with a 59 percent decline in the odds of marriage for whites, and the odds of marriage decreased 30 percent for blacks and 41 percent for Hispanics. Because marriage has proved a significant neutralizer of future criminality, the suppression effect on marriage that a prison sentence provides may help explain high recidivism rates.[133] And even if they do marry, former inmates may be restricted in their choice of mates. Their circumstances may force them to choose partners with equally checkered backgrounds, a circumstance that may enhance rather than reduce the likelihood of future criminality.

What about men who are married and then go to prison? Wives of inmates report that they had to face the shame and stigmatization of having an incarcerated spouse, while withstanding a barrage of calls from jealous husbands on the "inside," who tried to monitor their behavior and control their lives. Family visits to the inmate became traumatic and strained relationships because they often involved strip searches and other invasions of privacy.[134] Sensitive to these problems, some states have instituted support groups designed to help inmates' families adjust to their loneliness and despair.[135]

The specter of recidivism is especially frustrating to the American public: It is so

REALITY CHECK

MYTH OR REALITY? Most released inmates fail on parole.

REALITY: More than half of all released inmates return to prison shortly after their release.

What would you do, if you ran the correctional system, to reverse this trend?

difficult to apprehend and successfully prosecute criminal offenders that it seems foolish to grant them early release so they can prey on more victims. This problem is exacerbated when the parolee is a chronic, frequent offender. Research indicates that many of these returning prisoners are less prepared for reintegration and less connected to community-based social structures than in the past.[136] There seems to be a strong association between prior and future offending: The parolees most likely to fail on release are the ones who have failed in the past; chronic offenders are the ones most likely to reoffend. This issue takes on even greater importance when the community-level problems created by returning inmates are considered.

The Problems of Reentry

The problems of reentry are exacerbated now because of America's two-decade-long imprisonment boom, which has resulted in more than 500,000 inmates being released back into the community each year. As criminologist Joan Petersilia warns, there are a number of unfortunate consequences to this, because many of those being released have not received adequate treatment and are unprepared for life in conventional society.[137] The risks they present to the community include increases in child abuse, family violence, the spread of infectious diseases, homelessness, and community disorganization. Many have no way to cope and wind up in homeless shelters. A recent (2006) study of shelters in New York City found that 23 percent of the occupants had been released from New York prisons and jails in the past two years.[138]

The increased reentry risks can be tied to legal changes in how people are released from prison. In the past, offenders were granted early release only if a parole board believed they were rehabilitated and had ties to the community—such as a family or a job. Inmates were encouraged to enter treatment programs to earn parole. Changes in sentencing laws have resulted in the growth of mandatory release and limits on discretionary parole. People now serve a fixed sentence, and the discretion of parole boards has been blunted. Inmates may be discouraged from seeking involvement in rehabilitation programs (they no longer affect the chance of parole), and the lack of incentive means that fewer inmates leaving prison have participated in programs to address deficiencies in the areas of employment, education, and substance use. Nor does the situation improve upon release. Many inmates are not assigned to supervision caseloads once they are back in the community. About 200,000 released inmates go unsupervised each year, three-quarters of whom have been released after completing their maximum sentence and are therefore not required to be supervised.

Petersilia argues that most leave prison with no savings, no immediate entitlement to unemployment benefits, and few employment prospects.[139] Upon release, some find that they are no longer welcome in subsidized public housing complexes. This is a consequence of the U.S. Department of Housing and Urban Development's "one strike and you're out" policy, whereby all members of the household are evicted if one member is involved in crime. A year after release, as many as 60 percent of former inmates are not employed in the regular labor market, and employers are increasingly reluctant to hire ex-offenders. Ex-offenders are commonly barred from working in the fields in which most jobs are being created, such as child care, education, security, nursing, and home health care. More jobs are also now unionized, and many unions exclude ex-offenders.

Being barred from work opportunities produces chronic unemployment, a status closely related to drug and alcohol abuse. Losing a job can lead to substance abuse, which in turn is related to child and family violence. Mothers released from prison have difficulty finding services such as housing, employment, and child care, and this causes stress for them and their children. Children of incarcerated and released parents may suffer confusion, sadness, and social stigma, and these feelings often result in difficulties in school, low self-esteem, aggressive behavior, and general emotional dysfunction. If the parents are negative role models, children fail to develop positive attitudes about work and responsibility. Children of incarcerated parents are five times more likely to serve time in prison than children whose parents are not incarcerated.

Prisoners have significantly more physical and mental health problems than the general population. More than three-fourths of the inmates leaving prison report a history of drug and/or alcohol abuse in the next year. Inmates with mental illness are also increasingly being imprisoned—and then released. One recent study in New York State (2008) found that the number of prison inmates receiving mental health services had grown steadily, almost doubling from 4,500 in 1990 to 8,600. In the same four-year period there was a 22 percent increase in inmates who had a diagnosis of serious mental illness.[140]

Even when public mental health services are available, many mentally ill individuals fail to use them because they fear institutionalization, deny they are mentally ill, or distrust the mental health system. The situation will become more serious as more and more parolees are released into the same disorganized communities where deteriorated conditions may have motivated their original crimes.

THE EFFECT ON COMMUNITIES ● Parole expert Richard Seiter notes that when there were only a few hundred thousand prisoners, and a few thousand releasees per year, the issues surrounding the release of offenders did not overwhelm communities.[141] Families could house ex-inmates, job-search organizations could find them jobs, and community social service agencies could respond to their individual needs for mental health or substance abuse treatment. Today, the sheer number of reentering inmates has taxed the communities to which they are returning. Charis Kubrin and Eric Stewart have found that communities that already face the greatest social and economic disadvantages are ones that produce the highest recidivism rates.[142] Obviously, the influx of returning inmates can magnify their problems.

Resident Ed Hayes speaks during a town meeting on March 17, 2009, to voice his opposition to convicted child killer Raymon Guay serving his parole in Chichester, New Hampshire. The town of about 2,200 residents in south-central New Hampshire had been in an uproar since police announced that Guay would spend two months with the Reverend David Pinckney's family. Hayes lives on the same road as Pinckney. Such resentment makes it difficult for inmates to transition back into society. It is understandable that more than half of all parolees fail during the first three years of reentry.

© AP Images/Jim Cole

LOSING RIGHTS • Ex-inmates may also find that going straight is an economic impossibility. Many employers are reluctant to hire people who have served time. Even if a criminal record does not automatically prohibit employment, why would an employer hire an ex-con when other applicants are available? If they lie about their prison experience and are later found out, ex-offenders will be dismissed for misrepresentation. Research shows that former inmates who gain and keep meaningful employment are more likely to succeed on parole than those who are unemployed or underemployed.[143] One reason why ex-inmates find it so difficult to make it on the outside is the legal restrictions they are forced to endure. These may include prohibitions on certain kinds of employment, limits on obtaining licenses, and restrictions on their freedom of movement. One survey found that a significant number of states still restrict the activities of former felons.[144] Some of the more important findings are listed in Exhibit 12.3.

IMPROVING CHANCES ON REENTRY • Can something be done to ease reentry? Now that the scope of the problem has been recognized, both the federal and state governments have devoted energy to improving success at reentry. On April 9, 2008, the Second Chance Act was signed into law. This federal legislation authorized various grants to government agencies and nonprofit groups to provide a variety of services (including employment assistance, housing, substance abuse treatment, and family programming) that can help to reduce reoffending and violations of probation and parole.

State correctional agencies have made an effort to help inmates take advantage of these services. Take, for instance, the state of Maryland. In order to inform soon-to-be-released inmates of these services and help them to better prepare for reentry, the Maryland Correctional Education Libraries acquired two mobile units in April 2007. Equipped with computers and other educational tools, the mobile units are able to serve all the prerelease centers in Maryland.[145] Some private groups have obtained funding to provide postrelease counseling and support. One promising Virginia program, Women Inspired to Transform (WIT), uses volunteers to teach female returnees about anger management, job interviewing, communication, relationships, and parenting.[146]

EXHIBIT 12.3

Rights Lost upon Release from Prison

- Fourteen states permanently deny felons the right to vote; 18 states suspend the right until after the correctional sentence has been completed.
- Nineteen states terminate parental rights.
- Twenty-nine states consider a felony conviction to be legal grounds for a divorce.
- Six states deny felons the opportunity for public employment.
- Thirty-one states do not give convicted felons the right to serve on juries.
- Twenty-five states prevent convicted felons from holding public office.

- Federal law prohibits ex-convicts from owning guns. In addition, all states except Vermont employ additional legal measures to prevent felons from possessing firearms.
- Forty-six states require that felons register with law enforcement agencies. This requirement is up sharply in recent years; in 1986 only eight states required felons to register.
- Civil death, or the denial of all civil rights, is still practiced in four states.

Source: Kathleen Olivares, Velmer Burton, and Francis Cullen, "The Collateral Consequences of a Felony Conviction: A National Study of State Legal Codes Ten Years Later," *Federal Probation 60* (1996): 10–17.

ETHICAL CHALLENGES IN CRIMINAL JUSTICE

A WRITING ASSIGNMENT

Considering the reentry failure rate, some experts believe that early release from prison is bound to fail and create greater opportunities for crime. The solution is to keep people in prison as long as possible through mandatory minimum sentencing and "truth in sentencing" policies.

Comment on the failure of correctional treatment to make a dent in the recidivism rate. Come up with a "five-point plan" to ease reentry and reduce recidivism.

RealityCheck Revisited

To learn more about the myths and realities related to prison life that were raised in this chapter, visit the following websites.

Prison rape is a very serious issue. Learn more at

http://www.justdetention.org/

http://www.hrw.org/legacy/reports/2001/prison/

To learn more about women in prison, go to

http://www.wpaonline.org/

http://www.wpaonline.org/

Does correctional treatment work? To draw your own conclusions, go to

http://www.publicsafety.gc.ca/res/cor/sum/cprs200503_1-eng.aspx

http://www.ncjrs.gov/pdffiles1/nij/grants/184507.pdf

http://www.ojp.usdoj.gov/nij/pubs-sum/197018.htm

SUMMARY

© John Smierciak, *Chicago Tribune*/MCT/Landov

1. Discuss the problems of the adult correctional system

- There are more than 1,700 adult correctional facilities in the United States.

- A significant number of facilities are old and in ill repair.

- Institutions are overcrowded, and meaningful treatment efforts are often a matter of wishful thinking.

- The typical prison is often described as a "school for crime."

- Recidivism rates are shockingly high.

2. Know what is meant by the term "total institution"

- Prisons in the United States are total institutions.

- Inmates locked within their walls are segregated from the outside world.

3. Be familiar with the problem of sexual coercion in prison and with what is being done to help.

- Sexual coercion is a serious problem in contemporary prison institutions.

- Institutions with the highest sexual coercion rates have barracks-style housing, large prison populations, and lenient security.

- Young males may be raped and kept as sexual slaves by older, more aggressive inmates.

- The Prison Rape Reduction Act of 2003 established three programs to reduce rape in prison.

- However, many inmates refuse to report rape, and others may misunderstand what constitutes a "rape."

- It is estimated that 12 percent of all inmates are sexually victimized.

4. **Chart the prisonization process and the development of the inmate social code**

- Inmates go through classification.

- Part of living in prison involves learning to protect oneself and developing survival instincts.

- Younger inmates, gay men, and bisexual men are most often the targets of sexual assaults.

- Gangs are powerful in the larger prison systems.

- Each prisoner has his own method of coping.

- Inmates form their own world, with a unique set of norms and rules, known as the inmate subculture.

- Those who become the most "prisonized" will be the least likely to avoid criminal activity on the outside.

5. **Compare the lives and cultures of male and female inmates**

- Female prisons tend to be smaller than those housing male inmates, but female inmates may suffer from a lack of adequate job training and from inferior health, treatment, and educational facilities.

- Female inmates are young (most are under age 30), minority group members, unmarried, undereducated (more than half are high school dropouts), and either unemployed or underemployed.

- There are numerous reports of female prisoners being sexually abused and exploited by male correctional workers.

- Unlike male inmates, women usually do not present an immediate physical danger to staff and fellow inmates.

- Make-believe family groups contain masculine and feminine figures acting as fathers and mothers; some even act as children and take on the role of brother or sister.

6. **Be familiar with the different forms of correctional treatment**

- Almost every prison facility uses some mode of treatment for inmates.

- Counseling programs help inmates to control their emotions, communicate with others, deal with legal concerns, manage general life issues, and develop and maintain social relationships.

- Most prisons have programs designed to help inmates who suffer from alcohol and substance abuse.

- Inmate rehabilitation is also pursued through vocational and educational training.

- Most institutions provide vocational training programs.

- There has been considerable debate over the effectiveness of correctional treatment.

- Nonetheless, many experts still believe in the rehabilitative ideal.

7. **Discuss the world of correctional officers**

- Correctional officers are now viewed as dedicated public servants.

- Most are in favor of rehabilitation efforts.

- The correctional officer has been characterized as a "people worker."

- Correctional officers play a number of roles in their institutions.

- Correctional officers sit on disciplinary boards and escort inmates to hospitals and court appearances.

- There are few gender differences in the behavior of correctional officers.

8. *Understand the causes of prison violence*
- Conflict, violence, and brutality are sad but ever-present facts of institutional life.
- Violence can involve individual conflict: inmate versus inmate, inmate versus staff, or staff versus inmate.
- Prison violence is associated with overcrowding, lack of effective dispute resolution mechanisms, individual history of violence, and poor prison conditions.

9. *Know what is meant by prisoners' rights, and discuss some key privileges that have been granted to inmates*
- Before the early 1960s, it was accepted that upon conviction, an individual forfeited all rights not expressly granted by statutory law or correctional policy.
- Today inmates have the right to medical care, freedom from cruel and unusual treatment, the right to an attorney, and the right to practice their religion.

10. *Be knowledgeable about the parole process and the problems of prisoner reentry*
- At the expiration of their prison term, most inmates return to society and try to resume their lives.
- Most inmates are paroled either by mandatory release or parole board vote.
- Parole is generally viewed as a privilege granted to deserving inmates on the basis of their good behavior while in prison.
- More than half of all parolees return to prison shortly after their release.
- Recidivism may be a by-product of the disruptive effect a prison experience has on personal relationships.
- Parole failure has been linked to being barred from work opportunities.
- Ex-inmates may also find that going straight is an economic impossibility.

Key Terms

total institution, 410
inmate subculture, 413
inmate social code, 413
prisonization, 414
make-believe family, 419
anger management programs, 420
therapeutic communities, 420
work release, 423

furlough, 423
hands-off doctrine, 431
substantive rights, 431
jailhouse lawyer, 432
cruel and unusual punishment, 432
qualified immunity, 433
parole, 435
intensive supervision parole (ISP), 437

Review Questions

1. Considering the dangers that men face during their prison stay, should nonviolent inmates be placed in separate institutions to protect them from harm?

2. Should women be allowed to work as guards in male prisons? What about male guards in female prisons? Why or why not?

3. Should prison inmates be allowed a free college education while noncriminals are forced to pay tuition?

4. Define parole, including its purposes and objectives. How does it differ from probation?

5. What is the role of the parole board?

6. Should a former prisoner enjoy all the civil rights afforded the average citizen? Explain.

7. Should people be further penalized after they have paid their debt to society? Why or why not?

Part 5 | CONTEMPORARY CHALLENGES OF THE AMERICAN CRIMINAL JUSTICE SYSTEM

In 2008, Jesse Logan, an 18-year-old Ohio high school girl, made the mistake of using her cell phone to send nude pictures of herself to her boyfriend. When they later broke up, he emailed the pictures around to his schoolmates. As soon as the photos got into the hands of other students, they began harassing Jesse, calling her names and hurting her reputation. Jesse soon became depressed and reclusive, afraid to go to school. To fight back, her mother went on a Cincinnati television station to tell her story so that other teens could learn from Jesse's experience. The interview took place in May 2008; two months later, Jessica Logan hanged herself in her bedroom.

> Sending compromising photos has become a national issue, and what may seem like a harmless prank can have serious consequences.

Sexting, the act of sending compromising photos electronically, has become a national issue, and what may seem like a harmless prank can have serious consequences. In one case, female students at a Pennsylvania high school, all 14 or 15 years old, were charged with manufacturing, disseminating, or possessing child pornography, and the boys they sent the photos to, who were 16 and 17, faced charges of possession of pornography. In Pennsylvania, anyone convicted under these laws faces a possible 7-year sentence and a felony conviction on his or her record; such persons also must register as sex offenders for 10 years. The ACLU is helping the parents and teens fight the case.

Sexting between cell phones illustrates two special issues facing the justice system today: how to deal with young people who violate the law and how to deal with criminal acts that rely on technology (that is, cyber crime). Because of the salience of these and other issues for the contemporary justice system, Part 5 contains two chapters, one covering the juvenile justice system and the other addressing emerging crime patterns such as terrorism and cyber crime.

Chapter 13
Juvenile Justice in the Twenty-first Century

Chapter 14
Crime and Justice in the New Millennium: Terrorism and Cyber Crime

13

JUVENILE JUSTICE IN THE TWENTY-FIRST CENTURY

RealityCheck

MYTH or REALITY?

▶ Parens patriae is the guiding philosophy of juvenile justice today.

▶ All juveniles fall under the jurisdiction of the adult court at age 18.

▶ Juveniles enjoy the same legal rights as adults.

▶ Juvenile trials are identical to adult trials.

▶ Youths are more violent and criminally dangerous today than they were in the past.

Learning Objectives

1. Describe the nature and purpose of the juvenile justice system

2. Be familiar with the history and development of juvenile justice

3. Discuss the child savers and their vision of juvenile justice

4. Describe the efforts of the child savers to create an independent juvenile court

5. Describe the changes in juvenile justice that began in the 1960s and continue today

6. Discuss police processing of juvenile offenders

7. Distinguish between the adjudication of juvenile offenders and that of adult offenders

8. Discuss the problems and legal issues surrounding the waiver decision

9. Trace the juvenile trial and sentencing process

10. Compare efforts to treat troubled kids in the juvenile justice system with the belief that treatment is ineffective and should be abolished

Chapter Outline

© AP Photo/*The Oakland Press, Vaughn Gurganian*

Career Profile

Kevin Kellems is an intensive juvenile probation officer in Calhoun County, Michigan. He obtained a bachelor of science degree in Criminal Justice, with an emphasis on corrections, from Lake Superior State University, and a master of arts in Justice and Security Administration from the University of Phoenix. He feels his degree programs did a great

job of preparing him for his career in juvenile probation. "Having to take an internship class was also very helpful in [that I learned] the requirements of the position and the importance of networking," he says.

Kevin chose to work in the field of juvenile corrections in order to help change the youth in his community. "As a teenager, I ended up hanging around a much older and hard-core crowd. This led to more than a few brushes with law enforcement. Seeing that the future only held jail and prison if I continued on my path, I decided to change my course. In so doing, I wanted to help others do the same."

The biggest misconception about juvenile probation, according to Kevin, is that the probation officer is just there to lock up minors who behave improperly. "This misconception is common among law enforcement, schools, and parents," he says, but "the goal of the juvenile system is treatment, and in Michigan the law requires that treatment be attempted in the home and community if possible." This sets the juvenile justice system apart from the adult system.

Kevin's career, like others in criminal justice, can be challenging. "The stress comes from working with a population of young people and their families that are often highly chaotic and dysfunctional. Continued budget cuts also increase stress by reducing the services available to the children and families who need them. It can also be disappointing to see the same youth return to court time after time without making any changes or caring to."

Yet Kevin also finds being a juvenile probation officer rewarding. "The greatest rewards on this job are often very small baby steps that a family or client makes that you cannot really appreciate until you stop and look back on the case after closing it." One of his favorite cases involved a young lady whom he managed to get into foster care, where she was adopted. She came to visit him recently, after completing two years of college. She informed Kevin that she wanted to be a juvenile probation officer so that she could help others the way he had helped her.

I t is people like Kevin Kellems who make the juvenile justice system unique. Independent of (yet interrelated with) the adult criminal justice system, the juvenile justice system is primarily responsible for dealing with juvenile and youth crime, as well as with incorrigible and truant children and runaways. Conceived at the turn of the twentieth century, the juvenile justice system was viewed as a quasi-social welfare agency that was to act as a surrogate parent in the interests of the child; this is referred to as the **parens patriae** philosophy. Many people who work in the system still hold to the original social welfare principles of the juvenile justice system. In contrast, those who adopt a crime control orientation suggest that the juvenile justice system's parens patriae philosophy is outdated. They point to nationally publicized incidents of juvenile violence, such as the shootings at Columbine High School in Colorado, as indicators that serious juvenile offenders should be punished and disciplined rather than treated and rehabilitated. "Why should we give special treatment to violent young juveniles?" they ask. "After all, juveniles commit almost 9 percent of all the murders in the United States and about 15 percent of all rapes."[1]

parens patriae
Latin term meaning "father of his country." According to this legal philosophy, the government is the guardian of everyone who has a disability, especially children, and has a legal duty to act in their best interests until they reach the age of majority.

It remains to be seen whether the juvenile justice system will continue on its path toward deterrence, punishment, and control or return to its former role as a treatment-dispensing agency. This chapter reviews the history of juvenile justice and discusses the justice system's processing of youthful offenders.

The History of Juvenile Justice

The modern practice of legally separating adult criminals and juvenile offenders can be traced back to two developments in English custom and law that occurred centuries ago: the development of Elizabethan-era poor laws and the creation of the English chancery court. Both of these innovations were designed to allow the state to take control of the lives of needy but not necessarily criminal children.[2]

poor laws
Seventeenth-century laws in England that bound out vagrants and abandoned children as indentured servants to masters.

- **Poor laws.** As early as 1535 the English passed statutes known as **poor laws**, which (among other things) mandated the appointment of overseers who placed destitute or neglected children with families that then trained them in agricultural, trade, or domestic services; this practice was referred to as "indenture." The Elizabethan poor laws of 1601 created a system of church wardens and overseers who, with the consent of the justices of the peace, identified vagrant, delinquent, and neglected children and took measures to put them to work. Often this meant placing them in poorhouses or workhouses or, more commonly, apprenticing them until their adulthood. The indenture, or involuntary apprentice, system set the precedent, which continues today, of allowing the government to take control of youths who have committed no illegal acts but are deemed unable to care for themselves.

- **Chancery courts.** English chancery courts provided judicial relief to those who had no legal standing or could expect no legal relief because of the corruption and inadequacy of other common-law courts. People who felt their rights were being violated could take their cases to the chancery court for review. In this capacity, the chancery court protected the property rights and welfare of more minor children who could not care for themselves—children whose position and property were of direct concern to the monarch. The courts dealt with issues of guardianship and the use and control of property. Thus, if the guardian of an orphaned child wished to sell off his ward's inheritance, the chancery court might be asked to review the proceedings and determine whether the sale was in the child's best interest. Chancery courts operated under the parens patriae philosophy, which held that children were under the protective control of the state and that its rulers were justified in intervening in their lives.[3] In the famous English case *Wellesley v. Wellesley*, a duke's children were taken from him in the name of parens patriae because of his scandalous behavior.[4]

REALITY CHECK

MYTH OR REALITY? Parens patriae is the guiding philosophy of juvenile justice today.

MYTH: Parens patriae continues to influence juvenile justice, but there is increasing pressure to "get tough" with young offenders.

Many contemporary reforms are making the juvenile justice system resemble the adult system. It is also becoming more popular to try juveniles as adults. Fewer juveniles are processed informally today than in the past, and juvenile offenders enjoy less privacy than they once did. Are these moves in the right direction? What are the consequences of this progression?

The history of the juvenile justice system

To read more about **the history of the juvenile justice system**, go to

www.cengage.com/ criminaljustice/siegel

Care of Children in Early America

Poor laws and chancery courts were brought from England to colonial America. Poor laws were passed in Virginia in 1646, and in Connecticut and Massachusetts in 1678, and continued in force until the early nineteenth century. They

mandated care for wayward and destitute children. However, those youths who committed serious criminal offenses continued to be tried in the same courts as adults.

To accommodate dependent youths, local jurisdictions developed alms-houses, poorhouses, and workhouses. Crowded and unhealthy, these shelters accepted the poor, the insane, the diseased, and vagrant and destitute children. Middle-class civic leaders, who referred to themselves as **child savers**, began to develop organizations and groups to help alleviate the burdens of the poor and immigrants by sponsoring shelter care for youths, educational and social activities, and the development of settlement houses. In retrospect, their main focus seems to have been on extending governmental control over a whole range of youthful activities that previously had been left to private or family control, including idleness, drinking, vagrancy, and delinquency.[5]

child savers
Late nineteenth-century reformers in America who developed programs for troubled youths and influenced legislation creating the juvenile justice system.

The Child-Saving Movement

The child savers were responsible for creating a number of programs for indigent youths, including the New York House of Refuge, which began operations in 1825.[6] Its charter was to protect indigent youths who were at risk of crime by taking them off the streets and reforming them in a family-like environment.[7]

The New York House of Refuge, actually a reformatory, opened on January 1, 1825, with only six boys and three girls, but within the first decade of its operaion, 1,678 kids were sent there because of vagrancy and petty crimes. Once an adolescent was a resident, his or her daily schedule was devoted for the most part to supervised labor, which was regarded as beneficial to education and discipline. Male inmates worked in shops that produced brushes, cane chairs, brass nails, and shoes. The female inmates sewed uniforms, did laundry, and carried out other domestic work. The reformatory had the authority to bind out inmates through indenture agreements to private employers; most males so bound out were farm workers, and most females were domestic laborers.

Boys on the steps of an abandoned tenement building in New York City, about 1889. The child savers were concerned that, if left alone, children like these would enter a life of crime. They created the House of Refuge to care for poor and neglected kids. Critics accused them of class and race bias.

© The Granger Collection, New York

New York House of Refuge

To find out more about the
New York House of Refuge,
go to

www.cengage.com/
criminaljustice/siegel

Children's Aid Society

A child-saving organization begun
by Charles Loring Brace; it took
children from the streets in large
cities and placed them with farm
families on the prairie.

Charles Loring Brace

To learn more about **Charles
Loring Brace**, go to

www.cengage.com/
criminaljustice/siegel

juvenile court

A court that has original
jurisdiction over persons defined
by statute as juveniles and alleged
to be delinquents or status
offenders.

The Refuge Movement Spreads

When the House of Refuge opened, critics complained that the institution was run like a prison, with strict discipline and absolute separation of the sexes. Such a harsh program drove many children to run away, and the House of Refuge was forced to take a more lenient approach. Despite criticism, the concept enjoyed expanding popularity. In 1826, for example, the Boston City Council founded the House of Reformation for juvenile offenders.[8]

The child savers also influenced state and local governments to create independent correctional institutions to house minors. The first of these reform schools opened in Westboro, Massachusetts, in 1848 and in Rochester, New York, in 1849. Children lived in congregate conditions and spent their days working at institutional jobs, learning a trade where possible, and receiving some basic education. They were racially and sexually segregated, discipline was harsh and often involved whipping and isolation, and the physical care was of poor quality.

In 1853, New York philanthropist Charles Loring Brace helped develop the **Children's Aid Society** as an alternative for dealing with neglected and delinquent youths. Brace proposed rescuing wayward youths from the harsh environment of the city and providing them with temporary shelter and care. He then sought to place them in private homes in rural communities where they could engage in farming and agricultural work beyond the influence of the city. Although some placements proved successful, others resulted in the exploitation of children in a strange environment with few avenues of escape.

Establishment of the Juvenile Court

As the nation expanded, it became evident that private charities and public organizations were not caring adequately for the growing number of troubled youths. The child savers lobbied for an independent, state-supported **juvenile court**, and their efforts prompted the development of the first comprehensive juvenile court in Illinois in 1899. In his book *Juvenile Justice in the Making*, historian David Tanenhaus describes how the early child savers fought a long battle against legal and political opponents to get juvenile court legislation passed. He views the juvenile court as the forerunner of both public welfare and grassroots community organizing. He also views the court as the prototype for raising children using expert medical and psychological opinion, which has ranged from Dr. Spock to Dr. Phil.[9] Yet Tanenhaus finds that the early juvenile court also reflected some of the biases and prejudices of its time: Fatherless status offenders were allowed to stay in their homes; motherless ones were sent to institutions.

The Illinois Juvenile Court Act set up an independent court to handle criminal law violations by children under 16 years of age, as well as to care for neglected, dependent, and wayward youths. The act also created a probation department to monitor youths in the community and to direct juvenile court judges to place serious offenders in secure schools for boys and industrial schools for girls. The ostensible purpose of the act was to separate juveniles from adult offenders and to provide a legal framework in which juveniles could get adequate care and custody. By 1925 most states had developed juvenile courts. The enactment of the Illinois Juvenile Court Act of 1899 was a major event in the history of the juvenile justice movement in the United States.

The Development of Juvenile Justice

The juvenile court movement quickly spread across the United States. In its early form it provided youths with quasi-legal, quasi-therapeutic, personalized justice. The main concern was the "best interests of the child," not strict adherence to legal doctrine, constitutional rights, or due process of law. The court was paternalistic, rather than adversarial. Attorneys were not required; hearsay evidence, inadmissible in criminal trials, was commonly employed in the adjudication of juvenile offenders. Children were encouraged to admit their "guilt" in open court (in violation of their Fifth Amendment rights). Verdicts were based on a "preponderance of the evidence," instead of being "beyond a reasonable doubt." Juvenile courts then functioned as quasi-social service agencies.

REFORM SCHOOLS • Youngsters who were found delinquent in juvenile court could spend years in a state training school. Although they prided themselves on being nonpunitive, these early reform schools attempted to exercise control based on the concept of reform through hard work and discipline. In the second half of the nineteenth century, the emphasis shifted from massive industrial schools to the cottage system. Juvenile offenders were housed in a series of small cabins, each one holding 20 to 40 children, run by "cottage parents," who attempted to create a homelike atmosphere. The first cottage system was established in Massachusetts, the second in Ohio. The system was generally applauded for being a great improvement over the industrial training schools.[10] By the 1950s, psychological treatment was introduced in juvenile corrections. Group counseling techniques became standard procedure in most juvenile institutions.

LEGAL CHANGE • In the 1960s and 1970s, the U.S. Supreme Court radically altered the juvenile justice system when it issued a series of decisions that established the right of juveniles to due process of law. The Court established that juveniles had the same rights as adults in important areas of trial process, including the right to confront witnesses, notice of charges, and the right to counsel. Exhibit 13.1 lists some of the legal cases that were most important in bringing procedural due process to the juvenile justice process.

Besides the legal revolution brought about by the Supreme Court, Congress passed the Juvenile Justice and Delinquency Prevention Act of 1974 (JJDP Act) and established the federal Office of Juvenile Justice and Delinquency Prevention (OJJDP).[11] This legislation was enacted to identify the needs of youths and to fund programs in the juvenile justice system. Its main goal was to separate wayward, nondangerous youths from institutions housing delinquents and to remove adolescents from institutions housing adult offenders. In 1988, the act was amended to address the issue of minority overrepresentation in the juvenile justice system, and in 1996, in a move reflecting the growing national frustration with serious delinquent offenders, the act was again amended to make it easier to hold delinquents in adult penal institutions. The various stages in the history of juvenile justice are set out in Concept Summary 13.1.

EXHIBIT 13.1

Important Juvenile Justice Cases

- *Kent v. United States* (1966) determined that a child has the right to an attorney at any hearing to decide whether his or her case should be transferred to juvenile court (waiver hearings).
- *In re Gault* (1967) ruled that a minor has basic due process rights at trial, including: (1) notice of the charges, (2) right to counsel, (3) right to confront and cross-examine witnesses, (4) privilege against self-incrimination, and (5) the right to a transcript of the trial record.

- *In re Winship* (1970) determined that the level of evidence for a finding of "juvenile delinquency" is proof beyond a reasonable doubt.
- *McKeiver v. Pennsylvania* (1971) held that trial by jury in a juvenile court's adjudicative stage is not a constitutional requirement.
- *Breed v. Jones* (1975) ruled that a child has the protection of the double-jeopardy clause of the Fifth Amendment and cannot be tried twice for the same crime.

(continued)

Exhibit 13.1 (*continued*)

- *Fare v. Michael C.* (1979) held that a child has the protection of the *Miranda* decision: the right to remain silent during a police interrogation and to request that a lawyer be provided to protect his or her interests.
- *Schall v. Martin* (1984) allowed for the placement of children in preventive detention before their adjudication.
- *New Jersey v. T.L.O.* (1985) determined that although the Fourth Amendment protection against unreasonable search and seizure applies to children, school officials can legally search kids who violate school rules (e.g., smoking on campus), even when there is no evidence that the student violated the law.
- *Vernonia School District v. Acton* (1995) held that the Fourth Amendment's guarantee against unreasonable searches is not violated by drug testing all students choosing to participate in interscholastic athletics.
- *Roper v. Simmons* (2005) determined that juveniles who commit murder before they turn 18 cannot be sentenced to death.

Sources: *Kent. v. United States*, 383 U.S. 541, 86 S.Ct. 1045, 16 L.Ed.2d 84 (1966); *In re Gault*, 387 U.S. 1, 87 S.Ct. 1248 (1967); *In re Winship*, 397 U.S. 358 (1970); *McKeiver v. Pennsylvania*, 403 U.S. 528, 91 S.Ct. 1776 (1971); *Breed v. Jones*, 421 U.S. 519, 95 S.Ct. 1779 (1975); *Fare v. Michael C.*, 442 U.S. 707, 99 S.Ct. 2560 (1979); *Schall v. Martin*, 467 U.S. 253, 104 S.Ct. 2403 (1984); *New Jersey v. T.L.O.*, 469 U.S. 325, 105 S.Ct. 733 (1985); *Vernonia School District v. Acton*, 515 U.S. 646 115 S.Ct. 2386, 132 L.Ed. 2d 564 (1995); *Roper v. Simmons*, No. 03–633 (2005).

Concept Summary 13.1

© X Brand Images/Getty Images

Shifting Philosophies of Juvenile Justice

- **Before 1899:** Juveniles treated similarly to adult offenders. No distinction by age or capacity to commit criminal acts.
- **1899–1950s:** Children treated differently beginning with the Illinois Juvenile Court Act of 1899. By 1925, juvenile court acts had been established in virtually every state. Parens patriae philosophy dominates.
- **1950–1970:** Recognition by experts that the rehabilitation model and the protective nature of parens patriae had failed to prevent delinquency.
- **1970–1980:** Introduction of constitutional due process into the juvenile justice system. Experimentation with diversion and concern about stigma and labeling. Juvenile Justice and Delinquency Prevention Act of 1974 enacted.
- **1980–2000:** Rising juvenile crime rates, coupled with the perceived failure of rehabilitation to control delinquency, lead to a shift to a crime control and punishment philosophy similar to that of the adult criminal justice system. Focus on expanding the crime control capabilities of the juvenile justice system so that it resembles the adult system.
- **2000–today:** Balanced approach. Attempt to provide treatment to needy youths and get tough with dangerous repeat offenders.

Juvenile Justice Today

Today, the juvenile justice system has jurisdiction over two distinct categories of offenders: delinquents and status offenders.[12] **Juvenile delinquency** is a term applied to children who fall under a jurisdictional age limit, which varies from state to state, and who commit an act in violation of the penal code. **Status offenders** commit acts forbidden to minors, which include truancy and being a habitually disobedient and ungovernable child (see Figure 13.1). They are commonly characterized in state statutes as persons or children in need of supervision (PINS or CHINS). Most states distinguish such behavior from delinquent conduct to reduce the effect of any stigma on children, although in most jurisdictions, status offenders can be placed on probation much as delinquent offenders can. They are, however, in most instances barred from being placed in secure facilities that hold delinquent offenders. In addition, juvenile courts generally have jurisdiction over situations involving conduct directed at (rather than committed by) juveniles, such as parental neglect, deprivation, abandonment, and abuse. As Figure 13.2 shows, except for liquor violations, status offense cases peak at age 15 and then drop off dramatically.

The states have also set different maximum ages below which children fall under the jurisdiction of the juvenile court. Many states include all children under 18 years of age, others set the limit at 17, and still others at 16.

juvenile delinquency
Participation in illegal behavior by a minor who falls under a statutory age limit.

status offender
A juvenile who engages in behavior legally forbidden to minors, such as running away, truancy, or incorrigibility.

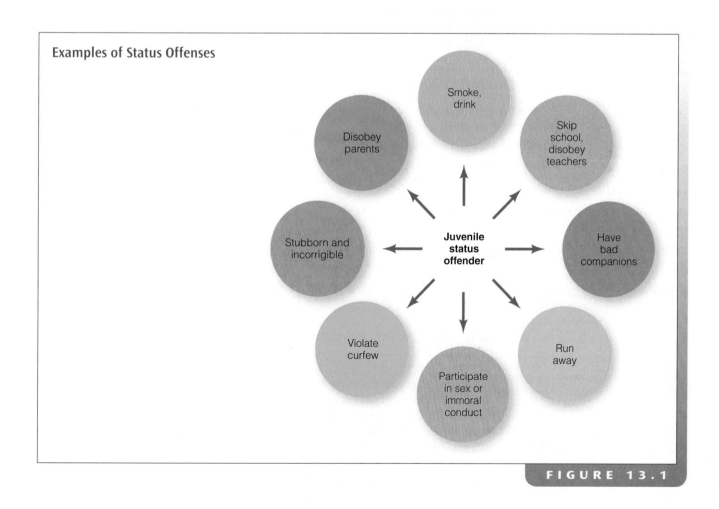

Examples of Status Offenses

- Smoke, drink
- Skip school, disobey teachers
- Have bad companions
- Run away
- Participate in sex or immoral conduct
- Violate curfew
- Stubborn and incorrigible
- Disobey parents

Juvenile status offender

FIGURE 13.1

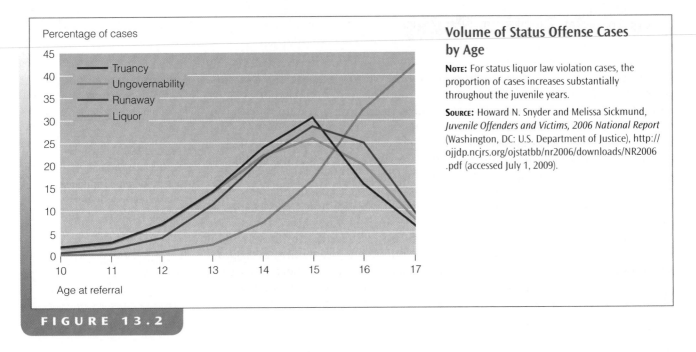

Volume of Status Offense Cases by Age

NOTE: For status liquor law violation cases, the proportion of cases increases substantially throughout the juvenile years.

SOURCE: Howard N. Snyder and Melissa Sickmund, *Juvenile Offenders and Victims, 2006 National Report* (Washington, DC: U.S. Department of Justice), http:// ojjdp.ncjrs.org/ojstatbb/nr2006/downloads/NR2006 .pdf (accessed July 1, 2009).

FIGURE 13.2

REALITY CHECK

MYTH OR REALITY? All juveniles fall under the jurisdiction of the adult court at age 18.

MYTH: There is considerable variation from state to state in terms of who is considered an adult for purposes of criminal prosecution.

In Connecticut, New York, and North Carolina, the oldest age for juvenile court jurisdiction in delinquency matters is 15. This means that youths 16 or older are tried as adults in those states. And there are exceptions to these rules. Sometimes younger individuals can be "waived" to adult court—a topic taken up later in the chapter.

Some states exclude certain classes of offenders or offenses from the juvenile justice system. Those youths who commit serious violent offenses such as rape or murder may be automatically excluded from the juvenile justice system and treated as adults on the premise that they stand little chance of rehabilitation within the confines of the juvenile system. Juvenile court judges may also transfer, or waive, to adult court repeat offenders whom they deem untreatable by the juvenile authorities.

Another trend has been to create family courts (see Exhibit 13.2 for an overview of Hawaii's family court system), which include a broad range of family- and child-related issues within their jurisdictions. Family courts are in use or are being considered in more than half of all U.S. states. They are designed to provide more individualized, client-focused treatment than traditional juvenile courts and to bring a holistic approach to helping kids and their families, rather than focusing on punishing and/or controlling delinquency.[13]

The juvenile justice system has evolved into a parallel yet independent system of justice with its own terminology and rules of procedure. Exhibit 13.3 describes the basic similarities and differences between the juvenile and adult justice systems. Exhibit 13.4 points out how the language used in the juvenile court differs from that used in the adult system.

Today, the juvenile justice system is responsible for processing and treating almost 2 million cases of youthful misbehavior annually. Each state's system is unique, so it is difficult to give a precise accounting of the justice process. Moreover, depending on local practice and tradition, case processing often varies from community to community within a single state. Keeping this in mind,

EXHIBIT 13.2

Hawaii's Family Court

Established by statute in 1965, the Family Court's mission is to provide a fair, speedy, economical, and accessible forum for the resolution of matters involving families and children.

Children

The Family Court hears legal matters involving children. These include
- Delinquency
- Status offenses
- Abuse and neglect
- Termination of parental rights
- Adoption
- Guardianships
- Detention

Domestic Relations

The Family Court also hears domestic relations cases, including

- Divorce
- Child support

- Paternity
- Uniform child custody jurisdiction cases
- Miscellaneous custody matters

Domestic Violence

Domestic violence cases include

- Requests for civil restraining orders involving family members
- Persons charged with the offense of abuse of family and household members
- Felony charges limited to offenses against household members

Source: Hawaii State Judiciary, http://www.courts.state.hi.us/page_server/Courts/Family/153E4A87ED63B9F8EBD8E1142F.html (accessed March 26, 2009).

EXHIBIT 13.3

Similarities and Differences between Juvenile and Adult Justice Systems

Similarities	Differences
Discretion used by police officers, judges, and correctional personnel	The primary purpose of juvenile procedures is protection and treatment; with adults, the aim is to punish the guilty.
Right to receive *Miranda* warning	Jurisdiction is determined by age in the juvenile system, by the nature of the offense in the adult system.
Protection from prejudicial lineups or other identification procedures	Juveniles can be apprehended for acts that would not be criminal if committed by an adult (status offenses).
Procedural safeguards when making an admission of guilt	Juvenile proceedings are not considered criminal; adult proceedings are.
Advocacy roles of prosecutors and defense attorneys	Juvenile court proceedings are generally informal and private; adult court proceedings are more formal and are open to the public.
Right to counsel at most key stages of the court process	Courts cannot release to the press identifying information about a juvenile, but they must release information about an adult.

(continued)

Exhibit 13.3 (*continued*)

Similarities	Differences
Availability of pretrial motions	Parents are highly involved in the juvenile process but not in the adult process.
Plea negotiation/plea bargaining	The standard of arrest is more stringent for adults than for juveniles.
Right to a hearing and an appeal	Juveniles are released into parental custody; adults are generally given bail.
Standard of proof beyond a reasonable doubt	Juveniles have no constitutional right to a jury trial; adults do. Some states extend this right to juveniles by statute.
Pretrial detention possible	Juveniles can be searched in school without probable cause or a warrant.
Detention without bail if considered dangerous	A juvenile's record is generally sealed when the age of majority is reached; an adult's record is permanent.
Probation as a sentencing option	A juvenile court cannot sentence juveniles to county jails or state prisons, which are reserved for adults.
Community treatment as a sentencing option	The U.S. Supreme Court has declared that the Eighth Amendment prohibits the death penalty for juveniles under age 18.

EXHIBIT 13.4

Comparison of Terms Used in Adult and Juvenile Justice Systems

	Juvenile Terms	Adult Terms
The person and the act	Delinquent child	Criminal
	Delinquent act	Crime
Preadjudicatory stage	Take into custody	Arrest
	Petition	Indictment
	Agree to a finding	Plead guilty
	Deny the petition	Plead not guilty
	Adjustment	Plea bargain
	Detention facility; child-care shelter	Jail
Adjudicatory stage	Substitution	Reduction of charges
	Adjudicatory or fact-finding hearing	Trial
	Adjudication	
Postadjudicatory stage	Dispositional hearing	Sentencing hearing
	Disposition	Sentence
	Commitment	Incarceration
	Youth development center; treatment center; training school	Prison
	Residential child-care facility	Halfway house
	Aftercare	Parole

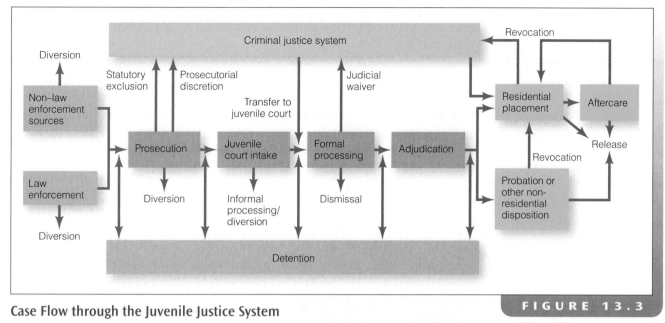

Case Flow through the Juvenile Justice System

SOURCE: Office of Juvenile Justice and Delinquency Prevention, http://ojjdp.ncjrs.org/ojstatbb/structure_process/case.html (accessed July 1, 2009).

FIGURE 13.3

the following sections provide a general description of some key processes and decision points in juvenile justice. Figure 13.3 presents a model of the juvenile justice process.

Police Processing of the Juvenile Offender

According to the Uniform Crime Reports, police officers arrest more than 1.6 million juveniles under age 18 each year, including almost 500,000 under age 15.[14] Most large police departments have detectives who handle only juvenile delinquency cases and focus their attention on the problems of youth. In addition to conducting their own investigations, they typically take control of cases after an arrest is made by a uniformed officer.

Most states do not have specific statutory provisions distinguishing the arrest process for children from that for adults. Some jurisdictions, however, give broad arrest powers to the police in juvenile cases by authorizing the officer to make an arrest whenever he or she believes the child's behavior falls within the jurisdiction of the juvenile court. Consequently, police may arrest youths for behavior considered legal for adults, including running away, curfew violations, and being in possession of alcohol.

Use of Discretion

When a juvenile is found to have engaged in delinquent or incorrigible behavior, police agencies are charged with the decision to release or to detain the child and refer her to juvenile court. Because of the state's interest in the child, the police generally have more discretion in the investigatory and arrest stages of the juvenile process than they do when dealing with adult offenders.

This discretionary decision—to release or to detain—is based not only on the nature of the offense but also on police attitudes and the child's social and personal conditions at the time of the arrest. The following is a partial list of factors believed to be significant in police decision making about juvenile offenders:

- The type and seriousness of the child's offense
- The ability of the parents to be of assistance in disciplining the child
- The child's past contacts with police
- The degree of cooperation obtained from the child and parents, along with their demeanor, attitude, and personal characteristics
- Whether the child denies the allegations in the petition and insists on a court hearing[15]

Legal Rights

Once a juvenile has been taken into custody, the child has the same right to be free from unreasonable searches and seizures as an adult does. Children in police custody can be detained prior to trial, interrogated, and placed in lineups. However, because of their youth and inexperience, children are generally afforded more protections than adults. Even though the Supreme Court has given juveniles the same *Miranda* rights as adults, police must ensure that the juvenile suspect understands his constitutional rights and, if there is some question, must provide access to a parent or guardian to protect the child's legal interests. Police should interrogate a juvenile without an adult present only if they are sure that the youth is unquestionably mature and experienced enough to understand his legal rights.[16] In a recent research study, however, Barry Feld found that police interrogation tactics with juveniles are quite similar to their questioning of adults. Once juveniles waived their *Miranda* rights, police used the same strategies and tactics

REALITYCHECK

MYTH OR REALITY?   Juveniles enjoy the same legal rights as adults.

MYTH: The Supreme Court has over the years extended more and more protections to juveniles (see Exhibit 13.1), but there are still rights that juveniles do not enjoy. One is the right to a jury trial.

Should juveniles have access to trial by jury? Why or why not? Juvenile proceedings are also usually closed to the public, unlike adult criminal trials. Is this advantageous or disadvantageous to the juvenile?

© AP Images/Matt Rourke

Juveniles are supposed to be accorded many of the same legal rights as adults. But the juvenile justice system, like the adult system, is not immune to mistakes and miscarriages of justice. Here Kurt Kruger, who spent three days in juvenile detention and another four months at a youth wilderness camp because his friend was caught shoplifting DVDs, poses for a photograph in Wilkes-Barre, Pennsylvania, on February 6, 2009. The northeastern Pennsylvania judge who sentenced Kruger and thousands of other youths has been charged, along with another judge, with pocketing millions of dollars to send kids to privately owned youth detention centers.

to question them, including the use of false statements and evidence. Juveniles responded to those tactics, cooperated or resisted, and provided incriminating evidence at about the same rate as did adults. Feld's conclusion: The law treats juveniles just like adults, and police question them just as they do older suspects. Although the questioning was somewhat more benign than Feld had expected, the danger of false confessions and convictions still exists.[17]

The Juvenile Court Process

After the police have determined that a case warrants further attention, they will bind it over to the prosecutor's office, which then has the responsibility for channeling the case through the juvenile court. In addition, cases may be petitioned to the court from non–law enforcement sources, such as when educational authorities ask the court to intervene in cases of truancy or when parents directly petition the court asking that their child be considered a status offender. The juvenile court plays a major role in controlling juvenile behavior and delivering social services to children in need.

U.S. juvenile courts process an estimated 1.6 million delinquency cases each year. The juvenile court delinquency caseload today is four times as large as it was in 1960.

The Intake Process

After police processing, the juvenile offender is usually remanded to the local juvenile court's intake division. At this juncture, court intake officers or probation personnel review and initially screen the child and the family to determine whether the child needs to be handled formally or the case can be settled without the need for costly and intrusive official intervention. Their report helps the prosecutor decide whether to handle the case informally or bind it over for trial. The intake stage represents an opportunity to place a child in informal programs both within the court and in the community. The intake process also is critically important because more than half of the referrals to the juvenile courts never go beyond this stage.

The Detention Process

After a juvenile is formally taken into custody, either as a delinquent or as a status offender, the prosecutor usually makes a decision to release the child to the parent or guardian or to detain the child in a secure shelter pending trial.

Detention has always been a controversial area of juvenile justice. Far too many children have been routinely placed in detention while awaiting court appearances. Status offenders and delinquents have been held in the same facility, and in many parts of the country, adult county jails were used to detain juvenile offenders. The Juvenile Justice Act of 1974 emphasized reducing the number of children placed in inappropriate detention facilities. Although the act was largely effective, there are places where the practice continues.

Despite such measures, hundreds of thousands of youths, most of whom are already living under difficult circumstances, are placed in pretrial detention each year. Many have suffered long histories of abuse and mental health problems.[18] The detention decision may reflect a child's personal characteristics and the quality of his or her home life rather than dangerousness or flight risk.[19] Detention is widely misapplied, according to the report by the Justice Policy Institute, a Washington, D.C.–based group, because even though detention facilities are meant to temporarily house those youths who are likely to reoffend before their trial or who are unlikely to appear for their court date, many of the youths in

Office of Juvenile Justice and Delinquency Prevention

The **Office of Juvenile Justice and Delinquency Prevention** website has a lot of information on the juvenile justice process. You can access the site at

www.cengage.com/
criminaljustice/siegel

detention
The temporary care of a child alleged to be a delinquent or status offender who requires secure custody, pending court disposition.

this country's 769 detention centers do not meet these criteria. Seventy percent of youths in detention are held for nonviolent charges. More than two-thirds are charged with property offenses, public order offenses, technical probation violations, or status offenses (such as running away or breaking curfew).[20]

The number of delinquency cases involving detention has increased significantly during the past decades. The largest relative increase was for drug offense cases. The data also shows that a disproportionate number of African American youths were detained before trial. Whereas less than 20 percent of delinquency cases involving white juveniles included detention at some point between referral and disposition, about 25 percent of cases involving black juveniles and 20 percent of cases involving youths of other races are detained. The disproportionate representation of minority youths in detention is a troubling aspect of juvenile justice.

LEGAL ISSUES • Most state statutes ordinarily require a hearing on the appropriateness of detention if the initial decision is to keep the child in custody. At this hearing, the child has a right to counsel and may be given other procedural due process safeguards, notably the privilege against self-incrimination and the right to confront and cross-examine witnesses. Most state juvenile court acts provide criteria to support a decision to detain the child. These include (a) the need to protect the child, (b) whether the child presents a serious danger to the public, and (c) the likelihood that the juvenile will return to court for adjudication. Whereas in adult cases most offenders are released if they can afford bail, juveniles may be detained for a variety of reasons, including their own protection. Normally, the finding of the judge that the child should be detained must be supported by factual evidence. In the 1984 case of *Schall v. Martin*, the U.S. Supreme Court upheld the right of the states to detain a child before trial to protect that child's welfare and the public safety.[21]

REFORMING DETENTION • There has been an ongoing effort to reform detention. The most important reform has been the successful effort to remove status offenders from lockups containing delinquents. After decades of effort,

© AP Images/Erik S. Lesser

Youthful offenders are often required to attend classes while in detention. Here Robert Harris, 17, left, listens to Fulton County Superior Court Judge Marvin Arrington, right, during Harris's high school graduation ceremony at the Metro Regional Youth Detention Center on May 15, 2009, in Atlanta. Harris is the first youth to graduate at the 11-year-old facility and has been accepted to enter Georgia Military College.

nearly all states have passed laws requiring that status offenders be placed in nonsecure shelters, rather than secure detention facilities, thereby reducing their contact with more dangerous delinquent youths.

Another serious problem is the detention of youths in adult jails. This practice is common in rural areas where there are relatively few separate facilities for young offenders.[22] The OJJDP has given millions of dollars in aid to encourage the removal of juveniles from adult lockups. These grants have helped jurisdictions develop intake screening procedures, specific release or detention criteria, and alternative residential and nonresidential programs for juveniles awaiting trial. By 1980, amendments to the act mandating the absolute removal of juveniles from jails had been adopted. Despite such efforts, many states are not complying with the removal provisions and still detain juveniles in adult jails. Adding to their numbers are youths who commit nonserious acts—such as runaways—but are apprehended in rural areas where there are no juvenile facilities. There are also states that define the age limit for delinquency as 16 or 17 and therefore treat minors of that age as legal adults. At the time of the last available jail census, more than 7,000 persons under age 18 were housed in adult jails. Jail stays are generally of short duration, so it is likely that hundreds of thousands of minors are held in adult jails each year.

Whatever the actual number jailed today, placing young offenders in adult jails continues to be a significant problem in the juvenile justice system. Juveniles detained in adult jails often live in squalid conditions and are subject to physical and sexual abuse. The practice is widely condemned, but eliminating the confinement of juveniles in adult institutions remains a difficult task.

Bail

If a child is not detained, the question of bail arises. Federal courts have not found it necessary to rule on the issue of a juvenile's constitutional right to bail, because liberal statutory release provisions act as appropriate alternatives. Although only a few state statutes allow release on money bail, many others have juvenile code provisions that emphasize the release of the child to the parents as an acceptable substitute. A constitutional right to bail that on its face seems to benefit a child may have unforeseen results. The imposition of money bail might create a serious economic strain on the child's family, while conflicting with the protective and social concerns of the juvenile court. Considerations of economic liabilities and other procedural inequities have influenced the majority of courts that have confronted this question to hold that juveniles do not have a right to bail.

Plea Bargaining

Before trial, prosecutors in the juvenile courts may attempt to negotiate a settlement to the case. For example, if the offender admits to the facts of the petition, she may be offered placement in a special community-based treatment program in lieu of a term in a secure state facility. Or a status offense petition may be substituted for one of

Kayla Hassall, 16, one of five teenagers accused of beating fellow teen Victoria N. Lindsay, weeps as she apologizes to the victim's mother Talisa Lindsay outside the courtroom on February 4, 2009, in Bartow, Florida. The attack was recorded on video and seen around the world via the Internet and television. Kayla pleaded no contest to misdemeanor battery. In exchange for her plea, prosecutors agreed to drop a related felony charge.

© AP Images/Michael Wilson, Pool

delinquency so that the adolescent can avoid being housed in a state training school and instead be placed in a more treatment-oriented facility.

If a bargain can be reached, the child will be asked to admit in open court that he did in fact commit the act of which he stands accused. State juvenile courts tend to minimize the stigma associated with the use of adult criminal standards by using other terminology, such as "agree to a finding" or "accept the petition" rather than "admit guilt." When the child makes an admission, juvenile courts require the following procedural safeguards: The child knows of the right to a trial, the plea or admission is made voluntarily, and the child understands the charges and consequences of the plea.

Waiver of Jurisdiction

waiver (juvenile)
A practice in which the juvenile court waives its jurisdiction over a juvenile and transfers the case to adult criminal court for trial. In some states, a waiver hearing is held to determine jurisdiction, whereas in others, juveniles may be automatically waived if they are accused of committing a serious crime such as murder.

transfer hearing
The hearing in which a decision is made to waive a juvenile to the criminal court. Waiver decisions are based on such criteria as the child's age, her or his prior offense history, and the nature of the offense.

Before development of the first modern juvenile court in Illinois in 1899, juveniles were tried for violations of the law in adult criminal courts. The consequences were devastating; many children were treated as criminal offenders and often sentenced to adult prisons. Although the subsequent passage of state legislation creating juvenile courts eliminated this problem, the juvenile justice system did recognize that certain forms of conduct require that children be tried as adults. Today, most American jurisdictions provide by statute for **waiver**, or transfer, of juvenile offenders to the criminal courts. Waiver is also widely used in juvenile courts in Europe and Great Britain.[23]

In its most basic form, the decision of whether to waive a juvenile to the adult, or criminal, court is made in a **transfer hearing**. The decision to transfer a juvenile to the criminal court is often based on statutory criteria established by the state's juvenile court act, so waiver provisions vary considerably among jurisdictions. Most commonly considered are the child's age and the nature of the offense alleged in the petition. Some jurisdictions require that children be over a certain age (typically, 14) before they can be waived. Others mandate that the youth be charged with a felony before being tried as an adult, whereas others permit waiver of jurisdiction to the criminal court regardless of the seriousness of the offense when a child is a chronic offender. In about 30 states, certain offenses, such as murder, have been excluded from juvenile court jurisdiction, creating a mandatory waiver provision for children who have committed those crimes.

LEGAL CONTROLS • Because of the nature of the waiver decision and its effect on the child in terms of status and disposition, the Supreme Court has imposed procedural protections for juveniles in the waiver process. In *Kent v. United States* (1966), the Court held that the waiver proceeding is a critically important stage in the juvenile justice process and that juveniles must be afforded minimum requirements of due process of law at such proceedings, including the right to legal counsel.[24] Then in *Breed v. Jones* (1975), the Court held that the prosecution of juveniles as adults in the California Superior Court violated the double jeopardy clause of the Fifth Amendment if they had previously been tried on the same charge in juvenile court.[25] The Court concluded that jeopardy attaches when the juvenile court begins to hear evidence at the adjudicatory hearing; this requires that the waiver hearing take place before any adjudication.

YOUTHS IN ADULT COURTS • Today, all states allow juveniles to be tried as adults in criminal courts in one of four ways:

1. *Direct file waiver.* The prosecutor has the discretion of filing charges for certain legislatively designated offenses in either juvenile or criminal court. About 15 states have this provision.

2. *Excluded offense waiver.* State laws exclude from juvenile court jurisdiction certain offenses that are either very minor, such as traffic or fishing violations, or very serious, such as murder. About 29 states now have such laws for certain crimes.

It is not uncommon for youths accused of serious and heinous crimes to be tried as adults. Here Alexander Alfaro, center, a juvenile arrested in connection with the killings of three college-bound youths, enters court in Newark, New Jersey, on February 6, 2008. Alfaro, 17, who was tried as an adult, pleaded not guilty to charges related to the three killings in a Newark schoolyard. His case recently went to trial.

© AP Photo/Mike Derer, Pool

3. *Judicial waiver.* After a formal hearing at which both prosecutor and defense attorney present evidence, a juvenile court judge may decide to waive jurisdiction and transfer the case to criminal court. This procedure is also known as "binding over" or "certifying" juvenile cases to criminal court.

4. *Reverse waiver.* State laws mandate that certain offenses be tried in adult court. Once the case is heard in the adult court, the trial judge may decide that the offender would be better served by the juvenile court and order a reverse waiver. About 25 states have this provision for certain circumstances.[26]

Every state has provisions for handling juveniles in adult criminal courts, and the trend is to make the waiver broader.[27] In 31 states, once a juvenile is tried in adult court, she is no longer eligible for juvenile justice on any subsequent offense.

THE EFFECT OF WAIVER • The problem of youths processed in adult courts is a serious one. About 8,000 juvenile delinquency cases are now being transferred to the adult courts each year. Supporters view the waiver process as a sound method of getting the most serious juvenile offenders off the streets. Kids are most likely to be transferred to criminal court if they have injured someone with a weapon or if they have a long juvenile court record.[28]

Waiver has its advocates, but many experts question its utility, arguing that it does more harm than good. One great fear is that juveniles will be forced to serve time in adult prisons, where they will be exposed to experienced criminals in what are essentially "schools for crime." In addition, children may be targets of adult predators if they are confined to adult institutions:

- Youths held in adult prisons and jails are five times more likely to be victims of attempted sexual attacks or rapes than those held in juvenile institutions.
- The suicide rate for juveniles in adult prisons and jails is nearly eight times higher than that for juveniles in youth detention centers.[29]

Not only are youths victimized if sent to adult prisons, but until relatively recently, waived youths could even be sentenced to death.[30] As noted earlier, in the 2005 case *Roper v. Simmons*, the Supreme Court ruled that no one could be executed for a crime committed before he or she was 18 years old.[31]

Although some youths who are transferred to adult court never spend a day in an adult prison, thousands do, and many of them become enmeshed in the daily life of an adult correctional facility. They miss out on being housed in juvenile facilities that are smaller, have much lower inmate-to-staff ratios, and place greater emphasis on treatment, counseling, education, and mentoring of inmates. Although some adult facilities do provide easy access to education and treatment, young inmates lose out on developing the relatively more supportive, mentoring-focused style of staff–inmate interactions that a juvenile facility provides.[32]

What is accomplished by treating juveniles as adults? Studies of the impact of the recent waiver statutes have yielded several interesting—and conflicting—results. Some recent (2006) research by Benjamin Steiner and Emily Wright on the effect of direct waiver laws found that they have little effect on juvenile violent crime rates in the states that have adopted them.[33] Other studies have found that juveniles waived to adult court receive harsher punishment and may be viewed as dangerous and incapable of being rehabilitated.[34] Waived juveniles may also spend more time in juvenile detention awaiting trial. In the end, what began as a "get tough" measure has had the opposite effect, while costing taxpayers more money.[35]

Transfer decisions are not always carried out fairly or equitably, and evidence indicates that minorities are waived to adult court at a rate that is greater than their representation in the population.[36] About 40 percent of all waived youths are African Americans, even though they represent less than a third (31 percent) of the juvenile court population.[37] No area of juvenile justice has received more attention recently than efforts to redefine the jurisdiction of the juvenile court.[38]

The Adjudication

initial appearance
A juvenile's first appearance before the juvenile court judge, in which the charges are reviewed and an effort is made to settle the case without a trial. If the child does not have legal counsel, an attorney is appointed.

There are usually two judicial hearings in the juvenile court process. The first, typically called an **initial appearance**, is similar to the arraignment in the adult system. The child is informed of the charges against him, attorneys are appointed, bail is reviewed, and in many instances cases are settled with an admission of the facts, followed by a community sentence. If the case cannot be settled at this initial stage, it is bound over for trial.

During the adjudicatory or trial process, which is often called the fact-finding hearing in juvenile proceedings, the court hears evidence on the allegations stated in the delinquency petition. In its early development, the juvenile court did not emphasize judicial rule making similar to that of the criminal trial process. Absent were such basic requirements as the standard of proof, rules of evidence, and similar adjudicatory formalities. Proceedings were to be nonadversarial, informal, and noncriminal. Gradually, however, the juvenile trial process became a target of criticism because judges were handing out punishments to children without affording them legal rights. This changed in 1967 when the Supreme Court's landmark *In re Gault* decision radically altered the juvenile justice system.[39] In *Gault*, the Court ruled that the concept of fundamental fairness is applicable to juvenile delinquency proceedings. The Court granted critical rights to juvenile defendants, most important among them the notice of the charges, the right to counsel, the right to confront and cross-examine witnesses, the privilege against self-incrimination, and the right to a transcript of the trial record.

REALITYCHECK

MYTH OR REALITY? Juvenile trials are identical to adult trials.

MYTH: Juveniles generally do not enjoy the right to a jury trial or a public hearing.

Juvenile trials are not really called trials at all, but rather "adjudicatory hearings." Adjudicatory hearings are less open and adversarial than adult criminal trials. The court hears evidence from both sides, but the judge renders the final decision. Why are juvenile "trials" called adjudicatory hearings?

The *Gault* decision completely altered the juvenile trial process. Instead of dealing with children in a benign and paternalistic fashion, the courts were forced to process juvenile offenders within the framework of appropriate constitutional procedures. And although *Gault* was technically limited to the adjudicatory stage, it has spurred further legal reform throughout the juvenile system. Today, the right to counsel, the privilege against self-incrimination, the right to treatment in detention and correctional facilities, and other constitutional protections are applied at all stages of the juvenile process, from investigation through adjudication to parole. *Gault* ushered in an era of legal rights for juveniles.

Once an adjudicatory hearing has been completed, the court is normally required to enter a judgment against the child. This may take the form of declaring the child delinquent or a ward of the court or possibly even suspending judgment to avoid the stigma of a juvenile record. After a judgment is entered, the court can begin its determination of possible **dispositions** for the child.

Some alternatives to the juvenile court trial are now in operation, and one of the more popular ones, the teen court, is discussed in the Policies, Programs, and Issues in Criminal Justice feature on pages 470 and 471.

Disposition and Treatment

At the dispositional hearing, the juvenile court judge imposes a sentence on the juvenile offender based on her offense, prior record, and family background. Normally, the judge has broad discretionary power to issue a range of dispositions from dismissal to institutional **commitment**. In theory, the dispositional decision is an effort by the court to serve the best interests of the child, the family, and the community. In many respects, this postadjudicative process is the most important stage in the juvenile court system, because it represents the last opportunity for the court to influence the child and control her behavior.

To ensure that only relevant and appropriate evidence is considered by the court during adjudication, most jurisdictions require a separate hearing to formulate an appropriate disposition. The bifurcated hearing process ensures that the adjudicatory hearing is used solely to determine the merits of the allegations, whereas the dispositional hearing determines whether the child is in need of rehabilitation.

In theory, the juvenile court seeks to provide a disposition that represents an individualized **treatment** plan for the child. This decision is normally based on the pre-sentence investigation of the probation department, reports from social agencies, and possibly a psychiatric evaluation. The judge generally has broad discretion in dispositional matters but is limited by the provisions of the state's juvenile court act. The following are typical juvenile court dispositions:

- Suspended judgment
- Probation
- Placement in a community treatment program
- Commitment to the state agency responsible for juvenile institutional care

In addition, the court may place the child with parents or relatives, make dispositional arrangements with private youth-serving agencies, or order the child committed to a mental institution.

DISPOSITION OUTCOMES • In dispositional hearings, juvenile court judges must determine the most appropriate sanction for delinquent youths. Disposition options include commitment to an institution or another residential facility; probation; and a variety of other dispositions, such as referral to an outside agency or treatment program, community service, fines, or restitution. Very often the court imposes some combination of these sanctions. What have been the trends in juvenile disposition? The number of adjudicated delinquency cases resulting in residential placement has increased significantly during the

disposition
For juvenile offenders, the equivalent of sentencing for adult offenders. The theory is that disposition is more rehabilitative than retributive. Possible dispositions include dismissing the case, releasing the youth to the custody of his or her parents, placing the offender on probation, or sending him or her to a state correctional institution.

commitment
Decision of judge ordering an adjudicated and sentenced juvenile offender to be placed in a correctional facility.

treatment
The rehabilitative method used to effect a change of behavior in the juvenile offender, in the form of therapy, or educational or vocational programs.

Policies, Programs, and Issues in Criminal Justice

Teen Courts

To relieve overcrowding and provide an alternative to traditional forms of juvenile courts, teen courts or youth courts are now in operation around the United States. According to the National Association of Youth Courts, there are 1,255 youth court programs in operation in 49 states and the District of Columbia. Agencies operating and administering youth court programs include juvenile courts, juvenile probation departments, law enforcement, private nonprofit organizations, and schools.

- Approximately 42 percent of youth court programs in operation are juvenile justice system–based programs.
- Approximately 22 percent of youth court programs are community based and are incorporated as, or operated by, private nonprofit organizations.
- Approximately 36 percent of youth court programs are school based.

These differ from other juvenile justice programs because in most instances young people, not adults, determine the disposition in a case. Cases handled in these courts typically involve young juveniles (ages 10 to 15), with no prior arrest records, who are being charged with minor law violations (such as shoplifting, vandalism, and disorderly conduct). Typically, young offenders are asked to volunteer to have their case heard in a teen court instead of the more formal court of the traditional juvenile justice system.

As in a regular juvenile court, teen court defendants may go through an intake process, a preliminary review of charges, a court hearing, and sentencing. In a teen court,

however, other young people are responsible for much of the process. Charges may be presented to the court by a 15-year-old "prosecutor." Defendants may be represented by a 16-year-old "defense attorney." Other youths may serve as jurors, court clerks, and bailiffs. In some teen courts, a youth "judge" (or panel of youth judges) may choose the best disposition or sanction for each case. In a few teen courts, youths even determine whether the facts in a case have been proven by the prosecutor (similar to a finding of guilt). Offenders are often ordered to pay restitution or perform community service. Some teen courts require offenders to write formal apologies to their victims; others require offenders to serve on a subsequent teen court jury. Many courts use other innovative dispositions, such as requiring offenders to attend classes designed to improve their decision-making skills, enhance their awareness of victims, and deter them from future illegal acts.

Although decisions are made by juveniles, adults are also involved in teen courts. They often administer the programs, and they are usually responsible for essential functions such as budgeting, planning, and personnel. In many programs, adults supervise the courtroom activities, and they often coordinate the community service placements, where youths work to fulfill the terms of their dispositions. In some programs, adults act as the judges while teens serve as attorneys and jurors.

Proponents of teen court argue that the process takes advantage of one of the most powerful forces in the life of an adolescent—the desire for peer approval and the reaction to peer pressure. According to this argument, youths

past decade, and today about 10 percent of all cases petitioned to juvenile court get some form of residential treatment. An additional 400,000 kids are put on probation each year.

Juvenile Sentencing Reform

Over the past decade, juvenile justice experts and the general public have become aroused about the serious juvenile crime rate in general and about violent acts committed by children in particular. As a result, some law enforcement officials and conservative legislators have demanded that the juvenile justice system take a more serious stand with dangerous juvenile offenders. Many state legislatures have responded by toughening their juvenile codes.

respond better to prosocial peers than to adult authority figures. Thus, teen courts are seen as a potentially effective alternative to traditional juvenile courts staffed with paid professionals such as lawyers, judges, and probation officers. Teen court advocates also point out that the advantages extend beyond defendants. Teen courts may benefit the volunteer youth attorneys and judges, who probably learn more about the legal system than they ever could in a classroom. The presence of a teen court may also encourage the entire community to take a more active role in responding to juvenile crime. In sum, teen courts offer at least four potential benefits:

1. **Accountability.** Teen courts may help to ensure that young offenders are held accountable for their illegal behavior, even when their offenses are relatively minor and would probably not result in sanctions from the traditional juvenile justice system.

2. **Timeliness.** An effective teen court can move young offenders from arrest to sanctions within a matter of days, instead of the months that may pass with traditional juvenile courts. This rapid response may increase the positive impact of court sanctions, regardless of their severity.

3. **Cost savings.** Teen courts usually depend heavily on youth and adult volunteers. If managed properly, they may handle a substantial number of offenders at relatively little cost to the community.

4. **Community cohesion.** A well-structured and expansive teen court program may affect the entire community by increasing public appreciation of the legal system, enhancing relationships between community and court, encouraging greater respect for the law among youths, and promoting volunteerism among both youths and adults.

The teen court movement is just beginning, and its effectiveness is still a matter of debate. Recent evaluations of teen courts have found that they did not widen the net of justice by handling cases that, in the absence of the peer court, would have been subject to a lesser level of processing. However, evaluations of effectiveness have been mixed. Evaluations by Kevin Minor and his associates of teen courts in Kentucky and by Paige Harrison and her colleagues in New Mexico indicate that recidivism levels range from 25 percent to 30 percent. In contrast, the Urban Institute's Evaluation of Teen Courts Project, which was based on four teen court programs (in Alaska, Maryland, Arizona, and Missouri), found that after six months, recidivism ranged from 6 percent to 9 percent, whereas cases sent to juvenile courts had an 18 percent recidivism rate. Considering that these cases typically involve offenses of only moderate seriousness, the findings do not suggest that the program can play a significant role in reducing teenage crime rates.

Critical Thinking

1. Could teen courts be used to try serious criminal acts such as burglary and robbery?
2. Is a conflict of interest created when teens judge the behavior of other teens? Does the fact that they themselves may one day become defendants in a teen court influence such judges' decision making?

Some jurisdictions have passed mandatory or determinate incarceration sentences for juveniles convicted of serious felonies. Not all jurisdictions have abandoned rehabilitation as a primary dispositional goal, however, and some still hold to the philosophy that placements should be based on the least detrimental alternative. This view requires that judges employ the least intrusive measures possible to safeguard a child's growth and development.[40]

A second reform has been the concerted effort to remove status offenders from the juvenile justice system and restrict their entry into institutional programs. Because of the development of numerous diversion programs, many children involved in truancy and incorrigible behavior who ordinarily would have been sent to a closed institution are now being placed in community programs. There are far fewer status offenders in detention or institutions than ever before.

REALITYCHECK

Youths are more violent and criminally dangerous today than they were in the past.

MYTH: Highly publicized juvenile crimes may give this impression, but the data tells a different story: Juvenile crime (and arrests) peaked in the early to mid-1990s.

During the latter part of the 1990s and into the early twenty-first century, juvenile crime declined. In 2004, the arrest rate for violent crimes committed by juveniles dropped to historic lows. Recently, juvenile crime and arrests have fluctuated, but they have yet to come close to their historic highs. What fuels the perception that juvenile crime is more serious and extensive than at any point in the past?

A third reform effort has been to standardize dispositions in juvenile court. As early as 1977, Washington passed one of the first determinate sentencing laws for juvenile offenders, resulting in other states adopting similar statutes.[41] All children found to be delinquent are evaluated on a point system based on their age, prior juvenile record, and type of crime committed. Minor offenders are handled in the community. Those committing more serious offenses are placed on probation. Children who commit the most serious offenses are subject to standardized institutional penalties. As a result, juvenile offenders who commit such crimes as rape or armed robbery are being sentenced to institutionalization for two, three, and four years. This approach is different from the indeterminate sentencing, under which children who have committed a serious crime might be released from institutions in less than a year if correctional authorities believe they have been rehabilitated.

The Juvenile Correctional Process

After disposition in juvenile court, delinquent offenders may be placed in some form of correctional treatment. Although many are placed in the community, more than 100,000 are now in secure facilities.

Probation

The most commonly used formal sentence for juvenile offenders is probation, and many states require that a youth fail on probation before being sent to an institution (unless the criminal act is quite serious). Probation involves placing the child under the supervision of the juvenile probation department for the purpose of community treatment. A juvenile may also be required to follow special rules, such as maintaining a curfew or attending substance abuse meetings. Alternative sanctions such as community service or monetary restitution may be ordered. Serious offenders can be placed in intensive supervision or under house arrest. Probation can be revoked if the juvenile violates the probation conditions. Just as in the adult system, probation can be revoked if the rules are not followed, and the court may impose stricter sanctions.

Juvenile probation is an important component of the juvenile justice system. It is the most widely used method of community treatment in juvenile court. Similar in form and function to adult probation, supervising juveniles in the community combines elements of treatment and control. Some probation officers maintain a social work orientation and want to provide needy kids with an effective treatment plan, but others maintain a law enforcement orientation, believing that their clients are offenders who need close monitoring.[42]

Institutionalization

The most severe of the statutory dispositions available to the juvenile court involves commitment of the child to an institution. The committed child may be sent to a state training school or private residential treatment facility. These are usually minimum-security facilities with small populations and an emphasis on treatment and education. Some states, however, maintain facilities with populations over 1,000.

State statutes vary in terms of the length of the child's commitment. Traditionally, many jurisdictions committed the child up to majority, which usually meant 21 years of age. This normally deprived the child of freedom for an extensive period of time—sometimes longer than an adult sentenced for the same offense would be confined. As a result, some states have passed legislation under which children are committed for periods ranging from one to three years.

To better handle violent juvenile offenders, some states have created separate or intermediate juvenile systems. Under such statutes, 14- to 17-year-olds charged with certain violent felonies are treated as adults and, if convicted, are sentenced to new intermediate prisons, separated from both adult and regular juvenile offenders, for terms of two to five years.

Today more than 100,000 juveniles are being held in either privately run or publicly managed juvenile correctional facilities.[43] About 35 percent are held for person-oriented offenses; the rest are held for property offenses (25 percent), drug offenses (9 percent), public order offenses (11 percent), technical violations (16 percent), and status offenses (5 percent).[44] The efforts made in recent years to keep status offenders out of institutions seem to have paid off.

The typical resident of a juvenile facility is a 15- to 16-year-old white male incarcerated for an average stay of five months in a public facility or six months in a private facility. Private facilities tend to house younger teens, whereas public institutions provide custodial care for older youths, including a small percentage of youths between 18 and 21 years of age.

Deinstitutionalization

Some experts in delinquency and juvenile law question the policy of institutionalizing juvenile offenders. Many believe that large institutions are too costly to operate and only produce more sophisticated criminals. This dilemma has produced a number of efforts to remove youths from juvenile facilities and replace large institutions with smaller, community-based facilities. The Commonwealth of Massachusetts closed all its state training schools more than 20 years ago (subsequently, however, public pressure caused a few secure facilities to be reopened). Many other states have established small residential facilities operated by juvenile-care agencies to replace larger units.

Despite the daily rhetoric on crime control, public support for community-based programs for juveniles still exists. Although such programs are not panaceas, many experts still recommend more treatment and less incarceration for juvenile offenders. Utah, Maryland, Vermont, and Pennsylvania, for example, have dramatically reduced their reform school populations while setting up a wide range of intensive treatment programs for juveniles. Many large, impersonal, and expensive state institutions with unqualified staff and ineffective treatment programs have been eliminated.

DEINSTITUTIONALIZING STATUS OFFENDERS • There has been an ongoing effort for almost 30 years to deinstitutionalize status offenders (DSO).[45] This means removing noncriminal youths from institutions housing delinquents in order to prevent them from interacting with violent or chronic offenders.

Since its inception, the DSO approach has been hotly debated. Some have argued that early intervention is society's best hope of forestalling future delinquent behavior and reducing victimization. Other experts maintain that legal control over status offenders is a violation of youths' rights. Still others have viewed status-offending behavior as a symptom of some larger trauma or problem that requires attention. These diverse opinions still exist today.

Since Congress passed the JJDP Act in 1974, all 50 states have complied with some aspect of the deinstitutionalization mandate. Millions of federal, state, and local dollars have been spent on the DSO movement. Vast numbers of programs have been created around the country to reduce the number of juveniles in secure confinement. What remains to be done, however, is to study the effect DSO has had on juveniles and the justice system.

Aftercare

Aftercare marks the final stage of the formal juvenile justice process. Its purpose is to help youths make the transition from residential or institutional settings back into the community. Effective aftercare programs provide adequate supervision and support services to help juvenile offenders avoid criminal activity. Examples of programs include electronic monitoring, counseling, treatment and community service referrals, education, work training, and intensive parole supervision.

Most juvenile aftercare involves parole. A juvenile parole officer provides the child with counseling, school referral, vocational training, and other services. Children who violate the conditions of parole may have their parole revoked and be returned to the institution. Unlike the adult postconviction process, where the Supreme Court has imposed procedural protections in probation and parole revocations, juveniles do not have such due process rights. State courts have also been reluctant to grant juveniles rights in this area, and those that *have* granted them generally refuse to require that the whole array of rights be made available, as they are to adult offenders. Since the *Gault* decision, however, many states have adopted administrative regulations requiring juvenile agencies to incorporate due process, such as proper notice of the hearing and the right to counsel in postconviction proceedings.

Preventing Delinquency

Although the juvenile justice system has been concerned with controlling delinquent behavior, important efforts are now being made to prevent delinquency before it occurs. "Delinquency prevention" refers to intervening in young people's lives before they engage in delinquency in the first place—that is, preventing any involvement in delinquency at all. In the past, delinquency prevention was the responsibility of treatment-oriented agencies such as day care providers, YMCA and YWCA, Boys and Girls Clubs of America, and other private and public agencies. Today, there are many community-based treatment programs involving a combination of juvenile justice and treatment agencies. Some programs focus on the educational experience and attempt to help kids maintain their bond to society by strengthening their

© Image Source/Getty Images

If juvenile delinquency can be prevented from occurring in the first place, young people stand the best chance of leading productive, law-abiding lives. Here Judge Alison Nelson Floyd, right, helps student Samuel Jordan, 10, from the W.E.B. Dubois Leadership Academy, navigate his way through his responsibilities as a judge in a mock trial in the courtroom of Judge Charles Patton at the Justice Center in Cleveland, Ohio, on March 21, 2009. Floyd, a juvenile court judge, volunteered to teach the boys, ages 10–13 years, about the workings of the criminal justice system.

© Lisa DeJong/The Plain Dealer/Landov

Careers in Criminal Justice

SOCIAL WORKER

Duties and Characteristics of the Job

- Social workers aid individuals or families who are disadvantaged or facing particular challenges.
- Social workers pick a specialization within one of several larger categories. Public health social workers help individuals and families dealing with the consequences of a serious illness. Child, family, and health social workers aid families dealing with issues of social functioning, such as child abuse or truancy. Clinical social workers help families deal with issues related to mental health and substance abuse through a rehabilitation program.
- Other social workers take positions where they do not deal with the public; instead, they may teach or may provide psychotherapy in private practices. There are also policy writers and advocates who attempt to find legislative solutions to social problems and lobby for funding.
- Social work is a demanding profession both intellectually and emotionally. Although social workers traditionally work a 40-hour office work week, working overtime or during evening hours to attend meetings or meet clients is not unusual.

Job Outlook

- The prospects for employment as a social worker are good, because jobs are expected to grow faster than average in the near future, and in many places there are more jobs than there are applicants.
- Because of the impending retirement of the baby boom generation, there will be many job opportunities in hospices and nursing homes for social workers specializing in care of the elderly.
- Jobs in school and private social service agencies will also increase.

Salary

- Median annual earnings of child, family, and school social workers is $37,480. The lowest 10 percent recently earned less than $24,480, and the top 10 percent earned more than $62,530. Social workers' salaries vary according to their specialization.
- Social twerkers who specialize in medical and public health have an average salary of $43,040.

(continued)

Careers in Criminal Justice (continued)

Opportunities

- Because of greater competition for jobs in urban areas, those with more education and some specialized experience stand a better chance of getting desirable positions and of career advancement.
- It may be considerably easier to find a job in a rural area, where educational requirements will be less stringent. Those who leave social work often successfully pursue careers in related fields such as counseling.

Qualifications

- Meeting the challenging education requirements and certification standards is the primary qualification necessary to become a social worker.
- Personal characteristics such as sensitivity, responsibility, and the ability to work independently are also very important.
- Potential social workers must have at least a bachelor's degree in social work to start at entry-level positions, and additional education for graduate-level degrees will prepare them for more advanced duties, such as clinical assessments and supervisory positions.
- In addition to being well educated, social workers must meet the particular licensing requirements of the state where they seek employment before they can begin to work.

Education and Training

- Applicants for entry-level positions will need a bachelor's degree in Social Work (B.S.W.) or a similar degree in fields such as sociology.
- Those who wish to advance further should earn a master's degree in Social Work (M.S.W.) or a doctorate (Ph.D. or D.S.W.).
- Those who wish to ascend to the highest-level positions in a social work organization or to design new social work policies or programs should pursue a Ph.D.
- Social workers' education is never truly complete; they must keep up on recent developments by attending conferences and reading the most recent literature.

Word to the Wise

- A majority of the social worker positions are in urban and suburban areas; potential social workers will find more competition for a limited number of jobs in urban areas.
- Education requirements can be intensive, particularly if one wishes to ascend to the highest-level positions.
- Applicants must have a strong desire to help improve people's lives.
- The work can be challenging because of understaffing and large caseloads.
- Burnout is not uncommon. At least one website is dedicated the problem (www.friedsocialworker.com). The site presents a humorous spin on social worker burnout, but there are some serious underpinnings.

attachments to school. Much of these efforts are conducted by social workers whose specialty is working with troubled youths. The Careers in Criminal Justice feature on page 475 describes this occupation.

Comprehensive community-based delinquency prevention programs are taking a systematic approach or using a comprehensive planning model to develop preventive interventions. This includes analyzing the delinquency problem, identifying resources available in the community, prioritizing delinquency problems, and identifying successful programs in other communities and tailoring them to local conditions and needs.[46] Not all comprehensive community-based prevention programs follow this model, but evidence suggests that this approach will produce the greatest reductions in juvenile delinquency.[47]

An example of the comprehensive community program is the Children At Risk (CAR) program funded by the federal government. CAR was designed to help improve the lives of young people at high risk for delinquency, gang involvement, substance abuse, and other problem behaviors. It was delivered to a large number of young people in poor and high-crime neighborhoods in five cities across the country. It involved a wide range of preventive measures, including case management and family counseling, family skills training, tutoring, mentoring, after-school activities, and community policing. The program was different in each neighborhood. The other beneficial results for those in the program included less association with delinquent peers, less peer pressure to engage in delinquency, and more positive peer support.[48]

The CAR program is now known as CASASTART, an acronym for the national Center on Addiction and Substance Abuse, Striving Together to Achieve Rewarding Tomorrows. Developed at Columbia University in New York, CASASTART is a neighborhood-based, school-centered program aimed at preventing substance abuse and delinquency among high-risk adolescents ages 8 to 13 and reducing drug-related crime in their neighborhoods. The program brings together different organizations, including schools, law enforcement, and social service agencies, to provide clients with eight different services: tutoring, after-school activities, mentoring, counseling, family services, community policing, juvenile justice intervention, and incentives.

Potentially eligible children are referred to CASASTART by school, social service staff, police, or juvenile court personnel. Staff members (called case managers) then determine whether children meet the criteria of being at high risk of substance abuse and crime. Each case manager works on a one-to-one basis with 15 families. In addition to seeking participants and coordinating services, CASASTART case managers engage in a full range of activities:

- Running after-school or recreation programs
- Arranging appointments and sometimes transporting family members to them
- Helping prevent homelessness and utility shutoffs
- Advocating for children and family members in court
- Helping parents resolve problems with schools or social service agencies

The program is now being used in 64 sites around the country, including Denver, Colorado, and San Antonio, Texas.[49]

Problems of Juvenile Justice

When Rasheed Stevenson's case was heard in a Baltimore juvenile court in 2006, no one doubted the severity of the crimes with which he was charged: choking a man until he was unconscious and then robbing him of six dollars and cigarettes. His public defender suggested sending Stevenson out of state for treatment. A prosecutor argued that the boy had no conscience. A judge wanted him under "strict control." A court-ordered evaluation recommended that he remain charged as an adult. But the judge ordered Stevenson sent back into the juvenile justice system, and several weeks later the case was dismissed because the victim didn't show up to testify. Back on the streets, Stevenson began hanging with a gang in the city's Harwood neighborhood off Greenmount Avenue. A little more than a month later, he was found stabbed to death.[50]

Stories such as Rasheed's indicate that the juvenile justice system is at a crossroads: Can it provide meaningful treatment to youths in an age of budget cutting and reductions in social services? Should it maintain the parens patriae

© Image Source/Getty Images

vision of its founders, or should it adopt a law and order approach to dealing with violent kids? Should the system be maintained, or should it be abolished?

Even those experts who want to retain an independent juvenile court have called for its restructuring.[51] Crime control advocates want to reduce the court's jurisdiction over juveniles charged with serious crimes and liberalize the prosecutor's ability to try them in adult courts. In *Bad Kids: Race and the Transformation of the Juvenile Court*, legal expert Barry Feld makes the rather controversial suggestion that the juvenile court system should be discontinued and replaced by an alternative method of justice.[52] During its history, various legal developments have undermined its purpose—most notably the *In re Gault* ruling, which ultimately led to juveniles receiving legal protections similar to those accorded adults and to children being treated like adults in all respects. Then, in the 1980s, the sudden rise in gang membership, gun violence, and homicide committed by juveniles further undermined the juvenile court mission and resulted in legislation creating mandatory sentences for juvenile offenders and mandatory waiver to the adult court. As a result, the focus of the court has been on dealing with the offense rather than treating the offender. In Feld's words, the juvenile court has become a "deficient second-rate criminal court." The welfare and rehabilitative purposes of the juvenile court have been subordinated to its role as law enforcement agent, so there is little purpose for retaining it in its current state. Feld's beliefs have been substantiated by research showing that at least in some jurisdictions, the focus of juvenile justice has shifted from individual needs to the seriousness of the crime, enhancing the prosecution's power to make decisions and the system's reliance on the adversarial process at the expense of parens patriae.[53]

Not all experts agree with Feld that the juvenile court has become redundant. Some, such as John Kerbs, believe that the "get tough" approach will force the criminal courts to provide harsher sentences and tougher treatment—and that the brunt of these draconian sentences will fall squarely on the shoulders of minority youths. Research efforts routinely show that African American adults are unduly punished in adult courts. Sending juvenile offenders to these venues is likely to enmesh them further in a system that is already unfair.[54]

Minority Overrepresentation in Juvenile Justice

In addition to controversies over its goals and values, another significant and enduring problem in juvenile justice is the overrepresentation of minority youths in the system and the inequitable treatment they receive. Minority youths accused of delinquent acts are less likely than white youths to be diverted from the court system into informal sanctions and are more likely to receive sentences involving incarceration. In some states, the ratio of minority custody to white custody is greater than 4 to 1.[55] Nationally, the ratio is 2.6 to 1, meaning that there are 2.6 members of minority groups in custody for every white juvenile in custody.[56]

Not only is the disproportionate minority representation in juvenile correctional facilities a very serious matter, but it also reflects the racial disparity that occurs at every stage of the juvenile justice process. A disproportionate number of minority youths suffer arrest, detention, waivers, and so on. It is not surprising, then, that they also face disparity in the probability of incarceration.

A recent (2007) report by the National Council on Crime and Delinquency highlights this problem. The council's "Treatment of Youth of Color in the Justice System" describes how minority youths receive differential treatment at every stage of the justice process.[57]

Among the findings from the council's report are these:

- Although African American youths are 16 percent of the adolescent population in the United States, they are 38 percent of the almost 100,000 youths confined in local detention and state correctional systems. They were overrepresented in all offense categories.

- Youths of color make up the majority of young people held in both public and private facilities.
- Youths of color, especially Latino youths, are a much larger proportion of the young in public facilities than in private facilities, which tend to be less harsh environments.
- Although they represent just 34 percent of the U.S. population, youths of color represent 62 percent of young people in detention, 66 percent of those committed to public facilities, and 55 percent of those committed to private facilities.
- Nationwide, youths of color were overrepresented in the detained population at 3.1 times the rate of white youths, among commitments to public facilities at 2.9 times the rate of white youths, and among private commitments at 2.0 times the rate of white youths.
- Overall, custody rates were four times greater for African American youths than for white youths. Custody rates for Latino and Native American youths were 1.8 and 2.6 times the custody rate for white youths, respectively.

Exhibit 13.5 illustrates some of the findings from this extensive national study. The council report concludes with this statement:

> While "Equal Justice Under the Law" is the foundation of our legal system, and is carved on the front of the U.S. Supreme Court, the juvenile justice system is anything but equal for all. Throughout the system, youth of color—especially African American youth—receive different and harsher treatment. This is true even when White youth and youth of color are charged with similar offenses. This report documents a juvenile justice system that is "separate and unequal." It is time for a nationwide effort to identify the causes of this differential treatment of youth of color and a concerted campaign to provide a fair and equal justice system for our youth.[58]

National Council on Crime and Delinquency

To read the report by the **National Council on Crime and Delinquency** in its entirety, go to

www.cengage.com/criminaljustice/siegel

To try to alleviate this problem, since 1988 the Juvenile Justice and Delinquency Prevention Act has required that in order to receive funding, states must monitor whether the proportion of juvenile minorities in confinement exceeds their proportion in the general population.[59] Achieving the goal of proportional representation has been elusive in actual practice. A number of strategies have been attempted, ranging from cultural competency training to providing increasing community-based detention alternatives.[60] But as the National Council report indicates, the problem of racial disparity has proved difficult to overcome.

EXHIBIT 13.5

Overrepresentation of Minority Youths in the Justice System

From 2002 to 2004, African Americans were represented in the following proportions:

- 16% of youths in the United States
- 28% of juvenile arrests
- 30% of referrals to juvenile court
- 37% of the detained population
- 34% of youths formally processed by the juvenile court
- 30% of adjudicated youths
- 35% of youths judicially waived to criminal court
- 38% of youths in residential placement
- 58% of youths admitted to state adult prison

Source: National Council on Crime and Delinquency, *And Justice for Some: Differential Treatment of Minority Youth in the Justice System,* January 2007.

ETHICAL CHALLENGES IN CRIMINAL JUSTICE

A Writing Assignment

You are a juvenile court judge. John M. has been arrested for robbery and rape. His victim, a young neighborhood girl, was seriously injured in the attack and needed extensive hospitalization; she is now in counseling. Because the charges are serious, John can be waived to the adult court and tried as an adult even though he is only 14 years old. Under existing state law, a hearing must be held to determine whether there is sufficient evidence that John cannot be successfully treated in the juvenile justice system and therefore warrants transfer to the adult system; the final decision on the matter is yours alone.

At the waiver hearing, you discover that John is the oldest of three siblings living in a single-parent home. He has had no contact with his father for more than 10 years. His psychological evaluations show hostility, anger toward females, and great feelings of frustration. His intelligence is above average, but his behavioral and academic records are poor. John is a loner with few friends. This is his first formal involvement with the juvenile court. Previous contact was limited to an informal complaint for disorderly conduct at age 13, which was dismissed by the court's intake department. During the hearing, John verbalizes what you interpret to be superficial remorse for his offenses.

Write an essay discussing whether you would waive John to the adult court or treat him as a juvenile, and give the reasons for your decision.

RealityCheck Revisited

To learn more about the myths and realities related to the juvenile justice system that were raised in this chapter, visit the following websites.

- For more information on state definitions of juvenile court jurisdiction, see page 103 of the report found here:

http://ojjdp.ncjrs.org/ojstatbb/nr2006/downloads/ chapter4.pdf

- For more information on juveniles' legal rights and the juvenile justice process in different states, see, for example,

Washington: **http://www.co.thurston.wa.us/ juvenilecourt/rights.htm**

New Hampshire: **http://www.nhbar.org/for-the-public/the-rights-of-juveniles.asp**

Oregon: **http://www.mbabar.org/docs/Juvrights.pdf**

Florida: **http://www.djj.state.fl.us/Parents/ juvenileprocess.html**

- For data on juvenile crime, including arrests, see

http://ojjdp.ncjrs.org/ojstatbb/

http://ojjdp.ncjrs.org/ojstatbb/nr2006/index.html

SUMMARY

© AP Photo/*The Oakland Press*, Vaughn Gurganian

1. Describe the nature and purpose of the juvenile justice system

- Conceived at the turn of the twentieth century, the juvenile justice system was viewed as a quasi-social welfare agency that was to act as a surrogate parent in the interests of the child.

- Juvenile justice was originally based on the parens patriae philosophy.

2. Be familiar with the history and development of juvenile justice

- The modern practice of legally separating adult and juvenile offenders can be traced back to the development of Elizabethan-era poor laws and the creation of the English chancery court.

- Poor laws and chancery courts were brought from England to colonial America.

- To accommodate dependent youths, local jurisdictions developed almshouses, poorhouses, and workhouses.

3. Discuss the child savers and their vision of juvenile justice

- The child savers were responsible for creating a number of programs for indigent youths, including the New York House of Refuge, which began operations in 1825.

- The child savers also influenced state and local governments to create independent correctional institutions to house minors.

- The first of these reform schools opened in Westboro, Massachusetts, in 1848 and in Rochester, New York, in 1849.

- In 1853, New York philanthropist Charles Loring Brace helped develop the Children's Aid Society, which placed neglected and delinquent youths in private homes in rural communities.

4. Describe the efforts of the child savers to create an independent juvenile court

- The child savers lobbied for an independent, state-supported juvenile court. Their efforts prompted the development of the first comprehensive juvenile court in Illinois in 1899.

- The Illinois Juvenile Court Act set up an independent court to handle criminal law violations by children under 16 years of age, as well as to care for neglected, dependent, and wayward youths.

- The main concern was the "best interests of the child," not strict adherence to legal doctrine, constitutional rights, or due process of law. Youngsters who were found delinquent in juvenile court could spend years in a state training school.

5. Describe the changes in juvenile justice that began in the 1960s and continue today

- In the 1960s and 1970s, the U.S. Supreme Court radically altered the juvenile justice system when it rendered a series of decisions that established the right of juveniles to due process of law.

- The term "juvenile delinquency" refers to children who fall under a jurisdictional age limit, which varies from state to state, and who commit an act in violation of the penal code.

- Status offenders commit acts forbidden to minors, which include truancy, running away, and being a habitually disobedient and ungovernable child.

- Another trend has been to create family courts, which include a broad range of family- and child-related issues within their jurisdictions.

6. Discuss the police processing of juvenile offenders

- According to the Uniform Crime Reports, police officers arrest more than 1.5 million juveniles under age 18 each year, including almost 500,000 under age 15.

continued

- Most states do not have specific statutory provisions distinguishing the arrest process for children from that for adults.

- Some jurisdictions give broad arrest powers to the police in juvenile cases by authorizing the officer to make an arrest whenever she or he believes that the child's behavior falls within the jurisdiction of the juvenile court.

- Police may arrest youths for behavior considered legal for adults, including running away, violating curfew, and being in possession of alcohol.

- When a juvenile is found to have engaged in delinquent or incorrigible behavior, police agencies are charged with the decision to release or to detain the child and refer her to juvenile court.

- Once a juvenile has been taken into custody, the child has the same right to be free from unreasonable searches and seizures as an adult has.

- After the police have determined that a case warrants further attention, they will bind it over to the prosecutor's office, which then is responsible for channeling the case through the juvenile court.

7. *Distinguish between the adjudication of juvenile offenders and that of adult offenders*

- After police processing, the juvenile offender is usually remanded to the local juvenile court's intake division.

- After a juvenile is formally taken into custody, either as a delinquent or as a status offender, the prosecutor usually decides whether to release the child to the parent or guardian or to detain the child in a secure shelter pending trial.

- There has been an ongoing effort to reform detention. The most important reform has been the successful effort to remove status offenders from lockups containing delinquents.

- Although only a few state statutes allow release on money bail, many others have juvenile code provisions that emphasize the release of the child to the parents as an acceptable substitute.

8. *Discuss the problems and legal issues surrounding the waiver decision*

- Before trial, prosecutors in the juvenile courts may attempt to negotiate a settlement to the case.

- Today, most U.S. jurisdictions provide by statute for waiver, or transfer, of juvenile offenders to the criminal courts.

- In *Kent v. United States* (1966), the Supreme Court held that the waiver proceeding is a critically important stage in the juvenile justice process and that juveniles must be afforded minimum requirements of due process of law at such proceedings, including the right to legal counsel.

- Waiver does not seem to influence crime rates or recidivism rates; one reason may be that juveniles whose cases are waived to criminal court are sentenced more leniently than they would have been in juvenile court.

- Although some youths who are transferred to adult court never spend a day in an adult prison, others become enmeshed in the daily life of an adult correctional facility.

9. *Trace the juvenile trial and sentencing process*

- There are usually two judicial hearings in the juvenile court process. The first, typically called an initial appearance, is similar to the arraignment in the adult system.

- During the adjudicatory or trial process, which is often called the fact-finding hearing in juvenile proceedings, the court hears evidence on the allegations stated in the delinquency petition.

- The *In re Gault* decision radically altered the juvenile justice system by applying due process to juvenile delinquency proceedings.

- *Gault* granted critical rights to juvenile defendants, the most important of these rights being notice of the charges, the right to counsel, the right to confront and cross-examine witnesses, the privilege against self-incrimination, and the right to a transcript of the trial record.

- At the dispositional hearing, the juvenile court judge imposes a sentence on the juvenile offender based on the offense, the youth's prior record, and his or her family background.

© AP Images/Suzanne Plunkett

Chapter Outline

Career Vignette

Mark O. is a special agent for the Department of Homeland Security. He works for the Immigration and Customs (ICE) Office of Investigations conducting criminal investigations into suspected, alleged, and/or known violations of federal law. Because of the secure nature of his work, we cannot reveal his real name or publish his photo. Why did he become a criminal investigator? Upon graduating from college with a degree in Psychology, he began working in a psychiatric hospital. A New York City native, he was personally affected

© AP Images/Suzanne Plunkett

RealityCheck

MYTH or REALITY?

▶ Terrorism began during the French Revolution and the reign of terror.

▶ Terrorists are cool and calculating.

▶ Terrorists are not a unified entity; they have a variety of goals and objectives.

▶ There is a single U.S. national entity/organization designed to accumulate all existing information on terrorism and to monitor terrorist activities.

▶ Antiterrorism law enforcement activities are under the jurisdiction of federal agencies such as the FBI and DHS.

▶ Cyber criminals are technologically sophisticated and can strike from anywhere in the world.

▶ It will be difficult to defeat cyber criminals without interagency and international cooperation.

Learning Objectives

1. Be able to define terrorism and cyber crime

2. Be familiar with the history of terrorism

3. Understand the factors that motivate terrorists

4. Be familiar with the various forms of contemporary terrorism

5. Discuss how the federal government has responded to terrorism

6. Recognize that state and local governments have created antiterror initiatives

7. Debate the utility and problems associated with the USA Patriot Act

8. Discuss the various forms of cyber crime

9. Define the concept of cyber terrorism

10. Know what is being done to thwart cyber criminals

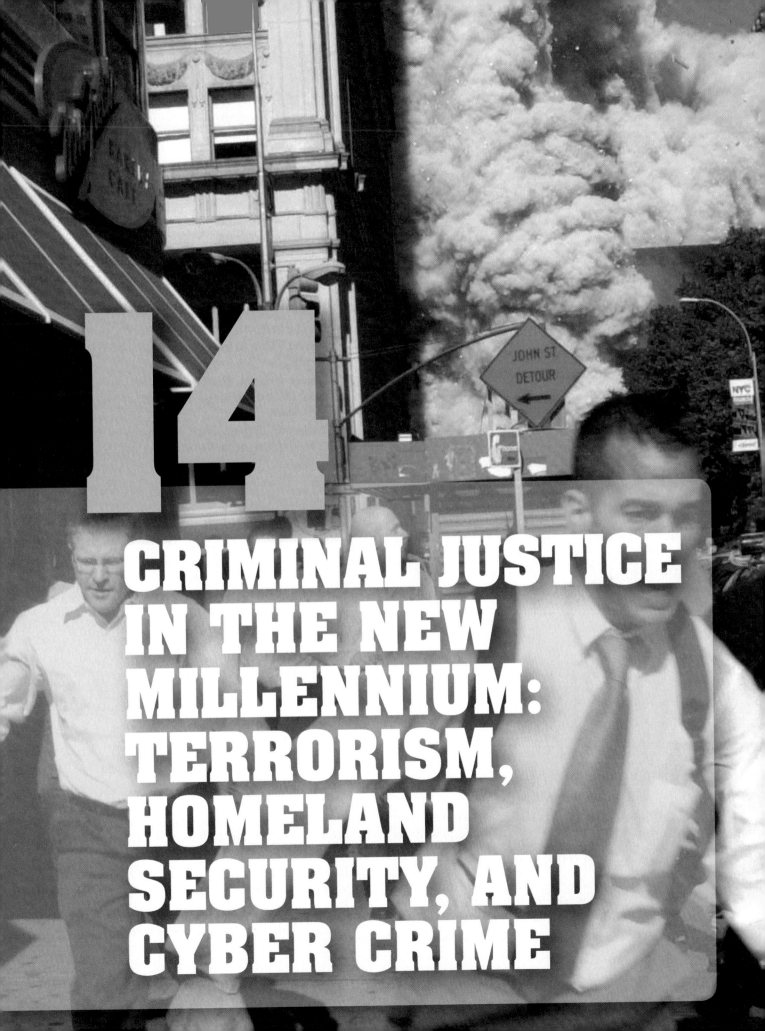

14

CRIMINAL JUSTICE IN THE NEW MILLENNIUM: TERRORISM, HOMELAND SECURITY, AND CYBER CRIME

- Some jurisdictions have passed mandatory or determinate incarceration sentences for juveniles convicted of serious felonies.

- A second reform has been the concerted effort to remove status offenders from the juvenile justice system and restrict their entry into institutional programs.

- Probation is the most commonly used formal sentence for juvenile offenders, and many states require that a youth fail on probation before being sent to an institution (unless the criminal act is quite serious).

- The most severe of the statutory dispositions available to the juvenile court involves commitment of the child to an institution.

- Some experts in delinquency and juvenile law question the policy of institutionalizing juvenile offenders.

- There has been an ongoing effort for almost 30 years to deinstitutionalize status offenders (DSO).

- The purpose of aftercare is to help youths make the transition from residential or institutional settings back into the community.

10. **Compare efforts to treat troubled kids in the juvenile justice system with the belief that treatment is ineffective and should be abolished**

- Although the juvenile justice system has been concerned with controlling delinquent behavior, important efforts are now being made to prevent delinquency before it occurs.

- Some experts question whether the juvenile justice system should exist in its present form.

- One ongoing problem has been minority overrepresentation in juvenile justice.

Key Terms

parens patriae, 451
poor laws, 452
child savers, 453
Children's Aid Society, 454
juvenile court, 454
juvenile delinquency, 457
status offender, 457

detention, 463
waiver (juvenile), 466
transfer hearing, 466
initial appearance, 468
disposition, 469
commitment, 469
treatment, 469

Review Questions

1. Should status offenders be treated by the juvenile court? Explain. Should they be placed in confinement for such acts as running away or cutting school? Why or why not?

2. Should a juvenile ever be waived to adult court with the possible risk that the child will be incarcerated with adult felons? Why or why not?

3. Do you support the death penalty for children? Explain.

4. Should juveniles be given mandatory incarceration sentences for serious crimes, as adults are? Explain.

5. Is it fair to deny juveniles a jury trial? Why or why not?

6. Do you think the trend toward treating juveniles like adult offenders is desirable? Explain.

by the terrorist attacks on September 11, 2001, and felt compelled to do something to help protect the country. Very shortly thereafter, he applied for, and was offered, his first federal law enforcement position. Eventually, he moved into the area of antiterrorism and counterterrorism.

While on the job, Mark has continued his education by pursuing a master's degree in Criminal Justice. As a criminal investigator, he finds that critical thinking and analytical skills are invaluable and that education is the best way to hone these skills. He believes that a criminal justice education is the best way to develop greater awareness of the complexities and prevalent issues facing law enforcement personnel and the entire criminal justice system. Instructors—and also peers—provide insight into varying points of view and current schools of thought across a wide spectrum of justice issues.

Although he loves his job, Mark believes that the general public hold many misconceptions about investigative work. Unlike what is often portrayed on television, investigations take time. Sometimes it may be several years before a single arrest is made. Often, solving a case depends not on the discovery of a single "smoking gun" but, rather, on the painstaking accumulation of evidence. Consequently, investigation requires a great deal of patience. Answers aren't always clear-cut, so an investigator must maintain a high level of alertness, flexibility, and focus. Yet the rewards are great. Mark gets to work alongside many dedicated colleagues who share a deep desire to do something to help their fellow citizens.

Department of Homeland Security

W hile efforts to control traditional crimes—murder, rape, robbery, drug trafficking—continue, emerging forms of criminal and illegal activity pose a significant threat to society and require the talent and experience of special agents such as Mark O. Because of their seriousness, potential for damage, and effect on public morale, two of these contemporary challenges stand out in importance: terrorism and cyber crime. Neither appeared on the radar screen 20 years ago; today they dominate the news. Criminal justice agencies at the federal, state, and local levels have been forced to adapt to the threats they present.

One reason why cyber crime and terrorism represent formidable challenges to the justice system is that both are evolving in complexity and seriousness. Terrorism consists of the illegal use of force against innocent people to achieve a political objective. Confronting terrorism is critical because of the lethal tactics now being used—such as bombings, killing hostages, chemical warfare, and spreading toxic biological agents. Terrorists' tactics are alien to most people, who refrain from violent solutions to their problems because they enjoy the benefits of living in a society with a secure economic and social system. Even when they wage war, stable governments abide by a standard code of conduct that spells out appropriate and inappropriate behaviors. Because they and their groups do not share in its benefits, terrorists not only have no stake in maintaining the economic, social, and political structure; they may be actively plotting its destruction. They obey few rules of combat and will use any tactic, no matter how violent, to achieve their goals.[1] Agencies of the justice system have little experience in dealing with such ruthlessness.

Cyber crime, the second contemporary challenge facing the justice system, is defined here as any illegal behavior that targets the security of computer systems and/or the data accessed and processed by computer networks. Included within this category of crime are attacks against computers themselves—computercrimes such as implanting a computer virus—and illegal acts that target computer networks, including Internet crimes such as identity theft.

Although at first glance cyber criminals seem to present law enforcement officials with a far different challenge than do terrorists, there is actually some common ground. Both groups rely on stealth and secrecy. And even though cyber crime and terrorism appear to be independent problems, cyber space may become an avenue for terrorist activity. Using the Internet as a theater of operations, cyber terrorists can mount attacks against an enemy nation's technological infrastructure, an action referred to as cyber terrorism.

This chapter looks at terrorism and cyber crime and reviews the efforts being made by the agencies of the criminal justice system to control such criminal behavior and bring offenders to justice.

Terrorism

Terrorism is sometimes viewed as a contemporary phenomenon, but terrorism and terrorists have been around for quite some time. The first terrorist activities were committed by members of minority religious groups who engaged in violence for one or more of three reasons: to gain the right to practice their own form of religion, to establish the supremacy of their own religion over others, and/or to meet the requirements of the bloodthirsty gods they worshipped.[2] In some instances, a conquered people used force and violence to maintain their right to worship in their own faith. Zealots, Hebrew warrior groups active during the Roman occupation of Palestine during the first century c.e., carried out attacks in broad daylight to send the message that the Roman authorities and those Jews who collaborated with them would not be safe.

REALITY CHECK

MYTH OR REALITY? Terrorism began during the French Revolution and the reign of terror.

MYTH: Terrorists and terrorism have been around at least since Roman times. However, the term "terrorist" was first used at the time of the French Revolution.

Were George Washington and Benjamin Franklin terrorists? Depends whom you ask.

The term "terrorist" first appeared at the time of the French Revolution, when Edmund Burke, a noted British political philosopher, referred to the violence he observed in Paris as the "reign of terror."[3] Terror was also associated with the unrest in Russia that led to the 1917 Bolshevik takeover. In May 1881, a terror group killed Czar Alexander II. After the revolution, Bolshevik leaders Vladimir Lenin and Leon Trotsky made terror an instrument of state policy. Terror has also been identified with the civil war in Ireland and the Irish Republican Army, which is considered to be the model for most contemporary terrorist organizations.[4]

Defining Terrorism

Despite its long history, it is often difficult to precisely define terrorism (the term is derived from the Latin *terrere*, which means "to frighten") and to separate terrorist acts from interpersonal crimes of violence. For example, if a group robs a bank to obtain funds for its revolutionary struggles, should the act be treated as terrorism or as a common bank robbery? In this instance, defining a crime as terrorism depends on the kind of legal response the act evokes from those in power. To be considered terrorism, which is a political crime, an act must carry with it the intent to disrupt and change the government; it must not be merely a common-law crime committed for greed or egotism.

Because of its complexity, an all-encompassing definition of terrorism is difficult to formulate. According to the U.S. State Department, the term "**terrorism**" means *premeditated, politically motivated violence perpetrated against noncombatant targets by sub-national groups or clandestine agents, usually intended to influence an audience.* The term "**international terrorism**" means terrorism involving the citizens or the territory of more than one country.[5] Terrorism can be distinguished from conventional warfare by its use of secrecy and clandestine operations to exert social control over large populations.[6]

terrorism
Premeditated, politically motivated violence perpetrated against noncombatant targets by sub-national groups or clandestine agents, usually intended to influence an audience.

international terrorism
Terrorism involving the citizens or the territory of more than one country.

Who Is the Terrorist?

Before terrorism can be effectively fought, controlled, and eradicated, it is important for agents of the justice system to understand something about the kind of people who become terrorists, what motivates their behavior, and how their ideas are formed. Unfortunately, this is not an easy task. Terrorism researchers have generally concluded that there is no single personality trait or behavior pattern that distinguishes the majority of terrorists or sets them apart so they can be easily identified and apprehended. Some seem truly disturbed, whereas many others have not suffered long-term mental illness or displayed sociopathic traits and/or tendencies (if that were so, bizarre or violent behavior in their early childhood would be a giveaway).[7] Consequently, there are a number of competing views of why terrorists engage in criminal activities such as bombings, shootings, and kidnappings to achieve a political end. Four stand out.

PSYCHOLOGICAL VIEW ● Not all terrorists suffer from psychological deficits, but enough do so that the typical terrorist can be described as an emotionally disturbed individual who acts out his or her psychoses within the confines of violent groups. According to this view, terrorist violence is not so much a political instrument as an end in itself; it is the result of compulsion or psychopathology. Terrorists do what they do because of a wide variety of emotional problems, including but not limited to self-destructive urges and disturbed emotions combined with problems with authority.[8]

SOCIALIZATION VIEW ● Terrorists have been raised to hate their opponents and learn at an early age that they have been victimized by some oppressor. Often, this socialization occurs in dysfunctional families in which the father was absent or, if present, was a distant and cold figure.[9] Terrorists report that they were estranged from their

MYTH OR REALITY? Terrorists are cool and calculating.

MYTH: The media portray terrorists as shrewd and devious, but many may be suffering from significant emotional problems.

Perhaps those terror suspects who suffer from emotional problems tend to be the ones who get caught, such as the lone wolf who engages in some off-the-wall terror act like shooting at soldiers in broad daylight. Perhaps the "real" terror masterminds are a different breed entirely. What do you think?

fathers, whom they viewed as economically, socially, or politically weak and in-effective. Because of this family estrangement, the budding terrorist may have been swayed to join a group or cult by a charismatic leader who serves as an alternative father figure. Thus terror groups, in a way similar to what happens in urban street gangs, provide a substitute family-like environment, which can nurture a heretofore emotionally underprivileged youth.

IDEOLOGICAL VIEW ● Terrorists hold extreme ideological beliefs that prompt their behavior. At first they have heightened perceptions of oppressive condi-tions, believing that they are being victimized by some group or government. Once these potential terrorists recognize that these conditions can be changed by an active reform effort that has not yet happened, they conclude that they must resort to violence to encourage change. The violence need not be aimed at a specific goal. Rather, terror tactics may help set in motion a series of events that enlists others in the cause and leads to long-term change. "Suc-cessful" terrorists believe that their "self-sacrifice" outweighs the guilt created by harming innocent people. Terrorism, therefore, requires violence without guilt; the cause justifies the violence.

ALIENATION VIEW ● Terrorist operatives are not poor or lacking in education. And yet lack of economic opportunity and recessionary economies are positively correlated with terrorism.[10] Terrorists may be motivated by feelings of alienation and failure to maintain the tools to compete in a post-technological society.[11] Some terrorists appear alienated from modern society, and some seem to feel that a suicide mission will cleanse them of the corruption of the modern world.

The Contemporary Terrorist

Al Qaeda
An international terrorist organization founded by Osama bin Laden that calls for the use of violence to battle Western governments and drive them from the Middle East.

On December 27, 2007, Pakastani political leader Benazir Bhutto was assas-sinated (this term is derived from the Arabic word *asāšīn*, which means "hash-ish users") while leaving an election rally in Rawalpindi. The exact cause of her death remains a mystery, but there is no question that she was shot at by gunmen who then set off a bomb, killing more than 20 people and injuring many others. Bhutto, the daughter of a former prime minister, was educated at Harvard and Oxford universities, had been elected prime minister in 1988 and again in 1993, and had just returned to Pakistan after years in exile in order to run once more for public office. Her death was linked to Baitullah Mehsud, a militant leader associated with **Al Qaeda** and other terror groups.

A woman weeping over the late Benazir Bhutto holds her portrait at the end of a 40-day Muslim mourning ritual in Islamabad, Pakistan, on Feb-ruary 7, 2008. On the same day, police arrested two more suspects in the suicide attack that killed Bhutto, an official said, as a team from Scotland Yard returned to Pakistan to report the conclusions of their probe into the former prime min-ister's assassination.

© AP Images/Wally Santana

As the death of Benazir Bhutto illustrates, terrorism encompasses many different behaviors and goals. It can be directed toward a foreign occupying power, a local politician, or even a corporation that produces something the terrorists find objectionable. Some of the more common forms of terrorism are described in Exhibit 14.1.

Homeland Security: The Criminal Justice Response to Terrorism

REALITY CHECK

MYTH OR REALITY? Terrorists are not a unified entity; they have a variety of goals and objectives.

REALITY: There are many forms of terrorism, and different groups of terrorists often have diverse goals, objectives, and motivations.

Do you consider someone who shoots an abortion provider while he is attending church services—which is what happened to Dr. George Tiller on May 31, 2009—a terrorist or a common criminal?

After the 9/11 attacks, agencies of the criminal justice system began to focus on combating the threat of terror. Even local police agencies created antiterror programs designed to protect their communities from the threat of attack. How should the nation best prepare itself to thwart potential attacks? The **National Commission on Terrorist Attacks Upon the United States** (also known as the 9/11 Commission), an independent, bipartisan commission was created in late 2002 and tasked with preparing an in-depth report on the events leading up to the 9/11 attacks. In response to the commission report, the position of **Director of National Intelligence (DNI)**, charged with coordinating data from the nation's primary intelligence gathering agencies, was created. The DNI serves as the principal intelligence adviser to the president and the statutory intelligence adviser to the National Security Council. The DNI is supported directly by the National Intelligence Council (NIC), which is the Intelligence Community's (IC's) center for strategic planning

National Commission on Terrorist Attacks Upon the United States
An independent, bipartisan commission created in late 2002 and tasked with preparing a report on the events leading up to the 9/11 attacks.

Director of National Intelligence (DNI)
Government official charged with coordinating data from the nation's primary intelligence-gathering agencies.

EXHIBIT 14.1

The Variety of Terror Groups

- **Revolutionary Terrorism.** These terrorists use violence to frighten those in power and their supporters, in an effort to replace the existing government with a regime that holds political or religious views acceptable to the terrorists.
- **Political Terrorism.** Political terrorism is directed at people or groups who oppose the terrorists' political ideology or whom the terrorists define as "outsiders" who must be destroyed.
- **Eco-Terrorism.** Political terror groups today are involved in violent actions to protect the environment.
- **Nationalist Terrorism.** These terrorists ostensibly promote the interests of a minority ethnic or religious group that has been persecuted under majority rule and/or wishes to carve out its own independent homeland.

- **Retributive Terrorism.** Such groups use violence as a method of influence, persuasion, or intimidation in order to achieve a particular aim or objective.
- **State-Sponsored Terrorism.** This form of terrorism is carried out by a repressive government regime to force its citizens into obedience, oppress minorities, and stifle political dissent.
- **Cult Terrorism.** The leaders of such cults demand that followers prove their loyalty through violence or intimidation.
- **Criminal Terrorism.** Criminal terrorist groups become involved in common-law crimes such as drug dealing, kidnapping, and even selling nuclear materials.

REALITYCHECK

MYTH OR REALITY? There is a single U.S. national entity/organization designed to accumulate all existing information on terrorism and to monitor terrorist activities.

REALITY: After 9/11, the federal government created the office of the Director of National Intelligence (DNI), and gave it the responsibility of coordinating all data on terrorism from the nation's primary intelligence-gathering agencies.

Do you feel safer now that there is a central government bureaucracy dedicated to gathering information on terrorist activity?

and analysis. Exhibit 14.2 contains an excerpt from the NIC's recent assessment of terrorist threats ranging to the year 2025.

In addition to the NIC, a number of other intelligence agencies report directly to the DNI, including the National Counterterrorism Center (NCTC), which is staffed by terrorism experts from the CIA, the FBI, and the Pentagon; the Privacy and Civil Liberties Board; and the National Counterproliferation Center. The NCTC serves as the primary organization in the United States government for analyzing and integrating all intelligence possessed or acquired by the government pertaining to terrorism and counterterrorism, except for purely domestic counterterrorism information.

National Counterterrorism Center (NCTC)

You can access the **National Counterterrorism Center (NCTC)** and the homepage for the **office of the Director of National Intelligence** at www.cengage.com/criminaljustice/siegel

Fighting Terrorism with Law Enforcement

In the aftermath of the September 11, 2001, attacks, and even before the 9/11 commission made its report, it became obvious that the nation was not prepared to deal adequately with the threat of terrorism. One reason is the very nature of American society. Because we live in a free and open nation, it is extremely difficult to seal the borders and prevent the entry of terrorists. In his book *Nuclear Terrorism*, Graham Allison, an expert on nuclear weapons and national security, describes the almost superhuman effort it would take to seal the nation's borders from nuclear attack. Every day, 30,000 trucks,

EXHIBIT 14.2

Prospects for Terrorism, Conflict, and Proliferation to 2025

Terrorism, proliferation, and conflict will remain key concerns even as resource issues move up on the international agenda. Terrorism is unlikely to disappear by 2025, but its appeal could diminish if economic growth continues and youth unemployment is mitigated in the Middle East. Economic opportunities for youths and greater political pluralism probably would dissuade some from joining terrorists' ranks, but others—motivated by a variety of factors, such as a desire for revenge or to become "martyrs"—will continue to turn to violence to pursue their objectives. In the absence of employment opportunities and legal means for political expression, conditions will be ripe for disaffection, growing radicalism, and possible recruitment of youths

into terrorist groups. Terrorist groups in 2025 will probably be a combination of descendants of long-established groups, which inherit the organizational structures, command-and-control processes, and training procedures necessary to conduct sophisticated attacks, and newly emergent collections of the angry and disenfranchised that become self-radicalized. For those terrorist groups that are active in 2025, the diffusion of technologies and scientific knowledge will place some of the world's most dangerous capabilities within their reach. One of our greatest concerns continues to be that terrorist or other malevolent groups might acquire and employ biological agents, or—less likely—a nuclear device, to create mass casualties.

Source: *Global Trends 2025: A Transformed World,* http://www.dni.gov/nic/PDF_2025/2025_Global_Trends_Final_Report.pdf.

6,500 rail cars, and 140 ships deliver more than 50,000 cargo containers into the United States. Fewer than 5 percent ever get screened, and those that do are inspected with external detectors, which may not detect nuclear weapons or fissile material. The potential for terrorists to obtain bombs is significant: There are approximately 130 nuclear research reactors in 40 countries. Two dozen of these have enough highly enriched uranium for one or more nuclear bombs. If terrorists got their hands on fissile material from these reactors, they could build a crude but working nuclear bomb within a year. But they might not have to build their own bomb. They might be able to purchase an intact device on the black market.

In response to 9/11, law enforcement agencies around the country began to realign their resources to combat future terrorist attacks. They undertook a number of steps: increasing the number of personnel engaged in emergency response planning; updating response plans for chemical, biological, or radio-logical attacks; and reallocating internal resources or increasing departmental spending to focus on terrorism preparedness.[12] Actions continue to be taken on the federal, state, and local levels.

FEDERAL LAW ENFORCEMENT • One of the most significant changes has been a realignment of the Federal Bureau of Investigation (FBI), the federal government's main law enforcement agency. The FBI has already announced a reformulation of its priorities, making protecting the United States from terrorist attack its number one commitment. At the center of this initiative, the Counterterrorism Division collects, analyzes, and shares critical information and intelligence on (a) international terrorism operations both within the United States and in support of extraterritorial investigations, (b) domestic terrorism operations, and (c) counterterrorism related to both international and domestic terrorism. In addition, the FBI, along with other government agencies such as the Central Intelligence Agency, the Department of Homeland Security and the Nuclear Regulatory Commission, participates in several joint antiterrorism centers:

- The **National Counterterrorism Center (NCTC)** integrates intelligence related to terrorism; conducts strategic operational planning; serves as the central repository for terrorism intelligence; provides intelligence support

The threat of terrorism has prompted the law enforcement community to train its members to deal with attacks and their after-math. Here, a trainee evaluates the hazards that first responders would encounter in the crash zone during an exercise simulating mass casualties resulting from the collision of a single-engine Cessna and a commercial airliner, with levels of radioactivity involved. The exercise was hosted by the California National Guard and is designed to promote interagency cooperation during a disaster or attack and to evaluate the performance of responding agencies. It is expected to be the first in a series of similar events at landmark sites.

© David McNew/Getty Images

government-wide; and makes possible connectivity and access to IT systems/databases of participating agencies. It also operates a secure website, NCTC On-Line, the primary dissemination system for terrorism information obtained by the NCTC and other counterterrorism mission partners, including international partners.

- The **Foreign Terrorist Tracking Task Force** provides information that helps keep foreign terrorists and their supporters out of the United States or leads to their removal, location, detention, surveillance, or prosecution.
- The **Terrorist Screening Center (TSC)** has created a single, comprehensive database of known or suspected terrorists (both domestic and international); it also manages a consolidated watch list available in real time to federal, state, and local officers.

To carry out its newly formulated mission, the FBI is expanding its force of agents. In addition to recruiting candidates with the traditional background in law enforcement, law, and accounting, the bureau is concentrating on hiring agents with scientific and technological skills, as well as foreign-language proficiency.

Department of Homeland Security (DHS)

Department of Homeland Security (DHS)
The mission of the Department of Homeland Security is to secure the nation from external and internal threats ranging from border security to emergency response.

As you may recall from Chapter 4, the **Department of Homeland Security (DHS)** was created soon after the 9/11 attacks and given responsibility for securing our nation's borders and transportation systems, which include 350 ports of entry. The department manages who and what enters the country, and it works to prevent the entry of terrorists and the instruments of terrorism, while simultaneously ensuring the speedy flow of legitimate traffic. The DHS also is in charge of securing territorial waters, including ports and waterways. The DHS incorporates existing agencies under a single administrative umbrella. Included are the following components:

- The **Directorate for National Protection and Programs** works to advance the department's risk-reduction mission, which involves addressing both physical and virtual threats and their associated human elements.
- The **Directorate for Science and Technology**, the primary research and development arm of the department, provides federal, state, and local officials with antiterror technology and advice.
- The **Directorate for Management** is responsible for budgets and appropriations, expenditure of funds, accounting and finance, procurement, and so on.
- The **Office of Policy** provides a centralized, coordinated focus to the development of department-wide, long-range planning.
- The **Office of Health Affairs** coordinates all medical activities to ensure appropriate preparation for and response to incidents that have medical significance.
- The **Office of Intelligence and Analysis** is responsible for using information and intelligence from multiple sources to identify and assess current and future threats.
- The **Office of Operations Coordination** is responsible for monitoring the security of the United States on a daily basis.
- The **Federal Law Enforcement Training Center** provides career-long training to law enforcement professionals to help them fulfill their responsibilities safely and proficiently.
- The **Domestic Nuclear Detection Office** works to enhance nuclear detection efforts.
- The **Transportation Security Administration (TSA)** protects the nation's transportation systems to ensure freedom of movement for people and commerce.

- **United States Customs and Border Protection (CBP)** is responsible for border protection while facilitating the flow of legitimate trade and travel.
- **United States Citizenship and Immigration Services** is responsible for administering immigration and naturalization adjudication functions and for establishing immigration services policies and priorities.
- **United States Immigration and Customs Enforcement (ICE)** is responsible for identifying and shutting down vulnerabilities in the nation's border, economic, transportation, and infrastructure security.
- The **United States Coast Guard** protects the public, the environment, and U.S. economic interests in the nation's ports and waterways, along the coast, on international waters, or in any maritime region as required to support national security.
- The **Federal Emergency Management Agency (FEMA)** prepares the nation for hazards, manages federal response and recovery efforts following any national incident, and administers the National Flood Insurance Program.
- The **United States Secret Service** protects the president and other high-level officials and investigates counterfeiting and other financial crimes, including financial institution fraud, identity theft, computer fraud, and computer-based attacks on our nation's financial, banking, and telecommunications infrastructure.[13]

Figure 14.1 illustrates the organizational structure of DHS and its various components. Within this structure the DHS is charged with identifying and

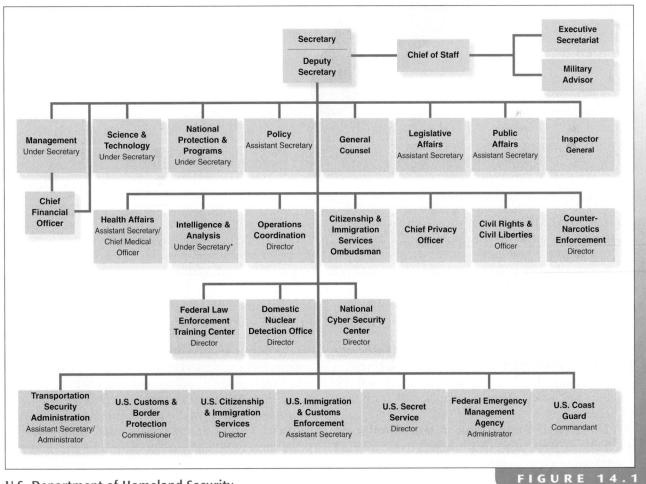

U.S. Department of Homeland Security

FIGURE 14.1

Source: Department of Homeland Security, Organizational Chart, http://www.dhs.gov/xlibrary/assets/ DHS_OrgChart.pdf.

dealing with potential threats to the nation's security. It focuses on the following 17 critical target areas:

- Agriculture and food
  - Banking and finance
  - Chemical
  - Commercial facilities
  - Commercial nuclear reactors, materials, and waste
  - Dams
  - Defense industrial base
  - Drinking water and water treatment systems
  - Emergency services
  - Energy
  - Government facilities
  - Information technology
  - National monuments and icons
  - Postal and shipping
  - Public health and health care
  - Telecommunications
  - Transportation systems

To protect these critical targets, DHS works to deny terrorists and terrorist-related weapons and materials entry into the country, while at the same time disrupting terrorists' efforts to operate within our borders, denying them future recruits, and defeating homegrown extremism. One approach is to develop and implement sophisticated screening techniques to identify and apprehend potential terror suspects. Exhibit 14.3 lists some of these techniques. One of the programs mentioned in Exhibit 14.3, the US-VISIT system, uses advanced biometric technology; it is discussed in detail in the Criminal Justice and Technology feature on page 497.

© Stockbyte/Getty Images

EXHIBIT 14.3

Screening People

- The **REAL ID Act** establishes federal standards for state-issued driver's licenses and nondriver's identification cards.
- **Secure Flight** will require airlines to submit passenger information to DHS for flights that operate to, from, and within the United States, as well as those that fly over the continental United States.
- The **Student and Exchange Visitor Information System (SEVIS)** is an Internet-based system that is improving America's ability to track and monitor foreign students and exchange visitors.
- The **United States Visitor and Immigrant Status Indicator Technology (US-VISIT)** program creates an entry and exit system that matches foreign travelers' arrival and departure records using biometrics to screen applicants for admission to the United States.
- The **Western Hemisphere Travel Initiative (WHTI)** reduces the number of identification and citizenship documents that may be used by persons entering or reentering the United States, from more than 8,000 documents to a few dozen secure documents. This expedites document review at ports of entry, while combating the use of fraudulent documents.
- The **Visa Waiver Program (VWP)** enables nationals of over two dozen countries to travel to the United States for tourism or business for stays of 90 days or less without obtaining a visa.

Source: Department of Homeland Security, *National Strategy for Homeland Security, 2007*, http://www.dhs.gov/xlibrary/assets/nat_strat_homelandsecurity_2007.pdf.

Criminal Justice and Technology

Using Biometrics to Fight Terrorism: US-VISIT

Is it possible to identify people by computer-based recognition of their facial characteristics or their fingerprints? Sounds like science fiction, or is it?

Biometrics, the science of using digital technology to identify individuals, has been installed in airports, land border points (border crossings), and seaports. The Department of Homeland Security's US-VISIT progam uses biometric scans to determine the identity of all travelers from foreign countries who attempt to enter the United States.

How It Works

Nearly all foreign citizens, regardless of country of origin, who wish to travel into the United States must comply with US-VISIT requirements. The process of registering for travel into the United States sometimes starts far from U.S. soil. Individuals who wish to travel to the United States must first visit the U.S. consular office in their country and apply for a visa. When they apply for the visa, they will have their biometrics collected in two separate ways. First, photographs will be taken of every applicant, and those photographs will be entered into the US-VISIT database, along with digital finger scans. The digital finger scans will be taken of both index fingers of the applicant. This information will be loaded into a database and then checked to see whether

the individual matches any criminal or suspected terrorist already in the system.

Once an applicant passes the database check, he or she can be issued a visa to travel to the United States. Upon arrival at a U.S. point of entry, the traveler will be required to scan her left and right index fingers to determine whether she is the same person who applied for the visa. This two-finger scanner is gradually being replaced by a more sophisticated 10-finger scanner.

Entry procedures were started in 115 airports at the beginning of 2004. US-VISIT entry procedures are now in place in 116 airports, 15 seaports, and the secondary inspection areas of 154 land points of entry.

Homeland Security believes that implementing these new security procedures will result in fewer criminals or terrorists entering the country and will also reduce the incidence of identity theft and fraud that may occur upon entry into or exit from the country. However, there are critics who say that the process makes too much personal information about travelers and U.S. citizens available to U.S. Customs and Immigration. Despite privacy concerns, the Department of Homeland Security is committed to using the US-VISIT program, in conjunction with other government programs, to increase the security of the United States.

Critical Thinking

1. Are you afraid that futuristic security methods such as biometric technology will lead to the loss of personal privacy and the erosion of civil liberties?

2. Would you want your personal medical information to be posted on a computer network where it could potentially be accessed by future employers and others?

State Law Enforcement Efforts to Combat Terrorism

In the wake of the 9/11 attacks, a number of states have beefed up their intelligence-gathering capabilities and aimed them directly at homeland security. One recent national survey found that state police organizations had adopted a number of homeland security roles, such as

- Coordinating homeland security at the state level
- Collecting, analyzing and sharing critical information and intelligence
- Protecting critical infrastructure and key assets
- Securing the nation's borders, airports, and seaports
- Collaborating with federal and local law enforcement on task forces
- Preparing for new response equipment, tactics, systems, and training[14]

Department of Homeland Security

Visit the **Department of Homeland Security** website at www.cengage.com/criminaljustice/siegel

A number of state initiatives are sprouting up. In Massachusetts, the Commonwealth Fusion Center works with federal, state, regional, and local law enforcement to collect and supply homeland security information to local law enforcement agencies. Intelligence analysts at the Fusion Center are assigned accounts that focus on terrorism, and each analyst develops contacts in her or his area of responsibility and is responsible for awareness in that subject area, focusing on threats to the Commonwealth.[15]

In a similar fashion, California has introduced the California Anti-Terrorism Information Center (CATIC), a statewide intelligence system designed to combat terrorism. It divides the state into operational zones, and it links federal, state, and local information services in one system. Trained intelligence analysts operate within civil rights guidelines and utilize information in a secure communications system; information is analyzed daily.[16] CATIC maintains a computerized database that is updated constantly with information coming from a variety of police agencies. The information is correlated and organized by analysts looking for trends. Rather than simply operating as an information-gathering unit, CATIC employs a synthesizing process. It combines open-source public information with data on criminal trends and possible terrorist activities. Processed intelligence is designed to produce threat assessments for each area and to project trends outside the jurisdiction. The CATIC system attempts to process multiple sources of information to predict threats. By centralizing the collection and analytical sections of a statewide system, California's Department of Justice may have developed a method for moving offensively against terrorism.

COUNTY LAW ENFORCEMENT ● Some counties are now engaging in antiterror and homeland security activities and employing a number of emergency response systems (see the Careers in Criminal Justice feature on page 499). For example, the Harris County Office of Homeland Security & Emergency Management (OHSEM), in Texas, is responsible for an emergency management plan that prepares for public recovery in the event of natural or humanmade disasters, catastrophes, or attacks. It works in conjunction with the state, federal, and local authorities, including the city of Houston and other municipalities in the surrounding Harris County area. When required, the Office of Homeland Security & Emergency Management activates an Emergency Operations Center to facilitate coordination of all support agencies and provide continuity of services to the public. OHSEM is responsible for advisement, notification, and assembly of services to deal with the crisis.[17]

Another approach is a multicounty approach. Two examples follow.

- **Upstate New York Regional Intelligence Center (UNYRIC)**. UNYRIC is a multiagency center that is responsible for the collection, analysis, and dissemination of intelligence information across the state of New York. Located in the Albany area, UNYRIC provides timely and accurate criminal intelligence to law enforcement agencies in the 54 counties outside of New York City. This center comprises representatives from various federal and state departments, including the Departments of Corrections and Parole, the Department of Motor Vehicles, the New York National Guard, the Office of Homeland Security, and the State Police.[18]
- **Central Florida Intelligence Exchange (CFIX)**. The stated goal of CFIX is to provide information and knowledge, in the form of actionable intelligence, to those who set policy and decision makers. CFIX collects, analyzes, produces, and reports intelligence in order to help law enforcement detect, deter, disrupt, and deny terrorist activity. CFIX combines the intelligence of sheriff's offices in Brevard, Indian River, Lake, Martin, Orange, Osceola, Seminole, St. Lucie, and Volusia Counties; the Orlando Police Department; and the Florida Department of Law Enforcement.[19]

Careers in Criminal Justice

EMERGENCY RESPONSE MANAGER

Duties

- Emergency management directors help communities prepare for and respond to natural, technological, and other disasters.
- Duties may vary, depending on where they are and which hazards are typical of their area.
- In the Northeast, flash flooding from melting river ice is a significant problem, whereas in the midlands, dealing with tornado damage may be the top priority.

Job Characteristics

- Emergency management directors work with and coordinate many different people and groups. Often, directors communicate with everyone from emergency response personnel to high-level officials.
- Planning and coordination with other state agencies is common. This might require combining forces with the departments of social services, public safety, transportation, or health and environmental control; the employment security commission; the state housing authority; and/or relief organizations such as the American Red Cross.
- Emergency management directors work long hours and often have irregular schedules.
- The travel and other demands of the work—which include maintaining a constant state of alertness and taking responsibility during a crisis—can take a toll.

Job Outlook

- The number of emergency management specialists of all kinds will grow more rapidly than the average for all occupations between now until 2014, adding more than 2,300 jobs over the decade.

Salary

- Emergency management specialists earned a median salary of more than $46,000, with the middle 50 percent earning between $33,390 and $62,370. The highest-earning 10 percent made more than $81,860, and the lowest earning 10 percent made less than $24,630.

Opportunities

- There will be many opportunities in the coming decade.
- Top employers of emergency management specialists are local governments, state governments, general medical and surgical hospitals, power generation and supply services, and emergency and other relief services.
- There is at least one emergency management director for each state, and there are other directors with similar functions throughout government and private industry.
- Other job titles for these workers include public safety director and emergency preparedness director.

Qualifications

- Management, leadership, and people skills are critical for emergency management directors. Experience in local government is valuable in emergency management.

Education and Training

- Many directors have a background in fire fighting, emergency medical services, or local law enforcement.
- People interested in emergency management may volunteer or serve as interns to get field experience and a feel for what the work is really like.
- A college degree in Criminal Justice, Public Policy, Business Administration, Public Administration, Professional Management, or a related field is preferred.

Word to the Wise

- Be prepared for a lot of stress and responsibility. When things go wrong, the buck stops at your desk.

LOCAL LAW ENFORCEMENT • Federal law enforcement agencies are not alone in responding to the threat of terrorism. And, of course, nowhere is the threat of terrorism taken more seriously than in New York City, one of the main targets of the 9/11 attacks, which has established a new Counterterrorism Bureau.[20] Teams within the bureau have been trained to examine potential targets in the city and are now attempting to insulate them from possible attack. Viewed as prime targets are the city's bridges, the Empire State Building, Rockefeller Center, and the United Nations. Bureau detectives are assigned overseas to work with the police in several foreign cities, including cities in Canada and Israel. Detectives have been assigned as liaisons with the FBI and with Interpol, in Lyon, France. The city is now recruiting detectives with language skills ranging from Pashtun and Urdu to Arabic, Fujianese, and other dialects. The existing New York City Police Intelligence Division has been revamped, and agents are examining foreign newspapers and monitoring Internet sites. The department is also setting up several backup command centers in different parts of the city, in case a terror attack puts headquarters out of operation. Several backup senior command teams have been created so that if people at the highest levels of the department are killed, individuals will already have been tapped to step into their jobs.

The Counterterrorism Bureau has assigned more than 100 city police detectives to work with FBI agents as part of a Joint Terrorist Task Force. In addition, the Intelligence Division's 700 investigators now devote 35 to 40 percent of their resources to counterterrorism, up from about 2 percent before January 2002. The department is also drawing on the expertise of other institutions around the city. For example, medical specialists have been enlisted to monitor daily developments in the city's hospitals to detect any suspicious outbreaks of illness that might reflect a biological attack. And the police are now conducting joint drills with the New York Fire Department to avoid the problems in communication and coordination that marked the emergency response on September 11, 2001.

REALITYCHECK

MYTH OR REALITY?   Antiterrorism law enforcement activities are under the jurisdiction of federal agencies such as the FBI and DHS.

MYTH: State, county, and local agencies have created a variety of antiterror centers that gather information and/or carry out antiterror activities.

Is this a dilution of resources? Would we be better off with a single entity run by the federal government?

Confronting Terrorism with the Law

Soon after the September 11 terrorist attacks, the U.S. government enacted several laws focused on preventing further acts of violence against the United States and creating greater flexibility in the fight to control terrorist activity. Most important, Congress passed the **USA Patriot Act (USAPA)** on October 26, 2001. The bill is over 342 pages long, creates new laws, and makes changes to over 15 different existing statutes. Its aim is to give sweeping new powers to domestic law enforcement and international intelligence agencies in an effort to fight terrorism, to expand the definition of terrorist activities, and to alter sanctions for violent terrorism. USAPA expands all four traditional tools of surveillance—wiretaps, search warrants, pen/trap orders (installing devices that record phone calls), and subpoenas. The Foreign Intelligence Surveillance Act (FISA) that governs domestic operations by intelligence agencies is also expanded. USAPA gives the FBI greater power to check and monitor phone, Internet, and computer records without first having to demonstrate that they were being used by a suspect or the target of a court order. The act also expands the

USA Patriot Act (USAPA)
A law designed to grant new powers to domestic law enforcement and international intelligence agencies in an effort to fight terrorism.

Jose Padilla is escorted by federal marshals on his arrival in Miami, Florida. Padilla was sentenced by Federal Judge Marcia Cooke on January 22, 2008 to 17 years and 4 months for conspiring to support Islamic extremists around the world. Padilla, a U.S. citizen, was part of a secret network that supported violent extremists. The government relied largely on wiretapped conversations when it put Mr. Padilla and others on trial as a "North American support cell" that sent money, goods, and recruits abroad to assist "global jihad." The Patriot Act makes it easier for U.S. agents to use wiretapping when investigating suspected terrorists in the interests of national security.

© AP Images/Alan Diaz

definition of "terrorism" and enables the government to monitor more closely those people suspected of "harboring" and giving "material support" to terrorists (Sections 803, 805). It increases the authority of the U.S. attorney general to detain and deport noncitizens with little or no judicial review. The attorney general may certify that he has "reasonable grounds to believe" that a noncitizen endangers national security and is therefore eligible for deportation. The attorney general and secretary of state are also given the authority to designate domestic groups as terrorist organizations and to deport any noncitizen who is a member of such an organization.

A reauthorization bill that left most of the act intact was passed by Congress on March 2, 2006, and was signed into law by President George W. Bush on March 9, 2006.

Civil Rights and the War against Terrorism

Civil libertarians are troubled by some of the actions taken by the various law enforcement agencies to combat terrorism, maintaining that the harshest measures are eroding civil rights. Some complain that there are provisions that permit the government to share information from grand jury proceedings and from criminal wiretaps with intelligence agencies. First Amendment protections may be violated because the Patriot Act authority is not limited to true terrorism investigations but covers a much broader range of activity involving reasonable political dissent. Even though many critics have called for its repeal, it was reauthorized in 2006 with a slew of provisions ensuring that the Act did not violate civil rights by limiting its surveillance and wiretap authorizations.[21]

There has also been significant controversy over the long-term detention of suspected terrorists without trial at the Guantanamo camp in Cuba. Although this complex issue is far from resolved, in *Boumediene v. Bush* the Supreme Court held that the Guantanamo prisoners had a right to habeas corpus protection under the United States Constitution.[22] *Boumediene*, along with similar cases, indicates that terror suspects are not denied the protection of the U.S. Constitution and that their indefinite detention without trial is not legally permissible. On January 22, 2009, President Barack Obama promised to shut down the Guantanamo prison within a year and also ordered a halt on all Guantanamo detainees' legal cases, pending a three-month review to decide whether to prosecute the suspects.

THE USE OF TORTURE • There has been much outcry over the revelation that United States intelligence agencies have used waterboarding in the interrogation of terror suspects. Waterboarding involves immobilizing a person on his or her back, with the head inclined downward, and pouring water over the face and into the breathing passages. It produces an immediate gag reflex and an experience akin to drowning; the subject believes that death is imminent.

Can the torture of a suspected terrorist determined to destroy the government and harm innocent civilians ever be permissible? Although most people loathe the thought of torturing anyone, and President Obama has vowed it will never happen again, some experts argue that torture can sometimes be justified in what they call the **ticking bomb scenario**: Suppose the government found out that a captured terrorist knew the whereabouts of a dangerous explosive device that was set to go off and would certainly kill thousands of innocent people. Would it be permissible to torture this single suspect if it would save the population of a city? The ticking bomb scenario is quite compelling, but opponents of torture believe that it can never be justified, no matter how much destruction its use may prevent. A number of arguments have been constructed:

ticking bomb scenario
A hypothetical case that involves the question, Would it be permissible, in order to save thousands of lives, to torture someone who was known to have planted a bomb somewhere?

1. There is a danger that the use of torture could become calculated and premeditated; torturers would have to be trained, ready, and in place for the ticking bomb argument to work. We couldn't be running around looking for torturers with a bomb set to go off, could we? Torture then might become routine, rather than being reserved for extreme cases.
2. What happens if a superior officer tells an enforcement agent to torture someone, but this subordinate believes the order is unjustified? Should he or she follow orders or risk punishment for being disobedient?
3. There is very little empirical evidence suggesting that torture provides any real benefits, and considerable evidence suggests that it can create serious problems. For example, it can undermine civil rights, damage democratic institutions, and cause the general public to have sympathy for the victims of torture, no matter what their evil intent.

Protestors demonstrate the use of waterboarding to volunteer Maboud Ebrahim Zadeh on November 5, 2007, in front of the Justice Department in Washington. The demonstration was performed to highlight the agony that waterboarding inflicts and to protest the nomination of Attorney General–designate Michael Mukasey, who had refused to characterize waterboarding as torture.

© AP Images/Manuel Balce Ceneta

4. The U.S. Constitution limits physical coercion by the government under the Fifth Amendment Due Process and Self-Incrimination Clauses and the Eighth Amendment prohibition against cruel and unusual punishments.

5. Intelligence is rarely, if ever, good enough to provide specific advance warning of a terror attack. If terrorists knew their plan could be foiled by information provided by a prisoner, why would they not change the plan?[23]

Although these arguments are persuasive, noted legal scholar Alan Dershowitz argues that torture can be justified under some circumstances, especially to prevent damaging terror attacks. Moreover, he believes that the "vast majority" of Americans would expect law enforcement agents to engage in time-honored methods of "loosening tongues" if the circumstances warranted. To ensure that torture is not used capriciously, Dershowitz proposes the creation of a "torture warrant" that can be issued by a judge only in cases where (a) there is an absolute need to obtain immediate information in order to save lives and (b) there is probable cause that the suspect has this information and is unwilling to reveal it to law enforcement agents. The suspect would be given immunity to prosecution based on information elicited by the torture; it would be used only to save lives. The warrant would limit the torture to nonlethal means, such as sterile needles being inserted beneath the nails to cause excruciating pain without endangering life.[24]

Cyber Crime

On May 15, 2008, a federal grand jury in Los Angeles indicted Lori Drew, a Missouri woman, for her alleged role in a MySpace hoax on a teen neighbor who later committed suicide. Drew, along with others, created a fake online boy named Josh Evans, who established a cyber romance with 13-year-old Megan Meier. Later, after being spurned by "Josh," Megan took her own life. She had received several messages from "Josh" suggesting that she kill herself

The nation abhorred the actions of Lori Drew, who used the Internet to harass a 13-year-old neighbor and encourage her suicide. Yet Drew was released on July 2, 2009, after a federal judge tentatively threw out, on technical grounds, the conviction of the Missouri mother for her role in a MySpace hoax.

© AP Images/Nick Ut

and that the "world would be better off without her." Drew was charged with one count of conspiracy and three counts of accessing protected computers without authorization to obtain information to inflict emotional distress. On November 26, 2008, Drew was found guilty on three lesser charges (reduced from felonies to misdemeanors by the jury); her conviction was later overturned on appeal.[25]

This cyber bully case, though unusual in its tragic outcome, illustrates one of the newest challenges facing the justice system. **Cyber crime**, a new breed of offenses that can be singular or ongoing, typically involves the theft and/or destruction of information, resources, or funds via computers, computer networks, or the Internet. This new category of crimes presents a compelling challenge for the justice system and the law enforcement community because (a) it is rapidly evolving, with new schemes being created daily, (b) it is difficult to detect through traditional law enforcement channels, and (c) to control it, agents of the justice system must develop technical skills that match those of the perpetrators.[26] It is even possible that the recent decline in crime is actually a result of cyber crime replacing traditional street crime. Instead of robbing a bank at gun point, a new group of contemporary thieves find it easier to hack into accounts and transfer funds to offshore banks. Instead of shoplifting from a bricks-and-mortar store, the contemporary cyber thief devises clever schemes to steal from retailers.

The Internet, coupled with ever more powerful computers, is now the medium of choice for providing a wide range of global services, from entertainment and communication to research and education. The cyber age has also generated an enormous amount of revenue. Spending on IT and telecommunications will grow by more than 6 percent each year, soon reaching about $2 trillion.[27] Today more than a billion people are using email, and 240 million are mobile Internet users. Magnifying the importance of the Internet is the fact that many critical infrastructure functions are now being conducted online, ranging from banking to control of shipping on the Mississippi River.[28] This vast network has now become a target for illegal activities and enterprise.

There are actually three forms of cyber crime (they are summarized in Concept Summary 14.1). Some cyber criminals use modern technology to accumulate goods and services. **Cyber theft** schemes range from illegally copying material under copyright protection to using technology to commit traditional theft-based offenses such as larceny and fraud.

Other cyber criminals are motivated less by profit and more by the urge to commit **cyber vandalism**, or technological destruction. They aim their malicious attacks at disrupting, defacing, and destroying technology they find offensive.

A third type of cyber crime is **cyber terrorism**, which consists of acts aimed at undermining the social, economic, and political sytem of an enemy nation by destroying its electronic infrastructure and disrupting its economy. This can range from stealing secrets from foreign nations to destroying an enemy's Web-based infrastructure.

Thus some cyber criminals are high-tech thieves and others are high-tech vandals; the property the latter destroy is electronic rather then physical. And some may combine theft and vandalism in cyber terror attacks.

Cyber Theft: Cyber Crimes for Profit

The new computer-based technology enables criminals to operate in a more efficient and effective manner. Cyber thieves now have the luxury of remaining anonymous, living almost anywhere on the planet, conducting their business

---

cyber crime
The theft and/or destruction of information, resources, or funds via computers, computer networks, or the Internet.

cyber theft
The use of computer networks for criminal profits. Illegal copyright infringement, identity theft, and Internet securities fraud are examples of cyber theft.

cyber vandalism
Malicious attacks aimed at disrupting, defacing, and destroying technology.

cyber terrorism
Politically motivated attacks designed to compromise the electronic infrastructure of the enemy and to disrupt its economy.

Typology of Cyber Crimes

Crime	Definition	Examples
Cyber theft	Use of cyber space either to distribute illegal goods and services or to defraud people for quick profits	Illegal copyright infringement, identity theft, Internet securities fraud, warez
Cyber vandalism	Use of cyber space for revenge, for destruction, or to achieve malicious ends	Website defacement, worms, viruses, cyber stalking, cyber bullying
Cyber terrorism	An effort by enemy forces to disrupt the intersection where the virtual electronic reality of computers meets the physical world	Use of logic bombs to disrupt or destroy "secure" systems or networks, use of the Internet to communicate covertly with agents around the world

© X Brand Images/Getty Images

during the day or at night, and working alone or in a group, while at the same time reaching a much greater number of potential victims than ever before. No longer are con artists and criminal entrepreneurs limited to fleecing victims in a particular geographic locale; the whole world can be their target. And the technology revolution has opened up novel avenues of attack for cyber theft—ranging from the unlawful distribution of computer software to Internet security fraud—that heretofore were nonexistent.

Cyber thieves conspire to use cyber space either to distribute illegal goods and services or to defraud people for quick profits. Some of the most common methods are described below.

REALITY CHECK

MYTH OR REALITY? Cyber criminals are technologically sophisticated and can strike from anywhere in the world.

REALITY: Cyber crime has no boundaries and is booming around the world.

Just a thought: Is it possible that the recent crime drop in America is a result of criminals giving up "traditional," common-law crimes for safer and more profitable cyber crimes?

Computer Fraud

Computer fraud is not a unique offense but, rather, a common-law crime committed using contemporary technology. Consequently, many computer crimes are prosecuted under such traditional criminal statutes as those prohibiting larceny and fraud. However, not all computer crimes fall under common-law statutes because the property stolen may be intangible—that is, electronic and/or magnetic impulse. Such crimes include

- *Theft of information.* This consists of the unauthorized obtaining of information from a computer (for example, "hacking"), including software that is copied for profit.
- *"Salami slice" fraud.* The perpetrator carefully "skims" small sums from the balances of a large number of accounts in order to bypass internal controls and escape detection.
- *"One-off kamikaze" fraud.* Similar to a "salami slice," this manipulation of accounts in the banking system occurs on a much larger and usually more complex scale.
- *Software theft.* The comparative ease of making copies of computer software has led to a huge illegal market, depriving authors of very significant revenues.
- *Corporate espionage.* Trade secrets are stolen by a company's competitors, which can be either domestic or foreign. The rival company's (or nation's) goal is to increase its competitive edge in the domestic or global marketplace.[29]

Pornography and Prostitution

The IT revolution has revitalized the "porn industry." The Internet is an ideal venue for selling and distributing adult material; the computer is an ideal device for storing and viewing it. Because of their vast number, it is difficult to estimate how many websites feature sexual content, including nude photos, videos, live sex acts, and Web-cam strip sessions, among other forms of "adult

© AP Images / Louis Lanzano

Sylvia Soto is led from the 112th precinct following her arrest on May 20, 2009, in the New York City borough of Queens. Seven people were indicted on charges of running a 24-hour prostitution ring on Craigslist. Internet prostitution is now a thriving business and has invigorated the sex trade in New York and elsewhere.

entertainment."[30] The number of pornography Web pages has soared during the past six years, and there are now over 1.3 million sites containing about 260 million pages of erotic content, all hoping to cash in on the billions in revenue spent on Internet porn annually.[31] The number of visits to pornography sites surpasses those made to Internet search engines.

Denial-of-Service Attack

A **denial-of-service attack** is an attempt to extort money from legitimate users of an Internet service by threatening to interfere with the user's access to that service.[32] Examples include attempts to "flood" a computer network, thereby preventing access by legitimate network traffic; attempts to disrupt connections within a computer network, thereby interrupting access to a service; attempts to prevent a particular individual from accessing a service; and attempts to disrupt service to a specific system or person.

Distributing Dangerous Drugs

In addition to offering sexual material, the Internet has become a prime purveyor of prescription drugs, some of which can be quite dangerous when they are used to excess or fall into the hands of minors. One national survey found that in a single year (2006–2007), the number of websites that advertise or sell controlled prescription drugs increased 70 percent. There was a 135 percent increase in websites advertising these drugs and a 7 percent increase in sites offering to sell them over the Internet.[33]

Copyright Infringement

For the past decade, groups of individuals have been working together to obtain software illegally and then "crack" or "rip" its copyright protections before posting it on the Internet for other members of the group to use. Its criminal purveyors refer to this pirated material as **warez** (pronounced like "wares," as in "software"). Frequently, these new pirated copies reach the Internet days or weeks before the legitimate product is commercially available. The government has actively pursued members of the warez community, and some have been charged and convicted under the Computer Fraud and Abuse Act (CFAA), which criminalizes accessing computer systems without authorization to obtain information,[34] and the Digital Millennium Copyright Act (DMCA), which makes it a crime to circumvent the antipiracy measures built into most commercial software and also outlaws the manufacture, sale, or distribution of code-cracking devices used to illegally copy software.[35] The United States Criminal Code provides penalties for a first-time offender of incarceration for five years and a fine of $250,000.[36] Other provisions provide for the forfeiture and destruction of infringing copies and all equipment used to make the copies.[37]

Internet Securities Fraud

Internet fraud involves using the Internet to intentionally manipulate the securities marketplace for profit. Three major types of Internet securities fraud are common today.

denial-of-service attack
Extorting money from an Internet service user by threatening to prevent the user having access to the service.

warez
Copyrighted software illegally downloaded and sold by organized groups without license to do so.

© Steffan Hill / Alamy

Cyber crime is an international phenomenon, and billion-dollar frauds have been uncovered around the world. Here, the founder and former chairman of Satyam Computer, B. Ramalinga Raju, is escorted from Chenchalguda Jail in Hyderabad, India, on April 9, 2009, en route to a court appearance. His arrest came after Indian police investigated a massive false-accounting scam at IT giant Satyam Computer. The Central Bureau of Investigation and India's market regulator have been conducting a joint probe into the billion-dollar scandal, which rocked the Hyderabad-based company in January. Nine people have been arrested in connection with the investigation, including Ramalinga's brother, Rama Raju.

© Noah Seelam /AFP/Getty Images

• ***Market manipulation.*** Stock market manipulation occurs when an individual tries to control the price of stock by interfering with the natural forces of supply and demand. There are two principal forms of this crime: the "pump and dump" and the "cyber smear." In a pump and dump scheme, erroneous and deceptive information is posted online to get unsuspecting investors interested in a stock while those spreading the information sell previously purchased stock at an inflated price. The cyber smear is a reverse pump and dump: Negative information is spread online about a stock, driving down its price and enabling people to buy it at an artificially low price before rebuttals by the company's officers reestablish the legitimate price.[38]

• ***Fraudulent offerings of securities.*** Some cyber criminals create websites specifically designed to sell securities fraudulently. To make the offerings look more attractive than they are, assets may be inflated, expected returns overstated, and risks understated. In these schemes, investors are promised abnormally high profits on their investments. No investment is actually made. Early investors are paid returns with the investment money received from the later investors. The system usually collapses, and the later investors do not receive dividends and lose their initial investment.

• ***Illegal touting.*** This crime occurs when individuals make securities recommendations and fail to disclose that they are being paid to disseminate their favorable opinions.

Identity Theft

identity theft
Using the Internet to steal someone's identity and/or impersonate the victim in order to conduct illicit transactions, such as committing fraud using the victim's name and identity.

Identity theft occurs when a person uses the Internet to steal someone's identity and/or impersonate the victim to open a new credit card account or conduct some other financial transaction. It is a type of cyber crime that has grown at startling rates over the past few years.[39]

Identity theft can destroy a person's life by manipulating credit records or depleting bank accounts. Some identity thieves create false emails and/or websites that look legitimate but are designed to gain illegal access to a victims' personal information; this is known as **phishing** (and also as *carding* and *spoofing*).

phishing
Also known as carding and spoofing, phishing consists of illegally acquiring personal information, such as bank passwords and credit card numbers, by masquerading as a trustworthy person or business in what appears to be an official electronic communication, such as an email or an instant message. The term "phishing" comes from the lures used to "fish" for financial information and passwords.

Phishing emails and websites have become even more of a problem now that cyber criminals can easily copy brand names, the names of corporate personnel, and their insignia directly into the email. The look is so authentic that victims believe the email comes from the advertised company. Most phishers send out spam emails to a large number of recipients, knowing that some of those recipients will have accounts with the company they are impersonating. Some phishing schemes involve job offers. Once the unsuspecting victims fill out the "application," answering personal questions and including their Social Security number, the phisher has them in his grasp.[40]

Etailing Fraud

New fraud schemes are evolving to exploit the fact that billions of dollars of goods are sold on the Internet each year. **Etailing fraud** can involve both illegally buying and selling merchandise on the Internet.

Some etailing scams involve failure to deliver on promised purchases or services, and others involve the substitution of cheaper or used material for higher-quality purchases.

etailing fraud
Using the Internet to illegally buy or sell merchandise.

Federal Trade Commission website on identity theft
The **Federal Trade Commission website on identity theft** can be found at www.cengage.com/criminaljustice/siegel

Cyber Vandalism: Cyber Crime with Malicious Intent

Some cyber criminals may be motivated not by greed or profit but by the desire for revenge, to inflict wanton destruction, and/or to achieve a malicious intent. Cyber vandalism ranges from sending destructive viruses to attack computer networks to bullying children on the Internet. Cyber vandals are motivated more by malice than by greed:

- Some cyber vandals target computers and networks, seeking revenge for some perceived wrong.
- Some desire to exhibit their technical prowess and superiority.
- Some wish to highlight the vulnerability of computer security systems.
- Some want to spy on other people's private financial and personal information ("computer voyeurism").
- Some want to destroy computer security because they believe in open access to all systems and programs.[41]

What forms of cyber vandalism currently exist?

VIRUSES AND WORMS ● A computer virus is one type of malicious software program (also called malware) that disrupts or destroys existing programs and networks, causing them to perform the task for which the virus was designed.[42] The virus is then spread from one computer to another when a user sends out an infected file through email, a network, or a disk. Computer worms are similar to viruses, but they use computer networks or the Internet to self-replicate and "send themselves" to other users, generally via email without the aid of the operator.

TROJAN HORSES ● Some hackers may introduce a Trojan horse program into a computer system. The Trojan horse looks like a benign application, but it contains illicit codes that can damage the system operations. Sometimes hackers with a sense of irony will install a Trojan horse and claim that it is an antivirus program. When it is opened, it spreads viruses in the computer system. Trojan horses do not replicate themselves as viruses do, but they can be just as destructive.

WEB DEFACEMENT ● Cyber vandals may target the websites of their victims. Web defacement is a type of cyber vandalism that occurs when a computer hacker intrudes on another person's website by inserting or substituting codes that expose visitors to the site to misleading or provocative information.

CYBER STALKING ● Traditional stalking involves repeated harassing or threatening behavior, such as following a person, appearing at a person's home or place of business, making harassing phone calls, leaving written messages or objects, or vandalizing a person's property. Cyber stalking is the use of the Internet, email, or other electronic communications devices to stalk another person.[43] Some cyber stalkers are sexual predators who contact a child in an online chatroom and then arrange a meeting with the unsuspecting victim. Today, Internet predators are more likely to meet, develop

cyber stalking
Using the Internet, email, or other electronic communications devices to stalk or harass another person. contact for the purpose of engaging in criminal sexual activities.

relationships with, and beguile at-risk adolescents and underage teenagers, rather than using coercion and violence.[44]

CYBER BULLYING ● Experts define bullying among children as repeated negative acts committed by one or more children against another.[45] These negative acts may be physical or verbal in nature—for example, hitting or kicking, teasing or taunting—or they may involve indirect actions such as manipulating friendships or purposely excluding other children from activities. Bullying is a problem that remains to be solved, it has now expanded from the physical environment to the virtual. Because of the availability of cyber space, physical distance is no longer a refuge from the frequency and depth of harm doled out by a bully to his or her victim.[46] Cyber bullying is willful and repeated harm inflicted through the medium of electronic text. Like their real-world counterparts, cyber bullies are malicious and cowardly aggressors who seek pleasure or profit through the mistreatment of other individuals. Although power in traditional bullying might be physical (stature) or social (competency or popularity), online power may simply stem from net proficiency. Cyber bullies who are able to navigate the net and utilize technology in a way that enables them to harass others are in a position of power relative to a victim. There are now four major formats that bullies can employ to harass their victims:

1. Bullies can send harassing emails or instant messages.
2. They can post obscene, insulting, and slanderous messages to online bulletin boards.
3. They can develop websites to promote and disseminate defamatory content.
4. They can send harassing text messages to the victim via cellular phones.[47]

cyber bullies

To learn more about **cyber bullies**, go to

www.cengage.com/ criminaljustice/siegel

Cyber Terrorism: Cyber Crime with Political Motives

The justice system must now also be on guard against attacks that integrate terrorist goals with cyber capabilities: cyber terrorism. Although the term may be difficult to define, cyber terrorism can be viewed as an effort by covert forces to disrupt the intersection where the virtual electronic reality of computers intersects with the physical world.[48]

Cyber terrorism has been defined as "the premeditated, politically motivated attack against information, computer systems, computer programs, and data which result in violence against noncombatant targets by sub-national groups or clandestine agents."[49] Cyber terrorism may involve the use of computer network tools to shut down critical national infrastructures or to coerce or intimidate a government or civilian population.[50]

Even though they come from a region where computer databases and the Internet are not widely used, terrorist organizations are beginning to understand the damage that cyber crime can inflict on their enemies. Terrorist organizations are now adapting IT into their arsenal, and agencies of the justice system have to be ready for a sustained attack on the nation's electronic infrastructure.

One form of attack is cyber espionage. This involves hacking secure computer networks at the enemy's most sensitive military bases, defense contractors, and aerospace companies in order to steal important data or to assess their defenses. Infrastructure attacks can also be aimed at water treatment plants, electric plants, dams, oil refineries, and nuclear power plants. These industries all provide vital services to society by allowing people to go about their daily lives. Terrorist computer hackers could make a dam overflow or cause real property damage to oil refineries or nuclear plants by shutting down safeguards in the system to prevent catastrophic meltdowns.

This undated web page image is from the Mujahedeen Electronic Net. Terrorist groups that have long used the Internet to spread propaganda are increasingly tapping the Web to teach Islamic extremists how to be hackers, recruit techies for cyber warfare, and raise money through online fraud. Intelligence reports indicate that extremist groups are seeking computer experts, including those capable of breaching government or other sensitive network systems. As a result, the United States is creating a cyber war czar who will have broad authority to protect the nation's government-run and private computer networks. The czar will be charged with establishing a strategy for defending critical national infrastructure systems, such as banking and utilities, from attack, as well as informing the various national security agencies (e.g. Department of Homeland Security) with threat assessments and cybersecurity strategies.

© AP Images/Associated Press

Controlling Cyber Crime

How common are cyber crimes and how costly are they to American businesses and the general public? The Internet has become a major source of illegal profits. Criminal entrepreneurs view this vast pool as a target for cyber crime, and although an accurate accounting of cyber crime will probably never be made because so many offenses go unreported, there is little doubt that its incidence is growing rapidly.

Thousands of breaches occur each year, but most are not reported to local, state, or federal authorities. Some cyber crimes go unreported because they involve low-visibility acts that are rarely detected, such as copying computer software in violation of copyright laws.[51] Some businesses choose not to report cyber crime because they fear revealing the weaknesses in their network security systems. However, the information that is available indicates that the profit in cyber crime is enormous and continually growing.[52] What is being done to control this growing social problem?

Cyber Crime Enforcement Systems

The proliferation of cyber crimes has created the need for new laws and enforcement processes. Because technology evolves so rapidly, enforcement presents challenges that are particularly vexing. Numerous organizations have been set up to provide training and support for law enforcement agents. In addition, new federal and state laws have been aimed at particular areas of high-tech crimes.[53] What are some of the new legislative initiatives designed to limit or control cyber crime?

SOFTWARE PIRACY • The government has actively pursued members of the warez community, and some have been charged and convicted under the Computer Fraud and Abuse Act (CFAA), which criminalizes accessing computer systems without authorization to obtain information.[54] The Digital Millennium Copyright Act (DMCA) makes it a crime to circumvent antipiracy measures built into most commercial software and also outlaws the manufacture, sale, or distribution of code-cracking devices used to copy software illegally.[55]

COPYRIGHT INFRINGEMENT • The United States Criminal Code provides penalties for a first-time illegal copyright offender of five years of incarceration and a fine of $250,000.[56] Infringing copies and all equipment used to make those copies are also subject to forfeiture and destruction.[57]

IDENTITY THEFT • To meet this increasing threat, Congress passed the Identity Theft and Assumption Deterrence Act of 1998 (the Identity Theft Act) to make it a federal crime when anyone knowingly transfers or uses, without lawful authority, a means of identification of another person with the intent to commit, or to aid or abet, any unlawful activity that constitutes a violation of federal law, or that constitutes a felony under any applicable state or local law.[58] Violations of the act are investigated by federal investigative agencies such as the U.S. Secret Service, the FBI, and the U.S. Postal Inspection Service. In 2004, the Identity Theft Penalty Enhancement Act was signed into law. The act increases existing penalties for the crime of identity theft, establishes aggravated identity theft as a criminal offense, and establishes mandatory penalties for aggravated identity theft. According to the new law, anyone who knowingly "transfers, possesses, or uses, without lawful authority" someone else's identification will be sentenced to an extra prison term of two years with no possibility of parole. Individuals committing identity fraud while engaged in crimes associated with terrorism—such as aircraft destruction, arson, airport violence, or kidnapping top government officials—will receive a mandatory sentence enhancement of five years.

INTERNET PORNOGRAPHY • As noted previously, it is difficult to detect and control Internet pornography. Opponents of any controls warn that the right of free speech may be violated. Congress has struggled to create legislation that will restrict objectionable use without violating First Amendment freedoms. For example, the Child Online Protection Act (COPA) (H.R. 3783), bans Web postings of material deemed "harmful to minors."[59] On May 13, 2002, the Supreme Court partly upheld the law when it ruled that the law's use of what it calls "community standards" to define what is harmful to children does not by itself make the law unconstitutional.[60] However, there may be future challenges to COPA on the grounds that it inhibits free speech.

COMPUTER CRIMES • Congress has treated computer-related crimes as distinct federal offenses since passage of the Counterfeit Access Device and Computer Fraud and Abuse Law in 1984.[61] The 1984 act protected classified United States defense and foreign relations information, financial institution and consumer reporting agency files, and access to computers operated for the government. The act was supplemented in 1996 by the National Information Infrastructure Protection Act (NIIPA), which significantly broadens the scope of the law.

Enforcing Cyber Laws

How has the justice system responded to cyber crime? Most of the efforts are being made at the federal level. The government is now operating a number of organizations that are coordinating efforts to control cyber fraud. One approach is to create working groups that coordinate the activities of numerous agencies involved in investigating cyber crime. The Interagency Telemarketing and Internet Fraud Working Group brings together representatives of numerous United States Attorneys' offices, the FBI, the Secret Service, the Postal Inspection Service, the Federal Trade Commission, the Securities and Exchange Commission, and other law enforcement and regulatory agencies to share information about trends and patterns in Internet fraud schemes. One of the most successful federal efforts is the New York Electronic Crimes Task Force (NYECTF), a partnership between the U.S. Secret Service and a host of other public safety agencies and private corporations. Today, the task force consists of over 250 individual members representing federal, state, and local law enforcement; the private sector; and computer science specialists from 18 different universities. Since 1995, the New York task force has charged over 1,000 individuals with causing electronic crime losses exceeding $1 billion. It has trained over 60,000 law enforcement personnel, prosecutors, and private industry representatives in cyber crime prevention. Its success has prompted Boston, Miami, Charlotte, Chicago, Las Vegas, San Francisco, Los Angeles, and Washington, D.C., to set up similar task forces.[62]

OTHER SPECIALIZED ENFORCEMENT AGENCIES ● Specialized enforcement agencies are being created to fight cyber crime. The Internet Fraud Complaint Center, based in Fairmont, West Virginia, is run by the FBI and the National White Collar Crime Center. It brings together about 1,000 state and local law enforcement officials and regulators. It then analyzes the fraud-related complaints for patterns, develops additional information on particular cases, and sends investigative packages to law enforcement authorities in the jurisdictions that seem likely to have the greatest investigative interest in the matter. In the first year of its operation, the center received 36,000 complaints, the majority involving auction fraud.

Law enforcement has made remarkable strides in dealing with the crime of identity theft over the last two years. Nonetheless, the problem is serious and may expand despite efforts to control it.

REALITY CHECK

MYTH OR REALITY? It will be difficult to defeat cyber criminals without interagency and international cooperation.

REALITY: No one federal or state agency can hope to control cyber crime by itself; interagency cooperation is essential.

If you were in charge, what would you do to combat cyber crime? Increase penalties? Create new enforcement agencies that employ cyber detectives?

What the Future Holds

The justice system's response to cyber crime and terrorism is constantly evolving, but all too often it is moved by events, being reactive rather than proactive. For example, before 9/11, most local law enforcement agencies had little experience with terrorist-related incidents, and most did little to prepare for attacks. After 9/11, the country went on high alert. State and local agencies began to develop antiterror strategies and responses. In response to 9/11, criminal justice agencies increased the number of personnel engaged in emergency response planning and antiterror activities. They have put in place updated plans for chemical, biological, or radiological attacks and, to a lesser extent, mutual aid agreements. They have reallocated internal resources and increased departmental spending to focus on terrorism preparedness.[63]

In the future, rather than merely reacting to events, the justice system may go on the offensive. Technological prowess may make it possible to identify terrorists and cyber criminals and bring them to justice before they can carry out their attacks. To meet this goal, greater cooperation between agencies ranging from the FBI and the Department of Homeland Security to the National Counterterrorism Center and the office of the Director of National Intelligence will be critical.

ETHICAL CHALLENGES IN CRIMINAL JUSTICE

A Writing Assignment

Because you are an expert on both terrorism and cyber crime, the president's national security adviser wants your opinion on a matter of national security. It has been suggested that all people seeking to enter the country for more than 30 days be biometically scanned so that they can be constantly monitored by surveillance devices now being set up all around the nation. The government could then keep tabs on their whereabouts and activities. The benefits are immense. Once people become suspected of committing a crime or are believed to be part of a terrorist cell, they can be easily monitored from a distance without danger to any government agent. They cannot hide or escape detection. The monitoring devices could be used to determine whether they are meeting with known terror suspects.

The National Security Agency wants your opinion on this device. Is its use a worthwhile precaution, considering the threats faced by America from terrorists and criminals? Or would it violate personal privacy and freedom?

RealityCheck Revisted

To learn more about the myths and realities related to the contemporary threats of terrorism and cyber crime that were presented in this chapter, visit the following websites.

- To investigate the diversity of terror groups, go to

http://www.terrorism.com/

http://www.cdi.org/program/index.cfm?programid=39

- Is cyber crime truly international in scope? To learn more, go to

http://www.cdt.org/international/cybercrime/

http://conventions.coe.int/Treaty/EN/Treaties/Html/185.htm

SUMMARY

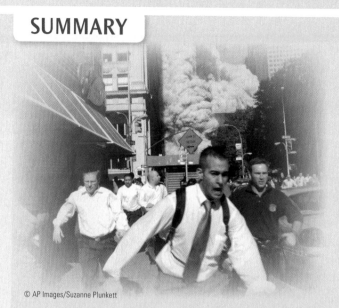

© AP Images/Suzanne Plunkett

1. Be able to define terrorism and cyber crime.

- Because of their seriousness, their potential for damage, and their effect on public morale, two challenges to the criminal justice system stand out in importance: terrorism and cyber crime.

- Terrorism involves the illegal use of force against innocent people to achieve a political objective.

- Cyber crime is any illegal behavior that targets the security of computer systems and/or the data accessed and processed by computer networks.

- Using the Internet as a theater of operations, cyber terrorists can mount attacks on an enemy nation's technological infrastructure, an action referred to as cyber terrorism.

2. Be familiar with the history of terrorism

- The term "terrorist" first appeared at the time of the French Revolution.

- Despite its long history, it is often difficult to precisely define terrorism.

- Terrorism is distinguished from conventional warfare by its use of secrecy and clandestine operations to exert social control over large populations.

3. Understand the factors that motivate terrorists

- Terrorists have been raised to hate their opponents and learn at an early age that they have been victimized by some oppressor.

- Terrorists hold extreme ideological beliefs that prompt their behavior.

- Terrorists may be motivated by feelings of alienation and failure to maintain the tools to compete in a post-technological society.

4. Be familiar with the various forms of contemporary terrorism

- Revolutionary terrorists use violence to frighten those in power and their supporters in order to replace the existing government with a regime that holds political or religious views acceptable to the terrorists.

- Political terrorism is directed at people or groups who are closely connected to the terrorists but who oppose the terrorists' political ideology or whom the terrorists define as "outsiders."

- Nationalist terrorism promotes the interests of a minority ethnic or religious group that believes it has been persecuted under majority rule and wishes to carve out its own independent homeland.

- Rather than fighting for a homeland, retributive terrorists fight for a cause.

- In state-sponsored terrorism, a repressive government regime forces its citizens into obedience, oppresses minorities, and stifles political dissent.

- Some cults may be classified as terror groups because their leaders demand that followers prove their loyalty through violence or intimidation.

- Sometimes terrorist groups become involved in common-law crimes such as drug dealing and kidnapping—or even selling nuclear materials.

5. Discuss how the federal government has responded to terrorism

- The Director of National Intelligence (DNI) is the government official charged with coordinating data from the nation's primary intelligence-gathering agencies.

- One of the most significant changes has been a realignment of the Federal Bureau of Investigation (FBI), the federal government's main law enforcement agency.

- The Department of Homeland Security (DHS) is the federal agency responsible for preventing terrorist attacks within the United States.

6. ***Recognize that state and local governments have created antiterror initiatives***

- Some counties are now engaging in anti-terror and homeland securities activities.
- New York City, one of the main targets of the 9/11 attacks, has established a new Counterterrorism Bureau.

7. ***Debate the utility and problems associated with the USA Patriot Act***

- The USA Patriot Act (USAPA) gives sweeping new powers to domestic law enforcement and international intelligence agencies in an effort to fight terrorism, to expand the definition of terrorist activities, and to alter sanctions for violent terrorism.

8. ***Discuss the various forms of cyber crime***

- Cyber crime typically involves the theft and/or destruction of information, resources, or funds via computers, computer networks, and the Internet.
- Cyber theft is the use of computer networks for criminal profits. Illegal copyright infringement, identity theft, and Internet securities fraud are examples of cyber theft.

- Cyber vandalism, or technological destruction, involves malicious attacks aimed at disrupting, defacing, and destroying technology.

9. ***Define the concept of cyber terrorism***

- Cyber terrorism consists of politically motivated attacks designed to compromise the electronic infrastructure of the enemy and to disrupt its economy.
- Cyber terrorism is an effort by covert forces to disrupt the place where the virtual electronic reality of computers intersects with the physical world.
- Cyber space is a handy battlefield for terrorists because an attack can strike at a target that bombs don't directly affect: the economy of their enemy.

10. ***Know what is being done to thwart cyber criminals***

- Numerous organizations have been set up to provide training and support for law enforcement agents. In addition, new federal and state laws have been enacted to help discourage particular types of high-tech crimes.
- In the future, technological prowess may make it possible to identify cyber criminals and bring them to justice before they can carry out their attacks.

Key Terms

Review Questions

1. Would you be willing to give up some of your civil rights in order to aid the war on terror?

2. Should people who illegally download movies or music be prosecuted for theft?

3. Should terror suspects arrested in a foreign land be given all the rights and privileges accorded to an American citizen accused of crime?

4. Should the Internet be more closely monitored and controlled to prevent the threat of cyber terrorism?

5. What groups in America might be a breeding ground for terrorist activity in the United States?

ABIS (Automated Biometric Identification System) Facial recognition system designed to sift through millions of images to find duplicates before issuing an ID or clearing a passport.

actus reus An illegal act. The actus reus can be an affirmative act, such as taking money or shooting someone, or a failure to act, such as failing to take proper precautions while driving a car.

adjudication The determination of guilt or innocence; a judgment concerning criminal charges. The majority of offenders charged plead guilty; of the remainder, some cases are adjudicated by a judge and a jury, some are adjudicated by a judge without a jury, and others are dismissed.

adversarial procedure The procedure used to determine truth in the adjudication of guilt or innocence in which the defense (advocate for the accused) is pitted against the prosecution (advocate for the state), with the judge acting as arbiter in accordance with legal rules. Under the adversary system, the burden is on the state to prove the charges beyond a reasonable doubt. This system of having the two parties publicly debate has proved to be the most effective method of arriving at the truth regarding a set of circumstances. (Under the accusatory, or inquisitorial, system, which is used in continental Europe, the charge is evidence of guilt that the accused must disprove; the judge takes an active part in the proceedings.)

al Qaeda A terrorist network strongly antagonistic to the United States that distributes money and tactical support and training to a wide variety of radical Islamic terrorist groups.

appellate court A court that reconsiders a case that has already been tried in order to determine whether the measures used complied with accepted rules of criminal procedure and were in line with constitutional doctrines.

assigned counsel A lawyer appointed by the court to represent a defendant in a criminal case because the person is too poor to hire counsel.

Auburn system The prison system developed in New York during the nineteenth century that stressed congregate working conditions.

augmented reality (AR) technology Wearable components that supply computer-generated virtual information.

bail The monetary amount for or condition of pretrial release, normally set by a judge at the initial appearance. The purpose of bail is to ensure the return of the accused at subsequent proceedings.

Bail Reform Act of 1984 Federal legislation that provides for both greater emphasis on release on recognizance for nondangerous offenders and preventive detention for those who present a menace to the community.

bench trial The trial of a criminal matter by a judge only. The accused waives any constitutional right to trial by jury.

bill of indictment A document created by a prosecuting attorney charging someone with the commission of a crime or other offense and presented to a grand jury for their review and endorsement.

Bill of Rights The first ten amendments to the Constitution.

biosocial theory The school of thought holding that human behavior is a function of the interaction of biochemical, neurological, and genetic factors with environmental stimuli.

bipolar disorder A psychological condition marked by mood swings between periods of wild elation and deep depression.

blameworthy Culpable or guilty of participating in a particular criminal offense.

blue curtain The secretive, insulated police culture that isolates officers from the rest of society.

boot camp A short-term militaristic correctional facility in which inmates undergo intensive physical conditioning and discipline.

broken windows model The term used to describe the role of the police as maintainers of community order and safety.

brutalization effect An outcome of capital punishment that enhances, rather than deters, the level of violence in society. The death penalty reinforces the view that violence is an appropriate response to provocation.

Bureau of Alcohol, Tobacco, Firearms, and Explosives (ATF) Federal agency with jurisdiction over the illegal sales, importation, and criminal misuse of firearms and explosives and the distribution of untaxed liquor and cigarettes.

challenge for cause Removing a juror because he or she is biased or has prior knowledge about a case, or for other reasons that demonstrate the individual's inability to render a fair and impartial judgment in a case.

charge In a criminal case, the judge's instruction to the jurors before deliberation.

child savers Late nineteenth-century reformers in America who developed programs for troubled youths and influenced legislation creating the juvenile justice system.

Children's Aid Society A child-saving organization founded by Charles Loring Brace; it took children from the streets in large cities and placed them with farm families on the prairie.

chivalry hypothesis The view that the low rates of female crime and delinquency are a reflection of the leniency with which police treat female offenders.

choice theory The school of thought holding that people will engage in delinquent and criminal behavior after weighing the consequences and benefits of their actions. Delinquent behavior is a rational choice made by a motivated offender who perceives that the chances of gain outweigh any perceived punishment or loss.

chronic offender A delinquent offender who is arrested five or more times before he or she is 18 and who stands a good chance of becoming an adult criminal; these offenders are responsible for more than half of all serious crimes.

circumstantial (indirect) evidence Evidence not bearing on the fact in dispute but on various indirect circumstances from which the judge or jury might infer the existence of the fact (for example, if the defendant was seen in the house with wet clothing, that is circumstantial evidence that the person had walked in the rain).

civil law All law that is not criminal, including torts (personal wrongs), contract, property, maritime, and commercial law.

classical theory of crime The view that people choose to commit crime after weighing the potential costs and benefits.

collective efficacy The ability of neighborhood residents to act cooperatively to maintain social control wtihin communities.

commitment Decision of judge ordering an adjudicated and sentenced juvenile offender to be placed in a correctional facility.

common law Early English law, developed by judges, that incorporated Anglo-Saxon tribal custom, feudal rules and practices, and the everyday rules of behavior of local villages. Common law became the standardized law of the land in England and eventually formed the basis of the criminal law in the United States.

community service restitution An alternative sanction that requires an offender to work in the community at such tasks as cleaning public parks or working with disabled children in lieu of serving an incarceration sentence.

community treatment The attempt by correctional agencies to maintain convicted offenders in the community instead of a secure facility; it includes probation, parole, and residential programs.

CompStat A program originated by the New York City police that uses carefully collected and analyzed crime data to shape policy and evaluate police effectiveness.

computer virus (malware) One type of malicious software program that disrupts or destroys existing programs and networks, causing them to perform the task for which the virus was designed.

computer worms Similar to viruses, worms use computer networks or the Internet to self-replicate and "send themselves" to other users, generally via email, without the aid of the operator.

concurrent sentences Prison sentences for two or more criminal acts, served simultaneously and run together.

conflict theory The view that human behavior is shaped by interpersonal conflict and that those who maintain social power will use it to further their own needs.

conflict view of crime (critical view of crime) The belief that the law is controlled by the rich and powerful, who shape its content to ensure their continued economic domination of society. The criminal justice system is viewed as an instrument of social and economic repression.

confrontation clause The constitutional right of a criminal defendant to see and cross-examine all the witnesses testifying against him or her.

congregate system The Auburn Prison, one of the nation's first correctional facilities, was a congregate system, because most prisoners ate and worked in groups.

consecutive sentences Prison sentences for two or more criminal acts, served one after the other.

consensus view of crime The belief that the majority of citizens in a society share common ideals and work toward a common good and that crimes are acts that are outlawed because they conflict with the rules of the majority and are harmful to society.

constable In medieval England, an appointed official who administered and supervised the legal affairs of a small community.

contingent exclusionary rule A plan that would allow evidence seized in violation of the Fourth Amendment to be used in a court of law.

contract system (attorney) Providing counsel to indigent offenders by having attorneys under

contract to the county handle all (or some) such cases.

contract system (convict) The system used early in the twentieth century by which private industry contracted with prison officials for convict labor and set up shops on prison grounds for them to work.

convict-lease system The system whereby the state leased its prisoners to a business for a fixed annual fee and gave up supervision and control.

court of general jurisdiction A state or federal court that has jurisdiction over felony offenses and more serious civil cases (i.e., involving more than a dollar amount set by the legislature).

court of last resort A court that handles the final appeal on a matter. The U.S. Supreme Court is the official court of last resort for criminal matters.

courtroom work group The phrase used to denote that all parties in the adversary process work together in a cooperative effort to settle cases with the least amount of effort and conflict.

crime A violation of societal rules of behavior as interpreted and expressed by a criminal legal code created by people holding social and political power. Individuals who violate these rules are subject to sanctions by state authority, social stigma, and loss of status.

crime control perspective A model of criminal justice that emphasizes the control of dangerous offenders and the protection of society. Its advocates call for harsh punishments such as the death penalty, as a deterrent to crime.

criminal justice process The decision-making points, from the initial investigation or arrest by police to the eventual release of the offender and his or her reentry into society; the various sequential criminal justice stages through which the offender passes.

criminal procedure The rules and laws that define the operation of the criminal proceedings. Procedural law describes the methods that must be followed in obtaining warrants, investigating offenses, effecting lawful arrests, conducting trials, introducing evidence, sentencing convicted offenders, and the review of cases by appellate courts.

cross-examination The process in which the defense and the prosecution interrogate witnesses during a trial.

cruel and unusual punishment Physical punishment or punishment far in excess of that given to people under similar circumstances and therefore banned by the Eighth Amendment. The death penalty has so far not been considered cruel and unusual if it is administered in a fair and nondiscriminatory fashion.

cultural transmission The passing of cultural values from one generation to the next.

culture of poverty The crushing lifestyle of slum areas produces a culture of poverty, passed from one generation to the next, marked by apathy, cynicism, feelings of helplessness, and mistrust of social institutions, such as schools, government agencies, and the police.

cyber bullying Willful and repeated harm inflicted on a victim through the medium of electronic text.

cyber crime Illegal behavior that targets the security of computer systems and/or the data accessed and processed by computer networks.

cyber stalking Using the Internet, email, or other electronic communications devices to stalk or harass another person.

cyber terrorism An attack against an enemy nation's technological infrastructure.

cyber theft The use of computer networks for criminal profits. Copyright infringement, identity theft, and Internet securities fraud are examples of cyber theft.

cyber vandalism Malicious attacks aimed at disrupting, defacing, and destroying technology.

cynicism The belief that most people's actions are motivated solely by personal needs and selfishness.

day fees A program requiring probationers to pay in part for the costs of their treatment.

day fine A fine geared to the average daily income of the convicted offender in an effort to bring equity to the sentencing process.

day reporting center (DRC) A nonresidential community-based treatment program.

decriminalization Reducing the penalty for a criminal act but not actually legalizing it.

deinstitutionalization The movement to remove as many offenders as possible from secure confinement and treat them in the community.

demeanor The way in which a person outwardly manifests his or her personality.

denial-of-service attack Extorting money from an Internet service user by threatening to prevent the user from having access to the service.

Department of Homeland Security (DHS) Federal agency responsible for preventing terrorist attacks within the United States, reducing America's vulnerability to terrorism, and minimizing the damage and recovering from attacks that do occur.

detention The temporary care of a child alleged to be a delinquent or status offender who requires secure custody, pending court disposition.

determinate sentence A fixed term of incarceration, such as three years' imprisonment. Many people consider determinate sentences too restrictive for rehabilitative purposes; the advantage is that offenders know how much time they have to serve—that is, when they will be released.

deterrent effect Stopping or reducing crime by convincing would-be criminals that they stand a significant risk of being apprehended and punished for their crimes.

developmental theory The view that social interactions developed over the life course shape behavior. Some interactions, such as involvement with deviant peers, encourage law violations; others, such as marriage and military service, may help people desist from crime.

direct examination The questioning of one's own (prosecution or defense) witness during a trial.

directed verdict The right of a judge to direct a jury to acquit a defendant because the state has not proved the elements of the crime or otherwise has not established guilt according to law.

director of national intelligence (DNI) Government official charged with coordinating data from the nation's primary intelligence-gathering agencies.

discretion The use of personal decision making and choice in carrying out operations in the criminal justice system. For example, police discretion can involve the decision to make an arrest; prosecutorial discretion can involve the decision to accept a plea bargain.

disposition For juvenile offenders, the equivalent of sentencing for adult offenders. The theory is that disposition is more rehabilitative than retributive. Possible dispositions may be to dismiss the case, release the youth to the custody of his or her parents, place the offender on probation, or send him or her to an institution or state correctional institution.

diversion A noncriminal alternative to trial, usually featuring counseling, job training, and educational opportunities.

DNA profiling The identification of criminal suspects by matching DNA samples taken from their person with specimens found at the crime scene.

double marginality The social burden African American police officers carry by being both minority group members and law enforcement officers.

Drug Enforcement Administration (DEA) The federal agency that enforces federal drug control laws.

due process perspective Due process is the basic constitutional principle based on the concept of the privacy of the individual and the complementary concept of limitation on governmental power; a safeguard against arbitrary and unfair state procedures in judicial or administrative proceedings. Embodied in the due process concept are the basic rights of a defendant in criminal proceedings and the requisites for a fair trial. These rights and requirements have been expanded by appellate court decisions and include (a) timely notice of a hearing or trial that informs the accused of the charges against him or her; (b) the opportunity to confront accusers and to present evidence on one's own behalf before an impartial jury or judge; (c) the presumption of innocence under which guilt must be proved by legally obtained evidence and the verdict must be supported by the evidence presented; (d) the right of an accused to be warned of constitutional rights at the earliest stage of the criminal process; (e) protection against self-incrimination; (f) assistance of counsel at every critical stage of the criminal process; and (g) the guarantee that an individual will not be tried more than once for the same offense (double jeopardy).

electronic monitoring (EM) Requiring convicted offenders to wear a monitoring device as part of their community sentence. Typically part of a house arrest order—enables the probation department to ensure that offenders are complying with court-ordered limitations on their freedom.

entrapment A criminal defense that maintains the police originated the criminal idea or initiated the criminal action.

equity The action or practice of awarding each person his or her just due; sanctions based on equity seek to compensate individual victims and the general society for their losses due to crime.

etailing fraud Use of the Internet to buy or sell merchandise illegally.

exclusionary rule The principle that prohibits using illegally obtained evidence in a trial. Based on the Fourth Amendment "right of the people to be secure in their persons, houses, papers, and effects, against unreasonable searches and seizures," the rule is not a bar to prosecution, because legally obtained evidence may be available that *may* be used in a trial.

Federal Bureau of Investigation (FBI) The arm of the U.S. Justice Department that investigates violations of federal law, gathers crime statistics, runs a comprehensive crime laboratory, and helps train local law enforcement officers.

felony A serious offense that carries a penalty of incarceration in a state prison, usually for one year or more. Persons convicted of felony offenses lose such rights as the rights to vote, hold elective office, or maintain certain licenses.

fine Levying a money payment on offenders to compensate society for their misdeeds.

First Amendment The U.S. constitutional amendment that guarantees freedom of speech, religion, press, and assembly, and the right of the people to petition the government for redress of grievances.

foot patrol Police patrols that take officers out of cars and put them on a walking beat in order to strengthen ties with the community.

forfeiture The seizure of personal property by the state as a civil or criminal penalty.

furlough A correctional policy that allows inmates to leave the institution for vocational or educational training, for employment, or to maintain family ties.

general deterrence A crime control policy that depends on the fear of criminal penalties. General deterrence measures, such as long prison sentences for violent crimes, are aimed at convincing the potential law violator that the pains associated with the crime outweigh the benefits.

Gideon v. Wainwright The 1963 U.S. Supreme Court case that granted counsel to indigent defendants in felony prosecutions.

good faith exception The principle of law holding that evidence may be used in a criminal trial, even though the search warrant used to obtain it is technically faulty, if the police acted in good faith and to the best of their ability when they sought to obtain the warrant from a judge.

grand jury A type of jury, responsible for investigating alleged crimes, examining evidence, and issuing indictments.

grass eaters A term for police officers who accept payoffs when everyday duties place them in a position to "look the other way."

halfway house A community-based correctional facility that houses inmates before their outright release so that they can become gradually acclimated to conventional society.

hands-off doctrine The legal practice of allowing prison administrators a free hand to run the institution even if correctional practices violate inmates' constitutional rights; ended with the onset of the prisoners' rights movement in the 1960s.

hearsay evidence Testimony that is not firsthand but related information told by a second party.

hot spots of crime Places from which a significant portion of all police calls originate. These hot spots include taverns and housing projects.

house arrest A form of intermediate sanction that requires that the convicted offender spend a designated amount of time per week in his or her own home—for example, from 5:00 P.M. Friday until 8:00 A.M. Monday.

hue and cry A call for assistance in medieval England. The policy of self-help used in villages demanded that everyone respond if a citizen raised a hue and cry to summon their aid.

hulk One of the mothballed ships used to house prisoners in eighteenth-century England.

hundred In medieval England, a group of 100 families responsible for maintaining order and trying minor offenses.

identity theft Using the Internet to steal someone's identity and/or impersonate the victim in order to conduct illicit transactions, such as committing fraud using the victim's name and identity.

incapacitation The policy of keeping dangerous criminals in confinement to eliminate the risk of their repeating their offense in society.

indeterminate sentence A term of incarceration with a stated minimum and maximum length, such as a sentence to prison for a period of from 3 to 10 years. The prisoner would be eligible for parole after the minimum sentence had been served. Based on the belief that sentences should fit the criminal, indeterminate sentences allow individualized sentences and provide for sentencing flexibility. Judges can set a high minimum to override the purpose of the indeterminate sentence.

indigent Without the means to hire an attorney.

inevitable discovery rule Evidence seized in violation of the Fifth Amendment's self-incrimination clause may be used in a court of law if a judge rules that it would have been found or discovered even if the incriminating statements had never been made.

in forma pauperis "In the manner of a pauper." A criminal defendant granted permission to proceed in forma pauperis is entitled to assistance of counsel at state expense.

initial appearance A juvenile's first appearance before the juvenile court judge in which the charges are reviewed and an effort is made to settle the case without a trial. If the child does not have legal counsel, an attorney is appointed.

inmate social code An unwritten code of behavior, passed from older inmates to younger ones, that gives guidelines for appropriate inmate behavior within the correctional institution.

inmate subculture The loosely defined culture that pervades prisons and has its own norms, rules, and language.

in-presence requirement The condition that in order to make an arrest in a misdemeanor, the arresting officer must have personally witnessed the crime being committed.

insanity A legal defense that maintains a defendant was incapable of forming criminal intent because he or she suffers from a defect of reason or mental illness.

intake The process in which a probation officer settles cases at the initial appearance before the onset of formal criminal proceedings; also, process in which a juvenile referral is received and a decision is made to file a petition in the juvenile court, release the juvenile, or refer the juvenile elsewhere.

intensive probation supervision (IPS) A type of intermediate sanction involving small probation caseloads and strict monitoring on a daily or weekly basis.

intensive supervision parole (ISP) A limited-caseload program for those parolees who need intensive surveillance. Parolees are required to meet more often with parole officers than routine parolees and may also have frequent drug testing, serve a term in a community correctional system, and be electronically monitored.

interactionist view of crime The belief that criminal law reflects the values of people who use their social and political power to shape the legal system.

intermediate sanctions The group of punishments falling between probation and prison ("probation plus"). Community-based sanctions, including house arrest and intensive supervision, serve as alternatives to incarceration.

internal affairs The branch of the police department that investigates charges of corruption or misconduct against police officers.

jail A place to detain people awaiting trial, to serve as a lockup for drunks and disorderly individuals, and to confine convicted misdemeanants serving sentences of less than one year.

jailhouse lawyer An inmate trained in law or otherwise educated who helps other inmates prepare legal briefs and appeals.

judicial reprieve The common-law practice that allowed judges to suspend punishment so that convicted offenders could seek a pardon, gather new evidence, or demonstrate that they had reformed their behavior.

jury nullification A defense tactic, suggesting that the jury acquit a defendant despite evidence that he actually violated the law, by appealing to the jury that the law was unjust or not applicable to the case.

jury trial The process of deciding a case by a group of persons selected and sworn in to serve as jurors at a criminal trial, often as a 6- or 12-person jury.

just desert The philosophy of justice asserting that those who violate the rights of others deserve to be punished. The severity of punishment should be commensurate with the seriousness of the crime.

justice of the peace Established in 1326 England, this office was created to help the shire reeve in controlling the county and later took on judicial functions.

justice perspective A view of justice that holds that all people should be treated equally before the law. Equality may best be achieved through the control of individual discretion in the justice process.

juvenile court A court that has original jurisdiction over persons defined by statute as juveniles and alleged to be delinquents or status offenders.

juvenile delinquency Participation in illegal behavior by a minor who falls under a statutory age limit.

Knapp Commission A public body that led an investigation into police corruption in New York and uncovered a widespread network of payoffs and bribes.

landmark decision A decision handed down by the U.S. Supreme Court that becomes the law of the land and serves as a precedent for similar legal issues.

Law Enforcement Assistance Administration (LEAA) Funded by the federal government's Safe Streets Act, this agency provided technical assistance and hundreds of millions of dollars in aid to local and state justice agencies between 1969 and 1982.

legalization The removal of all criminal penalties from a previously outlawed act.

lex talionis (Latin for "law as retaliation") From Hammurabi's ancient legal code, the belief that the purpose of the law is to provide retaliation for an offended party and that the punishment should fit the crime.

life history A research method that uses the experiences of an individual as the unit of analysis, such as using the life experience of an individual gang member to understand the natural history of gang membership.

make-believe family In women's prisons, some inmates adapt by creating substitute family groups with faux father, mother, and siblings.

mala in se A term that refers to acts that society considers inherently evil, such as murder or rape, and that violate the basic principles of Judeo-Christian morality.

mala prohibitum Crimes that are defined as such by legislative bodies and that this reflect prevailing moral beliefs and practices.

mandatory sentence A statutory requirement that a certain penalty shall be set and carried out in all cases up on conviction for a specified offense or series of offenses.

Manhattan Bail Project The innovative experiment in bail reform that introduced and successfully tested the concept of release on recognizance.

maximum-security prison A correctional institution that houses dangerous felons and maintains strict security measures, high walls, and limited contact with the outside world.

meat eaters A term for police officers who actively solicit bribes and vigorously engage in corrupt practices.

medical model A view of corrections holding that convicted offenders are victims of their environment who need care and treatment to transform them into valuable members of society.

medium-security prison A less secure institution that houses nonviolent offenders and provides more opportunities for contact with the outside world.

mens rea Guilty mind. The mental element of a crime or the intent to commit a criminal act.

meta-analysis Data gathered from a number of previous studies is pooled and analyzed to provide a more powerful and valid indicator of relationships than the results provided from a single study.

minimum-security prison The least secure institution; it houses white-collar and nonviolent offenders, maintains few security measures, and has liberal furlough and visitation policies.

Miranda warning The result of two U.S. Supreme Court decisions (*Escobedo v. Illinois* and *Miranda v. Arizona*) that requires police officers to inform individuals under arrest that they have a constitutional right to remain silent, that their statements can later be used against them in court, that they can have an attorney present to help them, and that the state will pay for an attorney if they cannot afford to hire one. Although aimed at protecting an individual during in-custody interrogation, the warning must also be given when the investigation shifts from the investigatory to the accusatory stage—that is, when suspicion begins to focus on an individual.

misdemeanor A minor crime usually punished by less than one year's imprisonment in a local institution, such as a county jail.

Missouri Plan A way of picking judges through nonpartisan elections as a means of ensuring judicial performance standards.

monetary restitution A sanction requiring that convicted offenders compensate crime victims by reimbursing them for out-of-pocket losses caused by the crime. Losses can include property damage, lost wages, and medical costs.

moral entrepreneurs People who wage moral crusades to control criminal law so that it reflects their own personal values.

National Commission on Terrorist Attacks Upon the United States An independent, bipartisan commission created in 2002, which prepared an in-depth report of the events leading up to the 9/11 attacks.

National Crime Victimization Survey (NCVS) The ongoing victimization study conducted jointly by the Justice Department and the U.S. Census Bureau that surveys victims about their experiences with law violation.

neighborhood-oriented policing (NOP) Community policing efforts aimed at individual neighborhoods.

no bill The action by a grand jury when it votes not to indict an accused suspect.

no-frills policy A correctional policy that stipulates that prisons are aimed at punishing and not coddling inmates. This usually means a strict regimen of work and discipline and reduced opportunities for recreation and education.

nolle prosequi The term used when a prosecutor decides to drop a case after a complaint has been formally made. Reasons for nolle prosequi include evidence insufficiency, reluctance of witnesses to testify, police error, and office policy.

nonintervention perspective A justice philosophy that emphasizes the least intrusive treatment possible. Among its central policies are decarceration, diversion, and decriminalization. In other words, less is better.

obitiatry Helping people take their own lives.

official crime statistics Compiled by the FBI in its Uniform Crime Reports, these are a tally of serious crimes reported to police agencies each year.

order maintenance (peacekeeping) The order-maintenance aspect of the police role involves peacekeeping, maintaining order and authority without the need for formal arrest, "handling the situation," and keeping things under control by using threats, persuasion, and understanding.

parens patriae Latin term meaning "father of his country." According to this legal philosophy, the government is the guardian of everyone who has a disability, especially children, and has a legal duty to act in their best interests until they reach the age of majority.

parental efficacy The ability of parents to provide support and discipline in a noncoercive manner.

parole The early release of a prisoner from imprisonment, subject to conditions set by a parole board. Depending on the jurisdiction, inmates must serve a certain portion of their sentences before becoming eligible for parole. The conditions of parole may require the individual to report regularly to a parole officer, to refrain from criminal conduct, to maintain and support his or her family, to avoid contact with other convicted criminals, to abstain from alcohol and drugs, to remain within the jurisdiction, and so on. Violations of the conditions of parole may result in revocation of parole, in which case the individual will be returned to prison. The concept behind parole is to allow the release of the offender to community supervision, where rehabilitation and readjustment will be facilitated.

Part I crimes Because of their seriousness and frequency, the FBI reports the incidence of these eight crimes in its annual Uniform Crime Reports. Part I crimes include murder, rape, assault, robbery, burglary, arson, larceny, and motor vehicle theft.

Part II crimes All crimes except the eight Part I crimes are referred to as Part II crimes. The FBI records all arrests made for these as well as for Part I crimes, including information on race, gender, and age.

penal harm The view that prison should be a punishing experience and that criminals will be deterred from crime and current inmates will be encouraged to go straight.

penitentiary A state or federal correctional institution for incarceration of felony offenders for terms of one year or more.

penitentiary house A secure correctional facility, based on the Quaker concept that incarcerated criminals should experience penitence.

Pennsylvania system The prison system developed during the nineteenth century that stressed total isolation and individual penitence as a means of reform.

penumbral crimes Criminal acts characterized by a high level of public noncompliance with the stated legal standard, an absence of stigma associated with violation of the stated standard, and a low level of law enforcement or public sanction.

peremptory challenge The dismissal of a potential juror by either the prosecution or the defense for unexplained, discretionary reasons.

phishing (carding, spoofing) Illegally acquiring personal information, such as bank passwords and credit card numbers, by masquerading as a trustworthy person or business in what appears to be an official electronic communication, such as an email or an instant message. The term comes from the lures used to "fish" for financial information and passwords.

plea bargaining Nonjudicial settlement of a case in which the defendant exchanges a guilty plea for some consideration, such as a reduced sentence.

police brutality Usually involves such actions as the use of abusive language, unnecessary use of force or coercion, threats, prodding with nightsticks, stopping and searching people to harass them, and so on.

police chief The top administrator of the police department, who sets policy and has general control over departmental policies and practices. The chief is typically a political rather than a civil service appointee and serves at the pleasure of the mayor.

poor laws Seventeenth-century laws in England that bound out vagrants and abandoned children as indentured servants to masters.

positive stage During the positive stage of human social development, people embrace rational scientific explanations for observed phenomena.

preponderance of the evidence The level of proof in civil cases; more than half the evidence supports the allegations of one side.

pre-sentence investigation An investigation performed by a probation officer attached to a trial court after the conviction of a defendant. The report contains information about the defendant's background, education, previous employment, and family; his or her own statement concerning the offense; prior criminal record; interviews with neighbors or acquaintances; and his or her mental and physical condition (that is, information that would not be made public record in the case of a guilty plea or that would be inadmissible as evidence at a trial but could be influential and important at the sentencing stage).

presentment The report of a grand jury investigation, which usually includes a recommendation of indictment.

pretrial detainees People who either are denied bail or cannot afford to post bail before trial and are kept in secure confinement.

pretrial detention Holding an offender in secure confinement before trial.

pretrial diversion A program that provides nonpunitive, community-based alternatives to more intrusive forms of punishment such as jail or prison.

pretrial procedures Critical pretrial processes and decisions, including bail, arraignment, and plea negotiation.

preventive detention The practice of holding dangerous suspects before trial without bail.

prison A state or federal correctional institution for incarceration of felony offenders for terms of one year or more.

prisonization Assimilation into the separate culture in the prison that has its own set of rewards and behaviors. This loosely defined culture that pervades prisons has its own norms, rules, and language. The traditional culture is now being replaced by a violent gang culture.

proactive policing A police department policy emphasizing stopping crimes before they occur rather than merely reacting to crimes that have already occurred.

probable cause The evidentiary criterion necessary to sustain an arrest or the issuance of an arrest or search warrant; less than absolute certainty or "beyond a reasonable doubt" but greater than mere suspicion or "hunch." Probable cause consists of a set of facts, information, circumstances, or conditions that would lead a reasonable person to believe that an offense was committed and that the accused committed that offense. An arrest made without probable cause may be susceptible to prosecution as an illegal arrest under "false imprisonment" statutes.

probation A sentence entailing the conditional release of a convicted offender into the community under the supervision of the court (in the form of a probation officer), subject to certain conditions for a specified time. The conditions are usually similar to those of parole. (*Note:* Probation is a sentence, an alternative to incarceration; parole is administrative release from incarceration.) Violation of the conditions of probation may result in revocation of probation.

probation rules Conditions or restrictions mandated by the court that must be obeyed by a probationer.

problem-oriented policing A style of police operations that stresses proactive problem solving, rather than reactive crime fighting.

proof beyond a reasonable doubt The standard of proof needed to convict in a criminal case. The evidence offered in court does not have to amount to absolute certainty, but it should leave no reasonable doubt that the defendant committed the alleged crime.

pro se The right of self-representation.

prosecutor Representative of the state (executive branch) in criminal proceedings; advocate for the state's case—the charge—in the adversary trial; for example, the attorney general of the United States, U.S. attorneys, attorneys general of the states, district attorneys, and police prosecutors. The prosecutor participates in investigations both before and after arrest, prepares legal documents, participates in obtaining arrest or search warrants, and decides whether to charge a suspect and, if so, with which offense. The prosecutor argues the state's case at trial, advises the police, participates in plea negotiations, and makes sentencing recommendations.

psychoanalytic view This position holds that criminals are driven by unconscious thought patterns, developed in early childhood, that control behaviors over the life course.

psychopathic (antisocial, sociopathic) personality Psychopaths are chronically antisocial individuals who are always in trouble and do not learn from either experience or punishment. They are loners who engage in frequent callous and hedonistic behaviors, are emotionally immature, and lack responsibility, judgment, and empathy.

public defender An attorney generally employed (at no cost to the accused) by the government to represent poor persons accused of a crime.

public safety doctrine Statements elicited by police violation of the Fifth Amendment's self-incrimination clause may be used in a court of law if a judge rules that the questioning was justified in order to maintain public safety. For example, it would be permissible for police to ask a suspected terrorist where he planted a bomb and then use his statement in a criminal trial even though he had never been apprised of his Fifth Amendment (*Miranda*) rights.

real evidence Any object produced for inspection at the trial (such as a weapon or photograph).

recidivism Repetition of criminal behavior; habitual criminality. Recidivism is measured by (1) criminal acts that resulted in conviction by a court when committed by individuals who are under correctional supervision or who had been released from correctional supervision within the previous three years and (2) technical violations of probation or parole in which a sentencing or paroling authority took action that resulted in an adverse change in the offender's legal status.

rehabilitation perspective A model of criminal justice that views its primary purpose as helping to care for people who cannot manage themselves. Crime is an expression of frustration and anger created by social inequality that can be controlled by giving people the means to improve their lifestyle through conventional endeavors.

release on recognizance (ROR) A nonmonetary condition for the pretrial release of an accused individual; an alternative to monetary bail that is granted after the court determines that the accused has ties in the community, has no prior record of default, and is likely to appear at subsequent proceedings.

residential community corrections (RCC) A nonsecure facility, located in the community, that houses probationers who need a more secure environment. Typically, residents are free during the day to go to work, school, or treatment, and they return in the evening for counseling sessions and meals.

restitution A condition of probation in which the offender repays society or the victim of crime for the trouble the offender caused.

restorative justice A view of criminal justice that focuses on crime as an act against the community rather than the state. Justice should involve all parties affected by crime—victims, criminals, law enforcement, and the community.

restorative justice perspective A view of criminal justice that advocates peaceful solutions and mediation rather than coercive punishments.

revocation An administrative act performed by a parole authority that removes a person from parole, or a judicial order by a court removing a person from parole or probation, in response to a violation on the part of the parolee or probationer.

risk classification Classifying probationers so that they may receive an appropriate level of treatment and control.

search warrant An order issued by a judge, directing officers to conduct a search of specified premises for specified objects or persons and bring them before the court.

self-defense A legal defense in which defendants claim that their behavior was legally justified by the necessity to protect their own life and property, or that of another victim, from potential harm.

sentencing circles A type of sentencing in which victims, family members, community members, and the offender participate in an effort to devise fair and reasonable sanctions that are ultimately aimed at reintegrating the offender into the community.

sentencing guidelines A set of standards that define parameters for trial judges to follow in their sentencing decisions.

sheriff The chief law enforcement officer in a county.

shire reeve In medieval England, the senior law enforcement figure in a county; the forerunner of today's sheriff.

shock incarceration A short prison sentence served in boot camp–type facilities.

shock probation A sentence in which offenders serve a short prison term before they begin probation, to impress them with the pains of imprisonment.

six-person jury The criminal trial of a defendant before a jury of 6 persons as opposed to a traditional jury of 12 persons.

Sixth Amendment The U.S. constitutional amendment containing various criminal trial rights, such as the right to public trial, the right to trial by jury, and the right to confront of witnesses.

social control The process of external regulation of individual and/or group behavior. Social control can be informal and applied through sanctions (or rewards) employed by families, neighbors, peers, and so on. There is also formal social control, which is applied by the justice system through the legal process.

social learning The view that behavior patterns are modeled and learned in interactions with others.

social process theory The view that an individual's interactions with key social institutions—family, school, peer group—shape behavior.

social structure theory The view that a person's position in the social structure controls behavior. Those in the lowest socioeconomic tier are more likely to succumb to crime-promoting elements in their environment, whereas those in the highest tier enjoy social and economic advantages that insulate them from crime-producing forces.

specific deterrence A crime control policy suggesting that punishment should be severe enough to convince convicted offenders never to repeat their criminal activity.

split sentence A practice that requires convicted criminals to spend a portion of their sentence behind bars and the remainder in the community.

spousal privilege exemption Spouses cannot be compelled to testify in court against one another.

stalking The willful, malicious, and repeated following and harassing of another person.

stare decisis To stand by decided cases. The legal principle by which the decision or holding in an earlier case becomes the standard by which subsequent similar cases are judged.

state courts of limited jurisdiction Generic term referring to courts that have jurisdiction over misdemeanors and conduct preliminary investigations of felony charges.

status offender A juvenile who engages in behavior legally forbidden to minors, such as running away, truancy, or incorrigibility.

sting operation An undercover police operation in which police pose as criminals to trap law violators.

stop and frisk The situation when police officers who are suspicious of an individual run their hands lightly over the suspect's outer garments, to determine whether the person is carrying a concealed weapon. Also called a patdown or threshold inquiry, a stop and frisk is intended to stop short of any activity that could be considered a violation of Fourth Amendment rights.

street efficacy Using one's wits to avoid violent confrontations and to feel safe.

strict liability crime Illegal act whose elements do not include the need for intent, or mens rea; usually, acts that endanger the public welfare, such as the illegal dumping of toxic wastes.

subculture A substratum of society that maintains a unique set of values and beliefs.

substantive criminal law A body of specific rules that declare what conduct is criminal and prescribe the punishment to be imposed for such conduct.

substantive rights Through a slow process of legal review, the courts have granted inmates a number of civil rights, including the rights to receive mail and medical benefits and to practice their religion.

suicide by cop A form of suicide in which a person acts in an aggressive manner with police officers in order to induce them to shoot to kill.

super-maximum-security prison The newest form of a maximum-security prison that uses high-level security measures to incapacitate the nation's most dangerous criminals. Most inmates are in lockdown 23 hours per day.

sureties During the Middle Ages, people who made themselves responsible for the behavior of offenders released into their care.

suspended sentence A prison term that is delayed while the defendant undergoes a period of community treatment. If the treatment is successful, the prison sentence is terminated.

systematic review Findings from previously conducted scientific studies of a particular problem are collected, appraised, and synthesized, and the collective evidence is used to address a particular scientific question.

terrorism Premeditated, politically motivated violence perpetrated against noncombatant targets by subnational groups or clandestine agents.

tier system The structure of early prisons having numerous floors or wings that stacked cells one over another.

time-in-rank system For police officers to advance in rank, they must spend an appropriate amount of time, usually years, in the preceding rank—that is, to become a captain, an officer must first spend time as a lieutenant.

tithing In medieval England, a group of ten families who collectively dealt with minor disturbances and breaches of the peace.

tort A personal injury or wrong for which an action for damages may be brought.

total institution A regimented, dehumanizing institution such as a prison in which like-situated people are kept in social isolation, cut off from the world at large.

transfer hearing The hearing in which a decision is made to waive a juvenile to the criminal court. Waiver decisions are based on such criteria as the child's age, any prior offense history, and the nature of the offense.

treatment The rehabilitative method used to effect a change of behavior in the juvenile offender, in the form of therapy, or educational or vocational programs.

Trojan horse Another type of malicious (computer) program that looks like a benign application but contains illicit codes that can damage the system operations.

true bill (of indictment) An indictment endorsed by a grand jury resulting in the person being bound over for trial.

truth-in-sentencing laws A sentencing scheme requiring that offenders serve at least 85 percent of their original sentence before being eligible for parole or other forms of early release.

Uniform Crime Report (UCR) The FBI's yearly publication of where, when, and how much serious crime occurred in the prior year.

USA Patriot Act (USAPA) The law designed to grant new powers to domestic law enforcement and international intelligence agencies in an effort to fight terrorism.

U.S. Marshals Service Federal agency whose jurisdiction includes protecting federal officials, transporting criminal defendants, and tracking down fugitives.

venire The group called for jury duty from which jury panels are selected.

verdict A finding of a jury or a judge on questions of fact at a trial.

vice squad Police officers assigned to enforce morality-based laws, such as those on prostitution, gambling, and pornography.

victim impact statement A postconviction statement by the victim of crime that may be used to guide sentencing decisions.

victimless crime An act that is in violation of society's moral code and therefore has been outlawed—for example, drug abuse, gambling, and prostitution. These acts are linked together because, although they have no external victim, they are considered harmful to the social fabric.

vigilantes Groups of citizens who tracked down wanted criminals in the Old West.

voir dire The process in which a potential jury panel is questioned by the prosecution and the defense in order to select jurors who are unbiased and objective.

waiver (juvenile) A practice in which the juvenile court waives its jurisdiction over a juvenile and transfers the case to adult criminal court for trial. In some states, a waiver hearing is held to determine jurisdiction; in others, juveniles may be automatically waived if they are accused of committing a serious crime such as murder.

Walnut Street Jail In 1790, a separate wing of Philadelphia's Walnut Street Jail was built to house convicted felons. This was the forerunner of the secure correctional system in the United States.

warez Refers to efforts of organized groups to download and sell copyrighted software in violation of its license.

watch system During the Middle Ages in England, men were organized in church parishes to guard at night against disturbances and breaches of the peace under the direction of the local constable.

Web defacement A type of cyber vandalism that occurs when a hacker intrudes on another person's website by inserting or substituting codes that expose visitors to the site to misleading or provocative information.

wergild Under medieval law, the money paid by the offender to compensate the victim and the state for a criminal offense.

widening the net of justice The charge that programs designed to divert offenders from the justice system actually enmesh them further in the process by substituting more intrusive treatment programs for less intrusive punishment-oriented outcomes.

work release A prison treatment program that allows inmates to be released during the day to work in the community and returned to prison at night.

writ of certiorari An order of superior court requesting that the record of an inferior court (or administrative body) be brought forward for review or inspection.

writ of habeas corpus A judicial order requesting that a person detaining another produce the body of the prisoner and give reasons for his or her capture and detention. Habeas corpus is a legal device used to request that a judicial body review the reasons for a person's confinement and the conditions of confinement. Habeas corpus is known as "the great writ."

zero tolerance The practice of seizing all instrumentalities of a crime, including homes, boats, and cars. It is an extreme example of the law of forfeiture.

Chapter 1,
Crime and Criminal Justice

1. This section relies heavily on Ted Robert Gurr, "Historical Trends in Violent Crime: A Critical Review of the Evidence," in *Crime and Justice: An Annual Review of Research*, vol. 3, ed. Michael Tonry and Norval Morris (Chicago: University of Chicago Press, 1981); Richard Maxwell Brown, "Historical Patterns of American Violence," in *Violence in America: Historical and Comparative Perspectives*, ed. Hugh Davis Graham and Ted Robert Gurr (Beverly Hills, Calif.: Sage, 1979), 18–29.

2. Samuel Walker, *Popular Justice* (New York: Oxford University Press, 1980).

3. Ibid.

4. For an insightful analysis of this effort, see Samuel Walker, "Origins of the Contemporary Criminal Justice Paradigm: The American Bar Foundation Survey, 1953–1969," *Justice Quarterly 9* (1992): 47–76.

5. President's Commission on Law Enforcement and the Administration of Justice, *The Challenge of Crime in a Free Society* (Washington, D.C.: Government Printing Office, 1967).

6. See Public Law No. 90-351, *Title I–Omnibus Crime Control Safe Streets Act of 1968*, 90th Congress, June 19, 1968.

7. For a review, see Kevin Wright, "Twenty-Two Years of Federal Investment in Criminal Justice Research: The National Institute of Justice, 1968–1989," *Journal of Criminal Justice 22* (1994): 27–40.

8. Bureau of Justice Statistics, http://www.ojp.usdoj.gov/bjs/sandlle.htm (accessed February 10, 2009).

9. Federal Bureau of Investigation, *Crime in the United States, 2007* (Washington, D.C.: Government Printing Office, 2006), Table 29.

10. Matthew R. Durose and Patrick A. Langan, *Felony Sentences in State Courts, 2002* (Washington, D.C.: Bureau of Justice Statistics, 2004).

11. For an analysis of this issue, see William Wilbanks, *The Myth of a Racist Criminal Justice System* (Monterey, Calif.: Brooks/Cole, 1987); Stephen Klein, Joan Petersilia, and Susan Turner, "Race and Imprisonment Decisions in California," *Science 247* (1990): 812–816; Alfred Blumstein, "On the Racial Disproportionality of the United States Prison Population," *Journal of Criminal Law and Criminology 73* (1982): 1259–1281; Darnell Hawkins, "Race, Crime Type, and Imprisonment," *Justice Quarterly 3* (1986): 251–269.

12. Court TV Crime Library, Marilyn Bardsley, Rachael Bell, and David Lohr, *BTK—Birth of a Serial Killer*, http://www.crimelibrary.com/serial_killers/unsolved/btk/index_1.html (accessed March 25, 2007).

13. Herbert L. Packer, *The Limits of the Criminal Sanction* (Stanford, Calif.: Stanford University Press, 1975), 21.

14. Matthew DuRose and Patrick Langan, *Felony Sentences in State Courts, 2002* (Washington, D.C.: Bureau of Justice Statistics, 2004).

15. James Eisenstein and Herbert Jacob, *Felony Justice* (Boston: Little, Brown, 1977); Peter Nardulli, *The Courtroom Elite* (Cambridge, Mass.: Ballinger, 1978); Paul Wice, *Chaos in the Courthouse* (New York: Praeger, 1985); Marcia Lipetz, *Routine Justice: Processing Cases in Women's Court* (New Brunswick, N.J.: Transaction Books, 1983).

16. Samuel Walker, *Sense and Nonsense About Crime* (Belmont, Calif.: Wadsworth, 1985).

17. Malcolm Feeley, *The Process Is the Punishment* (New York: Russell Sage, 1979).

18. John DiLulio, *No Escape: The Future of American Corrections* (New York: Basic Books, 1991).

19. Karen Parker and Patricia McCall, "Structural Conditions and Racial Homicide Patterns: A Look at the Multiple Disadvantages in Urban Areas," *Criminology 37* (1999): 447–448.

20. Francis Cullen, John Paul Wright, and Mitchell Chamlin, "Social Support and Social Reform: A Progressive Crime Control Agenda," *Crime and Delinquency 45* (1999): 188–207.

21. Jane Sprott, "Are Members of the Public Tough on Crime? The Dimensions of Public 'Punitiveness,'" *Journal of Criminal Justice 27* (1999): 467–474.

22. Packer, *The Limits of the Criminal Sanction*, 175.

23. "DNA Testing Has Exonerated 28 Prison Inmates, Study Finds," *Criminal Justice Newsletter*, June 17, 1996, 2.

24. Caitlin Lovinger, "Death Row's Living Alumni," *New York Times*, August 22, 1999, 1.

25. Eric Stewart, Ronald Simons, Rand Conger, and Laura Scaramella, "Beyond the Interactional Relationship Between Delinquency and Parenting Practices: The Contribution of Legal Sanctions," *Journal of Research in Crime and Delinquency 39* (2002): 36–60.

26. Cassia Spohn and David Holleran, "The Effect of Imprisonment on Recidivism Rates of Felony Offenders: A Focus on Drug Offenders," *Criminology 40* (2002): 329–359.

27. *Doe v. Pryor M.D. Ala*, Civ. No. 99-T-730-N, Thompson, J. 8/16/99.

28. This section is based on Paula M. Ditton and Doris James Wilson, *Truth in Sentencing in State Prisons* (Washington, D.C.: Bureau of Justice Statistics, 1999).

29. Herbert Bianchi, *Justice as Sanctuary* (Bloomington: Indiana University Press, 1994); Nils Christie, "Conflicts as Property," *British Journal of Criminology 17* (1977): 1–15; L. Hulsman, "Critical Criminology and the Concept of Crime," *Contemporary Crises 10* (1986): 63–80.

30. Larry Tifft, foreword to *The Mask of Love*, by Dennis Sullivan (Port Washington, N.Y.: Kennikat Press, 1980), 6.

31. Christopher Cooper, "Patrol Police Officer Conflict Resolution Processes," *Journal of Criminal Justice 25* (1997): 87–101.

32. Robert Coates, Mark Umbreit, and Betty Vos, "Responding to Hate Crimes Through Restorative Justice Dialogue," *Contemporary Justice Review 9* (2006): 7–21; Kathleen Daly and Julie Stubbs, "Feminist Engagement with Restorative Justice," *Theoretical Criminology 10* (2006): 9–28.

33. This section relies heavily on Joycelyn M. Pollock, *Ethics in Crime and Justice: Dilemmas and Decisions*, 4th ed. (Belmont, Calif.: Wadsworth, 2004).

34. International Association of Chiefs of Police, 2005.

35. Alex Roth, "Story of Plea Attempt Raises Ire of Many," *San Diego Union Tribune*, September 18, 2002, p. 1; "Did Westerfield's Attorneys Mislead the Jury?" Fox News Web page, http://www.foxnews.com/story/ 0,2933,63596,00.html (accessed October 15, 2002).

36. Allen Beck and Timothy Hughes, *Prison Rape Elimination Act of 2003, Sexual Violence Reported by Correctional Authorities, 2004* (Washington, D.C.: Bureau of Justice Statistics, 2005).

Box Source Notes
Careers in Criminal Justice: Municipal Police Officer

Bureau of Labor Statistics, U.S. Department of Labor, "Police and Detectives," *Occupational Outlook Handbook, 2008–2009 Edition*, http://www.bls.gov/oco/ocos160.htm (accessed February 10, 2009).

Policies, Programs, and Issues in Criminal Justice: Due Process in Action: Sattazahn v. Pennsylvania

Sattazahn v. Pennsylvania, 537 U.S. 101 (2003).

Chapter 2,
The Nature of Crime and Victimization

1. For a general discussion of Marxist thought on criminal law, see Michael Lynch, Raymond Michalowski, and W. Byron Groves, *The New Primer in Radical Criminology: Critical Perspectives on Crime, Power, and Identity*, 3rd ed. (Monsey, N.Y.: Criminal Justice Press, 2000).

2. Howard Becker, *Outsiders, Studies in the Sociology of Deviance* (New York: Macmillan, 1963).

3. The National Council on Alcoholism and Drug Dependence, www.ncadd.org (accessed June 20, 2007).

4. Federal Bureau of Investigation, *Crime in the United States, 2005* (Washington, D.C.: Federal Bureau of Investigation, 2006), http://www.fbi.gov/ucr/05cius/. Data comes from this report, updated when possible with data from the Preliminary Crime in the United States, 2006, http://www.fbi.gov/ucr/06prelim/index .html

5. Data from the NCVS used in this chapter comes from Shannan Catalano, *Criminal Victimization 2005* (Washington, D.C.: Bureau of Justice Statistics, 2006), which is hereinafter cited as *Criminal Victimization*. www.ojp.usdoj.gov/bjs/pub/ ascii/cv05.txt

6. Michael Rand, *Criminal Victimization, 2007* (Washington, D.C.: Bureau of Justice Statistics, 2008). http://www.ojp.usdoj.gov/bjs/pub/pdf/cv07.pdf

7. You can access the Monitoring the Future data and reports at http://monitoringthefuture.org/

8. Leonore Simon, "Validity and Reliability of Violent Juveniles: A Comparison of Juvenile Self-Reports with Adult Self-Reports" (paper presented at the meeting of the American Society of Criminology, Boston, November 1995), 26.

9. Stephen Cernkovich, Peggy Giordano, and Meredith Pugh, "Chronic Offenders: The Missing Cases in Self-Report Delinquency," *Criminology 76* (1985): 705–732.

10. See, for example, Spencer Rathus and Larry Siegel, "Crime and Personality Revisited: Effects of MMPI Sets on Self-Report Studies," *Criminology 18* (1980): 245–251; John Clark and Larry Tifft, "Polygraph and Interview Validation of Self-Reported Deviant Behavior," *American Sociological Review 31* (1966): 516–523.

11. Charles Katz, Vincent Webb, and Scott Decker, "Using the Arrestee Drug Abuse Monitoring (ADAM) Program to Further Understand the Relationship Between Drug Use and Gang Membership," *Justice Quarterly 22* (2005): 58–88.

12. Mallie Paschall, Miriam Ornstein, and Robert Flewelling, "African-American Male Adolescents' Involvement in the Criminal Justice System: The Criterion Validity of Self-Report Measures in Prospective Study," *Journal of Research in Crime and Delinquency 38* (2001): 174–187.

13. Alfred Blumstein, Jacqueline Cohen, and Richard Rosenfeld, "Trend and Deviation in Crime Rates: A Comparison of UCR and NCVS Data for Burglary and Robbery," *Criminology 29* (1991): 237–248.

14. Clarence Schrag, *Crime and Justice: American Style* (Washington, D.C.: Government Printing Office, 1971), 17.

15. Thomas Bernard, "Juvenile Crime and the Transformation of Juvenile Justice: Is There a Juvenile Crime Wave?" *Justice Quarterly 16* (1999): 336–356.

16. Rand, *Criminal Victimization*, 2007.

17. United States Census Bureau, Data Set: 2005–2007, American Community Survey 3-Year Estimates, http://factfinder.census.gov/servlet/STTable?_bm=y& -geo_id=01000US&-qr_name=ACS_2007_3YR_G00 _S0101&-ds_name=ACS_2007_3YR_G00_

18. James A. Fox, *Trends in Juvenile Violence: A Report to the United States Attorney General on Current and Future Rates of Juvenile Offending* (Boston: Northeastern University, 1996).

19. Steven Levitt, "The Limited Role of Changing Age Structure in Explaining Aggregate Crime Rates," *Criminology 37* (1999): 581–599.

20. Darrell Steffensmeier and Miles Harer, "Making Sense of Recent U.S. Crime Trend Composition Effects and Other Explanations," *Journal of Research in Crime and Delinquency* 36 (1999): 235–274.

21. Freda Adler, *Sisters in Crime* (New York: McGraw-Hill, 1975); Rita James Simon, *The Contemporary Woman and Crime* (Washington, D.C.: Government Printing Office, 1975).

22. Finn-Aage Esbensen and Elizabeth Piper Deschenes, "A Multisite Examination of Youth Gang Membership: Does Gender Matter?" *Criminology* 36 (1998): 799–828.

23. Daniel Mears, Matthew Ploeger, and Mark Warr, "Explaining the Gender Gap in Delinquency: Peer Influence and Moral Evaluations of Behavior," *Journal of Research in Crime and Delinquency* 35 (1998): 251–266.

24. Crime in the United States, 2007, http://www.fbi.gov/ucr/cius2007/data/table_43.html

25. David Jacobs and Katherine Woods, "Interracial Conflict and Interracial Homicide: Do Political and Economic Rivalries Explain White Killings of Blacks and Black Killings of Whites?" *American Journal of Sociology* 105 (1999): 157–190.

26. Robert Agnew, "A General Strain Theory of Community Differences in Crime Rates," *Journal of Research in Crime and Delinquency* 36 (1999): 123–155.

27. Bonita Veysey and Steven Messner, "Further Testing of Social Disorganization Theory: An Elaboration of Sampson and Groves's Community Structure and Crime," *Journal of Research in Crime and Delinquency* 36 (1999): 156–174.

28. Judith Blau and Peter Blau, "The Cost of Inequality: Metropolitan Structure and Violent Crime," *American Sociological Review* 47 (1982): 114–129.

29. Herman Schwendinger and Julia Schwendinger, "The Paradigmatic Crisis in Delinquency Theory," *Crime and Social Justice* 18 (1982): 70–78.

30. Michael Gottfredson and Travis Hirschi, "The True Value of Lambda Would Appear to Be Zero: An Essay on Career Criminals, Criminal Careers, Selective Incapacitation, Cohort Studies and Related Topics," *Criminology* 24 (1986): 213–234. Further support for their position can be found in Lawrence Cohen and Kenneth Land, "Age Structure and Crime," *American Sociological Review* 52 (1987): 170–183.

31. Marvin Wolfgang, Robert Figlio, and Thorsten Sellin, *Delinquency in a Birth Cohort* (Chicago: University of Chicago Press, 1972).

32. Marvin Wolfgang, Terence Thornberry, and Robert Figlio, *From Boy to Man, from Delinquency to Crime* (Chicago: University of Chicago Press, 1996).

33. Kimberly Kempf-Leonard, Paul Tracy, and James Howell, "Serious, Violent, and Chronic Juvenile Offenders: The Relationship of Delinquency Career Types to Adult Criminality," *Justice Quarterly* 18 (2001): 449–478.

34. Data in this section is from Michael Rand, *Criminal Victimization, 2007* (Washington, D.C.: Bureau of Justice Statistics, 2008), http://www.ojp.usdoj.gov/bjs/pub/pdf/cv07.pdf.

35. Centers for Disease Control, "Homicide among Young Black Males—United States, 1978–1987," *Morbidity and Mortality Weekly Report* 39 (1990): 869–873.

36. Janet Lauritsen and Kenna Davis Quinet, "Repeat Victimizations among Adolescents and Young Adults," *Journal of Quantitative Criminology* 11 (1995): 143–163.

37. Denise Osborn, Dan Ellingworth, Tim Hope, and Alan Trickett, "Are Repeatedly Victimized Households Different?" *Journal of Quantitative Criminology* 12 (1996): 223–245.

38. Terry Buss and Rashid Abdu, "Repeat Victims of Violence in an Urban Trauma Center," *Violence and Victims* 10 (1995): 183–187.

39. Graham Farrell, "Predicting and Preventing Revictimization," in *Crime and Justice: An Annual Review of Research*, vol. 20, ed. Michael Tonry and David Farrington (Chicago: University of Chicago Press, 1995), 61–126.

40. Cesare Beccaria, *On Crimes and Punishments and Other Writings* (*Cambridge Texts in the History of Political Thought*), trans. Richard Bellamy (London: Cambridge University Press, 1995).

41. David A. Ward, Mark C. Stafford, and Louis N. Gray, "Rational Choice, Deterrence, and Theoretical Integration," *Journal of Applied Social Psychology* 36 (2006): 571–585.

42. Brandon C. Welsh and David P. Farrington, *Making Public Places Safer: Surveillance and Crime Prevention* (New York: Oxford University Press, 2008).

43. Stephanie Carmichael and Alex Piquero, "Deterrence and Arrest Ratios," *International Journal of Offender Therapy and Comparative Criminology* 50 (2006): 71–87.

44. Ross Matsueda, Derek Kreager, and David Huizinga, "Deterring Delinquents: A Rational Choice Model of Theft and Violence," *American Sociological Review* 71 (2006): 95–122.

45. Alicia Sitren and Brandon Applegate, "Testing the Deterrent Effects of Personal and Vicarious Experience with Punishment and Punishment Avoidance," *Deviant Behavior* 28 (2007): 29–55.

46. Andrew Klein and Terri Tobin, "A Longitudinal Study of Arrested Batterers, 1995–2005: Career Criminals" *Violence Against Women* 14 (2008): 136–157.

47. Rudy Haapanen, Lee Britton, and Tim Croisdale, "Persistent Criminality and Career Length," *Crime and Delinquency* 53 (2007): 133–155.

48. Bernard Rimland, *Dyslogic Syndrome: Why Today's Children Are "Hyper," Attention Disordered, Learning Disabled, Depressed, Aggressive, Defiant, or Violent— And What We Can Do About It* (London: Jessica Kingsley Publishers, 2008).

49. Adrian Raine, "Biosocial Studies of Antisocial and Violent Behavior in Children and Adults: A Review," *Journal of Abnormal Child Psychology* 30 (2002): 311–327.

50. Todd A. Jusko, Charles R. Henderson Jr., Bruce P. Lanphear, Deborah A. Cory-Slechta, Patrick J. Parsons, and Richard L. Canfield, "Blood Lead Concentrations <10 μg/dL and Child Intelligence

at 6 Years of Age." *Environ Health Perspectives* 116 (2008); 243–248; Joel Nigg, G. Mark Knottnerus, Michelle Martel, Molly Nikolas, Kevin Cavanagh, Wilfried Karmaus, and Marsha D. Rappley, "Low Blood Lead Levels Associated with Clinically Diagnosed Attention-Deficit/Hyperactivity Disorder and Mediated by Weak Cognitive Control," *Biological Psychiatry 63* (2008), 325–331.

51. Lauren Wakschlag, Kate Pickett, Kristen Kasza, and Rolf Loeber, "Is Prenatal Smoking Associated with a Developmental Pattern of Conduct Problems in Young Boys?" *Journal of the American Academy of Child and Adolescent Psychiatry 45* (2006): 461–467; "Diet and the Unborn Child: The Omega Point," *The Economist*, January 19, 2006.

52. Rick Nevin "Understanding International Crime Trends: The Legacy of Preschool Lead Exposure," *Environmental Research 104* (2007): 315–336.

53. Alexandra Richardson and Paul Montgomery, "The Oxford-Durham Study: A Randomized Controlled Trial of Dietary Supplementation with Fatty Acids in Children with Developmental Coordination Disorder," *Pediatrics 115* (2005): 1,360–1,366.

54. Nandini Chakrabarti and V. K. Sinha, "A Study of Serum Lipid Profile and Serum Apolipoproteins A1 and B in Indian Male Violent Criminal Offenders," *Criminal Behaviour & Mental Health 16* (2006): 177–182; Adrian Raine, Kjetil Mellingen, Jianghong Liu, Peter Venables, and Sarnoff Mednick, "Effects of Environmental Enrichment at Age Three to Five Years on Schizotypal Personality and Antisocial Behavior at Ages Seventeen and Twenty-Three Years," *American Journal of Psychiatry 160* (2003): 1–9; Gloria McVeigh, "Calming Foods," *Prevention 77* (2005).

55. F. T. Crews, A. Mdzinarishvili, D. Kim, J. He, and K. Nixon, "Neurogenesis in Adolescent Brain Is Potently Inhibited by Ethanol," *Neuroscience 137* (2006): 437–445.

56. Gail Wasserman, Xinhua Liu, Faruque Parvez, Habibul Ahsan, Diane Levy, Pam Factor-Litvak, Jennie Kline, Alexander van Geen, Vesna Slavkovich, Nancy J. Lolacono, Zhongqi Cheng, Yan Zheng, and Joseph Graziano, "Water Manganese Exposure and Children's Intellectual Function in Araihazar, Bangladesh," *Environmental Health Perspectives 114* (2006): 124–129; Eric Konofal, Michel Lecendreux, Isabelle Arnulf, and Marie-Christine Mouren, "Iron Deficiency in Children with Attention-Deficit/Hyperactivity Disorder," *Archives of Pediatric and Adolescent Medicine 158* (2004) 1,113–1,115; Eric Konofal, Samuele Cortese, Michel Lecendreux, Isabelle Arnulf, and Marie Christine Mouren, "Effectiveness of Iron Supplementation in a Young Child with Attention-Deficit/Hyperactivity Disorder," *Pediatrics 116* (2005): 732–734; Paul Stretesky and Michael Lynch, "The Relationship Between Lead Exposure and Homicide," *Archives of Pediatric Adolescent Medicine 155* (2001): 579–582.

57. Alan Booth and D. Wayne Osgood, "The Influence of Testosterone on Deviance in Adulthood: Assessing and Explaining the Relationship," *Criminology 31* (1993): 93–118.

58. Celina Cohen-Bendahan, Jan Buitelaar, Stephanie van Goozen, Jacob Orlebeke, and Peggy Cohen-Kettenis, "Is There an Effect of Prenatal Testosterone on Aggression and Other Behavioral Traits? A Study Comparing Same-Sex and Opposite-Sex Twin Girls," *Hormones and Behavior 47* (2005): 230–237; Albert Reiss and Jeffrey Roth, ed. *Understanding and Preventing Violence* (Washington, D.C.: National Academy Press, 1993), p. 118.

59. Nathaniel Pallone and James Hennessy, "Brain Dysfunction and Criminal Violence," *Society 35* (1998).

60. Adrian Raine, Monte Buchsbaum, and Lori LaCasse, "Brain Abnormalities in Murderers Indicated by Positron Emission Tomography," *Biological Psychiatry 42* (1997): 495–508.

61. Kevin Beaver, John Paul Wright, and Matthew Delisi, "Self-Control as an Executive Function: Reformulating Gottfredson and Hirschi's Parental Socialization Thesis," *Criminal Justice and Behavior 34* (2007): 1345–1361.

62. Thomas Brown, *Attention Deficit Disorder: The Unfocused Mind in Children and Adults* (New Haven, Conn.: Yale University Press, 2005).

63. Leonore Simon, "Does Criminal Offender Treatment Work?" *Applied and Preventive Psychology* (Summer 1998); Stephen Faraone et al., "Intellectual Performance and School Failure in Children with Attention Deficit Hyperactivity Disorder and in Their Siblings," *Journal of Abnormal Psychology 102* (1993): 616–623.

64. B. Hutchings and S. A. Mednick, "Criminality in Adoptees and Their Adoptive and Biological Parents: A Pilot Study," in *Biosocial Bases of Criminal Behavior*, ed. S. A. Mednick and Karl O. Christiansen (New York: Gardner Press, 1977).

65. David Rowe, "Sibling Interaction and Self-Reported Delinquent Behavior: A Study of 265 Twin Pairs," *Criminology 23* (1985): 223–240; Nancy Segal, "Monozygotic and Dizygotic Twins: A Comparative Analysis of Mental Ability Profiles," *Child Development 56* (1985): 1,051–1,058.

66. Sara Jaffee, Avshalom Caspi, Terrie Moffitt, Kenneth Dodge, Michael Rutter, Alan Taylor, and Lucy Tully, "Nature × Nurture: Genetic Vulnerabilities Interact with Physical Maltreatment to Promote Conduct Problems," *Development and Psychopathology 17* (2005): 67–84.

67. August Aichorn, *Wayward Youth* (New York: Viking Press, 1965).

68. Paige Crosby Ouimette, "Psychopathology and Sexual Aggression in Nonincarcerated Men," *Violence and Victimization 12* (1997): 389–397.

69. Robert Krueger, Avshalom Caspi, Phil Silva, and Rob McGee, "Personality Traits Are Differentially Linked to Mental Disorders: A Multitrait-Multidiagnosis Study of an Adolescent Birth Cohort," *Journal of Abnormal Psychology 105* (1996): 299–312.

70. Seymour Halleck, *Psychiatry and the Dilemmas of Crime* (Berkeley: University of California Press, 1971).

71. Eric Elbogen and Sally Johnson, "The Intricate Link Between Violence and Mental Disorder," *Archives of General Psychiatry 66* (2009): 52–161.

72. John Bowlby, "Maternal Care and Mental Health," *World Health Organization Monograph*, WHO Monographs Series No. 2 (Geneva: World Health Organization, 1951).

73. Eric Wood and Shelley Riggs, "Predictors of Child Molestation: Adult Attachment, Cognitive Distortions, and Empathy," *Journal of Interpersonal Violence 23* (2008): 259–275.

74. Karen L. Hayslett-McCall and Thomas J. Bernard, "Attachment, Masculinity, and Self-Control: A Theory of Male Crime Rates," *Theoretical Criminology 6* (2002): 5–33.

75. David Eitle and R. Jay Turner, "Exposure to Community Violence and Young Adult Crime: The Effects of Witnessing Violence, Traumatic Victimization, and Other Stressful Life Events," *Journal of Research in Crime and Delinquency 39* (2002): 214–238. See also Albert Bandura, *Aggression: A Social Learning Analysis* (Englewood Cliffs, N.J.: Prentice-Hall, 1973); Albert Bandura, *Social Learning Theory* (Englewood Cliffs, N.J.: Prentice-Hall, 1977).

76. U.S. Department of Health and Human Services, *Television and Behavior* (Washington, D.C.: Government Printing Office, 1982).

77. George Comstock, "A Sociological Perspective on Television Violence and Aggression," *American Behavioral Scientist 51* (2008): 1184–1211.

78. Tom Grimes and Lori Bergen, "The Epistemological Argument against a Causal Relationship between Media Violence and Sociopathic Behavior among Psychologically Well Viewers," *American Behavioral Scientist 51* (2008): 1137–1154.

79. John Murray, "Media Violence: The Effects Are Both Real and Strong," *American Behavioral Scientist 51* (2008): 1212–1230.

80. Elizabeth Cauffman, Laurence Steinberg, and Alex Piquero, "Psychological, Neuropsychological, and Physiological Correlates of Serious Antisocial Behavior in Adolescence: The Role of Self-Control," *Criminology 43* (2005): 133–176.

81. Shadd Maruna, "Desistance from Crime and Explanatory Style: A New Direction in the Psychology of Reform," *Journal of Contemporary Criminal Justice 20* (2004): 184–200.

82. Donald Lynam and Joshua Miller, "Personality Pathways to Impulsive Behavior and Their Relations to Deviance: Results from Three Samples," *Journal of Quantitative Criminology 20* (2004): 319–341.

83. Tony Ward and Claire Stewart, "The Relationship Between Human Needs and Criminogenic Needs," *Psychology, Crime & Law 9* (2003): 219–225.

84. David Ward, Mark Stafford, and Louis Gray, "Rational Choice, Deterrence, and Theoretical Integration," *Journal of Applied Social Psychology 36* (2006): 571–585.

85. Coralijn Nas, Bram Orobio de Castro, and Willem Koops, "Social Information Processing in Delinquent Adolescents," *Psychology, Crime & Law 11* (2005): 363–375.

86. Elizabeth Kubik and Jeffrey Hecker, "Cognitive Distortions About Sex and Sexual Offending: A Comparison of Sex Offending Girls, Delinquent Girls, and Girls from the Community," *Journal of Child Sexual Abuse 14* (2005): 43–69.

87. Vincent Marziano, Tony Ward, Anthony Beech, and Philippa Pattison, "Identification of Five Fundamental Implicit Theories Underlying Cognitive Distortions in Child Abusers: A Preliminary Study," *Psychology, Crime & Law 12* (2006): 97–105.

88. David Lykken, "Psychopathy, Sociopathy, and Crime," *Society 34* (1996): 30–38.

89. Gisli Gudjonsson, Emil Einarsson, Ólafur Örn Bragason, and Jon Fridrik Sigurdsson, "Personality Predictors of Self-Reported Offending in Icelandic Students," *Psychology, Crime & Law 12* (2006): 383–393.

90. Rolf Holmqvist, Psychopathy and Affect Consciousness in Young Criminal Offenders, *Journal of Interpersonal Violence 23* (2008): 209–224.

91. Sue Kellett and Harriet Gross, "Addicted to Joyriding? An Exploration of Young Offenders' Accounts of Their Car Crime," *Psychology, Crime & Law 12* (2006): 39–59; Peter Johansson and Margaret Kerr, "Psychopathy and Intelligence: A Second Look," *Journal of Personality Disorders 19* (2005): 357–369.

92. Lykken, "Psychopathy, Sociopathy, and Crime," 30–38.

93. Jack Levin and James Alan Fox, *Mass Murder* (New York: Plenum, 1985).

94. Spencer Rathus and Jeffrey Nevid, *Abnormal Psychology* (Englewood Cliffs, N.J.: Prentice-Hall, 1991), 310–316.

95. Ibid.

96. Samuel Yochelson and Stanton Samenow, *The Criminal Personality* (New York: Jason Aronson, 1977).

97. Andreas Hill, Niels Habermann, Wolfgang Berner, and Peer Briken, "Sexual Sadism and Sadistic Personality Disorder in Sexual Homicide, *Journal of Personality Disorders 20* (2006): 671–684.

98. See, generally, Robert Nisbet, *The Sociology of Émile Durkheim* (New York: Oxford University Press, 1974).

99. Survey conducted by the Spectrem Group, 2006, http://today.reuters.com/news/articlenews .aspx?type=businessNews&storyid=2007-04 -17T175305Z_01_N17443462_RTRUKOC_0_US -MILLIONAIRES-SURVEY.xml&src=rss& (accessed June 15, 2007).

100. U.S. Census Bureau News, "Income Climbs, Poverty Stabilizes, Uninsured Rate Increases" (2006), www.census.gov/Press-Release/www/releases/ archives/income_wealth/007419.html (accessed June 15, 2007).

101. Ralph Taylor, *Breaking Away from Broken Windows: Baltimore Neighborhoods and the Nationwide Fight Against Crime, Grime, Fear, and Decline* (Boulder, Colo.: Westview Press, 2001).

102. Lincoln Quillian and Devah Pager, "Black Neighbors, Higher Crime? The Role of Racial Stereotypes in Evaluations of Neighborhood Crime," *American Journal of Sociology 107* (2001): 717–769.

103. William Julius Wilson and Richard Taub, *There Goes the Neighborhood: Racial, Ethnic, and Class Tensions in Four Chicago Neighborhoods and Their Meaning for America* (New York: Knopf, 2006).

104. Oscar Lewis, "The Culture of Poverty," *Scientific American 215* (1966): 19–25.

105. William Julius Wilson, *The Truly Disadvantaged* (Chicago: University of Chicago Press, 1987).

106. Xu Yili, Mora Fiedler, and Karl Flaming, "Discovering the Impact of Community Policing: The Broken Windows Thesis, Collective Efficacy, and Citizens' Judgment," *Journal of Research in Crime & Delinquency 42* (2005): 147–186.

107. C. L. Storr, C.-Y. Chen, and J. C. Anthony, "'Unequal Opportunity': Neighbourhood Disadvantage and the Chance to Buy Illegal Drugs," *Journal of Epidemiology & Community Health 58* (2004): 231–238.

108. Rebekah Levine Coley, Jodi Eileen Morris, and Daphne Hernandez, "Out-of-School Care and Problem Behavior Trajectories Among Low-Income Adolescents: Individual, Family, and Neighborhood Characteristics as Added Risks," *Child Development 75* (2004): 948–965.

109. Stacy De Coster, Karen Heimer, and Stacy Wittrock, "Neighborhood Disadvantage, Social Capital, Street Context, and Youth Violence," *Sociological Quarterly* (2006): 723–753.

110. Ibid.

111. Justin Patchin, Beth Huebner, John McCluskey, Sean Varano, and Timothy Bynum, "Exposure to Community Violence and Childhood Delinquency," *Crime & Delinquency 52* (2006): 307–332.

112. Catherine E. Ross, John Mirowsky, and Shana Pribesh, "Powerlessness and the Amplification of Threat: Neighborhood Disadvantage, Disorder, and Mistrust," *American Sociological Review 66* (2001): 568–580.

113. Michael Reisig and Jeffrey Michael Cancino, "Incivilities in Nonmetropolitan Communities: The Effects of Structural Constraints, Social Conditions, and Crime," *Journal of Criminal Justice 32* (2004): 15–29.

114. Steven Messner, Eric Baumer, and Richard Rosenfeld, "Dimensions of Social Capital and Rates of Criminal Homicide," *American Sociological Review 69* (2004): 882–903.

115. Paul Bellair, "Informal Surveillance and Street Crime: A Complex Relationship," *Criminology 38* (2000): 137–170.

116. Patrick Sharkey, "Navigating Dangerous Streets: The Sources and Consequences of Street Efficacy," *American Sociological Review 71* (2006): 826–846.

117. Ibid.

118. Ronald Simons, Yi Fu Chen, and Eric Stewart, "Incidents of Discrimination and Risk for Delinquency: A Longitudinal Test of Strain Theory with an African American Sample," *Justice Quarterly 20* (2003): 827–854.

119. Lisa Mufti, "Advancing Institutional Anomie Theory," *International Journal of Offender Therapy & Comparative Criminology 50* (2006): 630–653.

120. Ibid.

121. Joseph Rankin and L. Edward Wells, "The Effect of Parental Attachments and Direct Controls on Delinquency," *Journal of Research in Crime and Delinquency 27* (1990): 140–165.

122. John Paul Wright and Francis Cullen, "Parental Efficacy and Delinquent Behavior: Do Control and Support Matter?" *Criminology 39* (2001): 677–706.

123. Carter Hay, "Parenting, Self-Control, and Delinquency: A Test of Self-Control Theory," *Criminology 39* (2001): 707–736.

124. Eugene Maguin and Rolf Loeber, "Academic Performance and Delinquency," *Crime and Justice: An Annual Review of Research*, vol. 20, ed. Michael Tonry and David Farrington (Chicago: University of Chicago Press, 1996), 145–264.

125. David Fergusson, Nicola Swain-Campbell, and L. John Horwood, "Deviant Peer Affiliations, Crime, and Substance Use: A Fixed Effects Regression Analysis," *Journal of Abnormal Child Psychology 30* (2002): 419–431.

126. Karl Marx and Friedrich Engels, *Capital: A Critique of Political Economy*, trans. E. Aveling (Chicago: Charles Kern, 1906); Karl Marx, *Selected Writings in Sociology and Social Philosophy*, trans. P. B. Bottomore (New York: McGraw-Hill, 1956). For a general discussion of Marxist thought, see Michael Lynch and W. Byron Groves, *A Primer in Radical Criminology* (New York: Harrow and Heston, 1986), 6–26.

127. W. Byron Groves and Robert Sampson, "Critical Theory and Criminology," *Social Problems 33* (1986): 58–80.

128. Susan Ehrlich Martin and Nancy Jurik, *Doing Justice, Doing Gender* (Thousand Oaks, Calif.: Sage, 1996).

129. For a general review of this issue, see Sally Simpson, "Feminist Theory, Crime, and Justice," *Criminology 27* (1989): 605–632; James Messerschmidt, *Capitalism, Patriarchy, and Crime* (Totowa, N.J.: Rowman & Littlefield, 1986).

130. See, generally, Sheldon Glueck and Eleanor Glueck, *500 Criminal Careers* (New York: Knopf, 1930); Sheldon Glueck and Eleanor Glueck, *One Thousand Juvenile Delinquents* (Cambridge, Mass.: Harvard University Press, 1934); Sheldon Glueck and Eleanor Glueck, *Predicting Delinquency and Crime* (Cambridge, Mass.: Harvard University Press, 1967), 82–83.

131. Sheldon Glueck and Eleanor Glueck, *Unraveling Juvenile Delinquency* (Cambridge, Mass.: Harvard University Press, 1950).

132. Marvin Krohn, Alan Lizotte, and Cynthia Perez, "The Interrelationship Between Substance Use and Precocious Transitions to Adult Sexuality," *Journal of Health and Social Behavior 38* (1997): 88.

133. Norman White and Rolf Loeber. "Bullying and Special Education as Predictors of serious delinquency," *Journal of Research in Crime and Delinquency 45* (2008): 380–397.

134. G. R. Patterson, Barbara DeBaryshe, and Elizabeth Ramsey, "A Developmental Perspective on Antisocial Behavior," *American Psychologist 44* (1989): 329–335.

135. Michael Gottfredson and Travis Hirschi, *A General Theory of Crime* (Palo Alto, Calif.: Stanford University Press, 1990).

136. Jean McGloin and Lauren Shermer, "Self-Control and Deviant Peer Network Structure," *Journal of Research in Crime and Delinquency 46* (2009): 35–72.

137. Alex R. Piquero and He Len Chung, "On the Relationships Between Gender, Early Onset, and the Seriousness of Offending," *Journal of Criminal Justice 29* (2001): 189–206.

138. Rolf Loeber and David Farrington, "Young Children Who Commit Crime: Epidemiology, Developmental Origins, Risk Factors, Early Interventions, and Policy Implications," *Development and Psychopathology 12* (2000): 737–762.

139. Kevin Beaver, Matt Delisi, Michael Vaughn, John Paul Wright, and Brian Boutwell, "The Relationship Between Self-Control and Language: Evidence of a Shared Etiological Pathway," *Criminology 46* (2008): 939–970.

Box Source Notes
International Justice:
Crime Trends around the World

Chris Kershaw, Sian Nicholas, and Alison Walker, *Crime in England and Wales, 2007/2008 Findings from the British Crime Survey and Police Recorded Crime*, http://news.bbc.co.uk/1/shared/bsp/hi/pdfs/17_07_08_crime_statistics_200708.pdf James Finckenauer and Ko-lin Chin, "Asian Transnational Organized Crime and Its Impact on the United States" (Washington, D.C.: National Institute of Justice, 2007); Zhu Zhe, "Nationwide Crime Rate Shows Drop," *China Daily News* 1/20/2006, www.chinadaily.com.cn/english/doc/2006-01/20/content_513862.htm (accessed June 15, 2007); U.S. Government Interagency Working Group, "International Crime Threat Assessment," www.fas.org/irp/threat/pub45270index.html (accessed April 25, 2007); Mauro Marescialli, Crime in China: Some Statistics, Danwei Organization, www.danwei.org/ip_and_law/crime_in_china_some_statistics.php; Dag Leonardsen, "Crime in Japan: Paradise Lost?" *Journal of Scandinavian Studies in Criminology & Crime Prevention* 7 (2006): 185–210; Karen Joe Laidler, "The Rise of Club Drugs in a Heroin Society: The Case of Hong Kong," *Substance Use & Misuse 40* (2005): 1,257–1,279; Virendra Kumar and Sarita Kanth, "Bride Burning," *Lancet 364* (2004): 18–19; David P. Farrington, Patrick A. Langan, and Michael Tonry, *Cross-National Studies in Crime and Justice* (Washington, D.C.: Bureau of Justice Statistics, 2004); Pedro Scuro, *World Factbook of Criminal Justice Systems: Brazil* (Washington, D.C.: Bureau of Justice Statistics, 2003).

Careers in Criminal Justice: Criminologist

Bureau of Labor Sttistics, U.S. Department of Labor, "Social Scientists, Other," *Occupational Outlook Handbook, 2008–2009 Edition*, www.bls.gov/oco/ocos054.htm (accessed February 15, 2009); J. Pope, "Report: Some College Faculty Salaries Rise," *Associated Press Online Domestic News*; "Princeton Review Career Profiles: Criminologist," www.princetonreview.com/cte/profiles/dayInLife.asp?careerID=47 (accessed February 15, 2009).

Chapter 3,
Criminal Law: Substance and Procedure

1. See John Weaver, *Warren—The Man, the Court, the Era* (Boston: Little, Brown, 1967); see also "We the People," *Time*, July 6, 1987, 6.

2. *Kansas v. Hendricks*, 117 S. Ct. 2072 (1997); *Chicago v. Morales*, 119 S. Ct. 246 (1999).

3. *City of Chicago v. Morales et al.* 527 U.S. 41 (1999).

4. Daniel Suleiman, "The Capital Punishment Exception: A Case for Constitutionalizing the Substantive Criminal Law," *Columbia Law Review 104* (2004): 426–458.

5. *Calder v. Bull*, 3 U.S. 386 (1798).

6. See, for example, General Laws of Massachusetts, Part II: Real and Personal Property and Domestic Relations. Title III. Domestic Relations, Section 209 (June 30, 2002).

7. Sheldon Krantz, *Law of Corrections and Prisoners' Rights, Cases and Materials*, 3d ed. (St. Paul, Minn.: West, 1986), 702; Barbara Knight and Stephen Early Jr., *Prisoners' Rights in America* (Chicago: Nelson-Hall, 1986), chapter 1; see also Fred Cohen, "The Law of Prisoners' Rights—An Overview," *Criminal Law Bulletin 24* (188): 321–349.

8. See *United States v. Balint*, 258 U.S. 250, 42 S. Ct. 301, 66 L.Ed. 604 (1922); see also *Morissette v. United States*, 342 U.S. 246, 72 S. Ct. 240, 96 L.Ed. 288 (1952).

9. New York State Consolidated Laws, Article 270: Other Offenses Relating to Public Safety, Section 270.10: Creating a hazard (2002).

10. *Regina v. Dudley and Stephens*, 14 Q.B.D. 273 (1884).

11. For a history and analysis of these types of defenses, see Eugene Milhizer, "Justification and Excuse: What They Were, What They Are, and What They Ought to Be," *St. John's Law Review 78* (2004): 725–895.

12. William Blackstone, *Commentaries on the Law of England* vol. 1, ed. Thomas Cooley (Chicago: Callaghan, 1899), 4, 26. Blackstone was an English barrister who lectured on the English common law at Oxford University in 1753.

13. Henry Fradella, *From Insanity to Diminished Capacity: Mental Illness and Criminal Defenses of Excuse in Contemporary American Law* (Bethesda, Md.: Academic Press, 2007).

14. Samuel M. Davis, *Rights of Juveniles: The Juvenile Justice System* (New York: Boardman, 1974; updated 1993), chapter 2; Larry Siegel and Joseph Senna, *Juvenile Delinquency: Theory, Practice, and Law* (St. Paul, Minn.: West, 1996).

15. N.A. Criminal Law—Mutual Combat Mitigation—Appellate Court of Illinois Holds That Disproportionate Reaction to Provocation Negates Mutual Combat Mitigation—*People v. Thompson*, 821 N.E. 2d 664 (Ii. App. Ct. 2004), *Harvard Law Review 118* (2005): 2,437–2,444.

16. Florida Statutes, Home protection; use of deadly force; presumption of fear of death or great bodily harm, www.leg.state.fl.us/statutes/index.cfm? App_mode=Display_Statute&Search_String =&URL=Ch0776/SEC013.HTM&Title=->2005-> Ch0776->Section%20013#0776.013 (accessed February 15, 2009).

17. Patrik Jonsson, "Is Self-Defense Law Vigilante Justice? Some Say Proposed Laws Can Help Deter Gun Violence. Others Worry About Deadly Confrontations," *Christian Science Monitor*, February 24, 2006.

18. 356 U.S. 369, 78 S.Ct. 819, 2 L.Ed.2d 848 (1958); see also *Jacobson v. United States*, 503 U.S. 540, 112 S. Ct. 1535, 118 L.Ed.2d 174 (1992).

19. Matthew Lyon, "No Means No?: Withdrawal of Consent During Intercourse and the Continuing Evolution of the Definition of Rape. By: R." *Journal of Criminal Law & Criminology* 95 (2004): 277–314.

20. *Lawrence et al. v. Texas*, No. 02–102, June 26, 2003.

21. Marvin Zalman, John Strate, Denis Hunter, and James Sellars, "Michigan Assisted Suicide Three Ring Circus: The Intersection of Law and Politics," *Ohio Northern Law Review* 23 (1997): 230–276.

22. 1992 P.A. 270 as amended by 1993 P.A.3, M.C. L. ss. 752.1021 to 752. 1027.

23. *Michigan Code of Criminal Procedure*, Assisting a Suicide, Section 750.329a.

24. National Institute of Justice, *Project to Develop a Model Anti-stalking Statute* (Washington, D.C.: National Institute of Justice, 1994).

25. Environmental Protection Agency, Criminal Enforcement Division www.epa.gov/compliance/ criminal/index.html, accessed on May 8, 2005.

26. Jeffrey Rosen, "The Brain on the Stand," *New York Times*, March 11, 2007, http://www.nytimes. com/2007/03/11/magazine/11Neurolaw.t.html? _r=2&oref=slogin.

27. Ken Strutin, "Neurolaw and Criminal Justice," *Law and Technology Resources for Legal Professionals*, December 28, 2008.

28. 384 U.S. 436, 86 S. Ct. 1602, 16 L.Ed.2d 694 (1966).

29. Daniel Suleiman, "The Capital Punishment Exception: A Case for Constitutionalizing the Substantive Criminal Law," *Columbia Law Review* 104 (2004): 426–458.

30. *Baze and Bowling v. Rees*, 553 U.S. (2008).

31. See "Essay," *Time*, February 26, 1973, 95; also, for a tribute to the Bill of Rights and due process, see James MacGregor Burns and Steward Burns, *The Pursuit of Rights in America* (New York: Knopf, 1991).

32. 342 U.S. 165, 72 S. Ct. 205, 95 L.Ed. 183 (1952).

33. *Herring v. U.S.*

Box Source Notes
Careers in Criminal Justice: Attorney

"Lawyers, *Occupational Outlook Handbook, 2008–2009 Edition* (Bureau of Labor Statistics, U.S. Department of Labor), http://www.bls.gov/oco/ocos053.htm (accessed February 18, 2009); "Princeton Review Career Profiles: Attorney," www.princetonreview.com/cte/profiles/ dayInLife.asp?careerID=149 (accessed February 15, 2009).

Policies, Programs, and Issues in Criminal Justice: Gun Control and the Constitution

District of Columbia v. Heller, 554 U.S. (2008); E. R Vigdor and J. A. Mercy, "Do Laws Restricting Access to Firearms by Domestic Violence Offenders Prevent Intimate Partner Homicide?" *Evaluation Review* 30 (2006): 313–346; Gary Kleck and Jongyeon Tark, "Resisting Crime: The Effects of Victim Action on the Outcomes of Crimes," *Criminology* 42 (2005): 861–909; Robert Martin and Richard Legault, "Systematic Measurement Error with State-Level Crime Data: Evidence from the 'More Guns, Less Crime' Debate," *Journal of Research in Crime and Delinquency* 42 (2005): 187–210; Tomislav Kovandzic, Thomas Marvell, and Lynne Vieraitis, "The Impact of 'Shall-Issue' Concealed Handgun Laws on Violent Crime Rates: Evidence from Panel Data for Large Urban Cities," *Homicide Studies* 9 (2005): 292–323; Brady Handgun Violence Prevention Act, Pub. L. No. 103–159, 107 Stat. 1536 (November 30, 1993), codified at 18 U.S.C. § 921 et seq.

Chapter 4,
Police in Society: History and Organization

1. This section relies heavily on such sources as Malcolm Sparrow, Mark Moore, and David Kennedy, *Beyond 911: A New Era for Policing* (New York: Basic Books, 1990); Daniel Devlin, *Police Procedure, Administration, and Organization* (London: Butterworth, 1966); Robert Fogelson, *Big City Police* (Cambridge, Mass.: Harvard University Press, 1977); Roger Lane, *Policing the City, Boston 1822–1885* (Cambridge, Mass.: Harvard University Press, 1967); J. J. Tobias, *Crime and Industrial Society in the Nineteenth Century* (New York: Schocken Books, 1967); Samuel Walker, *A Critical History of Police Reform: The Emergence of Professionalism* (Lexington, Mass.: Lexington Books, 1977); Samuel Walker, *Popular Justice* (New York: Oxford University Press, 1980); John McMullan, "The New Improved Monied Police: Reform Crime Control and Commodification of Policing in London," *British Journal of Criminology* 36 (1996): 85–108.

2. Devlin, *Police Procedure, Administration, and Organization*, 3.

3. McMullan, "The New Improved Monied Police," 92.

4. Elizabeth Joh, "The Paradox of Private Policing," *Journal of Criminal Law & Criminology* 95 (2004): 49–132.

5. Wilbur Miller, "The Good, the Bad & the Ugly: Policing America," *History Today* 50 (2000): 29–32.

6. Phillip Reichel, "Southern Slave Patrols as a Transitional Type," *American Journal of Police* 7 (1988): 51–78.

7. Walker, *Popular Justice*, 61.

8. Christopher Thale, "Assigned to Patrol: Neighborhoods, Police, and Changing Deployment Practices in New York City Before 1930," *Journal of Social History 37* (2004): 1037–1064.

9. Ibid., 8.

10. Dennis Rousey, "Cops and Guns: Police Use of Deadly Force in Nineteenth-Century New Orleans," *American Journal of Legal History 28* (1984): 41–66.

11. Law Enforcement Assistance Administration, *Two Hundred Years of American Criminal Justice* (Washington, D.C.: Government Printing Office, 1976).

12. National Commission on Law Observance and Enforcement, *Report on the Police* (Washington, D.C.: Government Printing Office, 1931), 5–7.

13. Pamela Irving Jackson, *Minority Group Threat, Crime, and Policing* (New York: Praeger, 1989).

14. James Q. Wilson and George Kelling, "Broken Windows," *Atlantic Monthly 249* (1982): 29–38.

15. Frank Tippett, "It Looks Just Like a War Zone," *Time*, May 27, 1985, 16–22; "San Francisco, New York Police Troubled by Series of Scandals," *Criminal Justice Newsletter 16* (1985): 2–4; Karen Polk, "New York Police: Caught in the Middle and Losing Faith," *Boston Globe*, December 28, 1988, 3.

16. Staff of the *Los Angeles Times*, "Understanding the Riots: Los Angeles Before and After the Rodney King Case" (Los Angeles: *Los Angeles Times*, 1992).

17. David H. Bayley, "Policing in America," *Society 36* (December 1998).

18. Ronald Burns, Keith Whitworth, and Carol Thompson, "Assessing Law Enforcement Preparedness to Address Internet Fraud," *Journal of Criminal Justice 32* (2004): 477–493.

19. Edward R. Maguire, "Counting Cops: Estimating the Number of Police Departments and Police Officers in the USA," *Policing: An International Journal of Police Strategies and Management 21* (1998): 97–120.

20. Bruce Smith, *Police Systems in the United States* (New York: Harper & Row, 1960).

21. Brian Reaves and Matthew Hickman, *Census of State and Local Law Enforcement Agencies, 2000* (Washington, D.C.: Bureau of Justice Statistics, 2002).

22. Matthew Hickman and Brian Reaves, *Local Police Departments, 2003* (Washington, D.C.: Bureau of Justice Statistics, 2006).

23. Data in this section comes from Reaves and Hickman, *Census of State and Local Law Enforcement Agencies, 2000*.

24. Matthew Hickman and Brian Reaves, *Local Police Departments, 2003* (Washington, D.C.: Bureau of Justice Statistics, 2006).

25. See, for example, Robert Keppel and Joseph Weis, *Improving the Investigation of Violent Crime: The Homicide Investigation and Tracking System* (Washington, D.C.: National Institute of Justice, 1993).

26. Elizabeth E. Joh, "The Paradox of Private Policing," *Journal of Criminal Law and Criminology 95* (2004): 49–131.

27. Larry Coutorie, "The Future of High-Technology Crime: A Parallel Delphi Study," *Journal of Criminal Justice 23* (1995): 13–27.

28. This section is based on Derek Paulsen, "To Map or Not to Map: Assessing the Impact of Crime Maps on Police Officer Perceptions of Crime," *International Journal of Police Science & Management 6* (2004): 234–246; William W. Bratton and Peter Knobler, *Turnaround: How America's Top Cop Reversed the Crime Epidemic* (New York: Random House, 1998), 289; Jeremy Travis, "Computerized Crime Mapping," *NIJ News* (National Institute of Justice), January 1999.

29. Arthur Gordon and Ross Wolf, "License Plate Recognition Technology Innovation in Law Enforcement Use," *FBI Law Enforcement Bulletin 76* (2007), http://www.fbi.gov/publications/leb/2007/march07leb.pdf (accessed February 16, 2009).

30. "Spotlight on Computer Imaging," *Police Chief 66* (1999): 6–8.

31. See, generally, Laura Moriarty and David Carter, *Criminal Justice Technology in the Twenty-First Century* (Springfield, Ill.: Charles C Thomas, 1998).

32. Weipeng Zhang, Yan Yuan Tang, and Xinge You, "Fingerprint Enhancement Using Wavelet Transform Combined with Gabor Filter," *International Journal of Pattern Recognition & Artificial Intelligence 18* (2004): 1391–1406.

33. "LEO's National Dental Image Repository" *FBI Law Enforcement Bulletin 76* (2007), http://www.fbi.gov/publications/leb/2007/feb07leb.pdf (accessed February 16, 2009).

34. See, generally, Ryan McDonald, "Juries and Crime Labs: Correcting the Weak Links in the DNA Chain," *American Journal of Law and Medicine 24* (1998): 345–363; "DNA Profiling Advancement," *FBI Law Enforcement Bulletin 67* (1998): 24.

35. Ronald Reinstein, *Postconviction DNA Testing: Recommendations for Handling Requests* (Philadelphia: Diane Publishing Co., 1999).

36. "California Attorney General Endorses DNA Fingerprinting," *Criminal Justice Newsletter 1* (1989): 1.

37. *State v. Ford*, 301 S.C. 485, 392 S.E.2d 781 (1990).

38. "Under New Policy, FBI Examiners Testify to Absolute DNA Matches," *Criminal Justice Newsletter 28* (1997): 1–2.

39. "FBI's DNA Profile Clearinghouse Announce First 'Cold Hit,'" *Criminal Justice Newsletter 16* (1999): 5.

40. "South Side Strangler's Execution Cited as DNA Evidence Landmark," *Criminal Justice Newsletter 2* (1994): 3.

41. Elizabeth Joh, "Discretionless Policing: Technology and the Fourth Amendment," *California Law Review 95* (2007): 199–234.

42. Thomas Cowper, "Improving the View of the World Law Enforcement and Augmented Reality Technology," *FBI Law Enforcement Bulletin 74* (2004): 11–14.

43. "Facial AFIS Launched by Identix," *Biometric Technology Today 11* (2003): 4.

44. Ray Surette, "The Thinking Eye: Pros and Cons of Second-Generation CCTV Surveillance Systems," *Policing: An International Journal of Police Strategies and Management 28* (2005): 152–173.

Box Source Notes
Careers in Criminal Justice: Border Patrol Agent

http://www.cbp.gov/xp/cgov/careers/ (accessed June 10, 2009).

Criminal Justice and Technology: Crime Scene Investigation

Raymond E. Foster, "Crime Scene Investigation," *Government Technology* (March 2005), www.govtech.net/magazine/story.php?id=93225&issue=3:2005 (accessed June 17, 2005).

Chapter 5,
The Police: Role and Function

1. Brian Payne, Bruce Berg, and Ivan Sun, "Policing in Small Town America: Dogs, Drunks, Disorder, and Dysfunction," *Journal of Criminal Justice 33* (2005): 31–41.
2. Stacey Nofziger and Susan Williams, "Perceptions of Police and Safety in a Small Town" *Police Quarterly 8* (2005): 248–270.
3. James Willis, Stephen Mastrofski, and David Weisburd, "Making Sense of COMPSTAT: A Theory-Based Analysis of Organizational Change in Three Police Departments," *Law & Society Review 41* (2007): 147–188.
4. Matthew Durose and Patrick Langan, *Contacts Between Police and the Public, Findings from the 2005 National Survey* (Washington, D.C.: Bureau of Justice Statistics, 2007).
5. Brian A. Reaves and Pheny Smith, *Law Enforcement Management and Administrative Statistics, 1993: Data for Individual State and Local Agencies with 100 or More Officers* (Washington, D.C.: Bureau of Justice Statistics, 1995).
6. American Bar Association, *Standards Relating to Urban Police Function* (New York: Institute of Judicial Administration, 1974), standard 2.2.
7. Albert J. Reiss, *The Police and the Public* (New Haven, Conn.: Yale University Press, 1971), 19.
8. James Q. Wilson, *Varieties of Police Behavior: The Management of Law and Order in Eight Communities* (Cambridge, Mass.: Harvard University Press, 1968).
9. George Kelling, Tony Pate, Duane Dieckman, and Charles Brown, *The Kansas City Preventive Patrol Experiment: A Summary Report* (Washington, D.C.: Police Foundation, 1974).
10. Thomas Marvell and Carlysle Moody, "Specification Problems, Police Levels, and Crime Rates," *Criminology 34* (1996): 609–646; Colin Loftin and David McDowall, "The Police, Crime, and Economic

Theory: An Assessment," *American Sociological Review 47* (1982): 393–401.
11. For a thorough review of this literature, see John L. Worrall, "The Effects of Policing on Crime: What Have We Learned?" in R. Dunham and G. Alpert (eds.), *Critical Issues in Policing*, 6th ed. (Long Grove, IL: Waveland, 2009).
12. James Q. Wilson and Barbara Boland, "The Effect of Police on Crime," *Law and Society Review 12* (1978): 367–384.
13. Robert Sampson, "Deterrent Effects of the Police on Crime: A Replication and Theoretical Extension," *Law and Society Review 22* (1988): 163–191.
14. Richard Timothy Coupe and Laurence Blake, "The Effects of Patrol Workloads and Response Strength on Arrests at Burglary Emergencies," *Journal of Criminal Justice 33* (2005): 239–255.
15. Lawrence Sherman, James Shaw, and Dennis Rogan, *The Kansas City Gun Experiment* (Washington, D.C.: National Institute of Justice, 1994).
16. For a thorough review of this issue, see Andrew Karmen, *Why Is New York City's Murder Rate Dropping So Sharply?* (New York: John Jay College, 1996).
17. Robert Davis, Pedro Mateu-Gelabert, and Joel Miller, "Can Effective Policing Also Be Respectful? Two Examples in the South Bronx," *Police Quarterly 8* (2005): 229–247.
18. Mitchell Chamlin, "Crime and Arrests: An Autoregressive Integrated Moving Average (ARIMA) Approach," *Journal of Quantitative Criminology 4* (1988): 247–255.
19. Stewart D'Alessio and Lisa Stolzenberg, "Crime, Arrests, and Pretrial Jail Incarceration: An Examination of the Deterrence Thesis," *Criminology 36* (1998): 735–761.
20. Perry Shapiro and Harold Votey, "Deterrence and Subjective Probabilities of Arrest: Modeling Individual Decisions to Drink and Drive in Sweden," *Law and Society Review 18* (1984): 111–149.
21. William Spelman and Dale K. William, *Calling the Police: A Replication of the Citizen Reporting Component of the Kansas City Response Time Analysis* (Washington, D.C.: Police Foundation, 1976).
22. George Kelling and James Q. Wilson, "Broken Windows: The Police and Neighborhood Safety," *Atlantic Monthly 249* (1982): 29–38.
23. Catherine Coles and George Kelling, *Fixing Broken Windows: Restoring Order and Reducing Crime in Our Communities* (New York: Free Press, 1998).
24. Anthony A. Braga and Brenda J. Bond, "Policing Crime and Disorder Hot Spots: A Randomized Controlled Trial," *Criminology 46* (2008): 577–606.
25. Vincent Henry, *The Compstat Paradigm: Management Accountability in Policing, Business and the Public Sector* (New York: Looseleaf Law Publications, 2002).
26. See Belton Cobb, *The First Detectives* (London: Faber & Faber, 1957).
27. For a view of the modern detective, see William Sanders, *Detective Work: A Study of Criminal Investigations* (New York: Free Press, 1977).

28. Mark Pogrebin and Eric Poole, "Vice Isn't Nice: A Look at the Effects of Working Undercover," *Journal of Criminal Justice 21* (1993): 385–396; Gary Marx, *Undercover: Police Surveillance in America* (Berkeley: University of California Press, 1988).

29. Martin Innes, *Investigating Murder: Detective Work and the Police Response to Criminal Homicide* (Clarendon Studies in Criminology) (London: Oxford University Press, 2003).

30. John B. Edwards, "Homicide Investigative Strategies," *FBI Law Enforcement Bulletin 74* (2005): 11–21.

31. Robert Langworthy, "Do Stings Control Crime? An Evaluation of a Police Fencing Operation," *Justice Quarterly 6* (1989): 27–45.

32. Mary Dodge, Donna Starr-Gimeno, and Thomas Williams, "Puttin' on the Sting: Women Police Officers' Perspectives on Reverse Prostitution Assignment," *International Journal of Police Science & Management 7* (2005): 71–85.

33. Peter Greenwood and Joan Petersilia, *Summary and Policy Implications*, vol. 1, *The Criminal Investigation Process* (Santa Monica, Calif.: Rand, 1975).

34. Mark Willman and John Snortum, "Detective Work: The Criminal Investigation Process in a Medium-Size Police Department," *Criminal Justice Review 9* (1984): 33–39.

35. Janice Puckett and Richard Lundman, "Factors Affecting Homicide Clearances: Multivariate Analysis of a More Complete Conceptual Framework," *Journal of Research in Crime & Delinquency 40* (2003): 171–194.

36. Police Executive Research Forum, *Calling the Police: Citizen Reporting of Serious Crime* (Washington, D.C.: Police Executive Research Forum, 1981).

37. John Eck, *Solving Crimes: The Investigation of Burglary and Robbery* (Washington, D.C.: Police Executive Research Forum, 1984).

38. A. Fischer, "CopLink Nabs Criminals Faster," *Arizona Daily Star*, January 7, 2001; A. Robbins, *PC Magazine 22* (2003); M. Sink, "An Electronic Cop That Plays Hunches," *New York Times*, November 2, 2002.

39. Paul Johnson and Robin Williams, "Internationalizing New Technologies of Crime Control: Forensic DNA Databasing and Datasharing in the European Union," *Policing & Society 17* (2007): 103–118.

40. For a general review, see Robert Trojanowicz and Bonnie Bucqueroux, *Community Policing: A Contemporary Perspective* (Cincinnati, Ohio: Anderson, 1990).

41. Police Foundation, *The Newark Foot Patrol Experiment* (Washington, D.C.: Police Foundation, 1981).

42. John Worrall and Jihong Zhao. "The Role of the COPS Office in Community Policing," *Policing: An International Journal of Police Strategies & Management 26* (2003), 64–87.

43. Jihong Zhao, Nicholas Lovrich, and Quint Thurman, "The Status of Community Policing in American Cities," *Policing 22* (1999): 74–92.

44. Albert Cardarelli, Jack McDevitt, and Katrina Baum, "The Rhetoric and Reality of Community Policing in Small and Medium-Sized Cities and Towns," *Policing 21* (1998): 397–415.

45. Brian Renauer, "Reducing Fear of Crime," *Police Quarterly 10* (2007): 41–62.

46. Susan Sadd and Randolph Grinc, *Implementation Challenges in Community Policing* (Washington, D.C.: National Institute of Justice, 1996).

47. Donald Green, Dara Strolovitch, and Janelle Wong, "Defended Neighborhoods: Integration and Racially Motivated Crime," *American Journal of Sociology 104* (1998): 372–403.

48. Robin Shepard Engel, *How Police Supervisory Styles Influence Patrol Officer Behavior* (Washington, D.C.: National Institute of Justice, 2003).

49. Amy Halsted, Max Bromley, and John Cochran, "The Effects of Work Orientations on Job Satisfaction Among Sheriffs' Deputies Practicing Community-Oriented Policing," *Policing: An International Journal of Police Strategies & Management 23* (2000): 82–104.

50. Venessa Garcia, "Constructing the 'Other' Within Police Culture: An Analysis of a Deviant Unit Within the Police Organization," *Police Practice and Research 6* (2005): 65–80.

51. Kevin Ford, Daniel Weissbein, and Kevin Plamondon, "Distinguishing Organizational from Strategy Commitment: Linking Officers' Commitment to Community Policing to Job Behaviors and Satisfaction," *Justice Quarterly 20* (2003): 159–186.

52. Michael Palmiotto, Michael Birzer, and N. Prabha Unnithan, "Training in Community Policing: A Suggested Curriculum," *Policing: An International Journal of Police Strategies & Management 23* (2000): 8–21.

53. Lisa Riechers and Roy Roberg, "Community Policing: A Critical Review of Underlying Assumptions," *Journal of Police Science and Administration 17* (1990): 112–113.

54. Yili Xu, Mora Fiedler, and Karl Flaming, "Discovering the Impact of Community Policing: The Broken Windows Thesis, Collective Efficacy, and Citizens' Judgment," *Journal of Research in Crime and Delinquency 42* (2005): 147–186.

55. Ling Ren, Liqun Cao, Nicholas Lovrich, and Michael Gaffney, "Linking Confidence in the Police with the Performance of the Police: Community Policing Can Make a Difference," *Journal of Criminal Justice 33* (January/February 2005): 55–66.

56. Jihong Zhao, Ni He, and Nicholas Lovrich, "Value Change Among Police Officers at a Time of Organizational Reform: A Follow-up Study of Rokeach Values," *Policing 22* (1999): 152–170.

57. Herman Goldstein, "Improving Policing: A Problem-Oriented Approach," *Crime and Delinquency 25* (1979): 236–258.

58. Jerome Skolnick and David Bayley, *Community Policing: Issues and Practices Around the World* (Washington, D.C.: National Institute of Justice, 1988), 12.

59. Lawrence Sherman, Patrick Gartin, and Michael Buerger, "Hot Spots of Predatory Crime: Routine

Activities and the Criminology of Place," *Criminology* 27 (1989): 27–55.

60. Ibid., 45.

61. Dennis Roncek and Pamela Maier, "Bars, Blocks, and Crimes Revisited: Linking the Theory of Routine Activities to the Empiricism of 'Hot Spots,'" *Criminology* 29 (1991): 725–753.

62. Sherry Plaster Carter, Stanley Carter, and Andrew Dannenberg, "Zoning Out Crime and Improving Community Health in Sarasota, Florida: 'Crime Prevention Through Environmental Design,'" *American Journal of Public Health* 93 (2003): 1442–1445.

63. Anthony Braga, David Kennedy, Elin Waring, and Anne Morrison Piehl, "Problem-Oriented Policing, Deterrence, and Youth Violence: An Evaluation of Boston's Operation Ceasefire," *Journal of Research in Crime and Delinquency* 38 (2001): 195–225.

64. Bureau of Justice Assistance, *Problem-Oriented Drug Enforcement: A Community-Based Approach for Effective Policing* (Washington, D.C.: National Institute of Justice, 1993).

65. Ibid., 64–65.

66. William Doerner and Terry Nowell, "The Reliability of the Behavioral-Personnel Assessment Device (BPAD) in Selecting Police Recruits," *Policing* 22 (1999): 343–352.

67. See, for example, Richard Larson, *Urban Police Patrol Analysis* (Cambridge, Mass.: MIT Press, 1972).

68. Brian A. Reaves, *State and Local Police Departments, 1990* (Washington, D.C.: Bureau of Justice Statistics, 1992), 6.

69. Philip Ash, Karen Slora, and Cynthia Britton, "Police Agency Officer Selection Practices," *Journal of Police Science and Administration* 17 (1990): 258–269.

70. Dennis Rosenbaum, Robert Flewelling, Susan Bailey, Chris Ringwalt, and Deanna Wilkinson, "Cops in the Classroom: A Longitudinal Evaluation of Drug Abuse Resistance Education (DARE)," *Journal of Research in Crime and Delinquency* 31 (1994): 3–31.

Box Source Notes
Policies, Programs, and Issues in Criminal Justice:
Street Stories: The World of Police Detectives

Robert Jackall, *Street Stories: The World of Police Detectives* (Cambridge, Mass.: Harvard University Press, 2005).

Policies, Programs, and Issues in Criminal Justice: "Forensics under the Microscope"

Chicago Tribune, "*Forensics under the Microscope,*" http://www.chicagotribune.com/news/specials/chi-forensics-specialpackage,0,4244313.special (accessed June 10, 2009); National Academy of Sciences, National Research Council, *Strengthening Forensic Science in the United States: A Path Forward* (Washington, D.C.: The National Academies Press), http://www.nap.edu/catalog.php?record_id=12589#toc (accessed June 10, 2009).

Careers in Criminal Justice: Forensic Scientist

Hall Dillon, "Forensics: A Career In," *Occupational Outlook Quarterly 1* (Fall 1999), http://www.bls.gov/opub/ooq/1999/fall/art01.pdf (accessed June 10, 2009); U.S. Department of Labor, Bureau of Labor Statistics, "Forensic Science Technicians," *Occupational Employment and Wages, 2008,* http://www.bls.gov/oes/2008/may/oes194092.htm#ind (accessed June 10, 2009).

Chapter 6,
Issues in Policing: Professional, Social, and Legal

1. Eric Jefferis, Robert Kaminski, Stephen Homes, and Dena Hanley, "The Effect of a Videotaped Arrest on Public Perceptions of Police Use of Force," *Journal of Criminal Justice* 25 (1997): 381–395.

2. Richard Lumb and Ronald Breazeale, "Police Officer Attitudes and Community Policing Implementation: Developing Strategies for Durable Organizational Change," *Policing & Society* 13 (2003): 91–107.

3. Jihong Zhao and Nicholas Lovrich, "Determinants of Minority Employment in American Municipal Police Agencies: The Representation of African American Officers," *Journal of Criminal Justice* 26 (1998): 267–278.

4. Matthew Hickman and Brian Reaves, *Local Police Departments 2003* (Washington, D.C.: Bureau of Justice Statistics, 2006).

5. T. David Murphy and John Worrall, "Residency Requirements and Public Perceptions of the Police in Large Municipalities," *Policing* 22 (1999): 327–342.

6. Jack Kuykendall and David Burns, "The African American Police Officer: An Historical Perspective," *Journal of Contemporary Criminal Justice* 1 (1980): 4–13.

7. Ibid.

8. Nicholas Alex, *Black in Blue: A Study of the Negro Policeman* (New York: Appleton-Century-Crofts, 1969).

9. Kim Michelle Lersch, "Predicting Citizen's Race in Allegations of Misconduct against the Police," *Journal of Criminal Justice* 26 (1998): 87–99.

10. "Law Enforcement Seeks Answers to 'Racial Profiling' Complaints," *Criminal Justice Newsletter* 29 (1998): 5.

11. Stephen Rice and Alex Piquero, "Perceptions of Discrimination and Justice in New York City," *Policing: An International Journal of Police Strategies and Management* 28 (2005): 98–117.

12. Nicholas Alex, *New York Cops Talk Back* (New York: Wiley, 1976).

13. David Eitle, Lisa Stolzenberg, and Stewart J. D'Alessio, "Police Organizational Factors, the Racial Composition of the Police, and the Probability of Arrest," *Justice Quarterly* 22 (2005): 30–57.

14. Stephen Leinen, *African American Police, White Society* (New York: New York University Press, 1984).

15. Ni He, Jihong Zhao, and Ling Ren, "Do Race and Gender Matter in Police Stress? A Preliminary

Assessment of the Interactive Effects," *Journal of Criminal Justice 33* (2005): 535–547.

16. Joseph L. Gustafson, "Tokenism in Policing: An Empirical Test of Kanter's Hypothesis," *Journal of Criminal Justice 36* (2008): 1–10.

17. Robin Haarr and Merry Morash, "Gender, Race, and Strategies of Coping with Occupational Stress in Policing," *Justice Quarterly 16* (1999): 303–336.

18. For a review of the history of women in policing, see Dorothy Moses Schulz, "From Policewoman to Police Officer: An Unfinished Revolution," *Police Studies 16* (1993): 90–99; Cathryn House, "The Changing Role of Women in Law Enforcement," *Police Chief 60* (1993): 139–144.

19. Susan Martin, "Female Officers on the Move? A Status Report on Women in Policing," in *Critical Issues in Policing*, ed. Roger Dunham and Geoffery Alpert (Grove Park, Ill.: Waveland Press, 1988), 312–331.

20. *Le Boeuf v. Ramsey*, 26 FEP Cases 884 (9/16/80).

21. Michael Birzer and Delores Craig, "Gender Differences in Police Physical Ability Test Performance," *American Journal of Police 15* (1996): 93–106.

22. Hickman and Reaves, *Local Police Departments 2003*.

23. James Daum and Cindy Johns, "Police Work from a Woman's Perspective," *Police Chief 61* (1994): 46–49.

24. Mary Brown, "The Plight of Female Police: A Survey of NW Patrolmen," *Police Chief 61* (1994): 50–53.

25. Matthew Hickman, Alex Piquero, and Jack Greene, "Discretion and Gender Disproportionality in Police Disciplinary Systems," *Policing: An International Journal of Police Strategies & Management 23* (2000): 105–116.

26. Haarr and Morash, "Gender, Race, and Strategies of Coping with Occupational Stress in Policing."

27. Merry Morash and Jack Greene, "Evaluating Women on Patrol: A Critique of Contemporary Wisdom," *Evaluation Review 10* (1986): 230–255.

28. Ibid.

29. Cara E. Rabe-Hemp, "Female Officers and the Ethic of Care: Does Officer Gender Impact Police Behaviors?" *Journal of Criminal Justice 36* (2008): 426–434; Steven Brandl, Meghan Stroshine, and James Frank, "Who Are the Complaint-Prone Officers? An Examination of the Relationship between Police Officers' Attributes, Arrest Activity, Assignment, and Citizens' Complaints about Excessive Force," *Journal of Criminal Justice 29* (2001): 521–529.

30. Susan Martin, "Outsider within the Station House: The Impact of Race and Gender on Black Women Police," *Social Problems 41* (1994): 383–400 at 387.

31. Ibid., 392.

32. Ibid., 394.

33. Ibid., 397.

34. Ibid.

35. Eric Poole and Mark Pogrebin, "Factors Affecting the Decision to Remain in Policing: A Study of Women Officers," *Journal of Police Science and Administration 16* (1988): 49–55.

36. Hickman and Reaves, *Local Police Departments 2003*.

37. Jones, Jones, and Prenzler, "Tertiary Education, Commitment, and Turnover in Police Work."

38. Bruce Berg, "Who Should Teach Police? A Typology and Assessment of Police Academy Instructors," *American Journal of Police 9* (1990): 79–100.

39. David Carter and Allen Sapp, *The State of Police Education: Critical Findings* (Washington, D.C.: Police Executive Research Forum, 1988), 6.

40. John Krimmel, "The Performance of College-Educated Police: A Study of Self-Rated Police Performance Measures," *American Journal of Police 15* (1996): 85–95.

41. See, for example, Richard Harris, *The Police Academy: An Inside View* (New York: Wiley, 1973); John Van Maanen, "Observations on the Making of a Policeman," in *Order Under Law*, ed. R. Culbertson and M. Tezak (Prospect Heights, Ill.: Waveland Press, 1981), 111–126; Jonathan Rubenstein, *City Police* (New York: Ballantine Books, 1973); John Broderick, *Police in a Time of Change* (Morristown, N.J.: General Learning Press, 1977).

42. Gary R. Rothwell, "Whistle-Blowing and the Code of Silence in Police Agencies: Policy and Structural Predictors," *Crime and Delinquency 53* (2007): 605–632; Louise Westmarland, "Police Ethics and Integrity: Breaking the Blue Code of Silence," *Policing & Society 15* (2005): 145–165.

43. Malcolm Sparrow, Mark Moore, and David Kennedy, *Beyond 911: A New Era for Policing* (New York: Basic Books, 1992), 51.

44. M. Steven Meagher and Nancy Yentes, "Choosing a Career in Policing: A Comparison of Male and Female Perceptions," *Journal of Police Science and Administration 16* (1986): 320–327.

45. Venessa Garcia, "Constructing the 'Other' within Police Culture: An Analysis of a Deviant Unit within the Police Organization," *Police Practice and Research 6* (2005): 65–80.

46. Michael K. Brown, *Working the Street* (New York: Russell Sage, 1981), 82.

47. Stan Shernock, "An Empirical Examination of the Relationship between Police Solidarity and Community Orientation," *Journal of Police Science and Administration 18* (1988): 182–198.

48. John Crank, *Understanding Police Culture*, 2d ed. (Cincinnati, Ohio: Anderson, 2003).

49. Eugene Paoline, "Taking Stock: Toward a Richer Understanding of Police Culture," *Journal of Criminal Justice 31* (2003): 199–214.

50. Crank, *Understanding Police Culture*, 359–363.

51. Egon Bittner, *The Functions of Police in Modern Society* (Cambridge, Mass.: Oelgeschlager, Gunn & Hain, 1980), 63.

52. Richard Lundman, *Police and Policing* (New York: Holt, Rinehart & Winston, 1980); see also Jerome Skolnick, *Justice without Trial* (New York: Wiley, 1966).

53. Robert Regoli, Robert Culbertson, John Crank, and James Powell, "Career Stage and Cynicism among Police Chiefs," *Justice Quarterly 7* (1990): 592–614.

54. William Westly, *Violence and the Police: A Sociological Study of Law, Custom, and Morality* (Cambridge, Mass.: MIT Press, 1970).

55. Skolnick, *Justice without Trial*, 42–68.

56. Milton Rokeach, Martin Miller, and John Snyder, "The Value Gap between Police and Policed," *Journal of Social Issues* 27 (1971): 155–171.

57. Wallace Graves, "Police Cynicism: Causes and Cures," *FBI Law Enforcement Bulletin* 65 (1996): 16–21.

58. Larry Tifft, "The 'Cop Personality' Reconsidered," *Journal of Police Science and Administration* 2 (1974): 268; David Bayley and Harold Mendelsohn, *Minorities and the Police* (New York: Free Press, 1969); Robert Balch, "The Police Personality: Fact or Fiction?" *Journal of Criminal Law, Criminology, and Police Science* 63 (1972): 117.

59. Lowell Storms, Nolan Penn, and James Tenzell, "Policemen's Perception of Real and Ideal Policemen," *Journal of Police Science and Administration* 17 (1990): 40–43.

60. Skolnick, *Justice without Trial*.

61. Carroll Seron, Joseph Pereira, and Jean Kovath, "Judging Police Misconduct: 'Street-Level' versus Professional Policing," *Law & Society Review* 38 (2004): 665–710.

62. Peter Salovey and John D. Mayer, "Emotional Intelligence," *Imagination, Cognition, and Personality* 9 (1990): 185–211.

63. Michael E. Burnette, *Emotional Intelligence and the Police* (Germany: VDM Verlag, 2008).

64. Ivan Y. Sun, Brian K. Payne, and Yuning Wu, "The Impact of Situational Factors, Officer Characteristics, and Neighborhood Context on Police Behavior: A Multilevel Analysis," *Journal of Criminal Justice* 36 (2008): 22–32.

65. Kenneth Litwin, "A Multilevel Multivariate Analysis of Factors Affecting Homicide Clearances," *Journal of Research in Crime & Delinquency* 41 (2004): 327–351.

66. Robert Kane, "Patterns of Arrest in Domestic Violence Encounters: Identifying a Police Decision-Making Model," *Journal of Criminal Justice* 27 (1999): 65–79.

67. Gregory Howard Williams, *The Law and Politics of Police Discretion* (Westport, Conn.: Greenwood Press, 1984).

68. Dana Jones and Joanne Belknap, "Police Responses to Battering in a Progressive Pro-Arrest Jurisdiction," *Justice Quarterly* 16 (1999): 249–273.

69. Allison Chappell, John Macdonald, and Patrick Manz, "The Organizational Determinants of Police Arrest Decisions," *Crime and Delinquency* 52 (2006): 287–306.

70. Westly, *Violence and the Police*.

71. Peter Liu and Thomas Cook, "Speeding Violation Dispositions in Relation to Police Officers' Perception of the Offenders," *Policing & Society* (March 15, 2005): 83–88.

72. Joseph Schafer and Stephen Mastrofski, "Police Leniency in Traffic Enforcement Encounters: Exploratory Findings from Observations and Interviews," *Journal of Criminal Justice* 33 (2005): 225–238; Richard Lundman, "Demeanor or Crime? The Midwest City Police–Citizen Encounters Study," *Criminology* 32 (1994): 631–653; Nathan Goldman, *The Differential Selection of Juvenile Offenders for Court Appearance* (New York: National Council on Crime and Delinquency, 1963).

73. David Klinger, "Bringing Crime Back In: Toward a Better Understanding of Police Arrest Decisions," *Journal of Research in Crime and Delinquency* 33 (1996): 333–336; "More on Demeanor and Arrest in Dade County," *Criminology* 34 (1996): 61–79; "Demeanor or Crime? Why 'Hostile' Citizens Are More Likely to Be Arrested," *Criminology* 32 (1994): 475–493.

74. Ambrose Leung, Frances Woolley, Richard Tremblay, and Frank Vitaro, "Who Gets Caught? Statistical Discrimination in Law Enforcement," *Journal of Socio-Economics* 34 (2005): 289–309.

75. Jennifer Schwartz and Bryan D. Rookey, "The Narrowing Gender Gap in Arrests: Assessing Competing Explanations Using Self-Report, Traffic Fatality, and Official Data on Drunk Driving, 1980–2004), "*Criminology* 46 (2008): 637–671.

76. R. Steven Daniels, Lorin Baumhover, William Formby, and Carolyn Clark-Daniels, "Police Discretion and Elder Mistreatment: A Nested Model of Observation, Reporting, and Satisfaction," *Journal of Criminal Justice* 27 (1999): 209–225.

77. For a review, see Frank Schmalleger and John L. Worrall, *Policing Today* (Upper Saddle River, N.J.: Pearson, 2010), 319.

78. Brian Withrow, "Race-Based Policing: A Descriptive Analysis of the Wichita Stop Study," *Police Practice & Research* 5 (2004): 223–240.

79. Brian Withrow, "Race-Based Policing: A Descriptive Analysis of the Wichita Stop Study," *Police Practice & Research* 5 (2004): 223–240; Brian Withrow, "A Comparative Analysis of Commonly Used Benchmarks in Racial Profiling: A Research Note," *Justice Research and Policy* 6 (2004): 71–92; Amy Farrell, Jack McDevitt, Lisa Bailey, Carsten Andresen, and Erica Pierce, "Massachusetts Racial and Gender Profiling Final Report" (Boston: Northeastern University, 2004), http://www.racialprofilinganalysis .neu.edu/IRJsite_docs/finalreport.pdf (accessed May 21, 2008); Richard Lundman, "Driver Race, Ethnicity, and Gender and Citizen Reports of Vehicle Searches by Police and Vehicle Search Hits," *Journal of Criminal Law & Criminology* 94 (2004): 309–350; Michael Smith and Geoffrey Alpert, "Explaining Police Bias: A Theory of Social Conditioning and Illusory Correlation," *Criminal Justice and Behavior* 34 (2007): 1262–1283; Interim Report of the State Police Review Team Regarding Allegations of Racial Profiling (Trenton, N.J.: Office of the Attorney General, 1999).

80. David Eitle, Lisa Stolzenberg, and Stewart J. D'Alessio, "Police Organizational Factors, the Racial Composition of the Police, and the Probability of Arrest," *Justice Quarterly* 22 (2005): 30–57; Matt DeLisi and Robert Regoli, "Race, Conventional Crime, and Criminal Justice: The Declining Importance of Skin Color," *Journal of Criminal Justice* 27 (1999): 549–557; Jon Gould and Stephen Mastrofski, "Suspect Searches: Assessing Police Behavior Under the U.S.

Constitution," *Criminology & Public Policy 3* (2004): 315–362; Joseph Schafer, David Carter, and Andra Katz-Bannister, "Studying Traffic Stop Encounters," *Journal of Criminal Justice 32* (2004): 159–70; James Lange, Mark Johnson, and Robert Voas, "Testing the Racial Profiling Hypothesis for Seemingly Disparate Traffic Stops on the New Jersey Turnpike," *Justice Quarterly 22* (2005): 193–223; Geoffrey P. Alpert, Roger G. Dunham, and Michael R. Smith, "Investigating Racial Profiling by the Miami-Dade Police Department: A Multimethod Approach," *Criminology and Public Policy 6* (2007): 25–56.

81. Mathias Risse and Richard Zeckhauser, "Racial Profiling," *Philosophy and Public Affairs 32* (2004): 131–170.

82. Karen Kruger and Nicholas Valltos, "Dealing with Domestic Violence in Law Enforcement Relationships," *FBI Law Enforcement Bulletin 71* (2002): 1–7.

83. Lumb and Breazeale, "Police Officer Attitudes and Community Policing Implementation."

84. Donald Yates and Vijayan Pillai, "Frustration and Strain among Fort Worth Police Officers," *Sociology and Social Research: An International Journal 76* (1992): 145–149.

85. For an impressive review, see Richard Farmer, "Clinical and Managerial Implications of Stress Research on the Police," *Journal of Police Science and Administration 17* (1990): 205–217.

86. Lawrence Travis III and Craig Winston, "Dissension in the Ranks: Officer Resistance to Community Policing and Support for the Organization," *Journal of Crime and Justice 21* (1998): 139–155.

87. Francis Cullen, Terrence Lemming, Bruce Link, and John Wozniak, "The Impact of Social Supports on Police Stress," *Criminology 23* (1985): 503–522.

88. Morash, Haarr, and Kwak, "Multilevel Influences on Police Stress," *Journal of Contemporary Criminal Justice 22* (2006): 26–43.

89. Farmer, "Clinical and Managerial Implications"; Nancy Norvell, Dale Belles, and Holly Hills, "Perceived Stress Levels and Physical Symptoms in Supervisory Law Enforcement Personnel," *Journal of Police Science and Administration 16* (1988): 75–79.

90. Donald Yates and Vijayan Pillai, "Attitudes toward Community Policing: A Causal Analysis," *Social Science Journal 33* (1996): 193–209.

91. Harvey McMurray, "Attitudes of Assaulted Police Officers and Their Policy Implications," *Journal of Police Science and Administration 17* (1990): 44–48.

92. Lawrence Blum, *Force under Pressure: How Cops Live and Why They Die* (New York: Lantern Books, 2000).

93. Rose Lee Josephson and Martin Reiser, "Officer Suicide in the Los Angeles Police Department: A Twelve-Year Follow-Up," *Journal of Police Science and Administration 17* (1990): 227–230.

94. Yates and Pillai, "Attitudes toward Community Policing," 205–206.

95. Ibid.

96. Rosanna Church and Naomi Robertson, "How State Police Agencies Are Addressing the Issue of Wellness," *Policing 22* (1999): 304–312.

97. Farmer, "Clinical and Managerial Implications," 215.

98. Peter Hart, Alexander Wearing, and Bruce Headey, "Assessing Police Work Experiences: Development of the Police Daily Hassles and Uplifts Scales," *Journal of Criminal Justice 21* (1993): 553–573.

99. Scott R. Senjo and Karla Dhungana, "A Field Data Examination of Policy Constructs Related to Fatigue Conditions in Law Enforcement Personnel," *Police Quarterly 12* (2009): 123–136.

100. Bryan Vila and Dennis J. Kenney, "Tired Cops: The Prevalence and Potential Consequences of Police Fatigue," *NIJ Journal 248* (2002): 16–21.

101. Luenda E. Charles, Cecil M. Burchfiel, Desta Fekedulegn, Bryan Vila, Tara A. Hartley, James Slaven, Anna Mnatsakanova, and John M. Violanti, "Shift Work and Sleep: The Buffalo Police Health Study," *Policing 30* (2007): 215–227.

102. Ibid., 8.

103. Ibid., 17.

104. Sean Griffin and Thomas Bernard, "Angry Aggression among Police Officers," *Police Quarterly 6* (2003): 3–21.

105. Kim Michelle Lersch and Tom Mieczkowski, "Who Are the Problem-Prone Officers? An Analysis of Citizen Complaints," *American Journal of Police 15* (1996): 23–42.

106. Samuel Walker, Geoffrey P. Alpert, and Dennis J. Kenney, *Early Warning Systems: Responding to the Problem Police Officer, Research in Brief* (Washington, D.C.: National Institute of Justice, 2001).

107. Michael D. White, "Controlling Police Decisions to Use Deadly Force: Reexamining the Importance of Administrative Policy," *Crime and Delinquency 47* (2001): 131.

108. Kevin Flynn, "New York Police Sting Tries to Weed Out Brutal Officers," *New York Times*, September 24, 1999, 2.

109. Samuel Walker, *Popular Justice*, 2nd ed. (New York: Oxford University Press, 1997): 48–64.

110. Herman Goldstein, *Police Corruption* (Washington, D.C.: Police Foundation, 1975), 3.

111. Michael Johnston, *Political Corruption and Public Policy in America* (Monterey, Calif.: Brooks/Cole, 1982), 75.

112. Lawrence Sherman, *Scandal and Reform: Controlling Police Corruption* (Berkeley: University of California Press, 1978), 194.

113. Barbara Gelb, *Tarnished Brass: The Decade after Serpico* (New York: Putnam, 1983); Candace McCoy, "Lawsuits against Police: What Impact Do They Have?" *Criminal Law Bulletin 20* (1984): 49–56.

114. Samuel Walker, *Police Accountability: The Role of Citizen Oversight* (Belmont, Calif.: Wadsworth, 2001); Liqun Cao and Bu Huang, "Determinants of Citizen Complaints Against Police Abuse of Power," *Journal of Criminal Justice 28* (2000): 203–213; Peter Finn, "Getting Along with Citizen Oversight," *FBI Law Enforcement Bulletin 69* (2000): 22–27.

115. For a general review, see Tom McEwen, *National Data Collection on Police Use of Force* (Washington, D.C.: National Institute of Justice, 1996).

116. Matthew Durose and Patrick Langan, *Contacts between Police and the Public: Findings from the 2005 National Survey* (Washington, D.C.: Bureau of Justice Statistics, 2007).

117. Brad Smith, "The Impact of Police Officer Diversity on Police-Caused Homicides," *Policy Studies Journal 31* (2003): 147–162.

118. Brian Thompson and James Daniel Lee, "Who Cares If Police Become Violent? Explaining Approval of Police Use of Force Using a National Sample," *Sociological Inquiry 74* (2004): 381–410.

119. Sandra Lee Browning, Francis Cullen, Liqun Cao, Renee Kopache, and Thomas Stevenson, "Race and Getting Hassled by the Police: A Research Note," *Police Studies 17* (1994): 1–11.

120. Joel Garner, Christopher Maxwell, and Cedrick Heraux, "Characteristics Associated with the Prevalence and Severity of Force Used by the Police," *Justice Quarterly 19* (2002): 705–747.

121. William Terrill, "Police Use of Force: A Transactional Approach," *Justice Quarterly 22* (2005): 107–138.

122. Hannah Cooper, Lisa Moore, Sofia Gruskin, and Nancy Krieger, "Characterizing Perceived Police Violence: Implications for Public Health," *American Journal of Public Health 94* (2004): 1109–1119.

123. Lawrence Sherman and Robert Langworthy, "Measuring Homicide by Police Officers," *Journal of Criminal Law and Criminology 4* (1979): 546–560.

124. Ibid.

125. James Fyfe, "Police Use of Deadly Force: Research and Reform," *Justice Quarterly 5* (1988): 165–205.

126. Richard Parent and Simon Verdun-Jones, "Victim-Precipitated Homicide: Police Use of Deadly Force in British Columbia," *Policing 21* (1998): 432–449.

127. "10 Percent of Police Shootings Found to Be 'Suicide by Cop,'" *Criminal Justice Newsletter 29* (1998): 1.

128. Colin Loftin, David McDowall, Brian Wiersema, and Adam Dobrin, "Underreporting of Justifiable Homicides Committed by Police Officers in the United States, 1976–1998," *American Journal of Public Health 93* (2003): 1117–1121.

129. Sherman and Langworthy, "Measuring Homicide by Police Officers."

130. Brad Smith, "Structural and Organizational Predictors of Homicide by Police," *Policing 27* (2004): 539–557.

131. John MacDonald, Geoffrey Alpert, and Abraham Tennenbaum, "Justifiable Homicide by Police and Criminal Homicide: A Research Note," *Journal of Crime and Justice 22* (1999): 153–164.

132. Jonathan Sorenson, James Marquart, and Deon Brock, "Factors Related to Killings of Felons by Police Officers: A Test of the Community Violence and Conflict Hypotheses," *Justice Quarterly 10* (1993): 417–440; David Jacobs and David Britt, "Inequality and Police Use of Deadly Force: An Empirical Assessment of a Conflict Hypotheses," *Social Problems 26* (1979): 403–412; Smith, "Structural and Organizational Predictors of Homicide by Police."

133. David Jacobs and Jason Carmichael, "Subordination and Violence against State Control Agents: Testing Political Explanations for Lethal Assaults against the Police," *Social Forces 80* (2002): 1223–1252.

134. Fyfe, "Police Use of Deadly Force," 181.

135. John MacDonald, Patrick Manz, Geoffrey Alpert, and Roger Dunham, "Police Use of Force: Examining the Relationship between Calls for Service and the Balance of Police Force and Suspect Resistance," *Journal of Criminal Justice 31* (2003): 119–127; Matthew J. Hickman and Alex R. Piquero, "Organizational, Administrative, and Environmental Correlates of Complaints About Police Use of Force: Does Minority Representation Matter?" *Crime and Delinquency 55* (2009): 3–27.

136. *Tennessee v. Garner*, 471 U.S. 1, 105 S. Ct. 1694, 85 L.Ed.2d 889 (1985).

137. *Graham v. Connor*, 490 U.S. 386, 109 S. Ct. 1865, 104 L.Ed.2d 443 (1989).

138. Franklin Graves and Gregory Connor, "The FLETC Use-of-Force Model," *Police Chief 59* (1992): 56–58.

139. Frank Zarb, "Police Liability for Creating the Need to Use Deadly Force in Self-Defense," *Michigan Law Review 86* (1988): 1982–2009.

140. Warren Cohen, "When Lethal Force Won't Do," *U.S. News & World Report 122* (June 23, 1997): 12.

141. Richard Lumb and Paul Friday, "Impact of Pepper Spray Availability on Police Officer Use-of-Force Decisions," *Policing 20* (1997): 136–149.

142. Tom McEwen, "Policies on Less-than-Lethal Force in Law Enforcement Agencies," *Policing 20* (1997): 39–60.

143. *Miranda v. Arizona*, 384 U.S. 436 (1966).

144. *Colorado v. Connelly*, 107 S. Ct. 515 (1986).

145. *Minnick v. Mississippi* 498 U.S. 46, 111 S. Ct. 486, 112 L.Ed.2d. 489 (1990).

146. *Harris v. New York*, 401 U.S. 222 (1971).

147. *Nix v. Williams*, 104 S. Ct. 2501 (1984).

148. *Oregon v. Elstad*, 105 S. Ct. 1285 (1985).

149. *Colorado v. Connelly*, 107 S. Ct. 515 (1986).

150. *New York v. Quarles*, 104 S. Ct. 2626 (1984).

151. *Colorado v. Spring*, 107 S. Ct. 851 (1987).

152. *Moran v. Burbine*, 106 S. Ct. 1135 (1986).

153. *Davis v. United States*, 114 S. Ct. 2350 (1994).

154. *Missouri v. Seibert*, 542 U.S. 600 (2004).

155. *United States v. Patane*, 542 U.S. 630 (2004).

156. *Chavez v. Martinez*, 538 U.S. 760 (2003).

157. Marvin Zalman and Brad W. Smith, "Attitudes of Police Executives Toward *Miranda* and Interrogation Policies," *Journal of Criminal Law and Criminology 97* (2007): 873–942; Victoria Time and Brian Payne, "Police Chiefs' Perceptions about *Miranda:* An Analysis of Survey Data," *Journal of Criminal Justice 30* (2002): 77–86.

158. Ronald Allen, "*Miranda's* Hollow Core," *Northwestern University Law Review 100* (2006): 71–85.

159. G. Daniel Lassiter, Jennifer Ratcliff, Lezlee Ware, and Clinton Irvin, "Videotaped Confessions: Panacea or Pandora's Box?" *Law & Policy 28* (2006): 192–210.

160. *Chimel v. California*, 395 U.S. 752 (1969).

161. *Terry v. Ohio*, 392 U.S. 1 (1968).

162. *Illinois v. Wardlow*, 528 U.S. 119 (2000).

163. *Carroll v. United States*, 267 U.S. 132 (1925).

164. *United States v. Ross*, 102 S. Ct. 2147 (1982).
165. *Whren v. United States*, 116 S. Ct. 1769 (1996).
166. Drivers, *Pennsylvania v. Mimms*, 434 U.S. 106 (1977); passengers, *Maryland v. Wilson*, 117 U.S. 882 (1997) and *Arizona v. Johnson*, No. 07-1122 (2009).
167. Mark Hansen, "Rousting Miss Daisy?" *American Bar Association Journal* 83 (1997): 22; *Knowles v. Iowa*, 119 S. Ct. 507 (1998); *Wyoming v. Houghton*, 119 S. Ct. 1297 (1999).
168. *Thornton v. United States*, 541 U.S. 615 (2004).
169. *Bumper v. North Carolina*, 391 U.S. 543 (1960).
170. *Ohio v. Robinette*, 117 S. Ct. 417 (1996).
171. Limitations on the plain-view doctrine have been defined in *Arizona v. Hicks*, 107 S. Ct. 1149 (1987); the recording of serial numbers from stereo components in a suspect's apartment could not be justified as being in plain view.
172. *Warden v. Hayden*, 387 U.S. 294 (1967); *Minnesota v. Olson*, 495 U.S. 91 (1990); *Breithaupt v. Abram*, 352 U.S. 432 (1957).
173. *Weeks v. United States*, 232 U.S. 383, 34 S. Ct. 341, 58 L.Ed. 652 (1914).
174. *Mapp v. Ohio*, 367 U.S. 643, 81 S. Ct. 1684, 6 L.Ed.2d 1081 (1961).
175. William Greenhalgh, *The Fourth Amendment Handbook: A Chronological Survey of Supreme Court Decisions* (Chicago: American Bar Association Section on Criminal Justice, 1995).
176. *United States v. Leon*, 468 U.S. 897, 104 S. Ct. 3405, 82 L.Ed.2d 677 (1984).

Box Source Notes
Careers in Criminal Justice: Postal Inspector

U.S. Postal Inspection Service: Employment, https://postalinspectors.uspis.gov (accessed June 10, 2009).

International Justice: Interrogation Law in Three Other Countries

Yue Ma, "A Comparative View of the Law of Interrogation," *International Criminal Justice Review* 17 (2007): 5–26; Craig M. Bradley (ed.), *Criminal Procedure: A Worldwide Study* (Durham, N.C.: Carolina Academic Press, 1999); Stephen C. Thaman, "*Miranda* in Comparative Law," *Saint Louis University Law Journal* 45 (2001): 581–624.

Chapter 7,
Courts, Prosecution, and the Defense

1. Matthew Durose and Patrick Langan, *Felony Sentences in State Courts* (Washington, D.C.: Bureau of Justice Statistics, 2004).
2. Greg Berman and John Feinblatt, *Problem-Solving Courts: A Brief Primer* (New York: Center for Court Innovation, 2001).
3. Office of National Drug Control Policy, http://www.whitehousedrugpolicy.gov/enforce/drugcourt.html (accessed February 26, 2009).
4. Center for Court Innovation, http://www.courtinnovation.org/index.cfm?fuseaction=page.viewPage&pageID=511&documentTopicID=25 (accessed February 26, 2009).
5. Robert LaFountain, Richard Schauffler, Shauna Strickland, William Rafferty, and Chantal Bromage, *Examining the Work of State Courts, 2006* (Arlington, VA: National Center for State Courts, 2007), 69–71.
6. U.S. Constitution, Art. 3, Secs. 1 and 2.
7. David Klein and Robert Hume, "Fear of Reversal as an Explanation of Lower Court Compliance," *Law and Society Review* 37 (2003): 579–607.
8. Roy Schotland, "2002 Judicial Elections," *Spectrum: The Journal of State Government* 76 (2003): 18–20.
9. Sari Escovitz with Fred Kurland and Nan Gold, *Judicial Selection and Tenure* (Chicago: American Judicature Society, 1974), 3–16.
10. Judith McFarlane, Ann Malecha, Julia Gist, Kathy Watson, Elizabeth Batten, Iva Hall, and Sheila Smith, "Protection Orders and Intimate Partner Violence: An 18-Month Study of 150 Black, Hispanic, and White Women," *American Journal of Public Health* 94 (2004): 613–618.
11. Steven Perry, *Prosecutors in State Courts, 2005* (Washington, D.C.: Bureau of Justice Statistics, 2006).
12. Jessie Larson, "Unequal Justice: The Supreme Court's Failure to Curtail Selective Prosecution for the Death Penalty," *Journal of Criminal Law & Criminology* 93 (2003): 1009–1031.
13. Kenneth C. Davis, *Discretionary Justice* (Baton Rouge: Louisiana State University Press, 1969), 180; see also James B. Stewart, *The Prosecutor* (New York: Simon & Schuster, 1987).
14. Barbara Boland, *The Prosecution of Felony Arrests* (Washington, D.C.: Government Printing Office, 1983).
15. Newman Baker, "The Prosecutor—Initiation of Prosecution," *Journal of Criminal Law, Criminology, and Police Science* 23 (1933): 770–771; see also Joan Jacoby, *The American Prosecutor: A Search for Identity* (Lexington, Mass.: Lexington Books, 1980).
16. Jeffrey Spears and Cassia Spohn, "The Effect of Evidence Factors and Victim Characteristics on Prosecutors' Charging Decisions in Sexual Assault Cases," *Justice Quarterly* 14 (1997): 501–524.
17. Janell Schmidt and Ellen Hochstedler Steury, "Prosecutorial Discretion in Filing Charges in Domestic Violence Cases," *Criminology* 27 (1989): 487–510.
18. John Worrall, Jay Ross, and Eric McCord, "Modeling Prosecutors' Charging Decisions in Domestic Violence Cases," *Crime and Delinquency* 52 (2006) 472–503.
19. Rodney Kingsnorth and Randall Macintosh, "Domestic Violence: Predictors of Victim Support for Official Action," *Justice Quarterly* 21 (2004): 301–328.
20. Myrna Dawson and Ronit Dinovitzer, "Victim Cooperation and the Prosecution of Domestic Violence in a Specialized Court," *Justice Quarterly* 18 (2001): 593–622.
21. Rodney Kingsworth, John Lopez, Jennifer Wentworth, and Debra Cummings, "Adult Sexual Assault: The Role of Racial/Ethnic Composition in

Prosecution and Sentencing," *Journal of Criminal Justice 26* (1998): 359–372; *United States v. Armstrong* 517 U.S. 456 (1996).

22. Michael Edmund O'Neill, "Understanding Federal Prosecutorial Declinations: An Empirical Analysis of Predictive Factors," *American Criminal Law Review 41* (2004): 1439–1533.

23. Shaila Dewan, "Prosecutors Say Cuts Force Plea Bargains," *New York Times*, March 10, 2003, B3.

24. Charles D. Breitel, "Controls in Criminal Law Enforcement," *University of Chicago Law Review 27* (1960): 427.

25. Cassia Spohn, Dawn Beichner, and Erika Davis-Frenzel, "Prosecutorial Justifications for Sexual Assault Case Rejection: Guarding the 'Gateway to Justice,'" *Social Problems 48* (2001): 206–235.

26. "Prosecutor Conduct," editorial, *USA Today*, April 1, 1999, 14A.

27. American Bar Association, *Model Rules of Professional Conduct* (Chicago: ABA, 1983), rule 3.8; see also Stanley Fisher, "In Search of the Virtuous Prosecutor: A Conceptual Framework," *American Journal of Criminal Law 15* (1988): 197.

28. Stanley Fisher, "Zealousness and Overzealousness: Making Sense of the Prosecutor's Duty to Seek Justice," *Prosecutor 22* (1989): 9; see also Bruce Green, "The Ethical Prosecutor and the Adversary System," *Criminal Law Bulletin 24* (1988): 126–145.

29. *North Carolina v. Pearce*, 395 U.S. 711, 89 S. Ct. 2072, 23 L.Ed.2d 656 (1969).

30. *Blackledge v. Perry*, 417 U.S. 21, 94 S. Ct. 2098, 40 L.Ed.2d 628 (1974).

31. *Bordenkircher v. Hayes*, 434 U.S. 357, 98 S. Ct. 663, 54 L.Ed.2d 604 (1978).

32. American Bar Association, *Model Code of Professional Responsibility and Judicial Conduct* (Chicago: ABA, 1980), rule 3.8.

33. *Gideon v. Wainwright*, 372 U.S. 335, 83 S. Ct. 792, 9 L.Ed.2d 799 (1963).

34. *Argersinger v. Hamlin*, 407 U.S. 25, 92 S. Ct. 2006, 32 L.Ed.2d 530 (1972).

35. Carol J. DeFrances, *State-Funded Indigent Defense Services, 1999* (Washington, D.C.: Bureau of Justice Statistics, 2001).

36. Ibid.

37. Talia Roitberg Harmon and William Lofquist, "Too Late for Luck: A Comparison of Post-Furman Exonerations and Executions of the Innocent," *Crime and Delinquency 51* (2005): 498–520.

38. Data compiled by the Bureau of Justice Statistics, www.ojp.usdoj.gov/bjs/id.htm#conviction (accessed February 26, 2009); see also Arye Rattner, Hagit Turjeman, and Gideon Fishman, "Public versus Private Defense: Can Money Buy Justice?" *Journal of Criminal Justice 36* (2008): 43–49.

39. Radha Iyengar, "An Analysis of the Performance of Federal Indigent Defense Counsel," NBER Working Paper 13187 (Cambridge, Mass.: National Bureau of Economic Research, June 2007), http://ideas.repec.org/p/nbr/nberwo/13187.html (accessed February 27, 2009).

40. *Strickland v. Washington*, 466 U.S. 668, 104 S. Ct. 2052, 80 L.Ed.2d 674 (1984).

41. *Florida v. Nixon*, No. 03-931 (Decided: 12/13/04).

42. The following sections are based on Ron Bowmaster and John Cariotto, "Information Sharing in Nebraska," National Center for State Courts, 2003, www.ncsconline. org/D_Tech/ctc/showarticle. asp?id=69 (accessed June 19, 2007); Fredric I. Lederer, "The Road to the Virtual Courtroom? Consideration of Today's—and Tomorrow's—High-Technology Courtrooms," *South Carolina Law Review 50* (1999): 799; "Criminal Court Records Go Online," *The Quill 90* (2002), 39; Donald C. Dilworth, "New Court Technology Will Affect How Attorneys Present Trials," *Trial 33* (1997): 100–114.

Box Source Notes
Careers in Criminal Justice: Prosecutor

Bureau of Labor Statistics, U.S. Department of Labor, "Lawyers," *Occupational Outlook Handbook, 2008–09 Edition*, http://www.bls.gov/oco/ocos053.htm (accessed June 12, 2009); National Association for Legal Career Professionals: New Research on Attorney Salaries at Public Sector and Public Interest Organizations, http://www.nalp.org/2006octattorneysalaries (accessed June 12, 2009).

Criminal Justice and Technology: Improving Court Functions with Technology

James E. McMillan, *Using Technology to Improve Customer Service* (Williamsburg, Va.: National Center for State Courts, 2007), http://www.ncsconline.org/WC/Publications/Trends/2007/TecManTrends2007.pdf (accessed June 12, 2009).

Chapter 8,
Pretrial and Trial Procedures

1. *Stack v. Boyle*, 342 U.S. 1 (1951).

2. Data in this section comes from Thomas Cohen and Brian Reaves, *Felony Defendants in Large Urban Counties, 2002* (Washington, D.C.: Bureau of Justice Statistics, 2006).

3. Christopher Stephens, "Bail" section of the Criminal Procedure project, *Georgetown Law Journal 90* (2002): 1395–1416.

4. Traci Schlesinger, "Racial and Ethnic Disparity in Pretrial Criminal Processing," *Justice Quarterly 22* (2005): 170–192.

5. Bob Burton, Director of Training and Surety Corporation Liaison, National Institute of Bail Enforcement, personal contact, September 17, 2004.

6. Cohen and Reaves, *Felony Defendants in Large Urban Counties*.

7. Vera Institute of Justice, *1961–1971: Programs in Criminal Justice* (New York: Vera Institute of Justice, 1972).

8. Chris Eskridge, *Pretrial Release Programming* (New York: Clark Boardman, 1983), 27.

9. Public Law No. 89–465, 18 U.S.C., sec. 3146 (1966).

10. 18 U.S.C., sec. 3142 (1984).

11. See, generally, Fred Cohen, "The New Federal Crime Control Act," *Criminal Law Bulletin 21* (1985): 330–337.

12. *Schall v. Martin*, 467 U.S. 253 (1984).

13. *Demore v. Kim*, 538 U.S. 510 (2003).

14. This section leans on John Clark and D. Alan Henry, *Pretrial Services Programming at the Start of the 21st Century: A Survey of Pretrial Services Programs* (Washington, D.C.: Bureau of Justice Assistance, 2003).

15. Ric Simmons, "Reexamining the Grand Jury: Is There Room for Democracy in the Criminal Justice System?" *Boston University Law Review 82* (2002): 1–76.

16. John Gibeaut, "Indictment of a System," *ABA Journal 87* (2001): 34.

17. Kirke D. Weaver, "A Change of Heart or a Change of Law? Withdrawing a Guilty Plea Under Federal Rule of Criminal Procedure 32(e)," *Journal of Criminal Law and Criminology 92* (2001): 273–306.

18. Anne Piehl and Shaen Bushway, "Measuring and Explaining Charge Bargaining," *Journal of Quantitative Criminology 23* (2007): 105–125.

19. George Fisher, "Plea Bargaining's Triumph," *Yale Law Journal 109* (2000): 857–1058.

20. Fred Zacharis, "Justice in Plea Bargaining," *William and Mary Law Review 39* (1998): 1121–1189.

21. Nathaniel J. Pallone, "Without Plea-Bargaining, Megan Kanka Would Be Alive Today," *Criminology & Public Policy 3* (2003): 83–96.

22. William Stuntz, "Plea Bargaining and Criminal Law's Disappearing Shadow," *Harvard Law Review 117* (2004): 2548–2569.

23. Mike McConville, "Plea Bargaining: Ethics and Politics," *Journal of Law & Society 25* (1998): 526–555.

24. *Hill v. Lockhart*, 474 U.S. 52 (1985).

25. *Boykin v. Alabama*, 395 U.S. 238 (1969); *Brady v. United States*, 397 U.S. 742 (1970).

26. *Santobello v. New York*, 404 U.S. 257 (1971).

27. *Ricketts v. Adamson*, 483 U.S. 1 (1987).

28. *Bordenkircher v. Hayes*, 434 U.S. 357 (1978).

29. *North Carolina v. Alford*, 400 U.S. 25 (1970).

30. *United States v. Mezzanatto*, 513 U.S. 196 (1995).

31. Jeremy Ball, "Is It a Prosecutor's World? Determinants of Count Bargaining Decisions," *Journal of Contemporary Criminal Justice 22* (2006): 241–260.

32. Deirdre M. Bowen, "Calling Your Bluff: How Prosecutors and Defense Attorneys Adapt to Plea Bargaining Strategies to Increase Formalization," *Justice Quarterly 26* (2009): 2–29.

33. Stephen P. Lagoy, Joseph J. Senna, and Larry J. Siegel, "An Empirical Study on Information Usage for Prosecutorial Decision Making in Plea Negotiations," *American Criminal Law Review 13* (1976): 435–471.

34. William Stuntz, "The Uneasy Relationship between Criminal Procedure and Criminal Justice," *Yale Law Journal 107* (1997): 10–11.

35. Stephanos Bibas, "Plea Bargaining Outside the Shadow of Trial," *Harvard Law Review 117* (2004): 2464–2543.

36. Keith Bystrom, "Communicating Plea Offers to the Client," in *Ethical Problems Facing the Criminal Defense Lawyer*, ed. Rodney Uphoff (Chicago: American Bar Association Section on Criminal Justice, 1995), 84.

37. American Bar Association, Standards Relating to Pleas of Guilty, standard 3.3; *National Advisory Commission on Criminal Justice Standards and Goals, Task Force Report on Courts* (Washington, D.C.: Government Printing Office, 1973), 42.

38. American Bar Association, *Standards Relating to Pleas of Guilty*, 73; see also Alan Alschuler, "The Trial Judge's Role in Plea Bargaining," *Columbia Law Review 76* (1976): 1059.

39. American Bar Association, *Model Uniform Victims of Crime Act* (Chicago: ABA, 1992).

40. George P. Fletcher, *With Justice for Some—Victims' Rights in Criminal Trials* (New York: Addison-Wesley, 1995), 190–193.

41. *Santobello v. New York*, 404 U.S. 257 (1971).

42. Barbara Boland and Brian Forst, *The Prevalence of Guilty Pleas* (Washington, D.C.: Bureau of Justice Statistics, 1984), 3; see also Gary Hengstler, "The Troubled Justice System," *American Bar Association Journal 80* (1994): 44.

43. National Institute of Law Enforcement and Criminal Justice, *Plea Bargaining in the United States*, 37–40.

44. For a discussion of this issue, see Michael Tonry, "Plea Bargaining Bans and Rules," in *Sentencing Reform Impacts* (Washington, D.C.: Government Printing Office, 1987).

45. Candace McCoy, *Politics and Plea Bargaining: Victims' Rights in California* (Philadelphia: University of Pennsylvania Press, 1993).

46. Bibas, "Plea Bargaining Outside the Shadow of Trial."

47. Franklyn Dunford, D. Wayne Osgood, and Hart Weichselbaum, *National Evaluation of Diversion Programs* (Washington, D.C.: Government Printing Office, 1982).

48. Sharla Rausch and Charles Logan, "Diversion from Juvenile Court: Panacea or Pandora's Box?" in *Evaluating Juvenile Justice*, ed. James Kleugel (Beverly Hills, Calif.: Sage, 1983), 19–30.

49. John Hepburn, "Recidivism among Drug Offenders Following Exposure to Treatment," *Criminal Justice Policy Review 16* (2005): 237–259.

50. Ibid., p. 523.

51. See, for example, Minn. R. Crim. P. 26.03, subd. 13(4).

52. *Riggins v. Nevada*, 504 U.S. 127 (1992).

53. *Diaz v. United States*, 223 U.S. 442 (1912); *Taylor v. Illinois*, 484 U.S. 400 (1988).

54. *Illinois v. Allen*, 397 U.S. 337 (1970).

55. *Maryland v. Craig*, 497 U.S. 836 (1990).

56. *Washington v. Texas*, 388 U.S. 14 (1967).

57. *Baldwin v. New York*, 399 U.S. 66 (1970).

58. *Scott v. Illinois*, 440 U.S. 367 (1979).

59. *Shelton v. Alabama*, 122 U.S. 1764 (2002).

60. *Faretta v. California*, 422 U.S. 806 (1975).

61. See American Bar Association, *Standards Relating to Speedy Trial* (Chicago: ABA, 1995).

62. *Klopfer v. North Carolina*, 386 U.S. 213 (1967).

63. Ibid., at 223, 87 S. Ct. at 993.

64. *Doggett v. United States*, 505 U.S. 162 (1992).

65. *Nebraska Press Association v. Stuart*, 427 U.S. 539 (1976).

66. Ibid., at 547, 96 S. Ct. at 2797.

67. Ibid., at 370, 99 S.Ct at 2900.

68. *Press-Enterprise Co. v. Superior Court*, 478 U.S. 1 (1986).

69. *Wilson v. Layne*, 526 U.S. 603 (1999).

70. *Richmond Newspapers, Inc. v. Virginia*, 448 U.S. 555 (1980).

71. *Globe Newspaper Co. v. Superior Court for County of Norfolk*, 457 U.S. 596 (1982).

72. *Chandler v. Florida*, 449 U.S. 560 (1981); see also American Bar Association, *Criminal Justice Standards, Fair Trial, and Free Press* (Washington, D.C.: ABA, 1992).

73. See *Brinegar v. United States*, 338 U.S. 160 (1949); *In re Winship*, 397 U.S. 358, 90 (1970).

74. Ibid., at 174.

75. See *In re Winship*, at 397.

76. Ibid., at 371, 90 S. Ct. at 1076.

77. Brian Kalt, "The Exclusion of Felons from Jury Service," *American University Law Review 53* (2003): 65–189.

78. George Hayden, Joseph Senna, and Larry Siegel, "Prosecutorial Discretion in Peremptory Challenges: An Empirical Investigation of Information Use in the Massachusetts Jury Selection Process," *New England Law Review 13* (1978): 768.

79. *Batson v. Kentucky*, 476 U.S. 79 (1986); see also Alan Alschuler and Randall Kennedy, "Equal Justice—Would Color-Conscious Jury Selection Help?" *American Bar Association Journal 81* (1995): 36–37.

80. John Schwartz, "As Jurors Turn to Web, Mistrials Are Popping Up," *New York Times* (March 17, 2009), http://www.nytimes.com/2009/03/18/us/18juries.html?_r=1&emc=eta1 (accessed March 27, 2009).

81. Arie Rubenstein, "Verdicts of Conscience: Nullification and the Modern Jury Trial," *Columbia Law Review 106* (2006): 959–993.

82. David Pepper, "Nullifying History: Modern-Day Misuse of the Right to Decide the Law," *Case Western Reserve Law Review 50* (2000): 599–643.

83. *Chapman v. California*, 386 U.S. 18 (1967).

84. *Douglas v. California*, 372 U.S. 353 (1963).

Box Source Notes
Policies, Programs, and Issues in Criminal Justice: The *CSI* Effect

Donald E. Shelton, "The '*CSI* Effect': Does It Really Exist?" *National Institute of Justice Journal 259* (2008): 1–7; Donald E. Shelton, Young S. Kim, and Gregg Barak, "A Study of Juror Expectation and Demands Concerning Scientific Evidence: Does the '*CSI* Effect' Exist?" *Vanderbilt Journal of Entertainment and Technology Law 9* (2007): 331–368.

Careers in Criminal Justice: Court Reporter

S. E. Lambert and D. Regan, "Court Reporter," *Great Jobs for Criminal Justice Majors* (New York: McGraw-Hill, 2001), 159–161; Bureau of Labor Statistics, U.S. Department of Labor, "Court Reporters," *Occupational Outlook Handbook, 2008–09 Edition*, http://www.bls.gov/oco/ocos152.htm (accessed June 13, 2009).

Chapter 9, Punishment and Sentencing

1. Graeme Newman, *The Punishment Response* (Philadelphia: Lippincott, 1978), 13.

2. Michel Foucault, *Discipline and Punishment* (New York: Vintage Books, 1978).

3. Kathleen Auerhahn, "Selective Incapacitation and the Problem of Prediction," *Criminology 37* (1999): 703–734.

4. Kathleen Daly, "Neither Conflict nor Labeling nor Paternalism Will Suffice: Intersections of Race, Ethnicity, Gender, and Family in Criminal Court Decisions," *Crime and Delinquency 35* (1989): 136–168.

5. Among the most helpful sources for this section were Benedict Alper, *Prisons Inside-Out* (Cambridge, Mass.: Ballinger, 1974); Gustave de Beaumont and Alexis de Tocqueville, *On the Penitentiary System in the United States and Its Applications in France* (Carbondale, Ill.: Southern Illinois University Press, 1964); Orlando Lewis, *The Development of American Prisons and Prison Customs, 1776–1845* (Montclair, N.J.: Patterson-Smith, 1967); Leonard Orland, ed., *Justice, Punishment, and Treatment* (New York: Free Press, 1973); J. Goebel, *Felony and Misdemeanor* (Philadelphia: University of Pennsylvania Press, 1976); George Rusche and Otto Kircheimer, *Punishment and Social Structure* (New York: Russell & Russell, 1939); Samuel Walker, *Popular Justice* (New York: Oxford University Press, 1980); Newman, *The Punishment Response*; David Rothman, *Conscience and Convenience* (Boston: Little, Brown, 1980); George Ives, *A History of Penal Methods* (Montclair, N.J.: Patterson-Smith, 1970); Robert Hughes, *The Fatal Shore* (New York: Knopf, 1986); Leon Radzinowicz, *A History of English Criminal Law*, vol. 1 (London: Stevens, 1943), 5.

6. *Crime and Punishment in America, 1999*, Report 229 (Washington, D.C.: National Center for Policy Analysis, 1999).

7. Matthew DuRose and Patrick Langan, *Felony Sentences in State Courts, 2004* (Washington, D.C.: Bureau of Justice Statistics, 2007).

8. Patrick Langan and David Levin, *Recidivism of Prisoners Released in 1994* (Washington, D.C.: Bureau of Justice Statistics, 2002).

9. Faith Lutze, "The Influence of Shock Incarceration Program on Inmate Adjustment and Attitudinal Change," *Journal of Criminal Justice 29* (2001): 255–266.

10. Tomislav Kovandzic and Lynne Vieraitis, "The Effect of County-level Prison Population Growth on Crime Rates," *Criminology & Public Policy 5* (2006): 213–244.

11. Raymond Liedka, Anne Morrison Piehl, and Bert Useem, "The Crime-Control Effect of Incarceration:

Does Scale Matter?" *Criminology & Public Policy 5* (2006): 245–276.

12. Ibid.

13. Charles Logan, *Criminal Justice Performance Measures for Prisons* (Washington, D.C.: Bureau of Justice Statistics, 1993), 3.

14. Alexis Durham, "The Justice Model in Historical Context: Early Law, the Emergence of Science, and the Rise of Incarceration," *Journal of Criminal Justice 16* (1988): 331–346.

15. Andrew von Hirsh, *Doing Justice: The Choice of Punishments* (New York: Hill and Wang, 1976).

16. Shawn Bushway, "The Impact of an Arrest on the Job Stability of Young White American Men," *Journal of Research in Crime and Delinquency 35* (1998): 454–479.

17. Lawrence W. Sherman, David P. Farrington, Doris Layton MacKenzie, Brandon Walsh, Denise Gottfredson, John Eck, Shawn Bushway, and Peter Reuter, *Evidence-Based Crime Prevention* (London: Routledge and Kegan Paul, 2002); see also Arnulf Kolstad, "Imprisonment as Rehabilitation: Offenders' Assessment of Why It Does Not Work," *Journal of Criminal Justice 24* (1996): 323–335.

18. Francis Cullen, John Paul Wright, Shayna Brown, Melissa Moon, and Brandon Applegate, "Public Support for Early Intervention Programs: Implications for a Progressive Policy Agenda," *Crime and Delinquency 44* (1998): 187–204; Richard McCorkle, "Research Note: Punish and Rehabilitate? Public Attitudes Toward Six Common Crimes," *Crime and Delinquency 39* (1993): 240–252; D. A. Andrews, Ivan Zinger, Robert Hoge, James Bonta, Paul Gendreau, and Francis Cullen, "Does Correctional Treatment Work? A Clinically Relevant and Psychologically Informed Meta-Analysis," *Criminology 28* (1990): 369–404.

19. Paula Ditton and Doris James Wilson, *Truth in Sentencing in State Prisons* (Washington, D.C.: Bureau of Justice Statistics, 1999).

20. Jo Dixon, "The Organizational Context of Criminal Sentencing," *American Journal of Sociology 100* (1995): 1157–1198.

21. Michael Tonry, *Reconsidering Indeterminate and Structured Sentencing Series: Sentencing and Corrections: Issues for the 21st Century* (Washington, D.C.: National Institute of Justice, 1999).

22. *Blakely v. Washington*, 124 S. Ct. 2531 (2004).

23. *United States v. Booker*, No. 04–104, Decided January 12, 2005.

24. Michael Tonry, "The Failure of the U.S. Sentencing Commission's Guidelines," *Crime and Delinquency 39* (1993): 131–149.

25. Sean Nicholson-Crotty, "The Impact of Sentencing Guidelines on State-Level Sanctions: An Analysis Over Time," *Crime & Delinquency 50* (2004): 395–410.

26. United States Sentencing Commission, "Final Report on the Impact of *United States v. Booker* on Federal Sentencing," March 2006, www.ussc.gov/booker _report/Booker_Report.pdf (accessed March 24, 2009).

27. Jeffrey T. Ulmer, Megan C. Kurlychek, and John H. Kramer, "Prosecutorial Discretion and the Imposition of Mandatory Minimum Sentences," *Journal of Research in Crime and Delinquency 44* (2007): 427–458.

28. Henry Scott Wallace, "Mandatory Minimums and the Betrayal of Sentencing Reform: A Legislative Dr. Jekyll and Mr. Hyde," *Federal Probation 57* (1993): 9–16.

29. Marc Mauer, *Americans Behind Bars: The International Use of Incarceration, 1992–93: Part II* (Washington, D.C.: The Sentencing Project, 1994).

30. For a review of the literature, see John L. Worrall, *Crime Control in America: What Works?* 2nd, ed. (Boston, Mass.: Allyn and Bacon, 2008), 198–199.

31. Thomas B. Marvell and Carlisle E. Moody, "The Lethal Effects of Three-Strikes Laws," *Journal of Legal Studies 30* (2001): 89–106; Thomas Kovandzic, John J. Sloan, III, and Lynne M. Vieraitis, "Unintended Consequences of Politically Popular Sentencing Policy: The Homicide-Promoting Effects of 'Three Strikes' in U.S. Cities (1980–1999)," *Criminology and Public Policy 1* (2002): 159–201.

32. *Lockyer v. Andrade*, 538 U.S. 63 (2003).

33. *Ewing v. California*, 538 U.S. 11 (2003).

34. Ditton and Wilson, *Truth in Sentencing in State Prisons*.

35. Durose and Langan, *Felony Sentences in State Courts, 2002*.

36. Matthew Durose and Patrick Langan, *Felony Sentences in State Courts, 2004* (Washington, D.C.: Bureau of Justice Statistics, 2007); www.ojp.usdoj .gov/bjs/pub/pdf/fssc04.pdf (accessed March 24, 2009).

37. Brent Smith and Kelly Damphouse, "Terrorism, Politics, and Punishment: A Test of Structural-Contextual Theory and the Liberation Hypothesis," *Criminology 36* (1998): 67–92.

38. Stewart D'Alessio and Lisa Stolzenberg, "Socioeconomic Status and the Sentencing of the Traditional Offender," *Journal of Criminal Justice 21* (1993): 61–77.

39. Cecilia Saulters-Tubbs, "Prosecutorial and Judicial Treatment of Female Offenders," *Federal Probation 57* (1993): 37–41.

40. See, generally, Janet Johnston, Thomas Kennedy, and I. Gayle Shuman, "Gender Differences in the Sentencing of Felony Offenders," *Federal Probation 87* (1987): 49–56; Cassia Spohn and Susan Welch, "The Effect of Prior Record in Sentencing Research: An Examination of the Assumption That Any Measure Is Adequate," *Justice Quarterly 4* (1987): 286–302; David Willison, "The Effects of Counsel on the Severity of Criminal Sentences: A Statistical Assessment," *Justice System Journal 9* (1984): 87–101.

41. Cassia Spohn, Miriam DeLone, and Jeffrey Spears, "Race/Ethnicity, Gender, and Sentence Severity in Dade County, Florida: An Examination of the Decision to Withhold Adjudication," *Journal of Crime and Justice 21* (1998): 111–132.

42. Ellen Hochstedler Steury and Nancy Frank, "Gender Bias and Pretrial Release: More Pieces of the Puzzle," *Journal of Criminal Justice 18* (1990): 417–432.

43. Shimica Gaskins, "Women of Circumstance—The Effects of Mandatory Minimum Sentencing on

Women Minimally Involved in Drug Crimes," *American Criminal Law Review 41* (2004): 1533–1563.

44. Shawn Bushway and Anne Morrison Piehl, "The Inextricable Link between Age and Criminal History in Sentencing," *Crime & Delinquency 53* (2007): 156–183.

45. Dean Champion, "Elderly Felons and Sentencing Severity: Interregional Variations in Leniency and Sentencing Trends," *Criminal Justice Review 12* (1987): 7–15.

46. Darrell Steffensmeier, John Kramer, and Jeffery Ulmer, "Age Differences in Sentencing," *Justice Quarterly 12* (1995): 583–601.

47. Darrell Steffensmeier, Jeffery Ulmer, and John Kramer, "The Interaction of Race, Gender, and Age in Criminal Sentencing: The Punishment Cost of Being Young, Black, and Male," *Criminology 36* (1998): 763–798.

48. Tracy Nobiling, Cassia Spohn, and Miriam DeLone, "A Tale of Two Counties: Unemployment and Sentence Severity," *Justice Quarterly 15* (1998): 459–486.

49. Shawn Bushway and Anne Morrison Piehl, "Judging Judicial Discretion: Legal Factors and Racial Discrimination in Sentencing," *Law and Society Review 35* (2001): 733–765.

50. Michael Tonry, *Malign Neglect: Race, Crime, and Punishment in America* (New York: Oxford University Press, 1995), 105–109.

51. John Wooldredge, "Neighborhood Effects on Felony Sentencing," *Journal of Research in Crime and Delinquency 44* (2007): 238–263.

52. Cassia Spohn, "Thirty Years of Sentencing Reform: A Quest for a Racially Neutral Sentencing Process, in *Policies, Processes, and Decisions of the Criminal Justice System*, vol. 3, *Criminal Justice 2000* (Washington, D.C.: U.S. Department of Justice, 2000), 455–456.

53. Ibid.

54. Bruce Western, *Punishment and Inequality in America* (New York: Russell Sage Foundation, 2006).

55. *Payne v. Tennessee*, 111 S. Ct. 2597, 115 L.Ed.2d 720 (1991).

56. Robert Davis and Barbara Smith, "The Effects of Victim Impact Statements on Sentencing Decisions: A Test in an Urban Setting," *Justice Quarterly 11* (1994): 453–469; Edna Erez and Pamela Tontodonato, "The Effect of Victim Participation in Sentencing on Sentence Outcome," *Criminology 28* (1990): 451–474.

57. Rodney Kingsworth, Randall MacIntosh, and Jennifer Wentworth, "Sexual Assault: The Role of Prior Relationship and Victim Characteristics in Case Processing," *Justice Quarterly 16* (1999): 276–302.

58. *Coker v. Georgia*, 433 U.S. 584 (1977); see also *Lockett v. Ohio*, 438 U.S. 586 (1978).

59. For more on this issue, read Hugo Adam and Paul Cassell, *Debating the Death Penalty: Should America Have Capital Punishment? The Experts on Both Sides Make Their Best Case* (London: Oxford University Press, 2003).

60. Stephen Markman and Paul Cassell, "Protecting the Innocent: A Response to the Bedeau-Radelet Study," *Stanford Law Review 41* (1988): 121–170.

61. Tracy Snell, *Capital Punishment*, 2005 (Washington, D.C.: Bureau of Justice Statistics (2006), www.ojp.usdoj.gov/bjs/pub/ascii/cp05.txt (accessed March 24, 2009).

62. Stephen Layson, "United States Time-Series Homicide Regressions with Adaptive Expectations," *Bulletin of the New York Academy of Medicine 62* (1986): 589–619.

63. James Galliher and John Galliher, "A 'Commonsense' Theory of Deterrence and the 'Ideology' of Science: The New York State Death Penalty Debate," *Journal of Criminal Law & Criminology 92* (2002): 307.

64. Steven Stack, "The Effect of Well-Publicized Executions on Homicide in California," *Journal of Crime and Justice 21* (1998): 1–12.

65. David Friedrichs, "Comment—Humanism and the Death Penalty: An Alternative Perspective," *Justice Quarterly 6* (1989): 197–209.

66. Kathleen Maguire and Ann L. Pastore, eds., *Sourcebook of Criminal Justice Statistics, 2002*, www.albany.edu/sourcebook/ (accessed March 24, 2009).

67. For an analysis of the formation of public opinion on the death penalty, see Kimberly Cook, "Public Support for the Death Penalty: A Cultural Analysis" (paper presented at the annual meeting of the American Society of Criminology, San Francisco, November 1991).

68. Alexis Durham, H. Preston Elrod, and Patrick Kinkade, "Public Support to the Death Penalty: Beyond Gallup," *Justice Quarterly 13* (1996): 705–736.

69. See, generally, Hugo Bedau, *Death Is Different: Studies in the Morality, Law, and Politics of Capital Punishment* (Boston: Northeastern University Press, 1987); Keith Otterbein, *The Ultimate Coercive Sanction* (New Haven, Conn.: HRAF Press, 1986).

70. Michael Radelet and Hugo Bedau, "Miscarriages of Justice in Potentially Capital Cases," *Stanford Law Review 40* (1987): 121–181.

71. House Subcommittee on Civil and Constitutional Rights, *Innocence and the Death Penalty: Assessing the Danger of Mistaken Executions* (Washington, D.C.: Government Printing Office, 1993).

72. Samuel R. Gross, Kristen Jacoby, Daniel J. Matheson, Nicholas Montgomery, and Sujata Patil, "Exonerations in the United States: 1989 through 2003," *Journal of Criminal Law and Criminology 95* (2005): 523–560.

73. David Stewart, "Dealing with Death," *American Bar Association Journal 80* (1994): 53.

74. "The Innocence Protection Act," editorial, *America 187* (September 23, 2002): 2–3.

75. Erik Lillquist, "Absolute Certainty and the Death Penalty," *American Criminal Law Review 42* (2005): 45–92.

76. "A Victim's Progress," *Newsweek*, June 12, 1989, 5.

77. William Doerner, "The Impact of Medical Resources on Criminally Induced Lethality: A Further Examination," *Criminology 26* (1988): 171–177.

78. Elizabeth Purdom and J. Anthony Paredes, "Capital Punishment and Human Sacrifice," in *Facing the Death Penalty: Essays on Cruel and Unusual Punishment*, ed. Michael Radelet (Philadelphia: Temple University Press, 1989), 152–153.

79. Kimberly Cook, "A Passion to Punish: Abortion Opponents Who Favor the Death Penalty," *Justice Quarterly* 15 (1998): 329–346.

80. John Whitehead, Michael Blankenship, and John Paul Wright, "Elite versus Citizen Attitudes on Capital Punishment: Incongruity between the Public and Policy Makers," *Journal of Criminal Justice* 27 (1999): 249–258.

81. Julian Roberts, "Capital Punishment, Innocence, and Public Opinion," *Criminology & Public Policy* 4 (2005): 1–3.

82. Kathleen Maguire and Ann Pastore, *Sourcebook of Criminal Justice Statistics, 1995* (Washington, D.C.: Government Printing Office, 1996), 183.

83. James Unnever and Francis Cullen, "Executing the Innocent and Support for Capital Punishment: Implications for Public Policy," *Criminology & Public Policy* 4 (2005): 3–37.

84. Scott Vollum, Dennis Longmire, and Jacqueline Buffington-Vollum, "Confidence in the Death Penalty and Support for Its Use: Exploring the Value-Expressive Dimension of Death Penalty Attitudes," *JQ: Justice Quarterly* 21 (2004): 521–546.

85. Gennaro Vito and Thomas Keil, "Elements of Support for Capital Punishment: An Examination of Changing Attitudes," *Journal of Crime and Justice* 21 (1998): 17–25.

86. Denise Paquette Boots, Kathleen Heide, and John Cochran, "Death Penalty Support for Special Offender Populations of Legally Convicted Murderers: Juveniles, the Mentally Retarded, and the Mentally Incompetent," *Behavioral Sciences & the Law* 22 (2004): 223–238.

87. James Unnever and Francis Cullen, "The Racial Divide in Support for the Death Penalty: Does White Racism Matter?" *Social Forces* 85 (2007): 1281–1301.

88. Walter C. Reckless, "Use of the Death Penalty," *Crime and Delinquency* 15 (1969): 43; Thorsten Sellin, "Effect of Repeal and Reintroduction of the Death Penalty on Homicide Rates," in *The Death Penalty*, ed. Thorsten Sellin (Philadelphia: American Law Institute, 1959); Robert H. Dann, "The Deterrent Effect of Capital Punishment," *Friends Social Service Series* 29 (1935): 1; William Bailey and Ruth Peterson, "Murder and Capital Punishment: A Monthly Time-Series Analysis of Execution Publicity," *American Sociological Review* 54 (1989): 722–743; David Phillips, "The Deterrent Effect of Capital Punishment," *American Journal of Sociology* 86 (1980): 139–148; Sam McFarland, "Is Capital Punishment a Short-Term Deterrent to Homicide? A Study of the Effects of Four Recent American Executions," *Journal of Criminal Law and Criminology* 74 (1984): 1014–1032; Richard Lempert, "The Effect of Executions on Homicides: A New Look in an Old Light," *Crime and Delinquency* 29 (1983): 88–115.

89. Jon Sorenson, Robert Wrinkle, Victoria Brewer, and James Marquart, "Capital Punishment and Deterrence: Examining the Effect of Executions on Murder in Texas," *Crime and Delinquency* 45 (1999): 481–493.

90. Isaac Ehrlich, "The Deterrent Effect of Capital Punishment: A Question of Life or Death," *American Economic Review* 65 (1975): 397.

91. For a review, see William Bailey, "The General Prevention Effect of Capital Punishment for Non-Capital Felonies," in *The Death Penalty in America: Current Research*, ed. Robert Bohm (Cincinnati, Ohio: Anderson, 1991), 21–38.

92. Bijou Yang and David Lester, "The Deterrent Effect of Executions: A Meta-Analysis of Thirty Years after Ehrlich," *Journal of Criminal Justice* 36 (2008): 453–460.

93. Jonathan R. Sorensen and Rocky L. Pilgrim, "An Actuarial Risk of Assessment of Violence Posed by Murder Defendants," *Journal of Criminal Law and Criminology* 90 (2000): 1251–1271.

94. Rick Ruddell and Martin Urbina, "Minority Threat and Punishment: A Cross-National Analysis," *JQ: Justice Quarterly* 21 (2004): 903–931.

95. Marian Williams and Jefferson Holcomb, "Racial Disparity and Death Sentences in Ohio," *Journal of Criminal Justice* 29 (2001): 207–218.

96. Jon Sorenson and Donald Wallace, "Prosecutorial Discretion in Seeking Death: An Analysis of Racial Disparity in the Pretrial Stages of Case Processing in a Midwestern County," *JQ: Justice Quarterly* 16 (1999): 559–578.

97. Marian R. Williams, "Understanding the Influence of Victim Gender in Death Penalty Cases: The Importance of Victim Race, Sex-Related Victimization, and Jury Decision Making," *Criminology* 45 (2007): 865–891; Catherine Lee, "Hispanics and the Death Penalty: Discriminatory Charging Practices in San Joaquin County, California," *Journal of Criminal Justice* 35 (2007): 17–27.

98. Jefferson Holcomb, Marian Williams, and Stephen Demuth, "White Female Victims and Death Penalty Disparity Research," *JQ: Justice Quarterly* 21 (2004): 877–902.

99. Lawrence Greenfield and David Hinners, *Capital Punishment, 1984* (Washington, D.C.: Bureau of Justice Statistics, 1985).

100. Gennaro Vito and Thomas Keil, "Capital Sentencing in Kentucky: An Analysis of the Factors Influencing Decision Making in the Post-*Gregg* Period," *The Journal of Criminal Law & Criminology* 79 (1988): 483–508.

101. David Brown, "Man Is Executed in Carolina: Second of a White Who Killed a Black," *Boston Globe*, January 25, 1995, 3.

102. James Unnever and Francis Cullen, "Reassessing the Racial Divide in Support for Capital Punishment: The Continuing Significance of Race," *Journal of Research in Crime & Delinquency* 44 (2007): 124–158.

103. Geoffrey Rapp, "The Economics of Shootouts: Does the Passage of Capital Punishment Laws Protect or Endanger Police Officers?" *Albany Law Review* 65 (2002): 1051–1084.

104. William Bailey, "Disaggregation in Deterrence and Death Penalty Research: The Case of Murder in Chicago," *Journal of Criminal Law and Criminology* 74 (1986): 827–859.

105. Gennaro Vito, Pat Koester, and Deborah Wilson, "Return of the Dead: An Update on the Status of Furman-Commuted Death Row Inmates," in

The Death Penalty in America: Current Research, ed. Robert Bohm (Cincinnati, Ohio: Anderson, 1991), 89–100; Gennaro Vito, Deborah Wilson, and Edward Latessa, "Comparison of the Dead: Attributes and Outcomes of Furman-Commuted Death Row Inmates in Kentucky and Ohio," in *The Death Penalty in America: Current Research*, ed. Robert Bohm (Cincinnati, Ohio: Anderson, 1991), 101–112.

106. John Cochran, Mitchell Chamlin, and Mark Seth, "Deterrence or Brutalization? An Impact Assessment of Oklahoma's Return to Capital Punishment," *Criminology* 32 (1994): 107–134.

107. William Bailey, "Deterrence, Brutalization, and the Death Penalty: Another Examination of Oklahoma's Return to Capital Punishment," *Justice Quarterly* 36 (1998): 711–734.

108. *Hill v. McDonough*, 547 U.S. ____ (2006).

109. Robert Johnson, *Death Work: A Study of the Modern Execution Process* (Pacific Grove, Calif.: Brooks/Cole, 1990).

110. Joseph Schumacher, "An International Look at the Death Penalty," *International Journal of Comparative and Applied Criminal Justice* 14 (1990): 307–315.

111. Don Terry, "California Prepares for Faster Execution Pace," *New York Times*, October 17, 1998, A7.

112. See, for example, Ernest Van Den Haag, *Punishing Criminals: Concerning a Very Old and Painful Question* (New York: Basic Books, 1975), 209–211; Walter Berns, "Defending the Death Penalty," *Crime and Delinquency* 26 (1980): 503–511.

113. Thoroddur Bjarnason and Michael Welch, "Father Knows Best: Parishes, Priests, and American Catholic Parishioners' Attitudes toward Capital Punishment," *Journal for the Scientific Study of Religion* 43 (2004): 103–118.

114. Franklin Zimring, *The Contradictions of American Capital Punishment* (London: Oxford University Press, 2003).

115. Vance McLaughlin and Paul Blackman, "Mass Legal Executions in Georgia," *Georgia Historical Quarterly* 88 (2004): 66–84.

116. Austin Sarat, "Innocence, Error, and the 'New Abolitionism': A Commentary," *Criminology & Public Policy* 4 (2005): 45–53.

117. *Furman v. Georgia*, 408 U.S. 238 (1972).

118. *Gregg v. Georgia*, 428 U.S. 153 (1976).

119. Ibid., at 205–207, 96 S. Ct. at 2940–2941.

120. *Ring v. Arizona*, 536 U.S. 584 (2002).

121. *Coker v. Georgia*, 430 U.S. 349 (1977); *Kennedy v. Louisiana*, 554 U.S. __ (2008).

122. *Ford v. Wainwright*, 477 U.S. 399 (1986).

123. *Atkins v. Virginia*, 536 U.S. 304 (2002).

124. *Roper v. Simmons*, 543 U.S. 551 (2005).

Box Source Notes
Careers in Criminal Justice: Forensic Psychologist

The British Psychological Society, "Forensic Psychology," http://www.bps.org.uk/careers/what-do-psychologists-do/areas/forensic .cfm (accessed June 29, 2009); Bureau of Labor Statistics, U.S. Department of Labor, "Psychologists," *Occupational Outlook Handbook, 2008–2009 Edition*, http://www.bls.gov/oco/ocos056.htm (accessed June 29, 2009).

International Justice: International Use of the Death Penalty

Death Penalty Information Center, http://www.deathpenaltyinfo.org/abolitionist-and-retentionist-countries (accessed June 29, 2009).

Chapter 10, Community Sentences: Probation, Intermediate Sanctions, and Restorative Justice

1. Brandon Applegate, Hayden Smith, Alicia Sitren, and Nicolette Fariello Springer, "From the Inside: The Meaning of Probation to Probationers," *Criminal Justice Review* 34 (2009): 80–95.

2. For a history of probation, see Edward Sieh, "From Augustus to the Progressives: A Study of Probation's Formative Years," *Federal Probation* 57 (1993): 67–72.

3. Ibid.

4. David Rothman, *Conscience and Convenience* (Boston: Little, Brown, 1980), 82–117.

5. See, generally, Todd Clear and Vincent O'Leary, *Controlling the Offender in the Community* (Lexington, Mass.: Lexington Books, 1983).

6. Lauren Glaze and Thomas Bonczar, *Probation and Parole, 2007 Statistical Tables* (Washington, D.C.: Bureau of Justice Statistics, 2008). Data on probation comes from this source, herein cited as *Probation and Parole, 2007*.

7. Matthew Durose and Patrick Langan, *Felony Sentences in the United States, 2002* (Washington, D.C.: Bureau of Justice Statistics, 2004).

8. Tracey Kyckelhahn and Thomas Cohen, *Felony Defendants in Large Urban Counties, 2004* (Washington, D.C.: Bureau of Justice Statistics, 2008).

9. Heather Barklage, Dane Miller, and Gene Bonham Jr., "Probation Conditions vs. Probation Officer Directives," *Federal Probation* 70 (2006), www.uscourts.gov/fedprob/December_2006/probationconditions.html (accessed June 20, 2007).

10. Karl Hanson and Suzanne Wallace-Carpretta, "Predictors of Criminal Recidivism among Male Batterers," *Psychology, Crime & Law* 10 (2004): 413–427.

11. *Higdon v. United States*, 627 F.2d 893 (9th Cir., 1980).

12. *United States v. Lee*, No. 01-4485 01/07/03, United States v. Lee, PICS N. 03-0023.

13. *United States v. Gallo*, 20 F.3d 7 (1st Cir., 1994).

14. Todd Clear and Edward Latessa, "Probation Officers' Roles in Intensive Supervision: Surveillance versus Treatment," *Justice Quarterly* 10 (1993): 441–462.

15. Paul von Zielbauer, "Probation Dept. Is Now Arming Officers Supervising Criminals," *New York Times*, August 7, 2003, 5.

16. Jeffrey Lin, Joel Miller, Mayumi Fukushima, "Juvenile Probation Officers' Dispositional Recommendations: Predictive Factors and Their Alignment with Predictors of Recidivism," *Journal of Crime & Justice 31* (2008): 1–34.

17. Diana Wendy Fitzgibbon, "Deconstructing Probation: Risk and Developments in Practice," *Journal of Social Work Practice 22* (2008): 85–101.

18. Hanson and Wallace-Carpretta, "Predictors of Criminal Recidivism among Male Batterers."

19. Richard Sluder and Rolando Del Carmen, "Are Probation and Parole Officers Liable for Injuries Caused by Probationers and Parolees?" *Federal Probation 54* (1990): 3–12.

20. Lawrence Sherman, "Use Probation to Prevent Murder," *Criminology & Public Policy 6* (2007): 843–849.

21. James Byrne, "Introduction to Special Issue on Risk Assessment," *Federal Probation 70* (2006), www.uscourts.gov/fedprob/September_2006/index.html (accessed June 20, 2007).

22. James Austin, "How Much Risk Can We Take? The Misuse of Risk Assessment in Corrections," *Federal Probation 70* (2006), www.uscourts.gov/fedprob/September_2006/risk.html (accessed June 20, 2007).

23. Melinda Schlager, "Validity of the Level of Service Inventory—Revised (LSI-R) among African American and Hispanic Male Offenders," *Criminal Justice and Behavior 34* (2007): 545–554; Carolin Kröner, Cornelis Stadtland, Matthias Eidt, and Norbert Nedopil, "The Validity of the Violence Risk Appraisal Guide (VRAG) in Predicting Criminal Recidivism," *Criminal Behaviour & Mental Health 17* (2007): 89–100.

24. *Minnesota v. Murphy*, 465 U.S. 420, 104 S. Ct. 1136, 79 L.Ed.2d 409 (1984).

25. *Griffin v. Wisconsin*, 483 U.S. 868, 107 S. Ct. 3164, 97 L.Ed.2d 709 (1987).

26. *United States v. Knights*, 122 S. Ct. 587 (2001).

27. *Mempa v. Rhay*, 389 U.S. 128, 88 S. Ct. 254, 19 L.Ed.2d 336 (1967).

28. *Morrissey v. Brewer*, 408 U.S. 471, 92 S. Ct. 2593, 33 L.Ed.2d 484 (1972).

29. *Gagnon v. Scarpelli*, 411 U.S. 778, 93 S. Ct. 1756, 36 L.Ed.2d 656 (1973).

30. *Beardon v. Georgia* 33 CrL 3101 (1983).

31. *United States v. Granderson*, 114 Ct. 1259, 127 L.Ed.2d 611 (1994).

32. *Probation and Parole, 2006*.

33. M. Kevin Gray, Monique Fields, and Sheila Royo Maxwell, "Examining Probation Violations: Who, What, and When," *Crime and Delinquency 47* (2001): 537–557.

34. Nancy Rodriguez and Vincent Webb, "Probation Violations, Revocations, and Imprisonment: The Decisions of Probation Officers, Prosecutors, and Judges Pre- and Post-Mandatory Drug Treatment," *Criminal Justice Policy Review 18* (2007): 3–30.

35. Kevin Minor, James Wells, and Crissy Sims, "Recidivism among Federal Probationers—Predicting Sentence Violations," *Federal Probation 67* (2003): 31–37.

36. Cassia Spohn and David Holleran, "The Effect of Imprisonment on Recidivism Rates of Felony Offenders: A Focus on Drug Offenders," *Criminology 40* (2002): 329–359.

37. Joan Petersilia, Susan Turner, James Kahan, and Joyce Peterson, *Granting Felons Probation: Public Risks and Alternatives* (Santa Monica, Calif.: Rand, 1985).

38. Spohn and Holleran, "The Effect of Imprisonment on Recidivism Rates of Felony Offenders."

39. Paula M. Ditton, *Mental Health and Treatment of Inmates and Probationers* (Washington, D.C.: Bureau of Justice Statistics, 1999).

40. Kathryn Morgan, "Factors Associated with Probation Outcome," *Journal of Criminal Justice 22* (1994): 341–353.

41. Naomi Freeman, "Predictors of Rearrest for Rapists and Child Molesters on Probation," *Criminal Justice and Behavior 34* (2007): 752–768.

42. Kathryn Morgan, "Factors Influencing Probation Outcome: A Review of the Literature," *Federal Probation 57* (1993): 23–29.

43. Diana Wendy Fitzgibbon, "Deconstructing Probation."

44. Joan Petersilia, "Probation in the United States," in *Crime and Justice: A Review of Research 21* (Chicago: University of Chicago Press, 1997), 185.

45. "Law in Massachusetts Requires Probationers to Pay 'Day Fees,'" *Criminal Justice Newsletter*, September 15, 1988, 1.

46. Peter Finn and Dale Parent, *Making the Offender Foot the Bill: A Texas Program* (Washington, D.C.: National Institute of Justice, 1992).

47. State of Arizona, Senate Bill 1476 (2008), http://www.votesmart.org/billtext/18014.pdf

48. Nicole Leeper Piquero, "A Recidivism Analysis of Maryland's Community Probation Program," *Journal of Criminal Justice 31* (2003): 295–308.

49. Todd R. Clear, "Places Not Cases: Rethinking the Probation Focus," *Howard Journal of Criminal Justice 44* (2005): 172–184.

50. Andrew Klein and Ann Crowe, "Findings from an Outcome Examination of Rhode Island's Specialized Domestic Violence Probation Supervision Program," *Violence against Women 14* (2008): 226–246.

51. Private Probation Services, http://www.privateprobationservices.com/index.html (accessed June 5, 2008).

52. Christine Schloss and Leanne Alarid, "Standards in the Privatization of Probation Services: A statutory analysis," *Criminal Justice Review 32* (2007): 233–245.

53. "HOPE in Hawaii: Swift and Sure Changes in Probation," National Institute of Justice, 2008, http://www.ncjrs.gov/pdffiles1/nij/222758.pdf

54. Ariel Hart, "Runaway Bride Enters Plea and Is Sentenced to Probation," *New York Times*, June 3, 2005, A14.

55. Todd Clear and Patricia Hardyman, "The New Intensive Supervision Movement," *Crime and Delinquency 36* (1990): 42–60.

56. Norval Morris and Michael Tonry, *Between Prison and Probation: Intermediate Punishments in a Rational Sentencing System* (New York: Oxford University Press, 1990).

57. Ibid., 8.

58. For a thorough review of these programs, see James Byrne, Arthur Lurigio, and Joan Petersilia, eds.,

Smart Sentencing: The Emergence of Intermediate Sanctions (Newbury Park, Calif.: Sage, 1993). Hereinafter cited as *Smart Sentencing*.

59. Michael Tonry and Richard Will, *Intermediate Sanctions* (Washington, D.C.: National Institute of Justice, 1990).

60. Sally Hillsman and Judith Greene, "Tailoring Fines to the Financial Means of Offenders," *Judicature 72* (1988): 38–45.

61. George Cole, "Monetary Sanctions: The Problem of Compliance," in *Smart Sentencing*, 51–64.

62. *Tate v. Short*, 401 U.S. 395, 91 S. Ct. 668, 28 L.Ed.2d 130 (1971).

63. Pennsylvania Department of Corrections, *Day Fines, 2003*, www.cor.state.pa.us/stats/lib/stats/Day_Fines .pdf (accessed June 20, 2007).

64. Doris Layton MacKenzie, "Evidence-Based Corrections: Identifying What Works," *Crime and Delinquency 46* (2000): 457–472.

65. John L. Worrall, "Addicted to the Drug War: The Role of Civil Asset Forfeiture as a Budgetary Necessity in Contemporary Law Enforcement," *Journal of Criminal Justice 29* (2001): 171–187.

66. C. Yorke, *Some Consideration on the Law of Forfeiture for High Treason*, 2d ed. (1746), 26; cited in David Fried, "Rationalizing Criminal Forfeiture," *Journal of Criminal Law and Criminology 79* (1988): 328–436.

67. Fried, "Rationalizing Criminal Forfeiture," 436.

68. James B. Jacobs, Coleen Friel, and Edward O'Callaghan, "Pension Forfeiture: A Problematic Sanction for Public Corruption," *American Criminal Law Review 35* (1997): 57–92.

69. Worrall, "Addicted to the Drug War."

70. For a general review, see Burt Galaway and Joe Hudson, *Criminal Justice, Restitution, and Reconciliation* (New York: Criminal Justice Press, 1990); Robert Carter, Jay Cocks, and Daniel Glazer, "Community Service: A Review of the Basic Issues," *Federal Probation 51* (1987): 4–11.

71. Frederick Allen and Harvey Treger, "Community Service Orders in Federal Probation: Perceptions of Probationers and Host Agencies," *Federal Probation 54* (1990): 8–14.

72. Gail Caputo, "Community Service in Texas: Results of a Probation Survey," *Corrections Compendium 30* (2005): 8–12.

73. Sudipto Roy, "Two Types of Juvenile Restitution Programs in Two Midwestern Counties: A Comparative Study," *Federal Probation 57* (1993): 48–53.

74. Joan Petersilia, *The Influence of Criminal Justice Research* (Santa Monica, Calif.: Rand, 1987).

75. Ibid.

76. Jodi Brown, *Correctional Populations in the United States, 1996* (Washington, D.C.: Bureau of Justice Statistics, 1999), 39.

77. Jodi Lane, Susan Turner, Terry Fain, and Amber Sehgal, "Evaluating an Experimental Intensive Juvenile Probation Program: Supervision and Official Outcomes," *Crime and Delinquency 51* (2005): 26–52.

78. Greg Warchol, "Intensive Supervision Probation: An Impact Evaluation," *Justice Professional 13* (2000): 219–232.

79. James Byrne and Linda Kelly, "Restructuring Probation as an Intermediate Sanction: An Evaluation of the Massachusetts Intensive Probation Supervision Program," final report to the National Institute of Justice, Research Program on the Punishment and Control of Offenders, Washington, D.C., 1989.

80. James Ryan, "Who Gets Revoked? A Comparison of Intensive Supervision Successes and Failures in Vermont," *Crime and Delinquency 43* (1997): 104–118.

81. Angela Robertson, Paul Grimes, and Kevin Rogers, "A Short-Run Cost-Benefit Analysis of Community-Based Interventions for Juvenile Offenders," *Crime and Delinquency 47* (2001): 265–284.

82. S. Christopher Baird and Dennis Wagner, "Measuring Diversion: The Florida Community Control Program," *Crime and Delinquency 36* (1990): 112–125.

83. Linda Smith and Ronald Akers, "A Comparison of Recidivism of Florida's Community Control and Prison: A Five-Year Survival Analysis," *Journal of Research in Crime and Delinquency 30* (1993): 267–292.

84. Robert N. Altman, Robert E. Murray, and Evey B. Wooten, "Home Confinement: A 90s Approach to Community Supervision," *Federal Probation 61* (1997): 30–32.

85. Ronnie Garrett, "Home Monitoring System Boosts Victim and Community Safety," *Law Enforcement Technology 34* (2007): 120–124.

86. Omnilink Systems, http://www.omnilink.com/default .asp (accessed June 5, 2008).

87. Edna Erez and Peter Ibarra, "Making Your Home a Shelter: Electronic Monitoring and Victim Re-Entry in Domestic Violence Cases," *British Journal of Criminology, 47* (2007): 100–120.

88. Matthew DeMichele, Brian Payne, and Deeanna Button, "Electronic Monitoring of Sex Offenders: Identifying Unanticipated Consequences and Implications," *Journal of Offender Rehabilitation 46* (2008): 119–135.

89. Kathy Padgett, William Bales, and Thomas Blomberg, "Under Surveillance: An Empirical Test of the Effectiveness and Consequences of Electronic Monitoring," *Criminology & Public Policy 5* (2006): 61–91.

90. William Burrell and Robert Gable, "From B. F. Skinner to Spiderman to Martha Stewart: The Past, Present and Future of Electronic Monitoring of Offenders," *Journal of Offender Rehabilitation 46* (2008): 101–118.

91. See, generally, Edward Latessa and Lawrence Travis III, "Residential Community Correctional Programs," in *Smart Sentencing*, 65–79.

92. Updated with personal correspondence, Portland House personnel, September 22, 2005.

93. Dale Parent, *Day Reporting Centers for Criminal Offenders: A Descriptive Analysis of Existing Programs* (Washington, D.C.: National Institute of Justice, 1990); Jack McDevitt and Robyn Miliano, "Day Reporting Centers: An Innovative Concept in Intermediate Sanctions," in *Smart Sentencing*, 80–105.

94. David Diggs and Stephen Pieper, "Using Day Reporting Centers as an Alternative to Jail," *Federal Probation* 58 (1994): 9–12.

95. For information on the Atlanta program, see www.dcor.state.ga.us/Divisions/Corrections/ProbationSupervision/DayReporting.html (accessed June 20, 2007).

96. Michael Ostermann, "An Analysis of New Jersey's Day Reporting Center and Halfway Back Programs: Embracing the Rehabilitative Ideal Through Evidence Based Practices," *Journal of Offender Rehabilitation* 48 (2009): 139–153.

97. Dae-Young Kim, Hee-Jong Joo, and William McCarty, "Risk Assessment and Classification of Day Reporting Center Clients: An Actuarial Approach," *Criminal Justice and Behavior* 35 (2008): 792–812.

98. Amy Craddock, "Day Reporting Center Completion: Comparison of Individual and Multilevel Models," *Crime and Delinquency* 55 (2009): 105–133; Sudipto Roy and Shannon Barton, "Convicted Drunk Drivers in Electronic Monitoring Home Detention and Day Reporting Centers," *Federal Probation* 70 (2006), www.uscourts.gov/fedprob/June_2006/drunkdrivers.html (accessed June 20, 2007).

99. Kathleen Daly and Russ Immarigeon, "The Past, Present, and Future of Restorative Justice: Some Critical Reflections," *Contemporary Justice Review 1* (1998): 21–45.

100. John Braithwaite, *Crime, Shame, and Reintegration* (Melbourne, Australia: Cambridge University Press, 1989).

101. Gene Stephens, "The Future of Policing: From a War Model to a Peace Model," in *The Past, Present and Future of American Criminal Justice*, eds. Brendan Maguire and Polly Radosh (Dix Hills, N.Y.: General Hall, 1996), 77–93.

102. Kay Pranis, "Peacemaking Circles: Restorative Justice in Practice Allows Victims and Offenders to Begin Repairing the Harm," *Corrections Today 59* (1997): 74.

103. Carol LaPrairie, "The 'New' Justice: Some Implications for Aboriginal Communities," *Canadian Journal of Criminology 40* (1998): 61–79.

104. Robert Coates, Mark Umbreit, and Betty Vos, "Restorative Justice Systemic Change: The Washington County Experience," *Federal Probation 68* (2004): 16–23.

105. David R. Karp and Beau Breslin, "Restorative Justice in School Communities," *Youth & Society 33* (2001): 249–272.

106. Paul Jesilow and Deborah Parsons, "Community Policing as Peacemaking," *Policing & Society 10* (2000): 163–183.

107. Aidan Wilcox, Richard Young, and Carolyn Hoyle, "Two-Year Resanctioning Study: A Comparison of Restorative and Traditional Cautions" (British Home Office: 2004), www.homeoffice.gov.uk/rds/pdfs04/rdsolr5704.pdf (accessed June 1, 2007); Lynette Parker, "Evaluating Restorative Programmes: Reports from Two Countries" (Restorative Justice.org: June 2005), www.restorativejustice.org/'itions/2005/june05/evaluations (accessed June 1, 2007); Aidan Wilcox and Richard Young, "How Green Was Thames Valley? Policing the Image of Restorative Justice Cautions," *Policing & Society 17* (2007): 141–163.

108. Australian Institute of Criminology, *Restorative Justice: An Australian Perspective*, www.aic.gov.au/rjustice/australia.html (accessed May 16, 2007); Kathleen Daly and Hennessey Hayes, *Restorative Justice and Conferencing in Australia*, http://www.aic.gov.au/publications/tandi/tandi186.html (accessed May 15, 2008); Hennessey Hayes "Assessing Reoffending in Restorative Justice Conferences," *Australian and New Zealand Journal of Criminology 38* (2005): 77–101.

109. Gordon Bazemore and Curt Taylor Griffiths, "Conferences, Circles, Boards, and Mediations: The 'New Wave' of Community Justice Decision Making," *Federal Probation 61* (1997): 25–37.

110. Mark Umbreit and Rina Ritter, "Arab Offenders Meet Jewish Victim: Restorative Family Dialogue in Israel," *Conflict Resolution Quarterly 24* (2006): 99–109.

111. John Braithwaite, "Setting Standards for Restorative Justice," *British Journal of Criminology 42* (2002): 563–577.

112. Nancy Rodriguez, "Restorative Justice, Communities, and Delinquency: Whom Do We Reintegrate?" *Criminology & Public Policy 4* (2005): 103–130.

113. John Braithwaite, "Setting Standards for Restorative Justice."

114. David Altschuler, "Community Justice Initiatives: Issues and Challenges in the U.S. Context," *Federal Probation 65* (2001): 28–33.

115. Lois Presser and Patricia Van Voorhis, "Values and Evaluation: Assessing Processes and Outcomes of Restorative Justice Programs," *Crime and Delinquency 48* (2002): 162–189.

116. Sharon Levrant, Francis Cullen, Betsy Fulton, and John Wozniak, "Reconsidering Restorative Justice: The Corruption of Benevolence Revisited? *Crime and Delinquency 45* (1999): 3–28.

117. Dean Gromet and John Darley, "Restoration and Retribution: How Including Retributive Components Affects the Acceptability of Restorative Justice Procedures," *Social Justice Research 19* (2006): 395–432.

118. Michael E. Smith, *What Future for "Public Safety" and "Restorative Justice" in Community Corrections?* (Washington, D.C.: National Institute of Justice, 2001).

Box Source Notes
Careers in Criminal Justice: Probation Officer

Andrew Alpert, "Probation Officers and Correctional Treatment Specialists," *Occupational Outlook Quarterly 45* (2001), www.bls.gov/opub/ooq/2001/Fall/art05.pdf (accessed June 20, 2007); Bureau of Labor Statistics, "Probation Officers and Correctional Treatment Specialists—Working to Rehabilitate Offenders," www.bls.gov/opub/ted/2001/sept/wk4/art05.htm (accessed June 20, 2007).

Criminal Justice and Technology: Monitoring Probationers with Technology

National Law Enforcement and Corrections Technology Center, "Community Corrections Directions," *Tech Beat*, Spring 2007, http://www.nlectc.org/TECHBeat/spring2007/CommunityCorrections.pdf

Chapter 11, Corrections: History, Institutions, and Populations

1. Heather West and William J. Sabol, *Prisoners in 2007* (Washington, D.C.: Bureau of Justice Statistics, 2008). http://www.ojp.usdoj.gov/bjs/pub/ascii/p07.txt (accessed March 1, 2009).

2. See David Fogel, *We Are the Living Proof*, 2d ed. (Cincinnati: Anderson, 1978); Andrew von Hirsch, *Doing Justice: The Choice of Punishments* (New York: Hill and Wang, 1976).

3. Francis Cullen, "The Twelve People Who Saved Rehabilitation: How the Science of Criminology Made a Difference," *Criminology 43* (2005): 1–42.

4. Malcolm Feeley and Jonathan Simon, "The New Penology: Notes on the Emerging Strategy of Corrections and Its Implications," *Criminology 30* (2006): 449–474.

5. Thomas Stucky, Karen Heimer, and Joseph Lang, "Partisan Politics, Electoral Competition, and Imprisonment: An Analysis of States over Time," *Criminology 43* (2005): 211–247.

6. Among the most helpful sources in developing this section were Mark Colvin, *Penitentiaries, Reformatories, and Chain Gangs* (New York: St. Martin's Press, 1997); Benedict Alper, *Prisons Inside-Out* (Cambridge, Mass.: Ballinger, 1974); Harry Elmer Barnes, *The Story of Punishment*, 2d ed. (Montclair, N.J.: Patterson-Smith, 1972); Gustave de Beaumont and Alexis de Tocqueville, *On the Penitentiary System in the United States and Its Applications in France* (Carbondale: Southern Illinois University Press, 1964); Orlando Lewis, *The Development of American Prisons and Prison Customs, 1776–1845* (Montclair, N.J.: Patterson-Smith, 1967); Georg Rusche and Otto Kircheimer, *Punishment and Social Structure* (New York: Russell and Russell, 1939); Samuel Walker, *Popular Justice* (New York: Oxford University Press, 1980); Graeme Newman, *The Punishment Response* (Philadelphia: J. B. Lippincott, 1978); David Rothman, *Conscience and Convenience* (Boston: Little, Brown, 1980).

7. Frederick Pollock and Frederick Maitland, *History of English Law* (London: Cambridge University Press, 1952).

8. Marvin Wolfgang, "Crime and Punishment in Renaissance Florence," *Journal of Criminal Law and Criminology 81* (1990): 567–584.

9. John Howard, *The State of Prisons*, 4th ed. (1792; reprint, Montclair, N.J.: Patterson-Smith, 1973).

10. Alexis Durham III, "Newgate of Connecticut: Origins and Early Days of an Early American Prison," *Justice Quarterly 6* (1989): 89–116.

11. Dario Melossi and Massimo Pavarini, *The Prison and the Factory: Origins of the Penitentiary System* (Totowa, N.J.: Barnes & Noble, 1981).

12. Lewis, *Development of American Prisons and Prison Customs*, p. 17.

13. Ibid., p. 29.

14. See, generally, David Rothman, *The Discovery of the Asylum* (Boston: Little, Brown, 1970).

15. Leonard Orland, *Justice, Punishment, and Treatment* (New York: Free Press, 1973), 143.

16. Ibid., p. 144.

17. Walker, *Popular Justice*, p. 70.

18. Ibid., p. 71.

19. Beverly Smith, "Military Training at New York's Elmira Reformatory, 1880–1920," *Federal Probation 52* (1988): 33–41.

20. William Parker, *Parole: Origins, Development, Current Practices, and Statutes* (College Park, Md.: American Correctional Association, 1972); Samuel Walker, *Popular Justice*.

21. This section leans heavily on David Rothman, *Conscience and Convenience*.

22. Ibid., p. 23.

23. Ibid., p. 133.

24. 18 U.S.C. 1761.

25. Barbara Auerbach, George Sexton, Franlin Farrow, and Robert Lawson, *Work in American Prisons: The Private Sector Gets Involved* (Washington, D.C.: National Institute of Justice, 1988), p. 72.

26. See, generally, Jameson Doig, *Criminal Corrections: Ideals and Realities* (Lexington, Mass.: Lexington Books, 1983).

27. Bonnie Green, Jeanne Miranda, Anahita Daroowalla, and Juned Siddique, "Trauma Exposure, Mental Health Functioning, and Program Needs of Women in Jail," *Crime and Delinquency 51* (2005):133–151.

28. Sonia Alemagno and Jill Dickie, "Employment Issues of Women in Jail," *Journal of Employment Counseling 42* (2005): 67–74.

29. Rachel McLean, Jacqueline Robarge, and Susan Sherman, "Release from Jail: Moment of Crisis or Window of Opportunity for Female Detainees?" *Journal of Urban Health 83* (2006): 382–393.

30. Fred Heinzlemann, W. Robert Burkhart, Bernard Gropper, Cheryl Martorana, Lois Felson Mock, Maureen O'Connor, and Walter Philip Travers, *Jailing Drunk Drivers: Impact on the Criminal Justice System* (Washington, D.C.: National Institute of Justice, 1984).

31. Kevin Krause, "Inspectors Fault Medical Care at Dallas County Jail," *Dallas Morning News*, February 4, 2009, http://www.dallasnews.com/sharedcontent/dws/news/localnews/stories/DN-jailreport_05met.ART.State.Edition1.4c50f36.html (accessed March 1, 2009).

32. Caroline Wolf Harlow, *Prior Abuse Reported by Inmates and Probationers* (Washington, D.C.: Bureau of Justice Statistics, 1999).

33. Doris James and Lauren Glaze, *Mental Health Problems of Prison and Jail Inmates* (Washington, D.C.: Bureau of Justice Statistics, 2006).

34. NBC5.com, Chicago, "Suicides Top List of Lake County Jail's Problems, Federal Report: Inmates Killing Themselves at Alarming Rate," May 20, 2007, www.nbc5.com/news/13354500/detail.html (accessed June 24, 2007).

35. Brandon Applegate, Ray Surette, and Bernard McCarthy, "Detention and Desistance from Crime: Evaluating the Influence of a New Generation of Jail on Recidivism," *Journal of Criminal Justice 27* (1999): 539–548.

36. Ibid.

37. Christine Tartaro, "Watered Down: Partial Implementation of the New Generation Jail Philosophy," *Prison Journal 86* (2006): 284–300.

38. Kristen Hughes, *Justice Expenditure and Employment in the United States, 2003* (Washington, D.C.: Bureau of Justice Statistics, 2006).

39. Human Rights Watch, *Prison Conditions in the United States*, www.hrw.org/wr2k2/prisons.html (accessed September 14, 2005).

40. "Suit Alleges Violations in California's 'Super-Max' Prison," *Criminal Justice Newsletter*, September 1, 1993, 2.

41. Jody Sundt, Thomas Castellano, and Chad Briggs, "The Sociopolitical Context of Prison Violence and Its Control: A Case Study of Supermax and Its Effect in Illinois," *The Prison Journal 88* (2008): 94–122.

42. Daniel Mears, "An Assessment of Supermax Prisons Using an Evaluation Research Framework," *The Prison Journal 88* (2008): 43–68; Daniel Mears and Jennifer Castro, "Wardens' Views on the Wisdom of Supermax Prisons," *Crime and Delinquency 52* (2006): 398–431; Daniel Mears and Jamie Watson, "Towards a Fair and Balanced Assessment of Supermax Prisons," *Justice Quarterly 23* (2006): 232–270.

43. James Anderson, Laronistine Dyson, and Jerald Burns, *Boot Camps: An Intermediate Sanction* (Lanham, Md.: University Press of America, 1999), 1–17.

44. Ibid., 328–329.

45. Doris Layton Mackenzie, "Boot Camp Prisons: Components, Evaluations, and Empirical Issues," *Federal Probation 54* (1990): 44–52; see also "Boot Camp Programs Grow in Number and Scope," *NIJ Reports* (November/December 1990): 6–8.

46. Doris Layton Mackenzie and James Shaw, "The Impact of Shock Incarceration on Technical Violations and New Criminal Activities," *Justice Quarterly 10* (1993): 463–487.

47. Doris Layton Mackenzie, Robert Brame, David McDowall, and Claire Souryal, "Boot Camp Prisons and Recidivism in Eight States," *Criminology 33* (1995): 327–358.

48. Vanessa St. Gerard, "Federal Prisons to Eliminate Boot Camps," *Corrections Today 67* (2005): 13–16.

49. Correctional Research Associates, *Treating Youthful Offenders in the Community: An Evaluation Conducted by A. J. Reiss* (Washington, D.C.: Correctional Research Associates, 1966).

50. Kevin Krajick, "Not on My Block: Local Opposition Impedes the Search for Alternatives," *Corrections Magazine 6* (1980): 15–27.

51. "Many State Legislatures Focused on Crime in 1995, Study Finds," *Criminal Justice Newsletter*, January 2, 1996, 2.

52. Corrections Corporation of America, http://www.correctionscorp.com/about/; Palash Ghosh, "Private Prisons Have a Lock on Growth," *Business Week Online*, July 7, 2006, 5.

53. The Geo Group homepage, http://www.thegeogroupinc.com/index.html

54. West and Sabol, *Prisoners in 2007*.

55. Richard Harding, "Private Prisons," in *Crime and Justice: An Annual Edition*, ed. Michael Tonry (Chicago: University of Chicago Press, 2001), 265–347.

56. William Bales, Laura Bedard, Susan Quinn, David Ensley, and Glen Holley, "Recidivism of Public and Private State Prison Inmates in Florida," *Criminology & Public Policy 4* (2005): 57–82; Lonn Lanza-Kaduce, Karen Parker, and Charles Thomas, "A Comparative Recidivism Analysis of Releases from Private and Public Prisons," *Crime and Delinquency 45* (1999): 28–47.

57. Charles Thomas, "Recidivism of Public and Private State Prison Inmates in Florida: Issues and Unanswered Questions," *Criminology & Public Policy 4* (2005): 89–99; Travis Pratt and Jeff Maahs, "Are Private Prisons More Cost-Effective Than Public Prisons? A Meta-Analysis of Evaluation Research Studies," *Crime and Delinquency 45* (1999): 358–371.

58. Ira Robbins, *The Legal Dimensions of Private Incarceration* (Chicago: American Bar Association, 1988).

59. Danica Coto, "Medical Care Company Named in Numerous Jail Lawsuits," *Charlotte Observer*, August 30, 2004.

60. *Richardson v. McKnight*, 521 U.S. 399 (1997).

61. Ahmed A. White, "Rule of Law and the Limits of Sovereignty: The Private Prison in Jurisprudential Perspective," *American Criminal Law Review 38* (2001): 111–147; *Correctional Services Corp. v. Malesko*, 534 U.S. 61, 122 S. Ct. 515 (2001).

62. Lawrence Travis, Edward Latessa, and Gennaro Vito, "Private Enterprise and Institutional Corrections: A Call for Caution," *Federal Probation 49* (1985): 11–17.

63. Patrick Anderson, Charles Davoli, and Laura Moriarty, "Private Corrections: Feast or Fiasco?" *Prison Journal 65* (1985): 32–41.

64. Richard Culp, "The Rise and Stall of Prison Privatization: An Integration of Policy Analysis Perspectives," *Criminal Justice Policy Review 16* (2005): 412–442.

65. Heather West and William Sabol, *Prisoners in 2007* (Washington, D.C.: Bureau of Justice Statistics, 2008), http://www.ojp.usdoj.gov/bjs/pub/pdf/p07.pdf (accessed March 1, 2009).

66. Pew Foundation, 1 in 31, *The Long Reach of American Corrections*, http://www.pewtrusts.org/uploadedFiles/wwwpewtrustsorg/Reports/sentencing_and_corrections/PSPP_1in31_report_FINAL_WEB_2-27-09.pdf

67. West and Sabol, *Prisoners in 2007*.

68. Caroline Wolf Harlow, *Education and Correctional Populations* (Washington, D.C.: Bureau of Justice Statistics, 2003).

69. Greg Greenberg and Robert Rosenheck, "Homelessness in the State and Federal Prison Population," *Criminal Behaviour & Mental Health 18* (2008): 88–103

70. Seena Fazel and John Danesh, "Serious Mental Disorder in 23,000 Prisoners: A Systematic Review of Sixty-Two Surveys," *Lancet 359* (2002): 545–561.

71. West and Sabol, *Prisoners in 2007*.

72. Sean Nicholson-Crotty, The Impact of Sentencing Guidelines on State-level Sanctions: An Analysis over Time," *Crime and Delinquency 50* (2004): 395–411.

73. Todd Clear, *Harm in American Penology: Offenders, Victims, and Their Communities* (Albany: State University of New York Press, 1994).

74. Benjamin Steiner and John Wooldredge**,** "Comparing State- versus Facility-level Effects on Crowding in U.S. Correctional Facilities," Crime and Delinquency 54 (2008): 259–290.

75. Thomas P. Bonczar and Allen J. Beck, *Lifetime Likelihood of Going to State or Federal Prison* (Washington, D.C.: Bureau of Justice Statistics, 1997).

76. Andrew Lang Golub, Farrukh Hakeem, and Bruce Johnson, *Monitoring the Decline in the Crack Epidemic with Data from the Drug Use Forecasting Program, Final Report* (Washington, D.C.: National Institute of Justice, 1996).

Box Source Notes
Careers in Criminal Justice: Corrections Counselor

Bureau of Labor Statistics, U.S. Department of Labor, "Counselors," *Occupational Outlook Handbook, 2008–2009 Edition*; www.bls.gov/oco/ocos067.htm (accessed February 25, 2009); Bureau of Labor Statistics, Occupational Employment and Wages, May 2005, www.bls.gov/oes/current/oes_nat.htm (accessed June 24, 2007).

Criminal Justice and Technology: Technocorrections: Contemporary Correctional Technology

Corrections Assistance, Tech Beat, *The Office of Justice Programs' National Institute of Justice (NIJ) 20080*, http://www.nlectc.org/TECHBeat/winter2008/CorrectionsAssistance.pdf John Ward, "Jump-Starting Projects to Automate Correctional Processes," *Corrections Today 68* (2006): 82–83; Debbie Mahaffey, "Security and Technology: The Human Side," *Corrections Today 66* (2004): 8; Frank Lu and Laurence Wolfe, "Automated Record Tracking (SMART) Application," *Corrections Today 66* (2004): 78–81; Gary Burdett and Mike Retford, "Technology Improves Security and Reduces Staff in Two Illinois Prisons," *Corrections Today 65* (2003): 109–110; Tony Fabelo, *Technocorrections: The Promises, the Uncertain Threats, Sentencing & Corrections: Issues for the 21st Century Series* (Washington, D.C.: National Institute of Justice, 2000).

Chapter 12, Prison Life: Living in and Leaving Prison

1. Sarah Lawrence and Jeremy Travis, *The New Landscape of Imprisonment: Mapping America's Prison Expansion* (Washington, D.C.: Urban Institute, 2004), http://www.urban.org/UploadedPDF/410994_mapping_prisons.pdf.

2. James Stephan and Jennifer Karberg, *Census of State and Federal Correctional Facilities, 2000* (Washington, D.C.: Bureau of Justice Statistics, 2003). Updated 2008.

3. Timothy Hughes and Doris James Wilson, "Reentry Trends in the United States: Inmates Returning to the Community after Serving Time in Prison," Bureau of Justice Statistics, http://www.ojp.usdoj.gov/bjs/reentry/reentry.htm (accessed March 1, 2009).

4. Ros Burnett and Shadd Maruna, "So 'Prison Works,' Does It? The Criminal Careers of 130 Men Released from Prison under Home Secretary Michael Howard," *Howard Journal of Criminal Justice 43* (2004): 390–404.

5. Richard Berk, Heather Ladd, Heidi Graziano, and Jong-Ho Baek, "A Randomized Experiment Testing Inmate Classification Systems," *Criminology & Public Policy 2* (2003): 215–242.

6. James A. Paluch Jr., *A Life for a Life, Life Imprisonment (America's Other Death Penalty)* (Los Angeles: Roxbury Press, 2004), 4.

7. David Eichenthal and James Jacobs, "Enforcing the Criminal Law in State Prisons," *Justice Quarterly 8* (1991): 283–303.

8. Manop Kanato, "Drug Use and Health among Prison Inmates," *Current Opinion in Psychiatry 21* (2008): 252–254

9. Gresham Sykes, *The Society of Captives* (Princeton, N.J.: Princeton University Press, 1958).

10. Karen Lahm, "Inmate-on-Inmate Assault: A Multilevel Examination of Prison Violence," *Criminal Justice and Behavior 35* (2008): 120–137.

11. Thomas, Noll, "Sexual Violence in Prison" *International Journal of Offender Therapy and Comparative Criminology 52* (2008): 251–252.

12. Christopher Hensley, Mary Koscheski, and Richard Tewksbury, "Examining the Characteristics of Male Sexual Assault Targets in a Southern Maximum-Security Prison," *Journal of Interpersonal Violence 20* (2005): 667–679.

13. T. J. Parsell, *Fish: A Memoir of a Boy in a Man's Prison* (Cambridge, Mass., Da Capo Press, 2007).

14. S. 1435[108]: Prison Rape Elimination Act of 2003; Public Law No: 108–179.

15. Christopher Hensley and Richard.Tewksbury, "Wardens' Perceptions of Prison Sex," *Prison Journal 85* (2005): 186–197.

16. Tonisha Jones and Travis Pratt, "The Prevalence of Sexual Violence in Prison," *International Journal of Offender Therapy and Comparative Criminology 52* (2008): 280–295.

17. Allen J. Beck and Timothy A. Hughes, *Sexual Violence Reported by Correctional Authorities, 2004* (Washington, D.C.: Bureau of Justice Statistics, 2005).

18. Allen J. Beck and Paige M. Harrison, *Sexual Victimization in State and Federal Prisons Reported by Inmates, 2007* (Washington, D.C.: Bureau of Justice Statistics, 2007), http://www.ojp.usdoj.gov/bjs/pub/pdf/svsfpri07.pdf

19. John Wooldredge, "Inmate Lifestyles and Opportunities for Victimization," *Journal of Research in Crime and Delinquency* 35 (1998): 480–502.

20. Charles Schwaebe, "Learning to Pass: Sex Offenders' Strategies for Establishing a Viable Identity in the Prison General Population," *International Journal of Offender Therapy & Comparative Criminology* 49 (2005): 614–625.

21. Attapol Kuanliang, Jon Sorensen, and Mark Cunningham," Juvenile Inmates in an Adult Prison System: Rates of Disciplinary Misconduct and Violence," *Criminal Justice and Behavior,* 35 (2008): 1186–1201.

22. Mark Kellar and Hsiao-Ming Wang, "Inmate Assaults in Texas County Jails," *Prison Journal* 85 (2005): 515–534.

23. Benjamin Steiner and John Wooldredge, "Inmate versus Environmental Effects on Prison Rule Violations," *Criminal Justice and Behavior* 35 (2008): 438–456.

24. Robert Johnson, *Hard Time: Understanding and Reforming the Prison* (Monterey, Calif.: Brooks/Cole, 1987), 115.

25. John Gibbons and Nicholas de B. Katzenbach, *Confronting Confinement: A Report of the Commission on Safety and Abuse in America's Prisons* (New York: Vera Institute of Justice, 2006).

26. Wooldredge, "Inmate Lifestyles and Opportunities for Victimization."

27. John Irwin, "Adaptation to Being Corrected: Corrections from the Convict's Perspective," in *Handbook of Criminology*, ed. Daniel Glazer (Chicago: Rand McNally, 1974), 971–993.

28. Donald Clemmer, *The Prison Community* (New York: Holt, Rinehart & Winston, 1958).

29. Gresham Sykes and Sheldon Messinger, "The Inmate Social Code," in *The Sociology of Punishment and Corrections*, ed. Norman Johnston, Leonard Savitz, and Marvin Wolfgang (New York: Wiley, 1970), 401–408.

30. Ibid., 439.

31. James B. Jacobs, ed., *New Perspectives on Prisons and Imprisonment* (Ithaca, N.Y.: Cornell University Press, 1983); James B. Jacobs, "Street Gangs behind Bars," *Social Problems* 21 (1974): 395–409; James B. Jacobs, "Race Relations and the Prison Subculture," in *Crime and Justice*, vol. 1, ed. Norval Morris and Michael Tonry (Chicago: University of Chicago Press, 1979), 1–28.

32. Nicole Hahn Rafter, *Partial Justice* (New Brunswick, N.J.: Transaction Books, 1990), 181–182.

33. Kathryn Watterson and Meda Chesney-Lind, *Women in Prison: Inside the Concrete Womb* (Boston: Northeastern University Press, 1996).

34. Merry Morash, Robin Harr, and Lila Rucker, "A Comparison of Programming for Women and Men in U.S. Prisons in the 1980s," *Crime and Delinquency 40* (1994): 197–221.

35. Pamela Schram, "Stereotypes about Vocational Programming for Female Inmates," *Prison Journal* 78 (1998): 244–271.

36. Morash, Harr, and Rucker, "A Comparison of Programming for Women and Men in U.S. Prisons in the 1980s."

37. Vernetta Young and Rebecca Reviere, *Women behind Bars: Gender and Race in U.S. Prisons* (Boulder, Colo.: Lynne Rienner Publishers, 2006).

38. Seena Fazel and John Danesh, "Serious Mental Disorder in 23,000 Prisoners: A Systematic Review of 62 Surveys," *Lancet 359* (2002): 545–561.

39. Gary Michael McClelland, Linda Teplin, Karen Abram, and Naomi Jacobs, "HIV and AIDS Risk Behaviors among Female Jail Detainees: Implications for Public Health Policy," *American Journal of Public Health 92* (2002): 818–826.

40. Christine Grella and Lisa Greenwell, "Correlates of Parental Status and Attitudes toward Parenting among Substance-Abusing Women Offenders," *Prison Journal 86* (2006): 89–113.

41. Lee Ann Slocum, Sally Simpson, and Douglas Smith, "Strained Lives and Crime: Examining Intra-Individual Variation in Strain and Offending in a Sample of Incarcerated Women," *Criminology 43* (2005): 1067–1110.

42. "Sex Abuse of Female Inmates Is Common, Rights Group Says," *Criminal Justice Newsletter*, December 16, 1996, 2.

43. Meda Chesney-Lind, "Vengeful Equity: Sentencing Women to Prison," in *The Female Offender: Girls, Women, and Crime* (Thousand Oaks, Calif.: Sage, 1997).

44. General Accounting Office, *Women in Prison: Sexual Misconduct by Correctional Staff* (Washington, D.C.: Government Printing Office, 1999).

45. Candace Kruttschnitt and Sharon Krmpotich, "Aggressive Behavior among Female Inmates: An Exploratory Study," *Justice Quarterly 7* (1990): 370–389.

46. Candace Kruttschnitt, Rosemary Gartner, and Amy Miller, "Doing Her Own Time? Women's Responses to Prison in the Context of the Old and New Penology," *Criminology 38* (2000): 681–718.

47. Mark Pogrebin and Mary Dodge, "Women's Accounts of Their Prison Experiences: A Retrospective View of Their Subjective Realities," *Journal of Criminal Justice 29* (2001): 531–541.

48. Shanhe Jiang and L. Thomas Winfree Jr., "Social Support, Gender, and Inmate Adjustment to Prison Life," *Prison Journal 86* (2006): 32–55.

49. Edna Erez, "The Myth of the New Female Offender: Some Evidence from Attitudes toward Law and Justice," *Journal of Criminal Justice 16* (1988): 499–509.

50. Robert Ross and Hugh McKay, *Self-Mutilation* (Lexington, Mass.: Lexington Books, 1979).

51. Denise Huggins, Loretta Capeheart, and Elizabeth Newman, "Deviants or Scapegoats: An Examination of Pseudofamily Groups and Dyads in Two Texas

Prisons," *The Prison Journal 86* (2006) 114–139; Alice Propper, *Prison Homosexuality* (Lexington, Mass.: Lexington Books, 1981).

52. Dianna Newbern, Donald Dansereau, and Urvashi Pitre, "Positive Effects on Life Skills Motivation and Self-Efficacy: Node-Link Maps in a Modified Therapeutic Community," *American Journal of Drug and Alcohol Abuse 25* (1999): 407–410.

53. Steven D. Vannoy and William T. Hoyt, "Evaluation of an Anger Therapy Intervention for Incarcerated Adult Males," *Journal of Offender Rehabilitation 39* (2004): 40.

54. Retrieved from http://www.unisa.edu.au/psychology/ research/CAPR/FPRG.asp, May 15, 2008.

55. Byron R. Johnson, "Religious Programming, Institutional Adjustment and Recidivism among Former Inmates in Prison Fellowship Programs," *Justice Quarterly 21* (2004): 329–354.

56. Charles McDaniel, Derek Davis, and Sabrina Neff, "Charitable Choice and Prison Ministries: Constitutional and Institutional Challenges to Rehabilitating the American Penal System," *Criminal Justice Policy Review 16* (2005): 164–189.

57. Lawrence T. Jablecki, "A Critique of Faith-Based Prison Programs," *The Humanist 65* (2005): 11–16.

58. Ibid.

59. Dawn Daggett, Scott Camp, and Okyun Kwon, "Faith-Based Correctional Programming in Federal Prisons: Factors Affecting Program Completion," *Criminal Justice and Behavior 35* (2008): 848–862.

60. Kate Dolan, James Shearer, Bethany White, Zhou Jialun, John Kaldor, and Alex Wodak, "Four-Year Follow-up of Imprisoned Male Heroin Users and Methadone Treatment: Mortality, Re-Incarceration and Hepatitis C Infection," *Addiction 100* (2005): Issue 6, 820–828.

61. Clayton Mosher and Dretha Phillips, "The Dynamics of a Prison-Based Therapeutic Community for Women Offenders: Retention, Completion, and Outcomes," *Prison Journal 86* (2006): 6–31.

62. Daniel Werb, Thomas Kerr, Will Small, Kathy Li, Julio Montaner, and Evan Wood, "HIV Risks Associated with Incarceration among Injection Drug Users: Implications for Prison-Based Public Health Strategies," *Journal of Public Health 30* (2008): 126–132; Will Small, S. Kain, Nancy Laliberte, Martin Schechter, Michael O'Shaughnessy, and Patricia Spittal, "Incarceration, Addiction and Harm Reduction: Inmates Experience Injecting Drugs in Prison," *Substance Use & Misuse 40* (2005): 831–843.

63. Bill Conlon, Scott Harris, Jeffrey Nagel, Mike Hillman, and Rick Hanson, "Education: Don't Leave Prison without It," *Corrections Today 70* (2008): 48–52; David Wilson, Catherine Gallagher, and Doris MacKensie, "A Meta-Analysis of Corrections-Based Education, Vocation, and Work Programs for Adult Offenders," *Journal of Research in Crime and Delinquency 37* (2000): 347–368.

64. Karen Lahm, "Educational Participation and Inmate Misconduct," *Journal of Offender Rehabilitation 48* (2009): 37–52.

65. Howard Skolnik and John Slansky, "A First Step in Helping Inmates Get Good Jobs after Release," *Corrections Today 53* (1991): 92.

66. Federal Bureau of Prisons web page concerning UNICOR Federal Prison Industries, Inc. Retrieved from http://www.unicor.gov/fpi_contracting/ ?navlocation+Contracting

67. Courtesy of the Prison Industry Authority, 560 East Natoma Street, Folsom, California, 95630-2200.

68. Diane Dwyer and Roger McNally, "Public Policy, Prison Industries, and Business: An Equitable Balance for the 1990s," *Federal Probation 57* (1993): 30–35.

69. Douglas Lipton, Robert Martinson, and Judith Wilks, *The Effectiveness of Correctional Treatment: A Survey of Treatment Evaluation Studies* (New York: Praeger, 1975).

70. Charles Murray and Louis Cox, *Beyond Probation: Juvenile Corrections and the Chronic Delinquent* (Beverly Hills, Calif.: Sage, 1979).

71. Steven Lab and John Whitehead, "An Analysis of Juvenile Correctional Treatment," *Crime and Delinquency 34* (1988): 60–83.

72. James Wilson and Robert Davis, "Good Intentions Meet Hard Realities: An Evaluation of the Project Greenlight Reentry Program," *Criminology & Public Policy 5* (2006): 303–338.

73. Paula Smith, Paul Gendreau, and Kristin Swartz, "Validating the Principles of Effective Intervention: A Systematic Review of the Contributions of Meta-Analysis in the Field of Corrections," *Victims & Offenders 4* (2009): 148–169.

74. Paul Gendreau and Robert Ross, "Effective Correctional Treatment: Bibliotherapy for Cynics," *Crime and Delinquency 27* (October 1979): 463–489.

75. Robert Martinson, "New Findings, New Views: A Note of Caution Regarding Sentencing Reform," *Hofstra Law Review 7* (Winter 1979): 244.

76. Mark W. Lipsey and Francis T. Cullen, "The Effectiveness of Correctional Rehabilitation: A Review of Systematic Reviews," *Annual Review of Law and Social Science 3* (2007): 297–320.

77. Lucien X. Lombardo, *Guards Imprisoned* (New York: Elsevier, 1981); James Jacobs and Norma Crotty, "The Guard's World," in *New Perspectives on Prisons and Imprisonment*, ed. James Jacobs (Ithaca, N.Y.: Cornell University Press, 1983), 133–141.

78. Richard Tewksbury and Elizabeth Mustaine, "Correctional Orientations of Prison Staff," *The Prison Journal 88* (2008): 207–233.

79. Mike Vuolo and Candace Kruttschnitt, "Prisoners' Adjustment, Correctional Officers, and Context: The Foreground and Background of Punishment in Late Modernity," *Law & Society Review 42* (2008): 307–335.

80. Dana Britton, *At Work in the Iron Cage: The Prison as Gendered Organization* (New York: New York University Press, 2003), Chapter 6.

81. *San Antonio Express News*, March 28, 2008.

82. David Duffee, *Corrections, Practice and Policy* (New York: Random House, 1989), 305.

83. Randy Martin and Sherwood Zimmerman, "A Typology of the Causes of Prison Riots and an

Analytical Extension to the 1986 West Virginia Riot," *Justice Quarterly* 7 (1990): 711–737.

84. Benjamin Steiner, "Assessing Static and Dynamic Influences on Inmate Violence Levels," *Crime and Delinquency* 55 (2009): 134–161.

85. David Allender and Frank Marcell, "Career Criminals, Security Threat Groups, and Prison Gangs," *FBI Law Enforcement Bulletin* 72 (2003): 8–12.

86. Terri Compton and Mike Meacham, "Prison Gangs: Descriptions and Selected Intervention," *The Forensic Examiner* 14 (2005): 26–31.

87. Benjamin Steiner and John Wooldredge, "Inmate versus Environmental Effects on Prison Rule Violations," *Criminal Justice and Behavior* 35 (2008): 438–456.

88. Attapol Kuanliang, Jon R. Sorensen, and Mark Cunningham, "Juvenile Inmates in an Adult Prison System: Rates of Disciplinary Misconduct and Violence," *Criminal Justice and Behavior,* 35 (2008): 1186–1201.

89. Grant Harris, Tracey Skilling, and Marnie Rice, "The Construct of Psychopathy," in *Crime and Justice: An Annual Edition*, ed. Michael Tonry (Chicago: University of Chicago Press, 2001), 197–265.

90. For a series of papers on the position, see A. Cohen, G. Cole, and R. Baily, eds., *Prison Violence* (Lexington, Mass.: Lexington Books, 1976).

91. Lahm, "Inmate-on-Inmate Assault."

92. Scott Camp and Gerald Gaes, "Criminogenic Effects of the Prison Environment on Inmate Behavior: Some Experimental Evidence," *Crime and Delinquency* 51 (2005): 425–442.

93. Hans Toch, "Cumulative Default: The Cost of Disruptive Prison Careers," *Criminal Justice and Behavior* 35 (2008): 943–955.

94. Bert Useem and Michael Resig, "Collective Action in Prisons: Protests, Disturbances, and Riots," *Criminology* 37 (1999): 735–760.

95. Wayne Gillespie, "A Multilevel Model of Drug Abuse inside Prison," *Prison Journal* 85 (2005): 223–246.

96. *Shaw v. Murphy* (99–1613), 2001.

97. *Newman v. Alabama*, 92 S. Ct. 1079, 405 U.S. 319 (1972).

98. *Estelle v. Gamble*, 429 U.S. 97 (1976).

99. Ibid.

100. Lester Wright, "Health Care in Prison Thirty Years after *Estelle v. Gamble*," *Journal of Correctional Health Care* 14 (2008): 31–35.

101. *Trop v. Dulles*, 356 U.S. 86, 78 S. Ct. 590 (1958); see also *Furman v. Georgia*, 408 U.S. 238, 92 S. Ct. 2726, 33 L.Ed.2d 346 (1972).

102. *Weems v. United States*, 217 U.S. 349, 30 S. Ct. 544, 54 L.Ed. 793 (1910).

103. *Lee v. Tahash*, 352 F.2d 970 (8th Cir., 1965).

104. *Estelle v. Gamble*, 429 U.S. 97 (1976).

105. *Robinson v. California*, 370 U.S. 660 (1962).

106. *Gregg v. Georgia*, 428 U.S. 153 (1976).

107. *Jackson v. Bishop*, 404 F.2d 571 (8th Cir. 1968).

108. *Hope v. Pelzer*, et al., 536 U.S. 730 (2002).

109. L. A. Times, Report predicted violence at Chino prison dorm hit by race riots August 10, 2009 http://latimesblogs.latimes.com/lanow/2009/08 /report-warned-of-violence-at-chino-prison-baracks-hit-by-race-riots.html (accessed on August 11, 2009).

110. *Johnson v. California*, 543 U.S. 499 (2005).

111. *Bell v. Wolfish*, 99 S. Ct. 1873–1974 (1979); see "*Bell v. Wolfish*: The Rights of Pretrial Detainees," *New England Journal of Prison Law* 6 (1979): 134.

112. *Farmer v. Brennan*, 144 S. Ct. 1970 (1994).

113. *Rhodes v. Chapman*, 452 U.S. 337 (1981); for further analysis of *Rhodes*, see Randall Pooler, "Prison Overcrowding and the Eighth Amendment: The Rhodes Not Taken," *New England Journal on Criminal and Civil Confinement* 8 (1983): 1–28.

114. *Prison Escape Survey* (Lincoln, Neb.: Corrections Compendium, 1991).

115. Lauren Glaze and Thomas Bonczar, *Probation and Parole in the United States, 2007* (Washington, D.C. Bureau of Justice Statistics, 2008), Statistical Table 5, http://www.ojp.usdoj.gov/bjs/pub/pdf/ppus07st .pdf

116. Sandra Crockett Mack and Khalil Osiris, "Successful Reentry, One Case at a Time," *Corrections Today* 69 (2007): 50–55.

117. Carolin Kröner, Cornelis Stadtland, Matthias Eidt, and Norbert Nedopil, "The Validity of the Violence Risk Appraisal Guide (VRAG) in Predicting Criminal Recidivism," *Criminal Behaviour & Mental Health* 17 (2007): 89–100.

118. Kathryn Campbell and Myriam Denov, "The Burden of Innocence: Coping with a Wrongful Imprisonment," *Canadian Journal of Criminology and Criminal Justice* 46 (2004): 139–164.

119. Brian Parry, "Special Service Unit: Dedicated to Investigating and Apprehending Violent Offenders," *Corrections Today* 63 (2001): 120.

120. Thomas Hanlon, David N. Nurco, Richard W. Bateman, and Kevin E. O'Grady, "The Response of Drug Abuser Parolees to a Combination of Treatment and Intensive Supervision," *Prison Journal* 78 (1998): 31–44; Susan Turner and Joan Petersilia, "Focusing on High-Risk Parolees: An Experiment to Reduce Commitments to the Texas Department of Corrections," *Journal of Research in Crime and Delinquency* 29 (1992): 34–61.

121. Mario Paparozzi and Paul Gendreau, "An Intensive Supervision Program That Worked: Service Delivery, Professional Orientation, and Organizational Supportiveness," *Prison Journal* 85 (2005): 445–466.

122. Patrick A. Langan and David J. Levin, *Recidivism of Prisoners Released in 1994* (Washington, D.C.: Bureau of Justice Statistics, 2002).

123. Robyn L. Cohen, *Probation and Parole Violators in State Prison, 1991: Survey of State Prison Inmates, 1991* (Washington, D.C.: Bureau of Justice Statistics, 1995).

124. Stephen Duguid, *Can Prisons Work? The Prisoner as Object and Subject in Modern Corrections* (Toronto: University of Toronto Press, 2000).

125. James Bonta, Moira Law, and Karl Hanson, "The Prediction of Criminal and Violent Recidivism among Mentally Disordered Offenders: A Meta-Analysis," *Psychological Bulletin* 123 (1998): 123–142.

126. Roger Peters, Paul Greenbaum, John Edens, Chris Carter, and Madeline Ortiz, "Prevalence of DSM-IV Substance Abuse and Dependence Disorders among Prison Inmates," *American Journal of Drug and Alcohol Abuse* 24 (1998): 573–580.

127. Catherine Hamilton, Louise Falshaw, and Kevin D. Browne, "The Link between Recurrent Maltreatment and Offending Behavior," *International Journal of Offender Therapy & Comparative Criminology 46* (2002): 75–95.

128. Brent Benda, "Gender Differences in Life-Course Theory of Recidivism: A Survival Analysis," *International Journal of Offender Therapy and Comparative Criminology* 49 (2005): 325–342.

129. Bonnie Todis, Michael Bullis, Miriam Waintrup, Robert Schultz, and Ryan D'Ambrosio, "Overcoming the Odds: Qualitative Examination of Resilience among Formerly Incarcerated Adolescents," *Exceptional Children* 68 (2001): 119–140.

130. Pamela Schram, Barbara Koons-Witt, Frank Williams, and Marilyn Mcshane, "Supervision Strategies and Approaches for Female Parolees: Examining the Link between Unmet Needs and Parolee Outcome," *Crime and Delinquency* 52 (2006): 450–471.

131. J. E. Ryan, "Who Gets Revoked? A Comparison of Intensive Supervision Successes and Failures in Vermont," *Crime and Delinquency* 43 (1997): 104–118.

132. Hanlon, Nurco, Bateman, and O'Grady, "The Response of Drug Abuser Parolees to a Combination of Treatment and Intensive Supervision," 108.

133. Beth Huebner, "Racial and Ethnic Differences in the Likelihood of Marriage: The Effect of Incarceration," *Justice Quarterly* 24 (2007): 156–183.

134. Laura Fishman, *Women at the Wall: A Study of Prisoners' Wives Doing Time on the Outside* (New York: State University of New York Press, 1990).

135. Leslee Goodman Hornick, "Volunteer Program Helps Make Inmates' Families Feel Welcome," *Corrections Today* 53 (1991): 184–186.

136. Jeremy Travis and Joan Petersilia, "Reentry Reconsidered: A New Look at an Old Question," *Crime and Delinquency* 47 (2001): 291–313.

137. Joan Petersilia, *When Prisoners Come Home: Parole and Prisoner Reentry* (New York: Oxford University Press, 2003); Joan Petersilia, "Hard Time Ex-Offenders Returning Home after Prison," *Corrections Today* 67 (2005): 66–72; Joan Petersilia, "When Prisoners Return to Communities: Political, Economic, and Social Consequences," *Federal Probation* 65 (2001): 3–9.

138. Stephen Metraux and Dennis Culhane, "Recent Incarceration History among a Sheltered Homeless Population," *Crime and Delinquency* 52 (2006): 504–517.

139. Petersilia, "Hard Time Ex-Offenders Returning Home after Prison."

140. Bruce Way, Donald Sawyer, Stephanie Lilly, Catherine Moffitt, and Barbara Stapholz, "Characteristics of Inmates Who Received a Diagnosis of Serious Mental Illness upon Entry to New York State Prison," *Psychiatric Services* 59 (2008): 1335–1337.

141. Richard Seiter, "Prisoner Reentry and the Role of Parole Officers," *Federal Probation* 66 (2002): 50–54.

142. Charis Kubrin and Eric Stewart, "Predicting Who Reoffends: The Neglected Role of Neighborhood Context in Recidivism Studies," *Criminology* 44 (2006): 165–197.

143. Hanlon, Nurco, Bateman, and O'Grady, "The Response of Drug Abuser Parolees to a Combination of Treatment and Intensive Supervision."

144. Kathleen Olivares, Velmer Burton, and Francis Cullen, "The Collateral Consequences of a Felony Conviction: A National Study of State Legal Codes Ten Years Later," *Federal Probation* 60 (1996): 10–17.

145. Maryland State Department of Education, http://www.marylandpublicschools.org/msde (accessed June 11, 2008).

146. Stacy Adams, "Richmond Program Helps Former Female Inmates," *Crisis 113* (2006): 8.

Box Source Notes
Policies, Programs, and Issues in Criminal Justice: World Apart: Life in a Female Prison

Cristina Rathbone, *World Apart: Women, Prison, and Life Behind Bars* (New York: Random House, 2005); Cristina Rathbone, "Locked In: Ever Since America's First Women's Prison Opened Nearly 200 Years ago, Debate Has Raged over How to Treat Female Inmates," *Boston Globe*, May 29, 2005.

Careers in Criminal Justice: Correctional Officer

Bureau of Labor Statistics, U.S. Department of Labor, "Correctional Officers," *Occupational Outlook Handbook, 2008–2009 Edition*, www.bls.gov/oco/ocos156.htm (accessed February 24, 2009); Stephen Lambert and Debra Regan, "Corrections Officer," in *Great Jobs for Criminal Justice Majors* (New York: McGraw-Hill, 2001): 193–196.

Chapter 13,
Juvenile Justice in the Twenty-first Century

1. Federal Bureau of Investigation, *Crime in the United States, 2005* (Washington, D.C.: U.S. Government Printing Office, 2006).

2. David S. Tanenhaus, *Juvenile Justice in the Making* (New York: Oxford University Press, 2004); Lawrence Stone, *The Family, Sex, and Marriage in England: 1500–1800* (New York: Harper & Row, 1977); Philippe Aries, *Century of Childhood: A Social History of Family Life* (New York: Vintage Press, 1962); Douglas R. Rendleman, *"Parens Patriae*: From Chancery to the Juvenile Court," *South Carolina Law Review 23* (1971): 205–229; Anthony M. Platt, "The Rise of the Child-Saving Movement: A Study in Social Policy and Correctional Reform," *Annals of the American Academy of Political and Social Science 381* (1979): 21–38;

Robert S. Pickett, *House of Refuge: Origins of Juvenile Reform in New York State, 1815–1857* (Syracuse, N.Y.: Syracuse University Press, 1969).

3. Douglas Besharov, *Juvenile Justice Advocacy: Practice in a Unique Court* (New York: Practicing Law Institute, 1974), 2; see also Jay Albanese, *Dealing with Delinquency: The Future of Juvenile Justice* (Chicago: Nelson-Hall, 1993).

4. 4 Eng. Rep. 1078 (1827).

5. Anthony Platt, *The Child Savers: The Invention of Delinquency* (Chicago: University of Chicago Press, 1969), 11–38.

6. See, generally, Anne Meis Knupfer, *Reform and Resistance: Gender, Delinquency, and America's First Juvenile Court* (London: Routledge, 2001).

7. This section is based on material from the New York State Archives, *The Greatest Reform School in the World: A Guide to the Records of the New York House of Refuge: A Brief History 1824–1857* (Albany: New York State Archives, 2001); Sanford J. Fox, "Juvenile Justice Reform: A Historical Perspective," *Stanford Law Review 22* (1970): 1187.

8. Pickett, *House of Refuge*.

9. David S. Tanenhaus, *Juvenile Justice in the Making*.

10. LaMar T. Empey, *American Delinquency: Its Meaning and Construction* (Homewood, Ill.: Dorsey Press, 1978), 515.

11. Public Law 93–415 (1974).

12. For a comprehensive view of juvenile law, see, generally, Joseph J. Senna and Larry J. Siegel, *Juvenile Law: Cases and Comments*, 2d ed. (St. Paul, Minn.: West, 1992).

13. Erika Gebo, "Do Family Courts Administer Individualized Justice in Delinquency Cases?" *Criminal Justice Policy Review 16* (2005): 190–210.

14. Federal Bureau of Investigation, *Crime in the United States, 2007*, http://www.fbi.gov/ucr/cius2007/data/table_38.html (accessed March 26, 2009).

15. Richard J. Lundman, "Routine Police Arrest Practices," *Social Problems 22* (1974): 127–141; Robert E. Worden and Stephanie M. Myers, *Police Encounters with Juvenile Suspects* (Albany: Hindelang Criminal Justice Research Center and School of Criminal Justice, State University of New York, 2001).

16. *Fare v. Michael C.*, 442 U.S. 707 (1979).

17. Barry Feld, "Police Interrogation of Juveniles: An Empirical Study of Policy and Practice," *Journal of Criminal Law & Criminology 97* (2006): 219–316.

18. Ana Abrantes, Norman Hoffmann, and Ronald Anton, "Prevalence of Co-occurring Disorders among Juveniles Committed to Detention Centers," *International Journal of Offender Therapy & Comparative Criminology 49* (2005): 179–194.

19. Nancy Rodriquez, "Juvenile Court Context and Detention Decisions: Reconsidering the Role of Race, Ethnicity, and Community Characteristics in Juvenile Court Processes," *Justice Quarterly 24* (2007): 629–656.

20. Barry Holman and Jason Ziedenberg, *The Dangers of Detention: The Impact of Incarcerating Youth in Detention and Other Secure Facilities* (Washington, D.C.: Justice Policy Institute, 2006), http://www.cfjj.org/Pdf/116-JPI008-DOD_Report.pdf (accessed March 26, 2009).

21. *Schall v. Martin*, 467 U.S. 253 (1984).

22. See Juvenile Justice and Delinquency Prevention Act of 1974, 42 U.S.C., sec. 5633.

23. Catherine Van Dijk, An Nuytiens, and Christian Eliaerts, "The Referral of Juvenile Offenders to the Adult Court in Belgium: Theory and Practice," *Howard Journal of Criminal Justice 44* (2005): 151–166.

24. *Kent v. United States*, 383 U.S. 541 (1966).

25. *Breed v. Jones*, 421 U.S. 519 (1975).

26. John Burrow, "Reverse Waiver and the Effects of Legal, Statutory, and Secondary Legal Factors on Sentencing Outcomes for Juvenile Offenders," *Crime and Delinquency 54* (2008): 34–64.

27. Alan Karpelowitz, *State Legislative Priorities—1995* (Denver, Colo.: National Conference of State Legislatures, 1995), 10.

28. Howard N. Snyder, Melissa Sickmund, and Eileen Poe-Yamagata, *Juvenile Transfers to Criminal Court in the 1990s: Lessons Learned from Four Studies* (Washington, D.C.: Office of Juvenile Justice and Delinquency Prevention, 2000).

29. James Austin, Kelly Dedel Johnson, and Maria Gregoriou, *Juveniles in Adult Prisons and Jails* (Washington, D.C.: Bureau of Justice Assistance, 2000).

30. Victor Streib, *Death Penalty for Juveniles* (Bloomington: Indiana University Press, 1987).

31. Biko Agozino, "The Crisis of Authoritarianism in the Legal Institutions," *Journal of Contemporary Criminal Justice 19* (2003): 315–350; *Roper v. Simmons*, 543 U.S. 551 (2005).

32. Aaron Kupchik, "The Correctional Experiences of Youth in Adult and Juvenile Prisons," *Justice Quarterly 24* (2007): 247–270.

33. Benjamin Steiner and Emily Wright, "Assessing the Relative Effects of State Direct File Waiver Laws on Violent Juvenile Crime: Deterrence or Irrelevance?" *Journal of Criminal Law & Criminology 96* (2006): 1451–1477.

34. Benjamin Steiner, "The Effects of Juvenile Transfer to Criminal Court on Incarceration Decisions," *Justice Quarterly 26* (2009): 77–106; Megan Kurlychek and Brian Johnson, "The Juvenile Penalty: A Comparison of Juvenile and Young Adult Sentencing Outcomes in Criminal Court," *Criminology 42* (2004): 485–517.

35. Barry Feld, "The Juvenile Court Meets the Principle of the Offense: Legislative Changes in Juvenile Waiver Statutes," *Journal of Criminal Law and Criminology 78* (1987): 471–533; see also John Kramer, Henry Sontheimer, and John Lemmon, "Pennsylvania Waiver to Adult Court," paper presented at the annual meeting of the American Society of Criminology, San Francisco, November 1991; authors confirm that juveniles tried in adult courts are generally male, age 17 or older, and disproportionately minorities.

36. Jeffrey Fagan, Martin Forst, and T. Scott Vivona, "Racial Determinants of the Judicial Transfer Decision: Prosecuting Violent Youth in Criminal Court," *Crime and Delinquency 33* (1987): 359–386; J. Fagan, E. Slaughter, and E. Hartstone, "Blind Justice: The Impact of Race on the Juvenile Justice Process,"

Crime and Delinquency 53 (1987): 224–258; J. Fagan and E. P. Deschenes, "Determinants of Judicial Waiver Decisions for Violent Juvenile Offenders," *Journal of Criminal Law and Criminology 81* (1990): 314–347; see also James Howell, "Juvenile Transfers to Criminal Court," *Juvenile and Family Justice Journal 6* (1997): 12–14.

37. Anne L. Stahl, *Delinquency Cases in Juvenile Courts, 1997* (Washington, D.C.: Office of Juvenile Justice and Delinquency Prevention, 2000).

38. Parent, *Key Issues in Criminal Justice*.

39. *In re Gault*, 387 U.S. 1 (1967).

40. See Joseph Goldstein, Anna Freud, and Albert Solnit, *Beyond the Best Interest of the Child* (New York: Free Press, 1973).

41. See Michael Serrill, "Police Write a New Law on Juvenile Crime," *Police Magazine* (September 1979): 47; see also A. Schneider and D. Schram, *Assessment of Juvenile Justice Reform in Washington State*, vols. 1–4 (Washington, D.C.: Department of Justice, Institute of Policy Analysis, 1983); T. Castellano, "Justice Model in the Juvenile Justice System—Washington State's Experience," *Law and Policy 8* (1986): 479.

42. Emily Gaarder, Nancy Rodriguez, and Marjorie Zatz, "Criers, Liars, and Manipulators: Probation Officers' Views of Girls," *Justice Quarterly 21* (2004): 547–578.

43. Office of Juvenile Justice and Delinquency Prevention, *Juveniles in Corrections*, http://ojjdp.ncjrs .gov/ojstatbb/corrections/qa08201.asp?qaDate=2006 (accessed March 26, 2009).

44. Office of Juvenile Justice and Delinquency Prevention, *Custody Data, 1997–Present*, http://ojjdp. ncjrs.gov/ojstatbb/corrections/qa08301 .asp?qaDate=2006 (accessed March 26, 2009).

45. National Conference of State Legislatures, *A Legislator's Guide to Comprehensive Juvenile Justice, Juvenile Detention, and Corrections* (Denver, Colo.: National Conference of State Legislators, 1996).

46. J. David Hawkins, Richard F. Catalano, and associates, *Communities That Care: Action for Drug Abuse Prevention* (San Francisco: Jossey-Bass, 1992).

47. Richard F. Catalano, Michael W. Arthur, J. David Hawkins, Lisa Berglund, and Jeffrey J. Olson, "Comprehensive Community- and School-Based Interventions to Prevent Antisocial Behavior," in *Serious and Violent Juvenile Offenders: Risk Factors and Successful Interventions*, ed. Rolf Loeber and David P. Farrington (Thousand Oaks, Calif.: Sage, 1998).

48. Adele V. Harrell, Shannon E. Cavanagh, and Sanjeev Sridharan, *Evaluation of the Children At Risk Program: Results One Year after the End of the Program* (Washington, D.C.: NIJ Research in Brief, 1999).

49. You can find out more about CASASTART at the following website: www.casacolumbia.org/ absolutenm/articlefiles/203-203-casastart_field _guide_2003.pdf (accessed March 26, 2009).

50. Baltimore City Paper, "Murder Ink: Rasheed Stevenson," http://www.citypaper.com/news/

murderink.asp?name=Rasheed+Stevenson (accessed March 26, 2009).

51. David Smith, "The Effectiveness of the Juvenile Justice System," *Criminal Justice: International Journal of Policy & Practice 5* (2005): 181–195.

52. Barry C. Feld, *Bad Kids: Race and the Transformation of the Juvenile Court* (New York: Oxford University Press, 1999).

53. Alexes Harris, "Diverting and Abdicating Judicial Discretion: Cultural, Political, and Procedural Dynamics in California Juvenile Justice," *Law & Society Review 41* (2007): 387–428.

54. John Johnson Kerbs, "(Un)equal Justice: Juvenile Court Abolition and African Americans," *Annals, AAPSS, 564* (1999): 109–125.

55. Howard N. Snyder and Melissa Sickmund, *Juvenile Offenders and Victims: 2006 National Report* (Washington, D.C.: Office of Juvenile Justice and Delinquency Prevention, 2006). Available online: http://ojjdp.ncjrs.gov/ojstatbb/nr2006/downloads/ NR2006.pdf (accessed March 26, 2009).

56. Ibid.

57. National Council on Crime and Delinquency, *And Justice for Some: Differential Treatment of Minority Youth in the Justice System*, January 2007, http://www .nccd-crc.org/nccd/pubs/2007jan_justice_for_some. pdf (accessed March 26, 2009).

58. Ibid. p. 37.

59. Public Law 93–415, 42 USC 5601 et seq.

60. Emily Cabaniss, James Frabutt, Mary Kendrick, and Margaret Arbuckle, "Reducing Disproportionate Minority Contact in the Juvenile Justice System: Promising Practices," *Aggression & Violent Behavior 12* (2007): 393–401.

Box Source Notes
Policies, Programs, and Issues in Criminal Justice: Teen Courts

National Association of Youth Courts, *Youth Court List by State*, http://www.youthcourt.net/content/view/7/14/ (accessed July 1, 2009); Jeffrey Butts, Janeen Buck, and Mark Coggeshall, *The Impact of Teen Courts on Young Offenders* (Washington, D.C.: Urban Institute, 2002); Jeffrey A. Butts and Janeen Buck, "Teen Courts: A Focus on Research," *Juvenile Justice Bulletin October 2000* (Washington, D.C.: Office of Juvenile Justice and Delinquency Prevention, 2000); Kevin Minor, James Wells, Irinia Soderstrom, Rachel Bingham, and Deborah Williamson, "Sentence Completion and Recidivism among Juveniles Referred to Teen Courts," *Crime and Delinquency 45* (1999): 467–480; Paige Harrison, James R. Maupin, and G. Larry Mays, "Teen Court: An Examination of Processes and Outcomes," *Crime and Delinquency 47* (2001): 243–264.

Careers in Criminal Justice: Social Worker

Bureau of Labor Statistics, U.S. Department of Labor, "Social Worker," *Occupational Outlook Handbook, 2008–2009 Edition*, http://www.bls.gov/oco/ocos060.htm (accessed July 1, 2009); Princeton Review Career Profiles: Social Worker, http://www .princetonreview.com/Careers.aspx?page=1&cid=143 (accessed July 1, 2009).

Chapter 14,
Criminal Justice in the New Millennium: Terrorism, Homeland Security, and Cyber Crime

1. Thomas P. M. Barnett, *The Pentagon's New Map: War and Peace in the Twenty-first Century* (New York: G. P. Putnam's Sons, 2004), 43–46.
2. Walter Laqueur, *The New Terrorism: Fanaticism and the Arms of Mass Destruction* (New York: Oxford University Press, 1999).
3. Edmund Burke, *Reflections on the Revolution in France, 1790* (New York: Penguin Classics; reprint edition 1982).
4. Lindsay Clutterbuck, "The Progenitors of Terrorism: Russian Revolutionaries or Extreme Irish Republicans?" *Terrorism and Political Violence 16* (2004): 154–181.
5. Title 22 of the United States Code section 2656f (d) (1999).
6. Jack Gibbs, "Conceptualization of Terrorism," *American Sociological Review 54* (1989): 329–340, at 330.
7. Stephen J. Morgan, *The Mind of a Terrorist Fundamentalist: The Psychology of Terror Cults* (Awe-Struck E-Books, 2001); Martha Crenshaw, "The Psychology of Terrorism: An Agenda for the 21st Century," *Political Psychology 21* (2000): 405–420.
8. Andrew Silke, "Courage in Dark Places: Reflections on Terrorist Psychology," *Social Research 71* (2004): 177–198.
9. This section leans heavily on Anthony Stahelski, "Terrorists Are Made, Not Born: Creating Terrorists Using Social Psychological Conditioning," *Journal of Homeland Security*, March 2004, www.homelandsecurity.org/journal/Articles/displayarticle.asp?article=109 (accessed August 14, 2005).
10. Ethan Bueno de Mesquita, "The Quality of Terror," *American Journal of Political Science 49* (2005): 515–530.
11. Haruki Murakami, *Underground* (New York: Vintage Books, 2001).
12. Rand Corporation, "How Prepared Are State and Local Law Enforcement for Terrorism?" www.rand.org/publications/RB/RB9093/ (accessed June 28, 2005).
13. Read the Department of Homeland Security Strategic Plan, September 16, 2008, http://www.dhs.gov/xlibrary/assets/DHS_StratPlan_FINAL_spread.pdf
14. Chad Foster and Gary Cordner, *The Impact of Terrorism on State Law Enforcement* (Lexington, Kentucky: The Council of State Governments, 2005), http://www.csg.org/pubs/Documents/TheImpactofTerrorismonStateLawEnforcement-ChadFoster.pdf (accessed July 6, 2009).
15. Commonwealth Fusion Center, http://www.mass.gov/?pageID=eopsterminal&L=3&L0=Home&L1=Homeland+Security+%26+Emergency+Response&L2=Commonwealth+Fusion+Center&sid=Eeops&b=terminalcontent&f=msp_homeland_security_terrorism_fusion_center_fusion_center_overview&csid=Eeops (accessed March 5, 2009).
16. California Anti-Terrorism Information Center (CATIC), www.ag.ca.gov/antiterrorism/ (accessed February 25, 2009).
17. Harris County Homeland Security and Emergency Management, http://www.hcoem.org/ (accessed March 5, 2009).
18. Foster and Cordner, *The Impact of Terrorism on State Law Enforcement*, http://www.csg.org/pubs/Documents/Misc0504Terrorism.pdf
19. Sharon Gogerty, Florida Department of Law Enforcement News Release, "First Regional Intelligence Fusion Center Opens in Central Florida," August 24, 2007, http://www.fdle.state.fl.us/Content/News/August-2007/First-Regional-Intelligence-Fusion-Center-Opens-in.aspx (accessed July 6, 2009).
20. William K. Rashbaum, "Terror Makes All the World a Beat for New York Police," *New York Times*, July 15, 2002, B1; Al Baker, "Leader Sees New York Police in Vanguard of Terror Fight," *New York Times*, August 6, 2002, A2; Stephen Flynn, "America the Vulnerable," *Foreign Affairs 81* (January–February 2002): 60.
21. http://judiciary.house.gov/Printshop.aspx?Section=232
22. *Boumediene v. Bush*, 553 U.S. (2008).
23. Jessica Wolfendale, "Training Torturers: A Critique of the 'Ticking Bomb' Argument," *Social Theory & Practice 31* (2006): 269–287; Vittorio Bufacchi and Jean Maria Arrigo, "Torture, Terrorism and the State: A Refutation of the Ticking-Bomb Argument," *Journal of Applied Philosophy 23* (2006): 355–373; Elizabeth Sepper, "The Ties That Bind: How the Constitution Limits the CIA's Actions in the War on Terror," *New York University Law Review 81* (2006): 1805–1843.
24. Alan M. Dershowitz, *Shouting Fire: Civil Liberties in a Turbulent Age* (New York: Little, Brown, 2002); Dershowitz, "Want to Torture? Get a Warrant," *San Francisco Chronicle 22* (January 2002), A19, http://www.alandershowitz.com/publications/docs/torturewarrants2.html (accessed July 6, 2009.
25. Fox News, "Missouri Woman Indicted in MySpace Cyber-Bullying Case That Ended in Teen's Suicide," May 15, 2008, http://www.foxnews.com/printer_friendly_story/0,3566,356056,00.html.
26. Statement of Michael A. Vatis, director, National Infrastructure Protection Center, Federal Bureau of Investigation, on cyber crime before the Senate Judiciary Committee, Criminal Justice Oversight Subcommittee, and House Judiciary Committee, Crime Subcommittee, February 29, 2000, www.cybercrime.gov/vatis.htm (accessed March 17, 2007).
27. Ed Frauenheim, "IDC: Cyberterror and Other Prophecies," CNET News.com, December 12, 2002 (accessed August 14, 2005).
28. Giles Trendle, "An e-jihad against Government?" *EGOV Monitor*, September 2002.
29. VoGon International, http://www.vogon-international.com/ (accessed April 20, 2007).
30. Andreas Philaretou,"Sexuality and the Internet," *Journal of Sex Research 42* (2005): 180–181.
31. N2H2 communication, http://www.n2h2.com/index.php.

32. This section relies heavily on CERT®. Coordination Center Denial of Service Attacks, http://www.cert.org/tech_tips/denial_of_service.html (accessed September 8, 2005.

33. National Center on Addiction and Substance Abuse at Columbia University "You've Got Drugs!" IV: Prescription Drug Pushers on the Internet," May 2007, http://www.casacolumbia.org/absolutenm/articlefiles/380-YGD4%20Report.pdf

34. The Computer Fraud and Abuse Act (CFAA), 18 U.S.C. §1030 (1998).

35. The Digital Millennium Copyright Act, Public Law 105–304 (1998).

36. Title 18, United States Code, section 2319.

37. Title 17, United States Code, section 506.

38. Jim Wolf, "Internet Scams Targeted in Sweep: A 10-Day Crackdown Leads to 62 Arrests and 88 Indictments," *Boston Globe*, May 22, 2001, A2.

39. These sections rely on "Phishing Activity Trends Report," June 2005, Anti-Phishing Working Group, http://www.ncjrs.org/spotlight/identity_theft/publications.html#phishing (retrieved August 30. 2005); Special Report of "Phishing" (2004), U.S. Department of Justice Criminal Division, http://www.ncjrs.org/spotlight/identity_theft/publications.html#phishing (retrieved August 30, 2005).

40. Identity Theft Resource Center (ITRC), "Scams and Consumer Alerts," www.idtheftcenter.org (accessed April 15, 2008).

41. Anne Branscomb, "Rogue Computer Programs and Computer Rogues: Tailoring Punishment to Fit the Crime," *Rutgers Computer and Technology Law Journal 16* (1990): 24–26.

42. Heather Jacobson and Rebecca Green, "Computer Crimes," *American Criminal Law Review 39* (2002): 272–326.

43. United States Department of Justice, "Cyberstalking: A New Challenge for Law Enforcement and Industry," A Report from the Attorney General to the Vice President, Washington, D.C., 1999, http://www.usdoj.gov/criminal/cybercrime/cyberstalking.htm (accessed September 12, 2005).

44. Janis Wolak, David Finkelhor, Kimberly Mitchell, and Michele Ybarra, "Online 'Predators' and Their Victims: Myths, Realities, and Implications for Prevention and Treatment," *American Psychologist 63* (2008): 111–128

45. Jane Ireland and Rachel Monaghan, "Behaviours Indicative of Bullying among Young and Juvenile Male Offenders: A Study of Perpetrator and Victim Characteristics," *Aggressive Behavior 32* (2006): 172–180.

46. This section leans heavily on Justin Patchin and Sameer Hinduja, "Bullies Move beyond the Schoolyard: A Preliminary Look at Cyberbullying," *Youth Violence and Juvenile Justice 4* (2006): 148–169.

47. Patchin and Hinduja, "Bullies Move beyond the Schoolyard."

48. Barry C. Collin (2004), "The Future of CyberTerrorism: Where the Physical and Virtual Worlds Converge," http://afgen.com/terrorism1.html (accessed August 14, 2005).

49. Mark Pollitt, "Cyberterrorism—Fact or Fancy?" FBI Laboratory, http://www.cs.georgetown.edu/~denning/infosec/pollitt.html (accessed August 17, 2005).

50. James Lewis, "Assessing the Risks of Cyberterrorism, Cyber War, and Other Cyber Threats," Report submitted to the Center for Strategic and International Studies [CSIS], Washington, D.C., 2002), 1.

51. Clyde Wilson, "Software Piracy: Uncovering Mutiny on the Cyberseas," *Trial 32* (1996): 24–31.

52. Deloitte, 2005 Global Security Survey, http://www.deloitte.com/dtt/cda/doc/content/dtt_financialservices_2005GlobalSecuritySurvey_2005-07-21.pdf (accessed September 14, 2005).

53. Heather Jacobson and Rebecca Green, "Computer Crime," *American Criminal Law Review 39* (2002): 273–326; Identity Theft and Assumption Act of 1998 (18 U.S.C. S 1028(a)(7)); Bruce Swartz, Deputy Assistant General, Criminal Division, Justice Department Internet Fraud Testimony Before the House Energy and Commerce Committee, May 23, 2001; Comprehensive Crime Control Act of 1984, PL 98–473, 2101–03, 98 Stat. 1837, 2190 (1984), adding 18 USC 1030 (1984); Counterfeit Active Device and Computer Fraud and Abuse Act Amended by PL 99–474, 100 Stat. 1213 (1986) codified at 18 U.S.C. 1030 (Supp. V 1987); Computer Abuse Amendments Act 18 U.S.C. section 1030 (1994); Copyright Infringement Act 17 U.S.C. section 506(a) 1994; Electronic Communications Privacy Act of 198618 U.S.C. 2510–2520 (1988 and Supp. II 1990).

54. The Computer Fraud and Abuse Act (CFAA) 18 U.S.C. section 1030 (1998).

55. The Digital Millennium Copyright Act, Public Law 105–304 (1998).

56. Title 18, United States Code, section 2319.

57. Title 17, United States Code, section 506.

58. Identity Theft and Assumption Deterrence Act, as amended by Public Law 105–318, 112 Stat. 3007 (October 30, 1998).

59. ACLU, "*ACLU v. Reno*, Round 2: Broad Coalition Files Challenge to New Federal Net Censorship Law," news release, October 22, 1998.

60. *Ashcroft v. ACLU*, 00–1293, 2002

61. PL 98–473, Title H, Chapter XXI, [sections] 2102(a), 98 Stat. 1837, 2190 (1984).

62. Statement of Mr. Bob Weaver, Deputy Special Agent in Charge, New York Field Office, United States Secret Service, Before the House Financial Services Committee, the Subcommittee on Financial Institutions and Consumer Credit and the Subcommittee on Oversight and Investigations, U.S. House of Representatives, April 3, 2003.

63. Rand Corporation, Research in Brief, "How Prepared Are State and Local Law Enforcement for Terrorism?" www.rand.org/publications/RB/RB9093/ (accessed July 13, 2005).

Box Source Notes
Criminal Justice and Technology: Using Biometrics to Fight Terrorism: US-VISIT

"United States Visitor and Immigrant Status Indicator Technology" (Electronic Privacy Information Center), http://www.epic.org/privacy/us-visit (accessed March 5, 2009); "US-VISIT," (Travel and Transportation, U.S. Department of Homeland Security), http://www.dhs.gov/dhspublic/interapp/content_multi_image/content_multi_image_0006.xml (accessed March 5, 2009).

Careers in Criminal Justice: Emergency Response Manager

Office of Emergency Response, http://www.epa.gov/emergencies/index.htm (accessed March 3, 2009); Career Planner.com "Emergency Management Specialists" Job Description, http://www.careerplanner.com/Job-Descriptions/Emergency-Management-Specialists.cfm

This page constitutes an extension of the copyright page. We have made every effort to trace the ownership of all copyrighted material and to secure permission from copyright holders. In the event of any question arising as to the use of any material, we will be pleased to make the necessary corrections in future printings. Thanks are due to the following authors, publishers, and agents for permission to use the material indicated.

Title page

© Laurent Hamels/PhotoAlto/Corbis

Contents

xi: (top) © VCL/Chris Ryan/Taxi/ Getty Images, (bottom) © Janine Wiedel Photolibrary/Alamy, **xii:** (top) © AP Images/Joseph Kaczmarek, (bottom) © Molly Riley/Reuters/ Landov, **xiii:** (top) © AP Images/ Jacquelyn Martin, (bottom) © AP Images/*Tyler Morning Telegraph*, Tom Worner , **xiv:** © AP Images/*Galveston Daily News*, Jennifer Reynolds, **xv:** (top) © AP Images/Hector Mata, (bottom) © Reuters/Issac Brekken/ Pool, **xvi:** (top) © AP Images/Matt York, (bottom) © AP Images/Eric Risberg, **xvii:** © John Smierciak, *Chicago Tribune*/MCT/Landov, (bottom) © AP Images/*The Oakland Press*, Vaughn Gurganian, **xviii:** © AP Images/Suzanne Plunkett

Part 1

1: © Rick Friedman/Corbis

Chapter 1

2–3: © VCL/Chris Ryan/Taxi/Getty Images; **4:** (left) © VCL/Chris Ryan/ Taxi/Getty Images; **7:** (top, both) © Bettmann/Corbis; **7:** (bottom) © moodboard/Corbis; **15:** © AP Images/Marcio Jose Sanchez; **18:** © X-Brand Images/Getty Images; **20:** © BCarter/Demotix. com. Reproduced by permission; **23:** © AP Images/Andy Manis; **24:** © Mike Kemp/Rubberball Productions/Getty Images; **26:** © AP Images/Jeff Roberson; **28:** © AP Images/Mary Altaffer, Pool; **29:** © Jose Luis Pelaez, Inc./Blend Images/Corbis; **30:** © moodboard/ Corbis; **33:** © VCL/Chris Ryan/Taxi/ Getty Images

Chapter 2

36–37: © Janine Wiedel Photolibrary/ Alamy; **38:** (left) © Janine Wiedel Photolibrary/Alamy; **41:** © X-Brand Images/Getty Images; **42:** © AP Images/John Heller; **47:** (top) © X-Brand Images/Getty Images; **47:** (bottom) © AP Images/Daily Local News, Tom Kelly IV; **53:** (top) © Robert Wallis/Corbis; **53:** (bottom) © SuperStock RF/SuperStock; **56:** © AP Images/David Kohl; **61:** © AP Images/Josh Reynolds; **67:** © AP Images/The Citizens Voice, Mark Moran; **70:** © Mark Ludak/The Image Works; **71:** © SuperStock RF/ SuperStock; **72:** © Kris Legg/Alamy; **74:** (top) © X-Brand Images/Getty Images; **76:** (top) © X-Brand Images/ Getty Images; **77:** © Janine Wiedel Photolibrary/Alamy

Chapter 3

80–81: © AP Images/Joseph Kaczmarek; **82:** (left) © AP Photo/ Joseph Kaczmarek; **86:** © X-Brand Images/Getty Images; **87:** *Wager of Battel*, from Le Coutum de Mormandie, an illuminated manuscript (1450–1470); **90:** © UPI Photo/Landov; **92:** © Mike Kemp/ Rubberball Productions/Getty Images; **93:** © Mike Kemp/ Rubberball Productions/Getty Images; **94:** © Joe Raedle/Getty Images; **95:** © Radius Images/Alamy; **97:** © AP Images/Thomas Roy; **100:** © Blue Images Online/ Masterfile; **101:** © UpperCut Images/ Getty Images; **102:** © AP Images/Elise Amendola; **105:** © AP Images/Gloria Ferniz; **107:** © AP Photo/Joseph Kaczmarek

Part 2

111: © Rick Friedman/Corbis

Chapter 4

112–13: © Molly Riley/Reuters/ Landov; **114:** (left) © Molly Riley/ Reuters/Landov; **118:** © Print Collector/HIP/The Image Works; **120:** © AP Images/Boston Public Library; **123:** © Reuters/Richard Carson/Landov; **127:** Radius Images/ Alamy; **128:** © AP Images/*The Register-Mail*, Bill Gaither; **131:** (top) © AP Images/Mark Lennihan; **131:** (bottom) © PhotoLink/ Photodisc/Getty Images; **135:** (top) © AP Images/Mike Groll; **135:** (bottom) © Chris Stein/Getty Images; **137:** © Molly Riley/Reuters/Landov

Chapter 5

140–41: © AP Images/Jacquelyn Martin; **142:** (left) © AP Images/ Jacquelyn Martin; **147:** © Justin Sullivan/Getty Images; **148:** © Mandel Ngan/AFP/Getty Images; **151:** © Darryl Estrine/ UpperCut Images/Getty Images; **153:** © X Brand Images/Getty Images; **154:** © AP Images/*The Herald Mail*, Ric Dugan; **156:** © Mike Kemp/Rubberball Productions/Getty Images; **157:** © Mike Kemp/Rubberball Productions/Getty Images; **158:** © Gareth Fuller/PA Wire URN:7043754/Press Association via AP Images; **159:** © Mike Kemp/ Rubberball Productions/Getty Images; **160:** © AP Images/*The Plain Dealer*, Lynn Ischay; **163:** © imac/ Alamy; **164:** © Robert W. Ginn/ Alamy; **166:** © Paul J. Richards/AFP/ Getty Images; **169:** © AP Images/ Jacquelyn Martin

Chapter 6

172–173: ©AP Images/*Tyler Morning Telegraph*, Tom Worner; **174:** ©AP

Images/*Tyler Morning Telegraph*, Tom Worner; **178:** © AP Images/ Mike Derer; **180:** © AP Images/Matt Rourke; **182:** © UpperCut Images/ Getty Images; **185:** © AP Images/ Tracy Gitnick; **188:** © AP Images/*The Plain Dealer*, Peggy Turbett; **189:** © © UpperCut Images/ Getty Images; **192:** © AP Images/ Craig Ruttle; **193:** © David Hiller/ Photodisc/Getty Images; **196:** © AP Images/*Kokomo Tribune*, Tim Bath; **202:** © Li-Hua Lan/ Syracuse Newspapers/The Image Works; **206:** ©AP Images/*Tyler Morning Telegraph*, Tom Worner

Part 3

209: © Rick Friedman/Corbis

Chapter 7

210–11: © AP Images/*Galveston Daily News*, Jennifer Reynolds; **212:** (left) © AP Images/*Galveston Daily News*, Jennifer Reynolds; **214:** © AP Images/Steve Pope; **215:** © Tim Pannell/Corbis; **221:** © AP Images/Joe Giblin; **223:** © AP Images/ *The Daily Camera*, Mark Leffingwell; **228:** © AP Images/Cheryl Senter, Pool; **233:** © moodboard/Corbis; **235:** © AP Images/*Atlanta Journal-Constitution*, Joey Ivansco; **239:** (top) © AP Images/ PA; **239:** (bottom) © Guy Cali/Corbis; **240:** © AP Images/Gary C. Knapp; **244:** © AP Images/*Galveston Daily News*, Jennifer Reynolds

Chapter 8

248–49: © AP Images/Hector Mata; **250:** (left) © AP Images/Hector Mata; **252:** © Timothy A. Clary/AFP/Getty Images; **253:** © Guy Cali/Corbis; **259:** © AP Images/Bizuayehu Tesfaye, Pool; **263:** © Fred Prouser/ Reuters/Landov; **266:** © Elaine Thompson/Reuters/Landov; **269:** © AP Images/Toby Talbot; **270:** © Mike Kemp/Rubberball Productions/Getty Images; **273:** © AP Images/Dan Williamson, Pool; **275:** © Image Source/Corbis; **280:** © moorboard/Corbis; **282:** © AP Images/Nati Harnik, Pool; **283:** © Steve Marcus/UPI/Landov; **285:** © X Brand Images/Getty Images **288:** © AP Images/Hector Mata

Chapter 9

292–93: © Reuters/Issac Brekken/ Pool; **294:** (left) © Reuters/Issac

Brekken/Pool; **296:** The Granger Collection, New York; **301:** © AP Images/*Bristol Herald Courier*, Andre Teague; **305:** California Department Of Corrections/Getty Images; **308:** © Tim Boyles/Getty Images; **314:** © AP Photo/*The Idaho Statesman*, Darin Oswald; **318:** © moorboard/ Corbis; **319:** © moorboard/Corbis; **322:** © AP Images/Donna Carson; **323:** © Image Source/Corbis; **327:** © Reuters/Issac Brekken/Pool

Part 4

331: © Rick Friedman/Corbis

Chapter 10

332–33: © AP Images/Matt York; **334:** (left) © AP Images/Matt York; **339:** © Reed Saxton/UPI Photo/ Landov; **340:** © Thinkstock/Getty Images; **344:** © Yoon S. Byun/*Boston Globe*/Landov; **351:** © AP Images/ John Bazemore; **353:** © AP Images/ *Corpus Christie Caller-Times*, Michael Zamora; **356:** © AP Images/Mary Ann Chastain; **357:** © AP Images/*The Daily World*, Freddie Herpin; **359:** © VisionAmerica/Joe Sohm/ Getty Images; **360:** © X-Brand Images/Getty Images; **361:** © AP Images/*Daily Star*/Keri Wheeler; **366:** © AP Images/Matt York

Chapter 11

370–71: © AP Images/Eric Risberg; **372:** (left) © AP Images/Eric Risberg; **377:** van Gogh, Vincent: *Prisoners Round* (detail), 1890. Pushkin Museum of Art, Moscow, Scala/Art Resource, New York; **378:** © ShutterStock RF/ ShutterStock; **379:** © X-Brand Images/Getty Images; **380:** The Granger Collection, New York; **383:** © AP Images/Associated Press; **386:** © Scott Houston/Corbis; **387:** © Thinkstock/Getty Images; **394:** © Scott Goldsmith/Aurora; **396:** © AP Images/*The Maryland Gazette*/Andy Carruthers; **401:** © Ted Soqui/Corbis; **402:** © AP Images/ Eric Risberg

Chapter 12

406–07: © John Smierciak, *Chicago Tribune*/MCT/Landov; **408:** (left) © John Smierciak, *Chicago Tribune*/ MCT/Landov; **417:** © Sean Cayton/ The Image Works; **418–19:** © Mike Kemp/Rubberball Productions/

Getty Images; **421:** © Crime/Alamy; **422:** © AP Images/Eric Risberg; **427:** © AP Images/Pat Sullivan; **428:** © AP Images/*Pecos Enterprise*, Smokey Briggs; **433:** © AP Images/ Washington County Hospital; **435:** © Thinkstock/Getty Images; **437:** © Thinkstock/Getty Images; **439:** © AP Images/*The Annapolis Capital*, Joshua McKerrow; **441:** © AP Images/Jim Cole; **443:** © John Smierciak, *Chicago Tribune*/MCT/Landov

Part 5

Opener: 447: © Rick Friedman/ Corbis

Chapter 13

448–49: © AP Images/*The Oakland Press*, Vaughn Gurganian; **450:** © AP Photo/*The Oakland Press*, Vaughn Gurganian; **453:** The Granger Collection, New York; **456:** © X-Brand Images/Getty Images; **462:** © AP Images/Matt Rourke; **464:** © AP Images/Erik S. Lesser; **465:** © AP Images/Michael Wilson, Pool; **467:** © AP Photo/ Mike Derer, Pool; **473:** © Doug Menuez/Photodisc/Getty Images; **474:** © Image Source/Getty Images; **475:** © Lisa DeJong/*The Plain Dealer*/ Landov; **477:** © Image Source/ Getty Images; **481:** © AP Photo/*The Oakland Press*, Vaughn Gurganian

Chapter 14

484–85: © AP Images/Suzanne Plunkett; **486:** (left) © AP Images/ Suzanne Plunkett; **490:** © AP/Images/ Wally Santana; **493:** © David McNew/ Getty Images; **496:** © Stockbyte/ Getty Images; **501:** © AP Images/ Alan Diaz; **502:** © AP Images/Manuel Balce Ceneta; **503:** © AP Images/ Nick Ut; **505:** © X-Brand Images/ Getty Images; **506:** © AP Images/ Louis Lanzano; **507:** © Steffan Hill/ Alamy; **508:** © Noah Seelam/AFP/ Getty Images; **511:** © AP Images/ Associated Press; **512:** © Equinox Imagery/Alamy **515:** © AP Images/ Suzanne Plunkett

Career Profiles

Permission has been granted by each person whose photo appears at the beginning of each chapter as well as the Career Proiles page in frontmatter.